HOLMAN
New
Testament
Commentary

HOLMAN *New Testament* Commentary

Matthew

GENERAL EDITOR

Max Anders

AUTHOR

Stuart K. Weber

HOLMAN
REFERENCE

Nashville, Tennessee

Holman New Testament Commentary
© 2000 Broadman & Holman Publishers
Nashville, Tennessee
All rights reserved

ISBN 0-8054-0201-2

Dewey Decimal Classification: 227.87
Subject Heading: BIBLE. NT. Matthew
Library of Congress Card Catalog Number: 98-39365

Weber, Stuart.
        Matthew / Stuart Weber
            p.   cm. — (Holman New Testament commentary)
        Includes bibliographical references.
        ISBN 0-8054-0201-2 (alk. paper)
            1. Bible. N.T. Matthew—Commentaries.   2. Bible. N.T. Matthew—
Commentaries. I. Title.   II. Title: Matthew.   III. Series
BS2775.3.L43   1999   98.39365
226.6'07—dc21   CIP

                        4 5 6 7   05 04 03 02
                                D

*T*o my teacher…

Who made the Bible live for me…

Who absolutely loved the Gospel of

Matthew…

Who lived for its King and His

Kingdom…

And who today is in heaven with

the Author he adores…

• Stanley Ellisen, Th.D. •

Senior Professor of Biblical Literature
Western Seminary
Portland, Oregon

Acknowledgments

No project of any magnitude is a solo venture. Certainly not the writing of a book. Most certainly, not a biblical commentary. Numerous people, across many years, are a part of this one. To name just a few:

- My grandfather, William, a simple coal miner who owned only a handful of books, most of them commentaries.
- My grandmother, Rose, whose highest praise for any preacher was "he sure knows his Bible."
- My father, Byron, whose love for the Bible marked our whole family.
- My wife, Linda, who was so incredibly and sacrificially supportive of my entering and completing seminary.
- My fellow elders at Good Shepherd Church who loyally "put up" with my growing over the years.
- My fellow ministry staff colleagues who so skillfully tend our flock.
- And our entire flock at Good Shepherd who so faithfully allow us to "practice" the ministry.

One ministry staff member deserves special note in conjunction with this project—*Brian Smith*. Our staff "resident theologian" and pastor of small group ministries for more than a decade now, Brian has not only overseen hundreds of Growth Groups over the years, he has also written most of the curricula. Brian has worked hard for me throughout this project. He has done much deep plowing, turning over the rich soil with his characteristic great care and insight. His attention to scholarly detail and his eye for key principles can be felt throughout this work. "Thanks, Brian" seems so inadequate. We at Good Shepherd are grateful you have chosen to steward your gifts in our midst!

One family member deserves very special note as well—*Dr. Rick Taylor*. Rick is my brother-in-law. And so much more! We have worked together on writing projects before, and as always is his manner, on this project he has lifted my spirits more than I can express. Rick, you have meant the world to me. You define "trustworthy." With his mature love for Christ and His Word, his great pastor's heart, and his organizational mind (not to mention his computer dexterity), Rick has picked me up, dusted me off, and set me back on track on this project more than once. Thanks, brother.

And two deeply respected mentors:

Dr. Earl D. Radmacher. As an earnest undergraduate, I heard the compelling preaching of Dr. Radmacher. Following my military service I entered Western Seminary and came under his consistent teaching. I had the privilege of serving him as assistant to the president. Now retired, he graciously consented to read through this manuscript. As usual, his coaching has been incredibly insightful and his friendship exhilarating.

Dr. W. Robert Cook. Dr. Cook brought dignity to the seminary classroom, thoughtful system to theology, and great inspiration to his students. Thank you, Dr. Cook, for reading this manuscript and encouraging me in it.

Contents

Contents

Editorial Preface

Today's church hungers for Bible teaching, and Bible teachers hunger for resources to guide them in teaching God's Word. The Holman New Testament Commentary provides the church with the food to feed the spiritually hungry in an easily digestible format. The result: new spiritual vitality that the church can readily use.

Bible teaching should result in new interest in the Scriptures, expanded Bible knowledge, discovery of specific scriptural principles, relevant applications, and exciting living. The unique format of the Holman New Testament Commentary includes sections to achieve these results for every New Testament book.

Opening quotations from some of the church's best writers lead to an introductory illustration and discussion that draw individuals and study groups into the Word of God. "In a Nutshell" summarizes the content and teaching of the chapter. Verse-by-verse commentary answers the church's questions rather than raising issues scholars usually admit they cannot adequately solve. Bible principles and specific contemporary applications encourage students to move from Bible to contemporary times. A specific modern illustration then ties application vividly to present life. A brief prayer aids the student to commit his or her daily life to the principles and applications found in the Bible chapter being studied. For those still hungry for more, "Deeper Discoveries" take the student into a more personal, deeper study of the words, phrases, and themes of God's Word. Finally, a teaching outline provides transitional statements and conclusions along with an outline to assist the teacher in group Bible studies.

It is the editors' prayer that this new resource for local church Bible teaching will enrich the ministry of group, as well as individual, Bible study, and that it will lead God's people to truly be people of the Book, living out what God calls us to be.

Holman Old Testament Commentary Contributors

Vol. 1, Genesis
ISBN 0-8054-9461-8
Kenneth O. Gangel and Stephen Bramer

Vol. 2, Exodus, Leviticus, Numbers
ISBN 0-8054-9462-6
Glen Martin

Vol. 3, Deuteronomy
ISBN 0-8054-9463-4
Doug McIntosh

Vol. 4, Joshua
ISBN 0-8054-9464-2
Kenneth O. Gangel

Vol. 5, Judges, Ruth
ISBN 0-8054-9465-0
W. Gary Phillips

Vol. 6, 1 & 2 Samuel
ISBN 0-8054-9466-9
Stephen Andrews

Vol. 7, 1 & 2 Kings
ISBN 0-8054-9467-7
Gary Inrig

Vol. 8, 1 & 2 Chronicles
ISBN 0-8054-9468-5
Winfried Corduan

Vol. 9, Ezra, Nehemiah, Esther
ISBN 0-8054-9469-3
Knute Larson and Kathy Dahlen

Vol. 10, Job
ISBN 0-8054-9470-7
Steven J. Lawson and Kenneth O. Gangel

Vol. 11, Psalms 1-72
ISBN 0-8054-9471-5
Steven J. Lawson

Vol. 12, Psalms 73-150
ISBN 0-8054-9481-2
Steven J. Lawson

Vol. 13, Proverbs
ISBN 0-8054-9472-3
Max Anders

Vol. 14, Ecclesiastes, Song of Songs
ISBN 0-8054-9482-0
David George Moore and Daniel L. Akin

Vol. 15, Isaiah
ISBN 0-8054-9473-1
Trent C. Butler

Vol. 16, Jeremiah, Lamentations
ISBN 0-8054-9474-X
Fred M. Wood and Ross McLaren

Vol. 17, Ezekiel
ISBN 0-8054-9475-8
Mark F. Rooker

Vol. 18, Daniel
ISBN 0-8054-9476-6
Kenneth O. Gangel

Vol. 19, Hosea, Joel, Amos, Obadiah, Jonah, Micah
ISBN 0-8054-9477-4
Trent C. Butler

Vol. 20, Nahum, Habakkuk, Zephaniah, Haggai, Zechariah, Malachi
ISBN 0-8054-9478-2
Stephen R. Miller

Holman New Testament Commentary Contributors

Vol. 1, Matthew
ISBN 0-8054-0201-2
Stuart K. Weber

Vol. 2, Mark
ISBN 0-8054-0202-0
Rodney L. Cooper

Vol. 3, Luke
ISBN 0-8054-0203-9
Trent C. Butler

Vol. 4, John
ISBN 0-8054-0204-7
Kenneth O. Gangel

Vol. 5, Acts
ISBN 0-8054-0205-5
Kenneth O. Gangel

Vol. 6, Romans
ISBN 0-8054-0206-3
Kenneth Boa and William Kruidenier

Vol. 7, 1 & 2 Corinthians
ISBN 0-8054-0207-1
Richard L. Pratt Jr.

**Vol. 8, Galatians, Ephesians,
Philippians, Colossians**
ISBN 0-8054-0208-X
Max Anders

**Vol. 9, 1 & 2 Thessalonians,
1 & 2 Timothy, Titus, Philemon**
ISBN 0-8054-0209-8
Knute Larson

Vol. 10, Hebrews, James
ISBN 0-8054-0211-X
Thomas D. Lea

Vol. 11, 1 & 2 Peter, 1, 2, 3 John, Jude
ISBN 0-8054-0210-1
David Walls & Max Anders

Vol. 12, Revelation
ISBN 0-8054-0212-8
Kendell H. Easley

Holman New Testament Commentary

Twelve volumes designed for Bible study and teaching to enrich the local church and God's people.

Series Editor	Max Anders
Managing Editors	Trent C. Butler & Steve Bond
Project Editor	Lloyd W. Mullens
Marketing Manager	Greg Webster
Product Manager	David Shepherd
Page Composition	TF Designs, Mt. Juliet, TN

Introduction to

Matthew

Author Phillip Yancey spoke for me when he recalled the scene—General Norman Schwarzkopf's final briefing of the Gulf War. America was glued to its TV sets. The general personified a new national confidence. The man was utterly engaging! With a proper sternness he described the swift offensive operation that caught the elite Republican Guard asleep on duty. With obvious pride he described how his soldiers had routed the hordes of Iraqi troops. With emotion he described the liberating of little Kuwait. With unabashed humor he chuckled about his allied forces' abilities to drive all the way to Baghdad, had that been necessary. With compassion he thanked the Kuwaiti people for their patience. And with humility he thanked our allies, noting especially our traditional friends, the British. It was a grand moment. America was back.

Committed to his mission. Confident in his plan. Diplomatic in posture. Kind in attitude. Strong where necessary. And so utterly proud of his troops—the GIs who had gotten the job done. The general's performance touched me deeply. As a soldier from another, less proud war, I remember thinking out loud, "I would follow that man into the alleys of Baghdad any day!" Writer Yancey, watching that same performance said it best, "That's exactly the kind of man you want to lead a war!"

Flash back now to another scene. There you see another commanding figure reaching right into the heart of a lonely, embarrassed human being: "Ma'am, if you knew who it was who is speaking to you, you would have asked him and he would have given you living water." And find yourself saying, again in the reflective words of Phil Yancey, "That's exactly the kind of man you want to save the world!"

Yes. Jesus Christ is exactly the kind of man you want to save the world!

That is what the Gospel of Matthew is all about. Take a long, thoughtful look at Jesus! Here is the kind of man you would follow anywhere. The emperor Napoleon saw the incomparable Jesus:

Everything in Christ astonishes me. His spirit overwhelms me, and his will confounds me. Between him and . . . whoever else in the world . . . there is no possible comparison. He is truly a being by himself . . . I search in vain in history to find (anyone) similar to Jesus Christ, or anything which can approach the Gospel. Neither history, nor humanity, nor the ages, nor nature offer me anything with which I am able to compare (him) or explain (him). Here (in Christ) is everything extraordinary.

THE CRITICAL PLACE OF THE GOSPEL OF MATTHEW IN THE BIBLE

It is no accident that Matthew appears as the first book of the New Testament. Matthew serves as the *hinge* upon which the Testaments pivot. Matthew is the gateway to the New Testament with the strongest of closing connections to the Old Testament. Matthew explains in "mini-Bible" form God's entire plan of the ages from Genesis to Revelation. To misunderstand the Messiah as presented by Matthew is to misunderstand much of the plan of God as it unfolds in the New Testament.

Matthew looks back and refers to Hebrew prophecies about sixty times ("was fulfilled" and "might be fulfilled"). He also looks forward by dealing not only with Messiah's coming and his ministry, but also his future plan for the kingdom, and for the building of his church. Matthew is therefore an essential link between the Old and New Testaments. Without Matthew, neither testament can be easily or fully understood.

WHY FOUR GOSPELS?

You might ask yourself, "If Matthew is so important, why are there three other Gospels—Mark, Luke, and John?"

Four Gospels incorporate a variety of perspectives and so provide a more complete picture of Jesus. His uniqueness is part of the reason there are four different Gospels. Even the inspired writers of Scripture cannot exhaust his majesty. You might liken them to a symphony which has numerous melodic themes that are woven into a harmonious whole.

The following table summarizes some of the key differences between the four Gospels.

Writer	Written to Whom	About Jesus As	Method or Approach	Featuring
Matthew	Jews	King	Synthetic	Discourses
Mark	Romans	Servant	Chronological	Miracles
Luke	Greeks	Son of Man	Historical	Parables
John	All mankind	Son of God	Theological	Personal interviews

MATTHEW'S DISTINCTIVES

Matthew, a Jew, wrote to the Jewish nation (approximately thirty years after Jesus' ministry) about their long-expected Messiah-King. Naturally, a Jewish audience familiar with the Old Testament wanted some answers. How could Jesus be the Messiah and end up crucified? And, if Jesus really was the "King of the Jews," what happened to the kingdom? Matthew answered their questions, relying heavily on their Old Testament prophecies about the Messiah-King. Matthew's purpose was to demonstrate that Jesus, the carpenter from Nazareth was, in deed and truth, the promised Messiah of Old Testament prophecy.

Matthew proved with a careful genealogy, easily confirmed in temple records of the time, that Jesus was the only rightful heir to the throne through his earthly guardian-father Joseph. Matthew moved then through Jesus' life in a thematic or synthesizing way (rather than simply historical/chronological), drawing together similar thematic elements (e.g., many miracles are lumped together in chaps. 8–10) from different times in Jesus' ministry, in order to leave a systematic, comprehensive, and conclusive picture that Jesus was indeed the Messiah-King.

Matthew. Some called him Levi, but his friends knew him as Matthew. He was a tax collector for the Roman government. His status in Jewish society was even lower than a Gentile, for he robbed and betrayed his own people. No one could have guessed the Father was carefully preparing a writer of holy Scriptures.

Matthew recorded his own call to follow Jesus as one of the twelve disciples (Matt. 9:9–13). With his attention to detail, Matthew was probably the group journalist, keeping records of Jesus' teaching and actions. Some time in the A.D. 50s or 60s, two or three decades after Jesus had finished his work on earth, Matthew's record-keeping skills merged with his love for the Old Testament to produce his Gospel account—a solid argument for the identity of Jesus as the promised Messiah, written for Jewish readers throughout the Mediterranean world.

Matthew's Readers. In a sense, when you read the Bible you are reading someone else's mail. It is written *for* you but it was not written *to* you. So, if you are going to truly understand someone else's mail, you need to know something about them and their context. Matthew wrote primarily to a Jewish audience. Because the Old Testament was the Bible of the first-century Jews, all of Matthew's references to it were intended to show them that Jesus was the culmination of God's plan of all history, the completion and perfection of the Old Testament covenants.

Matthew's Central Message. Matthew wrote, above all else, to prove that Jesus of Nazareth was indeed the promised Messiah-King (the sovereign Son of David and the sacrificial Son of Abraham). Matthew was also deeply concerned with the restoration of God's kingdom. He made a point of using the phrase *kingdom of heaven* thirty-two times, and *kingdom of God* four times, and he frequently showed through Jesus' words and actions that Jesus had the royal authority of God Almighty. Kingdom (*basileia*) is a word and a concept at the very heart of Matthew's Gospel, for he wrote specifically to the chosen Jewish people about the kingdom.

Matthew's Key Verse. If we were to pick out one verse that captures the main message of Matthew, it would have to be Matthew 27:37, "THIS IS JESUS, THE KING OF THE JEWS." This man, Jesus, grew up in the middle of nowhere (Nazareth) with a couple of nobodies (Joseph and Mary who?). Yet, he was the sole legal and rightful heir to the throne of Israel!

Matthew's Basic Structure. The first four chapters of Matthew serve as the narrative introduction to Matthew's Gospel. The last three chapters (26–28) balance the first four as narrative conclusion and serve as a magnificent climax to the earthly ministry of the Messiah-King. The middle twenty-one chapters (5–25) trace Jesus' ministry, featuring his five discourses as major pillars. The pace of chapters 1–4 and 26–28 is quicker and is not interspersed with parables, conflicts, or the frequent short teachings found in the central chapters (5–25).

Matt. 1–4	Matthew 5–25 Jesus' Discourses (Sermon Teaching)					Matt. 26–28
Opening Narrative *or*	5–7 Sermon on the Mount *or*	10 Commission of the Twelve *or*	13 Kingdom Parables *or*	18 Teaching on the Church *or*	24–25 Olivet Discourse *or*	Closing Narrative *or*
The Introduction	The Kingdom Constitution	The Kingdom's Foundational Leaders	The Pursuit of the Kingdom (in the King's Absence)	The Relational Principles in the Kingdom	The Kingdom's Future	The Climax

Historical Setting of Matthew. In the development of God's plan over the centuries, he brought his people to a particular point of readiness, about 430 B.C., when Malachi, the last of the Old Testament books, was written. Then God simply stopped speaking. For four hundred years there was no prophet, no word from God! During this time between the Testaments, God's Jewish people (at least the faithful among them) had begun to wonder what had happened to the kingdom.

One world empire had succeeded another. Cyrus, the king of Persia, had released the Jews from captivity in 536 B.C., allowing them to return and restore their home and their national worship. Alexander the Great ended Persian domination of Israel in 333 B.C., extending the Greek Empire with its language and culture throughout most of the known world. Long after the Greek Empire had fallen, Greek was still the common language throughout the Mediterranean world. The result was that in the first century A.D. the truth of Jesus the Messiah was written in a literary form called Gospels in the Greek language—easily understood by persons of many nations.

Israel enjoyed more than a century of self-rule beginning in 167 B.C., after a successful revolt against Greece. During this time they developed their system of synagogues, where the faithful gathered each Sabbath to hear the Scriptures taught. Here also they provided formal education for young boys from devout Jewish families. The Pharisees were the theologically conservative leaders of the synagogues. At the other end of the Jewish religious spectrum were the Sadducees, the more politically-connected leaders of the temple system in Jerusalem.

In 63 B.C., the Roman general Pompey and his armies besieged and conquered Jerusalem. While Israel was allowed to continue their religious practices, they paid dearly in taxes and in the loss of national freedom. Some Jews, primarily the political opportunists, allied themselves with the civil powers and became known as the Herodians.

The next few decades were fearful and uncertain for the Jewish people. Herod the Great was appointed ruler of Judea (the portion of Israel around Jerusalem) in 40 B.C. and three years later firmly established his rule. During the thirty-six years of his rule, he was given to perversion and paranoia. In fits of jealous rage he killed his wife, two sons, and several other family members whom he perceived as threats to his throne. This was the Herod who was so upset over the Magi's report of a newborn king that he ordered the massacre of children in his search for Jesus (Matt. 2:1–18). Herod the Great died in 4 B.C. His son Herod Antipater was the one before whom Jesus stood trial (Luke 23:6–12).

Ruled by numerous warring pagan nations over the years, most recently Rome, Israel had lost track of its king and of the kingdom. Pagan political leaders ruled. False religious leaders held sway. And the people were languishing in disarray, particularly spiritual disarray.

But during those four silent centuries, God, though prophetically silent, had never stopped working. He was, in fact, setting the stage for the climax of his plan, the coming of his Son. With the passing of those four centuries "the time had fully come, God sent his Son, born of a woman . . . to redeem those under law" (Gal. 4:4–5). The fullness of time had come in the pagan world. The Greeks had spread their magnificent language far and wide; the

Romans had built their unifying roads and their legions provided their quieting peace. The fullness of time had come in the nation of Israel. The priesthood had hit an all-time low. The fullness of time had come. The world was about to hear from God like never before!

The life and ministry of Jesus was carefully orchestrated from the heavens. And it was Matthew who put it all together for us. In order to truly understand Matthew, we must see where this Gospel fits in God's plan of the ages. Let us look at a few highlights of God's plan as it unfolded, first in heaven and then on earth, during the centuries before Jesus was born. Remember, Matthew is all about Jesus the king and his kingdom. Let us take a little closer look at that kingdom.

The Kingdom of God. The larger context of Matthew's Gospel is a battle of cosmic proportion. From Genesis to Revelation, the great unifying theme of the Bible is the kingdom of God. In fact, Jesus told his disciples to pray, first and foremost, to his Father about his Father's kingdom.

> This, then, is how you should pray:
> "Our Father in heaven,
> hallowed be your name,
> your kingdom come,
> your will be done
> on earth as it is in heaven" (Matt. 6:9–10).

That is the fulfillment of the Father's dream on this planet among human beings—his kingdom realized on earth as it is in heaven. That is at the core of the Bible from beginning to end. There will come a day when God will actually rule on this planet as he does in heaven!

Almighty God rules the universe in sovereign authority. Like any kingdom, God's kingdom is a realm governed by a ruler who reigns over subject-citizens through governing principles or laws. And God's kingdom is multifaceted. He rules in time and space. He rules in eternity. He rules in the material world, and he rules in the spiritual world. But his rule on this planet and among a portion of the angel-spirit world has experienced a temporary rebellion.

Further, in his wisdom God often chooses to rule his kingdom through regents or subordinate rulers. In eternity past before creating the material world, he created intelligent beings, angels (Job 38:4–7), to exercise authority in his name. When he created our world, he indicated man should rule over the planet (Gen. 1:26).

Originally, in the primordial world God's will was never questioned and was always done. Certainly it was never challenged. It is this absolute sovereignty that is the critical heart of the kingdom of God. A great many scholars and theologians have spent significant time and energy wrestling over just how the kingdom is to be defined. Simply put, the kingdom of God is the realm over which he rules. It is his exercise of total sovereign authority over all his subjects and includes this earth and its inhabitants. It is this extension of God's actual sovereignty over all life on this planet (like it already is in heaven) that Jesus instructed his followers to pray into reality (Matt. 6:9).

God's kingdom is both eternal and universal. There is absolutely nothing outside the purview of his sovereign authority—"The LORD is king for ever and ever" (Ps. 10:16). "The LORD has established his throne in heaven, and his kingdom rules over all" (Ps. 103:19).

It is therefore also both temporal and material, or local. "The kingdom of the world has become the kingdom of our Lord and of his Christ, and he will reign for ever and ever" (Rev. 11:15).

But somewhere between the eternity past of Psalm 10 and the temporal future of Revelation 11, the kingdom experienced rebellion. These subordinate authorities, these mere lieutenants, both angelic and human, at different times and in different ways, demonstrated an incredible capacity for rebellion. Rebellion thus forms the backdrop for the dramatic conflict—the battle—that unfolds in the pages of Scripture. An overarching question is, How will God, this king of glory, defeat the minions of the Evil One in this battle between God and Satan, between good and evil, between life and death, between heaven and hell?

The Bible is the story of God's divinely determined plan to crush the rebellion and reclaim the kingdom in its entirety. The Gospel of Matthew is at the very center of this great story. And, as we will see, this term *kingdom* becomes a central and critical element in understanding the Gospel of Matthew.

The Cosmic Battle. Let us step back and put this all together in basic terms. Somewhere in the far reaches of eternity past there was only God. In his own wisdom, according to his own counsel, he added the first forms of created intelligence—angels, magnificent inhabitants of the spirit world, myriads of them. We know that the most magnificent of all these creatures, the chief angel, was Lucifer, sometimes referred to as the Star of the Morning, or the Son of the Dawn. These angelic beings were part of the great timeless and boundless kingdom of God.

We do not know a lot of details, but we do know the big picture. Many believe that the chief angel, the acting prime minister if you will, rebelled because of deep-seated pride: "Wickedness was found in you" (Ezek. 28:12–19). This mighty celestial being became enamored with himself and infatuated with the concept of his becoming independent of Almighty God. He decided he would become "like the Most High" (Isa. 14:12–15). Under his arrogant and usurping leadership, about a third of the angels rebelled against God (Rev. 12:1–9), forming a kingdom of their own, a counterfeit kingdom of darkness (Isa. 14:12). This evil angel became, of course, God's chief adversary, the very meaning of the name Satan.

The question naturally arises, If God is sovereign, why did he let this happen? Why did he not just destroy the devil and his kingdom of darkness? It is an appropriate question. And it has an excellent answer. God has a plan to do just that! It will be in his own time and in his own way. That is what the kingdom plan of God is all about! God sovereignly allowed the formation of this counterfeit kingdom of darkness, but it was formed through the voluntary initiative of Satan, not God's creation. These rebels are on a leash and God is using them for his own purposes—to glorify his own name, if by no other means than sheer contrast. The kingdom of darkness serves as an enticing alternative. Each human being has to make a choice between the two kingdoms. Ultimately, only those choosing to follow the true king will live with him forever.

Some time after the fall of Satan, God created the material world and planet earth as a temporal and material reflection (microcosm) of God's eternal and spiritual kingdom. The capstone of that creation was the human being made "in the image of God" and with the full capacity to choose for himself. Satan, God's cosmic adversary, and in direct competition with him, seized upon the opportunity to tempt the human beings to defy God even as he himself had done. And they fell for it. The devil's schemes have served ever since as a giant polarizing magnet to attract the self-serving.

Consequently, this dark kingdom seems often to be the dominating force on this planet. But only for a time. When our parents Adam and Eve sinned, two enormous consequences set in: (1) every human being was born a sinner separated from the very God they were to reflect, and (2) the planet fell under the dark rule of the great usurper himself, Satan, now known as "the ruler of the kingdom of the air" (Eph. 2:2). Satan succeeded temporarily in besmirching God's image and reputation.

The Bible then spells out God's battle plan for history—how he will meet and defeat the challenge of Satan by (1) redeeming the sinful people, and (2) reclaiming the tarnished planet. He will see to it, over thousands of years as it turns out, that the devil is destroyed, his insurrection is put down, and "the kingdom of the world . . . become[s] the kingdom of our Lord and of his Christ" (Rev. 11:15). Christ, the Father's Son and champion of righteousness, is King of kings and Lord of lords. No book of the Bible speaks so consistently of this kingdom as does the Gospel of Matthew.

Paradise Lost. The two major consequences of man's fall created two problems God would address in manifesting his glory. These two problems— (1) the need to redeem the people and (2) the need to reclaim the planet— were opportunities for him to show himself sovereign and to demonstrate, in ultimate terms, "the manifold wisdom of God . . . to the rulers and authorities in the heavenly realms, according to his eternal purpose which he accomplished in Christ Jesus our Lord" (Eph. 3:10–11). Just how would he redeem the people from sin? And how would he reclaim the planet from Satan? In a word, *covenants!*

The Covenants. Those two problems became the basis for the major promises, or covenants, in the Old Testament. Two covenants in particular stand out—the primary Abrahamic Covenant and its subsidiary Davidic Covenant. Those two promises, made to two men, became the two tracks which carry the weight of Old Testament history and New Testament hope. God made a covenant with Abraham. And he made one with David.

God promised Abraham that he would bless all nations through Abraham's descendants. A thousand years later, God promised David he would have a son—a descendant—through whom the planet would be reclaimed. David's son would be a sovereign Son who would rule over the planet. And when those two promises were completely fulfilled, earth's history would have run its course and become "the kingdom of our Lord." Those two covenants come together in one person, Christ Jesus. That is why the first verse of the Matthew's Gospel is so explosive! This is "A record of the genealogy of Jesus Christ the son of David, the son of Abraham" (Matt. 1:1).

Remember these two tracks as you study Matthew: (1) How to redeem the people from sin, and (2) How to reclaim the kingdom from Satan.

Let us take a closer look at these two covenants and embody God's plan to reclaim his perfect kingdom—that is, to bring everything back into subjection to his will.

God's Covenant with Abraham. The primary covenant of God was given about 2000 B.C. to a man named Abraham and is thus called the Abrahamic Covenant. Its terms are covered in Genesis 12–17. In this covenant, God unconditionally promised Abraham:

- offspring beyond number (a people),
- the fruitful land that was then occupied by the people of Canaan (a place), and
- a blessing on Abraham and on all nations through him (a right relationship with the perfect king).

This was the first step toward paradise regained!

There is one other episode in the life of Abraham that is critical to our understanding of Matthew and God's plan of history. In Genesis 22, God commanded Abraham to sacrifice his one and only son, the only rightful heir, whom he loved dearly. When Abraham demonstrated his willingness to make even this greatest of sacrifices in obedience, God stepped in and provided a ram to sacrifice in the place of Abraham's son. This event illustrated two aspects of God's plan for regaining paradise. First, while the sin of God's people requires death as its price, this price could be satisfied by the death of a substitute. Second, the redemption (buying back) of God's people would be accomplished by a sacrificial Son (descendant) of Abraham. When Christ ascended the mount of offering (Calvary), however, there was no substitute ram for the Son, for Jesus is the Lamb of God.

God's Covenant with David. Later, about 1000 B.C., in the unfolding of God's covenant, we come across a further detail respecting the king who is to rule. God revealed the information to Israel's second human king, David, in the form of a subsidiary covenant with him. This is called the Davidic Covenant. It is laid out for us in 2 Samuel 7:1–16. In it, God unconditionally promised David that he would have a son (descendant) on the throne of his kingdom forever, and that God himself would have a Father-Son relationship with the king who would descend from David.

It is important to ask a key question here in our understanding of Matthew. In the context of God's promise to David, the king of Israel, do you think David would have understood this promise to pertain to the throne of Israel? Of course, David would have understood it this way. It was a plain and literal statement. Israel would rule the world with David's descendant as king. God was clearly and literally promising David that his descendant, the king of the nation of Israel, would rule over the world. In the future, when this planet has fulfilled its purpose, it will be ruled by Christ, the king of Israel.

Yes, Jesus is also the Lord of the church, but the church is not Israel. The church has not replaced Israel. It is grafted into the future kingdom as part of it (Rom. 11:1–29), but it has not taken Israel's place. The church is not the fulfillment of the promise to David, though it is part of it. The church and Israel are two distinct entities, and God has not yet finished with the nation of Israel. Matthew's careful use of the two different terms—kingdom (*basileia*) and church (*ekklesia*)—is strong evidence that kingdom and church are distinct. Matthew will demonstrate this distinction clearly.

The Covenant Completed in Christ. One thousand years after David, and two thousand years after Abraham, Matthew set out to write his Gospel. However, Matthew knew he was writing more than a simple personal biography. Matthew pulled together all the strands of God's eternal plan—laid out over the preceding millennia—and demonstrated how they found their final completion in Jesus the Messiah.

So the New Testament opens with the electrifying words of Matthew 1:1: "A record of the genealogy of Jesus Christ the son of David, the son of Abraham."

Jesus Christ is the sovereign Son of David, the sacrificial Son of Abraham, the Lion of Judah, and Lamb of God! He is the only person in all the world who brings together in one person the two great promises of the Old Testament.

Matthew introduced Jesus as "the son of David, the son of Abraham" and he did it in that order, reversing their chronological appearance in history. The two titles can be seen as a basic outline of Matthew's Gospel. Basically, Matthew deals in chapters 1–12 with Jesus as the sovereign Son of David, the reclaiming king and Lion of Judah. In chapters 13–28 he presents Jesus as the sacrificial Son of Abraham, the redeeming Savior and Lamb of God—an astounding claim to the Jewish mind. So Matthew proceeded, in his very first chapter, to document Jesus' physical descent from both of these historic figures (Matt. 1:1–17). As Matthew goes on to demonstrate, Jesus alone could fulfill God's covenant promises as both the sovereign Son of David and the sacrificial Son of Abraham.

Only Jesus the God-Man, of all David's descendants, and of all people on earth, had the authority of God Almighty to bring the kingdom program to its proper order and perfection. Only he could reclaim the fallen planet.

Only Jesus the God-Man, of all Abraham's descendants, and of all people on earth, could live a sinless life, incurring no debt of his own, to offer himself as the object of God's righteous wrath, substituting himself in our place, and paying the debt we owe. Only he could redeem God's fallen people.

Paradise Regained. While we have yet to see the kingdom in its full restoration, we can rest assured that paradise regained is as good as done. Jesus came the first time as the sacrificial Son of Abraham to die for the redemption of the people. He will come a second time as the sovereign Son of David to reclaim the planet and rule perfectly over it. Earth will fulfill its original purpose. Under the new covenant, completed in Jesus, we who are his people by our faith in him are promised:

- a people, the family of all who have trusted Christ, the church,
- a place, the new heaven and new earth to enjoy for eternity, and, best of all,
- a restored relationship with the perfect king.

And that is the Gospel of Matthew!

Matthew 1–2

The King Arrives

I. **INTRODUCTION**
"I'm My Own Grandpa"

II. **COMMENTARY**
A verse-by-verse explanation of these chapters.

III. **CONCLUSION**
An overview of the principles and applications from these chapters.

IV. **LIFE APPLICATION**
Rightful Heir to the Throne
Melding these chapters to life.

V. **PRAYER**
Tying these chapters to life with God.

VI. **DEEPER DISCOVERIES**
Historical, geographical, and grammatical enrichment of the commentary.

VII. **TEACHING OUTLINE**
Suggested step-by-step group study of these chapters.

VIII. **ISSUES FOR DISCUSSION**
Zeroing these chapters in on daily life.

"*There is no king who has not had a slave among his ancestors, and no slave who has not had a king among his.*"

H e l e n   K e l l e r

Matthew 1–2

IN A NUTSHELL

In these first chapters Matthew identifies Jesus as Messiah-King through his lineage, birth, and childhood. Matthew's record of Jesus' genealogy shows that Jesus is the sacrificial Son of Abraham, a legitimate descendant of David, and the rightful heir to the messianic throne. The events surrounding Jesus' birth and childhood prove him to be the promised Savior.

The King Arrives

I. INTRODUCTION

"I'm My Own Grandpa"

We have all heard that old song-spoof at one time or another. It seems that a widow remarried. Her grown daughter later married her new husband's father. Each couple had a child. The song distorts it from there:

> This made my dad my son-in-law,
> my daughter was my "mother," cause she was my father's wife.
> Father's wife then had a son,
> he became my grandchild, for he was my daughter's son.
> My wife is now my mother's mother,
> now if my wife is my grandmother,
> then I'm her grandchild . . .
> as husband of my grandmother,
> I'm my own Grandpa.

But for all the giggling in it, the song does have a sting. Too often modern families are pulled apart. Like eggs unceremoniously scrambled in a frying pan, we are tossed about in the crucible of modern life. The heat and pain of divorce, dysfunction, and abandonment leave many of us with little idea who we are, or where we have come from.

But somewhere down deep inside we want to know. For some people it is a deep yearning. For others it is a healthy curiosity. Somehow we understand that at least part of who we are can be explained by our roots.

That yearning helps explain the incredible popularity of Alex Haley's *Roots,* the most popular miniseries in the history of television. For years, Haley, an African-American descendant of slaves, traveled thousands of miles across several continents to gain insight into his identity.

In recent years there has been a phenomenal surge of interest in genealogy. Today we find numerous books on the history of family names: how to discover your ancestors, how to write for official records, how to trace your pedigree, and how to search for your ancestry around the world.

There was no such "missing ancestry" problem in first-century Israel. Every Jewish citizen who cared to know could determine exactly who his or her ancestors were. These facts were all meticulously recorded and maintained in the temple records at Jerusalem. Lineage and careful records were important to a people determined to maintain their identity in the midst of the turmoil of the ancient world.

Those records were all the more important when it came to identifying the royal line of the ancient Hebrew kings. If lineage was important to anyone, it was especially so in the royal family.

We find such a lineage in Matthew 1. We might paraphrase verses 1–17 as "Hear, O Israel! Here is your king! Jesus, son of Joseph, is the only living legal heir to the throne of Israel. The records prove it. And if you have got a problem with it, check it out. The lineage is indisputable. This is Jesus of Nazareth, king of the Jews!"

II. COMMENTARY

The King Arrives

> **MAIN IDEA:** *Jesus is identified as Messiah-King through his lineage, birth, and childhood.*

A The King's Amazing Pedigree (1:1–17)

> **SUPPORTING IDEA:** *Jesus' lineage proves him to be both the sacrificial Son of Abraham and the sovereign Son of David.*

1:1. It is fitting that the first verse of the first book of the New Testament, Matthew 1:1, identifies Jesus as the **Christ, the son of David, the son of Abraham.** These few words sum up the culmination of the entire Old Testament, and in them are the seeds from which the New Testament plan will grow. The long-awaited, promised Messiah, the restorer of God's kingdom and the redeemer of his people, is Jesus himself. This is Matthew's central message, his purpose for writing his book.

In his first verse, Matthew made an amazing claim. At the time he was writing, many Jewish readers would have been skeptical about the idea that the man Jesus was indeed also the promised king or Christ. After all, he was merely a carpenter from a backwoods province, and they wanted a king just like other worldly kings—politically connected, militarily powerful, and personally charismatic, with all the accompanying pomp, circumstance, and credentials.

1:2–17. Jesus had credentials all right. Overwhelmingly so. But he was not interested in "pomp." As Exhibit A to substantiate Jesus' claim to the throne, Matthew presented Jesus' pedigree—the genealogy linking Jesus by blood to both Abraham and David (1:1–17). Because the promised Christ must be descended from both of those key historical figures, the documentation of Jesus' lineage was critically important. When it comes to kings, people want to know just where they come from. These first seventeen verses may at first seem a little boring. But they were not to Matthew's audience—first-century Jews! So put yourself in the place of the first readers. Look up the names listed here. Recall their stories. And worship the God who authors such creative grace!

These lists serve a practical purpose. In a day before the man on the street had his own copy of the Bible, people had to rely on memory and oral history. So Matthew traced Christ's genealogy in three sets of fourteen generations. The three sets are broken down into those generations: (1) before the monarchy, (2) during the monarchy, and (3) after the fall of the monarchy to Babylon. He did not mention every single ancestor, but traced the generations in systematic, memorable terms. If the reader wanted more detail, it was available through the temple records. But Matthew's undeniable point was that Jesus of Nazareth is legal heir to the throne of Israel! The king is on the scene.

Note one more memorable fact. In the course of tracing the generations, Matthew tossed in a few surprises to help his readers begin to see the mercy and grace of God. He included no less than four women in the lineage, a highly unusual approach for a Jewish genealogy! And some of them are Gentiles! From the outset, Matthew used indisputable documentation to show the first-century Jewish mind that even Gentiles are included prominently in this kingdom of the new covenant.

B The King's Amazing Birth (1:18–25)

SUPPORTING IDEA: *The circumstances and events surrounding Jesus' birth prove him to be the promised Savior.*

1:18. As Matthew launched the account of Jesus' birth, note that he was careful to highlight the title *Christ*—the title he used in the preceding passage that demonstrated Jesus had the right to claim deity. Watch for Matthew's use of this title throughout his Gospel. His purpose in writing was to make the case for Jesus as the promised king.

To understand the significance of some statements in this passage, it is necessary to understand the Jewish marriage customs of the day. The bride and groom went through a period of betrothal or engagement. In that culture and time, betrothal was virtually as binding as marriage. In this waiting period, Mary was found to be pregnant. Matthew was careful to protect the virtue of Mary and the supernatural origin of Christ.

Why is it so important that the Christ, the promised king, be born to a virgin? The virgin birth is more than a miracle to draw attention to the unique nature of this child. Because Mary was a virgin, only God could have been the father of Jesus, making Jesus the one and only God-Man in all the universe. God's plan would have been impossible if Jesus had been anything less.

1:19. A betrothed couple was as good as married, and breaking off the relationship was seen as divorce, even though the couple had not yet been married. It also helps us gain a better perspective of the emotional state of Mary and Joseph when we realize that she was probably in her teens at the time of these events. The minimum marriageable age in Israel was twelve for women and thirteen for men. To remain unmarried as late as one's twenties may have been cause for social embarrassment.

1:20–21. Imagine having to deal with the responsibility of parenting the promised Messiah at such a young age! We should let the faith of these two "kids" be an example to us. Mary, initially fearful of being an unwed mother, accepted God's revealed intentions for her. And Joseph, initially not all that sure himself about the "virgin birth," was originally thinking divorce, albeit quietly and with no public scandal. But when Joseph was approached by God through the angel, he accepted his role and did precisely as he was instructed by God. He kept Mary a virgin until after Jesus was born, after which their normal marital relations produced other children who were the half-brothers of Jesus. And Joseph, as the legal heir to the throne, named their son "Jesus" as he was told. Mary and Joseph learned that the only way to follow God was to "trust and obey" his word. The character of these two young adults reminds us that God fulfills his purposes by using people of strong character and unquestioning obedience.

The name **Jesus** chosen by God for his Son (1:21) was, in that day and for centuries before, a common name with special meaning. *Jesus* is the Greek equivalent of the Hebrew *Joshua,* meaning "Yahweh is salvation."

Jewish boys for centuries had been given this name Jesus with the frequency of today's John or Mike. This reflects, in part, the hope of Jewish parents for God's salvation from centuries of oppression under a succession of world powers. God's choice of such a common name, when he could have chosen something unique, also emphasized that Jesus came in a way that identified with "the average Joe." He came in love to become one of us, that we might be drawn to him and become one of his. Jesus was approachable and touchable. He was one of us. "We do not have a high Priest who is unable to sympathize with our weaknesses" (Heb. 4:15). Jesus did everything to build bridges to us.

Yet, while the name Jesus was common, only this child was qualified as the God-Man to **save his people from their sins** (1:21). Jesus came at the strategically appointed time to seal the eternal salvation of all whom the Father had chosen.

1:22–23. In these verses Matthew provided the first of many direct quotes from the Old Testament, and the first of many Old Testament prophecies fulfilled by the earthly life of Jesus. These Old Testament quotes and prophecies show, in part, the linkage and unity between the Old and New

Testaments, helping us understand how God was preparing the way for the Christ from centuries past. They also validate the identity of Jesus as the promised Messiah, strengthening our faith in him. And their perfect fulfillment in Jesus gives us confidence that God is faithful and mighty to keep his word to us today.

Matthew is quick to support the doctrine of the virgin birth, and his quote in 1:23 is from Isaiah 7:14, originally written by the prophet Isaiah over seven hundred years before Jesus' birth. This verse in its original Old Testament context seems to be referring to a child who was to be born in that setting of Isaiah's day, rather than centuries later. However, Matthew's inspired revelation fills the original statement out to its full intention. God is never so clearly present with his people as he is through his virgin-born Son, the Messiah of Israel. Jesus is Immanuel! The linguistic components of the name **Immanuel** and their individual translations—Im = "with," anu = "us," and el = "God"—make it clear that Isaiah's original prophecy could refer in its fullest sense only to the promised Messiah. This name of Jesus is a strong argument for his deity.

1:24–25. The dream that had begun for Joseph in verse 20 ends in these verses with him waking and choosing to obey everything the angel had told him to do. This fine man had learned to "trust and obey."

The King's Amazing Childhood (2:1–23)

> **SUPPORTING IDEA:** *The Father's protection of Jesus in his childhood proves him to be the promised Savior for all nations.*

2:1–6. The mention of Jesus' birthplace, Bethlehem of Judea, is significant in this passage especially because of the prophecy it fulfilled (see 2:4–6). Matthew is building his case. Jesus is the fulfillment of all the prophetic intentions of the long-awaited Jewish Messiah. All the details apply, including his birthplace.

The King Herod in this passage, one of many Herods, is Herod the Great, mentioned here and in Luke 1:5. His father, Antipater II, was a Jew of Idumaean descent (Edomite, related through Esau to Jacob) who gained influence under the Roman Empire. He was influential in his son Herod's rise to power, in a succession of positions over Galilee and ultimately Judea, where Herod ruled from 37–4 B.C. (Herod's death in 4 B.C. is one of the main reasons we know Jesus was born somewhat earlier than the traditional A.D. 1; cf. 2:19.) During this time Herod was given the title "king of the Jews" by the Roman senate. This in part explains his fear and aggressive murderous actions when he heard from the Magi that another **king of the Jews** had been born (2:2).

These **Magi from the east** (2:1) were likely from Babylon and were culturally influential students of the stars, not evil magicians of some sort. Their interest must have been aroused by the unusual star they observed. We do not know their number, but their entourage was probably substantial to make such a lengthy cross-continent trip and to cause such a noticeable stir in Jerusalem (2:3). How they came to connect the birth of the king of the Jews with the strange star is a matter of conjecture. Some scholars believe they may have been responding, in an amazing display of faith, to a scrap of Scripture brought to their people centuries before through Balaam (Num. 24:17), who was a Mesopotamian himself.

The important point here is that God brought the birth of the king to the attention of these Gentiles, who probably journeyed many months (possibly one to two years) from Mesopotamia to Jerusalem. Matthew included this information to alert his Jewish readers to several realities: (1) the event of Jesus' birth had worldwide impact; (2) the Messiah was coming through Israel as a gift from God to all nations of the world, not just to the Jews; and (3) in contrast to the indifference of Jewish chief priests and scribes who should have anticipated the king's birth (2:4), these Gentiles were overwhelmed with joy!

The quote in 2:6 comes from Micah 5:2. Micah prophesied around the time of the Northern Kingdom's fall in 722 B.C. Through this man, the Lord used the lesson of the Northern Kingdom's fall to confront Judah's own covenant disobedience. He warned of Judah's future judgment, but he also gave cause for hope, foretelling his restoration of the remnant. It is in this context of hope that the words quoted by Matthew are written in Micah.

2:7–12. Herod called the Magi into his chambers alone to try to determine when this new king, Jesus, was born. Because both the Magi and Herod seemed to identify the appearance of the star with the birthdate of the Messiah, Jesus must have been at least a year old when the Magi arrived. (This fact changes the traditional image of the Magi visiting the young family in the stable where Jesus was born. Certainly the shepherds found him there, but Joseph would have found his family a home to live in by the time the Magi arrived.)

Herod wanted to use the Magi to determine the exact location of this new king. This was a self-serving strategy, not a generous desire to aid the Magi in their quest. Herod had no desire to worship the new king. His goal was to locate him and eliminate this bud of growing messianic hope which he viewed as potential competition.

The Magi likely followed this star very much as a sailor follows the stars to get to his destination. The text does, however, give every indication that this star was a supernatural phenomena.

When the Magi found where Jesus and his family were living, they were overjoyed. Their destination was not just a place—but a person—Jesus. Their response was the same response that Matthew wanted for his readers; they worshiped him. The gifts they gave to Jesus—gold, frankincense, and myrrh—were the most common mediums of exchange in that day. The gold and two forms of incense made it possible for the Magi to cross through many different lands on their way to Bethlehem, much like people today use travelers checks when they are traveling. These gifts would come in handy later for Jesus' family as they traveled themselves (2:13–15).

The Magi chose not to go back to Herod as he had instructed. Instead they went a different way. For foreigners to disobey a king in that day was risky. But the Magi, by faith, followed the warning they had received in a dream. They clearly were more awed by God than by Herod.

2:13–15. When the Magi finally left to go back to their own land, an angel appeared to Joseph in a dream. The angel told Joseph to gather his family and move to a country that was the archenemy of Israel. Why Egypt and not some other location? Simple prophetic fulfillment of Hosea 11:1. We see in both Hosea 11:1 and Numbers 24:8 an allusion to the future, when God would call "him" out of Egypt. The scene was being set for those prophecies to be fulfilled by Jesus when he returned from Egypt.

It must have been frightening to move to enemy territory. God gave Joseph the reason for this drastic move. Herod was planning to find Jesus to kill him. Joseph recognized the dream as God speaking to him. He gathered his family and left immediately for Egypt, once again trusting and obeying. The family stayed in that country until Herod the Great died.

2:16–18. Herod would do anything to protect his own interests, including murdering children. Even though Herod the Great accomplished some wonderful achievements (such as major construction) during his reign, he is best known for his extreme paranoia and the bloodshed that ensued. The story of his slaughter of young boys in and around Bethlehem is consistent with the pattern of his life.

At the time of Herod's slaughter of infant boys, Jesus must have been around one and one-half to two years old. Herod, in his paranoia, would have allowed for a margin of error in the estimate of the child's age, ordering that the age range of those killed be high enough to include this king of the Jews (2:16). Demographers tell us there would have been perhaps two dozen boys two years old and under who were killed because of Herod's obscene order. The weeping would have filled the night from Bethlehem to Ramah. Consider the arrogance of this man. He was observant enough to recognize the truth of Old Testament prophecies about God's plan, but arrogant enough to think that he could thwart it! No created being, not even Lucifer, can thwart the plan of God. In this situation, God the Father intervened to protect his Son and to preserve our salvation.

The quote in 2:18 is from Jeremiah 31:15. Jeremiah prophesied during the decades leading up to and immediately following Judah's fall to Babylon in 586 B.C. His ministry was one of proclaiming doom and judgment. However, he, like most Old Testament prophets, included a message of hope of forgiveness and restoration. Jeremiah 30–31 gives us a lengthy oracle focused on the future restoration of Judah. Even in this oracle of hope, Jeremiah occasionally mentions the sorrow and devastation of Judah, by way of contrast with the joy that would follow. Jeremiah's specific prophecy relates to the captivity in Babylon and the killing of children during Babylon's conquest of Judea. Its parallel here is striking.

The verse Matthew quoted regarding the children slaughtered by Herod is one of these sorrowful notes common in Jeremiah's ministry. But in its original context it is immediately followed by, "This is what the LORD says: 'Restrain your voice from weeping and your eyes from tears, for your work will be rewarded,' declares the LORD. 'They will return from the land of the enemy. So there is hope for your future,' declares the LORD" (Jer. 31:16–17). Perhaps a number of bereaved parents in and around Bethlehem found comfort in the Lord's promise, trusting, without understanding, that there was some kind of meaning behind their tragedy. Matthew probably intended his readers, familiar as they were with the Old Testament, to understand the context of hope in which this tragic verse was originally planted, and so to be led one step closer to finding hope in the Messiah.

2:19–23. The threat to the young king did not end with his return to Israel after Herod's death. The Lord confirmed Joseph's fears of Herod's cruel son (2:22), and so Joseph took his family farther north to his and Mary's hometown, Nazareth in Galilee (see Luke 1:26–27; 2:39). At this time Galilee was an out-of-the-way province, far from the centers of religious and political power in Jerusalem. The Father wanted the king's beginnings to be quiet and unnoticed, where he would grow to maturity among the common people whom he had come to save.

Nazareth was a neighborhood with a dubious reputation (see John 1:46). It was a Roman military post with all the attendant and "disreputable" trappings. While Jesus grew up with strong convictions, keeping himself from giving in to the temptations that surrounded him, he learned in this setting to understand and have compassion on the sick and sinful people around him (see Luke 2:40). His ability to dine with the outcasts (Matt. 9:10–13) did not develop overnight. Although the turn of events in Joseph's return with his family to Israel may seem haphazard, God had a purpose in every detail.

Matthew uses the formula "in order to fulfill" thirteen times in his Gospel. Among them, Matthew 2:23 is unique. It refers to the **prophets**. This plural usage is helpful in explaining that this statement is not found verbatim in any one prophet in the Old Testament. Rather, it seems to be an indirect quotation summarizing the tenor of more than one prophet. What Matthew intended to communicate was not a word-for-word quote found in a specific location, but a theme supported in multiple locations in the Old Testament.

Why did Matthew highlight this negative anticipation of Messiah's ministry? A couple of reasons are likely. First, by the time Matthew wrote his account, the word *Nazarene* had become a household adjective describing anything despised and scorned. When Christ's followers were called members of "the Nazarene sect" by their enemies (Acts 24:5), the term was intended as an insult.

MAIN IDEA REVIEW: *Jesus is identified as Messiah-King through his lineage, birth, and childhood.*

III. CONCLUSION

As Matthew began to make his case for Jesus as the promised King-Messiah, he first established his unique pedigree in the genealogy, putting Jesus' birth into its historical context and setting him forth as the ultimate fulfillment of both the Abrahamic and Davidic Covenants. He then demonstrated the Father's supernatural intervention through the virgin birth, and through his protection of his Son from King Herod and Herod's son. While narrating these events, Matthew demonstrated over and over that Jesus uniquely fulfilled several messianic prophecies from the Old Testament. The overall message: "This child is something special!"

PRINCIPLES

- God protects his own.
- Jesus is the ultimate fulfillment of all God's promises to Israel and to us.
- God will use anyone for his purposes, no matter how unlikely.
- God often uses the humble and willing (Joseph and Mary) rather than the high and mighty (King Herod) to accomplish his greatest missions on earth.
- No one can thwart God's plans (not even the politically powerful Herod).
- Sometimes the brightest light grows in the darkest place (Nazareth).
- People with head knowledge (the scribes) may not have heart knowledge.

- Knowing God's Son in the right way brings unspeakable joy.
- The gospel is a message for people of all nations.

APPLICATIONS

- Respond to the king as the Magi did, with great joy and devotion.
- Humbly make yourself available and ready to be used by God, allowing him to accomplish his purposes through you.
- Seize opportunities to share your faith in Christ with others, exercising wisdom in reaching out toward those who are not believers.
- Serve the Lord with joy, even during the dark and difficult hours.
- Learn to place your trust in God's protective care and timing.
- Study Matthew's approach to communicating Jesus as Messiah to his audience.

IV. LIFE APPLICATION

Rightful Heir to the Throne

When Americans think of royalty and succession to thrones, the British Monarchy often comes to mind. Determining the rightful heir to the British throne is apparent to all. It's a cut-and-dried process. Succession to the throne is based on the principle of male primogeniture, according to which male heirs take precedence over daughters and the right of succession belongs to the eldest son. Daughters take precedence over the Sovereign's brothers. When a daughter succeeds, she becomes Queen Regnant and has the same powers as a king. Where a Sovereign has no children, the succession then lies with the Sovereign's eldest surviving brother and his children (sons, then daughters), as when William IV was succeeded by his niece Victoria. If a Sovereign has no brothers, or if those brothers have no children, then the line of succession passes to the Sovereign's sister(s) in age order, as when Edward VI was succeeded by his half-sisters Mary and Elizabeth. Succession in this case is not a matter of validating one's rightful candidacy to the throne.

The old days were a far cry from today's British Monarchy and others. Genealogies were important in biblical times for they were used to validate one's lineage. Matthew's genealogy of Jesus relates Joseph's genealogy. Luke presents Mary's genealogy, and reaches back to Adam and God.

Matthew made it a point to show Jesus' lineage, for his genealogy validated Jesus as the son of Abraham and of David. This gave Jesus' legal ancestry by which he was the legitimate successor to the throne of David.

What does all this mean to the individual believer? We celebrate the coming of the Messiah and his kingdom. Paul teaches that we are fellow heirs with Christ and will reign with him in his kingdom. Are you living a life of righteousness befitting of a fellow heir?

V. PRAYER

Lord God, thank you for sending your Son to be born into humble surroundings among ordinary people. Make me a witness of his salvation to people whom I meet each day in the normal patterns of life. Amen.

VI. DEEPER DISCOVERIES

A. The Messiah

The Old Testament contains numerous prophecies and images indicating that both the Davidic and the Abrahamic Covenants will find their final fulfillment in one man—who is also God's own Son. The sovereign Son of David, who will restore the kingdom, and the sacrificial Son of Abraham, who will redeem the people, is one and the same!

This one man, foreseen in numerous passages throughout the Old Testament, is known in the Hebrew language of the Old Testament as the Messiah, or literally "Anointed One" (e.g., see Dan. 9:25–26). The New Testament was written in Greek. Thus, when the New Testament writers referred to the Anointed One, they did not use the Hebrew term *Messiah,* but the equivalent Greek term *Christ.* Both are accurate. Neither term is more or less accurate or more or less spiritual. The Spirit-inspired word of the New Testament is "the Christ."

B. Prophet, Priest, and King

In Bible times, the great leaders of God's people normally held one of three offices. Three kinds of people were publicly anointed—prophets, priests, and kings. A *prophet* was one who represented God and spoke his message to the people. A *priest,* on the other hand, represented the people and brought sacrifices before God on the people's behalf. Matthew showed that Jesus, as the Christ or "Anointed One," fulfilled both the priestly and prophetic roles. However, Matthew placed his greatest emphasis on Jesus' role as the *king.*

C. Virgin Birth Significance

Jesus' miraculous conception, or virgin birth, is significant in Scripture. First, with God as his Father, he did not inherit Adam's sin nature, as have all other men and women in the world who have two human parents. Thus, he could be the "spotless lamb," the unblemished sacrifice that would satisfy God's judgment of sin. Anything less than perfect is not good enough as payment for our sin. Jesus was sinlessly perfect.

Second, because Jesus is God, his becoming a human, his perfect life, and his sacrificial death are actions of God involving himself personally in the solution to our problem. God did not just sit back and shout "I love you!" from the heavens. Nor did he send someone else as a messenger or servant to do the work. God himself became one of us! Only God himself could satisfy his own standards of perfection. Only God could offer himself as a full payment that would satisfy his own righteous demands, fully appeasing his own wrath against our sin. God, the judge, passed the death sentence against us; then God, the Savior, came down to stand in front of us and absorb that sentence himself. This could not have happened if Jesus had been born of a human father.

Third, because Jesus is human, he qualifies as a representative of the human race, a mediator, before God (see Heb. 4:14–5:3; also Rom. 5:12–21). It would have been meaningless for a nonhuman to die for the human race, because he would have had no connection or identity with those for whom he died. In order for Jesus the Christ to die in our place, he had to be one of us. This point of identification is critical to the success of God's plan. Without a human mother, Jesus could not have carried out God's plan to redeem (buy back) his own people. Nor could he have done it without a divine Father.

D. Significant Genealogical Insights

While the most important point to be learned from the genealogy of 1:1–17 is that it shows Jesus to be the promised son of David and the promised son of Abraham, there are a few interesting side lights that deserve some attention.

First, in addition to Mary (1:16), four women are mentioned among the long list of men.

Tamar (1:3) was actually Judah's widowed daughter-in-law. She tricked Judah into sleeping with her to produce offspring to carry on her dead husband's name (Gen. 38). Without this incident, the line to the promised king would have been broken.

Rahab (1:5) was a Canaanite prostitute who lived in Jericho and harbored Israelite spies before Joshua's conquest of the city (Josh. 2). Because of her faithfulness to God, he not only spared her family from destruction (Josh. 6:24–25), but he also made her part of the Messiah's ancestry.

Ruth (1:5) was a foreigner in Israel at a time when Israelites were commanded not to intermarry with other nationalities (see the Book of Ruth). But she demonstrated such strength of character and faithfulness to God that she was privileged to become an ancestor of the Messiah. In fact, she was the great-grandmother of King David (Ruth 4:13–22).

The mention of Uriah's wife, Bathsheba (1:6), calls to mind her adulterous relationship with David, leading first to David's murder of her husband Uriah, but also to the birth of Solomon, an ancestor of the Messiah.

Why are these four unlikely women mentioned in Matthew's genealogy, when the normal practice was to mention only the men's names? At least three of them were Gentiles, considered "unclean" by the standards of God's Old Testament law. Three of them were involved in illicit sexual relationships. God is sending a clear message that he can and will use anyone he wants to accomplish his purposes. He is willing to forgive the worst of sins and then go on to do amazing things through the faithful life he has restored. God loves to choose the "least likely" tools for his tasks (1 Cor. 1:26–29). How will he use you?

Throughout Matthew's genealogy, many generations are skipped over in the list. Some of the men listed are not literally the fathers of the men listed after them, but the grandfathers, great-grandfathers, and so on. However, this does not invalidate the genealogy, for the Greek wording for a father-son relationship can also mean an ancestor-descendant relationship, with several generations between the two. Matthew chose to shorten the list of names to those who stood out historically, in order to compile a list of three "fourteens" (1:17). This would be easier for people to remember.

Skeptics of the Bible point out that Matthew's genealogy is different than Luke's (Luke 3:23–38). They conclude that one of these Gospel writers has made a mistake. Indeed, while Matthew says that Jesus is descended through David's son Solomon (Matt. 1:6), Luke says he was descended through David's son Nathan (Luke 3:31). However, the apparent contradiction disappears when we consider the different purposes of Matthew's and Luke's books.

Matthew emphasized Jesus as the king, so his genealogy traced Jesus' *legal* lineage of record through Joseph, even though Joseph was really only the *adoptive* father of Jesus (see the wording of Matt. 1:16). On the other hand, Luke emphasized Jesus' physical, human side, so his genealogy traced Jesus' *physical* lineage through his physical mother Mary, and ultimately to Adam.

VII. TEACHING OUTLINE

A. INTRODUCTION

1. Lead Story: "I'm My Own Grandpa"
2. Context: Matthew wrote an account of the life, teachings, and reality of who Jesus Christ is. But he wrote primarily with his own countrymen in mind—the Jewish nation. The Hebrew Scriptures and traditions had long predicted that a Messiah or deliverer would come to rescue them and fulfill the promises of God. Matthew wrote to

demonstrate that Jesus is indeed the rightful promised king, the Messiah. Lineage was crucial in establishing this connection for the Jewish audience.

3. Transition: Matthew established Jesus' credentials as the promised Messiah by authenticating his legal lineage as the king, by showing that he is the Son of God, by supplying the three eastern witnesses to his supernatural birth, and by showing that even Herod the Great realized that this baby was the promised Messiah. These were strong evidences to the Jewish audience for whom Matthew wrote his Gospel.

B. COMMENTARY

1. The King's Amazing Pedigree (1:1–17)
2. The King's Amazing Birth (1:18–25)
3. The King's Amazing Childhood (2:1–23)

C. CONCLUSION

1. Wrap-up: Matthew was approached by Jesus to follow him. Matthew did just that and his life was never the same. Matthew was personally touched and changed forever by Jesus, the Messiah. In writing about Jesus, Matthew shared his personal testimony about Jesus and what he had said and done that impacted Matthew so much. He shared this testimony with his family, those of Jewish heritage. He wanted them to meet Jesus, to follow him, and to have their lives radically changed by the Messiah-King.

2. Personal Challenge: Like Matthew, you have met and responded to Jesus. Your life has been touched and changed. Like Matthew, you have family and friends who would benefit from hearing your testimony of who Jesus is and how he has changed your life.

VIII. ISSUES FOR DISCUSSION

1. What is the meaning of the *kingdom of God* in the Gospel of Matthew?
2. Who were the Magi who visited Jesus when he was a young child?
3. Why did Matthew use the phrase "in order to fulfill" so many times in his Gospel?
4. Why do you think Jesus grew up in Nazareth of Galilee, an out-of-the-way town and province, rather than a prestigious city such as Jerusalem?

Matthew 3—4

The King Is Introduced

I. INTRODUCTION
Announcing: A New Son Is Born

II. COMMENTARY
A verse-by-verse explanation of these chapters.

III. CONCLUSION
An overview of the principles and applications from these chapters.

IV. LIFE APPLICATION
No Substitute for Preparation

Melding these chapters to life.

V. PRAYER
Tying these chapters to life with God.

VI. DEEPER DISCOVERIES
Historical, geographical, and grammatical enrichment of the commentary.

VII. TEACHING OUTLINE
Suggested step-by-step group study of these chapters.

VIII. ISSUES FOR DISCUSSION
Zeroing these chapters in on daily life.

Quote

"*You cannot repent too soon, because you do not know how soon it may be too late*"

Thomas Fuller

Matthew 3–4

IN A NUTSHELL

In chapter 3, Matthew jumped from the events of Jesus' birth to his adult life. Preaching a message of repentance, John the Baptizer prepared the hearts of the people for the coming of the Messiah-King. In chapter 4, following his baptism, the Spirit led Jesus to the wilderness where he fasted for forty days and nights before being tempted by the devil. Chapter 4 also marks the calling of the first disciples and the beginning of Jesus' ministry of teaching, preaching, and healing.

The King Is Introduced

I. INTRODUCTION

Announcing: A New Son Is Born

*I*t was the shortest of nights. No sleep. It was the longest of nights. Hardest work. At least for his mother. Births are like that!

Ever since the doctor confirmed my wife's suspicions ("You are pregnant!"), we had been making preparations. We calculated the arrival date and converted the extra bedroom to a nursery. We collected diaper bags, bottles, sheets, receiving blankets, and a great deal of paraphernalia. We journaled our doctor appointments.

Linda studied volume after volume about the physical aspects of her pregnancy. I reviewed the route to the hospital time and again. There would be no wrong turns on this thirty-five-mile dash! We were ready—sort of.

One can never be truly ready. The event is simply too big. Mind-boggling. Eye-brimming. Lip-quivering. Simply overwhelming. How could something so common be so indescribable! Our son was here!

When he arrived, we drew incredible pleasure from announcing his birth. Nothing we had ever accomplished in either of our lives compared to giving birth to our child. We were going to let the world know! We nearly exhausted our next month's budget with telegrams, phone calls, and specially designed and printed birth announcements to our friends. This was our son! A unique human being, a very special child—with both a heritage and a destiny.

Somehow, with every child, parents believe with all their hearts this is so much more than a baby. This was a man of difference in the making. He would be the first of a new branch of our little Weber clan in this big world. He was the beginning of a new generation and an anchor in a continuing lineage. His birth just shouted to be announced. That is why it was hard for us to control ourselves and why we spared no expense in announcing his arrival.

Now multiply our feeble efforts by infinity. Multiply our son's birth by the birth of God's only Son! Can you imagine how the Father must have felt?

The Father had made all the preparations. The angels had been readied. The stars were arranged. The census was established to get the key players in position. His celestial light show was an extravaganza. And wise men came. The birth of Jesus Christ was no ordinary event. This was God's Son. And to cap off the announcement process, God arranged for a special trumpeter—a herald of prophetic proportions—John the Baptizer. John was the forerunner, the king's ambassador, sent ahead to lay out the red carpet and prepare the way. Messiah's arrival screamed to be announced. Everyone needed to respond to his arrival. And the appropriate response was, in a word, *repentance*. John's message was contained in that single word, *Repent,* which means "to change one's thinking and behavior." The Messiah is here!

II. COMMENTARY

The King Is Introduced

> **MAIN IDEA:** *God exercised great care in preparing Jesus' way, Jesus' character, and the foundations of Jesus' ministry.*

Ⓐ The King's Forerunner (3:1–12)

> **SUPPORTING IDEA:** *God prepared Jesus' way through John the Baptizer.*

3:1–2. For four hundred years, heaven had been silent. No more! Now to center stage strode a lone but powerful figure. Looking a lot like Elijah with his rough, camel-haired garment and leather belt, John the Baptizer was the first prophet of God to speak in four centuries, and his voice and message were loud and clear. According to Luke, both of John the Baptizer's parents were descended from Aaron (Luke 1:5–10), and his father Zechariah served as a priest. So John himself was qualified to serve as a priest after his father.

John was a miracle child, born of a barren womb to elderly parents (Luke 1:7). John was somehow related to Jesus through their mothers (Luke 1:36), so it is probably safe to call them cousins. Mary had such a strong relationship with Elizabeth that she traveled from Nazareth to Judea for a visit during Elizabeth's pregnancy (Luke 1:39–40). Thus, it is likely that Jesus and John had contact during their childhood and early adulthood. John would have been six months older than Jesus (Luke 1:36), so the two were probably friends (see Jesus' grief at John's death in Matt. 14:12–13).

John's message was like Elijah's. Both demanded change—repentance! **Repent, for the kingdom of heaven is near** (3:2). Jesus preached this same message when he began his public ministry after John's imprisonment (4:17). John fulfilled the role predicted by Isaiah to prepare Messiah's way (Isa. 40:3–5). John's message was very pointed. He confronted the false Jewish religious practices of his day. The Jews presumed they were God's children simply because they were descendants of Abraham. On the contrary, though the nation of Israel was indeed the recipient of the Abrahamic Covenant (and its subordinate Mosaic Covenant), the covenant people had abandoned the provisions of the covenant.

The condition of God's covenant people in Jesus' day was dismal. The priests who were supposed to represent the people to God were crooks! They were the wicked men that Isaiah (Isa. 28:1–29) had prophesied about. Completely out of touch with God and his covenant, they were a nation in need of repentance. The apostle Peter, who was close to Matthew, also acknowledged the nation's apostasy. Peter quoted Isaiah in describing Jesus' first coming to earth: "See, I lay a stone in Zion, a chosen and precious cornerstone, and the one who trusts in him will never be put to shame" (1 Pet. 2:6). The apostle Paul, in describing Israel's rejection of Jesus' ministry (Rom. 9:32–33), noted that the Jewish people "stumbled" over this same cornerstone. This was another reference to Isaiah's messianic prophecy: "And he will be a sanctuary; but for . . . Israel he will be a stone that causes men to stumble and . . . make them fall" (Isa. 8:14).

The nation could not walk with God if they were out of fellowship with him. They needed to change. That was precisely the message of the Old Testament prophet Amos: "Do two walk together unless they have agreed to do so?" (Amos 3:3). When John the Baptizer was speaking out, God and the nation of Israel were moving in two different directions. The "kingdom of heaven was at hand," the king was on the scene, but the people would have to change their direction (repent!) if the kingdom was to be realized.

Unfortunately, they had become so worldly they were spiritually blind. In fact, as John the apostle reported in his Gospel, Jesus "came to that which was his own [people], but his own did not receive him. Yet to all who received him, to those wo believed in his name, he gave the right to become children of God . . . born not of natural descent, nor of human decision or a husband's will, but born of God" (John 1:11–13).

It is precisely this question—How could the Jewish people reject their own Messiah-King?—that Matthew's Gospel answers. The covenant with Israel is not forgotten, but, as we shall see in the course of Matthew's Gospel, it will not be fulfilled in this first-century generation. A later generation of Jews (cf. Rom. 11:25–27) will respond to Jesus, and the unconditional covenant promise to Abraham and his seed will be fulfilled. But Matthew's Gospel will explain how the Jews of the first century missed it.

"Repent" was the first word of the ministry of both John and Jesus. If the kingdom of heaven was to be realized, some changes would have to be made. The people of Israel had been thinking wrongly about God, themselves, their sin, their righteousness, and the nature of the kingdom.

The word "repent" (*metanoeo*) literally means "to change the mind." However, a change of mind is suspect if it does not result in a change of behavior, as John made clear to the hypocrites in 3:8. This same principle is echoed in James 2:14–26. Just as "faith" without works is not faith at all, so "repentance" without its fruit is not authentic. Repentance in Scripture refers to a decision to turn from one's sins because of an inward "mind-change" which involves how we look at God as well as how we look at sin.

John the Baptizer was not so much calling individuals to eternal salvation as he was calling the nation to turn from its sins and back to God so the kingdom might come to Israel. The Bible insists that the Messiah-King will not set up his kingdom "on earth as it is in heaven" until the nation of Israel has come to faith in Messiah and turned from their sinful ways. The day will come when Israel will do both, but that will be during the "day of Jacob's trouble" (the Tribulation) yet to come. That great day of biblical covenant fulfillment will be followed by the Messiah-King's millennial kingdom on this earth.

The phrase **kingdom of heaven** (3:2) is found thirty-three times in Matthew. Matthew also uses the phrase "kingdom of God" a few times. Some scholars draw a distinction between the two phrases. However, practically speaking, "kingdom of heaven" is interchangeable with "kingdom of God" (also used in 12:28; 19:24; 21:31,43), as Jesus demonstrated in 19:23–24. Matthew preferred "kingdom of heaven," while the other Gospel writers preferred "kingdom of God." Matthew's preference reflects his writing for a Jewish audience. For centuries before Jesus' day, the Jewish superstition prohibiting the pronunciation of the name Yahweh had become firmly entrenched, to the point that even pronunciation of titles such as "God" were kept to a minimum. So "kingdom of heaven" is a euphemism in which heaven, the home of God, refers to God himself.

"Kingdom of heaven" is a comprehensive concept. Within this broad concept, we can see at least three distinct referents.

First, John the Baptizer referred to the kingdom of heaven as being "at hand" because of the earthly presence of its king, and because Jesus was about to present the kingdom to Israel and the world.

Second, following Israel's failure to repent and their opposition to him, Jesus in Matthew 13 revealed the kingdom as a reality perceived by some people but hidden from others. The kingdom, in this sense, exists between the first and second comings of its king. During this current "Christian era" (A.D./C.E.) prior to Christ's second coming, the kingdom is represented as the rule of God in the hearts of believers while the king is absent. This kingdom form (church) is a mystery in the sense that prior to Jesus' day it had not been revealed to the Old Testament prophets (Matt. 13:11). Before Jesus revealed these truths, they had been "hidden since the creation of the world" (Matt. 13:35).

Third, there is the kingdom in its comprehensive climax. Upon a day yet future—in fulfillment of Daniel's prophecies and innumerable other Old Testament prophetic passages which picture a grand and golden age of righteousness and peace on earth—the Son of David will reign over the entire world. Truly, that day will see his "kingdom come, [his] will be done on earth as it is in heaven" (6:10).

The Bible informs us (Rev. 20:3) that Christ's earthly kingdom reign will last a thousand years (a millennium). Certainly this earth has never yet experienced such peace and righteousness, and it never will until Christ sets foot on the earth as the Lion of Judah and ruling king.

3:3. The quote in 3:3 is from Isaiah 40:3. In Isaiah, this passage falls at the beginning of Isaiah's lengthy prophecy (chaps. 40–66) concerning the end-times restoration of Israel. In the Old Testament context, this message is one of comfort for those anticipating or experiencing the exile, assuring them that they would be restored to their land. But God went beyond the restoration of Israel to their land and foretold the complete scope of the end-times restoration of his kingdom throughout the world. This covers the time from the coming of his Son to die (Isa. 52–53) to the new heaven and the new earth (Isa. 66).

In Matthew, the verse is shown to apply to John the Baptizer as the person crying in the wilderness, preparing the way for the Lord. The Jewish reader, familiar with Isaiah, would understand Matthew to be saying, "All that Isaiah prophesied in Isaiah 40–66 is now available to you. If you choose to recognize your king, this is the beginning of the glorious end."

3:4. John's unusual clothing is intended to remind the reader of Elijah (2 Kgs. 1:8). As Elijah's ministry did, John addressed a spiritual crisis in Israel. Garments of hair were apparently a common type of garb for a prophet (Zech. 13:4). John is later identified more explicitly with Elijah in Matthew 11:14 and 17:12–13. In Malachi 4:5 we are told that Elijah will be the prophet sent "before that great and dreadful day of the LORD comes," that is, before Israel's tribulation and Daniel's seventieth week (Dan. 9:24–27). The Jews of Jesus' day were aware of the prophetic silence since Malachi (four hundred years), and the coming of John heralded the coming of God's voice out of silence. John was unconventional in his wardrobe and in his diet (cf. with Elijah in 1 Kgs. 17:1–6).

3:5. Notice that Matthew did not say, "Many people came out from Jerusalem." Rather, he said, **People went out to him from Jerusalem and all Judea and the whole region of the Jordan.** This is obviously hyperbole, but Matthew's point is that John was a major attraction. Some scholars argue that John's audience was in the six-figure range. When God chooses to move in a people, there is an enthusiasm or conviction that spreads through the hearts of many people. This can only be explained by the work of the Holy Spirit. Without a doubt, much of this sudden movement was motivated sincerely. However, we know by the presence of the Pharisees and Sadducees that there was some measure of hypocrisy in the crowd.

3:6. For centuries baptism had been one of the four steps necessary for a Gentile to become a Jew (the other three were sacrifice, circumcision, and memorization of portions of Moses' Law).

The word *baptize* means "to dip or to immerse." Ritual immersion for the purpose of converting proselytes and for other purposes was only one of many types of ritual washing in the centuries before Christ's advent. Nor was immersion or washing a ritual unique to the Jews. It was practiced in various forms in many cultures. The underlying theme behind ritual immersion was some kind of new identification.

The people of Israel were familiar with this change of identity because of the dyer's trade in the region. As a piece of cloth dipped into dye takes on the identifying color of the dye, so the immersion of new believers symbolized their taking on the identifying marks of Christ. When a Gentile was converted to the Jewish religion, from that point on he was identified no longer with the nationality of his birth, but with the Jewish nation. (Of course, the imagery of spiritual cleansing would also be a natural part of the significance of baptism in almost any setting.)

Just what did John's baptism mean? It signified a person's willingness to turn from his or her sins and from the false belief that being born a Jew automatically put a person in right relationship with God. John announced Israel was in spiritual crisis and about to be judged. When John came with the first prophetic message in four centuries, it was only natural that as people repented, they demonstrated the sincerity of their repentance by submitting to baptism, thus publicly identifying themselves with the faithful among God's people.

To *confess* (*homologeo*) is literally to "speak the same," meaning to acknowledge reality, or to agree with the truth (which means agreeing with God). A necessary part of the repentance process was to acknowledge before God what it was in one's life that needed to change ("repent" = "change the mind"). Confession required the penitent person to take his or her well-intentioned desire to do better, and focus it in on the specific sins that needed addressing in his or her life.

3:7. John noticed that **many** of the Pharisees (legalistic Jews) and the Sadducees (liberalized Jews) were coming out to the baptism. The presence of these hypocrites revealed that there were some among the crowds who were insincere in their participation. The NIV is probably accurate in translating this passage, **coming to where he was baptizing** (the phrase is literally, "coming to the baptism").

For the most part, these religious leaders were present only to observe (or possibly to confront John). John chose to confront the source of hypocrisy in Israel, in hopes that their true repentance might make them the leaders they should be, leading many others of Israel to true repentance. Or, possibly, John hoped that bystanders would take warning from his confrontation and be wary of the hypocritical leaders.

We may draw a practical lesson from John's example—he spoke the truth, even though it resulted in his arrest (4:12) and eventual death (14:1–12).

By addressing the religious hypocrites as **you brood of vipers** (see also Jesus' use of this insult in 12:34 and 23:33), John was warning others of their danger. Hypocrisy, especially among leadership, is not a victimless crime. The image of a poisonous snake connotes danger as well as stealth. The danger of the religious leaders was a subtle one that caught most people off guard. As to how specifically the hypocrites endangered their followers, see Jesus' confrontation in chapter 23.

3:8–10. John was not implying that the hypocrites had come to the baptism to show their own repentance. But he was confronting their consistent hypocrisy. They claimed one thing (to be repentant of the sins of which they acknowledged everyone to be guilty), but they lived another (continuance in sins of which they denied their guilt).

The religious leaders assumed they were "hereditarily holy"; that is, that their identification by blood with Abraham automatically brought them under the safety of God's covenant (3:8). John pointed out that mere Jewishness or nationality was not enough to make a person a true follower of God. In fact, he claimed that these hypocrites had no more in common with God's people than a rock does.

John continued to use the language of imminent judgment (**already** in 3:10). The **ax** of judgment was ready to cut them off. He was warning the hypocrites that the danger facing them was a very present danger, but that they were blind to it. John also returned to the imagery of fruit. He had already accused them of being fruitless, implying the insincerity of their repentance. He warned that their fruitlessness was an indication of their impending judgment (a judgment Jesus will discuss in 23:31–38 as well as chaps. 24–25).

3:10–12. In these verses, John used the imagery of fire as a means of judgment. The fruitless tree will be burned (3:10). The Messiah-King to come **will baptize you with the Holy Spirit and fire** (3:11). He will separate the wheat from the chaff, and he will burn up **the chaff with unquenchable fire** (3:12). Later in the New Testament we will see fire as a means of separating the eternal from the temporal (1 Cor. 3:12–15; 1 Pet. 1:6–7), thus testing the genuineness of such qualities as truth and faith. The fire here clearly refers to judgment.

3:11–12. The climax of John's powerful ministry was to point to Christ. With appropriate humility, John understood his place in the bigger picture. John's job was to serve as a marker, directing people's eyes past himself to the coming Messiah-King. John was indeed a great man (11:11–14), but he derived his greatness from the even greater One whom he served. To illustrate the contrast between himself and the Messiah, John thought of the lowest of all tasks (removal of another person's sandals), and then said he was even below that. He was voicing the impossibility of comparison between his humanity and the Messiah-King's deity.

Two elements of the Messiah's ministry are mentioned in 3:11–12, both in contrast with John's ministry of water baptism. The Messiah-King would baptize in two different elements (the Holy Spirit and fire). Fire is clearly associated with judgment and burning. The Holy Spirit is something else altogether. John stated that the king would identify (baptize) some people in the life of the Holy Spirit and others in the fire of judgment. For those who knew the Old Testament, this baptism in the Holy Spirit had to mean more than the temporary resting of the Holy Spirit's power on selected people of faith for a specific task of leadership (e.g., Judg. 14:6).

The concept of baptism in the Holy Spirit was much more than that. It had everything to do with God's promise of the new covenant age in Ezekiel 36:26–27, where God makes a promise of the permanent gift of his Spirit in the believer. John was referring to the coming identification of believers (the church) in the baptism and indwelling of the Spirit.

Second, the Messiah would baptize others in fire. The Messiah was coming as both a Savior and a judge. Anyone who overemphasized one of those two qualities at the expense of the other was seriously mistaken. The reason John emphasized the Messiah's role as judge in this passage was because those to whom he spoke had a warped view about this role that they needed to correct.

We conclude that baptizing in fire and the Holy Spirit are two separate and distinct baptisms. The baptism in the Spirit relates to the king's first coming, and the baptism in fire relates to his second coming. The baptism of the Spirit is mentioned only seven times in the Bible (four times in the Gospels as here, also in Acts 1:8; 11:16, 1 Cor. 12:13). Each reference views the baptism of the Spirit as a once-for-all historical corporate event, not an ongoing personal phenomenon for individual believers.

We now know that: (1) the baptism in the Holy Spirit was fulfilled at Pentecost after the king's ascension, and (2) that the baptism of fire, while foreshadowed in Israel's destruction in A.D. 70 with the leveling of Jerusalem by the Roman legions, will be ultimately fulfilled in final judgment at the king's second advent.

The **winnowing fork** (3:12) was used on a windy day to toss the trampled grain and chaff mixture into the air, allowing the wind to blow away the lighter chaff, and keeping the grain on the winnowing floor. The language of 3:12 indicates this is a thorough judgment that no one will be able to escape. The judge will make no mistakes in sorting the believer from the unbeliever.

Ⓑ The King's Baptism (3:13–17)

SUPPORTING IDEA: *God prepared Jesus' character through personal affirmation at his baptism.*

3:13–15. When we last saw Jesus at the end of Matthew 2, he was still a child, settling into the home of his upbringing in Nazareth. The placement of Jesus' name and the connecting word **then** immediately following John's description of the Messiah's ministry of judgment (and salvation) identifies Jesus as that very same Messiah, judge, and Savior. It also indicates that the messianic era characterized by judgment and salvation is now beginning, even as we watch Jesus walk up to John in the River Jordan.

To this point, Jesus has spent his nearly three decades of earthly life in quiet obscurity. Galilee was the backwater of Israel, so Matthew's choice of wording here implies a "coming out," and a readiness to begin public ministry.

The need for Jesus to be baptized, and thereby to serve as our representative and model, was not optional for him. It was important to the fulfillment of his mission on earth, in identifying with the "righteous remnant" of Israel. He said it was a necessary step in order **to fulfill all righteousness** (3:15). So Jesus' baptism was unique. It was not a "baptism of repentance" (as John's was) nor was it a "Christian baptism" (as ours is today). But it was an identifying step of obedience at the beginning of Jesus' public ministry. Jesus would not have been fully obedient if he had bypassed this step that seemed to John to be unnecessary for the Holy One (3:14).

3:16–17. When Jesus came up out of the water from being baptized by John, he received an immediate confirmation from his family. He saw the Spirit of God, and he heard his Father's approval. It was like having your family come and cheer for you at your graduation.

This scene is something like a family reunion—all three members of the Trinity manifesting their presence in such a way that bystanders could see or hear them. This was a testimony to human witnesses about the identity of Jesus, the Messiah. It serves as one of hundreds of exhibits in Matthew's Gospel for Jesus as the Messiah.

It was also a personal affirmation from the first and third members of the Trinity to the Son. This fact reminds us of the emotional-relational side of the Godhead, a side we often forget. Even God the Son enjoyed personal affirmation from his family. And certainly the people needed to hear from the Father (cf. John 11:42).

Twice in Matthew the Father speaks from heaven. In both cases he speaks in third person, addressing listeners other than Jesus (compare the second-person "you are" in Mark 1:11; Luke 3:22; and the third-person "this is" in Mark 9:7; Luke 9:35). The second instance is in Matthew 17, on the Mount of Transfiguration. The wording in this warm, fatherly statement is reminiscent of the threefold emphasis on Isaac's uniqueness and value to Abraham in Genesis 22:2. There has never been, nor will there ever be, a prouder father in all the universe than God the Father.

C The King's Testing (4:1–11)

SUPPORTING IDEA: *God tested Jesus' character through hardship and temptation in the wilderness.*

4:1. These verses describe the moral testing of the king. High moral character is essential to effective leadership. We perform much the same testing of people who present themselves for leadership positions. Unfortunately, our culture has lost its bearings in this regard. This is a foreshadowing of our ultimate fall and judgment if we do not repent. But Jesus' testing here is more of a powerful demonstration of his capacity than an "I-wonder-if-he will-pass" kind of test. God himself has recognized such testing as a necessary part of Messiah's ministry.

Jesus' preparation for ministry involved a combination of pleasant experiences (the affirmation at his baptism) and unpleasant experiences (his fasting and temptation). God uses the same pattern in our lives, and we should be surprised at neither great outward blessing nor great trials in our lives. Jesus faced forty days of direct confrontation with the archenemy whom his messianic ministry would destroy. Satan, the adversary, is always seeking to usurp God's place and oppose God's will.

One practical implication we may draw from this passage is that temptation itself is not a sin. Jesus was "tempted in every way, just as we are—yet was without sin" (Heb. 4:15; see also 2 Cor. 5:21). A misunderstanding of this defeats many people before they begin resisting temptation. A false (devilish) guilt grips them, and they begin to lose the battle before they begin to fight it. Jesus' temptation was a test not so much to see if he would fail (he could not!) but a "test" (much like the test drive of a new automobile) to demonstrate just how powerful the Son of God was, even in the face of the devil himself.

4:2. It is possible to fast forty days without food, but not without water, especially in an arid, hot climate like the Judean wilderness. The understatement about Jesus' hunger is intended to show that Jesus fought his battle with a serious handicap but still came out victorious.

4:3–4. Satan's words in Jesus' first temptation indicate that Jesus was indeed the Son of God, and Satan acknowledged the fact. This might be better translated, "Since you are the Son of God." See exactly the same wording used with sarcasm in 27:40. Satan was not questioning the fact of Jesus' sonship, but he was tempting him to misuse it.

In this first temptation Satan was tempting Jesus to rely on his own self-provision, rather than on the provision of God. Jesus often insisted he would do nothing of his own will. He came to do the Father's will only. This would have been a departure from the mission on which the Father had sent him. Jesus would have been exercising improper independence.

Satan's temptations follow the familiar pattern he used in Eden and which he has used ever since—the lust of the flesh, the lust of the eyes, and the pride of life (1 John 2:6). "Try this good food (flesh)." "It looks good (lust of the eyes)." "It will make you wise and in charge like God (pride of life)."

In a similar manner, Israel was tempted by their hunger in the desert to seek ways to provide for themselves. When they found they had no resources, they grumbled. God demonstrated their need to depend on him by providing manna. Even then they were tempted to take care of themselves by hoarding the food. But the extra manna was always spoiled the next day, so they were once again dependent on God's provision for that day. Through this concrete demonstration, God taught Israel to be dependent on him, in hopes that they would apply the same lesson concerning their dependence on God for truth, wisdom, and instruction.

Because of this parallel between Jesus and Israel, it is appropriate that Jesus quoted Moses' words from Deuteronomy 8:3. In the larger context of Deuteronomy 8, Moses was reminding Israel of their need to depend on God's provision. Jesus brought this truth to bear in his personal battle. Rather than launch out in independent self-provision, he entrusted his well-being to his Father. He refused to be improperly independent.

4:5–7. The **highest point** in Satan's second temptation refers to the high southeast corner of the temple platform that overlooked the great depth of the Kidron Valley. This was a temptation to be "showy," to do miraculous works to draw attention.

Again Satan used a conditional statement, **If you are the Son of God** (see 4:3). Again, he was not challenging Jesus' sonship, but he was using it as a basis to argue to a false conclusion—that it is appropriate to "force" God into supernatural demonstrations of his faithfulness to intervene for our good. In this temptation Jesus was tempted to exercise improper dependence to "force" divine intervention. That is sin.

Satan, in quoting Psalm 91:11–12, misused Scripture in his attempt to deceive and mislead. It was a subtle challenge to Jesus to prove his deity.

In response to Satan's second challenge, Jesus took the matter back to Scripture and quoted Moses from Deuteronomy 6:16, which prohibited testing God in this way. Jesus refused improper dependence.

4:8–10. The third temptation may have been the most appealing of the three to Jesus, not because of the anticipation of ruling the earth—that was already part of God's plan—but because Satan's offer would allow him to rule the earth without going through the sacrifice of the cross. God the Father had a plan for the certainty of the restored kingdom and great glory for Jesus. Satan offered an "even better" plan (both deceptive and impossible)—a kingdom and all its glory, minus the suffering. Satan tempted Jesus to believe that someone else could provide for him in a better way than God could. That is always the satanic appeal, whether it involves work, power, money, success, or some personal interest.

Again Jesus reached into Scripture, interpreted it accurately, and sent Satan on his way. We see a personal lesson here. The Bible is our *only* authority for right living. Old Testament Israel had bought the lie that God had competition. Jesus did not. He would be mastered by nothing and no one except the true God.

4:11. Satan's departure from Jesus followed the king's authoritative command, **Away from me, Satan!** (4:10). It is ironic that Satan had just offered to be the benevolent master to Jesus, but Jesus' authoritative response and Satan's cowering obedience demonstrated who was the real Master.

Thus the battle has begun. The rest of Matthew demonstrates its further development. Never again in this book do we see Satan openly engaging the king in warfare. But he has not gone away. From time to time Satan will try to turn Christ from the Father's will and the route to the cross. But we will also see the wisdom and moral courage of the king as he dodges every blow, even taking the offensive at times, and ultimately finishing with the decisive victory.

D The King's Early Ministry (4:12–25)

SUPPORTING IDEA: *God prepared the foundations of Jesus' ministry with the right message, the right men, and the right methods.*

4:12. John had publicly challenged Herod the tetrarch's adultery and was jailed for it. The atmosphere in Jerusalem became increasingly hostile to the prophetic message of repentance, and Jesus moved north to the countryside of Galilee.

There is both a continuity and a discontinuity between the ministries of John and Jesus. Matthew portrayed Jesus as picking up the baton from John when John was imprisoned (see 14:1–12 for more on John's imprisonment and death), preaching exactly the same message of repentance (4:17; cf. 3:2). But there is also a clear distinction between the ministries of John and Jesus. John himself described this distinction (3:11–12). And Matthew brings to bear the testimony of Isaiah in 4:15–16 to describe the beginning of a new era. Jesus moved into Galilee in fulfillment of a centuries-old prophecy (Isa. 9), which prophesied that the northern country so trampled by pagan armies and living in gloomy, depressed darkness, will now enjoy the messianic light!

4:12–13. Galilee was the region of Jesus' early ministry, contrasting significantly with the locations of his later ministry. The geographical flow of Jesus' ministry as portrayed in Matthew is very distinctly north-to-south, from Galilee to Jerusalem. Beginning with 4:12, and extending through chapter 18, Jesus' ministry takes place in the region around the Sea of Galilee, with two late ventures even farther north into the Gentile territory of Tyre and Sidon (15:21–28) and Caesarea Philippi (16:13–20.).

Beginning with chapter 19, Jesus moved resolutely south toward Jerusalem and his appointment with the cross. In the north, far from the center of religious power (John 4:1), the "little people" would hear and respond more readily to the Messiah. Zebulun and Naphtali were the two tribes whose territory was bordered by the Sea of Galilee—Zebulun to the south (including Nazareth), and Naphtali to the north (including Capernaum). Capernaum was the home of several of Jesus' disciples.

4:14–16. The quote is from Isaiah 9:1–2. Jesus' ministry in the north was anticipated by the prophet Isaiah, whom Matthew quoted here to stifle any criticism that Jesus was an uncivilized Galilean. Isaiah 9 is part of a larger prophetic statement concerning the coming of the Messiah. Matthew has already quoted from this portion. In the latter portion of Isaiah 8, Isaiah emphasized the Lord's judgment on errant Israel: "Then they will look toward the earth and see only distress and darkness and fearful gloom, and they will be thrust into utter darkness" (8:22). Israel was in trouble.

The first word of Isaiah 9 is "nevertheless," introducing the contrasting light and hope brought to Israel by the Messiah. The portion quoted by Matthew is a carefully selected segment of the larger message of hope for Israel. Any Jew familiar with his Bible would have recognized Matthew's quote and would have made the connection to the remaining, unquoted portions (Isa. 9:3–7). Among the promises made here are the renewed covenant blessing on Israel; the removal of the oppressor's yoke; the birth of the promised child, whose name will be called "Wonderful Counselor, Mighty God, Eternal Father, Prince of Peace"; and his reign on David's throne in justice and righteousness. There was no doubt who this Jesus is. Matthew clearly identified Jesus' move to Capernaum as the "official" beginning of his public ministry and as the fulfillment of Isaiah's prophecy.

"Galilee of the Gentiles" was a common designation for this region. It was Galilee, bordering on the Gentile nations, where the "light" shone. Although it is clear that Jesus' earthly ministry would be mainly to the Jews, Matthew went to great lengths to show the long-term implications of Jesus' coming for all nations. In Matthew 4:1–11, Jesus was portrayed as the faithful Son, paralleling Israel as the unfaithful son. It is clear from the Old Testament (e.g., Gen. 12:3) that Israel's purpose was to minister to all nations. They had failed, but the faithful Son would succeed.

4:17. Some scholars believe that the phrase **From that time** and an identical phrase in 16:21 provide the fundamental structure of Matthew, dividing the book into three portions. While this seems overstated, these key verses do indicate critical turning points in the ministry of Jesus, particularly regarding the themes of his preaching and teaching. The theme **Repent, for the kingdom of heaven is near** (4:17) underlies virtually everything Jesus taught in 4:17–16:20. The king made a legitimate offer of the long-promised kingdom to the long-promised people—Israel. By contrast, from 16:21 on, Jesus' teaching dealt predominantly with the preparation of his disciples for his coming death, resurrection, and ascension.

Jesus' preaching ministry here is one message: **Repent, for the kingdom of heaven is near** (4:17; cf. 3:2). This quotation, reflecting the essence of Jesus' message—"turn from your sins; the long-promised king is in your midst"—is identical to that of John the Baptizer in 3:2. The kingdom is at hand because its king is, and the potential for its full realization is near.

4:18–22. Peter, Andrew, James, and John were fishermen (all involved in a family business) living in Capernaum or nearby Bethsaida (see John 1:44). This was apparently also the home of Matthew at the time of his calling (9:1,9), and of Philip and possibly Nathanael (John 1:43–45). The fishing profession in that day probably carried with it the same kind of social stigma that "common laborer" does today. Three of the four (Peter, James, and John) would become Jesus' closest earthly friends. And Andrew played a significant role in his ministry more than once (Mark 13:3; John 1:40; 6:8; 12:22).

Matthew left his readers with the impression that this was Jesus' first encounter with these four men. However, John recorded that some of the Twelve (at least Andrew, Peter, Philip, and Nathanael) had been with Jesus during his earlier ministry (John 1:35–51; 2:2,12,17; 3:22; 4:1–2,27–33). Jesus had known his disciples for some time and had even seen them in ministry situations. Thus, their decision to follow him was not hastily made.

However, this does not decrease the significance of their commitment. In fact, quite the opposite. These men, in well-reasoned decisions, left both career and family to follow Jesus. And their confidence in him was such that, when he called, they all came **at once** (4:20) or **immediately** (4:22). They literally dropped their nets and left the boats in which they were standing. James and John left their father standing with his boats.

When Jesus said, **Come, follow me** (4:19), he was calling these men to a new career. In keeping with his skill as a teacher, he used terminology that would inspire them because of its relationship to their life experience. These men knew how to fish—for fish. So they had some concept of the task to which he was calling them. However, even though they had some familiarity with the concept of fishing, Jesus would still need to transform them into **fishers of men**. And that is the point of most of the teaching that follows, including the Sermon on the Mount—*Jesus taught his disciples!* He trained the Twelve whose names would one day mark the foundation "stones" (Matt. 16:18; Eph. 2:20; Rev. 21:14) of the New Jerusalem!

You will notice as Matthew's Gospel unfolds that, while Jesus did not ignore the crowds, he was primarily engaged in teaching the Twelve. Even when he ministered to the thousands, it was in the context of teaching the Twelve. For example, the feeding of the five thousand, while compassionately providing food for thousands, was about his attempt to impact the Twelve (Mark 6:30–44). (See discussion at Matthew 5:1–2.)

The one condition necessary to their becoming fishers of men was to **follow me**. Packed into this two-word command are many implications. Jesus was saying, "Live with me and learn by watching me. Own my values and priorities. Learn to become passionate for the things I live for. And follow my example by doing the ministry I have come to do."

4:23. A slight shift takes place, as Jesus took his new disciples and showed that following him meant serving the needs of others. Galilee was small but it had over two hundred villages, each with hundreds, or perhaps thousands, of people. This preaching tour **throughout Galilee** probably lasted several months.

We may summarize Jesus' ministry with three words: teaching, proclaiming or preaching, and healing. These words help us understand Jesus' threefold approach to ministry in Matthew's Gospel. He was always teaching the Twelve, often proclaiming to the people, and performing miraculous healing as a teaching and proclaiming tactic.

While there is much overlap between preaching and teaching, there is also a distinction. Preaching is the banner flying atop the castle (seen far and wide), and teaching is the body of bricks and mortar that supports it (sought out by the followers). Teaching fills out the proclamation, explaining both its support and its implications.

Furthermore, Jesus' healing ministry was subordinate to his preaching and teaching ministries. Throughout the Bible, the purpose of miracles is primarily to attest to the authority of the messenger and his message. The benefit to the person healed is secondary. Jesus' miracles validated his claim to be the Messiah, and they validated the message he preached.

Throughout the four Gospels, Jesus is shown frequenting the synagogues as a routine part of his teaching ministry (Matt. 4:23; 9:35; 12:9; 13:54). He used the platform available in Jewish culture to teach the true meaning of God's Word. Because of the respect he enjoyed among the people (even Jewish leaders referred to him as "Rabbi"), he often was given the place of the teacher.

The word *synagogue* is derived from a combination of words meaning "to lead together," and it literally means "meeting place." The synagogue's origin is a bit sketchy, but it was probably begun during the Exile several centuries before Christ. It became a central institution in Jewish society during the period between the close of the Old Testament and the beginning of the New Testament.

Jesus' activity was ceaseless as he went from one village and synagogue to the next, conducting his primary ministry of preaching. The phrase **the good news of the kingdom** is interchangeable with several other phrases used throughout the four Gospels (e.g., "the gospel," "the gospel of Christ," "the gospel of God"). In keeping with his emphasis on the kingdom and the king, Matthew used this terminology. Jesus' message is *good news* because it focuses on the forgiveness and restoration of God as opposed to the "bad news" or impossibility of "law-keeping."

4:23–24. Verse 23 tells us that Jesus went throughout Galilee **healing every disease and sickness among the people.** There was no illness too difficult for Jesus to heal. The list in 4:24 illustrates the breadth of Jesus' healing ministry. He healed "lesser" or trivial diseases, but he also faced off with the incurables. None were beyond his healing touch. His miracles were verifiable, not vague. The king's sovereignty was complete. Jesus' healing ministry was moving toward its climax in Matthew 8:17 where Isaiah 53:4 is quoted, indicating the Messiah-King's healing is only an outward symbol of the inner healing based on forgiveness of sins.

4:25. The people heard the king's message. They came not only from Galilee, but also from Jerusalem to the south and the Decapolis to the east. While we are unsure of precisely what **Syria** means in 4:24, any territory it might cover is likely included in the list of regions in 4:25. Matthew's point is that Jesus' teaching and miracles were so amazing that word spread fast and far. People came from hundreds of miles around to see him. In particular, the mention of **Galilee** and **the region across the Jordan** remind the reader of Isaiah's prophecy (Isa. 9:1) quoted in Matthew 4:15. Although the multitudes came, the king kept leaving them to spend quality time with his disciples.

MAIN IDEA REVIEW: *God exercised great care in preparing Jesus' way, Jesus' character, and the foundations of Jesus' ministry.*

III. CONCLUSION

Jesus took responsibility for making his disciples "fishers of men." He did not say, "Follow me, and make yourselves fishers of men." This is instructive to us in our witness today. Jesus promises to superintend the process of our growth into full-fledged fishers of men. But we have to take a small, yet significant, risk in order to initiate the process. We have to love and speak to unbelievers. We have to tell the Good News to others. As we tell the Good News, we must look to Jesus as our model for significant ministry. We should expect God to use both pleasant (affirming) experiences and unpleasant (stretching) experiences to prepare us for ministry. We must combat temptation by memorizing God's Word and by relying on God's total sufficiency. Our words and our deeds must be consistent to impact the lives of others.

PRINCIPLES

- Unnecessarily offending others is often a sign of callousness or carelessness.
- When God chooses to move in a people, there is an enthusiasm or conviction that spreads through the hearts of many persons. This can only be explained by the work of the Holy Spirit.
- Speaking truth is always right but seldom easy.
- There is no such thing as hereditary righteousness.
- Jesus identifies with sinful human beings.
- Jesus was tempted in every way that we are tempted, yet without sin.
- Jesus called and trained others to join him in kingdom work.
- Jesus has power over sickness and demons.

APPLICATIONS

- Be sensitive to how others will hear your words, and careful not to compromise your faith with your speech.
- Resolve to be truthful in both word and deed, in spite of circumstances and pressures to compromise.
- Trust God's righteousness that he offers in Christ and not your religious heritage.
- When tempted, trust Jesus who has been tempted in that way and stands ready to help you be victorious over your temptation.

IV. LIFE APPLICATION

No Substitute for Preparation

The scene was Yosemite National Park. The hiker was a midwesterner from Chicago. His backpack was light, he wore excellent hiking boots, and he carried a full canteen of water. His goal was the summit of Half Dome. He was game for the eight-and-a-half mile hike up Mist Trail, past Vernal Falls, Nevada Falls, and the steep, final ascent to the Half Dome summit.

The hike started with an effortless pace in the valley floor, but soon became a steep and arduous climb. Then, after several miles into the hike, things started to go wrong. Because of the summer heat, the water supply was taking a hit. The air was becoming rarefied, forcing a slower pace. Each step became a chore and was accompanied by muscle cramps in both legs. A sign appeared ahead on the trail: "Half Dome - 2 mi." The hiker looked up through the pine treetops and could see the Dome summit and what appeared to be specks moving up the mountainside. These "specks" were other hikers using a cable system that aided their climb up the final 900-foot granite face to the summit. Two more miles? No way. It was evident that this hiker's legs were spent. It was inevitable that this hiker would need to abort the hike and return to the valley floor. He had not properly prepared his body for the task.

This story does have a happy ending. After several months of exercise and conditioning, the Chicago hiker returned to Yosemite. After a couple of days of higher-elevation camping for acclimation, the man successfully made it to the summit of Half Dome. Hard work and preparation had paid off.

Never underestimate the value of preparation. We see God's method of preparing men and women for service throughout Scripture. Moses spent many years of character-building in the desert before God called him to lead his people out of Egypt. Daniel and Joseph similarly spent long periods of time in preparation for their God-given missions. Our ultimate example is Jesus, who invested the first thirty years of his life in preparation for three years of effective ministry. God is always more interested in development of the person into the image of Christ.

God prepares us for what he has prepared for us. Always submit to his leading and timing.

V. PRAYER

Dear Father, thank you for sending John the Baptizer as the forerunner for your Son. Make me a forerunner in the lives of others to help prepare their hearts for receiving Jesus Christ as their Lord and Savior. Amen.

VI. DEEPER DISCOVERIES

A. The Kingdom

The kingdom is a key concept throughout Matthew. Simply put, the kingdom means "God's reign." In his model prayer (6:9–13), Jesus indicated that God's reign is complete in heaven, but that it is not yet complete on earth. The prophets foretold a time when everything and everyone on earth would submit to the will of God. To date, this has not happened. This world's present mess is Satan's doing. Christ is allowing this testing to prepare his followers for the ultimate realization of the kingdom and to share in his reign. Speaking to Christians, he states it bluntly in Revelation 3:21: "He who overcomes, I will give him the right to sit with me on my throne, just as I over-came and sat down with my Father on his throne."

God chose to allow this current period of time during which the archen-emy of Jesus Christ, Satan, is the energizing force behind our current world system. Opposition to Christ is the result of people falling victim to Satan's dark schemes (John 8:44). First John refers to the fact that this "whole world is under the control of the evil one" (5:19). Human beings have been allowed the freedom to demonstrate what happens when the world goes its own way. The results of this experiment in rebellion have been disastrous, and we live with them today.

The larger reality is that God's reign over earth has always been absolute. Nothing happens that he in his sovereignty does not allow. But with the first coming (advent) of Jesus, another dimension of God's kingdom began on earth. This was the development of God's sovereign reign in and through his believing people, the church. To some people who expected the ultimate manifestation of God's reign on earth when Christ came the first time, this manifestation was a disappointment. Jesus confronted this misconception in Luke 17:21: "Because the kingdom of God is within you."

Before Jesus was born, died, and rose from the dead, this less visible king-dom manifestation was not possible, because there was not yet the means for God to enter and abide in the individual human. With the ratification of the new covenant through the blood of Jesus, the human heart was made a cleansed dwelling place for God, and he was able to sit enthroned in the human heart. The external law that people had been attempting to fulfill in the flesh was written on the hearts of all who believed, so that God's reign was brought to bear from within the individual, rather than from without (Jer. 31:33; Ezek. 36:26–27). But the best is yet to come.

The full reality of the message of John and Jesus, "The kingdom of heaven is near," does not stop with this inward manifestation. They were warning people that the ultimate manifestation of God's kingdom was com-ing with all certainty. We know now that the final advent of the kingdom is at least two thousand years removed from their warning, but its certainty makes the time span inconsequential. God does reign and he will reign, and there can be no doubt that every knee will bow and every tongue will confess the lordship of Jesus.

This current age serves as a time of preparation for a large army of God's soldiers who will reign with Christ (Rev. 19:7–16; 20:4–6). Therefore, this current, less-than-final manifestation of God's kingdom through Christ and his body of believers is far from a disappointment. It is the Christian's salva-tion and reward—the reason we will be allowed to be a part of reigning with him when his kingdom comes on earth as it is in heaven. In one sense, the kingdom is here already; and in another sense, it is not yet here.

B. Why Did Jesus Need to Be Baptized (3:13–15)?

Baptism is a rite of identification for us. It was also a step of identification for Jesus, but Jesus' baptism was not a Christian baptism *per se*. Jesus served in two roles during his earthly ministry.

First, he served as a representative for humanity. This was why he had to be fully human, so he could stand before God as one of us. He served as our representative when he took the full weight of God's wrath on the cross on our behalf, and he still serves as our representative today, interceding on our behalf at the Father's right hand (Rom. 8:34; Heb. 7:25). By submitting to baptism, Jesus expressed his identification with the family of the faithful, thus further validating his role as our representative.

Second, Jesus served as a model for believers. He did not expect his followers to do anything he had not already done himself, including submission to the rite of baptism. By so doing, he clarified the definition of a leader—one who leads not merely by instructing others, but by going before them as an obedient example. Such leadership requires deep, authentic humility. The leaders of God's people and the leaders of believing families would do well to heed this lesson about leadership. Jesus is identified with the "faithful remnant" who are coming out of religiously hypocritical Israel and into the righteousness of repentance as preached by both John the Baptizer and Jesus.

C. The Devil

While three different Greek words are used of the devil in Matthew 4, four times (4:1,5,8,11) he is called *diabolos,* meaning "slanderer, false accuser." This title reveals that Satan's goal in a person's life is not simply to make that person do evil, but to tempt the individual in order to accuse the person before the judge. He is more concerned with how God sees us than with what we actually do. If he can bring even an unsubstantiated charge against us (slander us) to achieve that end, he will do so.

D. Jesus' Pattern of Response to Temptation

One of the most obvious lessons from this passage is the example Jesus sets for us in response to temptation. Long before Jesus fought this battle, he spent years preparing for it by studying and memorizing God's Word. If he, being the God-Man, had to spend three decades in preparation, why should we expect to win our battles with temptation without any effort? Satan uses this world system to approach us through our sin nature (capacity for sin) to do his will. At any moment, as believers, we are either following the will of Satan or the will of the Spirit of God. There is no in-between. Notice how Peter pinpointed this in Acts 5:1–11.

It is what we absorb and apply during the uneventful periods of our lives that strengthens and equips us for spiritual warfare. Jesus, even though he was the author of Scripture, fell back on Scripture to answer Satan's attacks. He modeled for us how to use the authority of written Scripture rather than our own cleverness to combat temptation.

E. Summary

Matthew 1–4 serve as a unit to set the stage for the body of Matthew's work, which begins with chapter 5. In chapter 3, John the Baptizer prepared the hearts of Israel for the king. He also brought to the forefront the conflict with the hypocritical religious leaders that would continue throughout Matthew's Gospel. The baptism of Jesus is important in order for the reader to see Jesus' identification with us throughout the rest of the book. Jesus' baptism is also the setting for the Father's public affirmation of his Son before launching him into further testing and his public ministry.

In chapter 4, Jesus' testing provides a model for us to follow in resisting temptation. It is also a glimpse of the true battle that will be waged throughout Matthew's book. And it portrays the Jesus of Matthew as the faithful Son of God (contrasted with unfaithful Israel) who will now fulfill the twofold plan (redeem and reclaim) that Israel failed to implement.

We see that the launching of Jesus' public ministry in Capernaum is the fulfillment of Isaiah's prophecy about the Messiah (4:12–16). We learn the underlying theme of Jesus' teaching and ministry through the events of chapter 16 (4:17). We catch a glimpse of the relationship of authority and faith between Jesus and his disciples (4:18–22) And we see, in summary form (4:23–25), the ministry context in which the words and works of Jesus throughout the rest of the book are to be understood.

VII. TEACHING OUTLINE

A. INTRODUCTION

1. Lead Story: Announcing: A New Son Is Born

2. Context: The birth of Jesus Christ was no ordinary event. This was God's Son. To cap off the entire process, God arranged for a herald known as John the Baptizer to prepare the way and announce the arrival of Jesus. John's message was contained in a single word: *Repent!* This was an appropriate response to the birth of a king.

3. Transition: How natural it is to announce the arrival of someone important who will have a lasting impact. That is what Matthew is doing in these two chapters—announcing that a king has been born who will have an eternal impact on the entire world.

B. COMMENTARY

1. The King's Forerunner (3:1–12)
2. The King's Baptism (3:13–17)
3. The King's Testing (4:1–11)
4. The King's Early Ministry (4:12–25)

C. CONCLUSION

Just as Jesus was announced, ratified, and reaffirmed by others in that day, so we need to be a people today who announce, ratify, and reaffirm that Jesus is our Savior and Lord.

VIII. ISSUES FOR DISCUSSION

1. In what sense was John the Baptizer like the prophet Elijah?
2. What does it mean to repent? How do you know that a person has repented?
3. Why did Jesus consent to be baptized at the hands of John the Baptizer?
4. What does Jesus' resistance of Satan's temptation tell us about how we can overcome temptation?

Matthew 5

The King Speaks His Heart (Part I)

I. INTRODUCTION

Repentance Is Good for You—You Have to Change the Heart Attitude

II. COMMENTARY

A verse-by-verse explanation of the chapter.

III. CONCLUSION

An overview of the principles and applications from the chapter.

IV. LIFE APPLICATION

Seasoning for a Tasteless World

Melding the chapter to life.

V. PRAYER

Tying the chapter to life with God.

VI. DEEPER DISCOVERIES

Historical, geographical, and grammatical enrichment of the commentary.

VII. TEACHING OUTLINE

Suggested step-by-step group study of the chapter.

VIII. ISSUES FOR DISCUSSION

Zeroing the chapter in on daily life.

Quote

" *I* don't believe that the big men, the politicians and the capitalists alone are guilty of the war. Oh, no, the little man is just as keen, otherwise the people of the world would have risen in revolt long ago! There is an urge and rage in people to destroy, to kill, to murder, and until all mankind, without exception, undergoes a great change, wars will be waged, everything that has been built up, cultivated and grown, will be destroyed and disfigured, after which mankind will have to begin all over again."

Anne Frank

Matthew 5

I N   A   N U T S H E L L

*T*he first of Jesus' five discourses in Matthew, the Sermon on the Mount was a discourse on kingdom living. This sermon described the kind of righteousness he expected of his followers. This righteousness surpasses' the legalistic religion of the Pharisees and must be lived so as to impact the world.

The King Speaks His Heart (Part I)

I. INTRODUCTION

Repentance Is Good for You—You Have to Change the Heart Attitude.

We have all experienced life's "wake up calls." I can recall several powerful ones in my own life. And each has resulted in a significant change of heart and direction.

I am a fairly typical guy. I am task-oriented, goal-focused, and mission-driven. Like most men, generally speaking, I am not always as alert to the relational nuances involved. I tend to focus on "getting the job done" as opposed to wondering how everyone is feeling about it. Sometimes that is okay, but in a marriage it can be trouble.

About fifteen years after our wedding, I found out just how much trouble. In the early years of our marriage I had been focused on any number of "tasks"—finishing college, working hard in the military, completing seminary, founding a church—all good things. But each was a potentially significant distraction from our home and family life.

On the day in question, I was charging along focused on the task at hand (a tennis match, of all things; with my wife, of all persons!) when the proverbial two-by-four hit me. My normally gentle-spirited wife had had enough "task orientation." I saw it in her eyes. For the first time in all our years together, I saw anger there—deep, hot anger. I could not just shrug it off.

It became clear that some changes were needed in our relationship. I began to realize that I had been taking our relationship for granted. I had been treating her more like a trophy (conquered and on the shelf) than a companion. More like a contractual partner than an intimate friend.

I needed to repent. My attitude needed to change. My heart needed to change. My behavior needed to change. And my schedule needed to change.

I repented. I acknowledged that I had been walking down the wrong path. I turned around and began to work hard at our relationship. When that happened, Linda and I began to rediscover each other.

Here is the principle we must all understand and use: *personal heart change is a necessary first step toward personal life change.* That principle is at the core of Jesus' teaching. It provides the centerpiece of his well-known Sermon on the Mount. Matthew is telling his readers that Israel (and all mankind) needs to change its heart attitude toward self and God or there will be no hope.

II. COMMENTARY

The King Speaks His Heart (Part I)

MAIN IDEA: *The righteousness of Jesus' followers must impact the world because it surpasses mere "religiosity."*

A The Heart of a Kingdom Citizen (5:1–12)

SUPPORTING IDEA: *The righteousness of Jesus' followers will be rewarded in this life and in the next.*

5:1–2. Matthew is setting the stage for the first of five significant sermons (or discourses) by Jesus in his account. Matthew's purpose is to present Jesus as the long-awaited king. Because the coming kingdom is so central to the book, he inserts the Sermon on the Mount up front. This is the king's manifesto—his statement of the kingdom's moral principles. These are the guiding principles of the king's teaching, truths that he repeated many times. And they form the message which Israel's leaders reject in Matthew 8–12 which, in turn, leads to Jesus' second major discourse in Matthew 13 on the mysteries of the kingdom and the age between the king's two advents.

It is important to note the audience. When Jesus saw **the crowds**, he slipped away from them to the mountain. But **his disciples came to him** away from the multitudes, and Jesus sat down to speak directly to his own. This is an oft-repeated pattern (see 10:1; 11:1; 13:10). Sometimes it is very deliberate and direct (8:18). Apparently during this discourse others found them, joined the crowd (cf. 7:28) and listened in, but Jesus' intention was to sit down, much as Moses did in the interpretation of the Law in Deuteronomy, to instruct his disciples.

A. B. Bruce was right on target in his classic *The Training of the Twelve.* Matthew's entire gospel is discipleship training. The crowds were there, tagging along, but Christ was always training "the Twelve," who were marked for leadership in the kingdom (cf. Matt. 19:28; Rev. 21:14).

Throughout the Gospels, there were at least three different concentric circles of followers with Jesus, and he dealt with each of them differently.

First, and most centrally, there were the Twelve, sometimes referred to simply as the **disciples**. The term is a translation of the Greek verb meaning, "to learn" and to do so particularly by actual experience and *doing*. It is instructive to read through the Gospels assuming that almost everything Jesus did and said was for the purpose of training his twelve disciples. This assumption sheds new light on many of his otherwise puzzling statements and actions.

Jesus was wise in knowing that one man (even the God-Man) was limited in the number of lives he could directly influence. Modern sociological experts say that a person is limited to twelve truly significant relationships at a time, and only a maximum of three of these at most can go to the deepest levels of intimacy. (Note Jesus' even closer circle of three: Peter, James, and John.

Jesus maximized the potential of his human nature by carefully choosing twelve men who would not in themselves be dead-end products, but who would learn from his teaching and example and then reproduce themselves in others (2 Tim. 2:2).

Robert Coleman expands on this theme in his classic *The Master Plan of Evangelism*. It was the Twelve that Jesus trained and sent out to do his ministry in chapter 10. It was the Twelve to whom Jesus privately explained his parables (e.g., 13:10–23). And from the turning point of 16:21 on, Jesus' ministry focused even more exclusively on the Twelve, preparing them for his impending suffering and victory.

The second circle outwardly was also sometimes called "disciples" and included those who were serious followers of Jesus, but who were not among the Twelve. These likely numbered in the hundreds and may be part of the circle of followers mentioned in 5:1. We see clear glimpses of this circle in Acts 1:15, where 120 people hid in the upper room, expecting persecution because of their commitment to Christ. There were also the women who constantly ministered to the physical needs of Jesus and his disciples. However, even these followers had their limits and probably did not pass all the tests Jesus subjected them to (see John 6:66).

And third came **the crowds**. These comprised a cross section of all levels of faith and disbelief. These people kept their distance emotionally, either because they were genuinely curious but cautious, or because they were critical and simply watching for an opportunity to ambush Jesus. Sometimes Jesus addressed the multitudes (e.g., Matt. 23), and sometimes he huddled with his more committed followers (e.g., Matt. 5:1), where the multitudes would gradually collect (7:28). Primarily, Jesus' teaching focused on those who were serious about the kingdom.

5:3–12. This first section, the introduction of Jesus' message, is typically called the Beatitudes. It amounts to a description of the character of those who are in the kingdom, servants of the king. Jesus always starts with the heart. These verses are progressive, following logically one after another, and they form something of an outline for the sermon in Matthew 5–7. Verses 3–5 deal with the individual's heart personally, as does Matthew 5:13–20. Verse 6 deals with our genuine relationship with the Lord, as does

Matthew 6. And verses 7–12 deal with our relationships with others—how we may impact them, and how they might relate to us—as does Matthew 7.

Treating the internal character of the kingdom servant, these Beatitudes are not separate, little statements intended to be hung on wall plaques in our homes. They are so much more than cute, memorable phrases. They are rock solid truths for living. While each Beatitude stands on its own, each is linked progressively to the one following it. Like pearls in a necklace they are strung together; each builds on the previous one.

The Greek term for "blessed, happy" was not nearly as difficult to understand for Jesus' audience and Matthew's readers as it is for us. Matthew's Jewish listeners and readers were familiar with the term.

Our modern idea of "happiness" is a diluted version of the joy implied by the term Jesus used. Our idea of happiness is a dependence on circumstances. Instead, God's happiness or joy is dependent on the assurance of God's blessing (sometimes present, often future), not on current circumstances, and it abides deep and undisturbable within the believer.

The Beatitudes use terminology and concepts that draw from the Old Testament, usually reminding the listeners of passages describing the downtrodden and oppressed. Jesus identified kingdom servants as those who, by outward circumstances, were to be most pitied, but who, according to present and future reality, were to be most envied. Jesus' listeners were familiar with the iron fist of the Roman Empire. Rome's military presence was everywhere, curtailing freedoms and demanding taxes. Matthew's readers were probably on the verge of the first outbreak of worldwide persecution and would have been in desperate need of the eternal perspective and hope the Beatitudes provide. They needed to be assured there was an inheritance-reward coming.

5:3. In any century, a poor person has little reason to be happy, based on outward circumstances. Jesus, however, clarified in the first words of his sermon that he was not speaking of physical poverty, but spiritual poverty—**poor in spirit.** The beginning of repentance is the recognition of one's spiritual bankruptcy—one's inability to become righteous on one's own. The blessing or happiness that belongs to the poor in spirit is because such a person is, by his admission, already moving toward participating in God's kingdom plan, acknowledging his need for a source of salvation outside himself. Old Testament uses of this concept would have been familiar to Jesus' listeners and Matthew's readers. (Familiar Scriptures would have included Pss. 40:17; 69:29–30,33–34; Isa. 57:15; 61:1; 66:2,5.)

5:4. The penitent person who recognizes the weight of his or her sin and spiritual bankruptcy can only respond with sorrow. This has nothing to do with "feeling badly" over some unhappy event. This refers to the condition of the human heart. Only when we are truly sorrowful for our spiritual bankruptcy can the grace of God be introduced into the picture. It is through God's grace that we experience great joy and the comfort of the forgiveness he offers. (Old Testament parallels include Isa. 1:17,23; 2:11,17; 61:2.)

5:5. The "gentle" or **meek** are those who are powerful, but who have the maturity and grace to use their power for constructive rather than destructive purposes. The term Matthew used here is much misunderstood. Meekness is *not* weakness. Quite the opposite; it is "strength under control." Southern horse breeders used to have a phrase—"the meekest horse wins the race." The meek horse is the one who has most responded to his training. All his obvious and inherent strength is harnessed and brought under focused control. Moses was referred to as "more humble than anyone else on the face of the earth" (Num. 12:3). This is hardly a description of weakness when you consider the incredible personal strength required to lead over a million people on a camping trip through the wilderness for forty years.

The inheritance of the earth here looks ahead to reward in the coming kingdom reign with Christ, which will be the grand climax of history. Notice that future rewards, hinted at here, will be a consistently recurring theme throughout Matthew's Gospel. Note the progression thus far. Jesus' kingdom servants are those who: (1) recognize they are spiritually bankrupt; (2) are deeply sorrowful for it; and (3) have begun to respond humbly to their trainer. (Old Testament parallels for the concept of meekness-gentleness include Ps. 37:7–11; Isa. 57:15.)

5:6. Hunger and thirst are characteristics, again, of the oppressed and downtrodden. Jesus again clarified that the realm of which he spoke is the spiritual, not the physical. A person who is starving for righteousness, whether in one's own life or in one's environment, is not a happy person, if that person is focused on his or her immediate circumstances. Happiness comes from the assurance that all righteousness will some day be fulfilled. The believer will personally become perfected, never to sin again, and the kingdom will be purged of all unrighteousness.

Skeptics of Christianity argue that the Bible cannot be true because of all the evil in the world. "Why has not God done anything about that?" they sneer. One Christian responded, "Your skepticism only seeks to excuse yourself. For the moment, let us set aside the evil 'out there.' The question you should be asking is, 'What shall we do about the evil *in you*?'" For kingdom servants, there should certainly be a hunger and thirst for righteousness to be restored in our surrounding world. But there must be an even deeper hunger that such restoration begin within our own heart. (Old Testament parallels include Pss. 32; 37; 51; 73; 139:23–24; Prov. 8:22–36.)

5:7. Kingdom servants must reflect in their own hearts the heart of the king. That they are part of the kingdom implies that they are objects of mercy. They are "others-oriented." What we have received in such abundance, we must dispense abundantly. Jesus repeated the concept in different words in 6:14–15. Kingdom servants are compassionate toward others.

5:8. The term Matthew used here means **pure** or "clean." It can be used literally of physical cleanness, but Scripture often uses it for moral cleanness and purity. A simple but helpful way of looking at the word is to realize that it implies the absence of impurity or filth. It implies a singleness of purpose, without distraction (akin to the concept of "holiness," being set apart for a special purpose; see Jas. 4:8). Any distracting or corrupting influence a kingdom servant allows into his or her heart makes that person less effective as a servant. The kingdom servant has a heart that is undivided and unalloyed.

This quality is a natural by-product of the preceding blessings and character qualities. Purity of heart is not manufactured by the believer, but is granted by the God of mercy (5:7) to those who mourn their spiritual bankruptcy (5:3–4) and who seek his righteousness (5:6). When the king grants purity of heart, he gives not only judicial purity (forgiveness, absolution from guilt), but also the actual removal of corrupting impurities from the heart. This comes about through the empowerment of the believer to grow into holiness and out of these impurities.

Jesus may have had a dual meaning behind the phrase **see God**. First, the pure heart is unhindered in its ability to understand the heart and person of God in this life on earth and, in this sense, is better able to **see** God. Moreover, only the pure (forgiven) heart is able to enter heaven to enjoy the presence of God for eternity.

5:9. Peace is, first and foundationally, internal and spiritual. It is not primarily physical, military, or political. Peace for the nations flows from peace in the hearts of individuals. Peacemakers are not power brokers but people lovers. The promised kingdom is characterized by peace, as described in Isaiah 9:6–7; 66:12–13; Micah 4:3.

5:10–12. Persecution is familiar to all who are oppressed and downtrodden. However, Jesus did not offer the kingdom of heaven as a blanket blessing to all victims of persecution everywhere for all causes. He offered it only to those who are **persecuted because of righteousness** (5:10) and **because of me** (5:11). Kingdom honor is not granted as compensation for the unfairness of life, but as a blessing on those who have actively pursued true kingdom righteousness and have been persecuted for it.

The Old Testament prophets were regarded as heroes to the Jews (5:12; see also 2 Chron. 36:16; Matt. 23:29–36; Acts 7:51–53; Jas. 5:10). Their endurance of persecution elevated them further in the people's eyes. Jesus here showed the continuity between the ministry of the prophets and the ministry of the kingdom servant. Both are serving the same cause, advancing the same kingdom, and serving the same king. Jesus promised that both would suffer the same abuse, but that both would also receive indescribable reward in heaven. So both have cause for rejoicing in spite of their temporal circumstances.

Jesus wished to highlight this final Beatitude by expanding on it in a way that he did with none of the other seven. Persecution by the king's enemies was one of the most significant marks of a kingdom servant, and it will continue to be a theme throughout Matthew's Gospel. Jesus also went beyond the formula **Blessed are** to say, **Rejoice, and be glad**. He gave special hope and courage to those whose righteousness is of such tenacity and brilliance that the enemies of the kingdom are moved to snuff it out.

B The Influence of a Kingdom Servant (5:13–16)

SUPPORTING IDEA: *The righteousness of Jesus' followers must impact their world.*

In Matthew 5:13–16, before embarking on the body of the sermon, Jesus explained in two word pictures the impact that a truly righteous person will have on his or her world. The entire sermon, including the Beatitudes before and the many teachings after, shows us how to live as "salt and light" in the world as representatives of another kingdom. These word pictures also serve Matthew's purpose—to encourage believers to change their world (Matt. 28:18–20).

5:13. There are many lists of the uses of salt, most of them inspired by Jesus' statement here. However, among the many possible connotations, Jesus probably had two most centrally in his mind. First, salt preserves from corruption. In the centuries before modern refrigeration, salt was the method of choice for preventing bacteria from poisoning food. Salt was so vital for this purpose that wars were fought over salt, and entire economies were based on it. Salt could literally make the difference between life and death in a time when fresh food was unavailable.

Just as salt prevents or kills bacteria in food, the kingdom servant prevents or confronts corruption in the world. Notice that it is the **earth** that needs the salt, not the kingdom of heaven. If the kingdom servant did not have a function to perform on earth according to God's plan, he might as well go straight to heaven upon conversion. The reality is that the earth needs the influence of Christ's church in this age.

The second function of salt is to add flavor or interest (Col. 4:5–6). Jesus highlighted this purpose when he spoke of the danger of salt losing its **saltiness**. The kingdom and all associated with it are anything but boring. They are life! However, the kingdom servant is capable of living like a dead person. Part of the church's task on earth is to live according to its new nature—alive, purposeful, hopeful, joyful! Christians should be living in such a way that others will pause and consider what is different about them (1 Pet. 3:15).

Believers are different and should appear so, because the Father is different (holy; 1 Pet. 1:15–16).

The kingdom servant who does not live according to his nature as salt is useless to the king's advancement of the kingdom on earth. One might even question the genuineness of such a person's kingdom citizenship.

5:14–16. The picture of light is similar to salt, in that both describe the influence the believer is to have in the **world** ("world" here is synonymous with **earth** in 5:13). However, it reveals a different facet of the believer's influence. The function of light is to make reality or truth visible, thereby giving direction and guidance by what is seen. Light is a common theme throughout the Bible (e.g., Isa. 9:2; 42:6; Matt. 4:16; John 1:4–5,9; 12:46; Eph. 5:8; Phil. 2:15; 1 Thess. 5:5).

Jesus again used the emphatic "you," and again clearly stated that this is already what a believer *is*, not something he might *become*. It is the nature of a kingdom servant to be light in the world. Any believer who fails to function as light is going against his nature as God's new creation. The believer has no light inherent in himself. The believer's light is a reflected light. Believers are to make certain that nothing comes between them and their source of light (2 Cor. 3:18; Phil. 2:13–16).

Both **a city on a hill** (5:14) and the **lamp . . . on its stand** (5:15) fulfill their function by being elevated, so their light can be seen by many people over a broad area. Jesus himself explained the application of this principle in 5:16. The light represents our good works, which must be done with such integrity that all who see have no choice but to credit our Father in heaven. The Christian's life and influence is to be visible and obvious, not secret or hidden. We must not camouflage our devotion to Christ, but humbly do all we can to allow its truest colors to be seen where we live.

The term translated **praise** means "to make manifest or visible." When we **shine** our **light** before others by living righteously, we are making visible the character of the Father. Some people might claim a contradiction between the instruction here to **Let your light shine before men**, and in 6:1–6, **Be careful not to do your acts of righteousness before men, to be seen by them.** However, there is a great difference between the two passages, and it has to do with who is glorified by the good works. In one case attention is drawn to God; in the other, it is drawn to self. It is the Christian's commission to live in such a way as to make God visible in a world that is blind to him.

This is the first time Matthew calls God **Father.** It is a wonderful, new emphasis on personal intimacy for the believer. Matthew used this word forty-five times. And while the fatherhood of God was not unknown in the Old Testament, here it is endowed with a very personal sense (Mark 14:36; Rom. 8:15; Gal. 4:6). The king wants his people to know that his kingdom involves a deeply personal relationship with God. It is so much more than a religious or organizational connection.

C Standard of Righteousness (5:17–20)

SUPPORTING IDEA: *The righteousness of Jesus' followers must surpass mere "religiosity."*

5:17. The **Law or the Prophets** was one way of referring to the entire Hebrew Scriptures (our Old Testament). Jesus meant the same thing in 5:18 when he referred to **the Law**. Jesus was about to say some things that would strike the minds of the religious leaders like a sledgehammer. He would sound to their ears as though he were antilaw because he would insist the law can do nothing for them except define sin. It cannot save them even if they could (hypothetically) keep it perfectly (exceeding the Pharisees). So Jesus assured his Jewish listeners that he was not antilaw at all. On the contrary, he was going to **fulfill** it; that is, both keep and explain fully its original intention, which they had managed to miss over the centuries.

There is much debate over what Jesus meant by the word **fulfill**. The word means "to fill out, expand." It does not mean to bring to an end. Jesus was not taking away from the law, nor was he adding to it. He was clarifying its original meaning. After all, he was its author. And we must not forget that Jesus, as a Jew, related well to the law—not as it was commonly understood, but as it was originally intended.

All that Jesus said in 5:21–48 was within the intended meaning of the law when it was originally given fourteen centuries earlier. Certainly some righteous people throughout the centuries understood this, but as a whole, the nation of Israel was limited in the thoroughness of its understanding. This limited understanding was further warped and misguided by the perversions of the Pharisees and others who thought God's Word needed "completion" through the oral tradition.

Jesus' teaching here awakened his people to what the law meant from the beginning. He clarified God's longstanding desire that his creation be characterized by both internal (attitudes) and external (actions) obedience and holiness. Fulfilled law is written on the heart. Jesus himself fulfilled the law in several ways: (1) by keeping it perfectly; (2) by fulfilling the Old Testament messianic types and prophecies; and (3) by providing the way of salvation that meets all the righteous requirements of the law.

Two pivotal passages (Jer. 31:31–34; Ezek. 36:26–27) explain how, under the new covenant, the same law (the very character of God) is not to be an external standard, but its values are to become an intrinsic part of newly recreated people. In a way, Jesus was teaching something that was not yet completely possible for people to follow. It is good to say, "People should move from external obedience to an obedience motivated by the law written upon the heart." But this is an impossibility until the heart is transformed and the very person of God himself, along with his righteous character as expressed in the law, comes to abide in one's heart. What Jesus taught would become a reality in the lives of God's people after his death sealed the new covenant and made possible the promised internal transformation.

5:18. Whenever Jesus began a statement with **I tell you the truth**, it was time to get quiet and listen. The word *amen* is the transliteration of the Hebrew *'amen,* expressing affirmation that the associated truth is totally reliable. The Old Testament usage of the word is always as a response to a preceding statement. Jesus introduced the formula in which the word precedes the weighty statement in order to prepare the hearer to listen.

Jesus overwhelmed the Pharisees' charge that he was destroying the law. The Bible teaches that the law is both temporary (Gal. 3:19; Eph. 2:15; Heb. 7:12) and eternal (Rom. 3:31; 8:4).

The **least stroke** (5:18) of the Hebrew alphabet is the *yod.* It is no bigger than our apostrophe. The smallest stroke of a pen is a very tiny mark that is only one part of a single Hebrew letter, like the dot over our "i." Jesus was serious about the eternal quality of his written Word. We must never trifle with even the smallest part of Scripture. Jesus affirmed the inerrancy of Scripture and its absolute trustworthiness.

5:19. Once again Jesus affirmed the law as it stood (properly interpreted), but he began to shift his focus toward those who had changed its original meaning, while claiming to uphold it unchanged. Not only did he identify the Pharisees and other religious leaders by their tampering with the law, but he also focused on their responsibility to teach others.

One of the least of these commandments does not refer to any specific commandment or collection of commands. Rather, it has the same effect as the "jot and tittle" terminology in the preceding verse. Jesus used these words to say, "Do not toy or tamper with *any* of it."

5:20. After stating that no one—not even the Messiah himself—was to change the law in any way, Jesus proclaimed the thesis for the remainder of the sermon—**unless your righteousness surpasses that of the Pharisees and the teachers of the law, you will certainly not enter the kingdom of heaven.**

This is an enormous statement. It would have shocked Jesus' listeners, because the scribes and Pharisees were considered the ultimate example of righteousness. To the Jewish listener, Jesus' statement meant that no one could enter heaven. To the average person trying to eke out a living, the Pharisees were the truly holy people. Jesus claimed that even they were not good enough!

No amount of lawkeeping was good enough because the problem is the human heart. Jesus went on to illustrate how bankrupt their understanding of the law was by making comparison after comparison (**you have heard that it was said . . . but I tell you**; 5:21–22). For example, the Pharisees' teaching implied that if a man avoided having sex with someone other than his spouse, then he had kept that portion of the law. Jesus, understanding the universality of human lust, filled the law out to the full by pointing out God's original intention—because adultery is a matter of the heart, people regularly commit this sin through a single moment of lust in the mind.

A careful examination of the remainder of the Sermon on the Mount reveals that virtually every point Jesus made draws a contrast between the pseudo-righteousness of the religious leaders and the true righteousness that God desires. The person who discovers and appropriates true righteousness will manifest the character qualities described in the Beatitudes (5:3–12) and will impact the world as described in 5:13–16. The Pharisees did not.

Jesus drew attention to the gravity of his foundational premise with the formula, **I tell you.** He equated himself with the author of Scripture which, of course, he was. Jesus insisted his words bore all the authority of God himself which, of course, he was. Jesus claimed deity for himself.

Jesus was essentially declaring war on the false pharisaical religion. He insisted that no person could be saved by his or her own righteousness. This was something the law intended to indicate all along, but Israel had missed the point (Rom. 2:17–3:31; Gal. 3:17–29; 5:3–6). The point was hard for the self-righteous to swallow—no one, not even the super law-keeping Pharisees, could enter into heaven. All needed a Savior!

D Examples of True and False Righteousness (5:21–48)

SUPPORTING IDEA: *Every aspect of a true believer's conduct must be characterized by a righteousness that surpasses mere appearance.*

5:21–48. Note the pattern in these verses. Jesus gave six examples that contrasted pharisaical "righteousness" with true, "surpassing" righteousness. He began two of them with the formula, **You have heard that it was said to the people long ago.** He began three with, "**You have heard that it was said**; and one (5:31) with, "**It has been said.**"

All of these introductory formulae reflect the same implications. Jesus used variety as a way to keep his students' attention. Note the repeated emphasis on the words **heard, told,** and **said.**

Jesus' repeated use of these verbs reflected the belief of the Pharisees in the oral tradition. They believed that, in addition to the written law, rabbis of old had created additional clarification and detail, held to be as authoritative as the written word (not unlike some current religious traditions). All six examples that Jesus gave his listeners were either limited or warped understandings of written Old Testament law.

In contrast, in all six examples, Jesus followed with **But I tell you.** Because of the strength of contradiction and the sixfold repetition, commentators refer to 5:21–48 as "the six antitheses." First note the heightened emphasis on "I." Jesus contrasted his own authority, as the original author and ultimate interpreter of the law, with the false authority of the rabbinic oral tradition.

Second, note the immediacy Jesus attached through his repeated use of the phrase **tell you.** Rather than communicating what others had passed on secondhand, Jesus looked his audience in the eye and said, "You yourselves are hearing this directly from the source of truth." This also is the relationship that every believer has with the author of truth today. Certainly we need wise and experienced teachers to help us understand more fully, but the essence of biblical truth is within the grasp of everyone who is indwelt by the illuminating Spirit of God. Diligent study is the necessary ingredient (2 Tim. 2:15).

There is one more critical principle for us to understand in interpreting this sermon. As with the Old Testament law, these points in the Sermon on the Mount are presented as "samples." That is, the sermon was not intended to be an exhaustive list of every possible instance of application, but a *pattern* which is to be learned, and then generalized to all attitudes, words, and actions in our lives. In 5:21–48, Jesus presented six examples supporting his thesis (5:20). He could easily have provided more. But his purpose was not to teach every possible example, but *a way of thinking.* This approach would prepare believers for every possible situation they would face.

For instance, Jesus could have addressed the tithe as a seventh example. He could have explained how the percentages of the Old Testament were a basic guideline for growing believers, and that his kingdom citizens must actually seek to go beyond this "kindergarten level" of thinking about giving.

The insights to be gained here about murder, adultery, divorce, oaths, revenge, and love are valuable. But we miss the entire message of the sermon if we do not take the single underlying principle and learn how to apply it to the infinite number of decisions that we face throughout our lives. That underlying principle is: *Seek and apply the heart intention of God's instruction, not merely the letter of it.* This is impossible to do on a human level. But as we seek him with all our hearts, he will reveal it to us (Prov. 2:1–8; Jer. 29:13).

5:21–26. The command, **Do not murder,** comes straight from the Ten Commandments (Exod. 20:13). But from Jesus' contrasting clarification, we can surmise that the scribes and Pharisees limited their interpretation of murder to its most literal meaning—wrongly taking a human life. Jesus broadened their understanding of murder to include wrongful anger that might, in some cases, lead to literal murder. He included cutting, harmful words that can kill a person's spirit. To call a brother **Raca** ("empty-headed") was to cross the boundary. Essentially, Jesus instructed his kingdom servants to value every aspect of another person's well-being, and to treat each person in keeping with this valuation.

It is important to acknowledge the validity of righteous anger (Pss. 4:4; 139:19–24; Matt. 21:12–19; 23:17; Mark 3:1–5; Eph. 4:26–27). Traditional Christianity tends to squelch all anger as sinful. Such an attitude has caused many believers to grow up emotionally undeveloped, unable to be honest in their hearts with God, people, or even themselves. This attitude leads to some of the worst forms of hypocrisy. Anger is a valid human emotion, especially when it is felt because of some offense against God. Offenses against oneself and others can be valid causes for anger. In all cases, the anger must be short-lived, or it will turn into harmful and sinful bitterness (Ps. 4:4; Eph. 4:26–27). So we must present our hearts continually to God, so he can examine us and show us what is accurate and what is inaccurate in our perspectives (Ps. 139:23–24).

Anger can affect a person's relationship with God. For this reason, Jesus urged that all offenses be corrected quickly and person-to-person whenever possible (5:25–26). The longer a person waits to correct an offense, the weightier the consequences can become. We may find that the offended party will be much more gracious in settling matters than the impersonal justice of the courts (or the ultimate judgment of God).

Jesus gave more space to this first example than he gave to any of the others. This does not imply that it has more practical weight than the others. Rather, in this first example, Jesus showed the extent to which the implications of his law must be taken in our daily living.

5:27–30. Jesus drew the command concerning adultery directly from the Ten Commandments (Exod. 20:14). Again, however, we are led to assume that the pharisaical interpretation of **adultery** was the actual physical act. Jesus expanded our understanding of adultery to include a lustful attitude toward a spouse who is not one's own.

Also, as he did with murder, Jesus acknowledged the higher court of heaven (5:29–30) as the court we should be mindful of, since the thoughts of our hearts are difficult for a human court to judge.

In 5:25–26, Jesus urged the offender to settle an offense quickly at lesser cost, rather than delay and incur the judgment of higher authority. Similarly, in 5:29–30, he urged his students to pay the lesser costs that may be required to halt an adulterous heart early on, rather than allow the sin to develop fully and incur the final judgment of God. Because Jesus repeated this pattern twice, we may take from it another underlying principle: It costs less to address the root of a sin early on than to carry the weight of the consequences of the sin fully developed as well as the weight of judgment before God. The earlier sin is dealt with, the better.

The exhortation to gouge out one's eye or cut off one's hand is hyperbole, intended to communicate the point, "Do whatever it takes to correct your heart attitude." Some people have missed the figure of speech here—hyperbole. At least one early church leader who struggled with lust thought that castration was the answer. We realize, of course, that lust originates in a person's mind. Mutilating the body will not solve the problem.

5:31–32. Jesus' quote of the rabbinic thinking on divorce in 5:31 was drawn from Deuteronomy 24:1. The Old Testament instruction requiring a certificate of divorce was *not* commanding divorce. Rather, it provided protection to the woman when a divorce was chosen. It was actually Moses' effort to curtail the rampant practice of "easy divorce" among God's people. The legal certificate kept the husband from treating his wife capriciously, threatening her with abandonment one day, and taking her back the next. It protected her from abuse. The scribes and Pharisees were apparently using this instruction to excuse divorces for any reason. Jesus later explained that the purpose of Deuteronomy 24 and other such passages was not to allow divorce, but to keep his people within certain boundaries when they chose divorce (19:1–12).

In his corrective **But I tell you,** Jesus narrowed the allowable reasons for justifiable divorce. And even at that, he was not commanding that an adulterous spouse be divorced. He was *allowing* such recourse for the spouse offended by adultery. Like his Father (Mal. 2), Jesus hates divorce in every instance, but he permits it in extremely narrow circumstances. His will is always reconciliation except in the face of ongoing, unrepentant, adulterous destruction of the marriage covenant.

Jesus looked beyond the adulterous spouse even to the possible future partner of that man or woman. In effect, he was limiting the wrongly divorced person's future marriage options to one—remarriage only to his or her previous spouse. Essentially, Jesus was saying, "Marriage is intended to be an exclusive, one-on-one relationship—for life. The only excuse a person has for violating this principle through divorce is that the other partner has destroyed it through ongoing, unrepentant adultery."

Jesus' purpose in these two verses was not to explain every detail regarding divorce and remarriage, but to help people think differently about his law—to help them begin to see the heart intention behind the letter "of the law."

5:33–37. Jesus' quotes regarding oaths in 5:33 are derived from such passages as Leviticus 19:12; Numbers 30:2; and Deuteronomy 5:11; 6:13; 23:21–23. A biblical vow or oath in the Old Testament was an optional, above-and-beyond promise of an offering to God. Vows were never required, as were the basic tithes (Deut. 23:22). But once made, a vow was to be kept.

A promise must not be complicated, legalized, or reduced to technicalities. A broken vow was subject to God's punishment.

The Pharisees, in contrast to Jesus' insistence upon straightforward truthfulness, had expanded oaths to matters of technicalities, much like our own American legal system that often twists and turns the normal meaning of words. Legal technicalities can devolve to the point of destroying the justice they are supposed to serve. Truth loses itself in wordiness. The pharisaical system of oaths was expanded to cover all kinds of promises made to one another. "Levels of truth" emerged from the varieties of oaths. **Oaths . . . by heaven** were considered more binding than oaths **on the earth.** Like children crossing their fingers behind their backs, the Pharisees camouflaged reality in elaborate technicalities.

Beginning in 5:34, Jesus again used hyperbole when he instructed the people not to make any oaths. Oaths, properly understood and respectfully used, are a good thing. Jesus was saying that it is better just to make a promise and keep it (and prove by your track record that you are a promise keeper worth trusting) than to thoughtlessly use the powerful name of Yahweh to back up a promise that may or may not be kept. Simply put, Jesus insisted that his followers tell the truth always—not simply when "under oath." Citizens of his kingdom are to be truth tellers, in contrast to those who play with words and twist their meaning to their own selfish ends.

5:38–42. As many people do today, the scribes and Pharisees of Jesus' day must have taken the "eye for an eye" passages (Exod. 21:24; Lev. 24:19–20; Deut. 19:21) as justification for hurting others at least as badly as they had been hurt. The law was not given to exact revenge, but to legislate justice. Breaking the law has consequences, but personal vengeance has no place. These passages have often been wrongly taken as a minimum guideline for retaliation. What Jesus clarifies is that they were always intended as a maximum or a ceiling for retaliation, and that mercy was always an acceptable intention underlying these laws.

For the kingdom servant, legalistically "letting the punishment fit the crime" and insisting upon a "pound of flesh" falls short. We must actually consider blessing the repentant criminal. Mercy (withholding deserved punishment) and grace (giving undeserved gifts) are legitimate norms of conduct.

The **one mile** (5:41) refers to the practice of the Roman soldiers requiring civilians to carry their burden for one mile. By Roman law, the soldier could require no more than one mile of a single porter, but Jesus' kingdom servants (in representing the gracious spirit of their king) are to go beyond what is required of them.

5:43–48. The first part of Jesus' quote in 5:43, **Love your neighbor,** is one of the central commands of the Bible (Lev. 19:18; Matt. 22:34–40). But the mistaken thinking came with the second portion, **and hate your enemy.** Here again, the human inclination is retaliation or revenge. To human thinking, this might seem like a logical corollary flowing out of the first statement. But the reality is that "hate your enemy" is far removed from God's intended meaning in "love your neighbor." In the parallel passage in Luke (10:25–37), Jesus explained through the parable of the good Samaritan that every human in our sphere of influence is our **neighbor.** Therefore, by definition, Christians are to love everyone and hate no one.

Jesus used a different approach to make the same point. He emphasized two principles to urge his followers to love all people. First, he urged them to follow the example of their Father in heaven. The Father gives gifts (sun and rain) to good and evil alike, and so we, as believers, ought to love and pray for our enemies (Luke 23:34; Rom. 5:8). By this we will show ourselves **sons of your Father in heaven.** He teaches us to love everyone because God does.

The ultimate expression of this pattern is the command to imitate the Father in 5:48, **Be perfect, therefore, as your heavenly Father is perfect.** Jesus used *teleios,* a Greek word that means "having reached its end, mature, complete, perfect." The goal for the kingdom servant is to behave like his Father, and so to reach the mature level of supernatural transformation.

Second, Jesus urges us to show ourselves distinct from the rest of the world, the citizens of the earth. This is actually the flip side of the first argument, to be like the Father. If we show partiality and if we love only those who love us, we are like unbelievers. If, on the other hand, we show love impartially, guided by grace and mercy, then we show ourselves distinct, and we shine before the world (5:14–16), bringing glory to the Father.

All six examples are striking in their implications, but this one in particular stands out as a pinnacle exemplifying mercy and grace, the supernatural qualities of God's kingdom servants.

MAIN IDEA REVIEW: *The righteousness of Jesus' followers must impact the world because it surpasses mere "religiosity."*

III. CONCLUSION

From the Beatitudes we learn that we need to come to grips with who we *are* and who we are *not*. Until we accomplish this, we will not be able to relate to others or face persecution the way we should as part of Christ's kingdom.

PRINCIPLES

- Realizing one's spiritual bankruptcy is the first step in following Jesus.
- Jesus did not come to destroy the law but to fulfill it.

- Those in the kingdom will be marked by a number of distinguishing characteristics.
- Jesus' followers are called to an exceedingly high standard.
- God cares about our attitudes and motives for behaving as we do.

APPLICATIONS

- Ask Jesus to build character within you that will be salt and light to society.
- Don't measure your lives by others. Look to the exacting standards of Jesus.
- Ask for God's grace in meeting the high standards of discipleship.
- Be as mindful of motives and attitudes as you are of your public behavior. Ask Jesus for help in making corrections.

IV. LIFE APPLICATION

Seasoning for a Tasteless World

The analogies are probably endless. We sometimes hear, "He's not worth his salt!" "What a salty character he has."

Most people probably think of salt as simply that white, granular, food seasoning found on virtually every dining table. It is that, but it is far more. It is an essential element in the diet of not only humans but of animals, and even of many plants. It is one of the most effective and most widely used of all food preservatives. Today, salt has more than 14,000 known uses.

And it is abundant. The world's oceans contain an average of 2.6% (by weight) salt or 26 million metric tons per cubic kilometer, making salt an inexhaustible commodity.

Salt was of crucial importance in ancient times. A far-flung trade in ancient Greece involving exchange of salt for slaves gave rise to the expression, "not worth his salt." Special salt rations given early Roman soldiers were known as *salarium argentum,* the forerunner of the English word "salary."

We find more than thirty references to salt in the Bible. It was used as a seasoning for food (Job 6:6) and offerings (Lev. 2:13; Ezek. 43:24). As a preservative, salt was symbolic of covenants (Num. 18:19; 2 Chron. 13:5).

Both of those meanings are present in Jesus' comparison of the disciples to salt (Matt. 5:13). The Master calls us to be salt in a decaying, often tasteless world. Christians are to season or "flavor" their spheres of contact and activity with Christ's righteousness.

Christians are to have a preserving effect, slowing and holding at bay the decaying process brought on by the world's corrupt values and philosophies. It is a difficult assignment, for the world resists these efforts. But our efforts to be the salt of the earth are not fruitless. Progress is often gradual and not even observable. Resolve to be an influence for the cause of Christ wherever you are. Ultimately, you will make a difference and bring glory to God.

V. PRAYER

Lord, make me hunger and thirst after righteousness and after doing your will. Make the principles of your kingdom come alive in my heart, especially your exhortation to "love your neighbor."

VI. DEEPER DISCOVERIES

A. Interpreting the Sermon on the Mount

Very few passages in the Gospels have been more controversial than this sermon. Some see it as the way of salvation (as if we could live up to its standard). Others see it as not dealing with salvation at all. Still others see it as purely future-oriented with no bearing on contemporary Christian living; that is, when Jesus comes to reign, this is how the kingdom will look. So how should we regard it? Even a casual reader can see that the Sermon on the Mount does not spell out the gospel of salvation or clarify justification by faith. But it is certainly intended to be a careful statement of Christ's teaching to the first-century Jewish world he entered and those who responded to his message of repentance.

It comes to us from several angles. First, the sermon is without doubt a presentation of Jesus as the long-awaited king who offered Israel the prophesied kingdom. But as he offered it, it became increasingly evident that first-century Israel did not want it. Israel wanted a kingdom characterized more by political freedom from Rome and material freedom from want than by moral ethics and spiritual righteousness. Second, a thoughtful reading makes it clear that these principles of the kingdom are far more than simple rules limited to the millennial kingdom to come. While they are lofty principles, Jesus clearly expected an immediate and personal response from his hearers. They were to do something about his teachings in their hearts and lives.

So we must read the Sermon on the Mount with an eye to understanding: (1) its general truths, (2) its personal and present applications, and (3) its relationship to the future millennial kingdom program. The Sermon on the Mount is a treatise on God's expectations for his kingdom servants.

B. Disciple

Matthew uses the term "disciple" seventy-two times in sixty-nine verses. The word *disciple* begins to disappear from the Bible in the Book of Acts, and it never occurs in the Epistles. This reflects the transition to the "corporate discipling" of the church. This represents a clear contrast with the one-on-one, leader-to-follower approach of the Gospels.

C. Structure of the Sermon on the Mount

Whether we attribute the structure of the Sermon on the Mount to one message Jesus composed and preached one time, or to the inspired Matthew who collected the heart of Jesus' teaching from several messages delivered on more than one occasion, commentators generally agree that it falls into a beautifully balanced outline:

- Matthew 5:3–16 serves as an introduction to the entire sermon, presenting in lyrical form the basic characteristics of the kingdom servant and describing the impact that the righteousness of a true kingdom servant will have on the world.
- Matthew 5:17–20 presents the primary thesis of the entire sermon, stated most concisely in verse 20, "unless your righteousness surpasses that of the Pharisees and teachers of the law, you shall not enter the kingdom of heaven."
- Matthew 5:21–48 provides six examples or illustrations contrasting the "righteousness" of the Pharisees' oral tradition with the true intent of God's law.
- Matthew 6:1–7:12 continues to present examples of true versus false righteousness.
- Matthew 7:13–27 concludes the sermon with three presentations of the "only two ways" theme: two gates and paths (7:13–14), two kinds of fruit (7:15–23), and two ways of responding to Jesus' words (two builders; 7:24–27).
- Matthew 7:28–29 describes the results and reaction of the audience to the sermon.

D. Summary

Matthew 5 must be seen in two contexts: (1) within the context of the entire Sermon on the Mount; and (2) within the sermon as a part of Matthew's entire book. Matthew 5:20 provides the thesis for the entire sermon: God's kingdom servants will live by an internal supernatural righteousness that goes beyond the religious facade of the scribes and Pharisees.

VII. TEACHING OUTLINE

A. INTRODUCTION

1. Lead Story: Repentance Is Good for You—You Have to Change the Heart Attitude

2. Context: Chapter 5 of Matthew is the first of three chapters collectively called the Sermon on the Mount. These three chapters form a basic platform for the new king. He is letting the audience know what is expected of those who would be a part of his kingdom, and exactly what God intended from the beginning.

3. Transition: Chapter 5 specifically tells us that a servant of God's kingdom will have a change of heart and perspective from what he is accustomed to in his religion. Without a heart and perspective change, there can be no satisfying life change, which is what the king desires of his servants. Jesus then pointed out the process of this heart change in the Beatitudes and the need for the change in the rest of the chapter.

B. COMMENTARY

1. The Heart of a Kingdom Citizen (5:1–12)
2. The Influence of a Kingdom Servant (5:13–16)
3. The Kingdom Servant's Standard of Righteousness (5:17–20)
4. Examples of True and False Righteousness (5:21–48)

C. CONCLUSION

1. Wrap-up: Personal heart change is necessary if there is to be a personal life change on the part of people who would call themselves followers of Jesus.
2. Personal Challenge: Have you begun this heart change by being willing to give up your personal striving to please God with all you have to offer him? If not, why not?

VIII. ISSUES FOR DISCUSSION

1. Why did Jesus place such a high priority on training his disciples?
2. What is the meaning of the concept of *meekness* as Jesus expressed it in the Sermon on the Mount?
3. How can Christians be "salt" and "light" in the modern world?
4. How did Jesus use hyperbole in this section of the Sermon on the Mount?

Matthew 6

The King Speaks His Heart (Part II)

I. **INTRODUCTION**
Two Kinds of Presidents

II. **COMMENTARY**
A verse-by-verse explanation of the chapter.

III. **CONCLUSION**
An overview of the principles and applications from the chapter.

IV. **LIFE APPLICATION**
God Will Take Care of You

Melding the chapter to life.

V. **PRAYER**
Tying the chapter to life with God.

VI. **DEEPER DISCOVERIES**
Historical, geographical, and grammatical enrichment of the commentary.

VII. **TEACHING OUTLINE**
Suggested step-by-step group study of the chapter.

VIII. **ISSUES FOR DISCUSSION**
Zeroing the chapter in on daily life.

"*Hypocrisy in anything whatever may deceive the cleverest and most penetrating man, but the least wide-awake of children recognizes it, and is revolted by it, however ingeniously it may be disguised.*"

Leo Tolstoy

Matthew 6

 **I N   A   N U T S H E L L**

Matthew presents several distinctions that support the thesis of the Sermon on the Mount (Matt. 5:20). He contrasts religious masquerades and genuine spirituality, those who serve money and those who serve God, and those who worry about providing their own needs and those who trust in God's provision.

The King Speaks His Heart (Part II)

I. INTRODUCTION

Two Kinds of Presidents

*T*he first president of the United States had a legendary commitment to always telling the truth. He laid the foundation for a healthy and powerful republic. Some later presidents of the United States had a legendary capacity for lying. They shredded the soul of the republic.

The first president sacrificed self to serve the truth and the republic. Some later presidents sacrificed the truth and the republic to serve self. The first president walked the walk. Others only talked the talk. The first was an honorable man. Others were hypocrites. Even the enemies of the first held him in high regard. But even the supporters of some of our presidents, in the quietness of their closets, were nauseated by their disregard for truth.

Truthfulness breathes freedom into the spirit. Hypocrisy is a malignancy of the soul.

Hypocrisy, like the malignancy it is, eventually destroys everything it touches, including the hypocrite himself. That is why Jesus was so harsh with the false religious leaders of his day. From the beginning Jesus was the author and friend of truth and authenticity. He is the enemy of falsehood and hypocrisy.

II. COMMENTARY

The King Speaks His Heart (Part II)

MAIN IDEA: *Jesus' followers must be motivated by trust in God's provision rather than trust in any earthly source.*

A Seek Your Reward from God, Not from People (6:1–18)

SUPPORTING IDEA: *Jesus' followers must live for God's approval, not the praise of people.*

While 5:21–48 related most closely to the Sermon on the Mount thesis in 5:20, chapter 6 serves to support that thesis by drawing distinctions:

- between religious masquerades and genuine spirituality (6:1–18),
- between those who serve money and those who serve God (6:19–24), and
- between those who worry about providing for their own needs and those who trust God as the provider (6:25–34).

Jesus continued to indict the scribes and Pharisees for their hypocrisy and lack of true righteousness, while instructing his followers in the way of righteousness (5:20). The Pharisees had missed the point about how a person becomes righteous. They thought it was by works of law-keeping. Because the Pharisees had sought to establish their own righteousness, their self-righteousness could only produce hypocrisy. They were masquerading as something they were not. Jesus made it clear in 6:33 when he insisted that we seek **first his kingdom and his righteousness** from which all of life's resources flow.

Hypocrisy is, of course, true of all of us from time to time, but Jesus was encouraging genuineness and true spirituality as opposed to hypocritical self-righteousness. God despises appearance that is not reality (e.g., Ananias and Sapphira; Acts 5:1–10).

6:1. This first verse serves as an introduction to all of 6:1–18. It establishes the theme of doing **acts of righteousness** before men, and thus losing **reward from your Father in heaven.** Matthew recorded the term *Father* seventeen times in the sermon, something fresh to Jewish ears. Jesus was emphasizing the reality of a relationship. The Pharisees practiced a performance-oriented "works-righteousness" apart from any relationship. For Jesus, this was unacceptable. It was the same problem the rich young ruler would demonstrate. What humans consider "righteous" is worthless. Jesus' exhortation **Be careful** is the present tense form, and emphasizing the need to be on the alert to the temptation to seek our reward from men.

Jesus was not condemning the righteous acts themselves. Genuineness was his focus, not the acts themselves. His concern was the motivation behind the actions. The same act of obedience can be right or wrong, depending on *why* a person does the act.

We must recognize, however, that the line between right and wrong motives is not the same as that between private and public obedience. Not all public acts of obedience are done for the wrong motives. Jesus has already commanded us, "Let your light shine before men, that they may see your good deeds and praise your Father who is in heaven" (5:16). We are actually commanded to perform righteous acts of obedience before others. The difference is in whom others see as a result of our public righteousness. Do they see only us, or do they see our Father more clearly?

Some Christians have the mistaken notion that if their acts of righteousness become known, they will receive no reward in heaven for those deeds. We must seek a balance. We must relax in faith in a God who searches our hearts and is willing to reveal and to purify our hearts (Ps. 139:23–24; 1 John 1:7,9).

6:2–4. The opening **when** implies that this was a teaching which applied to any instance of giving. Jesus began by telling his hearers *not* to give alms, ascribing such ostentatious behavior to the hypocrites (referring to the scribes and Pharisees of 5:20). Key to the passage is the explanation of their motive: **to be honored by men.** In this first example, Matthew uses a verb meaning **praise** (5:16), whereas in the second and third examples, he uses another verb meaning "to make visible" (active), "to be seen" (passive). The meanings of the words overlap, but the concern is the tendency toward competition with God for glory.

"Giving" or "almsgiving" is the translation of terms meaning "perform an act of mercy." By the first century, the phrase came to mean specifically the act of giving to the needy. This kind of giving was not mandatory in Scripture, for it was above and beyond the three required tithes. The specific historical meaning of **trumpets** is unclear, but the intended point is clear: God's people are not to give to draw attention to themselves. The observation of this principle would change the face of much of Christian ministry in our day!

In classical Greek, the term *hypocrite* referred to an actor on stage, wearing a mask. In the New Testament, it came to have a negative connotation, referring to someone putting on an act (i.e., masking the truth). We find the foundational point in Isaiah 29:13, quoted in Matthew 15:8, "These people honor me with their lips, but their hearts are far from me." Genuine righteousness is a matter of belief in the heart (Rom. 10:10).

As we saw in 5:18,26, the introductory phrase, **I tell you the truth** (found thirty-two times in Matthew), prepares the listener for a statement of great importance. In this case, it is a statement intended to shock the listener. Jewish rabbis taught that almsgiving received especially high reward. How empty to know that, due to one's own pride, there was no reward remaining for an act of righteousness beyond the glory of the moment. This was shocking to a first-century Jewish audience.

Verse 3 begins with the strong adversative, **So when you.** The emphasis on "you" was intended to draw a stark contrast between the hypocrites just described and Jesus' kingdom servants, the disciples of 5:1–2. Jesus' instruction in 6:3 is exaggerated wording intended to make the point: "Do all you can to avoid drawing attention to yourself."

Since nothing escapes the eye of God, even the most private act is noticed and will be rewarded. Jesus' use of the title **Father** added warmth to his guarantee of reward. This is not to be seen as a mechanical kind of relationship. Rather, the gift from the heart is given out of love for the Father, and the reward is returned as to a dearly beloved Son.

The **reward** (6:4,6,18) is not unrelated to the concept of reward in 6:1. The first word leans more toward the idea of repayment; thus, the idea of reimbursement for our "expense" incurred in each act of righteousness. But the point is the Father rewarding his servants. We were "created . . . to do good works" (Eph. 2:10). In keeping with the instruction of 5:16 to "let your light shine," our Father in heaven will reward us for good works. The issue for the Pharisees was works apart from God's righteousness. The Pharisees were trying to establish their own righteousness by works.

6:5–6. Many of the comments in the preceding section on giving also apply to 6:5–6 on praying. **Love** in 6:5 is a word used also of the Pharisees in 23:6. **Standing** is from a verb implying the practice of taking a position and keeping it for a long time. And **street** is not just any street, but a *wide* street, implying one heavily traveled, thus a street where the most people would see a person praying. Again the emphatic **you** at the beginning of 6:6 separates the kingdom servant from the crowd of hypocrites.

Jesus was certainly not forbidding public prayer (see 14:19; 15:36; Acts 1:24; 3:1; 4:24–30). But it may be said that the person who prays only in public and never in private is praying for the wrong reasons.

6:7–8. It is ironic that this prohibition against meaningless repetition is issued immediately before the Lord's Prayer. This passage is, without doubt, the most-often-repeated-without-meaning passage in the Bible. Of course, this is actually the Disciples' Prayer as the Lord never prayed for forgiveness of his sin. He was teaching his *disciples* how to pray.

The first-century Greeks and Romans believed in a pantheon of gods, all of whom had their faults; each of whom controlled some aspect of nature. They attempted to appease as many of these gods as possible, to receive their blessing and to avoid their wrath. Because these gods were so much like humans, the pagan worshiper believed he needed to pray repetitively to get their attention. Once a worshiper got a god's attention, he continued to pray repetitively to ensure that he was heard correctly and to convince the god that his request was worth granting.

Worshipers of these pagan gods also believed that the words they used carried some kind of magical power. Thus, the more often these words were used, the more powerful the magic. It is possible that some well-meaning modern believers may fall into this same trap—as though repeating certain "power words" somehow induces the Lord to act in their behalf.

Prayer is not for the purpose of informing God. Rather, prayer expresses to him (and to ourselves) the fact of our impotence to meet our own needs. Biblical prayer is an act of faith, an expression of dependence on God. Meaningless repetition signifies dependence on oneself to manipulate or badger God into compliance.

When are believers guilty of meaningless repetition? For example, we add "in Jesus' name" as a mere punctuation mark at the end of our prayers. Would not it be better actually to *pray* in Jesus' name (with his authority, according to his will), instead of merely adding the phrase? We can pray in Jesus' name without using those words.

When we pray over meals or with our children at bedtime, do we really think about what we are saying? When we sing the words of a song of worship to the Lord, do we really mean them?

6:9–15. An important point to be made about the "Lord's Prayer" is that Jesus intended it to be a pattern for the servant of his kingdom, just as he intended much of his teaching in the Sermon on the Mount. It is not a magical formula. The specific words he used are not any more sacred than requests we might make expressing the same kinds of desires to the Father. We should seek to learn how to pray *like* Jesus prayed, not merely *what* Jesus prayed. That was his point when he said, **This, then, is how you should pray** (6:9). The pattern of meaningful prayer is to begin by majoring on the person and nature of God and his kingdom interests, coming to personal requests and needs only secondarily.

You in Jesus' introduction (6:9a) is grammatically unnecessary, and is therefore emphatic. It is also placed at the end of the sentence for emphasis. His implication is, "*You*, on the other hand (in contrast to both the pompous hypocrites and the thoughtless, superstitious Gentiles), are to pray simply and meaningfully, as follows."

Our Father in heaven. The plural pronoun *our* indicates that prayer should be an expression of corporate desires to God, and should often be prayed in fellowship with other believers. The words *Father* and *heaven* together demonstrate the loving closeness and awesome transcendence of God to his child.

Hallowed be your name. The verb *hallowed* means "to sanctify, make holy." Because the grammatic form here is unknown in English, we tend to take this line in Jesus' prayer as a statement of fact, when, in fact, it is a request. Jesus was teaching us to make the request, "Lord, may your name be sanctified." Why should we pray to God that he would sanctify his own name? Probably as a reminder to ourselves to live a life that advertises a holy God. Also, this kind of greeting was a form of blessing on the one addressed.

In both Old and New Testament thinking, a person's name was equivalent to his or her very person (thus the careful choice in those days of children's names for their *meaning*, not just their sound). For this reason, it is not important to know what **name** of God Jesus may have meant. To say that the word by which God is called is to be holy falls far short of Jesus' meaning. Jesus was asking that God himself be set apart as holy, and so Jesus also modeled the attitude we should have toward God during prayer.

Hallowed has to do with something or someone being different or set apart. We must come before God with an attitude of reverence for God's perfection (in contrast to our imperfection), his wisdom (in contrast to our foolishness), his power (in contrast to our impotence), and his love (in contrast to our selfishness). God's holiness is everything that sets him apart from us and all the rest of his creation. Addressing such a being should never be done casually or flippantly.

Your kingdom come. The kingdom servant sees God's kingdom as not yet completely fulfilled on earth. This prayer is not only for the future coming of Christ (although this can be included), but it is also for the spreading of God's kingdom around the world through his kingdom servants. Therefore, it is a prayer that we, his servants, would be faithfully obedient and effective in living his kingdom principles in our own lives and then spreading the kingdom through our actions and words.

Your will be done on earth as it is in heaven. This request assumes that God's will is done in heaven, but not yet on earth (in the same full way). Sin and rebellion are absent in heaven, but hindrances are present on earth. This is another request for the spreading of God's kingdom rule on earth, primarily through the church as the agent of the kingdom. Our prayers are to be continual reminders to ourselves to "get with" the kingdom program. Sadly, too many believers live for the weekends and not for Christ's kingdom.

Give us today our daily bread. This petition is probably best taken at face value—as a request for the food needed daily, and that it be provided *when* it is needed. Most of the people in Jesus' day lived hand-to-mouth. This was true particularly among the lower classes to whom Jesus' message appealed most. This request acknowledges God as the provider of every physical need, but it also reminds the petitioner to trust God to provide as the needs arise, and not necessarily in advance. Compare this with the lesson Israel had to learn during forty years of daily manna; any excess spoiled by the second day. They were always just one day away from starvation, and yet they ate well during all those decades.

Forgive us our debts, as we also have forgiven our debtors. The Greek word for *debts* in the New Testament appears only here and Romans 4:4. It is clear that Jesus and Matthew intended the word to mean "sins" here (Luke 11:4). The choice of this word reflects the fact that all sins place us in debt to God. In a more extended treatment and parable on this same concept in 18:21–35, Jesus used the idea of debt to teach about sin and forgiveness.

This is the only petition that seems to have a condition prerequisite to its fulfillment and two full verses of explanation following (6:14–15). The context is the relationship of a child to a father. This is "family forgiveness," not forensic or judicial forgiveness. Jesus is not saying that our forgiving is a necessary means to earning God's forgiveness. The Bible makes it clear that there is nothing we can do to merit God's judicial forgiveness, but that it is given freely (e.g., Rom. 5:6–8; Eph. 2:8–9).

One does not gain forgiveness by forgiving. But a person evidences his or her own forgiveness by forgiving others. Since this is family forgiveness, our sense of forgiveness is denied us when we deny forgiveness to others. As God's children, we are commanded to be forgiving. When we fail to forgive, we reap the consequences of spiritual and moral defeat.

6:14–15. These verses further exhort the kingdom servant concerning the necessity of forgiveness in human relationships if we expect God's forgiveness. These verses, and 18:21–35, explain 6:12. Receiving God's forgiveness motivates forgiveness toward others.

Jesus expects us to replace this specific petition with more personalized requests for forgiveness for the specific sins in our own lives. No "meaningless repetition" here. Jesus' intention might be better reflected if our Bibles printed his words of petition followed by a large white space, leaving room for us to "fill in the blanks" with our own personal sins. The petitions as he has given them guide us to the important themes for prayer, but he expects us to personalize these principles in our own lives.

And lead us not into temptation, but deliver us from the evil one. If the preceding request for forgiveness is curative spiritual medicine, then this request is the preventative medicine. Forgiveness is required to deal with guilt already incurred. Deliverance from temptation and evil is required to prevent our incurring future guilt. The kingdom servant's petition for both forgiveness and deliverance is a prayer dealing with the power of sin (1 John 1:7–9); both look forward to the day when we will escape the presence of sin.

The kingdom servant who matures and grows in purity and obedience should rely less and less on the prayer for forgiveness and more and more on the prayer for protection. In this life, the kingdom servant will have need for ongoing forgiveness, but the many lessons learned will help in avoiding the traps of temptation in later life. Believers must never let down their guard. We find many exhortations in the New Testament to stay awake and watchful (e.g., Matt. 24:42; 25:13; 26:41).

We will follow the Lord's example in prayer if we pray regularly for specific spiritual dangers of which we are aware. Perhaps there is a particular area of temptation to avoid, or a particular person who is a stumbling block, or a trial looming in our future. God is interested in the details, and we will recognize his answers more clearly if we have made specific requests.

6:16–18. After a long but meaningful departure, Jesus' sermon returned to the pattern established in 6:2–6. Again, what is most important is not that we learn specific techniques for fasting, but that we see Jesus' underlying message (seek the reward of God, not the approval of people) and apply it to every act of righteousness practiced by believers today.

In fact, we can make a scriptural case that fasting is not a critical discipline for believers today. Moses commanded it only on the Day of Atonement (Lev. 16:29–31; 23:27–32). Most often in the Old Testament it is associated with self-humiliation before God, frequently in connection with confession of sins (e.g., Neh. 9:1–2; Ps. 35:13; Dan. 9:2–20). Fasting may be a healthy personal practice for Christians, but even the Old Testament warns against its abuse (Isa. 59:3–7; Jer. 14:12).

In the Old Testament, fasts were required only occasionally. In the New Testament, we find no instructions pertaining to frequency, duration, or any other details about fasting. The only didactic New Testament teaching on fasting is in this passage, which focuses not on the fasting, but on the motive. Some people might even argue that Jesus chose this "act of righteousness" as one of three examples because of its practice among the Jews, not because he expected it to be a major part of the Christian's life (Pharisees fasted twice a week). In fact, he may have chosen an "act of righteousness" that was known to be above and beyond the requirement of the law to heighten the contrast between the hypocrite and the person who was truly righteous.

The exhortation to anoint one's head and wash one's face was basically saying, "Take great care to groom yourselves normally," perhaps even to take extra care to cover any public signs of discomfort from fasting. Only the Father is to know about the fasting.

The main point of this passage is not fasting, but the contrast between the hypocritically self-righteous and those who are truly righteous. While the practice of fasting is not commanded for New Testament believers, many saints who are prominent role models for us did practice fasting. Note especially Jesus' own example in Matthew 4:1–11.

The temporary deprivation of the body for the purpose of prayer and vigilance can have a profound spiritual impact, both on the person fasting and on the objects of their prayer. Further, consider the possibility that dietary fasting is only one example of a broader category of Christian discipline. For example, many families have benefited by rising to the challenge of a "TV fast." First Corinthians 7:5 seems to support the idea of a brief sexual fast. Even the discipline of solitude might fall in this category, as a "fast" from normal human interaction.

B Seek to Serve God, Not Money (6:19–24)

> **SUPPORTING IDEA:** *Jesus' followers must be motivated by their love relationship with God.*

The last half of Matthew 6 deals with wrong perspectives regarding the material realm. In a word, *money*. In 6:19–24 Jesus dealt with our greed, while in 6:25–34 he dealt with our anxiety over basic necessities. These two problems are actually cousins to each other, because both display a lack of trust in the Father and a lack of eternal perspective.

It is not as obvious in this portion of the sermon that Jesus was confronting the hypocritical religious leaders and contrasting them with the truly righteous kingdom servant. But in the context of the entire Sermon on the

Mount (especially the theme of 5:20—exceeding the "righteousness" of the Pharisees), we may assume that such a contrast was intended. This is clear in light of the greed of the religious leaders (see 21:12–17).

There is a connection between this portion of the Sermon on the Mount and its immediate context (6:1–18). In the preceding section, Jesus contrasted the earthly reward of men's attention with the heavenly reward from the Father. Now, beginning in 6:19, he contrasted the transience of earthly wealth with the permanence of heavenly wealth. Even the teachings on anxiety (6:25–34) climaxes with the exhortation to **seek first his kingdom and his righteousness** (6:33) in the assurance that the fulfillment of our earthly needs will naturally follow. All of Matthew 6 seems to be saying, "Look up!" when our natural tendency is to look at the world around us (see Col. 3:1–2).

6:19–21. Verses 19 and 20 are almost exact parallels, designed for easy understanding and easy memorization. This is a critical passage. Here the king drew an ultimate contrast between **on earth** and **in heaven**. He urged his followers to forget earth and think of heaven. We must not waste our time trying to get ahead in this world. It is the same idea he expounded in 16:24–27. What does it profit a person "if he gains the whole world"? Jesus was demanding that his disciples look up and ahead—"for the Son of Man is going to come in his Father's glory . . . and then he will reward each person according to what he has done" (Matt. 16:27).

Jesus was summarizing why the kingdom servant is motivated to practice righteous acts. It is not for temporary honor among men on earth, but for eternal reward before the Father in heaven. The point of this life is preparation for the world to come. The present tense verb here can best be translated, "Stop storing up treasures on earth!" But Jesus does specifically command us to **store up for yourself** in heaven. Moths were universally known as a destructive force (Job 4:19; Isa. 50:9; 51:8). Burglary was especially common in the day of mud-brick homes. **Break** is the Greek term meaning "break through." It literally means "dig through." There is no permanence in this world. You cannot take your treasure with you into the next world, but you can send it on ahead through kingdom-oriented stewardship.

Jesus not only saw nothing wrong with his followers working for reward; he went so far as to command it. The New Testament clearly encourages it (e.g., 1 Cor. 3:10–15; 9:24–27). Jesus' words in the last few verses of the Bible emphasize it: "Behold, I am coming soon! My reward is with me, and I will give to everyone according to what he has done" (Rev. 22:12).

This concept of storing up heavenly treasure by doing good works was common in rabbinic tradition, and so it would have been easily understood by Jesus' audience and Matthew's readers. (New Testament passages that expand on this concept, including specific examples of behaviors that have eternal significance, include Matt. 5:12,30,46; 6:6,15; 10:42; 16:24–27; 19:21,27–29; 25:40; Luke 12:16–21; 2 Cor. 4:17; 1 Tim. 6:13–19.)

6:22–23. The conditional "if" statements of 6:22b–23a are parallel, again using the form of poetic wisdom literature.

These two verses can be confusing until we look at them in the light of the preceding and following context. We have not departed from the theme of the person's attitude toward material wealth. Jesus spoke of a small part of the body as being very important to the body as a whole, much as James claimed that anyone who could tame his tongue could tame his whole body (Jas. 3:1–12). No muscle of the body can relax if the eye is uncomfortable. Both Jesus and James were speaking of the inner human control over one's attitude toward wealth and one's choice of words. These two limited aspects of human choice can have profound consequences for the entire person (the **whole body,** figuratively speaking).

In keeping with the figurative language, the **light** would be an accurate perspective on the value of material wealth, while **darkness** would be some warped distortion of this truth. The person with a generous **eye** can see clearly, and life can be guided in wisdom and safety by such **light.** The person with a covetous, selfish **eye** is walking in **darkness** and is bound for harm he cannot see." Poor perspective causes stumbling.

6:24. The center of this verse is, again, a symmetrical parallel pair of statements, poetically memorable. The term **Money** is from the Aramaic *mamon,* meaning "wealth" or "property." It is anything in which a person places confidence. Jesus carefully chose here the picture of a slave. There could be no doubt about the issue of control. No person can serve two masters.

Any compromise of allegiance in this issue reminds us of the Lord's attitude toward those who are "lukewarm" in Revelation 3:15–16. It seems to suggest he thinks even less of those who claim to serve him, but have other loyalties, than he does of those who claim no loyalty to him at all. The terms **hate** and **despise** should be taken to mean "be less devoted to," "disregard," or "love less." On the other hand, **love** and **be devoted to** would imply a higher priority commitment, not necessarily an exclusive commitment.

Trust God's Provision, Not Your Own (6:25–34)

SUPPORTING IDEA: *Jesus' followers must be motivated by confidence in the Father's provision for their basic needs.*

In this passage, we find the word *worry* or *worrying* six times. The word **Therefore** at the beginning of 6:25 is important in helping us understand the relationship between a kingdom servant and the king. In 6:19–24, the king expounded on his demand for unreserved devotion. Beginning in 6:25, he began to say, "Now, when you enter into this kind of total commitment to me, I am going to take care of you. Do not worry." Our commitment to him and his commitment to us go hand in hand. They are part of the covenant relationship he has established with his people. The person who is totally committed to the king has no need for worry.

This entire passage focuses almost exclusively on God's provision of (and our anxiety over) food and clothing. However, we must see these two items as simply two concrete examples used to teach a broader principle. We could just as easily insert any other basic need (shelter, a community of belonging, and so on) that can be a source of anxiety, which is also provided by the Father, and the principle applies equally. However, the examples of food and clothing are well chosen (particularly for the first-century world), because they are so foundational to our survival, and they illustrate so well the Father's provision for us.

6:25. Jesus' point could be translated as "stop worrying." The rhetorical questions in 6:25b imply, "If God is the provider of life and body, he will also provide for their sustenance."

6:26. In this verse Jesus came to the first of two illustrations, supporting his main theme in verse 25. Note the use again of the phrase **heavenly Father,** especially in this context of God's loving care. Jesus was not advocating waiting lazily for God's provision, but avoiding anxiety as we take responsibility for obtaining it.

6:27. This verse moves away from the specific example of food to the broader picture of anxiety in general, showing its utter futility. There is controversy over this verse's translation, but the NIV translates it as **add a single hour to his life.** Jesus was saying, "If you try to take your basic provision into your own hands, you will find you do not have the power over life and death. Only God has this power, and he will sustain you as long as his plan intends."

6:28–30. Here we are given a more fully developed picture of the second illustration supporting Jesus' main point in verse 25. Verse 30 is a conditional statement, assuming the truth of the condition. So it could just as easily be translated, "Since that is how God clothes the grass of the field." The qualifying phrase, **which is here today and tomorrow is thrown into the fire,** emphasizes the transience and worthlessness of the grass. If God cares so much for something of little value, he will certainly care even more for us who are of much greater value to him. This passage is not only an exhortation to trust the Father, but it is also an affirmation of our great worth in his eyes.

The words **you of little faith** in 6:30 should be translated literally "little faith ones" (and is used elsewhere in the New Testament only in Matt. 8:26; 14:31; 16:8; 17:20; Luke 12:28). While it can be a confrontational term, it may also be endearing. In this context, Jesus' tone was not scolding, but coaxing and reasoning. He was asking, "Do you trust your Father or not?"—

not with a slap in our face, but with an arm around our shoulder. Jesus was not belittling his disciples; he was encouraging them upward.

6:31–33. With these three verses, having illustrated and supported his theme, Jesus built his climax. In verse 32, he made two more points about anxiety. First, it was downright pagan; anxiety was the attitude of those who were not a part of God's kingdom. Second, it was totally unnecessary to worry about what to eat or drink or wear, because **your heavenly Father knows that you need them.**

If our life is not to be preoccupied with fretting over basic needs, what is our concern to be? The answer is, **his kingdom and his righteousness.** Those two terms are almost synonymous. God's kingdom means his sovereign rule in heaven and on earth, most particularly in and through the life of the individual believer. To seek his kingdom is to seek to ensure that his righteousness is done in heaven, on earth, and, most particularly, in and through our lives.

We are to seek *first* God's kingdom and righteousness. Everything starts here. This is to be our consuming priority. So it is important to remind ourselves of some basic kingdom realities. How does a person find God's righteousness that characterizes his kingdom? Jesus started his sermon by pointing out our utter spiritual bankruptcy. We have no righteousness of our own. Even our best attitudes and actions do not procure it. Righteousness comes as a merciful gift, grace through faith (Eph. 2:4–10).

The first reference to righteousness that we find in Scripture is Genesis 15:6. Abraham knew how a person received grace, and the apostle Paul confirmed it (Rom. 4:2–25). The New Testament makes it clear that the righteousness of God comes through faith in Jesus Christ (Rom. 3:22–24). That is the only way we may enter into God's kingdom. Jesus clarified this issue for Nicodemus (John 3:3). We cannot see the kingdom of God unless we are "born again."

So everything begins with our seeking his kingdom and righteousness. In fact, we are to keep on seeking God's kingdom and righteousness. But we are not to seek in the sense of looking for something hidden. Rather, we are to look for every opportunity to expand more fully his already established rule in our lives and in our world, in anticipation of the day when believers will reign with him (Matt. 19:27–29; Rom. 8:17; 2 Tim. 2:12; Rev. 2:26–27; 3:21) when he establishes his kingdom fully on this earth.

Notice how this passage (6:25–34), which seemed to be taking us in a new direction, actually returns us to the theme of 6:19–24—that we are not to allow anything to distract us from total devotion to God and his kingdom. This is the one priority we must embrace. Money and other concerns can distract us.

Three times in verses 32 and 33, we find the phrase **all these things.** We might imagine Jesus using it somewhat disparagingly. This was not to belittle the importance of basic necessities, but to place them at the back of the mind of his disciples, far behind his kingdom and righteousness in importance.

"All these things" are what pagans (and the Pharisees) scrambled after. "All these things" are thoroughly known by the Father. "All these things" will fall into place when we put God's kingdom and righteousness in its proper place and serve the kingdom's interests.

6:34. Jesus restated for the third time his command, **Do not worry**! This time he broadened it to include any possible anxieties we may have for tomorrow. As an expression of trust in his heavenly Father, the kingdom servant is to live in the present, trusting the Father for the grace to cover the needs of the present. "When tomorrow comes, the Father will provide the grace to cover its needs also," is the implied assurance.

> **MAIN IDEA REVIEW:** *Jesus' followers must be motivated by trust in God's provision rather than trust in any earthly source.*

III. CONCLUSION

Greed for material wealth can become so strong that it grows into a controlling influence in our lives. As believers, we can also be too concerned about daily necessities. Anxiety over daily needs is natural but not productive. The more we make God's kingdom the priority of our lives, the less we will worry about "things."

PRINCIPLES

- God sees the motives for our benevolent actions.
- God is a Father who cares about his children.
- God, who provides for plants and animals, cares even more for his children.
- Humans need to be forgiven and need to forgive those who have wronged them.
- God's kingdom is our first priority.

APPLICATIONS

- Pray to God according to his character as a generous Father.
- Build your prayer life on the simple but profound petitions of the Model Prayer.
- Seek reward from your Father in heaven, not the admiration of people on earth.
- Seek first to serve God and advance his kingdom. Do not allow any of the many possible distractions to pull this down on your priority list.
- When worry or anxiety intrudes, turn to God who cares for the flowers and provides food for the birds.

IV. LIFE APPLICATION

God Will Take Care of You

When the stock market crashed in 1929, J.C. Penney lost almost all of his material assets. Worry and anxiety set in. He became physically ill and deeply depressed. As a result, he had to be hospitalized.

Mr. Penney's illness became so severe that on one particular night he thought he was dying. When he woke up, he realized he was still alive. As he walked down the hospital corridor that day, he heard singing coming from the hospital chapel. The words were "God will take care of you, through every day, o're all the way."

These words kindled a spark of hope in his heart. He went into the chapel where the prayers and reading of Scripture directed his focus from his problems to God who cared about him and was able to deliver him from his difficult circumstances.

This was the turning point for J.C. Penney. He made a complete recovery from his illness and went on to build one of the most successful retail businesses in the United States. He had heeded Jesus' counsel to turn from worry to God.

V. PRAYER

Lord, teach me to seek first your kingdom and your righteousness, not being distracted by all the things of this world that compete for my loyalty and devotion.

VI. DEEPER DISCOVERIES

A. Key Thoughts about Prayer (6:5–15)

This passage is a good opportunity to correct some misconceptions about prayer. Prayer is fundamentally two things: (1) it is an expression of our powerlessness; and (2) it is an intimate conversation between Father and child. If we could see prayer in this light, we would long to pray more and we would pray more effectively. Prayer is tapping into the infinite resources of the living God.

This is an important point for those who view prayer as effective only if they "have enough faith"—implying that they must do some kind of "work" to get an answer from God. Faith is a total dependence on God. And prayer is the voice of faith. It shouts, *"Help! I need you!"*

This first clarification, that prayer is an expression of powerlessness, is also important for those who see prayer as a means for manipulating God.

God's will is far superior to ours. We need to become intimately acquainted with the heart of a loving Father and rest in the security of trusting him.

The second point of clarification—that prayer is an intimate conversation between Father and child—is essential. God provides for us the opportunity to enjoy him within a safe relational environment. Relationships can only be built through conversation.

Many people have tasted the intimacy of conversation with God and then entered the stale malaise of stifled growth. They need a fresh glimpse of the joy of coming boldly before the Father. They need to see prayer less as the words they speak and more as the continual awareness of the Father's presence and his involvement in their daily lives. Prayer is "words," but it is also a mind-set, an attitude that acknowledges the Father as a life partner and a loving authority.

The person who enjoys the most intimate communion with God is the one who lives on the edge of obedience to God's clear, revealed will.

B. Summary

We must view Matthew 6 in two contexts: (1) as part of the Sermon on the Mount; and (2) as part of the overall Gospel. Matthew 6 develops the theme established in 5:20, "unless your righteousness surpasses that of the Pharisees and the teachers of the law, you will certainly not enter the kingdom of heaven." This divine, surpassing righteousness is required for entering the kingdom. As the Beatitudes stated, the kingdom belongs to those who recognize their spiritual bankruptcy. This is the starting point. The kingdom servant seeks not a righteousness of his own (as the Pharisees did), but God's kingdom and righteousness.

Matthew 5:21–48 clarifies the extent or degree of the kingdom servant's commitment to righteousness, in contrast with that of the hypocrites. Matthew 6 clarifies the motivation behind the kingdom citizen's commitment to righteousness, again in contrast with the motives of the hypocrites. In chapter 7, Jesus will emphasize *the evidence* of the kingdom citizen's commitment to obedience, in contrast to the fruit of the hypocrites.

VII. TEACHING OUTLINE

A. INTRODUCTION

1. Lead Story: Two Kinds of Presidents
2. Context: Whereas Matthew 5 (esp. v. 5) focused on the fact that a kingdom servant has a changed heart, Matthew 6 talks about having a different perspective about our personal relationship with God. Much like the epistle to the Hebrews and 2 Peter 1:5–9, Christ is

teaching that those who have righteousness by faith alone now need to *add* to their faith what brings growth and reward.

3. Transition: Contrary to the way "religion" tells us to relate to God, the king is telling us that God wants us to relate to him personally, in secret. He does not want us to put on a religious performance for the sake of others. And in like manner, God wants us to realize that he cares about every detail of our lives, that we can trust him as we go through life.

B. COMMENTARY

1. Seek Your Reward from God, Not from People (6:1–18)
2. Seek to Serve God, Not Money (6:19–24)
3. Trust God's Provision, Not Your Own (6:25–34)

C. CONCLUSION

1. Wrap-up: God hates hypocrisy, but he cherishes an authentic personal relationship with his children.
2. Personal Challenge: Are there parts of your life that are shows or exhibits to get others to see how spiritual you are? Are you living in the confidence that God is overseeing your life and taking care of you in all circumstances?

VIII. ISSUES FOR DISCUSSION

1. What does it mean in practical terms for a person to "seek *first* the kingdom of God and his righteousness"?
2. Do you agree that the Lord's Prayer should really be called the Disciple's Prayer? Why or why not?
3. Should Christians today practice fasting? Why or why not?

Matthew 7

The King Speaks His Heart (Part III)

INTRODUCTION
Behavior That Is Golden

II. **COMMENTARY**
A verse-by-verse explanation of the chapter.

III. **CONCLUSION**
An overview of the principles and applications from the chapter.

IV. **LIFE APPLICATION**
Watch Out Who You Follow

Melding the chapter to life.

V. **PRAYER**
Tying the chapter to life with God.

VI. **DEEPER DISCOVERIES**
Historical, geographical, and grammatical enrichment of the commentary.

VII. **TEACHING OUTLINE**
Suggested step-by-step group study of the chapter.

VIII. **ISSUES FOR DISCUSSION**
Zeroing the chapter in on daily life.

I shall be telling this with a sigh

Somewhere ages and ages hence:

Two roads diverged in a wood, and I—

I took the one less traveled by,

And that has made all the difference.

Robert Frost

Matthew 7

 IN A NUTSHELL

Matthew challenges his readers to choose between obeying the will of God and disobeying the will of God. For the believer, this involves humility, self-examination, and dependence on him for everything.

The King Speaks His Heart (Part III)

I. INTRODUCTION

Behavior That Is Golden

I have one friend, betrayed by another, who managed to dig deep enough to apply the kingdom's Golden Rule to the betrayer. Let the forgiven betrayer tell the story of his "golden friend" in his own words:

Bill is one of my very few "soul mates" in life. That is not to say that we have very much in common or that we share any of the same interests or skills or hobbies. We are soul mates because we connect at the level of life values. We are passionate about building the same kingdom, and that cause is larger than the petty issues of our lives.

But several years ago I betrayed Bill. In my immaturity, I said some things that hurt him deeply, and would have provided any lesser man with reason to abandon the relationship. God used the resulting pain and confrontation to wake me up, and to cause me to see my error and to confess my sin. It was a hard moment for both of us, but perhaps the most significant time in defining our current relationship.

Bill never allowed my failure to destroy our relationship. He forgave me fully, accepting my sincere apology, and never mentioning the issue again. We are brothers in the battle of life.

Bill is the kind of golden friend we all need in this life. But, if the truth be known, we would all have to admit we like "the Golden Rule" when it benefits us. And we may not find ourselves so quick to offer its grace to another as Bill did.

It all boils down to a choice, a determination to go the extra mile for someone in need. The choice is made more difficult when the other person has deeply wounded us. Jesus made this choice, and he expects the same of his children. It is a golden road that can make all the difference in relationships.

II. COMMENTARY

The King Speaks His Heart (Part III)

MAIN IDEA: *The righteousness of Jesus' followers will be evident in their relationships and in their daily choices.*

This chapter contrasts the true way (doing the will of the Father) and the false way (not doing the will of the Father). Having exposed hypocrisy, Jesus pointed out our human tendency to judge others and not ourselves.

The Kingdom Servant Sees Self and Others Accurately (7:1–6)

SUPPORTING IDEA: *Jesus' followers discern their own faults before examining the faults of others.*

7:1–5. This is one of the most often misunderstood and misquoted passages in all the Bible. It is important to understand that Jesus was not making a blanket prohibition against all judgment and discernment, but only against that which is done in self-centered pride. A good summary of his meaning is, "Do not judge others until you are prepared to be judged by the same standard. And then, when you exercise judgment toward others, do it with humility."

A primary evidence for this interpretation is in 7:5. Jesus did command his listeners to help their brothers and sisters with the speck in their eye (exercise judgment concerning another person), but only *after* we have taken the log out of our own eyes. This presumes that we have acknowledged that we have at least as great an offending capacity as our brother or sister, and so have no cause to think of ourselves as better. Matthew 7:6 also denies a sweeping "no judgment whatsoever" interpretation in that it assumes we should have the good judgment to discern a "swine" when we see one. It is impossible to carry out many of the teachings of the Sermon on the Mount without exercising humble judgment concerning others (e.g., 5:6,7,9–11,20,39,44; 6:14–15; 7:6,15–20).

It is one thing to exercise judgment, and quite another to have a judgmental attitude. One is an action that might be carried out with right or wrong motives; the other is a negative character quality.

The theme of prideful judgment seems at first glance to be a radical departure from the flow of the sermon. However, when we consider some of the teaching Jesus had been giving his followers, we begin to understand why this warning is important. He had been challenging the people to rise above what had been wrongly considered the ultimate height of righteousness (5:20)—pharisaical self-righteousness. In fact, Jesus challenged them to perfection (5:48).

But Jesus also knew well our human tendency to take truth and use it to feed a new kind of hypocritical supremacy. He did not want the hypocritical followers of the Pharisees to become the hypocritical followers of Jesus. So he stopped and warned them to apply his teaching first to themselves, then to others.

This is the central application of 7:1–5. Our habitual response to Scripture must be to say, "What about me?" rather than, "What about others?"

The Greek word translated *judge, condemn, discern* is related to the English "critic" and "criticize."

The command at the beginning of 7:1 is present tense and, therefore, is best rendered as "stop judging." We are to get rid of a critical spirit, but seek to be a discerning person. (Passages that reinforce Jesus' teaching here are Rom. 2:1; 14:4,10–13; 1 Cor. 4:5; 5:12; Jas. 4:11–12.)

Verse 2 expands the principle stated in verse 1 with poetic parallelism. Some suggest that **measure** refers to charitable judgment. So verse 2 begins with a negative statement ("If you judge harshly, God will judge you harshly"), and ends with a positive statement ("If you judge generously, God will judge you generously").

In 7:3–5, the **speck** can mean a small speck of anything. The repeated reference to **your brother** refers to fellow disciples (5:1–2), meaning that Jesus had the Christian community primarily in mind. But the principle is also applicable to anyone. Jesus' own familiarity with the carpenter's shop and the frustration of sawdust and small particles in one's eye personalizes the illustration.

7:6. The second of Jesus' four final exhortations is another warning. This warning balances the first (7:1–5), and attempts to head off another misconception Jesus' listeners might have taken away from the sermon. At first glance, this verse is difficult to interpret because the terms **what is sacred, pearls, dogs,** and **pigs** are not explained. But the verse does guard against our tendency to oversimplify the **do not judge** (7:1) statement, instructing us to be discerning about the character of other people.

Dogs and **pigs** (wild and unclean) likely refer to people who are not only unbelievers but also active enemies of the gospel (15:14; Luke 23:8; 2 Cor. 6:14–18; 2 Pet. 2:22). The most likely interpretation is to take **what is sacred** and **pearls** to refer to the gospel or truth, and to take **pigs** and **dogs** to mean any person who persistently rejects the gospel or truth, whether Jew or Gentile. Jesus was teaching his people to use discernment when sharing the truth with others. To persist in sharing with a resistant person wastes time and energy. It can also destroy a relationship that might prove fruitful later. It could even (in the climate of growing persecution) result in harm to the believer; it could **tear you to pieces.**

Taking care with whom and how we share truth is an important principle for believers to grasp in their evangelistic efforts. When we share with our neighbors, we tend to feel we have failed if they do not accept the Lord on the spot. We need to be patient, giving our own lives a chance to speak as a testimony for Christ and allowing the Holy Spirit to take his time to work the truth we have shared into the heart and conscience of the unbeliever (John 16:8–11). However, we should not be lazy or inattentive to signs that the unbeliever might be ready for more. There is an art to walking the line between pushiness and apathy.

B The Kingdom Servant Sees the Father as His Provider (7:7–11)

SUPPORTING IDEA: *Jesus' followers are not afraid to make requests of their Father.*

7:7–8. The principle of persistent reliance on the Father as loving provider certainly applies to all these "good things." But Jesus probably had the disciples' temporal needs in mind. This is the simplest, most obvious meaning, and it would further underscore Jesus' teaching against anxiety over daily needs (6:25–34). This is Jesus' third of four "final exhortations" (7:1–12), addressing possible misconceptions people might take away from the sermon.

Verses 7 and 8 have six symmetrically arranged verbs paired first in a triplet of commands (7:7) and then in a triplet of affirmations (7:8). There is no need to try to distinguish different kinds of activity between **ask, seek,** and **knock.** Jesus was probably using the three verbs to refer to the same activity of petitioning the Father. His use of three different verbs added emphasis to his message. This three-pronged approach, together with the fact that all three verbs are in the present tense, conveys a clear picture of persistence in prayer.

The other three verbs in 7:7 (**will be given, will find,** and **will be opened**) are in the future tense, while in 7:8 **receives** and **finds** are in the present tense, and **will be opened** is in the future.

With these tenses in mind, we could translate 7:7–8 as, "Keep on asking, and it will be given to you; keep on seeking, and you will find; keep on knocking, and it will be opened to you. For everyone who keeps on asking will continually receive, and he who keeps on seeking will continually find, and to him who keeps on knocking it will be opened."

Some other passages on prayer (e.g., Matt. 21:22; Mark 11:24; John 14:13–14; 15:7), emphasize the manner in which the human activity is to be conducted. Here the emphasis is on the generosity and faithfulness of the Father. There is no condition placed on the promises (as "if you believe" in 21:22). James 4:2–3 gives some reasons why prayer sometimes does not "work." Other passages that teach persistence in prayer are Luke 11:5–8; 18:1–8.

7:9–11. Verses 9 and 10 are rhetorical questions, implying that no parent would pull such tricks on their sincere children. A stone can resemble a loaf of "bread" (4:3), and some "snakes" can resemble "fish."

In my experience as a pastor, I have come across several people who have a deeply rooted impression of God as a trickster. They view him as a kind of cosmic killjoy with a warped sense of humor. These individuals often come from an abusive background, so their ability to trust a father figure has been severely damaged. To them, God lives only to bring them some kind of grief, usually after stringing them along and lulling them into a sense of security. As a result, they withhold intimate trust from him. Ironically, these people also tend to have a firm conviction about the moral superiority of God, so they do not see his trickery as evil on his part, but as something they have come to deserve.

Throughout the Sermon on the Mount, Jesus set up stringent standards for his disciples, but he also went to great lengths to change people's picture of God the Father. In today's environment of parental abuse, transient relationships, and growing isolationism, this portion of Scripture provides comfort for the deepest needs of many adults who are, inwardly, abandoned children.

In 7:11, Jesus brought his argument of verses 9–11 to a point. Because even the most evil parents provide the basic necessities for their children, how much more can we trust the Father in heaven, who is free from sin. (Note the assumption here of universal sinfulness; see Rom. 3:23.)

C The Kingdom Servant Stands in Others' Shoes (7:12)

SUPPORTING IDEA: *Jesus' followers treat others with kindness.*

7:12. The "Golden Rule" needs to be seen in a fresh light. For those who know the Bible, this verse has the tendency to go the way of John 3:16, often quoted but seldom applied. Jesus gave his audience a simple and profound principle to guide them in relating to others. We are to treat them the way we would want them to treat us in the same circumstance.

Jesus indicated that this "Golden Rule" sums up much of the Old Testament teaching on interpersonal relationships. Leviticus 19:18, together with Deuteronomy 6:5, quoted by Jesus in Matthew 22:35–40, is essentially an equivalent statement (see also Rom. 13:8–10; Gal. 5:14).

D Conclusion: The Kingdom Or Destruction (7:13–27)

SUPPORTING IDEA: *Jesus' followers make choices each day that lead to life, not destruction.*

Jesus finished his sermon with a series of challenges to wise choice and obedient action. He provided no new ethical teaching; rather, he challenged the disciple to obey what had already been taught. It is probably best to see 7:15–20 and 7:21–23 together as one warning rather than as a series of different warnings. These warnings emphasize the same message: *Choose!*

Then throughout the conclusion, the basic choices are laid before us. We see contrasts between two choices: life or destruction. This passage is the New Testament equivalent of the blessings and curses of Leviticus 26 and

Deuteronomy 11:26–29; 28. We also see a strong parallel to Moses' parting challenge: "I call heaven and earth as witnesses against you that I have set before you life and death, blessings and curses. Now choose life, so that you and your children may live and that you may love the LORD your God, listen to his voice, and hold fast to him" (Deut. 30:19–20a; cf. Matt 16:24–27).

Another thread throughout the conclusion is the emphasis on doing God's will. Jesus prescribed the test of false prophets-teachers (Deut 13:1–11; 18:20–22). Every speaker and teacher of Scripture is to be tested against the truths in God's Word (Jude 3; Rev. 22:18–19). Note **fruit** (7:16–20), **he who does the will of my Father"** (7:21), **evildoers** (7:23), and **puts them into practice** (7:24). The difference between life and destruction boils down not to what a person hears and believes, but to what he *does*. The dividing line lies between doing right and doing wrong rather than between doing the spectacular and doing the ordinary (7:22–23).

Jesus made it clear that moral behavior is more important even than miraculous acts. Character matters. This warning must lead us to the conclusion that what may appear to be miraculous can be either: (1) convincingly faked or (2) imitated by evil powers. Miraculous acts in and of themselves guarantee nothing.

In the broader context, this emphasis on doing righteousness cannot be construed as a works-oriented gospel. Jesus placed obedience in the context of the picture of a helpless child (5:3–5,36; 6:11,25–34; 7:7–11) who is utterly dependent on the Father, even for the ability to do what is right (5:6; 6:12–13). Other New Testament passages that emphasize *doing* righteousness are Matthew 5:16,20,48; Romans 2:13; James 1:22,25; 2:14; 1 John 2:17.

A third thread found in the sermon's conclusion is the continual reference to final judgment. Note **life** and **destruction** (7:13–14), **fire** (7:19), **enter the kingdom of heaven** (7:21), **on that day** (7:22), **away from me** (7:23), and the foolish builder's house that **fell** (7:27). Jesus made it clear to his listeners that their present choices had eternal consequences, so *now* was the time to choose wisely. Jesus was concerned that his followers live every day alert to coming judgment.

7:13–14. In his first concluding warning—the "two ways"—Jesus talked about the rigors of true discipleship. The **narrow gate** is the way of personal faith in Christ. This is precisely what the Pharisees missed so badly (Matt. 5:20). The Pharisees used **the wide . . . gate**, which is the normal human tendency toward dependence on self-righteousness. The number of people who would, historically, find the narrow way has by now mounted into the millions, if not billions. But Jesus' **few** is a relative term. The true servant of the kingdom will always be in the minority.

7:15–20. Jesus began his second concluding warning with a clear statement of the kind of person he will be discussing in 7:15–23. They are **false**

prophets—people claiming to be mouthpieces for God. He also began with a single-statement metaphor—ferocious wolves in sheep's clothing—before switching to the metaphor of the two trees. The common theme between the two metaphors is the attempt to deceive, but the inability to do so. A wolf may get away with his deception for a time, but his true nature will become apparent when his hunger forces him to act like a wolf. In the same way, a thorn bush or thistle cannot keep up the deception of being a grapevine or fig tree, especially when the season for fruitbearing arrives.

Even though he spent most of his time on the tree metaphor, Jesus had an important reason for inserting the wolf metaphor (Acts 20:27-31)—to alert his listeners to the danger of a false prophet. If the false prophets were thought of as a source of bad fruit, then the disciples might think it was enough simply to recognize and ignore the false prophet, refusing to consume his bad fruit, and awaiting God's judgment on him. But the wolf metaphor attributes a more active and malicious motive to the false prophet. He is actually an enemy of the sheep, and, if not confronted, will get his way by destroying the sheep.

Although Matthew 7 distinguishes between true kingdom righteousness and hypocritical pseudo-righteousness (5:20), Matthew 17:15 comes closest to identifying the religious leaders as Jesus' target. Of all the people in Jewish culture, they were the ones most likely to be seen as spokesmen for God. And, of the three warnings of 7:13-27, Jesus reserved his strongest and most pointed language for this central warning. But Jesus' warning concerned not only the Jewish religious leaders of his day. He was preparing his followers (hence his church) to be able to discern those of any age who would profess to be disciples of Jesus, but who were really out for their own selfish purposes (also a major theme in Titus and 1 John). Jesus repeated his central theme twice in 7:16,20: **By their fruit you will recognize them.**

The expression **is cut down and thrown into the fire** implies the judgment of God (cf. with John's warning in 3:10,12; 13:40,42,50; 18:8-9; 25:41; Luke 13:6-9; John 15:6). The use of the present tense in both verbs implies that this was common practice among those who pruned orchards, but there is also an implied reference to future judgment, and the present tense intensifies the certainty of the future event.

This warning pertains primarily to those who were never believers in the first place. But believers would also do well to heed this as a warning against any kind of false or hypocritical obedience in our lives. It is possible for a believer, destined for eternal life, to experience some of the unhealthy fruit of death and destruction along the way (1 Cor. 3:1-4; 11:30-32).

7:21-23. This embellishment on the two-trees theme shares many similarities with Matthew 25 (note verses 11-12,41-44). As is true throughout the sermon's conclusion (7:13-27), the emphasis here is on *doing* God's will.

This time the doing is contrasted with lip service, calling Jesus **Lord, Lord.** This double usage of "Lord" is found elsewhere only in 25:11 (also a parabolic reference to the day of judgment) and Luke 6:46 (parallel to this verse). Since the occasion for these quotes is **on that day,** on the verge of entering the kingdom of heaven, we can safely assume that "Lord" is to be taken with the impact of the Old Testament *Adonai*. Jesus here indirectly acknowledged his deity.

But the point of the passage is that someone else's acknowledgment of Jesus' deity will not be sufficient for their entrance into the kingdom, if they have not done the will of the Father. Note that this does not imply that if a person did the will of the Father but did not acknowledge Jesus as Lord, he or she might still enter heaven (see Rom. 10:9–10; 1 Cor. 12:3; Phil. 2:11).

This is the first time in Matthew that Jesus has said, **my Father.** It is significant that Jesus so closely associated himself with the Father that he implied his own deity as well as his role as the final judge.

The evidence that the claimants brought before Jesus in 7:22 would seem quite spectacular and convincing to most of Jesus' listeners. In fact, these were the kinds of works Jesus had been doing for some time (4:23–25). They were validating his claims and drawing large crowds. Therefore, this was a startling statement for Jesus to make. His listeners must have thought, *If we cannot believe prophecy, exorcisms, and miracles—especially those done in the name of Jesus—as signs of a true prophet, then what* can *we believe?*

Jesus went to this length to demonstrate the importance of righteousness by faith alone in Christ alone (Rom. 4) as the criterion for entry into the kingdom. Even doing the activities that he was doing was not sufficient. We should be warned that counterfeits today will look very much like they are carrying on the work of Jesus. But we must look at their lives as well as their works. Our culture's compartmentalization between a person's personal life and his or her professional life was a foreign concept to Jesus.

In 7:21–23 we have seen at least three ways the counterfeits try to get by without actual obedience: (1) lip service, claiming loyalty to Jesus as Lord and God; (2) spectacular signs; and (3) performing these signs **in your name,** in essence claiming them to be the work of God. What would lead someone to such an elaborate subterfuge? It seems easier to obey than to go to all this trouble in an attempt to fool the Lord. *Pride* is the answer. In our efforts to protect the little god of "self," we humans can go to amazing lengths.

Jesus' response to the counterfeits was harsh, because he revealed that he had the power of the eternal judge. In the first part of his response, he used a verb meaning to "know by experience." The greatest blessing in life and eternity is to know the Lord personally, and to be known in the same way by him. The greatest curse is to have this relationship denied.

The second part of Jesus' response, **Away from me, you evildoers**, is a quote from Psalm 6:8. In this psalm, David warned evildoers of their judgment, subsequent to his petition to God. Matthew used the present tense with an imperative force of the verb, meaning "go away, depart." He also used **evildoers** as a synonym for those who practice evil. This is significant in light of Jesus' clarification of the original intent of the Old Testament law in 5:17–48. This is the bottom line of the sermon and kingdom righteousness. Even if a person performed works identical to those of Jesus, did those works in the name of Jesus, and called on Jesus as Lord and God, he would still be breaking God's law if his life was not lawful according to Jesus' definition throughout this sermon. True righteousness can be derived only from the Savior.

7:24–27. In this third and final challenge to choose between life and destruction, Jesus made it even clearer that the criterion for a righteous life is obedience to Jesus' teaching. His righteousness was diametrically opposed to pharisaical self-righteous works. Note **these words of mine** (7:24,26). The possessive pronoun **mine** is in the emphatic beginning position in that phrase. Jesus was equating his own words with the will of his Father (7:21). Jesus was claiming to have the same authority as the God who authored the Old Testament Scriptures—a claim he also implied in clarifying the original intent of the law in 5:17–48.

Jesus did not leave it to the crowd to perceive his authority (7:28–29). He claimed it openly. This is quite an audacious claim, unless he actually had the authority to make it. Jesus did not give his skeptics much room to maneuver in their opinion of who he was—he was either everything he says he was . . . or he was nothing at all. He must be fully accepted or fully rejected, for no "good moral teacher" would say the astonishing things Jesus did unless they were true. Jesus is God's Son.

Therefore in 7:24 refers to the preceding clarification (7:13–23), which justifies the generalizations Jesus made in 7:24–27. Anyone who knows of the coming judgment (7:21–23) but ignores Jesus' teaching is as foolish as a person who builds a house on sand.

The people represented by the two builders share one similarity and one difference. Both "keep on hearing" the words of Jesus. The present tense may imply that both hearers had been exposed to his teachings. In any case, both hearers were now accountable to obey what they had heard. However, the first person "keeps on doing" what Jesus taught, while the second "keeps on *not* doing" what Jesus taught.

The first man was wise; the second man was foolish. The first man found stability and blessing in this life and in eternity; the second experienced calamity in this life and in eternity (the rain, floods, and winds can represent both hardships in this life and God's final judgment).

Notice that wisdom (**the rock**) means to put the words of Jesus into practice.

Ⅲ The Crowd Recognizes the King's Authority (7:28–29)

SUPPORTING IDEA: *Jesus' followers recognize Jesus' authority in his demands for righteous character.*

7:28–29. Jesus began the Sermon on the Mount with only his intended audience (his disciples) present, but by the time he concluded a crowd had gathered. Matthew's closing comments to the sermon emphasize that the crowds were **amazed**. Matthew used the Greek imperfect tense to denote an ongoing effect in Jesus' listeners. They just could not get over it. But it says nothing about their commitment. This is the only one of five discourses Matthew recorded in which he commented on the crowd's response. This does not mean that this discourse was unique, for Matthew continued to use the same word of the crowd's response to Jesus' teaching in a more general way (13:54; 19:25; 22:33). Most likely, he wanted his readers to understand that the crowd had this kind of response to Jesus' teaching wherever he went and whatever he taught.

Both the content and manner of Jesus' teaching were overwhelming. Unlike other teachers, he taught with **authority** (7:29). Unlike them, he did not cite other authorities—only his own and his Father's. And it was he alone who decided who would enter the kingdom and on what basis they would do so—through a personal relationship with God.

Jesus' authority is one of the central themes in Matthew. Jesus anticipated the questions of his listeners, "Who is this man that he speaks with such authority?" Matthew is about to demonstrate, by his collection of miracles in chapters 8–9, that Jesus was precisely who he claimed to be. Matthew now transitioned from Jesus' teachings into a lengthy account of his early miracles (chaps. 8–9) and his delegation of authority to his disciples (ch. 10). Jesus' authority increased the tension between Jesus and the hypocrites that would grow throughout the remainder of the book.

MAIN IDEA REVIEW: *The righteousness of Jesus' followers will be evident in their relationships and in their daily choices.*

III. CONCLUSION

The Golden Rule is a profound principle for living in relationship with other people. If other people treated you the way you treat them, how would life be for you?

PRINCIPLES

- Human beings exaggerate their own virtues and minimize or ignore their faults.

- Humans are quick to judge others.
- Disciples are to be proactive and persistent in their relationship with God.
- Actions and attitudes have eternal consequences.
- False prophets are wolves disguised as sheep.

APPLICATIONS

- Keep on asking, seeking, and knocking.
- Take a close and accurate look at yourself before you judge others.
- Evaluate present actions and attitudes in light of God's judgment and the eternal consequences that result.
- Use discernment in timing and persistence when you share the gospel with unbelievers.
- Understand and accept the narrow road of hardship and persecution (7:13–14).
- Recognize false prophets by their fruit and realize they are malicious.

IV. LIFE APPLICATION

Watch Out Who You Follow

A man was walking through a cemetery and noticed a tombstone that caught his attention. The epitaph read:

As you are now, so once was I.

As I am now, you are sure to be.

So may I say, as now I lie,

Prepare yourself, to follow me.

The man took out a piece of chalk and wrote two more lines under the epitaph:

To follow you I'm not content,

Until I know which way you went.

V. PRAYER

Dear Father, make me gentle and loving, not harsh and critical, in my discernment and judgment of others. Help me to remove the log from my own eye before I search for the speck in the eye of another person.

VI. DEEPER DISCOVERIES

A. Summary

A lesser teacher might have finished the body of his sermon at the end of chapter 6, then added a suitable conclusion. But Jesus knew there were misconceptions people were likely to take away from what he said. Before closing, he added four final, balancing exhortations in an attempt to head off some of these misconceptions.

Verses 1–5 challenge people to humility and self-examination, lest Jesus' lofty teaching cause some to believe they are better than others. Verse 6, on the other hand, challenges people to be discerning, lest they become too tolerant of the kingdom's enemies. Verses 7–11 encourage God's beloved children to depend on him for everything, lest they fear his rejection after failing his high standards. And verse 12 sums up the entire sermon, lest people get caught up in the minute details of obedience, as a pharisaical mind is prone to do.

When Jesus closed the sermon, he did it with three parabolic warnings, challenging people to choose between the kingdom (obeying the will of the Father as revealed in Jesus' teachings) and destruction (disobeying the words of Jesus). Implicit in this warning was Jesus' claim that he was the source of Scripture and the judge of those who hear it.

B. The Authority Issue

Matthew 7 shows how Jesus prepared his followers for life in the church age. It raises the theme of authority, which will be key throughout the book. Who should the people follow—Jesus or the religious leaders? Who has the real authority of God behind him? How will we recognize it? Who will win the ultimate battle? Get ready for increasing conflict in the chapters ahead.

VII. TEACHING OUTLINE

A. INTRODUCTION

1. Lead Story: Behavior That Is Golden
2. Context: This is the third of three chapters that comprise the Sermon on the Mount—a message Jesus gave to his disciples. Overheard by the multitudes, it is also intended for us today.
3. Transition: This portion of the Sermon on the Mount has two main parts. First, the focus is on how a person should relate to others. This concludes with the Golden Rule as the principle for relating to others. Second, Matthew challenged his audience to make a choice, realizing his readers' choices would have eternal consequences.

B. COMMENTARY

1. The Kingdom Servant Sees Self and Others Accurately (7:1–6)
2. The Kingdom Servant Sees the Father as His Provider (7:7–11)
3. The Kingdom Servant Stands in Others' Shoes (7:12)
4. Conclusion: The Kingdom Or Destruction (7:13–27)

C. CONCLUSION

1. Wrap-up: Jesus challenged his listeners to make a choice at the end of his sermon. This challenge should send us back to review "these words of mine" to which he referred.
2. Personal Challenge: Have you actually heard Jesus' words and responded by choosing to enter into a personal relationship with him? Knowing Jesus—not just knowing about him and speaking his language—is the key to entering the kingdom of heaven.

VIII. ISSUES FOR DISCUSSION

1. What is the Golden Rule? How can we apply its principles in our relationships with others?
2. Which is more important in prayer—our persistence or asking in accordance with the Father's will?
3. What picture of God does Jesus paint in this section of the Sermon on the Mount?
4. What are some methods of subterfuge and trickery used by false prophets?
5. Why were the crowds amazed at Jesus' teachings in the Sermon on the Mount?

Matthew 8–9

The King Demonstrates His Authority

I. INTRODUCTION
Real Love and True Authority Go Together

II. COMMENTARY
A verse-by-verse explanation of these chapters.

III. CONCLUSION
An overview of the principles and applications from these chapters.

IV. LIFE APPLICATION
Counting the Cost

Melding these chapters to life.

V. PRAYER
Tying these chapters to life with God.

VI. DEEPER DISCOVERIES
Historical, geographical, and grammatical enrichment of the commentary.

VII. TEACHING OUTLINE
Suggested step-by-step group study of these chapters.

VIII. ISSUES FOR DISCUSSION
Zeroing these chapters in on daily life.

"*The capacity to give one's attention to a sufferer is a very rare and difficult thing; it is almost a miracle; it is a miracle. Nearly all those who think they have this capacity do not possess it. Warmth of heart, impulsiveness, pity are not enough.*"

Simone Weil

Matthew 8–9

IN A NUTSHELL

In these two chapters we see Jesus demonstrate his authority. Matthew balances this major theme with the theme of compassion. The three miracles in chapter 8 show Jesus' willingness to become unclean in order to make others clean. His works of healing and forgiveness were signs that God's kingdom was dawning.

The King Demonstrates His Authority

I. INTRODUCTION

Real Love and True Authority Go Together.

I tend to be my own worst enemy. You probably do, too. I remember as a kid getting all caught up in myself. Those terrible, horrible, prepubescent years. I made friends with a couple of seedy characters (for a few weeks before my dad got hold of me). I mean we were tough, at least in our own minds.

One time we crawled up in my tree fort with a pack of cigarettes one of the guys had stolen somewhere. When we ran out of matches, I ran into the house for a new supply. But my mother, with a nose like a bloodhound, smelled that cigarette smoke a block away. I was caught! She told Dad and "suggested" I report to the front steps where my father was reading the newspaper.

I approached Dad sheepishly from the back. But he would not turn around. He just kept reading the paper. I just stood there, slowly falling apart inside. He knew I was there. I knew he knew I was there. But he would not say anything to me. He just let me stand there and "stew in my own juice." When I was sufficiently undone, my father said simply, "Son, do you mean to tell me that, knowing how strongly and negatively I feel about smoking, you went ahead and did it anyway?" He then turned back to his paper. End of conversation.

It was in those desperate moments that I learned about the power of loving authority. Later, of course, Dad in fuller conversation forgave me for betraying his intentions for me. I knew he loved me. And I also knew he would not bend his standards. That day I learned a lesson for life. Authority and love are two of the most basic elements in the universe. And when they come together in the same person, they are an incredibly powerful combination. I learned that real fathers love enough not to compromise their values.

That is Jesus—love and authority personified. His love is deeper than any other love. His authority is higher than any other authority. And he compromises neither. He loves people. And he insists on upholding his principles of righteousness.

Who does Jesus think he is? That was undoubtedly the question running through the minds of the people who had just overheard the Sermon on the Mount. "Who is this man to speak so authoritatively?" Matthew regarded this as a legitimate question. He answered it in chapters 8–9 when he recounted miracle after miracle to demonstrate the power of the king. Jesus' loving compassion and his uncompromising authority came together in power. These compassionate, authoritative miracles demonstrate the power of the king. Observe Jesus very carefully in chapters 8–9 as he uses his power selectively.

Think about faith. What is faith? A source of great power from within ourselves? That is a concept many Christians have embraced from other religions, or from fleshly pride. But biblical faith is something quite different. In fact, faith is really an expression of power*less*ness that invites the true source of power to step in. Many times in chapters 8–9, powerless people demonstrated that the strength to do the miraculous was not in the believer, but it had its source in the One believed. Faith is our invitation to the Lord to do as he wishes, what we by ourselves find impossible. And prayer is the voice of faith. We must ask ourselves whether we truly understand how weak we are.

It is a common misconception that a Christian must "work up" to a certain level of faith in order to experience God's power in his or her life. This is a reversal of true faith. In reality, faith consists of giving up on our own lonely efforts and acknowledging our dependence on God. Throughout Matthew 8–9 we will see the helplessness of the people who received demonstrations of the king's power. Note the frequent use of the words *faith* or *believe* (both from the same Greek word *pisteuo*).

This is not to say that there is nothing for us to do in obedience. In fact, the "faith chapter" (Heb. 11) is packed with expressions of active faith. But faithful obedience is carried out with the knowledge that even that would be impossible without the enabling power of the king.

II. COMMENTARY

The King Demonstrates His Authority

MAIN IDEA: *Jesus demonstrates that he has absolute authority, exercised with compassion, proving himself to be Messiah.*

Springing directly out of his demonstration of authority through his teaching of the Sermon on the Mount (7:28–29), Jesus now proceeded to demonstrate that his authority extended to more than his teaching. In fact, he is the absolute authority, the complete sovereign—in a word, the Almighty. This is the next step in Matthew's methodical presentation of Jesus as the promised Messiah-King. Not only would observers and readers recognize Jesus as exercising the power of God, but, more specifically, they would see his miracles as fulfillment of messianic prophecies such as Isaiah 53:4 (quoted in Matt. 8:17) and Isaiah 35, especially verses 5–6.

Chapters 8–9, together with chapter 10, serve as a unit on the theme of Jesus' authority. In chapters 8–9, the king *demonstrates* his authority; in chapter 10, the king *delegates* his authority. The gemstone Matthew chose to place directly in the center of this three-chapter unit was the miracle of Matthew's own conversion.

There is a continuity between the Sermon on the Mount and Matthew 8–9. In chapters 5–7, the people marveled at the authority of Jesus' words (7:28–29); in chapters 9–10, the authority of Jesus' word continues as a key feature (8:3,8,13,16,26–27,32; 9:6,9,29). This reminds us of the power of the Creator, who spoke the universe into being with a word (Gen. 1).

It is important to see also, along with the major theme of authority, an interwoven balancing theme of *compassion*. Unlike most earthly leaders (the hypocritical Jewish leaders in particular), the king did not exercise his authority for selfish ends, but in compassion to meet the needs of others. Jesus amazed the pharisaical mind. He touched a leper. He honored a Gentile for his faith. He crossed the Sea of Galilee to the unclean tombs in Gentile territory to free two men from demons. He associated with the scum of society. He healed and reassured a woman unclean from her bleeding. He touched a dead body. And he was moved by the vulnerability of the crowds to spiritual predators.

Many times he broke cultural taboos to exercise mercy toward the needy. In this way, he shook up the conventional thinking to reveal the priority of mercy as his mission (9:13, quoting Hos. 6:6). Notice how many times Matthew mentions touch as a part of Jesus' compassionate ministry (e.g., 8:3,15; 9:21,25,29). There is something deeply personal and compassionate in a gentle touch.

One expression of Jesus' compassion and mercy in this chapter is his response to every level of faith. He responded to the **great faith** of the centurion (8:5–13), as well as to the **little faith** of the disciples (8:23–27). He even responded to people who were unable to give voice to their faith, such as the demon-possessed men (8:28–34; 9:32–33), or people merely *accompanied* by those who had faith (the friends of the paralytic, 9:2). Jesus was moved by helplessness of all kinds—physical and spiritual.

In the midst of many accounts of physical healing, notice that spiritual healing was Jesus' highest priority. While our physical needs are important to him, he is even more eager to repair our souls and our relationship with him. In these chapters he used physical miracles to highlight the importance of faith (8:10–12,26; 9:28–29). He made the paralytic walk to make obvious the reality of the greater miracle of forgiveness he had performed (9:1–8).

It is also important to understand the miracles of these chapters in light of the purpose of miracles throughout the Bible. Certainly miracles meet an immediate need, about which God cares very much (a disease, a demon possession, a threatening storm), but throughout the Old and the New Testaments, these immediate needs are always the secondary purpose for the miracle. In virtually every instance, the primary purpose of the miracle was to validate a messenger and his message. The healing was not the message itself.

More specifically, most miracles served to validate the message of those who were actually the writers of Scripture. The biblical "seasons" of great miracle working surround the human authors of God's written Word—Moses, the prophets, and the disciples-apostles. The reason miracles have become so rare since the apostolic age is because God's message has been transmitted in full, and the messengers he used for its transmission have lived and moved on. The miracles recorded in Matthew serve to validate Jesus as the Messiah from God and, therefore, they also validate his claims and his teachings.

In the midst of these two chapters packed with miracles, Matthew inserted three non-miracle paragraphs, each making a spiritual claim endorsed by the surrounding miracles. In 8:18–22, Jesus claimed the right to exclusive loyalty from his followers, that they might give up even their homes and their family obligations to follow him. In 9:9–13 (see also 9:6), he claimed the authority to forgive even the worst of sinners. In 9:14–17, he claimed center stage as Israel's guest of honor. These were audacious claims. Therefore, they were surrounded by validating miracles.

Even in Jesus' day, many paralytics stayed on their beds, many blind remained sightless, and many demons remained unexorcised. Jesus did as many miracles as necessary to validate his identity and his message, that the deeper spiritual need of mankind might be addressed—that we might believe and be restored to our Maker. But nowhere did he heal entire villages.

Now, turning our focus to the beneficiaries of Jesus' miracles, we see marked contrasts. The first two examples provide perhaps the greatest contrast of all. From a worldly viewpoint, how much farther apart can two people get than a despised leper and a mighty Roman centurion? We also see Gentile (the centurion, who displayed **great faith**) versus Jews (Jesus' disciples, who showed **little faith**), and the official (**ruler**) of 9:18. The one theme throughout chapters 8–9 is that all these people were helpless to address their own need. All of them needed someone outside themselves to help them. Our helplessness, whether recognized or not, is the great equalizer before God. Jesus loves helpless people.

Notice the frequent use of **faith** and **believe**. Faith is the mature attitude that recognizes our helplessness and seeks help from God. We see in chapters 8–9 many positive models of faith, but we also see two departures from it. First, the disciples in the storm (8:23–27) realized their helplessness, but they did not understand that Jesus was to be the object of their faith. Helplessness with no object for faith is despair. Second, the Pharisees (9:3,11,34) were oblivious to their helplessness, so they saw no need for faith.

Another theme of these chapters is Jesus' emphasis on the training of his disciples. Even when the disciples are not mentioned, we may picture them standing to the side, observing and learning. Jesus capitalized on their experiences in these chapters when he resumed his training of the disciples in chapter 10. As Matthew's Gospel progresses, Jesus increasingly directs his focus to his inner circle. Even as he deals with the crowds and with his enemies, the disciples are involved and learning.

A The King's Authority over Illness (8:1–17)

SUPPORTING IDEA: *Jesus exercises authority and compassion to heal physical diseases.*

8:1. This was the mountain Jesus climbed to teach the Sermon on the Mount, and these were the **large crowds** that followed him in 4:23–25 because of his teaching and healing ministry. Now they had all the more reason to follow him, because of the authority he demonstrated through his teaching in chapters 5–7. Before such an audience Jesus continued to reveal his authority.

8:2. The mention of the word **leprosy** made the first-century reader gasp. Leprosy was the AIDS of the ancient world. Everyone was terrified of this disease. Anyone who came in contact with a leper was ritually unclean (Lev. 13–14) and at risk of his or her life. Lepers were outcasts. They were to stay far away from healthy people and were obligated to warn anyone who might come near (Lev. 13:45–46). This man's willingness to approach Jesus and violate acceptable practice was an expression of his faith. His confident words— not necessarily confidence in Jesus' willingness, but primarily in his ability— further emphasize the man's faith.

Lord was used as a title of respect, like "sir." The leper was conveying respect to Jesus.

8:3. Jesus' willingness to touch the leper was an expression of his compassion. Matthew went to great lengths to emphasize Jesus' action. Instead of recording "Jesus touched him," Matthew used an expanded version: **Jesus reached out his hand and touched the man**. Jesus' touch was purposeful. He extended himself for the benefit of this man in need.

When touching an unclean leper, Jesus would normally have become ceremonially defiled himself (Lev. 13–14). Of course, at Jesus' touch nothing can be defiled. Jesus not only remained clean; he made the unclean clean! Touch in Jesus' ministry is important throughout Matthew—especially in these chapters (8:15; 9:20,25,29). And, of course, the man's restoration was a testimony to the power and authority of Jesus the Messiah-King.

8:4. Periodically throughout the Gospels, we see Jesus warning people not to spread the word about a miracle they have witnessed (9:30; 12:16;

16:20; 17:9). Primarily, this was to keep Jesus' public notoriety within bounds until the time was right for his public conflict with the Jewish leaders. He did not intend to hide from the crowds, but his focus was on the training of his disciples. He needed to guard enough time before his arrest and death to see them through to the necessary level of maturity.

In this verse, Jesus' warning to the man also serves to underscore the urgency of going directly to the priest. According to Leviticus 13–14, there was a strict procedure for people with skin diseases. It involved periodic inspection by the priests and offering of sacrifice to restore the healed person's ritual cleanness before God. But beyond this, Jesus wanted the man to go to the priests at the temple **as a testimony to them.** This man's miraculous recovery from leprosy was to be an indication to the religious leaders that "Messiah-King is here!"

8:5–6. Jesus established his base of operations in Capernaum in 4:13. As with the leper, the mention of a Gentile centurion was meant to challenge the social taboos of the Jews. Certainly, the centurion was aware of the Jews' repulsion toward him. But desperate, he approached Jesus.

Centurions commanded a unit known as a century, but as is often the case in active military units today, the actual numbers were somewhat lower—sixty to eighty men. Centurions were the backbone of the Roman legions. Every biblical reference to a centurion casts them in a positive light.

In ancient times, many servants became as close as family members to their masters. This centurion displayed great love for his servant in his request. Notice the intensity with which he begged Jesus for healing. He also displayed a sense of helplessness through his appeal. He knew that he was inadequate to address his need, and he had need of help from someone else.

8:7. Jesus' simple response packs a world of meaning. To offer to enter a Gentile's home was unthinkable for a Jew—especially for a respected Jewish teacher (Acts 10:27–29). Israel never seemed to understand that as God's chosen people, they were to be a medium of ministry to all nations of earth (Gen. 12:3; Deut. 4:6–8; Ps. 67; Isa. 42:6–7; 49:6). Israel took the Lord's prohibitions against any fraternization that might lead Israel into idolatry, and they applied it wholesale to any contact with Gentiles. They also held to an elitist attitude, because they were the people to whom God had revealed the law (Rom. 2:17–29). They should have realized that he was revealing the law (his heart) not to them, but also *through* them to the world.

8:8–9. The centurion was aware of the Jewish taboo against visiting Gentile homes. In response to Jesus' offer, he explained that he understood the concept of true authority. Whereas he commanded men, and the men obeyed (Roman soldiers were known for exacting discipline and prompt obedience), he recognized that Jesus could command anything in creation, and it would obey. **Say the word,** he told Jesus (see discussion of the power of Jesus' word at 8:27). He probably did not understand the full identity of Jesus, but he recognized God's power working through him.

8:10–12. Jesus was not above surprise. He had been looking for genuine faith throughout his ministry, and here he found it, of all places, in the heart of a Gentile! He **was astonished.** Jesus turned to the crowd, elevating this man as a model for them all, and challenged those who should know better to believe as this heathen man believed. He pointed to the coming day of the kingdom's full realization when many Gentiles would be gathered from east and west to **take their places at the feast with Abraham, Isaac and Jacob.** The coming kingdom is often portrayed in terms of a feast, particularly a wedding feast (Isa. 25:6; Matt. 22:1–14; Rev. 19:7–10).

The phrase **subjects of the kingdom** in 8:12 refers to the Jews, who had been given all the covenants and promises, and who should have known how to be heirs of the kingdom. This statement shocked Jesus' Jewish audience. The idea that Gentiles would even be in the coming kingdom, let alone take their place, was unimaginable to the average Jew. Peter (as well as others of the disciples) would not fully appreciate Jesus' words until much later (Acts 10). They had adopted the prejudice and exclusiveness of Israel.

8:13. Jesus turned back to the centurion and assured him that his request had been honored, connecting the answer with the centurion's faith—**as you believed it would.** It was not the faith alone that healed the servant, but the fact that the centurion's faith was placed in a worthy object—the Messiah-King. Matthew then recorded that the servant was healed at the very moment Jesus proclaimed him healed.

8:14–15. After telling the stories of an unnamed leper and an anonymous centurion, Matthew included a brief account regarding a family member of one of Jesus' own inner circle. At the time of Matthew's writing, critics might have been able to dismiss the former two stories. But the naming of a specific person to whom living eyewitnesses were more likely to attest would silence many of Jesus' critics.

Again Jesus ministered through touch (8:3; 9:20,25,29). Religious leaders seldom touched a woman at all. They wanted to avoid any possibility of becoming "unclean" because of her monthly menstrual cycle (Lev. 15:19). Peter's mother-in-law, previously immobilized by fever, recovered so miraculously that she had strength to prepare a meal for Jesus.

8:16. Long into the night Jesus ministered to everyone who came. There was not a demon too powerful to remove **with a word,** and no illness was too great for him to heal. The Messiah-King was the sovereign authority over all creation, and he extended himself sacrificially in compassion to the desperate masses.

8:17. To seal his case even tighter, Matthew chose the context of this summary statement about Jesus' day of healing to show that Jesus fulfilled the messianic prophecy of Isaiah 53:4. And since he **was to fulfill** it before the atonement on Calvary, we have no basis for claiming special acts of "healing in the atonement" today. Later Matthew demonstrated that Jesus' fulfillment of this prophecy went far beyond the healing of the body to the healing of the sinful soul. But some may have recognized the connection between the physical healings and the promised spiritual healing (Isa. 33:24; 53:5–6; Hos. 14:4; Matt. 1:21).

B The Cost of Following the King (8:18–22)

SUPPORTING IDEA: *As Messiah-King, Jesus claims the right to undivided loyalty.*

Jesus was about to make some lofty claims on the lives and loyalties of those who would follow him. These claims were placed in the context of his miracles to validate his right to make them.

8:18. Jesus felt it was time to get away from the crowd. As long as he was being mobbed, he could not give his disciples the attention they needed. His orders to cross the lake (the Sea of Galilee) narrowed the number who could accompany him to a committed few.

8:19. One person who wanted to follow Jesus was a teacher of the law. We have already seen these Jewish experts in the Old Testament Scriptures mentioned three times (2:4; 5:20; 7:29), twice in a negative light. They will be mentioned several times again, almost always lumped together with the Pharisees as part of the hypocritical Jewish leadership opposing Jesus.

Of all people, these experts of the Scriptures should have been the first to recognize the Messiah-King, but their pride and exclusivism blinded most of them. Here we meet an exception. His commitment was similar to that of Joseph of Arimathea and Nicodemus (John 3:1–21; 7:50–52; 19:38–42). The scribe's use of the title **Teacher** for Jesus probably demonstrated the man's submission to Jesus' authority, especially in the area of his expertise.

8:20. Jesus warned the man that following him would not be easy and might involve a life of deprivation and poverty. Jesus had recently taught that his Father would care for people better than he did for the birds and the flowers (6:25–34). Now he taught that those who follow him will have even less than the animals—no place to call home. While food and clothing are physical necessities for human survival, an established home is not. However, part of human emotional make-up is a strong drive for the security of a home. Jesus' demand for his followers was not impossible, but it was lofty enough that only the most committed would accept it. We are not told whether the teacher of the law followed Jesus.

This is the first of twenty-nine times that Matthew mentions the title **Son of Man**. Jesus used this messianic title more than eighty times to refer to himself. From clues solely within Matthew, such as the heavy use of the title in connection with Jesus' role as judge in the end times, we can discern that it connotes the identity and power of deity. This is in keeping with the meaning that most educated Jewish listeners and readers would give the title, knowing of its use of the glorified Messiah in Daniel 7:13–14. However, the wording itself (Son of Man) emphasizes Jesus' identification with humanity. By its use, Jesus was claiming to be the Messiah-King, but he also postponed confrontation with the Jewish leaders because of the human connotations of the title.

8:21–22. In this ancient culture, one of an eldest son's responsibilities was taking care of his father's final arrangements. It is likely this son's father had not yet died, and he was simply stalling indefinitely by appealing to family responsibilities. This was a typical stalling tactic, not unlike that for which Jesus chided the Pharisees in Mark 7:11. But whatever the cultural expectations, the point is clear—Jesus expects of his kingdom servants unqualified submission to his lordship. Commitment to Jesus is to be without reservation.

Ⓒ The King's Authority over Nature (8:23–27)

SUPPORTING IDEA: *Jesus exercises authority over nature, even in response to unbelief.*

8:23–24. Having filtered the curious and uncommitted from among his disciples by clarifying the price they would pay (8:18–22), Jesus and his disciples got into the boat he had ordered in 8:22. Matthew highlighted the leadership of Jesus by his language: "Then he got into the boat and his disciples followed him." Those who followed were the few who were willing to pay the price of 8:18–22.

The Sea of Galilee was well-known for sudden, unpredictable, and violent storms. It is about thirteen miles long from north to south, and nearly seven miles wide at its widest, from west to east. To travel from Capernaum (8:5) at the north end of the sea to the region of the Gadarenes (8:28) at the southeast end would have meant crossing the longest distance possible across the lake. Matthew pointed out that waves were sweeping over the boat. The natural reaction of anyone in this situation would be to bail out the water, so the disciples must have been working feverishly.

That Jesus managed to sleep at such a time attests to his humanity. He was exhausted from a long day of ministry. Even though the events of Matthew 8–9 are drawn out of chronological order into a thematic pattern, Matthew was showing that the Messiah was constantly ministering with compassion and authority and that he grew tired from his work.

8:25. The disciples were probably angry that Jesus was not contributing to the bailing effort or exercising his power to help save their lives. To these men **of little faith** (8:26), Jesus was at least another pair of hands to help man the bailing buckets. The fact that they were so amazed in 8:27 suggests that their plea to **save us** (8:25) meant they were looking for his participation and possibly his leadership in averting the crisis. But they apparently did not expect him to exercise such incredible supernatural power. It was one thing to heal leprosy, but quite another to control nature's fury.

Still, the disciples had at least one necessary ingredient for true faith—an awareness of their helplessness. They despaired for their lives: **We're going to drown!** Their cry for Jesus' help was more desperation than faith that he would actually stop the storm. Clearly, they did not yet have a full grasp of the nature of Messiah's mission and his unfinished business.

8:26. It was significant that Jesus rebuked his disciples *before* he rebuked the winds and sea. If Jesus had any uncertainty about the outcome of the situation, he would have calmed the sea first, and then saved the lecture for afterward. By his conscious choice, he spoke while the boat was pitching wildly and the rain and wind were lashing violently and the boat continued to sink. This was a teachable moment. We can imagine Jesus lingering in the midst of this violent scene, holding the disciples' eyes for a moment to let his rebuke settle in, and then getting up from where he had been sleeping to calm the sea.

Jesus' rebuke of his disciples was justified because of the many miracles they had already witnessed that attested to his identity and power. But they were slow to catch on to the implications of what they had witnessed. Just as Jesus was surprised by the centurion's faith (8:10), he was also disappointed at his own disciples' lack of faith.

Jesus literally called his disciples "little-faith ones," a single Greek adjective he used at times to rebuke his disciples (6:30; 14:31; 16:8; Luke 12:28). These "little-faith ones," like you and me, needed to be "adding" or "supplying" to their faith the kind of growth that ensured their greater reward (2 Pet. 1:5–9).

Matthew did not record the actual words Jesus used to rebuke the winds and the sea, but the words are not important. What is important is the identity and authority of Jesus over the natural world. Matthew chose wording that heightened his absolute authority over nature. Literally, "a great calm happened." The word *galene,* "a calm," is used only here and in the parallel Gospel passages, Mark 4:39 and Luke 8:24. Jesus proved himself to be the God of all nature, praised as sovereign over the mighty seas in Psalms 65:7; 89:9; 107:23–32.

8:27. Three times in chapters 8–9, observers **were amazed** (*thaumazo*) at Jesus' miracles (8:27; 9:8, *phobeo;* 9:33), and the same verb is used of Jesus' response to the centurion's faith (8:10). People in the first century had a much greater respect for the forces of nature than we do today (**even the winds and the sea** revealed the disciples' awe at nature's power). This respect for nature's power is reflected by the numerous Old Testament passages that praise God for his control over them. To see the winds and the sea respond instantly to the word of Jesus was a major contribution to their developing understanding of Jesus.

What kind of man is this? The disciples were trying to pigeonhole Jesus. They were now being forced to add a new category to their mental list. Not only were the Pharisees impacted by Jesus' actions; Jesus' disciples were getting some major wake-up calls themselves.

The King's Authority over Spiritual Forces (8:28–34)

SUPPORTING IDEA: *Jesus exercises authority and compassion to free people from demon possession.*

8:28. Previously, Jesus had conquered disease and nature. Now he conquered demons. We arrive with Jesus at the end of the journey that began in 8:18. Both Gadara and Gerasa (Mark 5:1) are cities of the Decapolis, south of the Sea of Galilee, but Gadara is only six miles southeast of the lake. It probably controlled the shoreline where these events happened. Gerasa was thirty miles southeast of the lake, but it was of greater importance than Gadara— thus Mark's use of its name. This entire region was predominantly Gentile, which explains the local residents' ability to raise pigs (8:31–33). Some Jews did live in the region.

Three things in this verse would have shocked the first-century Jewish reader. First, Jesus purposefully entered Gentile territory. Second, he went to a cemetery, thought to be unclean because of the dead bodies, and also thought to be inhabited by evil spirits. Third, he was met by two men possessed by demons. Just as first-century people treated natural forces with greater respect than we do, they also respected more highly the forces of the spirit world. The concept of going face-to-face with demons was frightful to the first-century reader. These two men were so violent and dangerous that people avoided them.

8:29. We learn several things about demons in this passage. They immediately recognized Jesus for who he was. They knew there would be an **appointed time** for their judgment by Christ (25:41; Jas. 2:19; 2 Pet. 2:4; Jude 6), and their eternal **torture** (25:41), but they clearly expected this to come much later.

Notice that only the demons spoke. The men probably had no ability to speak for themselves because of the power of the demons. This is an example of Jesus' compassion for those in need who were not able even to call out for help.

8:30–31. Mark's account revealed the large number of demons through the demons' own confession (Mark 5:9), but Matthew alluded to the number of demons by referring to the **large** herd of pigs they would inhabit. We learn at least three truths about these spirit beings from their request to go into the pigs. First, they either needed to inhabit a physical body or they found this preferable to existing on their own. Second, Jesus had the power to drive them out and leave them without a home if he so wished. Third, while demons are not physical beings, they seem to be bound by some of the same physical laws as physical beings (e.g., location has significance for them, and they can only be in one place at a time).

8:32. Jesus exercised his authority by forcing the demons to leave the men, and then he honored their request to enter the pigs. Notice once again the use of Jesus' *word* as the vehicle of his authority. Matthew recorded only a single, concise command: **Go!** That was enough to defeat the powerful beings of the spirit world.

8:33–34. What we have not been told until now is that there were witnesses to this event—the herdsmen in charge of the pigs. Their immediate response was to run into town and tell others what had happened. Matthew mentioned that their report included the exorcism of the demons. This should have been evidence that Jesus was a powerful being. When the **whole town** came back to Jesus, their request for him to leave may have been out of fear of his power. They may have been angry over the loss of their property and the pigs. In any case, they did not recognize the Messiah-King.

E The King's Authority to Forgive (9:1–13)

SUPPORTING IDEA: *Jesus exercises authority and compassion to heal.*

Although these next two related stories include a miracle, their central emphasis is on Jesus' authority to forgive sin, not primarily on the physical healing of the paralytic. Jesus' claim to have authority to forgive sins was validated by the healing of the paralytic, but also by the surrounding context of the series of miracles recorded in Matthew 8–9.

Notice that Matthew placed his own conversion at the heart of chapter 9. There was no outward, physical miracle recorded in 9:9–13. But Matthew's placement may indicate that he saw this as one of Jesus' greatest miracles—the rescue of a soul from the kingdom of darkness; the forgiveness of one of society's worst sinners, a traitorous tax collector (9:9).

9:1. Jesus and his disciples retraced the journey they had taken south across the Sea of Galilee (8:23–27). This time they traveled from the southern tip to the northern tip, to Capernaum, which was now Jesus' **own town,** his base of operations since 4:13. Note also that, in crossing the lake, Jesus was honoring the request of the Gentiles in 8:34.

9:2–3. The men who brought the paralytic to Jesus were the companions of the paralytic. (Matthew chose not to record the extent to which their faith took them; that is, tearing through the roof of the house, as Mark 2:3–4 and Luke 5:18–19 did.) All three Gospel writers note that Jesus saw **their** faith—not just the faith of the paralytic but the faith of the man's friends. This is significant today. We must realize that our faith or lack of faith has an impact upon the lives of others.

Jesus' words to the paralytic were probably even more surprising to the Jewish listeners and readers of the first century than they are to us today. We would expect his words to have something to do with the man's physical healing, but instead he started by talking about the man's spiritual healing. We might be surprised and puzzled, but the Jewish bystanders, especially the religious leaders (9:3), were shocked and offended. In claiming to do what only God could do, Jesus was blaspheming, in their opinion. To blaspheme was to insult God's name and honor by laying claim to an attribute or action that could be attributed to God alone.

The most fundamental tenet of the Jewish faith is found in Deuteronomy 6:4: "Hear, O Israel: The LORD our God, the LORD is one." The Lord is a jealous God, unwilling to "yield [his] glory to another" (Isa. 48:11). The Jews would have been justified in their condemnation of Jesus, if not for the fact that he was indeed the Messiah-King. His miracles and authoritative teaching had already testified to this fact.

Jesus' compassion was evident in his encouraging words, **Take heart**, and in his reference to the man as **son** (literally, "child"). The man was probably feeling intimidated in the presence of the great teacher and feeling unworthy of the attention, due to the humiliation of his physical condition and the sin in his heart.

Jesus did not say, "Your sins will be forgiven" (future tense), which would amount only to an exhortation of hope, looking ahead to God's future forgiveness. Nor did he say, "Your sins have been forgiven" (past tense), separating the forgiveness from this encounter. Jesus confidently used the present tense, **your sins are forgiven**. Jesus was boldly proclaiming his word as the means of forgiveness. This was an incredible claim to deity.

The scribes' thoughts about Jesus were **said to themselves**, that is, probably only silent thoughts in their own minds. This sets the stage for our appreciation of Jesus' insight in 9:4. It also emphasizes the fact that sin is not only what comes out of us, but also what is within our minds and hearts. An attitude can be as much a sin as an action or a word. Attitudes will inevitably come out as actions and words. This was already happening at least through the scribes' nonverbal expression.

9:4. We need not assume that Jesus literally read the minds of these scribes. He certainly had the capability to use supernatural mental powers when it was appropriate. But Jesus temporarily gave up the exercise of his divine omniscience during his visit to earth (e.g., recall his surprise at the centurion's faith; 8:10). It is not necessary to be a mind reader to know a person's thoughts under the right circumstances. When a pro-life advocate is in the presence of a pro-choice advocate, or a staunch Democrat is with a staunch Republican, both know much of what is on the other's mind. Jesus, the God-Man, was an astute student of humankind. He had at least as much insight into people as the wisest and most perceptive people do today. He knew his opponents would be thinking hostile thoughts when he claimed the authority to forgive sins.

Jesus was justified in declaring the scribes' thoughts **evil**. To conclude that Jesus was blaspheming ignored the significance of his authenticating miracles. They had hardened their hearts against God's truth.

9:5. Having confronted their obstinate disbelief, Jesus prepared them for proof that he had authority to forgive sins and to heal paralysis. Neither spiritual healing nor physical healing is "easier" than the other. But physical healing is easier to authenticate than spiritual healing, because physical healing happens in the visible realm. Spiritual healing occurs in the invisible spirit realm. If Jesus could prove he had authority to heal physically, he could also prove that he had authority to heal spiritually—to forgive sins.

9:6–7. Jesus put this reasoning into words: **But so that you may know that the Son of Man has authority on earth to forgive sins**. He proceeded, with the authority of his word, to reveal a visible truth—that he was able to heal the man's paralysis.

9:8. The crowd's reaction was awe and praise to God. There was no mistake that Jesus' authority came from God. What they praised God for was that he had **given such authority to *men*** (italics added). The crowd apparently saw Jesus as a God-ordained prophet, like Elijah or Elisha. They had not yet recognized Jesus' deity. They had heard the human side of the "Son of Man," but they had not recognized the divine implications from Daniel 7:13–14.

God's glory is the physical, visible demonstration of his nature and character. To "praise" God is to make him visible or to make him known to others. This was what the crowd was doing in their praise. They proclaimed what they had witnessed of God's nature and character, that he might be made known more fully.

9:9. Again Matthew showed Jesus violating a cultural taboo by associating with a tax collector. The Roman Empire's practice was to recruit tax collectors from among the people they had conquered. These natives worked for the hated oppressor. This made them traitors and outcasts among their countrymen. But it was common practice for tax collectors to demand more from their countrymen than was actually due in order to line their own pockets. If the people refused to pay, the tax collector had the threat of the Roman military to back him up. Tax collectors, in general, were known for their greed and lack of conscience, so they were thought of as the lowest form of humanity.

Not only did Jesus speak to such a vile sinner, but he invited Matthew, a tax collector, to become one of his closest followers. Implied here is the ultimate in forgiveness and unconditional acceptance. Matthew's conscience must have been in torment for him to accept the Master's invitation to spiritual cleansing and restoration, giving up the wealth and privilege of his position. Again the Messiah-King manifested the compelling authority of his word—turning the worst of sinners into disciples.

This brief passage is Matthew's only mention of himself. It is natural that he should hold up—as an exhibit in his case for the identity of Jesus as Messiah—the key turning point of his own life. Matthew placed this account at the heart of Matthew 8–10, possibly as the crowning miracle authenticating the authority of the Messiah-King. This passage also links directly with 9:1–8, because it demonstrates the king's authority to forgive sins.

9:10–11. Jesus proceeded to violate the cultural standards of acceptable behavior even further by visiting Matthew's home and by eating with him and many of his tax collector friends as well as many other **sinners.** Eating together was the deepest form of social intimacy. Normally no "sinner" was welcome at a **righteous** man's table, and no "righteous" man would consider eating at a sinner's table. Jesus had no such misgivings; he displayed his unconditional acceptance and impartiality by participating in this meal.

The Pharisees did not address Jesus directly. Perhaps they were trying to use the disciples' limited understanding to drive a wedge between them and Jesus. Their use of the title **teacher** may have been sarcastic. It was generally assumed that such a righteous man as a Jewish teacher would refrain from associating with society's undesirables. Their question was mocking and critical.

9:12–13. When he became aware of the question, Jesus rose to confront the hypocrites and their self-righteousness with righteous indignation. Jesus portrayed himself here, in the context of so many healing miracles, as a **doctor** for the human spirit. He defended his lack of association with the Pharisees (the **healthy**) by alluding to the fact that they saw no need for spiritual healing in themselves. He was not implying that the Pharisees were righteous, but only that they saw themselves that way, and so were not open to receiving his healing (forgiveness). It is safe to read some irony into Jesus' use of the word *healthy* in referring to the Pharisees.

Jesus also defended his association with the tax collectors and sinners by their own self-awareness regarding their spiritual illness (sin) and their hunger for his healing (forgiveness).

Also implied in Jesus' words was an affirmation of the basic equality of all people, a truth the Pharisees failed to grasp. This basic lack of understanding is why they needed to **go and learn** the lesson of Hosea 6:6. This Old Testament passage does not belittle sacrifice, but it elevates right treatment of the poor above it. By quoting the Old Testament, which the Pharisees knew well, Jesus shamed his opponents by confronting their misunderstanding of the spirit of the Lord's Word. The word **sacrifice** here represents all the religious motions and rituals the Pharisees observed that were meaningless and empty. But accompanied by a heart after God, particularly a heart of mercy and compassion, righteous deeds take on positive significance before God (Matt. 6:1–18).

Compassion or **mercy** is an attitude toward a need that is compelled to take action to meet that need. A compassionate and merciful heart finds it impossible to remain neutral when it sees a need of any kind.

Jesus was not blind to the faults of the sinners with whom he dined, but his mercy caused him to withhold judgment. The Pharisees had no right to exercise judgment, since they were just as sinful themselves. They should have been the first to withhold judgment and accept the other **sinners**. But in their pride, they were unmerciful, demonstrating they had no grasp of Jesus' statements in 6:14–15.

Finally, Jesus clarified his "physician" analogy by saying, **for I have not come to call the righteous, but sinners**. Again, we can read some sarcasm and irony into his use of the word **righteous** when referring to the Pharisees. They were not truly righteous, but they saw themselves as such. Thus, they were not willing to accept his forgiveness and respond to his call. The sinners, on the other hand, were aware of their sin (Matt. 5:3, "poor in spirit") and hungered for forgiveness. They responded to his call to true discipleship. Jesus' disciples were not perfect, but they accepted his forgiveness with humility and moved on toward maturity.

F Celebrate! The King Is Finally Here! (9:14–17)

SUPPORTING IDEA: *As Messiah-King, Jesus claims the right to be treated as Israel's guest of honor.*

In this passage, Jesus made another bold assertion that is supported by the context of validating miracles.

9:14. Both John the Baptizer's disciples and the Pharisees built fasting into their standard regimen, far beyond the requirements of Old Testament law. Although this was not bad in itself, they began to believe that any person who fell short of this standard of righteousness was less devout in his or her faith. Some Christians today do the same thing with "spiritual tests" of their own.

9:15. Jesus' response to John's disciples was that fasting while he—the bridegroom, the guest of honor—was present would be inappropriate. But a time would come when fasting among his followers would be appropriate—after he was **taken from them.** Jesus liked to use the analogy of a wedding or marriage to describe his relationship to his people (22:1–14; 25:1–13). This is a theme used elsewhere in both the Old and New Testaments (e.g., Hos. 2; Eph. 5:22–33; Rev. 19:7–9; 21:2,9; 22:17). Jesus is the bridegroom.

Jesus' statement about being **taken from them** is an early indication in Matthew that the king would not reign in this first coming. His choice of words, "taken from them" (also in Mark 2:20; Luke 5:35), provide a foreshadowing of his own suffering and death, as well as the loss and despair his followers would experience.

9:16. An old garment has shrunk after it has been worn a while. A new patch of cloth, when first washed, would shrink and pull away from the older cloth. Jesus was saying, "Something new and unusual is happening. A new era is dawning, and the old methods do not apply. They are inappropriate while I, the Messiah-King, am here."

By the use of these miniparables (unshrunk cloth and new wineskins), Jesus was alerting his disciples to the fact that he was about to move further away from Israel as the chosen recipient of his message. Jesus indicated that his message of the new covenant was too fresh and vital to be attached to an old garment. His **new wine** of the new covenant was too vibrant and potent to be placed in an old wineskin that is rigid and inflexible. The situation demanded a new vessel. Matthew recorded Jesus hinting at his coming announcement (16:18) of a new approach. He will deposit his message into a new wineskin—the church.

9:17. Jesus used this second parable to underscore the same message as the old garment. When wine ferments, it gives off gasses that stretch the wineskins. The fresh leather can stretch and expand, but older leather has already stretched as much as it can. Fresh wine in old wineskins would burst the old leather. Jesus indicated that pharisaical Israel will not be able to handle Jesus' truth. Israel was too rigid and unresponsive to carry his message to the world. God would use the church to accomplish that goal.

G The King's Authority over Life and Death (9:18–26)

SUPPORTING IDEA: *Jesus exercises authority and compassion to defeat death.*

After a stretch of non-miracle narratives in Matthew 8–9, Matthew recorded a flurry of miracle activity in 9:18–34.

9:18–19. Not all religious leaders were hostile toward Jesus. We do not know the attitude of this synagogue ruler before his daughter's illness and death, but desperation can soften even the strongest critics. This man, like all the rest of the seekers in Matthew 8–9, was at the end of his resources. He had no place to turn except to the king. The official showed reverence for Jesus. Recognizing him as a prophet from God, the official **knelt before him.**

His request revealed great faith. To this point, Jesus had performed all of his healing miracles on people who were still living. This is the first instance in Matthew where he ministered to a dead person. The official's confidence in Jesus is evident in his bold assertion that Jesus' touch would bring her back to life.

Touching a dead body was considered the most defiling kind of uncleanness (Num. 19:11–22). Most religious leaders and teachers would have refused to come anywhere near the dead.

9:20–21. Even as Jesus made his way to touch a dead girl, he came into contact with another threat to his ritual purity. According to Old Testament law, a woman having her monthly menstrual period was unclean for seven days, and anyone who touched her would be unclean "till evening" (Lev. 15:19–33). This woman, with her continual bleeding, would have been considered continually unclean, and was probably a social outcast. She acted boldly to come into close contact with a revered teacher. But she also limited her action, touching **the edge of his cloak** to minimize the likelihood of making Jesus unclean. In fact, she did not even want Jesus to know she had put him at risk.

This woman was another of the desperate, helpless people cataloged in Matthew 8–9. She was willing to go beyond the bounds of culturally acceptable behavior to draw on help from outside herself.

9:22. Jesus detected her presence and touch. The fact that he had to turn around and look for the woman further emphasizes that she tried to do this secretly.

In Jesus' initial words of comfort, **Take heart, daughter,** notice the parallel to his words to the paralytic, **Take heart, son** (9:2). Rather than becoming angry at an unclean woman for touching him, Jesus showed compassion toward the woman's need and expressed affirmation for her faith. She displayed both components of faith: she recognized her helplessness and she went to the appropriate person for help.

The power of Jesus' touch and the power of his word are highlighted in this account. **From that moment,** with his declaration of her healing, she stopped bleeding. Both the touch and the word of Jesus were instrumental in her healing.

9:23–24. Having postponed a mission of healing to deal compassionately with the bleeding woman, Jesus resumed his walk to the synagogue official's home. When he entered the official's house and saw the **flute players** (hired as part of the mourning process) and the **noisy crowd,** Jesus spoke to the mourners as though they were not necessary. They laughed at him as though he was crazy. The girl was dead, but death was no obstacle to Jesus. Because the girl would be alive soon, Jesus told the mourners she was **asleep.** He would awaken her.

9:25. Jesus was not interested in masses of witnesses for this miracle. As usual, he seemed to be most interested in the training and education of his disciples (9:19). In taking the hand of the dead girl, Jesus would have been seen as defiling himself, according to Old Testament law. But instead of death defiling him, he defied death: **she got up.** This is one of the most powerful examples of Jesus ministering through touch.

9:26. This miracle serves as a climax for Matthew 8–9. None of the enemies Jesus had conquered so far in these two chapters (illness, demons, nature) had been as formidable as death. The resurrection of a child would have reminded people of similar miracles by Elijah (1 Kgs. 17:17–24) and Elisha (2 Kgs. 4:18–37), and the prophecies about the return of the prophet Elijah (Mal. 4:5–6). It is no wonder that news of this miracle **spread through all that region.** Jesus' growing notoriety set the stage for the first major grumblings of the Pharisees (9:34). Things were going to get a bit rougher.

Ⅲ The King's Authority Begins to Provoke the Pharisees (9:27–34)

SUPPORTING IDEA: *The contrast between Jesus' authority and that of counterfeits is so obvious that conflict between them must occur.*

Healing of both the blind and the mute were given in Isaiah 35:5–6 as signs of the Lord's coming redemption. This and other Old Testament passages were in Matthew's mind as he chose these two miracles to report in quick succession at the end of Matthew 8–9 (cf. 11:2–6, Jesus' response to John's doubt). Messiah-King is here!

9:27. Jesus' reputation had spread throughout the region. In their helplessness and faith, two blind beggars persisted in crying out to him. There is irony in this verse. It was two blind men who recognized Jesus as the royal **Son of David.**

9:28–31. Jesus questioned their faith in his ability to heal them. The men were convinced of his power. Again Jesus ministered through touch, emphasizing their faith as the key to his ability and willingness to heal their blindness. **According to your faith** is not a statement of the quality of their faith (so much faith = so much sight) but of its presence.

Matthew recorded Jesus' warning to the men not to spread the news of their healing to others, much as he did with the leper in 8:4. However, with the leper account, we are not told whether the man obeyed Jesus; we can probably assume he did. In contrast, now that Jesus had established a sound basis of miracles to validate his identity, the men who had been blind could not contain themselves: **they went out and spread the news about him all over that region.** This heightened the stakes for Jesus' opponents, who began to voice their slander against Jesus just a few verses later (9:34).

9:32–33. Again Jesus faced the evil forces of the spirit world. But this time Matthew's purpose for recording the account, together with the preceding healing of the blind men, was probably as an allusion to the messianic ministry of Isaiah 35:5–6. And, as in 8:27, the witnesses were **amazed**. The crowd's words emphasized the uniqueness of Jesus and his actions: **Nothing like this has ever been seen in Israel**. The advent of the Messiah-King was a one-time, historical event. And the growing momentum was beginning to force the opposition's hand.

9:34. The implications about Jesus' identity were plain to the Pharisees, who tried to explain away the miracles as Satan's work rather than God's. This verse represents the early grumblings of the religious leaders. This would soon grow into a full-blown conflict.

▌ The King's Compassion for the Misguided Crowds (9:35–38)

SUPPORTING IDEA: *Jesus sees the peril of the misguided crowds and is moved to address their need through the ministry of his followers.*

This short but powerful passage provides insight into Jesus' motivation for extending the training of his disciples to the next level (their public preaching) in chapter 10. Jesus' compassion, evident throughout chapters 8–9, came to a great crescendo. Jesus saw beyond the physical diseases to the deeper tragedy of the people's spiritual aimlessness.

9:35. This summary statement of Jesus' ministry amounts to a repetition of 4:23 (see commentary on 4:23).

9:36. As Jesus conducted his itinerant ministry, he saw many crowds. He felt compassion for their lack of spiritual shepherding and the presence of spiritual abuse. A shepherd feeds, comforts, heals, guides, and protects his sheep (Ezek. 34). But Israel's religious leaders were harassing and abandoning their sheep, leaving them **harassed and helpless, like sheep without a shepherd**. "Harassed" is from a verb meaning "to trouble, distress." "Helpless" is from a verb meaning "to throw down." The past tense used here implies the thoroughness of their oppression and its persistent effect on the people. These people were completely and perpetually discouraged.

Remember from 9:13 that compassion or mercy is an attitude toward a need that grows into action in an effort to meet the need. Here Matthew used a different word, whose root meaning is "intestines, bowels." Jesus was physically moved by a stomach-wrenching empathy for the plight of his flock. He was literally sickened by the poor leadership of Israel's hypocritical religious leaders. We can read his words in 9:37–38 as an impassioned plea to his disciples, whom he proceeded to equip and commission to meet the people's need.

9:37–38. In these verses, Jesus' disciples begin to take a place of greater prominence in Matthew's narrative. Until now, Jesus had been training them primarily through their observations of his ministry, but his focus turned increasingly toward intensified teaching directed at them. These men and their spiritual offspring were Jesus' plan for continuing his ministry to a lost world. If he failed to prepare his workers, his ministry would die when he left. This is instructive to every spiritual leader today—mentor and multiply. Do not just "perform."

Jesus' passion for the needs of the crowds caused him to ask his disciples to pray for **workers** to go out into the **harvest**. Christ's workers gain courage from his assertion that the **harvest is plentiful**. The hurting people whom he saw and whom we see all around us are like fruit ripe for the picking. Christians today seem to view non-Christians with fear, but Jesus saw them with compassion. And so should we. If we hold out the truth—Jesus himself—they will come to him, for they hunger for guidance.

The workers are few, said Jesus as he turned from the distressed masses to the dozen men around him. Our job is to pray fervently for more people to come and help, as we are moving boldly to be involved with the harvest.

> **MAIN IDEA REVIEW:** *Jesus demonstrates that he has absolute authority, exercised with compassion, proving himself to be Messiah.*

III. CONCLUSION

Jesus can work miraculously in your life if you will depend on him—and sometimes he does this even if you do not.

PRINCIPLES

- Jesus has absolute authority to heal physical diseases. He is not only the healer of the physical body, he is also the healer of spiritual wounds.
- Jesus has absolute authority over nature.
- Jesus has absolute authority to forgive sin.
- Jesus has absolute authority over spiritual forces.
- Jesus is the ultimate example of compassion towards others.

APPLICATIONS

- Recognize the authority of Jesus in your life.
- Draw upon the authority of Jesus in your life.
- Seek healing of your wounds from Jesus the healer.
- Recognize Jesus' compassion toward you.
- Follow Jesus' compassionate example in your attitude and actions toward others.

- Be a devoted follower of Jesus; do not use excuses to postpone your devotion.
- Be a willing worker in God's harvest.

IV. LIFE APPLICATION

Counting the Cost

In the world of physics, particle accelerators have allowed physicists to explore sub-atomic particle collisions under controlled conditions. This research has revealed most of the matter particles and force carriers we know today.

The particle accelerators physicists use, however, are massive. The Tevatron, the world's most powerful particle accelerator, at Fermilab National Laboratory for Research in Batavia, Illinois, uses an underground circle that is four miles in diameter.

A new kind of accelerator is on the drawing board. It is called a *muon collider.* The feasibility study for the prospective muon collider project was enormous. The executive summary for the project report was fifteen pages long, and the report itself totaled into hundred of pages. Why? Before tackling such a massive project, it was necessary to count the cost. To do the project would require the commitment of millions of dollars, many years, and the efforts and careers of thousands of trained personnel would be essential to its success. Such a project would be extremely demanding. Those involved would not have the option of a half-hearted allegiance to the mission. They would need to commit their time, expertise, and lives to ensure the success of the project.

Jesus asked his followers to count the cost of being a disciple. Following Jesus is not an easy road, for there would be hardships and persecution. Have you counted the cost? Are you committed to obediently following Jesus in spite of circumstances and consequences?

V. PRAYER

Merciful Father, thank you for Jesus, the Great Physician and friend of sinners. Fill me with his love and compassion that I might be a medium of his healing in the lives of those in need. Amen.

VI. DEEPER DISCOVERIES

A. Increased "Demonic Activity" in the Gospels (8:28)

It is appropriate to mention the possible reasons for the heightened activity of demons in the Gospels. One explanation is that they had always been active, but Jesus' ministry revealed and thwarted their work. The satanic army knew the significance of Jesus' coming to earth. So they intensified their warfare during his ministry on earth.

B. Summary

We can consider Matthew 1–4 as prologue. Chapters 5–7 are the most powerful example of Jesus' authoritative teaching. Chapters 8–9 are the most powerful example of Jesus' authoritative actions. It is as though chapters 1–4 give us Jesus' calling card, but in chapters 5–9 we meet the real teacher. A good novel may start with a few pages of foundational material, then abruptly pick up and grab the reader's attention. This is the effect of Matthew's outline.

Chapters 8–9 serve as exhibits supporting Matthew's claim that Jesus was the Messiah. He showed this through his supernatural authority over every aspect of the natural, the supernatural, and the spiritual. These chapters also pave the way for Jesus' delegation of the same authority to his disciples in chapter 10.

VII. TEACHING OUTLINE

A. INTRODUCTION

1. Lead Story: Real Love and True Authority Go Together
2. Context: These chapters spring directly out of Jesus' pronouncement of authority through his teaching of the Sermon on the Mount (7:28–29). Now he proceeds to demonstrate that his authority extends to more than his teaching. In fact, he is the absolute authority, the complete sovereign—the Almighty. This is the next step in Matthew's methodical presentation of Jesus as the promised Messiah.
3. Transition: It is important to see, along with the theme of authority, an interwoven balancing theme of compassion. Unlike most earthly leaders (the hypocritical Jewish leaders in particular), the king did not exercise his authority for selfish ends but in compassion to meet the needs of others:
   - He touched a leper.
   - He honored a Gentile for his faith.
   - He crossed the Sea of Galilee to the unclean tombs in Gentile territory to free two men from demons.
   - He associated with the scum of society.
   - He postponed a resurrection to heal and reassure a woman unclean from her bleeding.
   - He touched a dead body.
   - He was moved by the crowds' vulnerability to spiritual predators.

Notice how many times Jesus broke cultural taboos to exercise mercy toward the needy. In this way he shook up the conventional thinking to reveal the priority of mercy as his mission (9:13, quoting Hos. 6:6). Notice how many times Matthew also mentions touch as a part of Jesus' compassionate ministry (8:3,15; 9:21,25,29).

B. COMMENTARY

1. The King's Authority over Illness (8:1–17)
2. The Cost of Following the King (8:18–22)
3. The King's Authority over Nature (8:23–27)
4. The King's Authority over Spiritual Forces (8:28–34)
5. The King's Authority to Forgive (9:1–13)
6. Celebrate! The King Is Finally Here! (9:14–17)
7. The King's Authority over Life and Death (9:18–26)
8. The King's Authority Begins to Provoke the Pharisees (9:27–34)
9. The King's Compassion for the Misguided Crowds (9:35–38)

C. CONCLUSION

1. Wrap-up: Jesus had all authority, absolute power to do whatever he wished. Jesus' words were recognized as having authority. His teaching was amazing. But words without actions can be suspect. Who was he to speak so authoritatively? In these two chapters Jesus showed his all-powerful authority by his acts of compassion and by his miraculous demonstration of loving power and authority.

2. Personal Challenge: We need to be people who recognize, respond to, and live under the absolute authority of Jesus, the Son of Man. Only when we live under his authority will we be able to live out the compassionate lifestyle that he demonstrated for us and which draws people to him.

VIII. ISSUES FOR DISCUSSION

1. What was the purpose of miracles in the ministry of Jesus?
2. Why did Jesus tell some of the people whom he healed not to spread the word about these miracles?
3. Why were the disciples shocked at Jesus' calming of the stormy sea? Why was this miracle so different than all the other miracles of Jesus they had witnessed?
4. What was the significance of *touch* in the healing miracles that Jesus performed?

Matthew 10

The King Delegates His Authority

Quote

"*S*urround yourself with the best people you can find,

delegate authority, and don't interfere."

R o n a l d   R e a g a n

Matthew 10

IN A NUTSHELL

*W*hereas Jesus demonstrated his authority in the previous chapters, he now delegates that same authority to his disciples so that they may carry out his ministry to the world. In this second of Matthew's five discourses, Jesus instructs, prepares, empowers, and encourages the twelve disciples for the immediate and distant future.

The King Delegates His Authority

I. INTRODUCTION

Go with Confidence

*T*oward the end of my tour of duty in Vietnam, I was given a special assignment by our commanding officer. The Green Berets were viewed with suspicion by certain career Army senior officers. In particular, General Abrams (the commanding general of all U.S. military forces in Vietnam) had little regard for Special Forces (Green Berets). He kept a close eye on the Fifth Special Forces Group of which I was a member. So close, in fact, that he required the group (headquartered far to the north of the general's location) to establish a second headquarters within shouting distance.

Just two months before I was scheduled to rotate home to the States, some special circumstances developed that required a change of command at this second location. The group commander called me to his office and informed me that I was being named the new commanding officer there. He stated that he had selected me because he had observed "a sense of integrity" in me. He told me that, given my familiarity with him and how he operated, I would be his personal representative there. He indicated he would expect me to act precisely as I anticipated he would do in my circumstances, and that the reputation of the group would be in my hands. I was to be alert to any action that would embarrass the group or its commander.

His appointment was humbling and terrifying. I would do my best. His confidence made it easier for me. And that is the way it is for the disciples in Matthew. Jesus' orders to them are humbling and terrifying. Still, they are orders and the men will do their best.

At the end of Matthew 9, Jesus told his disciples to pray that the "Lord of the harvest" would send out workers into his fields. Here in chapter 10, he called his disciples into his office, so to speak, and informed them that they were his personal representatives. He gave them authority. They were to act in his name and speak his message.

Just as soldiers or any other public officials have authority derived from a higher authority (the law), kingdom servants, as the king's personal representatives on earth, have authority delegated from the highest authority of all. We will see in this passage how the king intended his disciples to use such power.

II. COMMENTARY

The King Delegates His Authority

MAIN IDEA: *The king trains his disciples to carry out his ministry, giving them specific guidelines, realistic expectations of persecution, a clarified challenge, and hopeful reassurances.*

This chapter is the second of Jesus' five major addresses in Matthew (5–7; 10; 13; 18; 24–25). The first four verses provide the setting for the discourse, and Jesus' remarks actually begin in 10:5.

In Matthew 5–9, Jesus *demonstrated* his authority, first through his teaching (chs. 5–7), then through his actions (miracles; chs. 8–9). Now he will *delegate* this same authority to do exactly the same kinds of ministry (preaching, healing, casting out demons; 10:1,7–8) that he had been doing (4:23; 9:35). Jesus judged that the disciples were ready, for they had been with him long enough, observing his ministry and hearing his teachings, and probably participating in the ministry to a limited extent. Now it was time for their training to move to a new level.

Because Matthew is arranged thematically rather than chronologically, we should not assume that everything recorded before Matthew 10 had actually happened when Jesus gave this discourse. Then again, these stories are likely representative of a much larger number of such events, and there are certainly hundreds of other untold stories that the disciples had witnessed before the discourse of Matthew 10.

To equip someone to do a task, these are steps that must be taken:

- Talk about the task.
- Do the task while the learner observes.
- Let the learner help you do the task.
- Help the learner do the task.
- Let the learner do the task while you observe.
- Let the learner do the task on his own, under your supervision and guidance.
- The learner becomes a trainer, repeating the steps with someone else.

Jesus, the master teacher, probably followed a training method similar to this. Matthew did not systematically record all of the steps, but we do see glimpses of this process from time to time through Matthew and the other Gospels (e.g., 17:14–21). In Matthew 10, Jesus was preparing the Twelve to do a few central tasks at the upper level of this scale.

The historical period of Jesus' earthly ministry is, in many ways, unique. So some elements of Jesus' training of the Twelve are unique to them. They were the first generation of a two-thousand-year-long succession of mentors and disciples, in a world almost completely unaware of the Messiah. Here this first generation is trained. These are apostles. Here was unique New Testament revelation, Messiah himself training those who would actually be recording the Word of God.

Yet, there are many principles Jesus taught his disciples that can be generalized for every spiritual generation of disciples. One of the tasks of interpreting Matthew 10 is sorting out those principles that apply to us from those that do not (e.g., not every Christian has authority to heal every kind of disease and every kind of sickness). Still, we must keep in mind that we can learn from these examples.

Some of Jesus' training was also with a view to the years and decades ahead. The reason we know this is that there was no evidence of the severe level of persecution Jesus describes in 10:17–23 during Jesus' earthly ministry, or even during the years immediately following his ascension. But the apostles would experience it after he was gone. So his training was for both the immediate and the long-term in the lives of the disciples.

There is a thematic relationship between 9:36–38 and chapter 10, between Jesus' compassion for the people and his equipping of the Twelve.

Ⓐ The King Equips the First Kingdom Workers (10:1–4)

SUPPORTING IDEA: *The king empowers the twelve apostles.*

10:1. Because Jesus was just speaking to "his disciples" two verses earlier (9:37), we must make at least one of two assumptions in order to explain why he would be calling **his twelve disciples** so soon. Either (1) there was a time gap between 9:38 and 10:1, which is very likely, in light of Matthew's thematic construction of the book; or (2) Matthew meant some other grouping of "disciples" than the Twelve in 9:37. There is also room for both of these assumptions to be true. But the key point is this—it is *these twelve* whom he has named.

Whatever the chronological relationship between 9:36–38 and chapter 10, the argument of the book makes a clear connection to chapters 8–9. We have moved through the moral testing of the king (ch. 4), to the manifesto of the king (chs. 5–7), through the manifestation of the king's power (chs. 8–9); it is now time for the response of the people. There can be no doubt that Matthew intended us to see a cause-effect relationship between Jesus' compassion for Israel's need and his plea for prayer for workers (9:36–38), and his preparation of the Twelve to go out and multiply his ministry to Israel. Jesus' training in Matthew 10 is motivated by his heart-wrenching compassion for the shepherdless people (9:36; 10:6).

Verse 1 is the summary of chapter 10. The key word is **authority**. This is the same authority Jesus demonstrated through his teaching in chapters 5–7 and through his miracles in chapters 8–9. The authority to exorcise demons and heal illnesses is a summary encompassing all of the other actions mentioned later in the discourse, including preaching (10:7,14,26–27) and resurrecting the dead (10:8).

The authority Jesus delegated here was also the authority with which he would commission his followers in 28:18–20. He continued to be personally involved in making bold fishers of men (4:19). There is one major difference, however. In chapter 10 Jesus commissioned his disciples to go to **the lost sheep of Israel** alone. In chapter 28 his commission is to go to the Gentiles ("all nations"). This is a critical difference in understanding Matthew.

10:2–4. Here we have the second of three uses of the number twelve in this chapter (10:1,2,5). The general term now takes on a more specific meaning. Matthew wants us to know that the training of chapter 10 is meant for the Twelve.

We are not told what criteria Jesus used in selecting these disciples, but they may have been different criteria than most of us would have used. His selections prove to all spiritual generations to come that he will use anyone for his kingdom (1 Cor. 1:18–2:5; 1 Tim. 1:15–16), and that the credit for successful ministry goes to him, not to human beings (1 Cor. 1:29–31; 2 Cor. 12:7–10). It is probably safe to assume that he looked more at their *availability* than their *ability*. They really were "disciples of clay."

Verse 2 is the only place in all of Matthew where the word **apostle** is used. The word is the transliteration of the Greek word *apostolos* and means "one sent," usually with a specific message or to perform a specific task, often as a representative. The noun is most often used as a technical term referring specifically to the early church leaders, qualified by their first-hand contact with Jesus and their witness of his resurrection (Acts 1:21–22). Paul received the title by special dispensation (1 Cor. 15:8–10).

It is significant that Matthew's only use of "apostle" is in the context of the selection and training of the Twelve. These would be the twelve men on whom the future success of Jesus' world impact would rest. They were the foundation of the church (Matt. 16:18; Eph. 2:20). From a human standpoint, Jesus was taking a great risk. Recall the archetypal "hero story" we have heard so often, in which the future of an entire group rests in the hands of a small number of dubiously qualified individuals. This is the real-life crisis we see in the story of the human race and God's plan of redemption. All heaven must have held its collective breath.

We must also keep in mind that the plan of God to redeem the lost is always one generation away from extinction. In choosing each of us (Eph. 1:4,11–13; 3:2–9), God has made us as members of his church critical to the fulfillment of his redemption plan.

B The Method of the Kingdom Worker (10:5–15)

SUPPORTING IDEA: *The king gives specific guidelines for the immediate campaign.*

At the outset, Jesus gave the Twelve the basic criteria for their early ministry. The clarity and succinctness of these instructions reflects Messiah's strong expectations and his specific goals. We should not be surprised if Jesus sets an inflexible standard; novices in any area usually need a firm set of rules to guide them until they gain the experience to add their own creative variations to the theme. Jesus also had other reasons for each of his guiding criteria, explained in greater detail below.

10:5–6. The kingdom worker's target audience at this point was Israel alone. This is a critical point. Jesus certainly made the point emphatically. Some liberal thinkers have made much of this being the bigotry of Jesus in his early years, noting that later in the maturity of his "messianic consciousness" he opened it to all nations (28:18–20). Nothing could be further from the truth. Matthew made it perfectly clear that Jesus was still offering the long-promised kingdom to his own people, Israel (John 1:12).

The word *instructing* (used in the sense of the disciples being **sent out with the following instructions**; 10:5) means "to command, charge, give orders." This verb carries greater force and authority than "teaching," which is used to describe the teaching ministry of Jesus and the disciples. It is the verb used of an authority's instruction to a subordinate, as in a military setting. The point is emphatic. These are direct orders.

Jesus prohibited his disciples from going to the Gentiles or the Samaritans, not because they were not part of God's plan of redemption, but because the first step of God's plan was to offer the gospel to Israel (Acts 10:36; Rom. 1:16; 9–11), then through the Jewish nation to take it to all nations. But Israel wanted nothing to do with Jesus. What the apostle John took one verse to summarize in his Gospel (John 1:12), took Matthew, with his burden to communicate to the Jews, twelve chapters (Matt. 1–12). Still, God made it clear that he was offering Israel one more chance to be his representatives to the nations, as he had planned all along (Gen. 12:3; Deut. 4:6–8; Ps. 67; Isa. 42:6–7; 49:6).

Jesus referred to the Jews as **lost sheep**, in keeping with his compassion for their plight in 9:36. Their religious leaders had let them down. These lost sheep were of the house **of Israel**, meaning the family or offspring of Israel. Jesus looked back to God's covenant with the patriarchs of Israel. In Genesis 12:1–3 the Lord promised special blessing on Abraham, as well as blessing on all nations through him. In Genesis 28:10–15, the Lord passed on exactly the same blessing to Abraham's grandson Jacob (Israel). Jesus guided his small band to keep a two-thousand-year-old-promise to a nation first, and then to the world.

10:7–8. These verses focus on the kingdom worker's ministry and message. **Preach** is the present imperative and carries the force of "keep on preaching." The Twelve were given a simple message, practically identical to that of John the Baptizer (3:2) and Jesus (4:17). Only the command to repent is omitted here, but it is probably implied as the natural response to the impending kingdom.

As mentioned in 10:1, the Twelve were instructed to conduct virtually the same ministry of healing and exorcism that Jesus had been conducting, even to the point of raising the dead and cleansing lepers. Because these disciples had received Jesus' authority, they also received his "immunity" to defilement. His power in them would overwhelm any uncleanness. Even demons, those powerful spirit beings, would not stand before them.

It must have been exciting to have such authority and to see the wonders happening through their own words and touch. But this ministry was also hard and discouraging work. To motivate the Twelve to **freely give**, Jesus reminded them that they did nothing to earn all they had received from him. They had received their forgiveness and acceptance, their position and power, their authority freely from Jesus.

We today need to heed the same lesson. Believers today, in our comfortable lifestyles, tend to be hoarders of all we have received from the Lord—physical wealth, spiritual gifts for ministry, time, as well as the truth of the gospel and the authority to take it to others. We have earned none of this. It is all a gracious gift from the Father, given primarily so we might use it to further his kingdom. We must be careful stewards of what has been entrusted to us (1 Cor. 3:12–15; 9:24–27; 2 Cor. 5:10; Phil. 3:7–21).

10:9–10. The kingdom worker's provision is the theme of these verses. Having trained the disciples by example in chapters 8–9, Jesus took them another step forward. His command not to take any money or supplies for their journey was a great challenge to their faith in God's provision. Jesus wanted the Twelve to focus on *who* they represented as they ministered to those in need. If they would make his kingdom their sole focus, the Father would provide their daily needs through those to whom they ministered.

Furthermore, their mission was short. Basically, they were taking a census for the king. They were to travel light and to be relatively unconcerned for provision. But they were not to travel alone. This is an important ministry point. For all they were not to worry about, Jesus let them know they were not to travel without a close spiritual friend.

Let this be a lesson to us. This passage seems to support a consistent pattern in Jesus' ministry appointments. They were to go two-by-two (see Mark 6:7, Luke 10:1). The disciples were even named in pairs (10:2–4). Evidently, in Jesus' mind, they did not need a lot of equipment or personal gear, but they did need a ministry partner. Perhaps we should understand his intention to mean there are no "lone rangers" in the kingdom.

10:11–15. These verses emphasize the kingdom worker's local associates and sponsors. As the disciples entered a town, they were to choose their host carefully (10:11).

Jesus used the word **search** to mean "scrutinize, examine closely, inquire." It is used only two other times in the New Testament—in Herod's instructions to the Magi to search carefully for the newborn king (Matt. 2:8) and of the type of interrogation the disciples would conduct in order to confirm Jesus' post-resurrection identity (John 21:12).

Their host was to be a **worthy** person (literally, "weighty"). Their character, reflected in their receptiveness to Jesus' representatives, must consistently "stack up" against a high standard. Since the disciple would be dependent on this person as his sponsor during his stay in that town, it was important that the disciple not have any worry whether he would receive his daily meals or have a place to rest. It is not a matter of looking for a "comfortable home" but for a "worthy host," a person of commitment.

A disciple was not to move from home to home within a town, but to stay in one place (10:11). It was considered a privilege to show hospitality to an honored teacher, a representative of the king.

These visits were "the king's business." These disciples were on a unique and carefully commissioned trip of assessment. Their reception would measure how he would be received. Israel was hanging in the balance; they were looking for the "king's own."

Shaking the **dust** off their feet (10:14) was a symbolic gesture of God's rejection of the home or city—to the point that they did not want to touch even the dirt from that place.

Jesus introduced his warning against the rejecting city (10:15) with the formula, **I tell you the truth,** meaning, "Listen carefully. What I am about to say is of great significance" (5:18; 6:2; 8:10). This was a stern warning, because it was a serious offense to reject the Messiah-King. Because the city visited by the disciples had the opportunity to hear the truth and respond in repentance to the Messiah, their guilt on the day of judgment would be even greater than that of Sodom and Gomorrah (the epitome of sin and evil in Gen. 19). These two cities had no opportunity to respond to the truth of the Messiah.

Jesus gave the disciples authority to perform the same miracles he had been performing. We can assume that the rejecting cities had hardened their hearts so much that they were blind to the significance of the disciples' miracles (cf. with Jesus' denunciation of rejecting cities in 11:20–24, as well as his rejection in his hometown in 13:53–58).

Verse 15 implies there will be degrees of judgment and punishment for the lost. It insists that the message we take to the lost in our world is not only an invitation—it is also a warning. We must convey that warning with compassion to maximize the likelihood that it will be heard. But in the process we must be careful not to compromise its truth. Anyone today who has the opportunity to respond to the Messiah's offer of free forgiveness, and turns him away, must understand the fate they are choosing. Final judgment is very real.

Persecution of the Kingdom Worker (10:16–23)

SUPPORTING IDEA: *The king prepares his followers for persecution in the near and far future.*

At the end of Jesus' instructions regarding his disciple's basic guiding criteria (10:5–15), he began to touch on the rejection they would receive in some towns. This naturally flowed into the next segment of his discourse, preparing them for the persecution they would eventually encounter (most severely after his departure). His instruction applied not only to their ministry during this particular foray, but to all of their future ministry ventures (see 24:9).

10:16. This sentence is a true transition sentence, fitting just as easily with the preceding context as with the following. Jesus opened it with one word: **Therefore.** This had the effect of saying, "Observe carefully. Do not miss this. See for yourself." The truth of what he is saying is self-evident to the person who has eyes to see. Jesus knew that the king's message would face great opposition.

When we go out in obedience to Christ, we go with a message of love and compassion (**like sheep**) to an audience that includes those who violently oppose us and our Lord (**among wolves**). Because there are those in the audience who will respond to God's love and compassion, we must go. But we need not go blindly. We must go with a blend of grace—(**as innocent as doves**)—and truth—(**as shrewd as snakes**). Grace must govern our compassion toward others, as well as our own example of integrity through all circumstances.

But grace and truth are not mutually exclusive. They are the two sides of one eternal coin. Truth must govern our perceptions of danger and the faults of others. Jesus perfectly exemplified this blend of wisdom and love, and he coached his disciples to live by it.

10:17–20. Expanding on the "shrewd as snakes" part of his instruction (10:16), Jesus warned, **Be on your guard against men.** This warning seems, at first glance, to sweep too broadly, but Jesus intended it that way to convey the reality that all types of people would betray and persecute Christ's followers—even family (10:21–22,34–36).

While the trials and floggings of 10:17 involve persecution at the local level, Jesus warns that some of his followers would gain attention at higher levels of authority—even **governors and kings.** The phrase **On my account** means, "because of your association with me." But as intimidating as such high-level audiences would be, they served a good purpose toward the goals of Jesus' mission. How else would Jesus' followers be able to bear testimony **as witnesses** to these officials and many of the populations they oversaw?

The disciples, being largely uneducated and novice teachers, must have wondered how they would do credit to the Lord before a governor or a king. Jesus assured them not to worry about **what** to say. When they needed wise words, **at that time** they would be given the words to say (10:19). More specifically, just as the word of God was powerful through Jesus, in these hearings the word of God will speak through the disciple by **the Spirit of your Father speaking through you** (10:20).

What Jesus described was essentially a New Testament prophet, an authorized spokesman for God. While we see God literally keeping this promise in the Book of Acts, there is good reason to believe that this promise is not to be claimed as completely today. The apostles were the unique, first-time door openers for the gospel into the world. The impact of their testimony would pave the way for all later witnesses. At that time, the complete Scriptures had not yet been written, so God gave "special revelation" to select followers—knowledge they had no other way of knowing.

In contrast, we today have the complete Word of God. God will keep his promise to us in bringing to mind appropriate truths of Scripture that we have already learned as we need them. But we must be careful about claiming a promise that he will put into our mouths words that have never entered our minds before. The Spirit of God "will remind" (John 14:26) us of Jesus' teachings—presuming we have heard and learned them previously. Today's preachers must understand there is no substitute for careful preparation in speaking God's message.

Notice in 10:20 that Jesus chose the phrase **the Spirit of your Father** rather than "the Holy Spirit." The imagery of the accompanying Father must have been comforting to the persecuted follower. And it is a comfort to know that God will use Jewish rejection to bring the message to the Gentiles.

10:21–22. Some disciples would even die for their loyalty to Christ. Their complete loyalty to Christ might compete with the closest of family relationships (8:21–22; 10.34–37). Jesus was raising the stakes for the Twelve. If the thought of being betrayed by a brother, child, or parent was too much for them, they could turn back now. None of the Twelve did.

Jesus' sweeping warning of 10:17, **Be on your guard against men**, is further underscored in 10:22: **All men will hate you because of me.** This statement is hyperbolic, because some people would respond to the gospel and love the Lord and his disciples. But the statement is more than accurate in that people of all categories would hate the Lord and his disciples. The meaning is, "You [plural] will be continually being hated." The persecution and hatred would not end quickly; Jesus' followers must buckle down for a long ordeal. Thus the exhortation to **he**

who stands firm. But there will be an end, and the person who remains loyal to the end **will be saved.** Saved from what? This is not spiritual salvation but physical salvation. Endurance is never a condition of spiritual deliverance. **Because of me** means, "because of your association with me."

10:23. While Israel was a small nation (a territory 75 miles wide by 125 miles long), there was still a significant area to cover, and Jesus communicated a sense of urgency. When a disciple met with persecution in one city, he was to **flee** to another city, both for his own safety and to avoid wasting effort on a rejecting audience.

Jesus seemed to indicate in 10:23b that before the disciples had finished going through every city of Israel, the Son of Man would initiate the next step in the advancement of the kingdom. Some interpreters believe Jesus was referring to his kingdom's coming in "cameo" at the soon-to-be-witnessed Transfiguration (Matt. 17). Commentators universally acknowledge Jesus' statement in 10:23b as one of the most difficult in Matthew to interpret. There are innumerable numbers of variations among the proposed solutions.

How the disciples' survey went is revealed in the following chapters. In Matthew 11:12–19 Jesus announced that the response was negative. In Matthew 11:20 we arrive at something of a "high water" mark, and Jesus denounced the cities for their lack of response, indicating that even Gentile cities like Tyre and Sidon (11:21–24) would be more responsive than they had been.

By the end of chapter 12, the results of the national survey are completed. Israel's leaders had rejected Jesus, calling his ministry devilish (of Beelzebub; 12:24). At that time Jesus made his decision with respect to the kingdom and Israel (12:31–50). He indicated that the only remaining message (**sign;** 12:39) he will have for Israel will be his resurrection, and that at "the judgment" even the response of pagan Nineveh will condemn this generation of Israel. Jesus then announced that he chose to associate with people not on the basis of their Jewish blood, but on the basis of their choosing to do "the will of my Father" (12:50).

Some interpreters see Jesus in 10:23b referring specifically to his coming judgment upon Israel in A.D. 70 with the destruction of Jerusalem by the Roman legions. This destruction of Jerusalem was the result of the judgment that Jesus announced in Matthew 12 and confirmed in 23:31–39. This is supported by the fact that "coming" often involves judgment as well as deliverance. Furthermore, in the Olivet Discourse (Matt. 24–25), which seems to meld the A.D. 70 judgment with the end-time judgment, similar language is used ("he who stands firm to the end will be saved"; 24:13), and the central figure is Jesus the judge.

Ⅾ Comfort for the Kingdom Worker (10:24–33)

SUPPORTING IDEA: *The king alleviates his followers' fears.*

Having painted a bleak picture of the persecution his disciples would encounter, Jesus shifted over to words of comfort and encouragement. He talked about rewards for his followers.

10:24–25. Jesus' argument was that if the greater (a teacher or master) is mistreated, how can the lesser (a disciple or slave) expect better treatment? Jesus' exorcisms had already been attributed to Satan (9:34), and there may have been worse things said of him that are not recorded in Matthew. This is why he used a conditional statement ("if"), implying that, indeed, the statement was true: **If the head of the house has been called Beelzebub.** The latter part of this conditional statement is missing the verb. It reads, **how much more the members of his household!**

But Jesus obviously intended us to understand that we will be treated as poorly as he has been treated. Most modern American Christians find it hard to identify with this, but Christ's followers in other places find it as real as the morning news. Persecution of Christians throughout the world is a serious reality.

Jesus' notice of poor treatment is not an encouraging statement, further affirming the difficulty of being Jesus' follower. But his disciples probably found some encouragement, since such mistreatment implied close association with Jesus (Acts 5:41; 2 Cor. 11:16–12:10; Phil. 3:10–11). There is solace in camaraderie, especially when your comrade is the Messiah-King who is inviting you to share his throne (Rev. 3:21) and his reign (Rev. 2:26–28). They also recalled Jesus' exhortation to rejoice in persecution, because of their great reward in heaven (5:10–12).

Beelzebub is an Israelite term of mockery for a Philistine god. It means literally "lord of the flies."

10:26–27. Part of the fear of persecution is that the truth of the injustice may never become known, and justice may never be served. But Jesus encouraged the Twelve not to fear injustice from the persecutors. Ultimately, any concealed truth will break into the open. In fact, he exhorted his disciples to be instrumental in making the truth known (10:27), that justice might be done.

10:28–31. Another fear related to persecution is the fear of bodily harm and death. But Jesus helped his disciples to shift their focus. He told them, in essence, "Do not worry about your body. It is expendable. Concern yourself, instead, with the condition of your soul-life, which is eternal, and which, if invested rightly now, returns great reward" (16:34–27). A believer who adopts this perspective will not be afraid of those who can kill the body but will fear God, the Lord who has authority as judge to condemn the soul and the body to eternal destruction in hell. This healthy fear of God will cause a person to live by obedience, respecting the authority and power of the judge (Prov. 1:7).

To the stark truth of 10:28, Jesus added the comforting grace of 10:29–31, assuring the believer that the judge is also the Father, who values his children greatly and will always protect their souls.

Using a line of reasoning converse of that in 10:24–25, Jesus argued that because the Father cares what happens to the lesser (an insignificant sparrow), he will care much more deeply for the greater (a person made in his image—especially one who claims him as Father). The price of sparrows used in sacrifices (10:29), two for an *assarion* (the smallest copper coin), is intended to emphasize the insignificance of the bird; while the numbering of one's hairs (10:30) by the Father emphasizes how much the Father values and cares for his child.

So Jesus' **Do not be afraid** has multiple implications. We should not fear slander, because harm to our reputation (10:24–25) will be set right when the truth comes to light. We should not fear bodily harm, because harm to the body—even death—is endurable and insignificant compared to the value of the eternal soul. In fact, we have nothing to fear because our Father places such high value on us.

10:32–33. Because there is no reason to fear persecution from men (10:24–31), believers should have no hesitation in confessing Jesus before others. The person who can adopt the fearless perspective Jesus teaches and who confesses Jesus before men will find a willing advocate in heaven before the Father. But the person who gives into faithless fear and denies Jesus before men will find a just denial (of reward and reign; 2 Tim. 2:11–13) before the Father in heaven.

As the people turned away from him, Jesus focused on whether we are willing to associate with him under the public scrutiny of other people. We might say that Jesus was asking, "Will you really be my friends and loyal followers, no matter what other people think, say, or do to you?" If we will, we will find in him an even more faithful friend—in fact, a brother. And a rewarder. Every act of our lives will come under the scrutiny of the judgment seat of Christ (2 Cor. 5:10). If we should refuse to speak up for Christ because of fear or intimidation, we will suffer the loss of reward from him (2 Tim. 2:12).

E Single-Minded Devotion of the Kingdom Worker (10:34–39)

SUPPORTING IDEA: *The king clarifies the devotion expected of his followers.*

10:34–36. The king wanted his followers fully prepared for the difficulty they would face because of their loyalty to him, so he addressed a possible misconception. In 5:9, Jesus pronounced the "peacemakers" blessed. But here he announced that his mission on earth would cause not peace, but hostility (a sword)—even between the closest of family members (10:21). He was *not* saying that he would intentionally divide families. But he was saying that loyalty to him would cause some of his followers to be hated by their families, because of the disbelief of other family members. Jesus experienced those kinds of feelings at the deepest level when he was betrayed by Judas.

To further explain his prediction of hostility, Jesus quoted Micah 7:6 in 10:35–36. In Micah, this verse comes at the end of a lament about Israel's misery (Mic. 7:1–6), because of the Lord's judgment on them at the time of King Ahaz (Mic. 6). But the verse immediately following (Mic. 7:7) is a contrasting note of hope:

> "But as for me, I watch in hope for the LORD,
> I wait for God my Savior;
> my God will hear me."

The remainder of Micah (7:8–20) is prophecy and prayer about Israel's restoration. Those familiar with Jesus' quote in its original context would see the family hostility as a reference to God's judgment on unbelieving Israel and see the hopeful future beyond the devastating difficulties.

10:37–39. Jesus now moved from his warning about the divisions and hostility which his followers would encounter to clarify the standard for the follower **worthy** of him. First, the worthy follower will love Jesus more than anyone else—even one's own parent or child (10:37). Immediately following the quote of Micah 7:6, he issued this challenge: "If you find yourself faced with a choice between loyalty to an unbelieving and hostile family member and loyalty to me, I have to take priority." He was not assuming that everyone would have to leave his or her family. Jesus' demands here amount to one more declaration of his deity. One of the highest duties in all Judaism was to love family members, especially parents. Every faithful Jew knew and understood that only God himself could demand a higher love (Deut. 6:4–5; 13:6–11).

Second, the worthy follower will endure the mockery and suffering involved in following Jesus (10:38). Matthew referred here to the cross. The criminal had to carry the crossbeam—usually through an angry, chiding mob—to the site of the execution. Jesus stated that his faithful followers would experience some degree of suffering and shame. Jesus used this powerful imagery again in 16:24–27, after his first prediction of his death.

In addition, the worthy follower will give up all of his individual "rights" to the king, together with any possessions, passions, pastimes, or people that might distract from following him. In "losing" these lesser aspects of earthly life, the follower "finds" true worth—God's purpose, joy, and reward.

ⓕ Reward for Receiving a Kingdom Worker (10:40–42)

SUPPORTING IDEA: *The king assures his followers that their hosts will have incentive (and reward) to receive them well.*

10:40–42. Here Jesus returned to thoughts about the hosts of the disciples as they went from city to city (10:11–14) and continued his thoughts about reward.

An apostle was one who, if he conducted himself in a worthy manner, was to be treated exactly as the one he represented. He had the same authority and conveyed the same message as the person he represented. Jesus was an "apostle" from the Father, and the Twelve were apostles from Jesus. Through this chain of representation, the authority of God the Father was conveyed through the Twelve. And the response of those to whom they went was not a response to human beings, but a response to the Father whom they represented (10:40). Jesus focused on the positive response of "receiving" rather than on the negative response of rejection.

In the Old Testament, a person who accepted a prophet and his message had accepted God's will. Those who provided for the prophets were rewarded like the prophets. Similarly, to receive a righteous person or a disciple for Christ's sake would mean sharing in their reward for faithfulness. Matthew 10:41–42 has some characteristics of Hebrew poetry. In keeping with the rules of Hebrew parallelism, Jesus varied his wording for aesthetic value in the parallel statements about reward.

Little ones (10:42) was a term of affection that Jesus used toward his disciples, particularly when they followed him with the innocence and faith of a child (18:1–6; 19:13–15). He would use the same terminology in 25:31–46, asserting that those he sent represented him, and any kind of response to them was equivalent to a response to him in person. A cup of cold water was a gift that even the poorest person could give.

He will certainly not lose his reward (10:42) is not so much a statement allowing for the loss of reward as it is a different way to say that the person would be rewarded. Throughout this lengthy discussion (10:32–42), Jesus seemed to assume that the matter of rewards in his kingdom was understood by his disciples. But the vast majority of Christians today know little about rewards. We have lost this reality of kingdom service. Whether through simple ignorance or some kind of false piety, we have shied away from this biblical doctrine. Jesus will evaluate the service of every one of us, his servants. And our eternal reward is dependent upon our service in this life. How you serve him in this life determines how you will serve him in eternity (1 Cor. 3:10–15).

MAIN IDEA REVIEW: *The king trains his disciples to carry out his ministry, giving them specific guidelines, realistic expectations of persecution, a clarified challenge, and hopeful reassurances.*

III. CONCLUSION

We have been given authority from the king in this world. We represent him, and we have been commissioned to carry on his ministry. His authority and provision will give us all we need for success. We must trust him more than our preparations for success and provision in ministry.

PRINCIPLES

- Jesus suffered persecution during his time on earth.
- Hostility often comes from those closest to us because of our loyalty to the king.
- We need not fear bodily harm or death because the Father will guard our souls, which are eternal and more significant.
- Loyalty to the king is more important than loyalty to our closest family and friends.
- Letting go of this life is to gain the next life.

APPLICATIONS

- Do not fear damage to your reputation. The truth will ultimately vindicate you.
- Look for opportunities to aid other disciples of the king. We will share in their reward. And anyone who aids us will share in ours.
- Be prepared for long-term endurance of the same kinds of suffering the king endured.
- Publicly confess the king on earth. He will be our advocate before the Father in heaven.

IV. LIFE APPLICATION

The Kingdom Worker

Insects occupy a prominent place among the animals named in the Bible. The *ant* appears only in the book of Proverbs. It is a community creature, with communities sometimes as large as one-half million individuals. Ants mirror humans in the sense that they practice agriculture and conduct war on other ants.

Proverbs 6:6–8 praises the ant for its supreme example of industry. Proverbs 30:25 notes the ant's wisdom and ability to provide food. They are capable of finding the shortest path from a food source to the nest. They are also capable of adapting to changes in the environment. For example, they will find a new, shorter path once an old one is no longer feasible due to a new obstacle.

Ants are not thinking creatures; they are instinct-driven. Each is designed to accomplish a purpose in the ant kingdom. They are examples of efficiency because they unceasingly work and continue on their mission in spite of adversity, even to the point of sacrificing themselves for survival of the community.

The worker in God's kingdom can take a lesson or two from this small creature. Jesus has delegated his authority to every believer in the kingdom. He has also empowered each believer to live righteously.

First, as does the ant, kingdom workers must be prepared to endure adversity and hardship for the advancement of the kingdom. In fact, the follower of Jesus should not be surprised when persecution comes. Jesus promises that if we publicly confess his kingship on earth, he will be our advocate before the Father.

Second, we must not grow weary in well-doing. Those who are faithful in serving others in the kingdom will be rewarded. Christians of all ages need to follow the Messiah-King's teachings in Matthew 10 to lay hold of his guarantee of a future reward.

V. PRAYER

Gracious Father, send us out into the fields that are ready for the harvest, just as you sent your disciples. Thank you for the assurance of our reward in heaven if we remain faithful to your call. Amen.

VI. DEEPER DISCOVERIES

A. Further Insight into the Twelve Apostles

The Twelve are listed in pairs for easy memorization. The first two pairs are sets of brothers (Peter and Andrew, James and John), but there are no apparent connections between the other pairs. Of the twelve disciples, six are mentioned only here in Matthew (Philip, Bartholomew, Thomas, James the son of Alphaeus, Thaddaeus, and Simon the Zealot). Elsewhere in Matthew, Andrew and Matthew are mentioned only in the context of their original calling (4:18–20; 9:9–10). Judas Iscariot, although he played a critical role in the story, is mentioned only in the context of his betrayal (26:14–16,25–26,47–50; 27:3–5).

From Matthew's editorial comment in 10:2–4, we can assume that Matthew recalls his own corrupt past as a "tax collector" (9:9–13), emphasizing the life-changing power of Jesus' grace. Simon the Zealot was part of the sect called "Zealots," a group of political activists committed to freeing Israel from

Rome, sometimes by violent and subversive means. (Note the extreme contrast with Matthew, who was in the employ of the Roman Empire.) Judas Iscariot is, even this early, foreshadowed as the villainous traitor.

Only Simon Peter and the Zebedee brothers, James and John, receive any kind of extensive attention from Matthew. We see James and John in their original calling (4:21–22), in their mother's request for special treatment (20:20–24) and twice as part of Jesus' closest threesome (with Peter, 17:1–13, on the Mount of Transfiguration, and 26:37–45 at Gethsemane).

Simon Peter stands out as the disciple of note in Matthew. *Peter*, a nickname given him by Jesus (John 1:42), is the Greek word for "rock," which was the basis for a significant wordplay by Jesus in 16:18. (John used the Aramaic *Cephas*, meaning "rock," once in John 1:42; and Paul used it in 1 Cor. 1:12; 3:22; 9:5. Paul used *Peter* in 1 Cor. 15:5; Gal. 2:9.) Matthew labeled Peter "first," meaning that he was the leader of the Twelve, under Jesus. Peter was usually the spokesman for the Twelve, and he usually absorbed Jesus' rebuke, sometimes even when others were equally at fault. (Besides Matt. 10:2, we see Peter in 4:18–20; 8:14; 14:28–31; 15:15; 16:16–18,22–23; 17:1–13,24–26; 18:21, 19:27, 26:33–35,37–45,58,69–75.)

B. The Samaritans

In 722 B.C., Israel, the northern kingdom of ten Jewish tribes, was deported into exile by Assyria. The Assyrians repopulated the land with their own people. These people intermarried with the remaining Jews (2 Kgs. 17). Since Samaria was the capital of this territory, the offspring of these families became known as the Samaritans. Judah, the southern kingdom of two tribes, was also exiled in 586 B.C., but they returned to the land seventy years later without the large-scale intermingling with other ethnic groups.

The so-called "pure" Jews of Judah (later called Judea in Jesus' time) despised the Samaritans as "half-breeds," lower even than the Gentiles, because of the corruption of their bloodline and their form of worship (John 4:20). The region of Samaria was in the midst of Jewish territory, with the Jewish region of Galilee to the north and Judea (including Jerusalem) to the south. Jews traveling between Galilee and Judea usually crossed to the east side of the Jordan River to bypass Samaria.

C. Summary

Matthew 10 represents a significant step from the ministry of Jesus in the flesh toward the ministry of Jesus through his church. Here we see the first significant movement of the twelve apostles into their unique historical role as the foundation of the church (Eph. 2:19–22). Jesus delegated to his disciples (and through them to the rest of his church) the authority he demonstrated in word and deed in chapters 5–9.

The training discourse prepared the Twelve for all they would encounter in their ministry, including opposition and eventual eternal reward. It also provided clarity and reassurance to Matthew's readers, some of whom were probably experiencing the beginning of Roman persecution. Christians of all ages need the perspective provided by the king's teaching here and his encouraging guarantee of future reward.

VII. TEACHING OUTLINE

A. INTRODUCTION
1. Lead Story: Go with Confidence
2. Context: In Matthew 5–9, Jesus *demonstrated* his authority, first through his teaching (chs. 5–7), then through his actions (miracles; chs. 8–9). Now he will *delegate* this same authority to do exactly the same kinds of ministry that he has been doing (4:23; 9:35). Jesus judged that the disciples were ready because they had been with him long enough, observing his ministry and hearing his teachings, and probably participating in the ministry to a limited extent.
3. Transition: To equip someone to do a task, these are steps that must be taken:
   - Talk about the task.
   - Do the task while the learner observes.
   - Let the learner help you do the task.
   - Help the learner do the task.
   - Let the learner do the task while you observe.
   - Let the learner do the task on his own, under your supervision and guidance.
   - The learner becomes a trainer, repeating the above steps with someone else.

   Jesus, the master teacher, probably followed some training method similar to this. In Matthew 10, Jesus prepared the Twelve to do a few central tasks. Eventually, of course, they would be serving at the upper level of this scale.

B. COMMENTARY
1. The King Equips the First Kingdom Workers (10:1–4)
2. The Method of the Kingdom Worker (10:5–15)
3. Persecution of the Kingdom Worker (10:16–23)
4. Comfort for the Kingdom Worker (10:24–33)
5. Single-Minded Devotion of the Kingdom Worker (10:34–39)
6. Reward for Receiving a Kingdom Worker (10:40–42)

C. CONCLUSION

1. Wrap-up: Jesus saw his ministry from a multiplication point of view, not just from an addition perspective. He was powerful enough to demonstrate his authority over all things, but he was strategic also, in that he transferred this authority to those he had selected and prepared to carry on in his name. Jesus was not only thinking about the distant future but the nearer future of his departure to rejoin his Father and leave his work in the hands of others.

2. Personal Challenge: We need to realize that as a part of the body of Christ we have been commissioned by Christ, in his name, to carry out his work in his authority in this world. It is in the name of Jesus that we share his love and compassion with others. It is in the name of Jesus that we choose to abstain from certain things in life. It is in his power and authority that we share his forgiveness with others as we communicate the "Good News" of Jesus.

VIII. ISSUES FOR DISCUSSION

1. What methods did Jesus use to train his disciples to carry on the work of the kingdom after he was gone?
2. What criteria do you think Jesus might have used in selecting his twelve disciples?
3. What instructions did Jesus give his disciples when he sent them out to preach, teach, and heal?
4. What are the multiple implications of Jesus' exhortation to his disciples, "Do not be afraid"?

Matthew 11–12

The King Faces Opposition

I. **INTRODUCTION**
The Day the Lesbian Avengers Came to Church

II. **COMMENTARY**
A verse-by-verse explanation of these chapters.

III. **CONCLUSION**
An overview of the principles and applications from these chapters.

IV. **LIFE APPLICATION**
Denial in the Face of Evidence
Melding these chapters to life.

V. **PRAYER**
Tying these chapters to life with God.

VI. **DEEPER DISCOVERIES**
Historical, geographical, and grammatical enrichment of the commentary.

VII. **TEACHING OUTLINE**
Suggested step-by-step group study of these chapters.

VIII. **ISSUES FOR DISCUSSION**
Zeroing these chapters in on daily life.

Matthew 11–12

I N   A   N U T S H E L L

In chapter 11 Jesus begins to encounter open opposition from the hypocritical Jewish leaders. Because Israel has rejected the Messiah-King, Jesus invites the faithful remnant among the nation to enjoy his covenant blessings. Although the leaders try to slander Jesus, he refuses to play their game, warning them that their accusations will be their condemnation at the judgment. As they have refused to accept forgiveness from Jesus in the face of undeniable evidence that he is the Messiah, he condemns them for blasphemy against the Holy Spirit—the unforgivable sin.

The King Faces Opposition

I. INTRODUCTION

The Day the Lesbian Avengers Came to Church

*I*t was a gray, wet Sunday in January when our church was picketed by three groups with strange names and equally confused principles—the Lesbian Avengers, Radical Women, and Rockers for Choice. Our church people were known to be consistently active leaders in standing for pro-life causes, among them courteous sidewalk counseling at Portland's most active abortion clinic. We were, therefore, chosen as the "target." The three groups decided to stage a picket outside our services on the twenty-fifth anniversary of the infamous Roe v. Wade decision.

Through a variety of sources we were fortunate to have received prior notice, but we could not be certain the picket would be peaceful or respectful of our property or our services. The local sheriff, familiar with these groups' "tactics," had warned us that they could be a rough bunch, and that they had advertised in the metropolitan "underground" for busloads of followers to show up for the protest. The sheriff's S.W.A.T. team was strategically stationed out of sight nearby.

It was a tense situation, but none of our people stayed away from church. In fact, attendance was actually higher than average that morning. Our own people provided "security" on the property itself. We were as well prepared as we knew how to be with several layers of undercover but well-rehearsed security. But—most importantly—we enjoyed a potent concert of prayer during the week, and on the morning of the event a team of our people were in a large room near the sanctuary with one assignment only—to pray.

Out on the front lines where the picketers would be, our people were equally well prepared—providing tents for the picketers' protection from the rain, coffee and donuts for their appetites, and lots of compassionate personal conversation for their hearts.

As it turned out, it was an absolutely delightful morning! The protest was unfriendly but peaceful. The church property was respected. And the conversations with the picketers were careful, spiritual, and compassionate. So delightfully Christlike, in fact, that the picketers experienced real difficulty in maintaining their anger. Their leader even pleaded through a bullhorn, "Come on, girls, I know it is tough but you have got to stay focused and keep your anger up." Finding it impossible to do so, they simply began to wander back to their cars, meekly exiting the scene long before their planned departure. By the time our morning services were over, the picketers were gone.

But our people had the joy of faithfully representing Christ in the face of vocal opposition.

The point of this little story is straightforward. Jesus had said it himself, "Blessed are you when people insult you, persecute you and falsely say all kinds of evil against you because of me" (Matt. 5:11). In other words, your faithful Christlike stand will invite serious opposition. Count on it. Jesus experienced it in his day. And that is what we find in Matthew 11.

Chapter 11 highlights the growing tidal wave of pharisaical opposition to Jesus. In fact, this chapter marks the continental divide of Matthew's Gospel. From this point forward, Jesus no longer approached the lost people of Israel, the Jews, but turned his efforts dramatically to minister to the outcast Gentiles.

II. COMMENTARY

The King Faces Opposition

MAIN IDEA: *The king and his citizens will encounter opponents in this world who doubt his identity, even among those who should know better, and in spite of all the evidence supporting his identity as Messiah-King.*

Up to this point in Matthew's account, any opposition from the Pharisees and company had been subdued, often taking the form of critical questions (9:11) and defensive grumbling (9:3,34). Throughout Jesus' training in Matthew 10, he prepared his disciples for growing opposition. Now in Matthew 11–12, the conflict flamed into the open, and the hypocrites began to take the offensive. Still, we do not yet see the coordinated efforts we will see later (22:15–40), nor has the heat of the conflict yet reached a full boil, as it will in Matthew 22–23 and 26–27.

It is in the face of this opposition, reflecting the broader unbelief of much of the population (11:16–24), that the tone of Matthew's portrayal of the king shifts significantly. Up to Matthew 11:20, the emphasis had been on Jesus as the authoritative, sovereign Son of David. But from 11:20 on in Matthew's Gospel, the emphasis shifts toward a portrayal of Jesus as the rejected, sacrificial Son of Abraham. The opening statement of the book (Matt. 1:1) serves as a rough outline. Jesus played the role of the Son of David (reaching to Israel) in the first half, but shifted his role to that of the Son of Abraham (sacrificial lamb of God) and his reach to the Gentiles in the second half. By no means is either theme abandoned at any point in the book; we simply see a shift in emphasis. Indeed, there are signs of Jesus as the Son of Abraham early in the book (e.g., 1:21; 8:17; 9:12–13 34; 10:25), as well as signs of Jesus as the Son of David later in the book (e.g., 11:22,24; 12:8,23; 16:27–17:5; 20:30–31; 21:1–11; 22:40–46; 24:30–31; 26:64; ch. 28).

Both facets of Jesus' identity are critical to God's fulfillment of his twofold plan of salvation—the restoration of his prodigal kingdom (through the Son of David) and the redemption of his sinful people (through the Son of Abraham).

Much of the emphasis in Matthew 11–12 centers on Israel's rejection of Jesus, in spite of his many validating miracles (11:16–24; 12:22–24,38). Related to this is the question of his identity (11:1–6; 12:8,15–21).

A large part of Matthew 11–12 is devoted to Jesus' words, rebuking unbelieving Israel in general and the religious leaders in particular. The two miracles that are recorded serve a different purpose than those in Matthew 8–9. They serve not primarily to demonstrate the king's authority but as occasions for the hypocrites to criticize Jesus, in each case resulting in a resounding victory by Jesus.

A The King Responds to John's Uncertainty (11:1–6)

SUPPORTING IDEA: *Even the king's forerunner had his doubts about the king's identity.*

11:1. Upon completing his disciples' training for ministry, this verse says that **he departed** to minister from city to city. In the context of chapter 10, we understand that the Twelve also departed for the same purpose. While we are not explicitly told here that they went out in twos, as with the seventy-two in Luke 10:1, the listing of the Twelve in pairs (10:2–4) implies that this was also true here. It is difficult to imagine Jesus sending out such inexperienced teachers alone.

Jesus' (and the Twelve's) last-ditch campaign to Israel (and that of the Twelve) is described as teaching and preaching.

11:2–3. John's imprisonment in 4:12 had been the sign for Jesus to pick up the baton and continue the ministry John had announced. In 14:1–12 we learn that it was Herod the Tetrarch (or Herod Antipas), the son of Herod the Great, who imprisoned and then beheaded John. This was the same Herod who would interview Jesus in the midst of his trial before the Sanhedrin and Pilate (Luke 23:6–12).

Matthew is not saying that John knew Jesus was the promised Christ ("anointed One," equivalent to the Heb. "Messiah"). In fact, while John suspected this to be true, the fact that he sent his disciples to inquire of Jesus revealed his doubts. Perhaps John, in the hopelessness of his imprisonment, was swayed by the popular expectations of the promised Messiah-King—that he would come to rescue Israel from political oppression. John may have been genuinely asking, "If you are the king and I am your ambassador, how is it that I am in prison and opposition to you is growing?"

John literally asked if Jesus was "the coming one," referring to the Old Testament prophecies regarding the Messiah (Ps. 118:26; Heb. 10:37).

11:4–6. Rather than give a direct answer, Jesus challenged John's disciples to return to John as witnesses of the evidence for his identity. He told them to report what they **hear** (his teaching and preaching) and **see** (his miracles). Then he proceeded to outline his ministry, being careful to refer to messianic signs that are prominent in the Old Testament. References to the blind (9:27–31), lame (9:1–8) and deaf (possibly in 9:32–33) remind us of Isaiah 35:5–6 (cf. Isa. 29:18). Jesus had already used the healing of the leper as a testimony of his identity to the priests in 8:1–4. His raising of the dead (9:18–26; see Isa. 26:19) reminded observers of Elijah (1 Kgs. 17:17–24), Elisha (2 Kgs. 4:18–37), and Malachi's promise of the return of Elijah (Mal. 4:5–6).

The good news is preached to the poor is a reworded quote from Isaiah 61:1 (cf. Isa. 29:19).

Luke (4:14–30) portrays Jesus as inaugurating his public ministry by quoting the first one and one-half verses of Isaiah 61 (stopping short of the "day of vengeance") in the synagogue of his hometown Nazareth, and then announcing, "Today this Scripture is fulfilled in your hearing" (Matt. 11:21).

Jesus' brief allusion to Isaiah 61 in Matthew, and his more extended quote in Luke, convey the same message—Jesus is the Anointed One of Isaiah 61, speaking by the Spirit of the Almighty, bringing a message of healing, liberty, and vengeance. Certainly Jesus' preaching from town to town encompassed those themes. It brought hope to the spiritually poor (5:3), those who recognized their need for salvation.

In many ways Jesus was a contradiction to the people. They expected a Messiah who would overthrow Rome with military might, but instead they saw in Jesus a humble teacher and a quiet healer. By his choice of works, words, and timing, Jesus challenged the presuppositions of people about him. Most were confused, and many resolved their confusion by refusing to accept Jesus as Messiah. Instead, they "stumbled" over those aspects of his behavior that did not fit with their preconceptions. Only those who had "ears" to hear and eyes of faith to see (11:15; 13:9–17) would find the resolution to the apparent paradox in the true Messiah-King. These were the truly "happy" or "blessed" ones.

B This Generation (Israel) Rejects John and the King (11:7–19)

SUPPORTING IDEA: *The hypocrites of Israel were impossible to satisfy; neither the king nor his forerunner was credible in their eyes.*

This passage is a tribute to John the Baptizer. But Matthew's ultimate goal for this passage is to reveal the rejection of both the forerunner (John) and the Son of Man by **this generation** (11:16–19), building the picture of growing opposition in chapters 11–12.

11:7–8. Even as John's disciples were walking away, Jesus turned to the crowd, many of whom were probably familiar with John's ministry. He began to help them understand the contradiction that was John (similar to the contradiction that was Jesus; see above commentary on 11:6).

Matthew has already told us that John conducted his ministry in the desert of Judea. People had to go out of their way to see and hear him. They would not have gone to such trouble if they expected to find a weakling ("a reed"; Isa. 42:3; 1 Kgs. 14:15; 2 Kgs. 18:21; Ezek. 29:6). Nor would they have gone if they expected to find a wealthy teacher trying to take their money (**fine clothes** was a sign of wealth). In fact, such a shyster would not have bothered to go out into the wilderness, but would likely have found a place of notoriety as an advisor to a king.

11:9–10. Those who sought out John went to the desert only because they expected to see **a prophet.** Jesus confirmed that, whether they realized it or not, their expectations were fulfilled—and more. John was more than the typical prophet of the Old Testament. He was *the* prophet, the forerunner of the promised Messiah-King.

In the quote of 11:10, Jesus identified John as the messenger of Malachi 3:1. The Book of Malachi takes the form of a dialogue or a series of question-and-answer exchanges between hypocritical Israel (particularly the corrupt leaders) and the Lord. At the end of Malachi 2, the Lord says he is wearied with Israel's complaints about injustice (when, in reality, they themselves were guilty of causing much injustice). They asked, "Where is the God of justice?" In response to their complaints, the Lord answers: "See, I will send my messenger, who will prepare the way before me. But who can endure the day of his coming? Who can stand when he appears? For he will be like a refiner's fire or a launderer's soap. He will sit as a refiner and purifier of silver. So I will come near to you for judgment" (Mal. 3:1–5).

Jesus' quote of Malachi 3:1 made a statement about John the Baptizer. But for those who knew its context, the quote made an even more significant statement about Jesus himself. The messenger would prepare the way for One who would bring justice that the complainers of Israel would not welcome. He would come to the temple (Matt. 21:1–17,23–27). He would be "the messenger of the covenant," proclaiming judgment on them as the breakers of the covenant (Matt. 23).

11:11. Jesus used the formula, **I tell you the truth,** to draw attention to a significant statement. Of all mankind (**those born of women**), none was greater than John the Baptizer. John was the greatest because of his role as the Messiah's forerunner.

But here Jesus introduced a paradox that he would revisit in 19:30; 20:16,26–28. Prominence and greatness in human eyes do not necessarily equate to greatness in God's eyes. God measures greatness by a different yardstick—the willingness of the heart to yield itself to him and his will, so that his true greatness can manifest itself through the yielded heart. Therefore, the humblest (**least**) in the kingdom is even greater, by God's standard, than the great John the Baptizer. Jesus did not intend this to demean John or John's faith. He intended it, instead, as a parenthetical comment reinforcing the kingdom values that were so difficult for his audience to accept—values that run contrary to the world's values.

11:12. Jesus' statement, **The kingdom of heaven has been forcefully advancing, and forceful men lay hold of it**, is difficult to interpret. We may not be able to know with perfect precision what Jesus meant by this statement, but we can grasp his major point. The context indicates that Christ's advancing kingdom would be forcibly opposed by violent, hostile people. As Christ's kingdom advances, the opposition to it would increase. In fact, from the time John started announcing it, until this very day, the false leaders of Israel had done nothing but object.

11:13–15. John's appearance on the stage of history was a key turning point. It was the end of one era and the beginning of another. With his arrival, the period of the Old Testament came to an end. **The Prophets and the Law** is a variation on a phrase used often in the New Testament to represent the whole of the Old Testament. There is debate about whether John himself belonged to the old era or the new. Actually, John could be considered the last martyr among the prophets of old, and the first martyr of the New Testament order.

To **prophesy** (*propheteuo*) is not just to foretell the future. Rather, it is to make known or to reveal the mind of God. While this sometimes has to do with the future, more often it is simply God's perspective on the present or the past. If we inserted this definition into verse 13, it would read, "For all the Prophets and the Law revealed God's mind until John." Now there is coming a turning point in God's revelation—in the person of Jesus, the one for whom John prepared the way. Not only did Jesus bring a message; he *was* a message, revealing God's mind and heart and his person and presence.

The last two verses of the Old Testament (Mal. 4:5–6) foretell the coming of Elijah before the day of God's judgment. Before the final days of judgment upon the nation, one who is representative of Elijah's ministry would provide opportunity for the children of Israel to return to the faith of their fathers. Now that Messiah was present, John (representing the office of Elijah) offered Israel that opportunity to experience the long-awaited kingdom. **If you are willing to accept it** means that it was theirs for the taking.

But first-century Israel was not willing to accept John or Jesus or his kingdom. For Jesus to identify John as the promised Elijah further emphasized John's appearance as the marker of the end of the Old Testament age. The four silent centuries between the writing of Malachi and the appearance of John the Baptizer were a time of longing and hoping for the answers to the questions raised by the Old Testament.

Even though John's fulfillment of Malachi 4:5–6 is absolute truth, not all would accept it. So Jesus preceded the claim with **if you are willing to accept it,** and followed it with **He who has ears, let him hear.**

Throughout his teaching ministry, Jesus said many things that were difficult. He did this to sift out those who were truly teachable from those whose hearts were hardened to the truth, no matter how plainly it was explained.

11:16–19. Jesus concluded what began as a tribute to John by getting to his true purpose for launching into this exposition. He condemned the current generation of Israelites for ignoring the messages of John the forerunner and Jesus the Messiah.

To what begins the contrast between the one **who has ears** (11:15) to hear and the generation he is about to describe. He may already have chosen the simile he would use, but he used a question (**To what can I compare this generation?**) to prepare his listeners for it, identifying what he was about to say as a word picture and creating a brief moment of suspense.

Jesus compared disbelieving Israel to children, because their disbelief was so immature and childish. Referring to common children's games, which required responsiveness in participation, Jesus indicated that Israel had "refused to play" no matter what the tune. Neither John nor Jesus turned out the way Israel expected of the forerunner and the Messiah. Because of their presuppositions, Israel's response was the proverbial, "Our mind is made up; do not confuse us with the facts." Out of their hardened hearts the skeptics looked for any reason to reject John and Jesus in order to justify their disbelief.

They rejected John because he did not have enough fun (wandering in the desert) and they rejected Jesus because he had too much fun (eating with sinners). John took the hard-line approach (the funeral dirge). Jesus took the more positive approach (the inviting flute). Neither evoked response. Nothing would satisfy them. These children would not play, no matter what one might do for them.

In verses 18 and 19, Jesus clarified the complaints Israel had against John and himself. John's ascetic lifestyle (3:1,4; cf. with Elijah, 1 Kgs. 17:2–6; 2 Kgs. 1:8) became their excuse to reject him. "No man in his right mind would behave in such an eccentric way," went their reasoning. "Only a **demon** could have caused such insanity!"

Jesus the bridegroom, on the other hand, had reason to celebrate, and he invited those around him to do so as well (9:14–17). We have already seen the skeptics' criticism of his behavior (specifically, his failure to endorse fasting among his disciples; 9:14). This, combined with his association with sinners (9:9–13), was their justification for rejecting him as **a glutton and a drunkard, a friend of tax collectors and "sinners."**

Jesus' closing comment to this segment, **But wisdom is proved right by her actions,** is the same as saying, "Anyone who observes my behavior and John's behavior with an honest heart will see clearly our righteousness."

The King Denounces Unrepentant Cities (11:20–24)

SUPPORTING IDEA: *Because Israel continued to reject the king, even when presented with miraculous proof of his identity, he warned them of their greater accountability and their harsher judgment.*

Jesus pronounced strong judgment (**woe**) upon Israel because of the hardness of their hearts. He chose two cities in particular, Korazin and Bethsaida, which were within a couple of miles of his own headquarters at Capernaum. Both these Galilean villages would have witnessed Jesus' ministry firsthand. They are judged, as representative of the nation, for having seen the Messiah and having rejected him outright.

Matthew portrayed Jesus' caustic denunciation of the unrepentant cities of Israel as flowing directly out of his description of that generation's resistance (11:7–19). He used the words of Jesus in 11:7–24 to build to a climactic turning point in verses 20–24. In this passage, Jesus confronted Israel's disbelief more openly than ever. Prior to this denunciation, Matthew had been emphasizing Jesus as the sovereign Son of David, displaying his authority and minimizing his opposition. From this point on, through the rest of the book, Matthew emphasizes Jesus' role as the sacrificial Son of Abraham. Matthew begins with some minor confrontations in chapter 12, builds to the climax of condemning the Pharisees in chapter 23, and then walks us through the resolution of chapters 26–28 (Jesus' tragic death and his triumphant resurrection). This passage brings the reader to the final disillusionment concerning Israel's attitude toward the Messiah-King, preparing the reader for the growing conflict and the final resolution.

11:20. It is likely that Jesus concentrated his ministry within a limited geographical area, while occasionally venturing to other cities. Matthew referred to the cities in which Jesus did **most of his miracles.** He mentioned only three cities by name, all most likely within a few miles of one another. **Began to denounce** may indicate that these three were only a representative sampling of the cities Jesus visited and denounced.

In this context, Jesus challenged the cities of Israel to "change their minds" (**repent**) concerning his identity and their own sin, and to prove their change of thinking and belief by a change in behavior. Because they did not respond with repentance to such an obvious demonstration of the truth about him, they earned his curse, rather than his blessing (contrast 11:20–24 with the covenant blessing of 11:28–30).

11:21–24. Because the Jewish cities had more evidence to cause them to repent—Jesus' miracles—and therefore more accountability, they would incur a stricter judgment. Jesus did not lessen the severity of judgment on the Gentile cities, but used the severity of their judgment to heighten even further the sinfulness of the Jewish cities. The Jews had the promises and prophecies of the Old Testament, as well as their fulfillment before their eyes in Jesus. To reject the Messiah-King in the face of such evidence was a greater offense than the worst offenses of Sodom, Tyre, and Sidon, who were ignorant in their sin. Jesus stated that if these ignorant Gentiles had been presented with the same evidence, they would have repented and shown greater character than God's chosen people. **Sackcloth and ashes** (11:21) are the traditional symbols of mourning.

Even though Tyre, Sidon, and Sodom had received God's judgment through the course of history (**it would have remained to this day**; 11:23), the eternal souls of their inhabitants await the final **day of judgment** (11:23–24). And their judgment, though harsh, will not come close to that exacted upon the hardened Jewish hearts who witnessed Jesus' miracles. Rather than receiving the covenant blessing of heaven, they would receive the eternal covenant curse of **the depths** (11:23; cf. Jesus' language with Isa. 5:14; 14:14–15).

More bearable indicates there are degrees of punishment in the ultimate judgment to come, and suggests the same is true in terms of heaven's rewards.

D The King Invites the Weary to Himself (11:25–30)

SUPPORTING IDEA: *In the midst of a faithless generation, there remains a faithful remnant who will enjoy the covenant blessings of rest in the Messiah-King.*

After Jesus' righteous indignation (11:7–24) toward the disbelieving majority ("this generation," 11:16) had reached its peak, he subsided into an expression of gratitude and compassion (9:36) toward the **little children** (11:25)of Israel, and the **weary and burdened** (11:28) who came to him. We are reminded of the recurring theme of the faithful remnant in the midst of an unbelieving nation (e.g., 1 Kgs. 19:14–18; Isa. 1:9; 6:9–13; 10:20–22; 11:1). Though the majority of Israel had rejected God's gracious offer of a covenant relationship (1 Kgs. 19:10,14), a few from their midst were demonstrating the characteristics of kingdom servants (Matt. 5:3–12), humbling themselves before God, and accepting his provision for their restoration into the kingdom.

11:25–27. In these verses, Jesus was speaking to his Father. He praised his sovereign Father for his wisdom and his grace—wisdom in his discretion regarding who should receive revelation of the truth and who should not, and grace toward those who received the revelation (1 Cor. 1:18–31). Implied here, and stated clearly in verse 27, is the fact that no person on his own has the ability to know or understand the supernatural realities that only God can reveal (2 Cor. 4:3–4). Jesus would continue to manifest the same type of wisdom as he transitioned into his later style of teaching (beginning in Matt. 13), presenting truth in such a way that those who had "ears to hear" would understand it, and those with hardened hearts would not.

God takes an active hand in the blindness of the hard of heart, as an act of judgment. He hides the truth from the proud of heart (11:25; cf. 13:14–16).

Those with "ears to hear" were the "little children" (11:25); those who came to Jesus with the humility and simple faith of a child (18:1–4; 19:13–15). Those whose ears and hearts were closed to the truth were the **wise and learned** (skilled, wise, and intelligent). These are those who, in their own eyes, are too knowledgeable and mature to stoop to childlike humility. Those who think they know truth do not, and those who realize they do not know the truth will have it revealed to them (cf. Prov. 3:5–7; 12:15). It is the same today. As usual, Jesus turned the world's value system on its head, for it was exactly opposite from that of the Creator.

These things (11:25) refers to the knowledge of Jesus' authority and identity, based on his teaching and miracles. Jesus himself was at the heart of what was being revealed or hidden.

The Father was pleased that only those who recognized their own spiritual poverty (5:3) would receive revelation regarding Jesus' authority and identity (11:26; cf. God's pleasure and will in Eph. 1:5,9,11).

The Father, who is **Lord of heaven and earth** (11:25), has delegated **all things** to Jesus, his Son (v. 27). Jesus has total authority and discretion on earth about who will find true knowledge of the Father (cf. 28:18, as Jesus empowered the disciples to fulfill the Great Commission).

Only the Son and the Father truly know each other. The word for *know* here is *epiginosko,* which takes the root word *ginosko,* "to know intimately by experience" (a term of relationship, as opposed to *oida,* "to know factually"), and intensifies it with the prefix *epi-*. The resulting verb implies thorough, intimate, experiential knowledge, as in a very close relationship. This is the nature of the Father-Son relationship. Incredibly, those **to whom the Son chooses to reveal him** [the Father] can also participate in this divine intimacy, but no one else has a clue, being excluded by their lack of faith. The Christian can revel in his walk with Christ, while the arrogant unbeliever does not know it exists.

11:28–30. The Jewish people struggled under an enormous load of religious expectations and legalities that were laid on them by their false religious leaders. Jesus was saying, "Come, take on yourself the light burden of obedience under the covenant I will seal with my own blood, and I will give you the covenant reward of deep-down, peaceful rest—freedom from guilt, the power of sin, and self-striving. If you continue carrying the heavy burden of works-oriented, self-serving Pharisaism, you will never find rest. You were designed by God to carry my load, not man's" (cf. 23:4).

Jesus' quote in 11:29 from Jeremiah 6:16 ("you will find rest for your souls") further connects this blessing to a right covenant relationship with God. In Jeremiah 6, Jerusalem was experiencing disaster as a result of its disobedience. History was about to repeat itself. Here is the immediate context of Jesus' quote: "This is what the LORD says: 'Stand at the crossroads and look; ask for the ancient paths, ask where the good way is, and walk in it [comparable to Jesus' "light burden"], and you will find rest for your souls [Jesus' covenant promise]. But you said, 'We will not walk in it' . . . Hear, O earth: I am bringing disaster on this people" (Jer. 6:16–20).

Jesus is the source of covenant blessing. Notice he did not say, "Come to my teaching" or "Come to my miracles," but "Come to me." Jesus is the fulfillment of Jeremiah 31:25, where Yahweh announced the new covenant (Jer. 31:31; in contrast to the old Mosaic Law broken by the people) and its refreshing rest for the people. This new covenant will reconstitute faithful Israel, following its tribulation, in preparation for the king's millennial rule from the throne of David.

The tense in the first verb of the phrase, **weary and burdened**, conveys the idea of continual weariness and exhaustion, without a minute of relief. The perfect tense in the second verb implies that the people were completely loaded up at some time in the past, and the load remains perpetually on them. These people needed a break! Pharisaical legalism surrounding the Mosaic Law had ground them to spiritual powder. The Lord offered himself to them.

In that agrarian culture, everyone knew that a **yoke** (11:29,30) went across the necks of two beasts of burden, just in front of their shoulders, and connected them to the plow or wagon they were to pull. Under the covenant relationship, the believer is not relieved of all work or burden, but is given work that is appropriate to his abilities, within his limitations. In fact, the believer will find the work fulfilling and rewarding rather than toilsome and exhausting. Jesus' yoke is **easy** (suitable, good, reasonable), and his burden is **light** (easy to bear, insignificant).

Jesus instructed his followers to **take my yoke** at their own initiative. Jesus will not put it on us without our consent. But to refuse Jesus' yoke is not to be burden-free, but to retain a much heavier burden. Everyone in life must carry a burden; the question is whether we will carry one that is within our capacity, or one heavier than we were designed for.

To **learn from me** goes hand in hand with taking on Jesus' yoke. What Jesus will teach us is how to live under the light burden he offers and to enjoy his rest. As our teacher, he will deal with us with sensitivity and compassion.

The rest Jesus offered contrasts with the burden of the Pharisees' Sabbath rules in the following context (12:1–14).

E The Hypocrites Confront the King of the Sabbath (12:1–14)

SUPPORTING IDEA: *In contrast to the rest the Messiah-King offers, the hypocrites only demand impossible burdens of the people, and they will go so far as to destroy the king in order to keep the people subject to them.*

Keeping the Sabbath was a big deal to the Jewish religious leaders. It was a religious trump card. The way Jesus observed the Sabbath was always a point of contention for them. It is significant that Matthew chose a series of two conflicts (12:1–14) over the issue of the Sabbath (in Heb., literally, "the rest day") immediately following Jesus' promise of covenant rest to his followers. Not only do these two conflicts serve to heighten the tension that will build to a climax later in the book, but they also identify Jesus as the "Lord of the Sabbath," and therefore the only one qualified to offer the rest of 11:28 and to determine what is permissible on the Sabbath. Jesus' compassion and his authority are highlighted in this passage.

12:1. As in 11:25, Matthew again made a connection between this event and the preceding context: **At that time.** Because it was Jesus' practice to depend on God's provision while traveling (10:9–10), he and his disciples often had to draw upon their right to eat from other people's fields what they needed for the moment (Deut. 23:24–25).

Matthew mentiond that this happened **on the Sabbath** to set up his description of the conflict that follows. According to the Jewish clock, a day began and ended at sunset. So the Sabbath began at sunset Friday evening, and ended at sunset Saturday evening.

12:2. The Pharisees saw Jesus' disciples rubbing the heads of grain between their palms to separate the kernels from the hulls. According to their rules, this was considered work (reaping), and therefore, forbidden on the Sabbath (Exod. 20:8–11). In Israel, a teacher was responsible for the behavior of his students, so the Pharisees complained to Jesus that his disciples were breaking the Sabbath law. The Sabbath was established by Yahweh for a good purpose, and he took it seriously. Violation of the Sabbath was punishable by death (Exod. 31:14; 35:2).

12:3–6. Jesus' question **Haven't you read?** marks a continuing pattern on his part. Jesus regularly highlighted a pharisaical neglect of Scripture as opposed to their conformity to tradition. In defense of his disciples' behavior, Jesus cited the example of David in 1 Samuel 21:1–9, when he fled from Saul to the city of Nob, where the tabernacle was kept at the time. There David and his men ate the consecrated bread that was set apart for the priests to eat after it had been brought to the Lord as an offering (Lev. 24:8–9).

Jesus was not citing a specific Old Testament quote in 12:5, but he was making a general observation. Throughout the Old Testament law, the Lord prescribed work for the priests on the Sabbath to facilitate the worship of others (e.g., Num. 28:9–10), and yet the priests were never declared guilty for such practices.

Jesus argued that—based on those two examples and based on the fact that he himself, the architect of the temple and the one for whose worship the temple existed—he was **greater than the temple** (12:6). It was, therefore, beyond reproach for him and his disciples to "work" on the Sabbath to satisfy their hunger. If the servants of the temple could break the Sabbath for good reason, then so could the Almighty, who was worshiped in the temple and who stood before them as the Son of Man.

12:7. Jesus again demanded that the Pharisees look in their own Scriptures. For the second time, Matthew recorded Jesus as quoting Hosea 6:6 in response to the hypocrites. Previously we saw the quote in 9:13, where the Pharisees asked the disciples why Jesus ate with tax collectors and "sinners." Here Jesus used the quote to correct their misconception regarding the priority of mercy (the true spirit of the Sabbath law) over the letter of the law. God's command to observe the Sabbath is an expression of mercy, recognizing the limits of the human makeup, and requiring us to care for the bodies and minds he has entrusted to us.

The Pharisees had actually demeaned the Sabbath by robbing it of its "rest" and weighting it with overwhelming religious requirements. This is what Jesus meant in Mark 2:27 when he said, **The Sabbath was made for man, not man for the Sabbath.** So mercy is wrapped up in the heart of the Sabbath law. Jesus' actions, then, were consistent with this central thrust—to break the letter of the law to fulfill its true intent through an expression of mercy and compassion.

Jesus proclaimed his innocence, not defensively, but authoritatively. If the Pharisees had understood the centrality of mercy and compassion in the Sabbath law, they would not have attacked Jesus as a lawbreaker. Rather, they would have praised him for his consistency with the law's true meaning.

12:8. Jesus completed this conversation with an authoritative claim: **For the Son of Man is Lord of the Sabbath.** This is the reason he had the right to determine what was appropriate and inappropriate on the Sabbath, as well as the right to offer covenant rest in 11:28–30. As author of the law, he had authority to clarify its correct application. Jesus used the title "Son of Man" for himself to claim the prophetic authority that accompanied this messianic title.

12:9–10. These verses begin a new episode which Matthew intended to be a continuation of the theme from the preceding context (12:1–8). The issue is exactly the same.

Now Jesus was moving from the fields, where his disciples had been picking grain, into **their synagogue**—the synagogue where Pharisees were leaders. He was now on their home turf, in front of their followers and students. They probably planted the man with the withered hand to trap Jesus into breaking the Sabbath **to accuse Jesus.**

We can imagine the Pharisees of 12:2 accompanying Jesus to the synagogue, ensuring that he walked into their trap, while others awaited the group at the synagogue with the man. Their question was ready on their lips, **Is it lawful to heal on the Sabbath?** Healing, in their eyes, would be work, and work was prohibited on the Sabbath.

Jesus' enemies had taken the next step in escalating the conflict. Prior to this, they had reacted with criticism to his actions and teachings. Now they were taking the initiative to trap Jesus.

12:11–12. Jesus' response was a variation on the Hosea 6:6 quote, emphasizing mercy and compassion as the heart of the Sabbath law. He did not appeal to written law, but to common sense and common practice (the Sabbath law was always intended to be applied with common sense). Even the hypocrites to whom he spoke acted mercifully toward an animal in trouble on the Sabbath. Then Jesus used again the **how much more** argument to show that mercy toward a person on the Sabbath was even more appropriate than mercy toward an animal.

Before actually healing the man, Jesus came back to the Pharisees' question, **Is it lawful to heal on the Sabbath?** (12:10). His answer was essentially a "yes," but he worded it in such way that the Pharisees were embarrassed by the self-evident nature of the answer. Because everyone accepted the practice of mercy toward animals, and therefore people, on the Sabbath, **It is lawful to do good on the Sabbath.** This implied that everyone should know that healing is good, and therefore acceptable, even on the Sabbath.

12:13. Having brought the common sense of God's original intent for the law into view, Jesus proceeded to act in consistency with his words. He practiced compassion toward the man with the withered hand. The power of the king's word was again displayed, for the man's hand was restored even as he stretched it out. There was no indication that Jesus used touch in this case. This method was even more dramatic than if he had used touch. Jesus commanded, **Stretch out your hand,** and the man's compliance probably happened within a second or two. This brought into the scene the element of surprise, displaying the authority of Jesus' word. He was authenticating his right to the title, "Lord of the Sabbath."

12:14. In spite of such a display of power and authority, the Pharisees rejected this evidence of Jesus' identity. They were blinded by their presuppositions and vested interests. They began to work privately in closer coordination than ever, searching for the best method to **kill** Jesus. They expected to embarrass and accuse him in their synagogue filled with their followers. But Jesus embarrassed them instead, condemning them for their lack of mercy. Many more public interchanges such as this could undermine the people's trust in the Pharisees. Realizing they could not control Jesus, they decided to have him removed.

F The Servant King Tries to Minister Quietly (12:15–21)

SUPPORTING IDEA: *In contrast to the murderous hypocrites, the King serves his people gently and humbly.*

12:15–16. The verb **withdrew** may be another indication by Matthew that the chasm between Jesus and the false religious leaders was growing wider. Jesus now moved physically away from their presence and opposition. He knew the impact of the preceding confrontation, both on the crowd and on his enemies. Because the time for his death was yet future, and there was much more to do (especially the preparation of the Twelve to carry on his ministry), Jesus avoided further open conflict for a time, withdrawing to a more private place, away from the scrutiny of the hypocrites.

Many followed him, because of their growing faith in him and their decreasing trust in the hypocrites, **and he healed all their sick**, presumably at least some on the Sabbath. As in 8:4, 9:30, and 17:9, Jesus warned these people **not to tell who he was**. His ministry was not a show; he truly cared for the needy. The healing of the first man's hand was an act of true compassion and a public demonstration of Jesus' identity and authority. In these further healings, mercy became the more prominent element of his motivation.

12:17–21. By the act of withdrawing and conducting ministry quietly, Jesus proclaimed the truth of his identity by fulfilling another Old Testament messianic prophecy: "My servant . . . will bring justice to the nations. He will not shout or cry out" (Isa. 42:1–3). This prophecy pointed out the humble, quiet nature of the Messiah's ministry (cf. "gentle and humble in heart," Matt. 11:29). Matthew wanted to be sure his readers saw this side of the Messiah-King.

This passage, as much as any other in Matthew, confronted the popular expectations of the Messiah. Those who had hardened hearts would hold to their expectations of a political or military savior and reject the humble man they saw. But those with "ears to hear" would allow the reality of Jesus to change their expectations. This passage further reinforces Matthew's dramatic theme—the shift from hard-hearted Israel to believing Gentiles. Jesus withdrew from the religious hypocrites as personified by the Pharisees. This move was based on Old Testament prophecy: "In his name the nations will put their hope" (12:21).

Matthew, in his longest Old Testament quote, quoted only the first three verses of Isaiah 42:1–9. These verses deal with the meekness of the servant, although Matthew 12:21 is probably a very liberal paraphrase of Isaiah 42:4c. The song goes on in Isaiah 42:4–9 to describe the servant as one who would be the bearer of justice, the law, and the covenant, "as a light for the Gentiles." He would "open eyes that are blind" and "free captives." This would be a new era in God's plan. But all of this will spring from the humble, quiet ministry of the Suffering Servant described in Isaiah 42:1–3.

This song describes God's original intention for Israel. The nation was chosen not to remain separate from the other nations, but to be Yahweh's servant in taking the truth to the nations. The passage describes even more accurately the ministry of Yahweh's other servant, Jesus the Messiah-King, who initiated the plan to take the truth throughout the world.

The servant is one whom Yahweh has **chosen** (12:18a). He is not self-appointed, but willingly cooperates with Yahweh's will. In poetic parallel with the first line, the servant is loved by God (Heb., "my chosen one") and is the delight of the Lord (12:18b; cf. "my Son . . with him I am well pleased," 3:17; also the Transfiguration, 17:5). This is a significant connection. God's love and his choice are never separated. In fact, they are almost synonymous.

Yahweh will put his spirit on his servant so the servant will speak and act according to Yahweh's will and authority (12:18c). Out of this authority, by Yahweh's Spirit, the servant will **proclaim** (Heb., "bring forth") **justice to the nations** (12:18d). Jesus had already alluded to God's plan for nations besides Israel (8:11). God's kingdom will go beyond Israel, but Israel had lost sight of that vision.

Beginning in 12:19, the quote connects Isaiah's servant with the conduct of Jesus. **He will not quarrel or cry out; no one will hear his voice in the streets.** Jesus was not ready to begin the open conflict that would come later in his ministry, so he tried to stay out of the public eye during this period. Throughout every phase of Jesus' ministry, he behaved meekly, unleashing his wrath only on occasion, as a loving shepherd will lash out at a predator that threatens the flock.

Even those who are worthless and useless in the eyes of the world will be accepted by God's Suffering Servant (12:20a). **Reeds** were the stems of a variety of species of plants. They were carved into ink pens or walking sticks, or their fibers were used for weaving or making into parchment for writing on. Reeds were one of the most common materials in everyday life. Damaged reeds were discarded without thought because more were readily available. A wick on an oil lamp might smolder because it was low on oil or trimmed improperly. Usually a smoldering wick would be put out, because it would produce smoke but no light. The Messiah, who was "gentle and humble in heart" (11:29) would welcome and use in ministry those whom the world deemed worthless and useless.

The servant's purpose is **justice**, and his justice will lead **to victory** (12:20b; the Hebrew text means, "He will faithfully bring forth justice"). Even though the servant comes meekly, he is also the judge (11:27; 28:18), and he will bring justice and fairness to the people.

Verse 21 is not found in Isaiah 42 in the wording Matthew used. Most likely Matthew skipped the first two lines of 42:4 and paraphrased the third line: "And the coastlands [Gentile territory along the Mediterranean] will wait expectantly for his law." Matthew's purpose in paraphrasing the wording was to leave lingering in the reader's mind the role that Jesus the Messiah-King was to play in the world. No one of any nationality had any hope apart from him. And he was taking his message of hope to all the nations, not just chosen Israel.

The King Responds to Slanderous Accusations (12:22–37)

> **SUPPORTING IDEA:** *Rather than succumbing to the hypocrites' slander, the king warns them that their accusations will be their condemnation at the judgment.*

In the first portion of this conflict (12:22–29), we see Jesus on the defensive, fending off the Pharisees' accusation that he works for Satan. But in the second (12:30–32) and third (12:33–37) segments of the conflict, Jesus went on the offensive, revealing the depth of corruption and sin behind the Pharisees' accusation.

12:22. The restoration of the demon-possessed man serves as the kindling for the confrontation in 12:22–37. The details that the man was blind and mute are not critical to the story, but they provide a sense of historical authenticity to the account, and they subject the account to verifiability. They also echo again Jesus' fulfillment of Isaiah 35:5–6, with two of the illnesses from that passage being healed in the same man. The man was probably **brought** to Jesus as one of the many he was healing routinely (12:15), not as another trap by the Pharisees. The Pharisees were apparently not aware of the event until some time later (12:24).

12:23. As we saw frequently in Matthew 8–9, the crowd was **astonished** at his healing.

This is Matthew's only use of the Greek word *existemi* (**astonished**), meaning "to displace, put outside, stand aside from." Matthew used the middle voice, which gives the word a reflexive meaning; they were literally "beside themselves." He also used the imperfect tense, which implies continuous action in the past; the crowd's astonishment was perpetual. They kept on being astonished.

Note the crowd's question: **Could this be the Son of David?** They were not convinced, but the evidence was beginning to make them suspect the truth about Jesus. Most importantly in this context, their ponderings reached the ears of the Pharisees.

12:24. The Pharisees were disturbed at Jesus' power over demons (see their similar retort in 9:34), but when they heard the crowds speculating about his identity as the **Son of David** (12:23), they tried to discredit the idea by attributing Jesus' authority to Satan. Their argument was that Beelzebub, **the prince of demons**, was casting out those under his authority to perpetuate the "illusion" that Jesus was deriving his power from God. They tried to convince the crowd that Jesus was Satan's counterfeit Messiah.

12:25–27. But Jesus exposed the flaw in their reasoning. Satan's kingdom was obviously thriving, as evidenced by the flurry of demonic activity during the time of Jesus' public ministry. This could not be happening if there was division and civil war within Satan's kingdom. Jesus illustrated this principle twice, using the analogy of a human kingdom, and then the analogy of a city or a household (12:25). Then, in 12:26, he stated more clearly that division within Satan's kingdom would cause it to fall.

Jesus then turned their own argument against the Pharisees, saying, "I could make the same accusation against your followers. How do you know *they* are not performing exorcisms by Satan's power?" (12:27). **They will be your judges** means, "Your own followers will tell you that your accusation against me is false."

12:28. Having eliminated the possibility that his authority came from Satan, Jesus now turned to the only other alternative—that his authority came **by the Spirit of God.** This statement is a first-class condition in the Greek language, meaning that it should be translated, "But *since* I cast out demons by the Spirit of God." Since, indeed, God was the authority behind Jesus' authority, this was evidence that **the kingdom of God has come upon you.** The Messiah-King was in their presence and doing battle with the counterfeit kingdom of Satan. The anticipation of thousands of years—Messiah's presence—had come upon them.

12:29. Jesus added an additional supportive argument to his statement that his authority came from God. His plundering of Satan's **house**, robbing him of the souls he had taken captive, demanded that he had to be able to bind Satan, **the strong man.** Jesus had to come with an authority higher than Satan's. Otherwise, Satan would have been free to hinder Jesus' ministry. It was obvious to any observer that Jesus' ministry against Satan was proceeding unhindered. Jesus was overwhelming Satan in every incident, but it was just a foreshadowing of his second coming when he would bind Satan and establish his kingdom (cf. Rev. 20:1–6).

12:30. Having defended himself against the Pharisees' accusation, Jesus went on the offensive and turned the attack back on the hypocrites. In 12:30–32, he condemned them for **blasphemy against the Spirit.**

In 12:30, Jesus eliminated the possibility of anyone remaining "neutral" toward him. Anyone who was not seeking to live for Jesus was, by default, Jesus' enemy.

12:31–32. We now arrive at another difficult saying of Jesus, one that causes anxiety among believers. "How do I know I have not committed the 'unforgivable sin'?" is an oft-repeated chorus among believers. In light of the gracious heart of God as revealed throughout Scripture, and in light of the doctrine of eternal security (e.g., John 10:28–30), we can say that if a person is concerned that he may have committed the "unforgivable sin," this concern is proof that he has not committed it. There would be no concern if the Holy Spirit had ceased conviction. Anyone who desires God's forgiveness for anything will receive it. Therefore, the only truly unforgivable sin is one for which the sinner refuses to seek forgiveness.

Jesus' introductory **I tell you** causes the listener to stop and pay close attention to something of special importance. The Pharisees were slandering God by attributing the work of his Spirit to Satan. To speak in this manner about Jesus ("the Son of Man") would be forgiven. This was true because of Jesus' human nature and appearance (veiled deity), and the confusion this must have caused people as they grew to understand that Jesus was also thoroughly divine. But to slander the Holy Spirit of God was much worse, because there could be no confusion over the scriptural source of his works.

The essence of the "unforgivable sin" is a refusal to accept forgiveness from Christ in the face of evidence that Jesus is the Christ. The unforgivable sin is deliberately and knowingly attributing the works of the Holy Spirit in the Messiah-Christ to Satan. The unrepentant person actually condemns himself, and God only confirms what that person has already determined. It also follows that the unforgivable sin exists only for the person who maintains his refusal of God's forgiveness throughout his lifetime. If at any time he changes his mind and desires forgiveness, Jesus' warning no longer applies to him.

The sin that can actually never be forgiven is the consistent, lifelong refusal to bow to the Holy Spirit's conviction of sin and to accept the forgiveness that Christ offers. These religious leaders, like so many people today, refused to take an open-minded look at the evidence regarding Jesus as Messiah. They refused an honest consideration of the Christ and insisted on their own works-righteousness to justify them before God.

In his confrontation with the Pharisees, Jesus was able to discern the hardened hearts of his opponents. He knew they would persist in their disbelief for life. Thus, he announced that they were guilty of the unforgivable sin. Under Mosaic Law, blasphemy incurred a death sentence (Lev. 24:10–23).

One of the major themes in these chapters is Jesus' judgment on Israel. This "unforgivable" incident demonstrated the seriousness of that judgment—**will not be forgiven, either in this age or in the age to come**. They had rejected the Messiah-King as well as God's last word about Messiah-King in the witness of the Spirit. This generation of religious rejecters had put themselves beyond redemption. This serves as a warning for any others who reject God's last word about Jesus.

12:33–35. Finally, Jesus concluded his confrontation of the hypocrites by pointing out that their own words were their worst enemy. Those words would testify against them in the eternal courtroom of heaven. There is a major lesson here for us. Words are important. They come out of the heart. They expose the heart and therefore are a clue to final justification or judgment.

Jesus used the same argument as in 7:16–20—that no tree can produce any fruit other than its own kind of fruit, and that any tree can be identified as good or bad by examining its fruit. Specifically, the Pharisees' fruit was their words. Because Jesus had just demonstrated the deep evil in their words against the Holy Spirit, the natural implication was that these men were evil to the core. A good heart cannot produce evil words.

In verse 35, Jesus was referring to the inner, unseen person—equivalent to the **heart** in 12:34. The **good** or **evil** illustration restated what Jesus had already said in different words—the outside is only reflective of the inside.

12:36–37. Again Jesus emphasized the seriousness of what he was about to say, introducing it with **I tell you**.

Not only do a person's words demonstrate his inner character in the present day, but they will be either his defense or his incrimination in **the day of judgment**. Words are so easy to produce that we can forget how powerful they are. They have great potential for building up as well as tearing down. They can be used to advance God's kingdom, or to attack it, sometimes subtly, in ways even the speaker does not realize. Words must be used with care. **Careless** words are like loaded guns that are handled recklessly. Just as the handler of a gun would have to explain any damage done by his weapon, so every person with a tongue (cf. Jas. 3:2–12) will be held responsible for how he or she has used it.

The Pharisees had responded to Jesus' exorcism carelessly. Their only interest was in keeping their status and power over the people, and their speech attempted to protect their selfish interests. They spoke out of total disregard for the truth, so their words would return to condemn them on the day of judgment. Judgment would come not only because what they said was false, but also because their words led many of their followers astray. We see similar abuse of words among misleading preachers today.

The King Denies the Hypocrites a Sign (12:38–45)

SUPPORTING IDEA: *The king refuses to play the hypocrites' game, denying them more fuel for their opposition and denial.*

12:38. It would be natural to ask a person who claims to be God's representative for some sign of his authority. In fact, the Old Testament warns against false prophets, and gives criteria by which to determine a prophet's validity (Deut. 18:14–22). By addressing Jesus as **Teacher**, the hypocrites attempted to mask their hostility with civility to appear reasonable in their request. Jesus had already provided abundant signs for anyone with ears to hear and eyes to see. He unmasked the hypocrites by confronting them directly. Their demand for signs was an indication of unbelief, not faith. Jesus never performed miracles for the purpose of impressing others. Miracles were part of his proclamation, never a performance.

Matthew had arranged the many miracle accounts prior to this passage so that when we see the scribes and Pharisees demanding a sign from Jesus, we also see the deep irony in their request. If these hypocrites had used their eyes with an open heart, they would have been overwhelmed with the signs that validated Jesus' identity as the Messiah-King. But they were so blinded by their narrow, selfish interests that they missed the obvious.

12:39–40. Jesus responded that their request revealed the evil in their hearts. He was not saying it was wrong to test the validity of a person who claims to be God's prophet—only that it was wrong to test him when he had already proven his validity. Such continued testing demonstrated the hardened hearts of the persons seeking the sign.

Jesus refused their request for a sign. However, he did promise the ultimate miracle one day in their future. Quoting Jonah 1:17, Jesus paralleled Jonah's three days in the belly of a huge fish with his own three days in **the heart of the earth** (the tomb). The attesting miracle was not Jesus' burial, but the fact that there would be an end to the period of the burial. It was only three days! Implied here is the miracle of the resurrection (28:1–10), paralleled by the miracle of Jonah's escape from the fish's stomach (Jon. 2:10).

By Jewish reckoning, a part of a day was considered to be a whole day. And it was common Jewish idiom to refer to even a part of a day as "a day and a night." So **three days and three nights** might refer to as much as seventy-two hours, or as little as twenty-six hours (one full twenty-four-hour day, together with one hour of the preceding day and one hour of the following day). This explains why Jesus could be said to be in the tomb "three days and three nights," when he was buried late Friday and arose early Sunday.

Jesus again used the veiled messianic title **Son of Man**, so that those with "ears to hear" would understand he was speaking of himself. By the same token, the hardened heart would be confused by this title.

12:41–42. Continuing his comparison of the current situation with the story of Jonah, Jesus drew attention to the fact that Nineveh, the idolatrous city that Jonah hated, actually repented at Jonah's message (Jonah 3), while **this generation,** who should have known better, having been privileged with God's revealed Scriptures, was rejecting the Messiah-King. Heathen Nineveh repented before Jonah, God's prophet. Privileged Israel was rejecting the manifestation of God himself (**one greater than Jonah**). Thus, Nineveh had every right to **condemn** unbelieving Israel **at the judgment.**

Switching to a different example (12:42), Jesus compared **this generation** with **the Queen of the South** (the queen of Sheba, 1 Kgs. 10:1–13; 2 Chron. 9:1–12), who, though Gentile and alien to Yahweh's written revelation, praised Yahweh for his work through Solomon (1 Kgs. 10:9). Heathen Sheba believed in Yahweh because of his anointed king. Privileged Israel was rejecting God's Anointed—the Christ or Messiah-King (**one greater than Solomon**). Thus, Sheba had every right to **condemn** unbelieving Israel **at the judgment.**

12:43–45. This is a difficult analogy to interpret. Jesus' parable seemed to emphasize that Israel had a limited window of time in which to respond to him. His limited time on earth paralleled the period during which the man in the parable was free of demons (perhaps Jesus was holding off the forces of evil during this time). This period would be long enough for Israel, particularly their leaders, to repent and believe in him. But if they persisted in their conscious disbelief until this "limited-time" offer expired, their **final condition** would become **worse than the first.** They would be even more hardened by their rejection of the obvious, and they would be held even more accountable because they had abundant opportunity to repent.

Jesus was not saying that there was literally a demon that had been cast out of Israel, nor that there would be more literal demons controlling Israel after they had finally rejected him. What Jesus meant to carry over from the parable is that Israel was in danger of an even worse condition than before he came, if it did not take advantage of the window of opportunity presented by his coming.

What we learn here about demons and demon possession is secondary in importance to Jesus' message in the parable. The demon's wandering **through arid places seeking rest** served as the demon's motivation for returning to the man. This heightened Israel's awareness that they were in imminent danger. Israel's former condition was their desperate need of the Messiah. If they persisted in their unbelief, they would have no Messiah and they would be held responsible for rejecting him.

The condition of the man (the demon's "house")—being **unoccupied, swept clean and put in order**—parallels the short period of time during which Israel's options were open. Even those who continued to "sit on the fence" were rejecting Jesus: **He who is not with me is against me** (12:30). An active, affirmative decision for the Messiah was what was required—nothing less. If the demon had returned to the man and found him occupied by Christ, there would have been no room for the demon.

The **seven other spirits** likely parallel the deeper state of disbelief and the greater judgment incurred after the window of opportunity has closed.

Jesus closed his confrontation with the Pharisees as he began, declaring **this . . . generation** to be **wicked** (12:45; cf. 12:39) because they refused God's gracious gift, the Messiah and his salvation. Jesus' mention of **this . . . generation** is the clue that convinces us that the story about the demons is an analogy describing Israel (or at least the rebellious portion represented by the Pharisees).

■ The King Defines a New Family (12:46–50)

SUPPORTING IDEA: *The king clarifies the identifying mark of those who are truly his.*

In the preceding context (12:39–45) Jesus challenged the assumptions about who would comprise his kingdom and who would not. It was assumed that Israel was already in this kingdom, and that the Gentile nations would be left out. On the contrary, declared Jesus, repentant Nineveh and the believing queen of Sheba would pass through the judgment into the kingdom and disbelieving Israel would not.

He then used the idea of family to challenge the same kind of false assumption. He was not disowning his physical family in this passage but showing that believing covenant faith is the criterion for entrance into his spiritual family and kingdom, no matter what blood runs in a person's veins. In fact, his spiritual family is even more important than any physical blood relationships. This amounts to a pronouncement of judgment upon unbelieving Israel.

12:46–47. The interruption of Jesus' teaching by the arrival of his mother and brothers is significant. It was a graphic occasion for him to proclaim how a person must relate to him in order to participate in his spiritual family.

12:48–50. Jesus loved and honored his physical family (e.g., John 19:25–27), and he intended no insult to them. However, their presence gave him the opportunity to define an even more significant family. The head of this new family is God, the heavenly Father. Membership in this family is determined not by blood but by a relationship with the Father through covenant faith, evidenced by obedience to his will. Some of these spiritual family members were present—his disciples, those who had placed their faith in him and were showing true obedience to the Father. Jesus was finished with Israel for the moment. He was emphasizing his rejection by Israel and his withdrawal to outcasts and Gentiles. In Matthew 13 Jesus will explain his rejection of Israel and his new emphasis on Gentiles.

> **MAIN IDEA REVIEW:** *The King and his citizens will encounter opponents in this world who doubt his identity, even among those who should know better, and in spite of all the evidence supporting his identity as Messiah-King.*

III. CONCLUSION

Doubts are natural, and the Lord understands them, but our response to doubt should be to "check it out," accepting the solid answers when we find them. If we choose to disbelieve, nothing will change our minds, even if the truth stares us in the face. Willful disbelief, in the face of God's obvious truth, sets up the disbeliever for even stricter judgment. With greater knowledge and opportunity, there is greater accountability. Believing obedience to the Father's will is the identifying characteristic of a kingdom family member, demonstrating the fruit of a faith relationship with the King.

PRINCIPLES

- The only way to know God is by his own decision to reveal himself—particularly through Jesus.
- The blessing of living in right relationship with Jesus is rest from the burden of selfish living and prideful self-striving.
- Living in right relationship with Jesus does not mean a burden-free life, but carrying a burden which is reasonable and meaningful.
- In God's kingdom, compassion and mercy are higher priorities than keeping the rules.
- The King is a humble, gentle servant to his subjects, not a harsh overlord. He gives hope and victory to all who will trust him.
- Anyone who does harm to the kingdom of Satan by the power of God is doing good for the kingdom of heaven.
- It is impossible to take a "neutral" position with respect to Jesus.
- It is possible to live in permanent refusal to acknowledge and trust Jesus the King, thus making his forgiveness inaccessible.

- The quality of a person's words reveal the quality of his heart; our words will be evidence for or against us at the final judgment.

- For a person who is stubbornly set against Jesus, no evidence will change his or her heart.

APPLICATIONS

- Never allow pride to take root in your life.
- Exercise humility toward others.
- In everything, acknowledge and trust Jesus, the Messiah-King.
- Avoid a legalistic approach to the life of faith. Rather, actively exercise compassion and mercy toward others.

IV. LIFE APPLICATION

Denial in the Face of Evidence

Harry Truman was the friendly, 84-year-old owner of the rustic Mount St. Helens Lodge on the old south shore of Spirit Lake. The lodge was his home, and his sixteen cats were like family. He had spent a lifetime on the slopes of Mount St. Helens and considered the mountain a friend. Thus, when the volcano awoke early in 1980, Harry and his cats would not leave. As spring progressed, volcanic activity grew terrifyingly violent and the Governor of the State of Washington established restricted entry zones around the mountain with the intent of evacuating everyone except a few scientists and security personnel. Even then, Harry would not leave. On Saturday afternoon, May 17, 1980, state officials tried for what turned out to be the last time to get Harry to leave. He would not go. Early the next morning, Mount St. Helens exploded. The whole north side of the mountain collapsed in a giant avalanche of rock and debris that roared across the lodge at speeds near 100 m.p.h., obliterating the lodge and burying the site to a depth of about 50 meters. No trace was ever found of Harry or his cats.

Some of us read this and think, *How foolish! How tragic!* The evidence was overwhelming. The mountain was going to blow. Mr. Truman's refusal to leave and denial of the truth brought a heavy price.

We see in these two chapters of Matthew a similar situation with the religious leaders of Jesus' day. In spite of the overwhelming evidence (Jesus' authoritative teaching and his miracles), the religious leaders remained in denial of Jesus' identity. Theirs went beyond a case of willful disbelief; they actively opposed Jesus. Ultimately, their denial and opposition would lead them to crucify the Son of God.

V. PRAYER

Lord, give me ears to hear and eyes to see the truth about Jesus as the Messiah-King. Grant that I may follow him in faith and loving obedience. Amen.

VI. DEEPER DISCOVERIES

A. Matthew's Use of the Title "Christ" (11:2)

The careful observer of Matthew's Gospel will realize that we have not seen this title for some time in Matthew. In fact, it was used four times in the introductory chapter (1:1,16–18) and once when Herod the Great consulted the chief priests and teachers of the law to ask them "where the Christ was to be born" (2:4). Since then, throughout the entire account of Jesus' ministry to this point, the title has been absent. We will see it next in Peter's confession (16:16), and then nine more times through the rest of the book, as Jesus becomes more open about his identity, especially with his disciples.

B. The Concept of "Rest"

The idea of "rest" in Scripture is often closely related to covenant fulfillment (e.g., Isa. 40:28–31). Israel experienced rest in the land—fulfillment of God's covenant promise—when they began to live consistently by faith and obedience through the conquest of the land (Josh. 11:23; 21:43–45). Hebrews 4 creates a bridge between the experience of Old Testament Israel and the New Testament believer. This passage shows that there is a similar "rest" available to us if we believe and obey God, not following the example of the unbelieving first generation of Israel out of Egypt (Heb. 3:7–19).

C. Summary

Matthew 11–12 begins to demonstrate the denial of Israel (the religious leaders and those allied with them) in the face of the evidence of Jesus' identity (his authoritative words and works; Matt. 5–9). The evidence against Israel in these chapters provides the rationale for Jesus' change in teaching style in Matthew 13, justifying his application of the prophetic judgment of Isaiah 6:9–10 to them (13:13–15). Because they have proven willfully faithless, he will now begin to raise the bar to test and sift out those who want to believe from those who do not.

VII. TEACHING OUTLINE

A. INTRODUCTION

1. Lead Story: The Day the Lesbian Avengers Came to Church

2. Context: Up to this point in Matthew's account, any opposition from the Pharisees and allied opponents has been subdued, taking the form of critical questions (9:11; cf. 9:14) and defensive grumbling (9:3,34). Throughout Jesus' training in Matthew 10, he prepares his diciples for growing opposition. Then in Matthew 11–12, the conflict flames into the open, and the hypocrites begin to take the offensive.

3. Transition: Much of the emphasis in Matthew 11–12 centers around Israel's rejection of Jesus, in spite of his many validating miracles (11:16–24; 12:22–24,38). Related to this is the question of his identity (11:1–6; 12:8,15–21).

A large part of Matthew 11–12 is devoted to Jesus' words of judgment, rebuking unbelieving Israel in general and the religious leaders in particular. The two miracles recorded serve a different purpose than those in Matthew 8–9. They serve not to demonstrate the king's authority, but as occasions for the hypocrites to criticize Jesus. This results in each case in a resounding victory by Jesus and a greater condemnation of their false religion.

B. COMMENTARY

1. The King Responds to John's Uncertainty (11:1–6)
2. This Generation (Israel) Rejects John and the King (11:7–19)
3. The King Denounces Unrepentant Cities (11:20–24)
4. The King Invites the Weary to Himself (11:25–30)
5. The Hypocrites Confront the King of the Sabbath (12:1–14)
6. The Servant King Tries to Minister Quietly (12:15–21)
7. The King Responds to Slanderous Accusations (12:22–37)
8. The King Denies the Hypocrites a Sign (12:38–45)
9. The King Defines a New Family (12:46–50)

C. CONCLUSION

1. Wrap-up: The authority of Jesus that has been evident in the preceding chapters is a threat to those who have been in authority. Because of this and their natural selfishness and greed, the religious leaders begin to confront Jesus to diminish his authority and hold on to their own.

2. Personal Challenge: Does the authority of Jesus give you comfort and rest, or does it serve as a threat to your own sense of ultimate authority? This is why humbling ourselves is a prerequisite to accepting him as our Lord and Master—the One with all authority.

VIII. ISSUES FOR DISCUSSION

1. Why did John the Baptizer begin to have doubts about whether Jesus was the Messiah? What answer did Jesus give to John about his identity?
2. Why and how did Jesus compare disbelieving Israel to children?
3. What did Jesus mean when he said, "My yoke is easy and my burden is light"?
4. In what sense is Jesus "Lord of the Sabbath"?
5. What is the "unforgivable sin"?

Matthew 13

The King Reveals a Secret

I. **INTRODUCTION**
On Building a House or a Kingdom

II. **COMMENTARY**
A verse-by-verse explanation of the chapter.

III. **CONCLUSION**
An overview of the principles and applications from the chapter.

IV. **LIFE APPLICATION**
More Than the Eye Sees
Melding the chapter to life.

V. **PRAYER**
Tying the chapter to life with God.

VI. **DEEPER DISCOVERIES**
Historical, geographical, and grammatical enrichment of the commentary.

VII. **TEACHING OUTLINE**
Suggested step-by-step group study of the chapter.

VIII. **ISSUES FOR DISCUSSION**
Zeroing the chapter in on daily life.

Quote

"Jesus of Nazareth could have chosen simply to express Himself in moral precepts; but like a great poet He chose the form of the parable, wonderful short stories that entertained and clothed the moral precept in an eternal form. It is not sufficient to catch man's mind, you must also catch the imaginative faculties of his mind."

D u d l e y   N i c h o l s

Matthew 13

IN A NUTSHELL

This chapter begins the third major discourse of Jesus' teaching. It is a sermon comprised of seven interrelated parables with an added eighth. The kingdom must endure in the midst of opposition from the world. All the while, however, it will grow in power and influence. The kingdom will prevail and its citizens may look ahead to justice and reward at the final judgment.

The King Reveals a Secret

I. INTRODUCTION

On Building a House or a Kingdom

*N*ot too long ago, my wife Linda and I did something we had never done before. We built a new home. Throughout the process she was busy collecting sample materials she planned to use. She had boxes full of paint swatches, wall coverings, carpet samples, cabinet styles, and window coverings. She had her own copy of the architectural drawings, which she filled with little scale models of couches, desks, tables, and chairs. She so perfectly understood and visualized what she wanted that on one occasion the workers, professionals at reading drawings, had to be corrected by the more perfect drawings in her mind. After all, it was her home—not theirs.

More than once I found myself chuckling at the expression of some of our male-female differences. Sure, I was concerned about a few basics like the heating system or the quality of insulation. But she carried every tiny detail in her heart and mind, including what I considered unimaginable minutiae.

Unimaginable is the key word. I had a vague picture in my mind of what the home would look like. But I did not know exactly how it was going to turn out. I had not imagined certain developments and bottom-line goals. On the other hand, Linda knew every nook and cranny of the house. When the home ultimately came together, it was like a new revelation to me. It was so much more than I had anticipated.

The disciples in Matthew 13 might be compared to me. Their confusion about the kingdom might be (at least superficially) compared to mine about the house. For years they had made assumptions about Messiah's kingdom, and they were in for a surprise. Matthew 13 might be said to represent Jesus' attempt to walk the disciples through the changes. The disciples could not figure out what was happening. They had questions. If Jesus was the Messiah-King, then why all this nasty opposition? If Jesus was the Messiah, why did the religious leaders not get it? If Jesus was the Messiah, why were people not following him in droves? If Jesus was the king, then what happened to the kingdom?

Jesus was going to help his followers understand by telling them some stories. But there was a further twist. The stories would be parables. In these parables, Jesus told his disciples some family secrets, but with other bystanders overhearing. By using parables, the truly interested (believers) would understand, but the others, only vaguely curious (unbelievers), would not. Something similar often takes place inside families. Mom and Dad sometimes talk in code to one another in front of the children, communicating only to each other while protecting the topic from the "unready ears" of the kids. And that is what Jesus' parables were—kingdom truths for believers worded in such a way that the skeptics would not understand. This was kingdom truth for kingdom followers only.

Today, as then, those who accept God's truth with open hearts are able to understand even deeper truths. They pass through the doorway of initial receptiveness into a treasure of wisdom and insight. Meanwhile, those who resist opening themselves to introductory truths (such as the existence of a holy God and the reality of our sin and need for a Savior) go through life blindly ignorant to principles that the faithful easily see.

This highlights a danger for believers. Even we are capable of coming to a point where we resist God's truth in some area of our lives. This makes us blind to the riches of further insight and wisdom (cf. 2 Pet. 1:5–11). We cannot afford to resist him for long. The true believer will not lose his or her salvation, but there can certainly be spiritual loss and loss of eternal reward, all as a result of a hardened heart.

A word of caution is appropriate here. The Holy Spirit of God will always conform to the Word of God. He will never contradict it. Be sure the "further insight" you find corresponds to the Word of God and not some other word. Paul reminds us that absolutely everything we need to be—everything God wants us to be—is revealed to us in his Word (2 Tim. 3:16–17).

II. COMMENTARY

The King Reveals a Secret

MAIN IDEA: *Kingdom citizens must endure in the midst of evil and opposition, while the kingdom grows in power and influence, until justice and reward are dispensed in the final judgment.*

Matthew 13:1–52 is the third of five discourses by Jesus recorded in Matthew. The time cues given by Matthew (13:1–3,10,36,53) lead us to believe that Jesus spoke these things during a single teaching event.

Several features make this chapter important but somewhat difficult to interpret. It features a new teaching method for Jesus (parables). It also falls in the center of Matthew's Gospel and explains a major shift in the emphasis of the book from Jesus' role as the sovereign ruling Son of David to that of the sacrificial redeeming Son of Abraham (Matt. 1:1). Furthermore, it reveals for the first time some critical truths that never appeared anywhere in the Old Testament.

Anticipating Christ's coming death, resurrection, and ascension, Matthew 13 deals with the question, "What will happen to the kingdom when the rejected king goes back to heaven without having actually ruled over the earth?" To answer the question, Jesus used a somewhat unusual word in the Bible. He spoke of **secrets** (13:11) and indicated he was revealing to his disciples truths **hidden since the creation of the world** (13:35). In the Bible, a mystery or secret is not something hard to understand, as we commonly use the word. Rather, it refers to a truth that was never revealed in the Old Testament but now is made plain in the New Testament. The apostle Paul defined it as truth "that has been kept hidden for ages and generations, but is now disclosed to the saints" (Col. 1:26).

Of course, the concept of kingdom "postponement" until a second coming only describes what it looks like from the human perspective. The kingdom is not postponed at all, but advances in a different form—the church. There is no delay in the advance of God's purpose. Everything simply had not been revealed in the Old Testament. Human responsibility for the rejection of the Messiah-King and the "apparent postponement" of the kingdom stands, but in God's sovereign all-knowing plan, there are no surprises. The death and resurrection of Christ are essential elements of the redemptive plan.

The Old Testament has revealed the earthly reign of Christ on the throne of David. But Matthew 13 introduces a different form of the kingdom—the spiritual reign of the king over his own servants while he is physically absent before his second coming. That is the **secret**—how his kingdom program will unfold in the period between his two advents. That is the subject of Matthew 13.

The word *parable* (*parabole*) comes from the combination of the verb *ballo* ("to throw, cast") and the prefix *para-* ("alongside"). The idea is that of placing two things side by side for comparison. A parable uses something with which the learner is familiar from everyday life (farming, the marketplace, fishing) and compares it with something that is unfamiliar (in this chapter, various realities about the kingdom of heaven). The student learns something about the unfamiliar by its similarity to the familiar.

A The Kingdom: For Listeners Only (13:1–23)

> **SUPPORTING IDEA:** *Many people will reject the truth because of Satanic opposition, their own hard hearts, and because God will blind them further. But some will receive the truth and bear spiritual fruit.*

Jesus' first parable might be thought of as a parable about parables. It explained the need for parables, because of the varying responses God's Word receives from different people. For this reason, the parable of the sower is a suitable introduction to the discourse. It reveals a secret about the kingdom and justifies Jesus' use of parables.

The question that the parable of the sower answers is, Why do some respond in faith to the Messiah while others do not? The disciples may have been asking themselves, What went wrong? Why are people not accepting the king and his kingdom? Is there a problem with the king? Or his message? Jesus' first parable suggested there was no problem with the farmer (Messiah), or the seed (his message), but the problem was with the soil (the people hearing).

The parable placed people—all of whom have been exposed to the truth—in more than the two categories of "faithful" and "faithless." Jesus used the parable to demonstrate the variety of reasons the faithless avoid trusting or fall away from faith. Again, the problem was not with an ineffective teacher or his truth, but with the condition of the hearts of the listeners. And opposition from the kingdom's adversary, Satan, and his counterfeit kingdom cannot be discounted. Jesus stated that the devil himself was involved in this process (13:19).

Verses 10–17 are not an arbitrary interruption, separating the parable (13:3–9) from its explanation (13:18–23), but an integral part of the message of the parable. It contains Jesus' explanation as to why he used this new parabolic teaching method.

13:1–2. That same day provides both a chronological and thematic connection between this discourse and the preceding context of Jesus' rejection of Israel. Another connection with the preceding context is found in the mention of **the house**, meaning the one in which Jesus was teaching when his family came to speak to him (12:46–50). This was the same house to which Jesus would return for the private portion of the discourse (13:36)—probably Peter's house in Capernaum (8:14).

Jesus sat by the Sea of Galilee (**lake**, 13:1) and in **a boat** (13:2), because sitting was the posture a teacher assumed in that culture, reflecting the respect he received from his listeners. In contrast, the crowd **stood** (13:2). In many cultures, this is a sign of honor to the teacher and the sacred Scriptures he is teaching, but in this instance it was also necessary because of the pressing crowd.

13:3–8. The **many things** Jesus spoke in parables certainly included what was written in 13:3–52. It is possible that there were other parables that Matthew did not record.

The parable of the sower requires little comment, because Jesus himself explained the parable in 13:18–23. Note that the farmer sowed seed on several different kinds of soil. The soil **along the path** (13:4) would likely have been hard-packed from much traffic. There would be little or no vegetation or loose soil to hide or bury the seeds, so the birds could easily find them. **The birds** represent the devil, "the evil one" (13:19). Note also the variable quality of even the good soil (13:8); even among that which is conducive to fruit bearing, some soils do better than others.

As is common in storytelling today, Jesus used patterns of threes—three bad soils and three variations on the good soil. Usually the first two examples set a pattern, and the third example departs from that pattern, revealing the central message of the story. In this parable, the first three soils set the pattern of poor response to the seeds, and the fourth soil was the contrasting positive example.

13:9. Jesus repeated the challenge that Matthew first recorded in 11:15, after identifying John the Baptizer with "Elijah, who was to come." He will repeat the same wording in 13:43, and the challenge is explained thoroughly in the following context (13:10–17).

In fact, the distinction between those who have **ears** to hear and those who do not is central to understanding all of Matthew 11–13. In chapters 11–12, the conflicts revealed the contrast between those who willfully chose to disbelieve in the face of overwhelming evidence, and those who humbly accepted the evidence and responded in faith and obedience to the Messiah. Those who had **ears** to hear would not only find understanding about the parable, but would realize that the parable was talking about their willingness to hear. Those who did not have "ears to hear" would go on in denial about the parable's implications about their own unwillingness to hear.

13:10. The disciples noticed Jesus' shift in teaching style. He was changing over to parables as his primary method of public teaching, so they inquired about his reasons. He took this opportunity to explain to the disciples, in plain language, the root problem of Israel's disbelief.

13:11–12. Jesus' answer implied that the **secrets** about the kingdom are unknowable apart from God's determination to reveal them. Just as Jesus had complete authority about who would receive knowledge of the Father (11:27), he also had complete discretion as to who would receive the secrets about the kingdom of heaven.

Those who already had some knowledge—because they responded with humble faith to what had already been revealed—had been good stewards of this information. They would be entrusted with more (particularly through their understanding of the parables). These people, because of their faith, had received God's gracious favor. However, those who had consciously rejected the Messiah would receive only judgment, beginning with Jesus' withholding of insight by the use of parables. These outsiders had enough knowledge of the truth to be hostile against Jesus, but even that insight would be further clouded by their disbelief. Jesus' teaching style was designed to give them little help as long as they persisted in their rebellion.

This has application even today. It is a dangerous thing to hear and understand God's truth, and then to consciously choose to disbelieve it. Such people will become less and less aware of their own doom, as they slide deeper into denial of the Messiah. However, those who respond to God's word with open hearts will find an ever-widening road to further insight and reward.

13:13–15. Because of God's determination to bless those who believe and to judge those who disbelieve, Jesus changed his public teaching style to parables—teaching tools that would further polarize believers and skeptics. To further explain his use of parables, Jesus described the condition of the skeptics. The paradox of **seeing**, but not seeing, and **hearing**, but not hearing, is resolved when we realize that the first reference to each sense has to do with their physical senses. The second reference to each sense is figurative, referring to the eyes and ears of their hearts—their capacity to accept or reject the truth laid before them.

By adding **they do not hear or understand** (13:13), Jesus clarified this distinction, but he also hinted that part of God's judgment on the outsiders was a growing unawareness even of their own willful disbelief. The human heart is amazing in its capacity to convince itself of a falsehood—even one it has perpetrated itself. We are capable of lying to ourselves and coming to a point where we believe our own lies.

In them implies that the following prophecy from Isaiah did not apply to those who believed—only to the willfully disbelieving who bring this judgment on themselves.

The prophecy of Isaiah 6:9–10 comes from Isaiah's vision of Yahweh in his throne room. In Isaiah 6, in the face of Yahweh's glorious perfection, Isaiah fell on his face and proclaimed his uncleanness. An angel cleansed Isaiah's lips, qualifying him for his task as messenger to rebellious Israel. Isaiah then volunteered for the job of messenger, in response to Yahweh's invitation.

Isaiah was instructed to go to Judah with the truth. But because of Judah's rebellious disbelief, Isaiah's teaching would serve as God's instrument of judgment, causing the people to galvanize their hearts even more against the truth. Judah had gone beyond the point of being able to avoid judgment. So Yahweh sealed his case against them by taking them even farther from any possibility of restoration.

In the Isaiah context after Jesus' quote, Yahweh described the results of his judgment—the devastation of the land and the exile of the population—but left Judah with the hope of the faithful remnant, the "stumps" of the tree of Judah, from which the "holy seed" would grow back (Isa. 6:13). The period of judgment would purge and purify Judah, restoring the nation to its original purpose and ultimately producing the Messiah, who would be the final solution to Israel's rebellion.

While Jesus' parables would serve the same purpose as Isaiah's teaching—to further harden the hearts of willful disbelievers—the hardening of first-century Israel's heart was already well-advanced, and their judgment well-deserved.

The Lord's heart remains open, even as disbelieving hearts grow colder and harder. Verse 14 uses the Greek double negative *ou me* twice, meaning Israel would "by no means, absolutely not" understand or perceive the truth they had been continually seeing and hearing.

Both times the word **heart** (*kardia*) or **hearts** is used, it refers to the collective "heart" of all Israel. The concept of corporate solidarity was much better understood and accepted in first-century Israel than it is today in Western culture, with our emphasis on the individual. God does deal with whole peoples and nations at a time. Israel as a whole was characterized as having a **calloused** heart, and God would judge the nation accordingly. But he had not forgotten the remnant of the faithful (11:25–30; 12:48–50).

The figurative closing of Israel's ears and eyes is voluntary; they are not victims of some "disease" or "injury." Note especially that **they have closed their eyes.**

At any time Israel could have "turned" (*epistrepho*) for healing (i.e., forgiveness and spiritual restoration), by seeing, hearing, and believing God's message. But the mission of Isaiah and Jesus was to speak the truth, further galvanizing the resistant hearts of the unbelieving people and driving them further from repentance and healing, as an act of God's judgment. God had given Israel many chances, but now his patience had run out. Judgment was beginning.

13:16–17. In contrast with calloused Israel (the emphatic placement of **your** heightens the contrast), the disciples' eyes and ears were open, accepting God's message and his Messenger. They were therefore **blessed** (*makarios*, "happy"; cf. 5:3–12). The disciples' eyes and ears were also blessed because of the privilege they enjoyed, **which many prophets and righteous men** of past ages longed for. Those past heroes remained faithful, even though they never saw the ultimate fulfillment of the promises they claimed. The disciples claimed these promises and were eyewitnesses to their fulfillment in Jesus. **I tell you the truth** adds emphasis to the greatness of the disciples' privilege (13:17).

13:18–19. These verses connect Jesus' explanation of the parable of the sower and the soils (13:18–23) with the disciples' privilege as hearers of the truth. Jesus was saying to them, "Because you have responded to what you have already seen with eyes, ears, and hearts of faith and humble obedience, I will show you even more. You have proven faithful with little, so I will trust you with much."

Jesus identified the **seed** as **the message about the kingdom**—its arrival in Jesus and the way to participate in this kingdom. The "message about the kingdom" is probably identical to the "good news of the kingdom" in 4:23; 9:35; 24:14.

The soils were the issue. Throughout the parable's explanation, Jesus compared the four kinds of soil with various kinds of people who had been exposed to his teaching. The first soil, that "along the path" (13:4), was packed and hardened by traffic. It represented the person who **does not understand** the word he had heard. The person represented by the hardened soil is one who chooses not to understand rather than a person who wants to understand but cannot. Such a person may actually understand Jesus' teaching in a literal sense but refuse to accept its truth. The biblical concept of "understanding" goes beyond the idea of mental comprehension. It sometimes includes volitional acceptance. In 21:45, the chief priests and Pharisees knew the meaning of Jesus' parable concerning them, but they refused to accept its truth.

The person who refuses to accept the word of God will fall victim to the **evil one** (Satan, represented by the birds in 13:4), who **comes and snatches away what was sown in his heart.** If given even the slightest opportunity, Satan and his evil forces—archenemies of the kingdom of God—are able to remove or distort the truth, thus making that person even less likely to accept the truth in the future. This is one manifestation of the principle Jesus taught in 12:30: "He who is not with me is against me." To refuse to accept his word is to move away from him. There can be no objective neutrality.

Many people who were exposed to the words and works of the Messiah (especially the religious leaders) fell into this category. They rejected him without any second thoughts.

13:20–21. The rocky soil (13:5–6) receives extra attention in both the parable and its explanation because this person's response to the truth follows a two-stage pattern. His initial response is unreserved and emotional—joyful acceptance—but only because the circumstances are favorable. The cost of commitment is not yet obvious. This person's commitment is not deeply rooted. We might say that the truly committed "pay their dues up front," but the marginally committed cancel their membership when payment comes due. The cost of commitment to the Messiah comes in the form of **trouble** (*thlipsis*, "tribulation") or persecution (*diogmos*) that come **because of the word.** As quickly as this individual had committed, just as quickly he defected, distancing himself from the **word** or message.

There is debate as to whether such a person is truly saved. This question cannot be answered from Jesus' words, because it is not related to his purpose in the parable, and he does not make the answer clear. It is doubtful that the person was expressing true faith from the start.

13:22. The soil with **thorns** (13:7) is also assumed to produce some initial growth, as did the **rocky places** (13:20). But the influence which draws this person away from a sustained interest is not persecution but competing "gods"—**the worries of this life and the deceitfulness of wealth.** Rather than being driven from the truth by hardship, this person is lured away from the truth by promises of something better. Of course, these promises will never be fulfilled, because these competing gods or masters are deceitful.

Is this kind of person saved? The language may lean somewhat toward believing that this person had responded initially with sincere faith, for the seedling is not said to die (as we can presume with the rocky soil, 13:21), but rather to become choked and **unfruitful.** Still, without perseverance, there is no final evidence of salvation.

We have already seen in Matthew an example of a person who started following Jesus, but then began giving excuses for why he needed to postpone his commitment (8:21–22). But even more prominent in this category would be Judas Iscariot, who sold out Jesus for thirty coins (26:14–16,20–25,48–50; 27:1–10).

13:23. All three of the preceding "soils" had heard the word. So also the fourth **good soil** hears the word, but this one also **understands.** This person *chooses* to understand and accept the truth, also accepting the One who is truth (John 14:6). None of the other soils bore any fruit, but this soil yielded much fruit. Jesus did not clarify what caused the variability between the fruitfulness of various faithful followers. One factor may be the degrees of faith. Perhaps another factor has to do with the variety of tasks given to different believers by God. Some may have greater potential for bearing fruit than others (cf. the different number of talents and different levels of return in 25:14–30). **Crop** represents the tangible results of a life of faith, including godly character (Gal. 5:22–23) and other souls brought into the kingdom (Matt. 9:37–38; cf. John 15:1–17).

In Matthew, where the focus is primarily on Jesus, we are given little opportunity to see examples of the disciples' responses of faith. The rest of the New Testament, however, is filled with stories about the fruit of faithful hearts. Prominent examples include Peter, John, Philip, Stephen, Paul, and Timothy.

B The Kingdom: The Faithful Must Coexist with Evil until Judgment (13:24–30)

SUPPORTING IDEA: *Kingdom servants should take courage in the midst of an evil world, finding hope in the justice and reward of the final judgment.*

The parable of the weeds (or tares) answers two questions from the context of Matthew. First, why must the faithful kingdom servants live in the midst of evil on earth? Second, is there any hope of justice and freedom from the surrounding evil of the world? The concept that the weeds, in their early stages, were indistinguishable from the young wheat also points to the likelihood of counterfeits within the kingdom community (7:15–23). This parable offered assurance that even these convincing imposters would be "weeded out" in the end.

The meaning of this parable is virtually identical to the meaning of the parable of the dragnet (13:47–50). Both Jesus and Matthew felt a burden to help the faithful understand why they must tolerate evil for a time, and to give hope of ultimate justice and reward.

13:24–26. The theme of sowing continues in this parable, as Jesus described what the farmer did with what grew. The weeds or tares were *zizania,* a type of ryegrass, from among the types today known collectively as darnel. Until they mature, these weeds are indistinguishable from wheat, so they must be left to steal water and nutrients from the wheat until the two can be separated at harvest. Because Jesus himself explained this parable, we need not comment here on its meaning (see comment on 13:36–43).

13:27–30. Farmers were probably concerned with the purity of their seed when they bought it or set it aside from the previous year's harvest. They were anxious to avoid the decreased fruitfulness that is assured when weed seeds are mixed in with the wheat seeds. Because this particular farmer had been sure of the purity of the seed he had sown, the only explanation was that an enemy had sown the weeds. The most important elements are the enemy and the weeds.

To the farmer, it was more important to save the good wheat than to get rid of the weeds. He instructed his workers to leave the weeds until the harvest, when the two could be sorted out. Notice the verbal emphasis on the side-by-side existence of the wheat and the weeds. They are **both** to **grow together.** But when the two are separated, the weeds are burned, and the wheat is gathered into the farmer's barn. Jesus was careful to put into the farmer's mouth the words **my barn,** rather than simply, "the barn." Jesus hinted here at the loving, personal possessiveness the Lord has for his faithful.

The Kingdom: Surprising Impact (13:31–33)

SUPPORTING IDEA: *While God's kingdom appears to start small—almost invisible—we can take hope in the assurance that it is growing steadily and will achieve its promised glory and power out of all proportion to its small beginnings.*

This couplet of short parables answers two closely related questions. First, how can such a small beginning—a handful of uneducated, inexperienced men—be referred to as a "kingdom" that will have the impact prophesied by the Old Testament? Second, since Jesus' kingdom was not the powerful military and political takeover so widely expected, how can such a quiet, humble beginning be referred to as the powerful, world-changing "kingdom of heaven"?

Jesus was helping the faithful to see that outward appearances count for very little. In contrast, the power of God—who chooses to work through humble instruments, often in ways that are not obvious—is what will bring about the glorious and pervasive influence of the kingdom.

13:31–32. Here we come to a third parable about a sower and a seed. As with the parable of the weeds, the focus is on the thing growing, but this time the listener is struck by the contrast between the beginning and the end product. The mustard seed was the smallest of the commonly used garden seeds in that culture. Thus, the mustard seed was commonly used throughout the ancient world as a symbol of small size. Jesus chose to use it because it also produces a full-grown bush that is large, when compared to the size of the original seed. The plant can sometimes reach as high as ten or fifteen feet, but its normal height is about four feet.

Jesus' followers must have lost more and more sleep as the hostility of the powerful Jewish religious establishment grew. Jesus' mustard seed parable encouraged them to keep up hope in the power of God to work through these humble instruments and small beginnings.

13:33. The key to understanding the parable of the yeast (or leaven) is to note that Jesus said that the woman **mixed** the yeast into **a large amount of flour until it worked all through the dough.** The little bit of yeast worked its way unseen through the entire lump, radically changing its size and shape. And that is the point—the pervasive, internal, unseen power of the yeast that stimulates enormous internal growth.

The yeast has nothing to do with evil. The point Jesus made is the internal dynamic of rising as opposed to outward, physical organization. His kingdom will grow through an internal, unseen, spiritual dynamic.

The idea is that the kingdom, in some ways, is hidden from sight. Jesus had attempted to conduct his ministry quietly (8:4; 9:30; 12:15–21). But more significantly, the change brought about by the king's coming was not the military, political takeover that most Jews expected. Instead, the change the king caused was one that happened within the inner, unseen person. Jesus' kingdom took spiritual territory away from the unseen enemy. Jesus rescued souls; he did not capture land or seats of civil power. Nevertheless, the message of the kingdom would pervade the entire world.

Even today, when we look back on two thousand years of the gospel's progress throughout the world, we can become discouraged because of the kingdom's hidden nature. Consider what encouragement was necessary for Jesus' first small band of followers, when the gospel was brand new and they were its sole custodians.

The King Begins to Speak Only in Parables to the Crowds (13:34–35)

SUPPORTING IDEA: *The Lord makes his truth accessible to those who seek it but difficult to find for those who resist it.*

13:34–35. Even though Jesus had already explained why he was speaking in parables to the crowd (13:10–17), Matthew again emphasized the shift in Jesus' teaching style. Matthew was not intending to say that Jesus departed completely from any other style of teaching from this point on (e.g., 15:3–9; 19:3–12), but that on this particular occasion Jesus spoke only in parables to the crowds.

Matthew again quoted from the Old Testament to support Jesus' use of parables. This time he demonstrated Jesus' fulfillment of yet another prophecy. The original text of Psalm 78:2 reads: "I will open my mouth in parables, I will utter hidden things, things from of old."

It is unlikely a student would know that this was a messianic prophecy apart from the revelation of God (see comment on Ps. 78 below). The biggest change Matthew made was to change "of old" to **since the creation of the world.** The **things hidden** were probably not conceptually related to the hidden yeast (13:33) or the hidden treasure (13:44). In those parables, it was the kingdom itself that was hidden in some way. Rather, the "things hidden" of this quote are the same as "the secrets of the kingdom of heaven" in 13:11. They are previously unrevealed truths *about* the kingdom.

Matthew portrayed Jesus as the Messiah who, for the first time, opened the doors of understanding to eternal realities long kept secret. But he provided understanding only for those who had ears to hear. This is only one of many changes the king implemented in his inauguration of his kingdom on earth (9:14–17).

Often when a New Testament author quoted from the Old Testament, he intended to bring to the minds of his educated readers the larger original context of the quotation. Psalm 78 is by Asaph, the leader of choral worship under David (1 Chron. 15:17,19; 16:4–5). Verse 2 is part of a lengthy introduction, calling Israel to learn from the lessons of the nation's past, which he will put into story form. (One term he used to describe the story was *parables*.)

Then he launched into one of the longer psalms in the Psalter, weaving a sobering tale out of themes of God's faithfulness to Israel, Israel's disobedience, God's judgment and then forgiveness and love, and Israel's continued rebellion. Most of the historic recitation is focused on Israel's continued resistance against a pursuing God. Finally, in the last stanza (Ps. 78:65–72), Asaph resolved the dissonance of the psalm with God's provision of "David his servant . . . to be the shepherd of his people Jacob, of Israel his inheritance. And David shepherded them with integrity of heart, with skillful hands he led them" (78:70–72).

If Matthew's intended impact by use of this quotation went beyond the one isolated verse, then he was reminding his readers of Israel's past cycles of rebellion. He was showing them that the cycle was again repeating itself in first-century Israel, even in the face of God's repeated offer of restoration and forgiveness. He was also alluding to the solution to the problem through God's provision of a king, indeed the Son of David who would rule the nation again one day (Matt. 1:1–17; 12:23; 22:41–46).

The major point here is Jesus' explanation of the change, not only in his teaching style to the crowds, but the change in the direction the kingdom is taking in light of Israel's unbelief and Messiah's rejection of the nation. The nation would be set on the shelf while he worked through a new vessel.

E The Kingdom: Judgment on Evil, Exaltation of the Righteous (13:36–43)

SUPPORTING IDEA: *Kingdom citizens should take courage in the midst of an evil world, finding hope in the justice and reward of the final judgment.*

Here, at the heart of the discourse, Matthew placed Jesus' private and detailed explanation of the parable of the weeds (see 13:24–30). The central themes here are patient perseverance while evil is allowed to persist and hope of final justice and reward. The fact that this message was emphasized in three different locations in the discourse (13:24–30,36–43,47–50) and given so much text must give it high priority in discerning Jesus' central message.

13:36. Up to this point, Jesus had been speaking publicly to the crowds, but now he continued in private with only his disciples. **The house** is likely the house in which Jesus defined his new family (12:46–50), and which he left to come to the shore and present this discourse (13:1). It was probably Peter's home in Capernaum (8:14–15). There his disciples requested an explanation of the parable of the weeds.

13:37–39. Jesus identified what each key element in the parable represented in kingdom realities. Then in 13:40–43 he would explain the implications of the parable for both the faithless and the faithful.

This is the only one of Matthew's three "sowing" parables where Jesus identified who the sower represented. Here the sower was the "Son of Man." Note the way Jesus again used the title in 13:41, describing his authority over angels at the final judgment. Because the good seed represents **the sons of the kingdom**, and the field represents the **world** (13:38), the **Son of Man** in 13:37 is no less than the king himself, who "plants" and "grows" kingdom citizens in his world, at his discretion, and by his sovereign authority. In the parables many Old Testament images that apply only to God himself now represent Jesus.

The **devil**, on the other hand, had planted **sons of the evil one** in the world, among the kingdom citizens. These evil people included Jesus' opponents, who had been challenging him and his followers since 9:36. Jesus' followers are encouraged to persevere in the midst of evil until the **end of the age**. When God's plan of history—the restoration of his sovereign kingdom and the sacrificial redemption of his people—reaches completion, he will send his angels to sort out the evil and the good.

13:40–42. The word *end* (Gr., *sunteleia*) means "completion," as in 13:39. The gathering and burning of the weeds represent the gathering of all evil men and women **out of his kingdom** for punishment in the fire of hell. Jesus again used the title **Son of Man** (see comment at 3:37), this time describing himself in the role of the judge at the completion of earth's history.

The evil people are described as those who cause **sin** and continually **do evil**. Not only do these people break God's laws, but they also snare others into sin.

Hell is described as a **fiery furnace, where there will be weeping and gnashing of teeth** (cf. this passage with Isa. 32:13–15; Jer. 31:27–28; Hos. 2:21–23; 6:11).

13:43. In contrast to the evil people who had been sent to eternal torment, **the righteous**—those who had trusted and followed the Messiah—will enter into a glorious eternity with their Father. Matthew paraphrased Daniel 12:3: "Those who are wise will shine like the brightness of the heavens, and those who lead many to righteousness, like the stars for ever and ever." Not only had these people performed righteous deeds, but they had led others into righteousness also, in contrast to those who were punished. The context of Daniel 12 describes the final judgment and resurrection of both the good and the evil ("to shame and everlasting contempt").

Throughout Scripture, the picture of brightly shining light (here **like the sun**) often refers to God's perfect righteousness and glory, sometimes as it is imputed to his saints (e.g., Exod. 13:21,22; Matt. 17:2; Phil. 2:15; Rev. 1:14–16). Here, finally, is the hope of the kingdom as it was meant to be. Evil has been purged, and the Father is present in person with his children. They have been purified of sin so that they shine with his perfect righteousness.

Again Jesus issued the challenge of 11:15 and 13:9. Some would have **ears** to hear—a willing attitude of submission to the truth—so they would understand and accept what Jesus was saying about the final judgment and reward.

▣ The Kingdom: Surprising Value (13:44–46)

SUPPORTING IDEA: *Despite its appearance to human eyes, the kingdom is well worth the investment of a person's life.*

This couplet of short parables is, in some ways, parallel to 13:31–33, but the message of these parables has to do with the surprising value of the kingdom of heaven. These parables answer two closely related questions from the surrounding context. First, why should we give our lives for a kingdom we cannot see? Second, can the kingdom truly be the answer to our search for ultimate fulfillment?

Even at this early point in Jesus' ministry, he was demanding much of his followers. They had already given up the security of a quiet life at home (8:19–20), abandoning family priorities (8:21–22), risking the threat of imprisonment and torture (10:17–19; 11:2), and enduring the critical questioning of the powerful religious leadership (9:11,14; 12:2). In Matthew 10, Jesus projected even farther into the future, predicting even worse happenings for those who stayed by him. These timid souls needed assurance that the price they were paying was worth the kingdom they would receive. Believers today need exactly the same reassurance. The rewards are worth the price!

13:44. As with the yeast (13:33), here also the kingdom is portrayed as being **hidden** from view. It was a kingdom of the spirit realm and human souls, which cannot be seen with physical eyes. This parable makes four points: (1) there is an "accidental" aspect to our discovery of the kingdom's value, because each of us is so absorbed in going his own way that God must take the initiative to show us the kingdom (cf. Isa. 53:6; Matt. 18:12–14; Rom. 5:6–8; 1 John 4:10,19); (2) when we do realize the value of the invisible kingdom, its value is cause for great joy; (3) the kingdom is worth everything we have and are; (4) to own the kingdom, we must accept all that comes with it. The field in the parable that cost everything the man owned represents the losses, hardships, and persecution a follower of Jesus is called on to endure for him.

Even though Jesus said that the joyful person hid the **treasure** again, he did not mean to say that believers should hide and hoard the kingdom. He included this detail to make the parable realistic. If the man had made known to others what was hidden in the field, someone else might have made a higher bid to the landowner, and the original finder would have lost the field and the treasure. The comparison between the treasure and the kingdom breaks down at this point, because there is only one field with the treasure. But the kingdom is available to any who will come. The point is the incredible value of the kingdom.

13:45–46. While the man who found the "treasure" discovered the kingdom's worth by accident, the pearl merchant was searching for something of value. We need not take this as a contradiction of the "accidental" element of our discovery of the kingdom. Even though we are going our own way, oblivious to the kingdom apart from God's revelation, every human being is on a quest. Every choice a person makes is somehow guided by his or her search for ultimate fulfillment. Before God breaks in, we simply do not know what we are searching for. Most people search in the wrong places, seeking fulfillment through deceitful, worldly means (wealth, pleasure, power, fame), yet never finding it in those places. When, by God's gracious guidance, we find the kingdom, we realize that it is what we have been searching for all along.

The pearl merchant recognized instantly the value of the one pearl, because he had measured the value of many lesser pearls throughout his life. He, like the treasure finder, went and sold everything he owned in order to possess the pearl.

G The Kingdom: The Faithful Must Coexist with Evil until Judgment (13:47–50)

> **SUPPORTING IDEA:** *Kingdom citizens should look forward to the justice and reward of the final judgment.*

The parable of the net teaches the same lesson as the parable of the weeds—that the righteous must endure some period of coexistence with evil, until God's final judgment brings justice and reward.

13:47–50. Since the action that places the **bad** fish alongside the **good** is not attributed to the Evil One, there may be a slightly different emphasis in this parable than that in the parable of the weeds. Jesus drew a following comprised of both the faithful and the faithless, but they were sorted out through various tests he placed before them. He has continued throughout history to draw all sorts of people toward the kingdom, but these will be judged or sorted out in the end.

Here, as in the parable of the weeds, we find the coexistence of evil alongside the righteous, the discarding and burning of the evil, and the treasuring and protection of the righteous. Again, the angels are the agents of judgment whom Jesus will use. The description of hell (13:50) is identical to that in 13:42.

H The Kingdom: Valuing the Old, Committing to the New (13:51–52)

> **SUPPORTING IDEA:** *The New Testament kingdom of heaven is not a replacement for the Old Testament realities; rather, the kingdom of heaven brings the old covenant to its intended fulfillment.*

13:51–52. There may be an intended parallel between this brief question and answer and that in 13:10–23. Here the roles are reversed. Jesus asked the question, and the disciples answered. Both questions had to do with under-standing of the parables. In light of the meaning packed into the Greek verb *suniemi*, "to understand," in 13:14–15, Jesus may have been inquiring about more than mental comprehension. He was helping the disciples personalize his teaching. His question likely had the force of, "Have you chosen to accept all these things? Will you truly give up your life for my kingdom—for me?"

These are the kinds of healthy questions Christians should ask them-selves. Will we commit fully to the kingdom, not being driven away by hard-ship, not being lured away by competing masters? Will we endure evil and hold onto the hope of final justice? Will we refuse to lose sight of the final kingdom realities, even though the kingdom can seem overwhelmed at times in this evil world?

The disciples' affirmative answer to his question amounted to an expres-sion of volitional faith—a carefully considered choice to place their faith in the king and his teaching.

Jesus left the disciples with one more brief parable. Not many scribes had become disciples of the kingdom, especially because of their investment in the Jewish religious establishment. But any scribe who could say, "Yes, I com-mit," as did the disciples in the preceding verse, would bring with him a rich knowledge of the treasures of the Old Testament. A scribe was a specialist in the knowledge and teaching of the Hebrew Scriptures. At the same time, as a disciple of the kingdom that Jesus proclaimed, he would acknowledge the new covenant inaugurated by Jesus the king. He would embrace it while still appreciating the value of the old. Jesus' arrival on the stage of history and his death and resurrection would complete God's covenant, offered to any who would respond in faith.

It is important for Christians today to become familiar with both the Old and the New Testaments in order to reflect God's full revelation. The kingdom servant (and Christian disciple) is to be like the scribe who has become a disci-ple of the kingdom—continually opening the treasures of both old and new.

█ The King Is Rejected in His Hometown (13:53–58)

SUPPORTING IDEA: *Even those who should know best may reject the king and his kingdom.*

13:53. This formula may be thought of as the final verse of the discourse, since all five discourses end with similar formulae. At the same time, it tran-sitions into the action that follows.

13:54–56. From the site on the Galilean shore (probably Capernaum), Jesus decided to pay a visit to his hometown Nazareth, a village of perhaps 1,500 people in that day. Jesus entered the synagogue and began to teach, apparently also performing miracles. As in other settings, his hearers were

amazed (literally, "to be struck," also in 7:28; 19:25; 22:33), but theirs was amazed disbelief rather than a realization that would shock them into believing. They had no explanation for Jesus' wisdom and miraculous powers. But whatever the explanation, they would not consider the truth.

13:57. Because of the puzzle Jesus represented in these people's minds, they would not believe him. However, they could not honestly dismiss him. In their confusion, they became angry, looking for someone to blame for their uncomfortable mental state (**they took offense at him**). Familiarity truly does breed contempt. Jesus' relatives and neighbors proved his statement about his true family in 12:48–50.

13:58. Jesus' performance of miracles was associated with the faith of the people (see 8:13; 9:2,22,28–29). In this context, however, it was Jesus' lack of miracles that was associated with the people's lack of faith. This has to be one of the most sorrowful statements in the Bible. Imagine Jesus leaving his hometown, with many people whom he has loved, unable to find the faith that he found in a Gentile centurion (8:13). His own family and close friends were fulfilling Matthew 13:14–15—hearing, but not understanding.

> **MAIN IDEA REVIEW:** *Kingdom citizens must endure in the midst of evil and opposition, while the kingdom grows in power and influence, until justice and reward are dispensed in the final judgment.*

III. CONCLUSION

Believers are privileged with insight into God's truth, but even they must beware of the danger of a resistant heart. Many people resist God's truth because of their own pride and self-centeredness. Others may appear to commit to Christ, but their lack of faith is revealed at the first sign that their commitment will cost them something. Still other people may seem to commit to Jesus, but their heart is lured away from Christ by worries and competing gods such as money and lifestyle.

PRINCIPLES

- The person who receives God's truth and commits to Christ will live a fruitful life for the kingdom.
- Satan and sin are the causes of evil in the world.
- Believers must endure in the midst of evil until the final judgment.
- At the final judgment, God's justice will punish the evil and reward the righteous.
- Even though the kingdom is largely "hidden" today, it is worth our lives.

- Even though the kingdom seems to be small and insignificant, it is of great value, and it is worth our lives.
- The Old Testament serves a critical purpose in God's plan; it must be understood, valued, and taught as the foundation of God's plan, which comes to completion in the New Testament.
- The people whom we know best may become most resistant to our attempts to share the gospel.
- God will not work supernaturally in the lives of people who consciously disbelieve him.

APPLICATIONS

- Cultivate your Christian character. Grow in the grace of the Spirit.
- Be a student of the Scriptures. Study the Old Testament to understand the foundation of God's plan in the New Testament.
- Trust God genuinely, avoiding Satan's temptations to disbelieve.
- Live your life according to kingdom values.
- Don't be discouraged about your seemingly small contributions to the kingdom. God will use them to build toward his ultimate, glorious kingdom.
- Don't be discouraged if you don't see the kingdom growing as rapidly as you wish it would.

IV. LIFE APPLICATION

More Than the Eye Sees

When was the last time you quietly gazed into a clear night sky? The night sky seems full of celestial objects. Depending on when you are viewing the heavens, you may see the moon, stars, and planets. You might even catch a glimpse of a meteor streaking across the Milky Way. Surprisingly, we are viewing very little of the real universe. That is because what we see in the night sky as visible light is only a fraction of the light spectrum.

There is far more to the universe than can be seen with the human eye. To "see" other light wavelengths, one must use a different kind of instrument—an X-ray telescope. NASA's Chandra X-ray Observatory, the world's most powerful X-ray telescope, circles the Earth and observes the universe that exists beyond the spectrum of visible light. It allows scientists to obtain unprecedented X-ray images and spectra of violent, high-temperature events and objects to help us better understand the structure and growth of our universe. With the power and strength packed into this instrument, one could read a newspaper from half a mile away or see the letters of a stop sign from twelve miles. Astronomers are using this technology to uncover amazing phenomena such as black holes, exploding stars, rapidly rotating stars, and far-away exploding galaxies. In this way, they are "seeing" the real universe.

When Jesus taught with parables, he was delivering more than mere stories for his listeners. He was communicating important spiritual truths for those who had "eyes to see" and "ears to hear." Those with limited vision and understanding heard only a story. Those who had "eyes to see" and "ears to hear" understood much more. They were able to understand deep spiritual truths and mysteries of the kingdom. With one's spiritual eyes, the full spectrum of truth becomes visible. Are you viewing the world with an earthly, temporal vision, or are you seeing with far-reaching spiritual vision?

V. PRAYER

Gracious Father, thank you for the wonderful kingdom which you have established through your Son, and thank you for including me as a kingdom citizen. Amen.

VI. DEEPER DISCOVERIES

A. Interpreting Parables

There have been a wide range of approaches to interpreting the parables. At one extreme is the allegorical approach, which reads meaning into every detail of the parable and even finds different "levels" of meaning in each parable. Such interpreters take the parable to mean one thing to Jesus' immediate listeners, another to Matthew's readers, another as it applies to national Israel, another as it applies to the church, and yet another as it applies to the final judgment. This "method" stretches the parable beyond the limits of its purpose. It violates many hermeneutical guidelines making Scripture mean almost anything the reader wants it to mean.

In the last several decades, in an attempt to correct these abuses, certain authors have brought the interpretation of parables back to an opposite extreme. According to them, each parable makes only one point, and it is the interpreter's task to determine what that point is. According to this method, we should allow allegorical detail only when Jesus or the inspired author provides it.

In recent years, a healthy balance has emerged. Some interpreters have taken a stance that is close to the "one-point" method, but which allows that Jesus may have intended some allegorical detail that is not clearly defined as such by Jesus or the author. The parable should be taken to answer a question that has been raised elsewhere in the surrounding context. Some details in the parable are not meant to have parallels in the spiritual side of the comparison, but they serve to fill out the word picture (e.g., the birds perching on the branches of the mustard tree may be taken simply to emphasize the size of the tree). In general, this seems to be the most authentic method for interpreting the parables.

As we seek Jesus' meaning in the parables, we should look in the surrounding context for clues about the questions Jesus is answering by the parable. Because Matthew 13 is clearly connected with the preceding context (the Sabbath controversy, 12:1–14; the Beelzebub controversy, 12:22–37; the "sign" controversy, 12:38–45; the criteria for membership in Jesus' family, 12:46–50), we know that the parables in this discourse will answer one or more questions raised in the preceding context.

The theme of Matthew 11–12 dealt with conscious, volitional disbelief (blind eyes and deaf ears, 13:13–15) versus humble, obedient faith (seeing eyes and hearing ears, 13:9,16,43). This gives us a clue about the specific purpose and meaning of the Matthew 13 parables. In light of the growing opposition to Jesus and his judgment and rejection of Israel in the preceding chapters (9–12), Jesus explained in Matthew 13 through parables just how the kingdom could be so ignored or abused by so many in Israel. He also described how his kingdom would proceed from this point during his upcoming absence before his second coming.

B. The Structure of Matthew 13:1–52

Two prominent characteristics define the structure and the interpretation of this discourse. First, the discourse is divided into two halves. The first half (13:1–35, except possibly the private explanation in verses 10–23) was spoken to the crowds on the shore of the Sea of Galilee; the second half (13:36–52) was spoken in private, in "the house," to Jesus' disciples. A speaker's audience is a significant clue to the speaker's meaning, so we must keep this in mind as we come to each parable.

Second, the discourse also displays many of the features of a poetic form sometimes called "inverted parallel" or "chiasm." Trying to picture the discourse as a whole, then, we see it opening broadly, narrowing in the middle at its key point, and opening again toward the end (like an hourglass in appearance).

The structure of a literary piece is important in guiding its interpretation. For example, in a chiasm, the most important idea is found at the heart of the series of nested pairs. In Matthew 13, this would mean that both 13:34–35 (Jesus' revelation of things hidden since the creation of the world) and 13:36–43 (his rejection was a problem with the soil of Israel, not the Messiah-King-Sower) guide us to the central message of the discourse. The disciples were learning things from the Messiah-King that their predecessors, the Old Testament prophets, knew nothing about!

For example, the parable of the soils explained how the king could be rejected by Israel. The soil was bad! The nation had experienced a partial hardening (cf. Rom. 11:25). But the seeds would grow fruitfully in some people (the willing hearers and disciples)! The parable of the leavening process explains just how the kingdom will grow (internally and spiritually; cf. Rom. 16:25–26) until Israel finally does come around and accept its king (at his second coming, cf. Rom. 11:25–27).

C. The Secrets of the Kingdom

At the heart of Jesus' purpose in this discourse is the revealing of "the secrets of the kingdom of heaven" to his disciples, while hiding these developments from the faithless (13:11). "Mystery" is the transliteration of the Greek *musterion*. In English usage, a secret or mystery is usually understood as something we can understand only in a limited way.

However, this is not the New Testament meaning of the word *musterion*. In the Bible it means a fully understandable truth that has been unknown in the past simply because it had not yet been revealed. But it is now something that has been revealed. Jesus was revealing for the first time truths about the kingdom that not even the Old Testament prophets knew about. The Old Testament prophets did not visualize two comings for the Messiah. Therefore, they did not visualize any period between these two comings. To them, when the king came, Israel would rule.

For the "secrets of the kingdom" to be "given" to the disciples indicates that to them certain realities are being revealed for the first time. It had never been known before that the nature of the kingdom's growth would be in a more hidden inner form. The kingdom would not immediately, at Messiah-King's initial coming, take on its full outer reality. The kingdom has been planted by Jesus the Messiah-King, but it would grow now by an inner spiritual dynamic until he comes again to bring it to full realization.

D. Summary

After the demonstrations of disbelief in Matthew 9–12, Jesus' disciples were left with a question: What now? If Israel's king is here but is rejected, how will the long promised kingdom be pursued? Several related and unanswered questions flow from this most basic question: (1) Why do not more people respond to the Messiah? (2) Why do the righteous kingdom citizens still have to live with evil and oppressive people? (3) How long will kingdom citizens have to endure evil? (4) How can we be assured of final justice? (5) How can the kingdom of heaven emerge from such small beginnings? (6) Is this kingdom worth my life? (7) If the kingdom of heaven has experienced this unexpected delay, how should we think about the Old Testament Scriptures?

In Matthew 13, Jesus' discourse answers those questions in such a way that those who are genuinely seeking the answers will find them. But those who ask the same questions mockingly will not understand or accept the truth of Jesus' answers, so they will fall deeper into disbelief.

VII. TEACHING OUTLINE

A. INTRODUCTION

1. Lead Story: On Building a House or a Kingdom
2. Context: Matthew 13:1–52 is the third of five discourses by Jesus recorded in Matthew. The time cues given by Matthew (13:1–3,10,36,53) lead us to believe that Jesus spoke these things during a single teaching event.
3. Transition: The parables in Jesus' teaching served both to reveal and to hide the truth. In Matthew 11–12, the hardened hearts of most of Israel, particularly its leaders, were revealed. From chapter 13 on, Jesus began his predominant use of parables as the vehicle for public teaching, because those whose hearts are hardened will choose not to accept or understand the truth behind the parables. Jesus explained his use of parables in terms of judgment. Because they chose to disbelieve, he would make his teaching even harder to understand and believe.

   In the first twelve chapters of this Gospel, Jesus played his prophetic role as the sovereign Son of David, Israel's king, offering the long-awaited kingdom. In light of Israel's rejection of the king and his judgment of Israel, Matthew 13 explains a significant change in Jesus' role emphasis as well as the manner in which the kingdom will be pursued. The second half of Matthew's Gospel will portray Jesus more clearly as the sacrificial Son of Abraham who has come to take away the sins of the world.

B. COMMENTARY

1. The Kingdom: For Listeners Only (13:1–23)
2. The Kingdom: The Faithful Must Coexist with Evil until Judgment (13:24–30)
3. The Kingdom: Surprising Impact (13:31–33)
4. The King Begins to Speak Only in Parables to the Crowds (13:34–35)
5. The Kingdom: Judgment on Evil, Exaltation of the Righteous (13:36–43)
6. The Kingdom: Surprising Value (13:44–46)

7. The Kingdom: The Faithful Must Coexist with Evil until Judgment (13:47–50)
8. The Kingdom: Valuing the Old, Committing to the New (13:51–52)
9. The King Is Rejected in His Hometown (13:53–58)

C. CONCLUSION

1. Wrap-up: Jesus' parables teach us a significant lesson. They challenge us to trust the king enough to yield to him everything we are. This is an investment that will pay rich dividends.
2. Personal Challenge: Believers are privileged with insight into God's truth, but even we must beware of the danger of a resistant heart and seek the king and his kingdom with all our strength.

VIII. ISSUES FOR DISCUSSION

1. What did Jesus mean when he spoke of "secrets" or "mysteries" in this chapter of Matthew?
2. Why did Jesus teach in parables?
3. What is the central meaning of the parable of the sower?
4. What truth about the kingdom did Jesus emphasize through the parable of the yeast?
5. What is the central meaning of the parable of the net?

Matthew 14–15

The King Broadens His Ministry . . . Reaching Beyond Israel

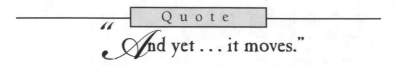

Quote

"*And* yet ... it moves."

Galileo Galilei, referring
to the rotation of the earth

Matthew 14–15

IN A NUTSHELL

Following Israel's rejection of Jesus as the Messiah-King, our Lord broadens his ministry to include the Gentiles. The feeding of the five thousand Jews, and the later feeding of the four thousand Gentiles, portrays Jesus as God's provision of miraculous, life-giving bread to all people. When confronted by the Pharisees about his failure to observe their standards of "cleanness," Jesus calls them blind guides, contrasting true, worshipful obedience with false, outward hypocrisy.

The King Broadens His Ministry ... Reaching Beyond Israel

I. INTRODUCTION

Blind Tradition Misses the Point

$\mathcal{W}$e have all heard the story of the woman whose baked ham was legendary for its taste and quality. As part of her careful regimen, she always cut both ends of the ham off before placing it in the oven. People assumed this strange procedure was a critical part of her "secret." One observer asked, "What is the purpose of cutting the ends off the ham?" The cook replied, "Mother always did it that way." She had always assumed it was a necessary part of the family secret. But it was a good and reasonable question. She would ask her mother from whom she had learned it. Her mother indicated that her mother, too, had always done it that way. Determined to get to the bottom of this technique, both mother and daughter approached the aged grandmother to learn the secret before she died. "Grandma, why did you always cut both ends off the ham before baking it?" Grandma replied, "My pan was too small."

Traditions can be like that. Unthinking repetition of meaningless behavior. Serving no purpose. Accomplishing nothing.

In the same way Jesus introduced in Matthew 14–15 an unconventional thought—God is pleased with faith, not tradition.

Israel's religious faith had become incredibly rigid. The pharisaical religious system had become so far removed from the original purpose of the Old Testament "laws" that the people were tied to meaningless repetition. And they experienced no personal relationship with God. John the Baptist had played the dirge. Jesus had played the flute. But there was no movement.

Jesus, however, was about to move—away from Israel and away from the false traditions. He was looking for people of faith. And he was about to find them among the Gentiles.

Meaningful interpersonal relationships are built primarily on love and trust, not rules. Meaningful religious faith is the same. The faith that Jesus espoused consisted of an intimate personal relationship with the living God. It was an intense, personal faith built upon love and trust. It was not rigid institutional tradition.

II. COMMENTARY

The King Broadens His Ministry . . . Reaching Beyond Israel

MAIN IDEA: *True, biblical faith is not the outward religiosity many people believe it to be, but submission to God's truth.*

Matthew 13 explained the pursuit of the new kingdom until Jesus comes a second time. Jesus was moving toward the announcement of his church (16:18). The Jewish nation would be temporarily shelved. The contrast between Jews and Gentiles is prominent in Matthew 14–15. After his debate with the hypocrites over what was clean and unclean (15:1–20), Jesus ministered in Gentile territory, where he found an enthusiastic reception. His ministry to the Gentiles made the point that the Jewish leaders were wrong in their assessment of what was clean and unclean. Jesus' actions spoke more loudly than words, redefining the popular idea of what was "clean" and acceptable to God.

Further demonstrating God's acceptance of both Jews and Gentiles are two pairs of parallel stories: (1) the miraculous feeding of the five thousand Jews (14:13–21) and the miraculous feeding of the four thousand Gentiles (15:32–39); and (2) the miraculous healing of many Jews (14:34–36) and the miraculous healing of many Gentiles (15:29–31). Possibly standing in parallel contrast are the stories of the disciples' disbelief (14:22–33) and the Gentile woman's persistent faith (15:21–28).

The three Jewish stories mentioned in the preceding paragraph are clustered together, as are the three Gentile stories, with the debate over cleanness and uncleanness separating the two clusters.

A The King Loses His Friend and Forerunner to Kingdom Opposition (14:1–12)

SUPPORTING IDEA: *The faithful believer will live by the truth, although it costs him his life; the faithless will always take the path of least resistance.*

Flowing out of a story that dealt with Jesus' identity and the kingdom opposition (13:53–58) even in his own hometown, this story began with the question of Jesus' identity (14:1–2) and shifted quickly into another example of kingdom opposition (14:3–12). In the former story, it was the Messiah-King himself who was rejected; here it is the Messiah's forerunner.

14:1–2. The phrase **at that time** connects the two stories. It means "at about that time." We know from the broader context that Herod Antipas had a fearful and superstitious respect for John and Jesus (14:5,9; Mark 6:19–20; Luke 23:8). So the news of Jesus' miracles, validating him as a prophet from

God, caused Herod to identify Jesus with John, whom he knew also to be God's prophet. Herod was obsessed with guilt over John's execution and may have seen John's "ghost" around every corner. So it is not surprising that he jumped to the conclusion that Jesus was John, back from the dead to torment him.

14:3–5. To explain Herod's confusion about Jesus' identity, Matthew provided a flashback (John had already been beheaded; here we learn how it happened), telling how John's execution came about. This story flows naturally into the account of Jesus' feeding of the five thousand (see 14:13) as Jesus left the "center of power" and moved to the "little people."

John followed the pattern of many Old Testament prophets in confronting the civil rulers of their day (e.g., 1 Kgs. 17:1; 18:1–46; 20:35–43; 22:1–28; 2 Kgs. 1). Herod had gone to Rome, where he met Herodias, the wife of his half-brother Philip. John warned Herod that his adulterous relationship with his brother's wife was "unlawful" (Lev. 18:6,16; 20:21). Both Herod and Herodias had divorced their spouses to marry each other. To silence John, Herod arrested him. In spite of his superstitious respect for John, Herod's grudge was strong enough that he would have preferred to execute John immediately, but he knew John was popular with the Jewish people. They saw John as a prophet from God. Herod suspected this was true, but his primary motivation for not killing John sooner was fear of the people.

14:6–8. But Herod was ambushed by his own lust and the trickery of Herodias, who despised John without sharing Herod's respect for John or the people. When John confronted Herod, he was also confronting Herodias, Herod's partner in adultery. There was no reason for her not to execute John. At Herod's birthday celebration, he was so impressed by the dancing of his niece, the daughter of Herodias, that he made an oath before his dinner guests to give the girl anything she asked. Herodias was hoping for just such a promise, and she prompted her daughter to ask for John's head **on a platter**. Such a ceremonial presentation of John's head symbolized Herodias's victory in her moral battle against John. Like many modern "death merchants," she thought she had won. But another day is coming (cf. Heb. 11, esp. vv. 32–40).

14:9–11. Because of Herod's superstitious respect for John and his fear of the people, he was **distressed** at the idea of executing John. But his oath before witnesses bound him to keep his promise or lose face. So he commanded that John be beheaded, thereby bypassing the Jewish requirement of a trial before an execution. Verse 9 refers to Herod as **the king** (even though his primary title was "tetrarch") perhaps with sarcasm, and possibly comparing him to the evil kings of the Old Testament who martyred God's prophets (cf. also with Jesus' prediction that his followers would be arrested and brought before "governors and kings"; 10:18–19).

John's head was given to Herod's niece, who then presented it to her mother, revealing Herodias's role in the trickery that led to John's death. She had "won," and this was her prize. John, the last of the Old Testament prophets, passed from the scene.

14:12. Meanwhile, John's disciples were given custody of John's body, and they buried him. The loss of their teacher must have taken them beyond the end of hope. Who would they follow now? In their despair, they came to Jesus, knowing he would want to know about this tragic development. Perhaps they looked to Jesus to fill the leadership vacuum left by John's death. After all, John's entire ministry had been to lead people to the Messiah.

B The King Feeds Five Thousand Jews (14:13–21)

> **SUPPORTING IDEA:** *Our gracious God will provide abundantly for those of the household of faith, thus assuring us that we can risk complete obedience.*

This account of Jesus' miraculous feeding of five thousand Jews is the parallel counterpart to his later feeding of four thousand Gentiles (15:32–39). It also launches a series of accounts that may be intended to portray Jesus as the second Moses and as God's provision of miraculous, life-giving bread to all people (14:13–16:12). On the "bread" theme, the life-saving manna that God provided for forty years comes to mind. Again, God was providing miraculous sustenance for his people, symbolized in the food provided by Jesus for the five thousand. John was much more forthright in his presentation of Jesus as the Bread of Life (John 6:30–35,47–58), but the imagery can be found in Matthew's two miraculous feedings. It is also stated clearly later at the Lord's Supper (26:26–29).

The story also represents Jesus as the Messiah who will fulfill the future salvation promises. For example, as in 8:11, people will recline at the messianic banquet. The same verb is used here of the people "reclining" on the grass (14:19). The people's hunger was completely satisfied, just as all their needs will be in eternity (Isa. 25:6–8; 66:11).

This miracle is significant because it compared Jesus to Moses, highlighted his ability to provide the needs of his people, and confirmed his ability to provide the messianic banquet (Ps. 132:15; Isa. 25:6).

Jesus may have intended this event to be, above all else, a training opportunity for his disciples. Notice how he challenged their faith by saying, **You give them something to eat** (14:16), before proceeding with the miracle. He also saw to it that the disciples distributed the bread to the thousands. It must have left an impression. His preparation of his disciples was a task of great importance. On them rested the future of the kingdom.

14:13–14. While we cannot be certain of the specific reason Jesus withdrew, it seems to fit the context if we understand him to be moving further from the centers of opposition to the countryside. It is also possible that Jesus had heard Herod was beginning to focus attention on him (14:1–2), so he withdrew to avoid the kind of treatment John had received.

Matthew's language gives a fourfold emphasis to Jesus' desire for solitude: (1) he **withdrew**; (2) he went **by boat** so the crowds on foot could not follow him; (3) he went **to a solitary place**; and (4) he went **privately**, emphasizing separation from the crowds, not from his disciples. If we assume that Jesus withdrew to mourn John's death, we see that Jesus had a deep emotional side and desired to be alone with his circle of friends.

In Luke 9:10 we are told that the "solitary place" was near Bethsaida, which was most likely on the northeast coast of the Sea of Galilee. The people, in such desperate need of a shepherd, and perhaps also being shaken by John's execution, followed by foot when they learned of Jesus' departure. **From the towns** emphasizes the desolate setting to which they followed Jesus.

Verse 14 implies that the crowd arrived at Jesus' destination ahead of him (clearly stated in Mark 6:33–34). It is possible that his journey by boat never took him out of sight of land. Those on land could have watched as they ran, anticipating where he would land. The crowd was **large**, and the crowd was needy. Even though he had not had a chance to process his grief over John, the Messiah-King **had compassion** on the people, and he went back to work, healing their sick. So strongly motivated was he to fulfill his mission of compassion that he put aside his deep personal needs until later that evening (14:23).

14:15–16. But his compassion did not stop at healing their sick. As evening came the people grew hungry. Jesus acted on their need for food, but not before setting his disciples up for an important lesson.

Dinnertime had come and gone, and the disciples drew Jesus' attention to the **solitary place**, with no food sources present. Apparently this location was not as remote as that in the second feeding (15:32–33), because the walk to a nearby village market was not unreasonable. The disciples urged Jesus to send the people away to buy food.

This was not an unreasonable request, assuming there was no food source present. However, there *was* another food source present, so Jesus treated their request as ridiculous. "Why should they go away? Provide them with food yourselves," is the impact of Jesus' challenge (the "you" is emphatic in **You give them**). He knew the disciples would not understand, but he issued the challenge to get their attention and to make it obvious how far they had to go in learning faith. This entire miracle is a lesson in the disciples' training.

14:17–20. Matthew got right to the point by abbreviating the story, leaving out details such as the boy who provided the loaves and fish (John 6:9) and the additional objections the disciples put forth in Mark 6:37.

The five loaves and two fish were probably so small (John 6:9) that one or two men could have eaten them in a single meal. This crowd needed a recipe that would feed ten thousand or more (the **five thousand** of 14:21 are only the men; we must estimate the additional women and children). The possibility of a feast arose when Jesus said, **Bring them here to me** (14:18). He himself would be the provider.

Jesus ordered the people to **sit down** on the grass. With the loaves and fish in his hands, he looked **up to heaven** (heaven represents God himself) and **gave thanks**, which means "speak well of, praise." There is no object for "gave thanks," but this was the common way to speak of giving thanks for one's food.

A good Jew would thank God for providing each meal, but this prayer was even more significant. It acknowledged the God of heaven as the source of authority and power behind the miracle that was about to happen. However, this act of provision was no more difficult for God than his normal, daily provision of food. We should not minimize the miracle of this passage, but let it raise our awareness of God's constant provision for our daily needs.

Jesus then broke the loaves and fish and began distributing the pieces to the crowd through his disciples. We do not know if Jesus kept giving arm-loads to the disciples or whether he gave each of them a small portion that multiplied as they handed it out. All Matthew tells us is the result: **They all ate and were satisfied.** And, as is characteristic of our gracious God, he provided more than was needed. The twelve baskets indicate the abundance of provision. These baskets may also relate to the fact that this was a feeding of Jews (represented by twelve tribes), in contrast to the Gentile feeding (15:32–39), where there were seven baskets of leftovers.

14:21. To this point, one might assume the crowd was a few score or possibly a few hundred. This would be miracle enough. But now we learn one last astounding fact—the crowd was far more than five thousand, very possibly ten thousand or more, if women and children were counted. Choose some stadium or arena and picture what fraction of the seating would be filled by ten thousand people. Then imagine these people all being satisfied by five loaves of bread and two fish. Then you will begin to comprehend the impact of this miracle—and, by extension, the impact of God's provision of our every need through Jesus, the Messiah-King. And, by personalizing it, the impact upon those twelve disciples.

The King Tests His Disciple's Faith (14:22–33)

SUPPORTING IDEA: *God appreciates our baby steps of faith, but as we grow he expects more than baby steps.*

Jesus probably intended the feeding of the five thousand to be primarily a lesson in faith for his disciples. Here, on the heels of the first lesson of the day comes the second lesson. The disciples had demonstrated no confidence in Jesus' ability to feed the crowd, but at least Peter began to show the first flicker of true faith. With much yet to learn, the disciples came closer than ever to an understanding of who Jesus was (14:33).

14:22–23. It was already evening when the people were fed. Jesus had not yet had his time of solitude for which he had come to this secluded spot. As soon as the miraculous feeding was completed (**immediately**), Jesus ordered his disciples back into the boat to precede him to their next destination.

Few people went up on the hilly terrain overlooking the lake. Nothing grew there and the roads used lower-lying routes. So Jesus was assured of solitude **up on a mountainside** above the site of the feeding. He used this solitude for conversation with his Father. This was a frequent practice for Jesus, but,because he was so popular and so much in demand, privacy was rare for him. Jesus must have had to work hard at protecting time to pray.

14:24. Meanwhile, the disciples were having some difficulty making the five-mile journey that cut across the northern tip of the lake from Bethsaida toward Gennesaret (14:34). They were fighting contrary winds, which implies they were having to row. Not only were they having to row into the wind, but they were also being **buffeted** by high waves. We have already seen (8:23–27) that violent storms could descend on the Sea of Galilee without warning. Apparently the disciples did not fear for their lives this time. But the going was far from easy, and there was some degree of danger. By now they had rowed **a considerable distance** from land.

14:25–26. According to Jewish time reckoning, the day begins at sunset (about 6:00 P.M.). The Jews divided the twelve-hour night into three watches, but the Gospel writers used the Roman custom of four three-hour watches—6 to 9 P.M., 9 P.M. to midnight, midnight to 3 A.M., and 3 to 6 A.M. It was during this last period, in the dark hours before dawn—after the disciples had battled the waves and Jesus had prayed through the night—that Jesus decided it was time to catch up with his disciples by walking across the tossing sea.

The disciples had no reason to expect him to come across the water. In fact, they had no reason to believe such a thing could be done (except to extrapolate from the power they saw in Jesus' other miracles, an unlikely prospect given their immaturity). So, naturally, they were **terrified** (from a verb meaning "to stir up, trouble") and gave voice to their fear in two ways. They gave each other the only explanation that made sense in light of their prior experience: **It's a ghost!** They could not imagine anyone or anything with physical form walking across water. And they **cried out in fear**. They had been through a long, busy day and an even longer, torturous night on the stormy water. Fatigue, combined with superstition and lack of faith-filled insight, set them up for a response of pure terror when they saw Jesus.

14:27. Jesus, the compassionate and patient teacher, **immediately** spoke three statements of comfort and encouragement: (1) **Take courage**, (2) **It is I**, and (3) **Don't be afraid**. This may not have been a rebuke but an effort to comfort the disciples. Jesus knew their faith was still in its infancy. Still, he would issue a rebuke to Peter in 14:31.

14:28–29. Peter's statement to the Lord took the form of a first-class condition (a construction in the original language that assumes the truth of the condition). Peter was at least beginning to be convinced that the figure on the waves was indeed Jesus, and he was beginning to be convinced that he and the other disciples could do some incredible things in his power. Was Peter running a bit of an experiment here? Probably so, but the realities of the moment—wind, water, waves—still overwhelmed him. This seems consistent with his impulsive enthusiasm.

Peter is to be commended for his belief that Jesus could make him walk on water, but his confidence was that of a baby just learning to walk. Twice in Matthew, the hypocrites would ask for a sign to back up Jesus' claims (12:38–45; 16:1–4). Both times Jesus denied them, because he knew they would not believe him even if he provided the sign. He had not come to put on impressive shows in an attempt to create faith where none existed. However, faith did exist in Peter, although it was small. Jesus, like a patient parent teaching a baby to walk, allowed Peter this demonstration of his power to nurture Peter's faith to the next level of maturity. He commanded Peter, **Come.** Both Peter and the water obeyed the Messiah-King, and Peter walked toward Jesus on the water.

14:30–31. But only a moment later, what Peter could see with his physical eyes (the violent, stormy sea) became larger in his mind than what can be seen only through the "eyes" of a faith-filled heart. There is a healthy, respectful fear we need to have before the Lord (Prov. 1:7), but the fear we feel toward anything that seems bigger than the Lord is a sign of small faith. Peter's underdeveloped faith feared the storm more than the Lord, so the Lord allowed him to sink into a dark, angry sea. Jesus was always teaching his disciples. Every moment, every conversation, and every demonstration were intended to develop his church's foundational leaders.

In that moment of terror, Peter called out with the most basic expression of faith possible: **Lord, save me!** (cf. 8:25). The Lord loves that kind of cry, because it is a sign that the person has come to the end of self-reliance and realizes there is nowhere else to turn but to the Lord. Whether from the unbeliever who knows he is helpless on his own or from the believer who has been self-striving for years and has only met with frustration and failure, the simple cry, "Save me!" is music to the Father's ears (cf. Pss. 18:16; 69:1–3; 144:7).

The Messiah answered Peter's cry **immediately** by reaching out and grabbing him. Then Jesus said calmly, **You of little faith . . . why did you doubt?** The issue here was not the *amount* of Peter's faith, but Peter's culpability. The smallest faith in the right object is effective. Jesus was chiding Peter, not his faith. The problem was that his faith was supplanted by doubt. In all this time, even Peter, one of Jesus' closest friends, had not learned to trust the king fully.

Jesus had also used the phrase **you of little faith** to address the disciples when he calmed the storm in 8:23–27 (also in 6:30; 16:8; Luke 12:28). Two important tests of faith for Jesus' disciples have now happened on a stormy sea. Given the awe with which most cultures view the power of nature, Jesus knew that if they could see him as greater than nature, they would be closer to mature faith.

14:32–33. God had evidently sent a storm primarily for this test, for the wind stopped as soon as Jesus and Peter climbed into the boat. This a sign of Jesus' authority, and it indicated the lesson was over. Now they could proceed without difficulty to their destination.

This entire series of events was a cluster of miracles (Jesus walking on the water, Peter walking on the water, the wind stopping) that brought the disciples to a greater understanding of Jesus than they had ever had before. Their response was to worship Jesus. This was more than the respect of a student for a teacher. The word implies awe and adoration. **Truly you are the Son of God** was their confession. In that moment, there was no doubt in their minds, although doubt would return to plague them several times before their faith was fully grown. This storm experience was great encouragement for the followers of a king who had been rejected by the leaders of Israel. Jesus was the king!

🄳 Many Jews Place Healing Faith in the King (14:34–36)

> **SUPPORTING IDEA:** *The Lord will graciously reward any expression of true faith.*

This summary of Jesus' healing ministry among the Jews is a contrasting parallel with the similar summary of his healing ministry among the Gentiles in 15:29–31.

14:34–36. Jesus and his disciples completed their journey to Genneseret in Jewish territory. As soon as the people there realized who had come to their town, word spread quickly. Once again Jesus was inundated with the sick seeking his healing. These people had the same kind of faith as the bleeding woman of 9:20–22. They sought only to touch the **edge of his cloak**, probably meaning the tassels on the edge of his garment. In fact, they **begged** him to let them touch his cloak. This touch brought healing to all who touched him. Such was the compassion and authority of the Messiah-King. The crowd's begging may have been intensified because they knew other leaders who would not allow themselves to be touched. Many of the

Pharisees, for example, would have been horrified at the thought of rubbing shoulders in a crowd like this.

E The King Versus the Hypocrites: What Is Clean and Unclean? (15:1–20)

SUPPORTING IDEA: *Superficial, artificial "faith" is actually the enemy of true, biblical faith.*

To this point Jesus had focused on ministry to the Jews. Now he was confronted by the Pharisees and scribes over the controversy of what is clean and unclean. This debate served as one of three or four turning points for Jesus. In the following context (beginning with 15:21) and through the end of Matthew 15, Jesus went directly into Gentile territory. He wanted to prove the point that the hypocrites were wrong in their standards of "cleanness." Perhaps he also went out of exasperation because of the persistent rejection he had received among the Jews. This foreshadows his announcement in 16:18 of the "new wineskin," the church. The "cleanness" debate served as a bridge between Jesus' Jewish ministry and his opening of ministry to the Gentiles.

15:1–2. For some time, Jesus had attracted a following from regions far and near, including Jerusalem. But this was the first time Matthew specifically recorded a confrontation between Jesus and any of the religious leaders from Jerusalem—the spiritual capital of Israel and the authoritative center of Judaism. It is possible that some of the religious leaders in previous encounters had been from Jerusalem, but this was the first time Matthew made specific mention of them and where they were from.

Many of Jesus' previous conflicts had probably been with local synagogue leaders in the various cities he had visited. His notoriety and the Pharisees' frustration with him had grown to the point that Jesus' opponents were now calling in the "big guns."

These men were concerned about **the tradition of the elders**. This was fitting for both the Pharisees and the scribes. Both held a fascination with the detailed implications of the Old Testament Law in every aspect of life. Through the centuries the Jewish authorities had put into spoken and written form what the law would mean in every possible situation. This oral law was not the Law of Moses but "the tradition of the elders." The Jewish scholars had gone far outside God's intended meaning for the Law, creating thousands of man-made regulations that were irrelevant or burdensome. Some of these traditions actually contradicted the original intent of God's Law.

The specific regulation in question here was the ceremonial washing of one's hands before eating. Even if Jesus' disciples had washed with soap and water, but had not used the acceptable procedure, they were not considered ritually clean by the Pharisees.

The New Testament refers to a variety of authoritative man-made traditions as "the tradition of the elders"(Matt. 15:2), "human tradition" (Col. 2:8), and "the traditions of my fathers" (Gal. 1:14). Most often in view, at least with the Jewish opposition, was a body of oral teachings known as the Talmud and Mishnah. These teachings consisted of comment on the Law, interpretation of the Law, and detailed rules of behavior.

Elevating human interpretation or tradition to a place of authority alongside Scripture is a plague that has infected every generation. Jesus' conflict with man-made tradition was often at the forefront of his ministry. Unfortunately, he might well regard many of our modern "authorities" the same way. What Jesus confronted here was not so different from the unwritten traditions of every denomination. We tend to put great stock in our traditions. Unfortunately, many of them are far removed from the teachings of Scripture.

15:3. Rather than defend his disciples' handwashing practices, Jesus went on the offensive, showing that the Pharisees' original question was foolish and did not warrant primary attention. He addressed their question (15:10–11,15–20), but there was a more important issue that he addressed first. Jesus expressed greater concern over their *transgression* (a word that literally means "to turn aside from the path") of **the command of God for the sake of your tradition.** Note the strong contrast between *God's* commandment and *your* tradition. While the hypocrites claimed to enhance God's Law through their tradition, Jesus claimed that God's Law and their tradition were mutually exclusive. When their man-made regulations took precedence, those regulations took a person astray from the straight path of God's Law (cf. the wide and narrow gates and roads of 7:13–14).

15:4–6. Having leveled the general accusation in verse 3, Jesus gave a specific example of their betrayal of God's commandment, beginning with a statement of the commandment in verse 4. He then explained their departure from it in verses 5–6.

For indicates that Jesus was about to provide supporting evidence for the accusation of 15:3. Jesus drew on two separate instructions from four passages in the Pentateuch to emphasize the principle that God's people are to honor their parents. The commandment, **Honor your father and mother,** is one of the Ten Commandments, found in Exodus 20:12 and Deuteronomy 5:16. Jesus chose a commandment that was central to the Jewish faith, well-known and unmistakable in its intent. Then he reinforced the commandment by referring to additional Mosaic legislation specifying the punishment for anyone who broke this commandment: **Anyone who curses his father or mother must be put to death** (Exod. 21:17; Lev. 20:9). By adding this quote, Jesus drove home the gravity of transgressing this particular commandment.

But indicates the contrast between what followed and what preceded between God's Law and the hypocrites' tradition. Note also the contrast between **God said** (15:3) and **you say** (15:4; *you* is emphatic). Jesus was shaming the hypocrites for pitting human words against God's Word.

Jesus was referring to a Jewish practice in which a person gave a **gift** that was **devoted to God** so it could be kept for oneself and not used for the good of others. Part of an adult child's obligation in honoring his parents was to care for them financially when they were in need, particularly as they grew older and were no longer able to make an adequate living. Widowed mothers or grandmothers were especially desperate for help. There was little opportunity for them to earn money, and they were unlikely to find a new husband to support them (1 Tim. 5:8). The Pharisees' loophole ("sorry, it is all 'devoted' to God") kept the younger generation from having to take care of their parents in their old age, and thus contradicted the Word of God.

By this means, said Jesus, the hypocrites **nullify** ("make void, revoke;" only here and Mark 7:13; Gal. 3:17) God's word **for the sake of your tradition.** Very possibly the ancient Jewish scholars who came up with this regulation had elderly parents they did not want to support. Or perhaps they were concocted by leaders who wanted to keep people's gifts "to God" that would otherwise have gone to the people's parents. Over time the "gifts" were allowed to stay in the hands of the "givers."

15:7–9. Jesus then showed how the Pharisees and scribes had fulfilled Isaiah's eighth-century B.C. prophecy (Isa. 29:13) concerning the hypocrisy of Judah. In fact, Jesus' statement was quite pointed, saying that Isaiah was prophesying about **you.** There was a clear continuity between the hypocrites then and in Jesus' day.

Jesus addressed the Pharisees and scribes here as **hypocrites.** The English word is transliterated from the earlier classic Greek term for "one who wears a mask" on stage in a Greek drama—an actor or pretender—although, by Jesus' day the language used the term exclusively for its present negative meaning. A hypocrite is a person who puts on an outward display that is not representative of what is truly inside. (See comment at 6:2.) As Jesus had demonstrated in 15:3–6, the religious leaders were putting on a show of spirituality and devotion to God and his Word. In reality, they were in rebellion against God and his Word.

Isaiah 29 is the second of four "woe oracles" (Isa. 28–31). In Isaiah 29:1–8, Yahweh describes the punishment he will bring down on Jerusalem. Beginning in Isaiah 29:9, he begins to transition into the reasons why he is judging Jerusalem. It must have been fearsome for these Pharisees to hear the words of condemnation by their great prophet Isaiah leveled at them: "Blind yourselves and be sightless . . . [your] worship of me is made up only of rules taught by men" (Isa. 29:9,13). The language Jesus used heightened the contrast between true, worshipful obedience and false, outward hypocrisy.

15:10–11. Having dealt with the real issue that stood between him and the hypocrites, Jesus returned to their original questions about handwashing (15:2). Instead of addressing the Pharisees and scribes, Jesus summoned the crowd, as though to invite them into the debate and to evaluate who was right about ritual handwashing. He then addressed the crowd.

Listen and understand is essentially the same as, "He who has ears, let him hear" (11:15; 13:9,43). Only those who would "hear" with a heart of faith and "understand" would accept Jesus' answer to the question of the Pharisees and scribes.

Jesus responded to the question of 15:2 with a "parable" (cf. 15:15) which reversed the assumption underlying the original question. The Pharisees and scribes assumed that ritual defilement came from unclean things outside the body, entering through the mouth. Jesus said that defilement comes because of unclean things from *within* a person's body, exiting out through the mouth.

Unclean is from a word meaning "to make common," as opposed to ceremonially holy and pure. Jesus was not denying that people can become unacceptable before God. He differed with the religious leaders on how a person becomes defiled before God. They said God evaluated what goes into a person from outside, but Jesus said God evaluated what comes out of a person from inside.

15:12. Some time after this confrontation, the disciples tried to point out to the Lord that the Pharisees were **offended** at Jesus' words. They were probably referring to the entire sequence, including the confrontation over oral tradition (15:3–9) and Jesus' parabolic defense of his disciples' ceremonial hygiene practices (15:10–11). This began another of Jesus' private conversations for his disciples' ears only, continuing through 15:20 and including Jesus' explanation of the parable.

15:13–14. Of course, Jesus was aware of the Pharisees' offense; he had intended to trip them up. His response, **Leave them,** did not deny the real danger involved in angering the Jewish leaders. His best course of action was to stand by the truth, not trying to pacify the Pharisees and not trying to convince them further about their faults.

Jesus' calm confidence came out of the assurance that the Pharisees would be judged justly—both by God (15:13) and by the natural consequences of their own blindness (15:14). The plant terminology (15:13) brings to mind the parable of the weeds (13:24–30,36–43). The hardened hearts of the Pharisees were not products of God's work. Although they claimed to represent God, they were actually some of the "weeds" planted by the Evil One. They were among those who, in rebellion against God, did evil themselves and caused others to do evil as well (13:41). So they would experience God's judgment. We will always have false religion in this world.

Using another illustration, Jesus said that the Pharisees were **blind guides** (15:14; also 23:16,24). He may have been referring to a title the Pharisees had given themselves—"guide of the blind" (Rom. 2:19). Any effective guide must know where he is going to guide another person. The foolishness of the situation is self-evident; only seeing people can guide blind people. A blind guide would be both arrogant and in serious denial about his own condition—both of which were true of the Pharisees.

The Pharisees thought they understood the law, but they were really ignorant of the law's meaning and guilty of contradicting it. Thinking they were leading those under them along the right path, they were actually leading themselves and their followers into eternal danger (**into a pit**). They were unwittingly bringing judgment on themselves.

15:15–16. Peter, acting as the spokesman for the disciples, asked Jesus to **explain the parable.** The disciples needed the explanations, but their "ears to hear" allowed them to accept the truth of the parable.

Jesus expressed disappointment in the disciples' lack of understanding. The word **still** compares Peter's lack of understanding with that of the Pharisees. If the disciples had understood the superiority of cleansing of the heart over ritual outward cleansing, they would have understood the parable. It was their inability to understand this principle that prompted Jesus' disappointment more than their inability to understand the parable. Their perspective, like that of many Christians today (more "politically correct" than biblical), was shaped and influenced more by their culture and peers than by their Lord and his Word. Though loyal and open to being taught, the disciples were often as far off the mark as the Pharisees were.

15:17. Jesus began explaining the parable by showing the things that go into a person's body from outside are harmless to his standing before God. We must distinguish carefully between washing for practical health purposes and the ceremonial washing that was at issue here.

If a person eats food with hands that are not ceremonially washed, the food is, in reality, no more or less clean (spiritually) than if that person had ceremonially washed. The body treats it the same either way. A person's decision one way or the other on ceremonial washing has no bearing on his or her standing before God. Even if the food or a person's hands are physically contaminated, and he becomes ill from the contamination, does not indicate he is unacceptable before God.

15:18–20. Jesus then revealed that it is not the mouth of a person that is the source of defilement, but the heart. The heart represents the invisible, "inner person." The inner person includes the mind and will—those components that determine moral character. The heart (not any external influence) is the source of all evil character, not the physical or spiritual "dirt" on a person's hands. The "renewing of your mind" (Rom. 12:2) is critical for every believer. Christ detailed here the principle that a person is as he thinks in his heart. Entry into the heart is through the eye and the ear, not the mouth.

Jesus listed seven defiling sins that begin in a person's heart. Some of these manifest themselves through avenues other than one's mouth (e.g., murder, theft), but Jesus was not inconsistent here. Although the debate began over eating and washing, Jesus now began to broaden the discussion to encompass the whole-person expression of the evil in one's heart. The mouth happened to be one of the most prominent tools for good and for evil (Jas. 3:1–12). Jesus' list of sins was not meant to be comprehensive, but he gave a series of examples.

Jesus mentioned **adultery**, a sexual sin that defiles a marriage vow. **Sexual immorality** is a broader category that includes all kinds of sexual sin. **Slander** includes all abusive speech, whether against God or other people.

▐F▐ The King Finds Faith in a Gentile Woman (15:21–28)

SUPPORTING IDEA: *True faith persists, guided by humility and truth.*

In the midst of the Pharisees' incessant spiritual whining, Jesus found incredible faith in a Gentile woman. Devout Jews would not have considered entering a Gentile's home, because they deemed such an act to be ceremonially defiling. Jews avoided Gentile territory out of prejudice and fear. Jesus' journey into Gentile territory took place immediately after the debate with the Jerusalem Jewish leaders. Matthew's account follows a chronological order in these later chapters. Jesus wanted to send two messages by this sequence of events.

First, he was backing up his challenge to the popular misconception regarding ceremonial cleanness and defilement (15:10–20). In 15:21–39, Jesus would demonstrate that it was the inner character (a heart of faith) that determined acceptability before God, not a person's nationality (an outward trait). A Gentile woman and thousands of other Gentiles (15:21–31) would express greater faith in Jesus than the Jews (cf. the centurion in 8:5–13). And the Father would manifest his acceptance of their hearts by performing the healings and the miraculous feeding of the four thousand (15:32–39).

Second, Jesus was demonstrating his frustration with disbelieving Israel (11:16–24; 13:10–17; 15:7–9). Jesus decided that the "washing" controversy of 15:1–20 was to be the "last straw." He was not abandoning Israel entirely, for there would continue to be a faithful remnant, but he demonstrated to Israel that their faith was inadequate. Their faithlessness was accented when compared to ignorant Gentiles, who did not have the privileged revelation of God's mind and heart through the Scriptures. Jesus stopped treating Israel with "favored nation status." But because of God's promise to Abraham, Israel would always play a special role in his plan.

15:21. The place which Jesus departed from was probably Gennesaret, on the northwest shore of the Sea of Galilee (14:34). This was probably the location of the "washing" debate (15:1–20). From Gennesaret it would have been a forty-mile journey northwest to Tyre on the Mediterranean coast, and another twenty miles or so farther north along the coast to Sidon. How long Jesus was there and where exactly he went in **the region of Tyre and Sidon** is not stated in the text. The two cities, the epitome of Gentile "uncleanness," showed just how far into non-Jewish territory Jesus was willing to go to find such persistent faith. Jesus shook the dust of Israel off his feet as he reached out to the Gentiles.

15:22. Of all the Gentile nationalities, those of Canaanite descent would have been among the most abhorred by the Jews. The Canaanites were one of the idolatrous nations Israel was instructed to exterminate when they entered the Promised Land (Deut. 7:1–2). In fact, this particular group was so prominent in Palestine that the entire area was frequently called "the land of Canaan" (e.g., Gen. 12:5; Lev. 18:3). When the Canaanite woman heard of Jesus' arrival, she **came to him**—she pursued Jesus in her desperation.

This woman's cry was virtually identical to that of the two pairs of blind men in 9:27 and 20:30–31: "Son of David, have mercy on us!" Matthew's imagery in these three passages is unmistakable. In all three places, people who were perceived by others to be blind (figuratively blind in the case of this woman, because she, a Gentile, supposedly could not have known God's revealed Scriptures)—these people were the ones who "saw" Jesus clearly enough to proclaim his messianic title, "Son of David" (see comment on 1:1–17). In contrast, those who had the capacity to see physically with healthy eyes and spiritually through knowledge of the Scriptures were the ones who refused to acknowledge the identity of Jesus.

15:23–24. But Jesus ignored the woman, walking along the road without answering a single word. The disciples noticed. Was Jesus deliberately letting the woman's persistence sink in? She persisted so loudly that the disciples became annoyed. They repeatedly **urged** Jesus to send her away, **for she keeps crying out after us**. The woman was following Jesus and his disciples along the road.

Jesus finally stopped and gave a reason why he should not honor her request. **The lost sheep of Israel** was exactly the same phrase Jesus used in 10:6, instructing the Twelve to go only to the Jews. (See comment on 10:6 for the implications of this phrase.) Two thousand years earlier, God had made a promise to his friend Abraham, as well as to Abraham's son Isaac, and then Abraham's grandson Israel (Gen. 28:13–15; 32:28). Now he had come down in human form to keep his promise. But he had made no such promise to the descendants of Canaan, or anyone else outside of Israel (yet he had promised blessing on all nations through Israel, Gen. 12:3; 28:14). On this basis, Jesus could say he was sent by the Father to Israel only.

The disciples were aware of these covenant implications for the children of Israel. But it appeared that Jesus was going overboard to emphasize the contrast between this ignorant foreign woman's faith and lack of faith on the part of the arrogant teachers of Israel. They had the covenants and they should have known better. We can almost see Jesus asking the disciples, "Can you *see* this woman? Do you understand?"

15:25. The woman came close to Jesus and **knelt before him**. The verb *knelt* is the common word that means "to worship" (e.g., 15:9). In this vivid account, there is probably an emphasis on the literal meaning of the word, "to bow down," but there is also a deliberate contrast between this woman's genuine, heart-felt response to Jesus and Israel's false, superficial "worship" in 15:9. This woman knew she needed a Savior, but Israel thought they were doing fine on their own.

This is true worship in its most basic form—to cast ourselves on God in helplessness, acknowledging the Lord's power, love, and wisdom as our only source of help.

15:26. In that day, dogs as pets were far less common than today. Most dogs were wild, filthy, dangerous animals that roamed the streets. Jews commonly referred to Gentiles as "dogs," meaning "unclean, wild dogs." This single word explained the Jews' attitude toward Gentiles. Jesus referred to house dogs, alluding to the election of the Jews over the Gentiles, but in a much less derogatory manner.

Jesus was not denying the dogs their keep; he was saying it was not **right** for the **children's** portion to go to the **dogs**. While the Lord had demonstrated that he valued and loved the Gentiles, he was seeking to drive home to the disciples that he was shifting away from Israel as the national carrier of faith in the age between his two advents.

The promise to Abraham and Israel to bless all nations through them certainly *affected* the Gentiles, but it was not a *promise to* the Gentiles. This would change under the new covenant, in which there would no longer be a distinction between Jew and Gentile (1 Cor. 12:13; Eph. 2:11–3:6). God's covenant blessings would be equally available to both. The Gentiles had now been grafted into God's covenant with Israel (Rom. 11), but even this picture assumed some kind of priority for the Jews. The promise of the king's reign from the throne of David (cf. Rom. 11:29) had not been revoked. Jesus had come to bring believers of all nations into one kingdom and one church, but he had come first to keep his promise to Abraham, Isaac, and Jacob (Rom. 1:16).

15:27. Matthew began to show his readers the contrast between Jesus' statement and the woman's response. **Yes, Lord**, she began, humbly acknowledging her place in the household of faith. Then, with surprising wisdom, she continued, **but even the dogs eat the crumbs that fall from their master's table**. She worded her response not as a contradiction of what Jesus had just said but as an extension of the argument Jesus had presented. She seemed to grasp more of the reality of the moment than the disciples did.

Moreover, she displayed mature humility by continuing to refer to herself and other Gentiles as **dogs** and to Israel as **their masters**. At the same time, she called on the compassion of God, who promised blessings on all nations.

15:28. Finally, having seen ample proof of this dear woman's heart of faith, and having "rubbed it in" for the disciples, Jesus broke his feigned "resistance" with this enthusiastic response: **Woman, you have great faith!** Clearly, he was deeply touched by such mature and persistent faith in this Gentile woman.

There was no longer any reason to test the woman's faith, so Jesus assured her that her deepest desire had been granted. Just as with the centurion's servant (8:13), Jesus performed a long-distance healing. Matthew records that the woman's daughter was healed **that very hour**.

Ⓖ Many Gentiles Place Healing Faith in the King (15:29–31)

SUPPORTING IDEA: *True faith can be found in even the most unlikely people.*

This summary is a contrasting parallel to the earlier summary of Jesus' healing ministry among the Jews (14:34–36). Matthew wanted his readers to know that the Lord accepted and loved the Gentiles as much as the Jews and that the Gentiles were responding with at least as much faith as the faithful remnant of the Jews. In fact, contrasting the centurion and the Canaanite woman with the religious leaders, Matthew tells us that some Gentiles responded with even *greater* faith than most of the Jews.

15:29–31. Jesus traveled down the east side of the Sea of Galilee into the Gentile territory around the Decapolis, southeast of the lake. He chose a mountainside as a stopping place, and he sat down in the posture of a teacher. As usual, **great crowds** came because of his widespread reputation, bringing their sick for him to heal. **The lame, the blind, the crippled,** and **the mute** were representative of the many ailments Jesus healed. Note that Matthew finished the list with this phrase, **and many others**. The wording of 15:31 reminds us of Jesus' response to John the Baptizer in 11:4–6. Both are intended to remind us of the messianic promises of Isaiah 29:18–19 and 35:5–6.

The crowd marveled at Jesus' healings and **praised the God of Israel**. These people, like most pagans of that day, believed there were many gods—a worldview held by both Greek and Roman cultures as well as the ancient cultures that inhabited Palestine before Joshua. These people never doubted that the God of Israel existed, but now they had seen such a display that they praised him as superior to all the gods.

The King Feeds Four Thousand Gentiles (15:32–39)

SUPPORTING IDEA: *Our gracious God will provide abundantly even for those outside the household of faith, thus assuring that all can risk complete obedience.*

This passage is a contrasting parallel to the feeding of the five thousand Jews (14:13–21), further illustrating God's acceptance of the Gentiles. In addition to the geography, a clue to the different constituencies of the two audiences (one Jew, one Gentile) is found in the use of two different Greek words for "basket" used in the two passages. The term in Matthew 14 is the word commonly used among the Jews. The term used in Matthew 15 is the word used in the Gentile community.

15:32. The crowd was the same Gentile people who had been with Jesus on the mountainside near the Decapolis throughout three days of teaching and healing ministry (15:29–31). Jesus expressed privately to his disciples his compassion for the people's hunger. "They are patiently waiting with me" is the force of the Greek. The Greek verb used here means "to remain a long time" (also in Mark 8:2; Acts 11:23; 13:43; 18:18; 1 Tim. 1:3; 5:5).

Most of the people must have prepared in haste when they heard Jesus was nearby. At the prospect of seeing, speaking, or walking for the first time, hunger seemed a minor consideration. If they brought any food, it was probably very little. The people must have lingered for days, hanging on Jesus' every word, unable to walk away from his teaching and healing. Jesus seemed to be more concerned about their nutritional deprivation than they were. He did not want them to **collapse** from hunger on the road home. Jesus' comments imply that he desired to feed the people before they left.

15:33. We might wonder how the disciples could have forgotten the feeding of the five thousand (14:13–21). Perhaps they assumed that such a miracle could only be done among the Jews, since the symbolism of the messianic banquet applied only to Israel. Or, more likely, they truly did not understand the teaching purpose of the feedings (see 16:5–12).

The disciples started calculating how much bread they would need to feed the eight thousand or more people (see comments on 14:21; 15:38). This location was apparently even more isolated than the location near Bethsaida in the earlier feeding ("remote place").

15:34–38. At Jesus' inquiry, the disciples reported that they had **seven loaves** and **a few small fish**—more food than they had at the feeding of the five thousand, but still inadequate.

Jesus directed the people to sit on the ground. Then he took the food and gave thanks. Again Jesus broke the loaves and fish and distributed them through his disciples to the people. The results were exactly the same. **They all ate and were satisfied.** In this case, the leftover pieces filled seven baskets. Perhaps this was symbolic of the fact that this was not a Jewish audience (in 14:20 there were twelve baskets of leftovers, possibly symbolizing the twelve tribes of Israel).

Matthew again saved the count of the people for the end of the story to preserve its impact on the reader. The **four thousand** men is representative of at least twice that number of people, when including women and children (see comment on 14:21).

15:39. Now Jesus was assured that the people would be able to travel home without collapsing from hunger, so he declared his work finished by sending them away. Then he and his disciples returned to their boat and traveled to **the vicinity of Magadan.** Its location is uncertain, but Magadan may have been a variation on "Magdala," the home of Mary Magdalene on the west shore of the sea. Wherever this region was, it was almost certainly in Jewish territory. Awaiting Jesus there were the Pharisees and Sadducees (16:1), spoiling for the next battle. What a refreshing vacation from hypocrisy Jesus' Gentile detour must have been.

MAIN IDEA REVIEW: *True, biblical faith is not the outward religiosity many people believe it to be, but submission to God's truth.*

III. CONCLUSION

Sometimes it is appropriate to set aside our own needs to meet the deeper needs of others, but the time comes when we are useless to others unless we attend to our own needs.

PRINCIPLES

- Those who are faithful to Christ may be called to give their lives for his kingdom.
- Rash, foolish vows can cause us to do things we will later regret.
- Solitude and prayer are essential to a vibrant spiritual life.
- God honors our baby steps of faith.
- Faith is as good as the One we trust.
- God evaluates the quality of a person's heart.
- God loves the simple, humble, helpless cry "Lord, help!"
- True faith will persist in seeking God.
- God provides abundantly for believers and unbelievers alike.
- We may be surprised who are believers and unbelievers.

APPLICATIONS

- Beware of man-made regulations that contradict God's Word.
- Trust God for all of your needs.
- Be guided by humble submission to the truth about yourself and God.
- Persistently seek God.
- Pray for the courage to be faithful to death.

IV. LIFE APPLICATION

Jesus, Our Great Provider

In the *Biography of James Hudson Taylor* by Dr. & Mrs. Howard Taylor (London: China Inland Mission, 1965), we find a story about a man who truly trusted God for provision. As a young man Taylor was preparing to go to China to be a missionary, but he had determined to learn to live by faith alone while he was still in England. His resolve was to use prayer alone.

At the time he worked for a doctor and was paid a wage quarterly. As the time to receive his salary drew near, Taylor was disturbed that his employer said nothing about it. Taylor was nearly broke, but would not break his resolution and ask for the salary. While visiting a needy home on the Lord's Day, Taylor felt led of God to give his last coin to the needy family. The next day he received an anonymous gift through the mail, four times what he had given to the poor!

The following Saturday, the doctor finished up his work and said, "Taylor, is not your salary due again?" Taylor confirmed that it was and became disappointed when he learned that the doctor had completely forgotten about Taylor's salary and sent all his funds to the bank! He prayed about the matter (for he had bills of his own to pay) and left it with the Lord. That evening, the doctor visited him and said that one of his richest patients came over *after hours* to pay his bill! He gave the money to Taylor, who rejoiced. He had learned he could trust God for the provision of his needs, both in England and China.

Jesus' feedings of the five thousand Jews and the four thousand Gentiles miraculously provided life-giving sustenance for all. He showed his ability to provide for our needs. We find the "bread" theme throughout Scripture. God provided manna for the wandering Israelites in the wilderness. In the model prayer, he promises to give us our daily bread (Matt. 6:11). Jesus is truly the Bread of Life (John 6:30–35; 47–58). We may confidently trust him to provide for our every need.

V. PRAYER

Lord, thank you for sending Jesus as the Bread of Life. I look to him for sustenance and strength as a child of his kingdom. Amen.

VI. DEEPER DISCOVERIES

A. Review and Preview

Matthew chapters 14–15 are part of a larger unit of Matthew's thought. We should consider Jesus' rejection at Nazareth (13:53–58) as the beginning of this unit. The religious leaders' second request for a sign (16:1–4) and Jesus' warning to the disciples concerning the Pharisees and Sadducees (16:5–12) definitely belong to this unit as well. Peter's confession of Jesus and Jesus' announcement of his church (16:13–20) serve to break through into the remainder of the book.

The overall flow of this large unit of thought goes something as follows: After the hardening of the heart of corporate Israel (Matt. 11–12) and the insight Jesus gave his disciples regarding the reasons for this resistance and the hope of the kingdom (13:1–52), Jesus continued to encounter increasing polarization between himself (and his followers, including John) and Israel, especially as represented by its leaders, lumped together with Herod (13:53–15:20).

So Jesus departed for a time from the Jews and traveled among the Gentiles, finding greater faith and no opposition among them (15:21–39), and hoping this lesson was not wasted on his disciples. They would become the foundation stones of the church (16:18) and rulers over the twelve tribes in the kingdom (19:27–29). But throughout both tours (among the Jews and the Gentiles, Matt. 14–15), Jesus' own disciples were slow to catch the significance of Jesus' miracles, his identity, and his greater intentions.

Upon returning to Jewish territory, Jesus was immediately confronted by the Jewish leaders and their deliberate disbelief (16:1–4). After this he issued a stern warning to his confused disciples concerning the danger of the hypocrites (16:5–12). Finally, his disciples made a significant breakthrough in their understanding of Jesus' identity (16:13–20), triggering a major turning point in Jesus' ministry (16:21). But as the following context will show, the disciples' understanding was still limited (16:21–17:23).

At the heart of this larger unit of thought (13:53–16:20) is a smaller subunit that is tied together by the theme of Jesus providing life-giving bread for both Jews and Gentiles (14:13–16:12). Matthew may have intended for us to see in this sub-unit multiple allusions to the miraculous provision of manna in the wilderness (beginning at Exod. 16; ending at Josh 5:10–12; explanation at Deut. 8:3). We will see several possible parallels between Jesus and Moses, Israel's deliverer and prophet (Deut. 18:15,18).

Certainly, Jesus' warning about the "yeast of the Pharisees and Sadducees" is tied to the two feedings, since Jesus referred to both of them there (16:5–12). Even the debate over what is clean and unclean was tied to food (15:1–20). So also was the question of whether the Gentile woman and her daughter should be able to eat from Israel's table (15:21–28), as well as the question of whether the many Gentiles Jesus visits were clean or unclean (15:29–31).

Three basic questions are woven throughout all of 13:53–16:20: (1) Who is Jesus? (2) Who will be willing to come to him for life-giving sustenance? (3) Whom will he accept at his table?

B. The Audience Included Great Crowds in Matthew 15:29–31

Mark's parallel for this brief summary (Mark 7:31–37) states the location as "the region of the Decapolis" (Mark 7:31) on and around the southeast shore of the Sea of Galilee, thereby also telling us that the crowd in the healing passage and the four thousand who were fed were Gentiles. Jesus' journey from Tyre and Sidon took him north of the Sea of Galilee, and then down along the east side of the lake in Gentile territory.

However, Matthew chose not to state that this was a Gentile crowd. Evidently, it was obvious to his first-century readers. When we look carefully, we see several clues that Matthew's readers would not have missed.

First, Matthew tells us this was a Gentile crowd through his wording of the crowd's response in 15:31: "They praised the God of Israel." Such a description of the response would most likely concern a Gentile audience. Second, the isolation of the place (v. 33) suggests the unpopulated eastern side of the lake. Third, the Greek term for *basket* is an indicator. Fourth, if the number of baskets of leftovers in the first feeding ("twelve," 14:20) is tied to the fact that this miracle was for the Jews, then the different number of baskets in the second feeding ("seven," 15:37) would seem to indicate that this miracle was not for Israel. These clues, together with Mark's clear statements, show that Matthew intended the reader to see a Gentile crowd here.

C. Summary

In Matthew 11–12, Israel proved to be faithless. In Matthew 13, Jesus explained this phenomenon, gave hope to the faithful, and outlined the kingdom's future development. At this point, the faithless and the faithful began to polarize further. Moreover, we learn here that the lines between the faithless and the faithful were not where we would commonly believe them to be. What we may have been taught to believe is "clean" or "religious" may, indeed, be the exact opposite. And those whom we think to be unapproachable with the truth may actually prove to be the most receptive.

Challenging the popular assumptions through his words and actions, Jesus further angered the religious leaders. This set the scene for the more heated confrontations to come, beginning immediately in Matthew 16. Of course, these confrontations would climax in the crucifixion.

Possibly most significantly of all, these chapters reveal the slow progress of the disciples' faith, making the limited breakthrough of 16:13–20 even more significant. As the disciples prepared to graduate from "primary" to "middle school," Jesus exulted in their immature grasp of his actual identity. He then launched an intense preparation of them for their leadership roles in the church (Matt. 16–20), and began to take the road leading to the cross (16:21).

VII. TEACHING OUTLINE

A. INTRODUCTION

1. Lead Story: Blind Tradition Misses the Point
2. Context: Matthew chapters 14–15 are part of a larger unit of Matthew's thought. We should consider Jesus' rejection at Nazareth (13:53–58) as the beginning of this unit. The religious leaders' second request for a sign (16:1–4) and Jesus' warning to the disciples concerning the Pharisees and Sadducees (16:5–12) definitely belong to this unit as well. While Peter's confession of Jesus and Jesus' announcement of his church (16:13–20) serve to break through into the next unit of the book, this general theme of opposition continues to rise to its culmination in the crucifixion.

   The overall flow of this large unit of thought, in its context, goes something like this: After the hardening of the heart of corporate Israel (Matt. 11–12) and the insight Jesus gave his disciples regarding the reasons for this resistance and the hope of the kingdom (13:1–52), Jesus continued to encounter increasing polarization between himself (and his followers, including John) and Israel, especially as represented by its leaders and Herod (13:53–15:20). So Jesus departed from the Jews and traveled among the Gentiles, finding greater faith and no opposition among them (15:21–39).

   Throughout both tours (among the Jews and the Gentiles, Matt. 14–15), even Jesus' own disciples failed to grasp the full significance of Jesus' miracles and his identity. Upon returning to Jewish territory, Jesus was immediately confronted by the Jewish leaders and their deliberate disbelief (16:1–4), after which he issued a stern warning to his confused disciples concerning the danger of the hypocrites (16:5–12). Finally, his disciples made a significant breakthrough in their understanding of Jesus' identity (16:13–20), triggering a major turning point in Jesus' ministry (16:21) and Matthew's Gospel. But the disciples' understanding was still limited (16:21–17:23).

3. Transition: The contrast between Jews and Gentiles is prominent in Matthew 14–15. After his debate with the hypocrites over what was clean and unclean (15:1–20), Jesus traveled into Gentile territory and ministered there throughout the remainder of Matthew 15, finding an enthusiastic reception. The "cleanness" debate and the ministry to the Gentile made the point that the Jewish leaders were wrong in their assessment of what was clean and unclean. Jesus' actions spoke louder than words, redefining the popular idea of what was "clean," that is, what was acceptable to God.

Further demonstrating God's acceptance of both Jews and Gentiles are two pairs of parallel stories: (1) the miraculous feeding of the five thousand Jews (14:13–21) and the miraculous feeding of the four thousand Gentiles (15:32–39); and (2) the miraculous healing of many Jews (14:34–36) and the miraculous healing of many Gentiles (15:29–31). The three Jewish stories mentioned in the preceding paragraph are clustered together, as are the three Gentile stories, with the debate over cleanness and uncleanness separating the two clusters.

B. COMMENTARY

1. The King Loses His Friend and Forerunner to Kingdom Opposition (14:1–12)
2. The King Feeds Five Thousand Jews (14:13–21)
3. The King Tests His Disciples' Faith (14:22–33)
4. Many Jews Place Healing Faith in the King (14:34–36)
5. The King Versus the Hypocrites: What Is Clean and Unclean? (15:1–20)
6. The King Finds Faith in a Gentile Woman (15:21–28)
7. Many Gentiles Place Healing Faith in the King (15:29–31)
8. The King Feeds Four Thousand Gentiles (15:32–39)

C. CONCLUSION

1. Wrap-up: Jesus was seeking followers who were characterized by true biblical faith as opposed to meaningless tradition based on human works.
2. Personal Challenge: Are you counting on the institutional traditions of your church to make you acceptable to Jesus, or are you coming to Jesus by personal faith? Are you going through the "motions"

because they are the conventional wisdom and the customs of your day, or are you coming to Jesus by faith through your own personal decision? Living by faith in Jesus does involve some social risks.

VIII. ISSUES FOR DISCUSSION

1. In his feeding of the five thousand, how might Jesus be compared to Moses?
2. What example did Jesus cite when he accused the Pharisees of transgressing "the command of God for the sake of your tradition"?
3. Why was Jesus so impressed with the faith exhibited by the Canaanite woman?
4. What clues did Matthew give to demonstrate that the four thousand whom Jesus fed were probably Gentiles?
5. In what sense is Jesus the Bread of Life for his followers?

Matthew 16

The King Turns Toward the Cross

I. **INTRODUCTION**
I Was Made for This

II. **COMMENTARY**
A verse-by-verse explanation of the chapter.

III. **CONCLUSION**
An overview of the principles and applications from the chapter.

IV. **LIFE APPLICATION**
The Art of Perseverance

Melding the chapter to life.

V. **PRAYER**
Tying the chapter to life with God.

VI. **DEEPER DISCOVERIES**
Historical, geographical, and grammatical enrichment of the commentary.

VII. **TEACHING OUTLINE**
Suggested step-by-step group study of the chapter.

VIII. **ISSUES FOR DISCUSSION**
Zeroing the chapter in on daily life.

Q u o t e

"The working method of God at any given time is to carry out His purpose through the members of the Body of Christ . . . the local church is God's agency in the world transacting God's business."

E a r l   D .   R a d m a c h e r

Matthew 16

I N   A   N U T S H E L L

To test Jesus and possibly diminish his influence with the people, the Jewish leaders demanded a sign to prove that Jesus' authority was from God. Jesus had already given abundant proof of the source of his ministry through his miracles and teachings. But the Pharisees and Sadducees could not interpret the signs of the times. Jesus continued to train the disciples and increase their understanding of his authority and who he is.

The King Turns Toward the Cross

I. INTRODUCTION

I Was Made for This

*E*very now and then in the course of our lives, we come to identifiable moments so intensely fulfilling that we feel like shouting: "I was made for this!" Great moments of personal accomplishment are like that. Maybe it is a moment of great achievement in sports. Or the moment in the life of a scientist when the elements all come together to complete a project.

Jesus came to such a moment in Matthew 16. He was now well into his public ministry, and about to turn his eyes toward Jerusalem and the cross. In preparation, he called a retreat for his disciples. His purpose was to evaluate his ministry, to test whether the disciples were grasping the overall picture, and then to announce the future strategy.

In the north country, not far from the slopes of Mount Hermon, he reviewed the game plan. He began by asking his disciples a few questions. "Who do people say the Son of Man is?" More importantly, "Who do you say I am?" Peter answered clearly and succinctly, "You are the Christ, the Son of the living God." In essence Peter said, "You are our king. We will follow you anywhere."

It was the correct answer, and much more. It was the key to a divine plan that had been in effect for centuries. It was the dream of the Father that his Son would bring the brothers and sisters home to the eternal family table. Jesus could not contain his pleasure. He replied, "Blessed are you, Simon son of Jonah, for this was not revealed to you by man, but by my Father in heaven."

Jesus then took his disciples to the next level when he made an announcement like few the world would ever hear. With his jaw set and his eyes full of joy and intensity, Jesus spoke his vision and his heart. Loud and clear, in five little words—five words that would change the course of human history: "I will build my church."

This was his plan, and this was his team. This was his body. It would look like him, sound like him, and reflect him. No one else called the signals. It was Jesus' church, and it would impact the entire world.

II. COMMENTARY

The King Turns Toward the Cross

MAIN IDEA: *In a world of opposition, true disciples must realize that submission to the king means following him to victory—through hardship and suffering.*

The people who decided where to put the chapter and verse divisions in our Bible were not inspired by God. Some times they placed a division right in the middle of what we see today as a cohesive unit of thought. At other times, a turning point or breaking point in the author's flow of thought is ignored, leaving a break in the middle of a chapter.

This is the case with Matthew 16. As we saw in our discussion of Matthew 14–15, Matthew's unit of thought extends all the way from 13:53 through 16:12. The chapter division would have been better placed between 16:12 and 16:13.

I mention this to emphasize that one of the two or three most significant turning points in Matthew (many would say *the* most important) is in the middle of chapter 16.

- Through the first part of Matthew 16, the disciples had limited understanding of Jesus' identity and mission. From the latter part of Matthew 16 forward, their understanding grew rapidly.
- Through the first part of Matthew 16, Jesus had generally avoided mentioning his death and resurrection, focusing instead on laying the foundation of his disciples' understanding. From the latter part of Matthew 16 forward, Jesus spoke clearly and often of his coming suffering, death, and resurrection.
- Through the first part of Matthew 16, Jesus had spoken in general fashion about the kingdom he was advancing. From the latter part of Matthew 16 on, he gave more specific instruction regarding the church he would build.
- Through Matthew 16:20, Jesus had been content to stay in the "backwater" around Galilee, far from the hotbed of religious hypocrisy in Jerusalem. Beginning with 16:21, he took the road toward Jerusalem and the cross (see also 19:1; 20:17,29; 21:1,10).

We will treat all of Matthew 16 together in this commentary chapter to avoid confusion, but we must realize that the first twelve verses of the chapter are actually the conclusion of one large unit of Matthew's thought, whereas the rest of the chapter begins the next unit of thought.

The King Again Denies the Pharisees (and Others) a Sign (16:1–4)

> **SUPPORTING IDEA:** *The world will remain blind and critical to the obvious truth.*

This passage is similar to 12:38–45. In both passages:

- Jesus' previous contact with the religious leaders had included a scathing condemnation of the hypocrites for serious sins (blaspheming the Holy Spirit in 12:22–37; replacing God's commands with human tradition in 15:1–20).
- the religious leaders challenged Jesus' authority by demanding to see a miraculous sign, proving his authority to be from God.
- Jesus called the hypocrites "a wicked and adulterous generation" (12:39,45; 16:4) because of their desire for a sign from him.
- Jesus denied their request for a sign.
- Jesus told them they would only receive the "sign of Jonah."

16:1. In Matthew 12:38–45, the Pharisees and teachers of the law challenged Jesus. Now the Pharisees teamed up with the Sadducees. In chapter 12 and this passage, the use of a single article in front of the list of two religious groups implies that they came in cooperation. That would raise the eyebrows of those who knew the two groups. The Pharisees and Sadducees, the two Jewish sects that represented essentially the entire Sanhedrin, were theological enemies. For these two adversarial groups to come together as allies against Christ demonstrated just how heated and widespread the growing opposition to Jesus had become. The Pharisees enjoyed the support of the people; the Sadducees controlled the political power in Jerusalem. Together, they were formidable opponents of Jesus.

Even though the Greek verb **tested** has a somewhat different meaning here, Matthew may have intended us to see a continuity between Satan in 4:1–11 and the hypocrites here. Both were bent on defeating Jesus, and both attempted to use twisted reasoning to trap him.

The Pharisees and Sadducees requested **a sign from heaven**; that is, from God, to demonstrate that Jesus' authority was from God. (For more on the "sign," see comment on 12:38.)

16:2–3. Jesus replied that his challengers had already been given abundant proof of the source of his authority (his many miracles and authoritative teachings), but they refused to interpret the evidence accurately. He described how well they could interpret the sky in discerning the upcoming weather, but they could not interpret **the signs of the times.** These were more obvious even than the indicators of the next day's weather. The use of the word *signs* (plural) in 16:3 is a reference back to the challengers' request for a "sign" (same word). Jesus was saying, "You want a sign? You know nothing about signs. I have already given you many signs. Why should I believe you will heed another sign any more than you have heeded those you have already received?"

16:4. Jesus condemned this **generation** of Israel, particularly its leadership, by using exactly the same words as in 12:39: **a wicked and adulterous generation.** Again he denied them any sign, except the **sign of Jonah,** Jesus' resurrection from the bowels of the earth (see comment on 12:39–41). With that, Jesus walked away from his critics.

Jesus did not haggle any longer than necessary with those who were opposed to the truth. He did not ignore them or avoid them, but neither did he get into a long and fruitless debate. When it was clear they were more interested in debating than in learning, Jesus went another direction. We would do well to follow his example with such people, praying for the Holy Spirit to soften their hearts and watching for signs of openness.

B The Disciples Still Do Not Fully Understand the King (16:5–12)

SUPPORTING IDEA: *Even we who are trying to follow the king will experience limitations in our understanding. This causes us to overlook dangers from the world.*

This passage brings to a close the sub-unit (14:13–16:12; within Matthew's larger unit of thought, 13:53–16:20) that centers on the theme of God's abundant provision (the two feedings) versus the hypocrites' desire to deprive and poison the people (replacing God's law with man's, rejecting as unclean that which God has accepted as clean, and rejecting God's Messiah). Matthew used Jesus' reference to the two feedings as another affirmation that God would provide abundantly for his people.

16:5. Jesus and his disciples again crossed the Sea of Galilee, apparently from Magadan (on the west shore) to somewhere on the east or northeast shore. In 16:13, we find them in **the region of Caesarea Philippi,** twenty-five miles north and slightly east of the lake. Apparently, Jesus once again withdrew from his opponents (12:15; 14:13) to postpone the final conflict and to further train his disciples with a minimum of distractions.

16:6–7. Once they were away from the challengers of 16:1–4, Jesus warned his disciples to **be on your guard against the yeast of the Pharisees and Sadducees.** Jesus meant "yeast" here as a figurative reference to the corrupting influence of the teachings of the Pharisees and Sadducees. The hypocrites' teachings were so subtle, and their spiritual power so intimidating, that Jesus foresaw a real danger that his own disciples might be led astray by the Pharisees and Sadducees. In fact, the most persuasive arguments of Jesus' critics were yet to be presented. If the disciples thought the heat was turned up high before now, they had not yet understood how hot the frying pan would become. Jesus knew his disciples might buckle under such pressure.

Jesus used the picture of yeast, because of yeast's ability to grow invisibly within the lump of dough, just as the poisoned teaching of the hypocrites might grow in the hearts of the disciples without their awareness. Jesus drew upon this same quality of yeast in 13:33 to describe the kingdom's growth.

The disciples did not understand Jesus' meaning. Like we are so often, they were not tuned in to the larger picture. Their concern for their stomachs had hindered their spiritual development. Because they had forgotten bread, they were preoccupied with the question of where they would buy their next meal. From the strength of Jesus' rebuke (16:8–11), they must have been very worried about how they would be fed. This concern was contrary to Jesus' teaching in 6:25–34 and contrary to the lesson of God's abundant provision. There were a variety of vendors from whom they could have bought bread, and their worry led them to misinterpret Jesus. They thought he was telling them which vendors to avoid—those who held to the teachings of the Pharisees and Sadducees.

The role of "remembrance" is critical in Scripture (Deut. 8). The disciples in this instance, much like their forefathers in the wilderness, had already forgotten God's dramatic provision in the past. So they floundered in the present. They worried about food, supposedly out of the hearing of Jesus (**they discussed this** [over and over] **among themselves**; imperfect tense of the verb "to consider"). Either they did not want to bother Jesus with such mundane matters, or they knew they were acting from out of a lack of faith and they did not want Jesus to be aware of their deliberations.

16:8–11. Jesus knew exactly what they were doing. **You of little faith** (little-faith ones) he called them, as he had done twice in Matthew (8:26; 14:21; see also 6:30). His question was rhetorical. He did not expect them to explain their discussion of bread. He was helping them to see the foolishness of their worry as well as their inability to understand the true meaning of his warning. The verb "to consider, discuss," is in the present tense, carrying the meaning, "Why do you keep on endlessly discussing?"

In verses 9–10, Jesus reviewed the lesson the disciples should have learned from the two miraculous feedings. In both cases, he highlighted the small quantity of bread (representing the whole meal, including the fish), in contrast to the size of the crowds. To heighten the lesson of God's abundant provision, he reminded them of the many baskets of leftovers. His message was, "You should know that my warning has nothing to do with physical bread, because the Father will provide all we need and more. You should have known I was not talking about physical bread."

In verse 9, the word *still* implies the disciples had been offered ample opportunity to learn these lessons. Jesus was disappointed that it was taking them so long. **Understand** means "rational reflection" or "reasoning." Jesus was amazed at the disciples' inability to reason out the lesson from what they had experienced!

16:12. This time they understood that Jesus was warning them about the teaching of the Pharisees and Sadducees. This understanding was built on the minor breakthrough in understanding the disciples made in 14:33. This further laid the foundation for the major breakthrough of 16:16.

ⓒ The Dawn of Understanding in the Disciples (16:13–20)

SUPPORTING IDEA: *A disciple must understand the king's identity and the authority we derive from him.*

We have arrived at a major turn in the road. This passage serves as the climax and the culmination of Jesus' ministry to this point. At 16:12 Jesus took his disciples further north, away from the crowds into a retreat setting. His purpose was to review his ministry and to clarify his own identity and his expectations of them.

The question of Jesus' identity had been there all along: "What kind of man is this?" (8:27). "Are you the one who was to come?" (11:2). "Could this be the Son of David?" (12:23). Now all of those questions came to a climax in this focused, intense retreat with the disciples.

This passage serves as a transitional section in Matthew's Gospel. Peter's confession summarized Jesus' ministry up to this point. And Jesus' announcement of the church began Jesus' preparation of the disciples for their leadership roles in his absence. Jesus' intention to build his church marks a major transition in God's pursuit of his great plan of the ages. The old wineskin of Israel had been set on the shelf temporarily, while the new wineskin of the church was introduced.

The disciples' breakthrough in understanding also opened the door for Jesus to initiate them into the next level. Verse 21 begins a series of detailed predictions by Jesus concerning his suffering, death, burial, and resurrection.

16:13. There is no reason not to believe the events of Matthew 16 happened in chronological order and in close succession. Jesus' arrival in **the region of Caesarea Philippi**, twenty-five miles north of Capernaum, represented his efforts at withdrawal from his critics in 16:1–4. He chose this site, far from the distractions and interruptions of desperate crowds and hypocritical questioners, to settle the critical question of his identity with his disciples. It was a quiet place at the headwaters of the Jordan River, a place long associated with idol worship and pagan deities.

Standing beneath the idols of a so-called deity, Pan, carved into the cliff-side, Jesus knew the timing was right to raise and settle this question. It was time to lead his disciples into a clear proclamation of his deity.

Jesus apparently had to ask his first question of the disciples more than once (**asked** is in the imperfect Greek tense, and delivers the meaning, "he asked repeatedly"). Perhaps he went around the circle, asking each disciple individually. This question prompted the disciples to share what they had heard from the **people**. By the parallel with 16:15, we know that **the Son of Man** here is a substitute for the personal pronoun "I." But in the context of the following verses (esp. vv. 16,20,27–28), it also foreshadowed the divine revelation of Jesus' messianic identity and mission.

16:14. During the two years the disciples had been with Jesus, they had overheard many rumors, speculations, and questions from the thousands of people who had seen Jesus. Virtually all of them assumed Jesus to be a pro-phetic forerunner to the Messiah rather than the Messiah himself. If any of those guesses were true, they would have implied a prophet coming back from the dead to minister in Israel. And all the guesses revealed some degree of accurate perception on the part of the people. All recognized God's author-ity behind the words and works of Jesus, because all the prophets listed here were known to be God's mouthpieces.

Some people, like Herod (14:1–2), thought Jesus was John the Baptizer reincarnated. Others saw Jesus' miracles, especially the resurrection of the dead (9:18–26), and they thought of Elijah the miracle worker (1 Kgs. 17–2 Kgs. 2; esp. 17:17–24). Also, since John was "Elijah who was to come" (11:14; 17:12; Mal. 4:5), this would explain why these two names were next to each other, both in this conversation and in the people's minds. Elijah was seen as a forerunner of the Messiah, as was John.

Still others thought Jesus was Jeremiah, the prophet of doom who proph-esied during the final decades before Judah was exiled to Babylon. The list included several of the other prophets, including Isaiah, whose prophecies Jesus fulfilled in Matthew and from whom Jesus quoted quite often.

16:15–16. In these verses Jesus asked a second, more pointed question: **But what about you? . . . Who do you say I am?** Notice that Jesus did not ask who the disciples *thought* he was, or who they *believed* he was, but who they *said* he was. Jesus wanted to know what they were ready to confess verbally about his identity. This was the point at which they needed to step across the line and commit to the reality of him as Christ or stay behind with the rest of the blind speculators.

Although Jesus asked all the disciples, it was Simon Peter—the forthright spokesman for the Twelve—who answered for them all. (We are to assume that the other eleven agreed with Peter's confession.) Peter, who stepped out of the boat with wavering faith in 14:28–31, now stepped out again with much more steady faith to confess the truth about Jesus.

In Peter's answer, the pronoun "you" is emphatic: "*You* are the Christ" (the Greek title equivalent to the Hebrew "Messiah," both meaning "Anointed One"). By the utterance of the word *Christ,* Peter attributed to Jesus all the hopes and promises, all the prophecies and all the messianic honor of the entire Hebrew Scriptures. No longer was Jesus merely a miracle-working prophet from God. He was now the king himself, the Savior who was promised. He was truly the one and only **Son of the living God**.

Here before the disciples stood the hope and salvation of Israel and all the earth. Certainly the Twelve had not been totally ignorant of this reality in the preceding weeks and months, but they finally had reached a degree of certainty. Now they were able to articulate the truth with confidence. Even as the reality took form in their minds, they must have felt a compulsion to bow down in awe before Jesus.

There were many false gods in the secular cultures surrounding the Jews, but only one God was **living**. The rest were dead and inactive. This included those gods carved into the high rock wall where they were standing. When Peter confessed Jesus as this "living" Son of God, he recognized Jesus as the unique, promised Son of prophecy (e.g., Isa. 7:14; 9:6–7). He was the *true* God as opposed to the dead deities of this world (cf. Deut. 5:26; Pss. 42:2; 84:2; Rom. 9:26; 1 Tim. 3:15; 1 Pet. 1:23; Rev. 7:2; 15:7).

16:17. We can read into Jesus' words his relief and joy that his disciples had finally been gripped by this reality. They had passed the test. He immediately pronounced Peter **blessed**, meaning that Peter had been the recipient of God's favor or blessing in the form of truth revealed to Peter's mind. It was not **man** who **revealed** this to Peter. The truth of Jesus' identity is one of the "secrets" of 13:11, easily understandable once it is revealed. But it is undiscoverable by natural, human means until God chooses to make it known. Only **my Father in heaven** was the source of such understanding about the Son. Here "my Father" took on extra significance in light of Peter's confession of Jesus as "the Son of the living God."

16:18. Parts of Jesus' declaration about Peter were intentionally parallel to Peter's declaration about Jesus. Jesus began with the emphatic **I tell you**, drawing a parallel between what he was about to say and Peter's confession.

You are Peter parallels **You are the Christ**. Peter's given name was Simon, but Jesus had nicknamed him Peter, meaning "rock" (John 1:42). Peter was actually the Greek equivalent of the Aramaic "Cephas." The New Testament authors, under the inspiration of the Spirit, translated "Cephas" to "Peter" for their Greek-speaking readers.

Jesus' words presented a deliberate wordplay in the text, and it is probably the most controversial statement in Matthew: **You are Peter** (Greek,

Petros, "rock"), **and on this rock** (Greek, *petra*) **I will build my church.** Upon this statement the Roman Catholic church has based its doctrine of Peter being appointed the first in a long line of popes. Jesus' statements of Peter's authority in the next verse provide the basis for the Roman Catholic church's erroneous teachings regarding the authority of the papal office.

And, equally in error, many Protestants have reacted against the Roman Catholic interpretation by going to the other extreme, allowing the "rock" (*petra*) to mean anything *but* Peter himself.

Matthew's record of Jesus' wordplay on Peter's name is significant. *Petros* is a masculine singular noun. *Petra* is feminine. And while clearly related, they represent a distinction. The masculine singular form refers to Peter as one singular rock. The feminine form may be understood to represent bedrock or a rock quarry. It is reasonable to understand Jesus' statement to mean that Peter was one rock among a rock quarry (the disciples). It was upon this quarry of disciples (cf. "living stones," 1 Pet. 2:5) and their understanding of Peter's confession that Jesus would build his church.

This interpretation fits with the apostle Paul's statement in Ephesians 2:19–22—that the church is "God's household, built on the foundation of the apostles and prophets, with Christ Jesus himself as the chief cornerstone. In him the whole [stone] building is joined together and rises to become a holy temple in the Lord . . . a dwelling in which God lives by his Spirit."

What Jesus was saying is that Peter would be a "first among equals" in the history of Jesus' church. Peter would be the initial spokesman among those who would become the custodians of the revealed truth about Jesus' identity—the heart of the revealed gospel. Peter was the first to proclaim the truth about Jesus. In fact, in the Book of Acts, Peter is the first spokesman for the fledgling church before the entire world.

But we lose sight of Peter almost completely after Acts 12 (when Paul gains prominence). This shows that Peter, while unique as the outspoken leader of the first church builders, was not any more significant than other devoted followers of Jesus. In fact, Peter was called into account more than once by other church leaders and by Paul himself (Acts 11:1–8; Gal. 2:11–14).

The Greek word for **church,** *ekklesia*, means "gathering." It comes from a verb meaning literally "call out from," and was used in a variety of ways in the first century. It could refer to any gathering of people for any purpose, including synagogue gatherings. This was *Jesus'* church as opposed to any other assemblies. *His* church would take on *his* characteristics.

We must be careful not to read into this exchange of Jesus with his disciples our own understanding of the word *church*. Certainly Jesus had in mind what the Christian church would begin to look like. In fact, he began to define it and set its guidelines for operation here and in Matthew 18. But when he spoke to the disciples here at Caesarea Philippi, he did not expect them to have the fully developed picture of "church" that believers would have even a few decades later—after the fuller plan was revealed by God in the Book of Acts and in the epistles of the New Testament. What the disciples heard from Jesus that day was, "On this rock quarry of disciples, I will build my community of believers."

It is significant that Jesus called the church **my church**. Jesus took his place as the center and owner of this community of followers. It is he who would be their means of entrance into the community, and it is he whom they would follow. His name, his character, his person, and his principles are to be represented by the church.

It is critical to understand that the words *church* and *kingdom* are two different words referring to two different realities. They are not synonymous or interchangeable. And the one (church) does not replace the other (kingdom). "Church" refers to a *people;* "kingdom" refers to a *reign.* Furthermore, the church does not subsume the kingdom, although it is part of it. Nor does the church replace the nation of Israel in the unfolding of the kingdom. Any attempt to make it so must require major allegorizing of the covenants (rather than interpreting them consistently and literally), which results in significant doctrinal error.

The church does not render God's covenant with David (2 Sam. 7) and David's kingdom obsolete. The Son of David will rule from David's throne (Israel) over the earth, and the church (the king's bride) will share in it, but the church cannot replace it. "God's gifts and his call are irrevocable" (Rom. 11:25–29). A study of the usages of the words *basileia* (kingdom) and *ekklesia* (church) will demonstrate a great difference between the two.

The gates of Hades was a phrase which referred to death, particularly the power of death. The gates of a city were a symbol of the city's strength. Jesus was saying, "My church is unstoppable. Satan cannot corral it. Nothing can overpower or silence my community of faith, not even the power of death itself. My church will go on, even if its individual members should die."

16:19. Jesus declared that to Peter (and the disciples) he would give **the keys of the kingdom of heaven**. It is likely that Jesus was referring to the keys commonly held by the scribes as a symbol of their teaching function. They were the "teachers" of Scripture. In this sense, Jesus was appointing the disciples as the initial teachers in his church. As elsewhere in Matthew, "heaven" is a euphemism for "God," so "kingdom of heaven" means "kingdom of God." Those who were the teachers of Scripture were the gatekeepers for all humanity. They were at the threshold of God's expanding kingdom as revealed in his Word.

The verbs **bound** and **loosed** (in the Greek future perfect tense) indicate the process was not yet complete. Jesus seems to have been instructing these teachers to be certain that before they taught some doctrine, it was something that had already been determined in heaven.

What are these **keys** by which the disciples, or subsequent teachers, open the way for people's understanding of the kingdom? From the immediate context as well as the broader context of the New Testament, we are safe in saying that these keys represent the supernaturally revealed truth of God, which Peter and the other disciples had just begun to receive.

If we conduct ourselves according to God's guidelines here on earth, we can take it on faith that our actions and decisions on earth are in accord with what has already been decided in heaven. We do not need specific direction or confirmation in each situation; we have God's word on it that his instruction, given to us in the Bible and properly carried out with a right heart, will achieve his will on earth.

16:20. The disciples had become confident enough to verbalize a confession of Jesus' true identity, but then Jesus warned them not to tell anyone else. This was not for the purpose of keeping his identity a secret. He wanted people to come to a knowledge of his identity based on the right motive—personal repentance rather than political zeal. Furthermore, while Jesus was headed for Jerusalem and the cross, he may have been guarding against the possibility of uninformed enthusiasm on the part of the multitudes interfering with his intentions.

D The King Takes the Road to the Cross (16:21–23)

SUPPORTING IDEA: *The king is our model of victory through suffering.*

These verses represent perhaps the most significant turning point in Matthew. The **from that time** statement of 16:21 is similar to that in 4:17 where Jesus began his preaching career upon the imprisonment of John the Baptizer. With the dawning of real understanding in his disciples, the king turned toward Jerusalem and the cross.

Peter's rebuke (16:22) also revealed that, although Jesus' disciples had passed a significant milestone in their understanding, they still had far to go. They knew him to be the Messiah-King, but they had not yet grasped an understanding of his suffering, death, and resurrection.

16:21. The theme of Jesus' suffering had already been anticipated in Matthew to a limited extent. From this point on in Matthew, Jesus referred to his coming death and resurrection numerous times. This explains Matthew's use of the Greek present infinitive, "point out, show, make known": **From that time on Jesus began to explain** (or *repeatedly* show). As always, the king was concerned with training his disciples.

To this point, Jesus generally had avoided conflict with his opponents. But to fulfill his and the Father's plan, he **must** ("it is necessary") go to Jerusalem, the heart of hypocritical Judaism, where there would be open conflict. The verb form "must" applies not only to Jesus' going to Jerusalem, but also to the other three verbs in this list: he must **suffer**, he must **be killed**, he must **be raised**. This sequence of events was according to God's plan.

Jesus indicated he would suffer **many things** at the hands of the religious leaders, because this suffering was an integral part of the price Jesus paid. The **elders** were synagogue officials in various cities, but in Jerusalem the term probably meant members of the Sanhedrin. The **chief priests** were the highest spiritual leaders of Israel who oversaw the temple sacrifices and other ceremonies (headed by the high priest, at this time Caiaphas, 26:3,57). The **teachers of the law** were the Jewish legal experts, steeped in the Old Testament and all the man-made regulations or traditions (15:1–9).

By listing all three groups and avoiding sectarian distinctions, such as Pharisees and Sadducees, Jesus focused on their functions in the spiritual leadership of Israel. He was saying that he would undergo persecution and rejection by the entire spiritual leadership of Israel.

At the heart of the plan, Jesus must **be killed**—as the sacrificial lamb, the Son of Abraham, for the sake of Israel and all nations (Gen. 12:3; Matt. 1:2,17). By this means he would redeem a sinful people. But he would **be raised** as the triumphant lion of Judah (Gen. 49:9), the sovereign Son of David (Gen. 49:10; Matt. 1:6,17). Thus, he would restore his entire kingdom to its proper place, under his authority.

The **third day** took on its precise meaning in Matthew 28, but Jesus had already alluded to the three days between his death and resurrection in "the sign of Jonah" (12:40).

16:22. The disciples, still with limited understanding, focused on the tragedy of Jesus' suffering and death. They seemed to overlook the triumphant ending of his resurrection. They had just come to their fullest realization yet that Jesus was the central figure toward whom all history pointed. Suddenly, they were blindsided by talk of this Messiah enduring suffering and death. Even though the suffering of the Messiah was foretold in the Old Testament (e.g, Isa. 53), the Jews did not know what to do with these prophecies. They had seen the Messiah only as triumphant.

Peter and the other disciples understood that persecution of their teacher implied persecution of them as well. Perhaps they responded, in part, out of fear for themselves. This realization made Jesus' teaching in 16:24–28 on rewards (Matt. 5:10–12) all the more significant.

Peter, the spokesman for the Twelve, pulled Jesus away from the others and talked to him in private. Peter launched into what he intended to be a lengthy rebuke. His first exclamation was **Never, Lord!** (literally, "Merciful to you!). This was a common expression, meaning, "May God be so merciful as to keep you from this," or, more concisely, "God forbid!" It has the force of a very strong *Never!*

Even as Peter spoke so brashly, he maintained a degree of respect, addressing Jesus as **Lord.** As we are prone to do, Peter made a great statement at one moment about truth and Jesus, but then turned around immediately and acted inconsistently, as though he knew more than Christ.

16:23. Jesus met Peter's rebuke with righteous rebuke. Peter had tried to correct Jesus' thinking, but Jesus showed Peter that it was his thinking that was inaccurate. In fact, in the following context (16:24–28), Jesus' teaching targeted the misconception that Peter needed to change—that the Messiah-King could never suffer. On the contrary, he *must* suffer if he was to accomplish the Father's will.

By addressing Peter as **Satan,** Jesus was saying that Peter's remark was representative of the kind of thinking Satan used. Therefore, Satan was using Peter's lack of understanding to tempt Jesus, much as Satan did in 4:8–9, when he offered Jesus a kingdom without suffering. **Get behind me!** has the same impact as "Away from me!" in 4:10.

In 16:18, Peter was a "rock" on which Jesus would build his church, but now Peter was a **stumbling block** in Jesus' way, interfering with Jesus' necessary, painful, but victorious destiny.

Peter's confession in 16:16 was revealed by God (16:17). But in 16:23, Peter did **not have in mind the things of God, but the things of men.** It was human nature to look for the easy road to triumph, but God's plan involved a deep valley on the way to victory.

In 16:24–28, Jesus attempted to fill the disciples with God's thoughts regarding the necessity of suffering. He wanted to replace their incorrect thoughts. In the process, he insisted that they look to the far side of victory and his future evaluation and reward for their actions (Matt. 5:10). There is great reward for serving the king.

E The King Explains the Cost of Following Him (16:24–28)

SUPPORTING IDEA: *A true disciple will follow the king to victory through suffering and receive great reward for it.*

Now that Jesus was on the road to Jerusalem and the cross, it would be critical for his disciples to understand the place that suffering and death would play in God's plan. It would play a part in their lives as well, and they must look beyond it to the rewards ahead.

16:24. These teachings followed immediately upon the heels of the interchange between Peter and Jesus. Peter's statement demanded another mentoring session. Many people wanted to follow Jesus, but most wanted to do it on their own terms. Jesus said that only those who followed on his terms could be disciples. And they would be rewarded for their loyalty.

Jesus defined a true follower in three ways. All three verbs he used are third-person imperatives in the Greek language, for which there is no exact English translation. The closest we can come to a proper translation is "let him," but even this is not forceful enough. **He must** carries the force of the commands.

First, the true follower **must deny himself.** The New Testament writers commonly used the verb *arneomai* to mean "say not, deny" (notably in Matt. 10:33). However, the emphatic verb *aparneomai*, "to deny utterly," is used only by the four Gospel writers, and then almost exclusively in the quotes parallel to this one (Mark 8:34; Luke 9:23), Jesus' prediction of Peter's denial (Matt. 26:34–35; Mark 14:30–31; Luke 22:34; John 13:38), and Peter's actual denial of Jesus (Matt. 26:75; Mark 14:72; Luke 22:61).

This verb is reserved to convey only the most conclusive denial. To deny oneself with this depth of denial is to live without a single thread of self-centered thought, devoted exclusively to Jesus and his work. Jesus was not saying that we need to create pain or deprivation for ourselves, but that we need to be prepared to let go of anything that competes with his kingdom.

Second, a devoted follower must **take up his cross** (see comment on 10:38). In this context, this phrase takes on new significance. In 10:38, Jesus used this phrase to clarify the follower's commitment in the context of the disciples' ministry training. Here he used it for much the same purpose, but with the shadow of his own cross drawing closer (Matt. 20:20–23).

Third, the true disciple must **follow me** (see comment on 10:38). Jesus commanded his disciples to follow him in 4:19, but the suffering that went with such following was not clarified until Jesus' statement in 10:38, where **follow me** comes after **take up his cross.** Again, this time the command was more ominous than ever. The disciples were being challenged to follow Jesus to Jerusalem, and then on to their own "crosses."

16:25–26. This paradoxical statement is almost identical to that in 10:39. The most important difference is the substitution of the verb **save** in the place of **find.** The meaning is very similar, but stronger here, with **save** and **lose** implying the higher possibility of physical death.

Jesus was talking about saving one's *life.* But his focus was on life's fulfillment in the next world. His point was profound. If a disciple spent all his energy focusing on this *life here and now,* he would lose the entire point of this life, which is investing in the *life to come.* And the difference between the two is the Messiah-King's cause. If the disciple tries to protect his life for himself in this life, he squanders the opportunity to increase his reward in the life that really matters—the eternal kingdom.

If a person does not accept the challenge of true discipleship, he will forfeit both true quality life now and full reward in eternity. There are no **gains** if a person wastes this life on himself. Matthew 16:27 confirms the subject here to be rewards rather than deliverance from hell.

16:27. Jesus then explained the wisdom of following and accepting the suffering and loss implicit in following him. Using the title **the Son of Man** in its eschatological, messianic sense, Jesus foretold the day when all the losses of his obedient followers would be abundantly compensated. In contrast to his first coming to earth in humility, the next coming would be **in his Father's glory with his angels.** Now he has come as the sacrificial Son of Abraham; then he will come as the sovereign Son of David.

Although Jesus' intention in the context of Matthew 16 was to give hope to his followers, the word **reward** does include the "repayment" or judgment of those works that do not honor Christ. **Each person** does not mean only those disciples who will be rewarded, but also those who seek the world and end up forfeiting their lives (Col. 3:23–25). Therefore, "repay" or "recompense" is a preferable translation over "reward."

The repayment will be **according to what he had done.** Christ was seeking to motivate his followers to work hard and invest their lives for eternity. Scripture makes it very clear that there are differing degrees of reward for believers, based on their stewardship of life opportunities (Matt. 25:14–30; Rom. 2:6; 14:12; 1 Cor. 3:13; 2 Cor. 5:10; Eph. 6:8; Col. 3:23–25; Rev. 2:23; 20:12; 22:12). In 2 Timothy 2:10–13, the apostle Paul summed up the basis of the disciple's reward as *endurance.*

16:28. Jesus grabbed his disciples' attention with another, **I tell you the truth.** Since the conversation on suffering and death may have been overwhelming to the disciples, Jesus assured them that some of those **standing here** would not **taste death** until they had seen firsthand the power of **the Son of Man coming in his kingdom.**

Jesus assured his followers that their suffering would not be without purpose or hope. They would be the tools the king would use to bring about the growth of his kingdom over the next few explosive decades. Such growth would be impossible without followers who were willing to deny themselves, take up their crosses, and follow Jesus through their own dark valleys.

> **MAIN IDEA REVIEW:** *In a world of opposition, true disciples must realize that submission to the king means following him to victory—through hardship and suffering.*

III. CONCLUSION

Jesus is the unique Messiah, God's promised king. Our recognition of his identity is critical to our success as followers. We must follow Peter's example by boldly acknowledging God's revealed truth about Jesus. The king's purpose on earth was to achieve victory through suffering and death. We, his followers, will also be victorious through hardship and suffering.

PRINCIPLES

- Those whose minds are made up through conscious unbelief will not believe the obvious.
- Preoccupation with the mundane and earthly can keep us from understanding what God is trying to teach us.
- False teaching can have subtle but profound effects if it gets a foothold in our hearts.
- Ultimately, only God can make the identity of Jesus clear to a person's mind.
- Death is no obstacle to God's purpose through his church.
- To his followers Jesus has entrusted the authority by the Word of God to open the door to eternal salvation.
- As we follow the guidelines of Scripture by depending on the Holy Spirit, we can be assured that we are acting in accord with God's will.
- Jesus demands our total obedience.
- Disciples of Jesus must be prepared to follow him everywhere he has gone—including the "cross."
- We receive life through believing. We receive reward through endurance.
- Any sacrifice we make now will be richly repaid when Jesus returns.

APPLICATIONS

- Beware of resisting God's truth, lest you become numb to it.
- Measure teaching by the truth of God's Word. Reject false teaching.
- Endure hardship in the life of faith, knowing that God will reward your faith.
- Concentrate on God's thinking above human thinking.
- Invest your life in the eternal values and purposes of God.

IV. LIFE APPLICATION

The Art of Perseverance

John Wesley was one of the great preachers of the Great Awakening. Few are probably aware of the difficulties John Wesley endured as he went about his work of preaching the gospel. Estimates are that he traveled by horseback more than a quarter of a million miles and preached more than 40,000 sermons! The difficulties and problems he encountered during his years of ministry were countless. But he would always keep his appointments, even at the risk of life and limb.

In their book, *The Wycliffe Handbook of Preaching & Preachers* (Chicago: Moody, 1984), Warren Wiersbe and Lloyd Perry tell this story about Wesley:

"While crossing a bridge in London, John Wesley stumbled and sprained his ankle. Some friends carried him to the house of Mrs. Mary Vazeille on Threadneedle Street. She was a widow with several children. She cared for Wesley and his response to her concern was to ask her to marry him.

"If we were writing fiction we might say that the sprained ankle was God's providential way to bring those people together. But the marriage was a disaster, and Mary finally left John. Had Wesley consulted with his brother Charles, and asked for the prayers of the brethren, he might have avoided that unfortunate situation. Mary was accustomed to her quiet home, and it was difficult for her to travel with her husband and stay in uncomfortable inns.

"It is unfortunate that Mary was not content just to ignore John's ministry; she actually opposed it. She gave certain personal letters to his enemies and even made additions to them that made them worse! Once she even pulled her husband around on the floor by his hair! 'I felt as though I could have knocked the soul out of her!' one of Wesley's friends said.

"Wesley concluded that his unhappy marriage encouraged him to work harder and not complain about missing the comforts of a home. Certainly it encouraged him to be away from home more!"

Here was a man who was not deterred by difficulty, but who stayed true to his mission. There will be times when God will call on us to endure difficulty and suffering for his sake. What motivated John Wesley is what should also motivate us. Because we are Christ's, we share in his suffering.

Are you going through a difficult period of your life? Submission to the king means following him to victory, even through hardship. Fully trust Jesus to see you through. He knows of your suffering and will reward your sacrifice and endurance when he returns.

V. PRAYER

Lord, we praise you for who you are. Thank you for revealing yourself to us. Grant us the strength to be obedient to our calling as Christians so that we can bear witness to your faithfulness, even in the midst of life's trials. Amen.

VI. DEEPER DISCOVERIES

Summary

Matthew 16 (particularly 16:13–20) answers the questions regarding Jesus' identity which are raised throughout the preceding chapters, beginning with the denial at Jesus' hometown (13:53–58), then Herod's speculation (14:1–2), the disciples' declaration (14:33), and the questions in the miracle passages. This represented a clear understanding and formal declaration of Jesus' deity by his disciples.

But most importantly, this chapter introduces a major element around which the New Testament will unfold—the concept of the new community of the saved, the church, which will be built on later, especially in Matthew 18.

This chapter also marks the point at which Jesus determined it was time to turn toward the cross. First, Jesus appeared to have based his timing of this turning point on the breakthrough in his disciples' understanding of his identity. Now they were ready to be educated and challenged to the next level of discipleship. Second, the further introduction of the new community, the church, will be interwoven with Jesus' teaching about his followers' suffering. Jesus' timing on announcing the church was related to his progression toward the cross. This community of faith will be built stronger as his followers trust him through their hardship, even through death.

VII. TEACHING OUTLINE

A. INTRODUCTION

1. Lead Story: I Was Made for This
2. Context: Although all of Matthew 16 is treated together in this commentary, it is important to realize that the first twelve verses of the chapter are actually the conclusion of one large unit of Matthew's thought, while the rest of the chapter begins the next unit of thought.
3. Transition: Matthew 16 (particularly 16:13–20) answers the questions regarding Jesus' identity which are raised throughout the preceding chapters, beginning with the denial at Jesus' hometown

(13:53–58), then Herod's speculation (14:1–2), the disciples' declaration (14:33), and the questions in the miracle passages.

This passage introduced the concept of the new community of the saved, the church. In the flow of Scripture from Genesis to Revelation, this is a major announcement. This new church will be the entity around which the dream of the Father (Gen. 12; Acts 1:4) unfolds and the New Testament is built.

This chapter also marks the point at which Jesus announces it is time to turn toward the cross. Chapter 16 may be summarized in these three vignettes: it (1) settles Jesus' identity; (2) announces his body—the church; and (3) launches his march to the cross.

B. COMMENTARY

1. The King Again Denies the Pharisees (and Others) a Sign (16:1–4)
2. The Disciples Still Do Not Fully Understand the King (16:5–12)
3. The Dawn of Understanding in the Disciples (16:13–20)
4. The King Takes the Road to the Cross (16:21–23)
5. The King Explains the Cost of Following Him (16:24–28)

C. CONCLUSION

1. Wrap-up: In a world of opposition, true disciples must realize that submission to the king means following him to eventual victory—through hardship and suffering.
2. Personal Challenge: Are you a fair-weather follower of Jesus Christ, or do you recognize the authority of the King of kings? Are you willing to follow him through hardship and suffering as well? Do you have a sober respect for the responsibility Christ has given you? Will you be motivated by the prospect of reward? Or will you simply bide your time here, living a decent life but making no real impact for the kingdom? Do you look forward to Jesus' return to reward his followers for their faithfulness?

VIII. ISSUES FOR DISCUSSION

1. Why did Jesus ask his disciples what other people were saying about him before he asked them what *they* thought about him and his true identity?
2. Who were the various personalities with whom Jesus had been identified by the people? Who were they saying that Jesus was?
3. Why did Jesus condemn Peter for stating that Jesus would not have to suffer and die?
4. What role did Jesus say his disciples were destined to fill in the building of his church?

Matthew 17

The King Reveals His Glory

I. INTRODUCTION
It Is Even Better Than I Had Hoped

II. COMMENTARY
A verse-by-verse explanation of the chapter.

III. CONCLUSION
An overview of the principles and applications from the chapter.

IV. LIFE APPLICATION
Turn on the Power!
Melding the chapter to life.

V. PRAYER
Tying the chapter to life with God.

VI. DEEPER DISCOVERIES
Historical, geographical, and grammatical enrichment of the commentary.

VII. TEACHING OUTLINE
Suggested step-by-step group study of the chapter.

VIII. ISSUES FOR DISCUSSION
Zeroing the chapter in on daily life.

Quote

"*O*ur brains are no longer conditioned for reverence and awe. We cannot imagine a Second Coming that would not be cut down to size by the televised evening news, or a Last Judgment not subject to pages of holier-than-Thou second-guessing in *The New York Review of Books.*"

John Updike

Matthew 17

IN A NUTSHELL

*T*he Transfiguration gives the disciples a glimpse of Jesus' future glory. Not only is it a foreshadowing of Jesus' resurrection and return, but the Father speaks and affirms the true identity of his Son—the Messiah. Immediately following this mountaintop experience, Jesus chastises the other nine disciples for their small belief. It is here that Jesus makes his second formal presentation about his coming suffering, death, and resurrection.

The King Reveals His Glory

I. INTRODUCTION

It Is Even Better Than I Had Hoped

At Good Shepherd Church we have worked hard to foster healthy interpersonal friendships on our pastoral staff. We believe the spirit of the New Testament must first be modeled by the leaders before the people can grasp it. And it has been a wonderful process. Staff longevity is amazing as we "learn together to live like Christ." But our joy in working together is difficult for people to believe.

At a pastor's conference, one of our newer staff pastors, who had been with us only a year or so, was approached by a colleague from a previous ministry. "We hear all the time about the quality of team ministry at Good Shepherd Church," this person said. "Now that you are on the inside, tell us what it is really like."

It was clear that he did not believe a word of what he had heard. This young ministerial skeptic had apparently been around the church-staff block a bit. Evidently, he had seen his share of professional jealousy, competition, and backbiting in the ministry. And he had allowed what he had seen to harden him. He had obviously bought into this world's adage, "If it seems too good to be true, it probably is." He will be in for a real surprise when he walks through the gates of heaven. Like one of my experienced ministry colleagues says, he will probably stand there with his lower jaw on the floor and say, "But you cannot be God. You are too nice!"

It is unfortunate that life on this planet is not all it should be. But we do not have to give in to the world. We do meet fine Christian people who are just as good as they seem. Unfortunately, our experience is often the opposite—the more you get to know people, the less you are able to respect them. But it ought to be the other way around—the longer you are together, the deeper the love and respect.

That is certainly the way it was with Jesus and his disciples. The more they were around him, the more amazing and glorious they found him to be. Matthew is about to make that point in chapter 17. The disciples' minds were about to explode in love, joy, and respect. They would get a glimpse of Jesus as he really is. We call it the Transfiguration.

II. COMMENTARY

The King Reveals His Glory

MAIN IDEA: *Kingdom citizens must live confidently in the supremacy of the king's glorious power and the truth of the king's teachings. This gives them the faith to follow him to the cross.*

Matthew 17 moves the story along from the transition of chapter 16 toward the teaching on the new community, the church, in chapter 18. Chapter 17 also serves to advance the continuing movement of conflict to its climax through the rest of the book. It does this in several ways:

The story of Jesus' transfiguration (17:1–8) gave Peter, James, and John a glimpse of eternal perspective and Jesus' true glory. It was an encouragement that followed some of the difficult sayings of chapter 16 (esp. 16:21,24–26).

Building on the confession of 16:16, the transfiguration of Jesus further advanced these three disciples' understanding of the identity and power of Jesus. Twice (17:9,12 and 17:22–23), Jesus referred to his suffering, death, and resurrection, fulfilling the pattern set in 16:21 and preparing for the fulfillment of all the predictions at the end of Matthew's Gospel.

The episode with the demonized boy (17:14–18) and the subsequent teaching on faith (17:19–20) showed that the disciples still had a long way to go in their faith, even after the breakthrough of 16:16.

The discussion of the temple tax (17:24–27) began to turn the reader's mind toward the privileges and responsibilities of being a part of the community of faith—the church. This is the theme of Matthew's fourth discourse in chapter 18.

The imagery of the mountain as the setting for the Transfiguration may serve to illustrate the "higher" level of understanding and faith of those with proper perspective on the Messiah. In contrast, when Jesus came down and returned to the normal events of life, he met with the usual lack of faith, even from his own disciples. Matthew intended us to see irony in the nine remaining disciples who were unable to cast out a demon (even after being given authority to do so in 10:1,8), while Jesus' awesome power and glory was revealed in the Transfiguration. The reality of power was there, but those without faithful understanding failed to tap into this source of strength.

Two more of Jesus' public miracles are recorded in this passage, but they served a much different purpose than those catalogued in Matthew 8–15. Rather than further validating Jesus as the Messiah, the healing of the demonized boy (17:18) showed up the disciples' lack of genuine faith. The provision of the temple tax in the mouth of a fish (17:27) highlighted God's provision for his children.

Ⓐ Up on High: A Glimpse of the King's Glory (17:1–13)

SUPPORTING IDEA: *Kingdom citizens must maintain a vision of the king's glorious identity and power and heed his teaching.*

Jesus had just finished a sobering and motivational discussion with his disciples. They were aware of his upcoming suffering and death. They had been made to realize that suffering and pain was also part of their calling as his disciples. They were probably puzzled and disillusioned. Jesus indicated that at least some of them would not experience death before they saw him in his power and kingdom. What did Jesus mean? Matthew 17 is our answer.

Six days after making the statement that some of them would "see" the kingdom, Jesus took his inner group of three disciples—Peter, James, and John—up on a mountain. There they were amazed by what they witnessed. As overwhelmed as they were, what they saw was only a glimpse of the kingdom. The Old Testament saints represented by Moses and Elijah were there. The New Testament saints were represented by the three disciples. And, most significantly, the Son of Man was transfigured in a demonstration of his awesome glory.

One purpose of Jesus' transfiguration (17:1–8) was to give these three disciples an encouraging glimpse of eternal reality. This experience had an unforgettable impact on Peter (2 Pet. 1:16–18) as well as James and John.

If Jesus was intentionally compared to Moses in this passage, it was for the purpose of showing how Jesus surpassed Moses as a prophet, a leader, and a Savior. While Moses' face shone with the reflected light of Yahweh's glory, Jesus was Yahweh himself, allowing his own glory to show through his Son. Moses went up on the mountain to meet with Yahweh, but Jesus brought Moses to him, and the Father's presence further affirmed the supremacy of the Son. The same kind of comparison may have been intended with Elijah, but, if so, it is not as obvious as the comparison with Moses.

17:1. This is one of the few precise time references in Matthew connecting the Transfiguration with Jesus' statement in 16:28. The events and teaching of the preceding chapter are clearly linked to this experience on the Mount of Transfiguration.

Peter, James, and John were Jesus' inner circle among the Twelve. They, together with Andrew, were the first four disciples whom Jesus called (Matt. 4:18–22; Mark 1:16–20; Luke 5:10–11). They are listed as the first three of the Twelve in four different lists (Matt. 10:2; Mark 3:16–17; Luke 6:14; Acts 1:13). These three alone witnessed Jesus raising the dead girl (Matt. 9:25), witnessed the Transfiguration (Matt. 17:1), and accompanied Jesus at Gethsemane (Matt. 26:37). These three and Andrew questioned Jesus privately about the end times (Mark 13:3; cf. Matt. 24:3), and these four may have been the only ones of the Twelve present at the healing of Peter's mother-in-law (Mark 1:29; cf. Matt. 8:14–15).

Peter and John played prominent roles early in Acts. They were groomed by Jesus as key leaders for the church. James may have had a similar role, but he was not as prominent because he was one of the earliest martyrs in church history, killed by Herod shortly after the stoning of Stephen (Acts 11:19; 12:1–2).

Jesus had used mountains as retreat locations before (Matt. 14:23). This **high** mountain may have been Mount Hermon, 9,200 feet in altitude, northeast of Caesarea Philippi, the location of Peter's confession (16:13–20). It is unlikely that it was Mount Tabor to the south, the traditional setting most frequently visited by modern tourists.

Matthew emphasized that Jesus and these three disciples were **by themselves.** Jesus entrusted this glimpse of his glory only to his three closest friends, who would also be the key church leaders to pass on the vision to the rest of the believers after the Resurrection (17:9). This experience would be a source of encouragement to the church through difficult and uncertain times. Peter was struck by the magnificent display, but he indicated in his second epistle that those who were not present need not feel slighted. They had the Scriptures "made more sure" (2 Pet. 1:19) than if they had been eyewitnesses.

17:2. Without further preamble, Matthew came right to the point. Jesus was **transfigured before them.** The three disciples observed the entire process. Matthew's emphasis here is important, because they would be the only eyewitnesses of the event for others. Regarding Jesus' shining face, Moses' face also shone, but with reflected and transient glory (Exod. 34:29–35; 2 Cor. 3:7–18; also Matt. 13:43, which takes wording from Dan. 12:3). Compare Jesus' shining garments with the white clothing of the angels in 28:3. This was not simply "white." This was of such brilliance that it partook of the very nature of light itself. To understand the Transfiguration, we must stretch our minds to another dimension beyond earthly white (Mark 9:3).

The word **transfigured** is the passive form of the Greek verb *metamorphoo,* meaning "to transform." It is the word from which we derive our English term *metamorphosis.* Aside from the parallel passage in Mark 9:2, this verb is used only in Romans 12:2 and 2 Corinthians 3:18, both describing the inner transformation that takes place in a believer. It is noteworthy that 2 Corinthians 3 also compares this transformation with that of Moses when he met with God. But in that instance, it was the transience and superficiality of Moses' outer transformation that was emphasized, compared with our deep and lasting inner transformation.

17:3. As if the dazzling transformation of Jesus' appearance was not enough, Matthew drew attention to the appearance of two additional figures with the phrase **just then.** Moses and Elijah may represent the two most prominent of the prophets from two divisions of the Old Testament—the Law and the Prophets. Although there is a third division, the wisdom books, "the law and the prophets" was a common phrase summarizing the whole of the Old Testament. The presence of Moses and Elijah with Jesus indicated their complete unity with him.

We know from Scripture that Elijah did not die but was taken directly into heaven (2 Kgs. 2:11–12). But Deuteronomy 32:50; 34:5–6 states that Moses died and was buried by God, although the site of his grave was unknown. Both men had prophetic roles beyond their lifetime. Moses was a model future prophet (Deut. 18:18) and Elijah was a model for Jesus' fore-runner (Mal. 4:5–6).

Those two revered historical figures must have loomed high over Jesus in the disciples' minds because of their limited understanding of Christ. The reality was that Jesus was the one who loomed over the rest, for he was their Creator and the mighty God who gave Moses and Elijah the prophetic words they spoke and wrote. "Listen to him," the Father commanded (Matt. 17:5). One purpose of the Transfiguration was to rearrange the order of priority that Jesus and the human prophets had in the disciples' minds. Note that the theme in Peter's recounting of the Transfiguration (2 Pet. 1:12–21) was the accuracy and reliability of God's inspired Word.

The fact that Moses and Elijah were **talking with** Jesus (Greek present tense participle) indicates familiarity, which would further heighten Jesus' stature in the eyes of the three disciples and Matthew's readers.

17:4. Peter, consistent with his character, did not know what to do. But he wanted to do something. **It is good for us to be here!** is an expression of his amazement and joy. Any Jew would have recognized the privilege of being in the presence of the glorious Messiah as well as Moses and Elijah. Feeling the need to do something, Peter offered (**if you wish**) to show reverence to Jesus and the two prophets by building three **shelters**.

Evidently, what Peter had in mind was not protection from the sun or weather, but sacred shrines, like the tabernacle or other Old Testament memorials. Jesus apparently did not wish for such an expression of rever-ence, because he did not respond to Peter's offer.

17:5. Peter's offer was interrupted by the appearance of the Father him-self. There is a connection between the cloud's appearance and the Father's voice and Peter's offer to build the shelters. Matthew says the cloud envel-oped them **while he** [Peter] **was still speaking.** God recognized Peter's good intention in wanting to honor Jesus, Moses, and Elijah, but he corrected Peter's misperception by elevating his Son above the others.

In addition to Jesus' dazzling transformation and the appearance of Moses and Elijah, the awesome display drew to its climax as the cloud of the Shekinah glory came down and the voice of God spoke from the cloud.

The cloud was **bright**, with the same glory that shone from Jesus' face and clothes, reminding us of the cloud of God's presence during Israel's wanderings (Exod. 13:21–22), and his indwelling of the tabernacle (Exod. 40:34–38) and the temple (1 Kgs. 8:10–13).

The Father's words were identical to those spoken at Jesus' baptism (3:17, see comment there), with the addition of **Listen to him** (the Greek present imperative, which means "keep on listening" or "always listen"). When the Father affirmed Jesus as his Son, the disciples gained a better idea of Jesus' true identity—the glorious and suffering Messiah. When the Father expressed his love for his Son, the disciples had a more complete idea why Jesus was pleasing to the Father. He had been and would be obedient to the Father, even to death.

The command to the disciples was "Listen to him," elevating the word of Jesus above the words of Moses and Elijah. Indeed, Moses himself commanded God's people to heed the prophet "like me" who would come (Deut. 18:15). This reminds us of Jesus' repeated challenge, "He who has ears, let him hear" (11:15; 13:9,43). The disciples had heard all of Jesus' teachings, but the "ears" of their hearts were not fully open to the meaning of what had been revealed to them.

17:6–8. The Father's proclamation was so frightening that the three disciples were unable to stand and face him, so **they fell facedown to the ground, terrified**.

There was a real element of worship in this action, even though it was motivated by fear. This fear of the Lord is much more than some vague form of respect or reverence. It is real fear. The command to fear the Lord (e.g., Prov. 1:7; 1 Pet. 1:17) includes the idea of literal fear at the awesome power and holiness of God. For a similar effect, see Daniel 10:7–9.

Jesus ministered to his disciples through the ministry of touch (see introductory thoughts on Matthew 8–9). Jesus also calmed the fears of the disciples after they had witnessed his glorious, awesome power (14:27; cf. 9:2,22). Because the glory of God was something his people could witness without shrinking away, and because the theophany (appearance of God) had ended, Jesus instructed the disciples to **Get up.**

As they raised their faces from the ground and looked around, the scene was restored to normal. The cloud and voice were gone. Moses and Elijah had vanished. Jesus stood alone. The brilliant light from his face and clothes had faded. But the memory would be theirs for life.

17:9. Jesus knew that such a revelation would be misused and misunderstood by others—even among the Twelve. His purpose in the Transfiguration had been to provide a striking testimony to and through Peter, James, and John after his resurrection. But in the wrong hands, this testimony could turn into a show, distracting from Jesus' purpose while the cross still loomed in the future. For this reason Jesus **instructed** the disciples not to tell anyone what they had seen, **until the Son of Man has been raised from the dead.**

17:10–13. Jesus' command for silence grew out of his realization that the multitudes of Israel had a wrong concept of the Messiah. They wanted a conquering king. They did not anticipate a suffering Messiah. Jesus did not want this magnificent display to encourage the masses to interfere with his suffering. He must go to Jerusalem, and he must die. And he did not want to encourage anyone to follow him for the wrong reason.

As the vision of Moses and Elijah lingered in the three disciples' minds, their heads must have been filled with questions. **Then** indicates that their question was a reaction to something they had witnessed or to Jesus' warning. They had just seen Elijah on the mountain. They knew the scribes anticipated Elijah's presence in association with Messiah's arrival. They did not understand why the Lord forbade them to tell anyone that Elijah had come.

Jesus assured them (17:11) that they had understood the Old Testament promise correctly. Jesus' promise that Elijah **will restore all things** was Jesus' paraphrase of Malachi 4:6: "He will turn the hearts of the fathers to their children, and the hearts of the children to their fathers; or else I will come and strike the land with a curse." He was using the future tense as though quoting the words of Malachi, for whom John's coming was future.

Then, with his **I tell you,** Jesus went on to explain that the prophecy had already been fulfilled in John the Baptizer—a fact he had already made known in 11:14. **They** (v. 12) means Israel, particularly as represented by the hypocritical leaders, who did not recognize John as God's coming **Elijah** because of their stubborn blindness and hardness of heart. Out of their hatred and ignorance, the enemies of the kingdom—Herod in particular—did to John **everything they wished,** rather than responding in the way God wished (see the Jewish leaders' rejection of John in 21:24–27). Just as they had mistreated the Messiah's forerunner, so they would also mistreat the Messiah. The same group of rebels would reject and persecute both John and Jesus (11:18–19).

With this, the three disciples' understanding was complete. They had come to realize that the prophecy of Elijah was fulfilled in John, and that it was John whom Jesus referred to in 17:11–12. In spite of Jesus' announcement in 11:14, it had taken them this long to realize more fully John's place in God's plan. Now they knew that God's plan was further along in its fulfillment.

B Meanwhile, Down Below: The Disciples' Continued Lack of Faith (17:14–21)

> **SUPPORTING IDEA:** *True dependence on God's power will give the kingdom citizen all he or she needs to do the kingdom work successfully.*

The failure of the nine disciples, who had remained below at the foot of the mountain, happened as the glory and authority of Jesus was being revealed on the mountain. In spite of the power available to them (17:2–5; also 10:1,8) and in spite of the truth about Jesus that they had confessed (16:16), their understanding and faith were still limited.

17:14–16. There was always a crowd near Jesus. We are probably to assume that this crowd was at or near Caesarea Philippi, awaiting his return from Mount Hermon and the Transfiguration. If this was the case, then this crowd was made up primarily of Gentiles.

As with the Canaanite woman (15:25), this man knelt before Jesus in desperation, begging for his help. Addressing Jesus with the title of respect, **Lord** (similar to "Sir" in English), the father explained that his son had **seizures.**

This Greek word for *seizures* (used only here in the New Testament) means literally, "to be moon-struck." The similarity between the backgrounds of the Greek and English words reveals the belief, common to many cultures, that insanity waxed and waned with the phases of the moon. The symptoms described by the boy's father were similar to those of epilepsy, but the context makes it clear that the boy's self-destructive behavior (falling into fire or water) was due to the influence of a demon (17:18–19).

While Jesus was experiencing his transfiguration on the mountain, the father had brought his son to the nine disciples. They had failed to draw on their delegated authority to cast out the demon and cure the boy. In 17:19, they expressed their puzzlement over this failure.

17:17–18. Jesus' harsh rebuke was directed toward the disciples. It was not surprising to hear him call them **unbelieving,** for he had already confronted their lack of faith many times. But for Jesus to address the disciples as part of an **unbelieving and perverted generation** was to lump them together with obstinate Israel and its hypocritical leaders (cf. 11:16; 12:39; 16:4).

The word **perverted** is the perfect passive participle of a Greek verb meaning "to make crooked, misshapen." It implies corruption or distortion of something to the point that the object is no longer useful. The disciples of the Messiah were empowered to draw upon his authority to advance the kingdom of heaven. Instead they failed miserably because of their lack of dependence on his power. This was symbolic of the failure of Israel.

At Jesus' command, the boy was brought to him. Jesus exercised the power of his word, rebuking the demon, who obeyed immediately. Matthew's wording that the boy was **healed from that moment** is parallel to the healing of the demonized girl in 15:28 (cf. 8:13). Jesus knew the power available to him. Although he was different than the disciples in that he was the Messiah-King, nevertheless he had delegated to them the same power and authority he had. Their failure to have enough faith to use this power frustrated Jesus.

17:19–21. Privately, the chastised disciples expressed their puzzlement over their failure (see comment on 17:16). Jesus' answer shed new light on the issue of a believer's faith. After grabbing their attention with **I tell you the**

truth, Jesus stated that their faith was so tiny that it was almost nonexistent. Even **faith as small as a mustard seed** (see comment on 13:31–32) was enough to move **this mountain** (possibly 9,200-foot Mount Hermon, looming above as Jesus pointed toward it) **from here to there** at a word (cf. this with 21:21, where Jesus taught that faith could enable the disciples to move another mountain). If such limited faith could give a follower of Jesus the same power he had exercised with his words, then the same power should be available to the follower to command a demon to leave a boy. In fact, with even this limited faith in God's infinite power, **nothing will be impossible for you.** The issue was not quantity of faith but quality of faith.

Attempting to quantify faith can be misleading. There is a common misperception today that "faith" in itself is the source of power, when true faith is actually an admission of powerlessness and a dependence on God's power. When Jesus spoke of **faith as small as a mustard seed,** he was encouraging us to let go of our own efforts and to rely instead on God's power.

A believer's lack of faith affects his or her ability to appropriate God's power to do God's work—to advance God's kingdom in the world. We are his instruments in this world. But if we choose to act without his power, we become useless to him.

Many people misinterpret the promise, "nothing will be impossible for you," and similar statements in the New Testament (e.g., John 14:13–14). This is not a blanket coverage of any desire we might express to God in prayer. Biblical faith taps into God's power and authority, but it can be exercised only in accordance with God's will (cf. 1 John 5:14). Biblical faith assumes not only a belief in God's power, but also a heart after God's own heart, which desires and asks for the things of God—not personal "wants." This is an important caution in light of the erroneous "name it and claim it" theology we hear so often today.

C The King's Second Prediction of His Death and Resurrection (17:22–23)

> **SUPPORTING IDEA:** *The road to the cross is the most difficult work of the kingdom servant. To take this road, we need the vision of the king's glory and the truth of the king's teaching.*

17:22–23. Jesus and his disciples were together in Jewish territory, before starting on the road to Jerusalem (19:1). Jesus made the second formal prediction of his suffering, death, and resurrection. This time he used the title **the Son of Man.** This clarified even further the suffering aspect of the Son of Man, the Messiah.

Even though Jesus was not yet literally moving toward the cross, Matthew's narrative is definitely moving in that direction, building the tragic picture in small bits.

The disciples' response to Jesus' prediction was deep distress and grief. Matthew used the extreme adverb (see comment on 17:6) to modify the verb "to distress, grieve." Their hopes were dashed because their preconceptions about the promised Messiah were so deeply ingrained in their Jewish hearts. They also feared the repercussions of such persecution upon them as the followers of Jesus. They overlooked the strong note of hope in Jesus' mention of the Resurrection.

D The Privileges and Responsibilities of Royal Sonship (17:24–27)

SUPPORTING IDEA: *Even though the king's death exempts his servants from obligations under the old covenant, we must be willing to give up our privileges for the ministry of the kingdom in the lives of others.*

In 16:17–19, Jesus introduced the church, together with some basic information about its invincibility, authority, responsibility, and mission. Beginning with this brief passage, Matthew turns our mind back to the church—the community of faith. This passage serves as a transition into Jesus' fourth discourse, Matthew 18, which clarifies the guidelines by which believers are to conduct their relationships with each other within the church. These verses emphasize the qualities of humility, purity, and mercy.

This introductory passage shares with Matthew 18 an emphasis on "children" of God in the community of faith, but it is also different from Matthew 18 in some significant ways. Matthew 18 deals with relationships within the church, while 17:24–27 deals with relationships between believers and unbelievers. Matthew 18 deals primarily with responsibilities, while 17:24–27 describes both the responsibilities and privileges of believers.

The central message of this passage is that the children of the king are no longer under the old covenant (temple tax of Exod. 30:13) but the new covenant. Modern believers are free from certain old covenant obligations. But we do have a responsibility to the king to live without sacrificing godly character. In this way, we may live at peace with others (Rom. 12:18 and context; 1 Tim. 2:1–2), and win as many as possible into the kingdom (1 Cor. 9:19–23). While sonship has its advantages, they are to be sacrificed to bring others to Christ.

17:24. Jesus had returned to Capernaum on the north shore of the Sea of Galilee, his base of operations after his withdrawal into Gentile territory throughout the events of 16:5–17:20. By the quick succession of events, Matthew gives us the impression that Jesus had not had much time to settle in before he was being harassed by those representing the Jewish religious establishment. This time it was the collectors of the temple tax.

17:25–27. Peter answered the tax collectors in the affirmative, either based on assumption or on Jesus' previous practice of paying the tax. But he did not have the means to pay this tax at the moment.

Jesus asked Peter to consider an analogy. Everyone knew that an earthly king's family was exempt from the king's taxes. This was part of the privilege of royalty. But all the commoners outside the royal family were obligated to pay taxes to the king. We must not become distracted from the main point of the passage concerning the payment of the temple tax.

Jesus was not teaching a lesson about civil taxes. Rather, he was paralleling the temple tax with the civil tax. The **kings of the earth** are parallel to God, and the **sons** represent true believers and children of God (5:9,45). The customs or poll tax paralleled the temple tax. Jesus left the implications for members of God's family unstated, but it is clearly implied: God's royal children are free from old covenant obligations that have been nullified by the new covenant.

In order **not to offend them** (literally, "causing them to stumble"), Jesus gave up the privilege for a higher value. The miraculous means by which God provided the tax money makes two points: (1) it underscored Jesus' point that the children of God are free from this kind of obligation; and (2) it testified again to the Father's faithfulness to provide for his children (6:19–34). The actual fulfillment of the miracle was not recorded. This has the effect of deemphasizing the miracle and drawing attention to the main lesson of the passage.

Jesus' payment of the unnecessary tax by supernatural means highlighted his humility. This will be an important theme in the discourse of chapter 18. The king did not have to pay the tax, but he sought to avoid causing offense to others.

> **MAIN IDEA REVIEW:** *Kingdom citizens must live confidently in the supremacy of the king's glorious power and the truth of the king's teachings. This gives them the faith to follow him to the cross.*

III. CONCLUSION

As children of God, we are responsible to follow the example of Jesus, relinquishing our privileges when they conflict with the ministry of redemption in the lives of people. (By extension, note that Jesus himself, the unique Son of God, relinquished his greatest privilege and right—uninterrupted life in glory with the Father—for the ministry of redemption to us, who are the most unworthy.)

PRINCIPLES

- Jesus is the Son of God and the supreme Prophet whose word all believers must heed.
- Reverence and even fear are appropriate responses to the awesome glory of God.
- God is compassionate.
- Believers have an obligation to civil authorities.

APPLICATIONS

- Submit always to the authoritative Word of God.
- Revere God. Praise him continually.
- Maintain a clear vision of the glory and power of God. This helps the believer remain faithful even through hardship to the kingdom.
- Understand that righteous suffering occurs within the framework of God's purposes and power.
- Avoid adopting the mind-set and values of the world.
- Pay the taxes you owe.

IV. LIFE APPLICATION

Turn on the Power!

We are attracted to displays of power. The forces of nature—hurricanes, tornadoes, earthquakes, and so on—get our attention, especially when they affect us directly. And rightly so. The damage these natural phenomenon cause is staggering. They demand a healthy respect.

Even beyond that direct involvement, we are awed by the power we see in nature. And, we are creative in capturing what natural power we can for our benefit. Dams store water that have energy potential. Nuclear power plants span our nation.

We are so quick to recognize and understand physical power, and quick to harness it. We need power to live our lives on this earth. That same principle applies to the spiritual world and kingdom living. But too often we fail to harness the spiritual power God makes available to us for kingdom living. God has delegated to us the power we need to be citizens of his kingdom.

An understanding of the truth of Jesus' teaching and a grasp on God's power will enable us to live righteously in God's kingdom, in spite of difficulties we may face. It was the vision of Jesus' power and glory in the Transfiguration that gave sustenance to the disciples and motivated them to persevere through persecution.

Without his strength and the power he provides for kingdom living, we will fail. Are you living by the power God provides, or trying to generate your own?

V. PRAYER

Lord, forgive us when we fail to exercise the power you have delegated to us as citizens of your kingdom. Make us bold witnesses to others of your love and grace and life-changing power. Amen.

VI. DEEPER DISCOVERIES

A. "Nothing Will Be Impossible for You" (17:19–21)

Several other New Testament passages state this condition more clearly in various ways. For example, we find that answered prayer is dependent on:

- our abiding in Jesus and his word abiding in us (John 15:7),
- our motives being right, not selfish (Jas. 4:3),
- our righteous character (Jas. 5:16),
- our consistent obedience (1 John 3:21–22), and
- our asking according to God's will (1 John 5:14–15).

All such promises in Scripture assume that God will answer all prayers that are according to his will, and that we can exercise his authority to do anything that is according to his will (the equivalent of praying "in his name"). However, from this truth comes yet another misconception—that we must be able to discern God's will before we ask for anything or draw upon his authority to act in the world. The prayer lives of many believers have been paralyzed by such assumptions.

None of the passages above prohibit making requests that are contrary to God's will. The New Testament simply tells us that such requests will not be granted. This should give the believer great freedom and security. We can ask for literally anything, and then trust our wise and loving Father to sort out that which is according to his will (and also in our best interest; 7:9–11).

Where we are likely to stray is in expecting something that we have no right to expect. If we ask in faith for something clearly promised in Scripture (e.g., wisdom, Jas. 1:5–8), then we are guaranteed to receive it (although not necessarily in the way or at the time we expect). If we ask for something that is contrary to God's will (e.g., harm to a person), then we are either guaranteed not to receive it, or we will receive it as an act of God's judgment (cf. "they have received their reward in full," 6:2,5,16).

Finally, in the many areas where God's will is unclear, we must search our hearts for right motives, ask God for wisdom, and then come to the Father as a child and place our request before him. The Father delights to please his children. He will grant our requests whenever he can and refuse them whenever he must—for our good and his glory.

As we grow in our knowledge of the Father and in our faith in him, we will develop a mind and heart more and more like his. Out of this heart will flow fewer of our selfish desires and more of his desires. Our prayers will reflect this transformation (Ps. 37:4; 1 Cor. 2:6–16, esp. v. 16; Rom. 12:2).

B. Summary

Without this chapter, we would not understand an important motivation for the disciples' spiritual sustenance through persecution—their vision of Jesus' transfiguration. Nor would we understand Jesus' supremacy over all holy men of history, or his continuity with or fulfillment of the Old Testament. Without this chapter, we would miss an important lesson on the abundant power of God (17:1–8) and our freedom to tap into it for success in kingdom work (17:20). And finally we would miss an important key to understanding our privileges and responsibilities under the new covenant (17:24–27).

VII. TEACHING OUTLINE

A. INTRODUCTION

1. Lead Story: It Is Even Better Than I Had Hoped
2. Context: Matthew has turned his Gospel away from the supernatural demonstrations of Jesus' authority in chapters 8–15 toward the purposes of: (1) highlighting the disciples' progress in faith; (2) developing the understanding of the new community, the church; and (3) escalating the conflict between Jesus and his opponents.

   Matthew 17 moves the story along from the transition of chapter 16 toward the teaching on the new community in chapter 18 and the climaxing conflict through the rest of Matthew's Gospel.

3. Transition: The story of Jesus' transfiguration (17:1–8) gave Peter, James, and John a glimpse of eternal perspective and Jesus' true glory. The Transfiguration further advanced these three disciples' understanding of the identity and power of Jesus, building especially on the confession of 16:16.

   Twice (17:9,12 and 17:22–23), Jesus referred to his suffering, death, and resurrection, fulfilling the pattern set in 16:21 and preparing for the fulfillment of all the predictions at the end of the Gospel.

   The episode with the demonized boy (17:14–18) and the subsequent teaching on faith (17:19–20) showed that the disciples still had room to grow in their faith, even after the breakthrough of 16:16.

The discussion of the temple tax (17:24–27) turned the reader's mind toward the privileges and responsibilities of being a part of the New Testament community of faith—the church. This is the theme of Matthew's fourth discourse in chapter 18.

B. COMMENTARY

1. Up on High: A Glimpse of the King's Glory (17:1–13)
2. Meanwhile, Down Below: The Disciples' Continued Lack of Faith (17:14–21)
3. The King's Second Prediction of His Death and Resurrection (17:22–23)
4. The Privileges and Responsibilities of Royal Sonship (17:24–27)

C. CONCLUSION

1. Wrap-up: Kingdom citizens must live confidently in the supremacy of the king's glorious power and the truth of the king's teachings. This gives them the faith to follow him to the cross.
2. Personal Challenge: The more we get to know Jesus, the more we will be awed by the glorious, humble, compassionate person he is. Are you taking regular, disciplined time to get to know Jesus better? He is even better than you had hoped!

VIII. ISSUES FOR DISCUSSION

1. Who were the three disciples before whom Jesus was transfigured?
2. Who were the two Old Testament personalities who appeared with Jesus at his transfiguration? What significance might be attached to their appearance?
3. Why did Jesus tell his disciples not to tell anyone about the transfiguration event, "until the Son of Man has been raised from the dead"?
4. Why were the disciples not able to cast the demon out of the boy with seizures? Why did Jesus rebuke the disciples?

Matthew 18

The King Explains Christian Personal Relationships

I. **INTRODUCTION**
You Are Asking the Wrong Question

II. **COMMENTARY**
A verse-by-verse explanation of the chapter.

III. **CONCLUSION**
An overview of the principles and applications from the chapter.

IV. **LIFE APPLICATION**
That God May Be Exalted

Melding the chapter to life.

V. **PRAYER**
Tying the chapter to life with God.

VI. **DEEPER DISCOVERIES**
Historical, geographical, and grammatical enrichment of the commentary.

VII. **TEACHING OUTLINE**
Suggested step-by-step group study of the chapter.

VIII. **ISSUES FOR DISCUSSION**
Zeroing the chapter in on daily life.

Quote

"*Humility must always be the portion of any man who receives acclaim earned in the blood of his followers and the sacrifices of his friends.*"

D w i g h t   D .   E i s e n h o w e r

Matthew 18

IN A NUTSHELL

Jesus weaves three themes throughout his discourse on the ethics of Christian relationships—humility, purity, and mercy. Those who are humble will be the greatest in the kingdom. The Father protects his "little ones," and will make every effort to restore those who stray. Christians must mercifully forgive sinning brothers and sisters.

The King Explains Christian Personal Relationships

I. INTRODUCTION

You Are Asking the Wrong Question

*H*ave you ever made a fool of yourself? We all have at one time or another. And it often happens when we have not been paying much attention to our surroundings. It is sometimes called "sleeping on the job."

I recall one such incident that took place during a class at a Bible college. It seems one of the students held a night job and always found it difficult to stay awake during his early morning, first-hour class. In fact, one day he fell asleep in his seat before the beginning of class. The other students arrived and took their seats. The instructor walked in, opened his notes, and began teaching. Virtually no one noticed our sleepy friend . . . until a student nudged him and whispered, "Quick—the professor just asked you to lead in prayer!"

Reacting to what his brain had barely registered, the sleeping student snapped straight up in his seat and began praying. Of course, all this was to the complete surprise of everyone in the room.

It was an unforgettable moment, prompting every person in the room to ask, "Where have you been?" Jesus likely felt like asking the same question of his disciples on more than one occasion. As Matthew 18 opens, the disciples had evidently been sleeping on the job. They were out of touch with their surroundings and their Master.

Chapter 18 opens with the disciples asking Jesus a question. That they asked this particular question indicates they still did not understand the heart of Christ's instruction and the appropriate relationships in his kingdom. Like the groggy student, they were "asleep on the job" and spouting off the wrong questions at the wrong time. The disciples asked, "Who is the greatest in the kingdom of heaven?" Jesus spent the rest of the Matthew 18 discourse telling them, "You are asking the wrong question."

II. COMMENTARY

The King Explains Christian Personal Relationships

> **MAIN IDEA:** *The Father esteems and protects each of his precious children—even when they sin. We must esteem and protect them with the same loving mercy.*

Matthew 18, the fourth of Jesus' five discourses in Matthew, is about life in the church—the king's new community. The placement of this discourse in Matthew is determined by two factors: (1) the readiness of the disciples to think toward the church age; and (2) the nearness of Jesus' death and departure, motivating him to prepare his disciples for the church's proper operation and its members' proper attitudes toward one another.

The disciples needed to overturn their concept of "greatness." So do we. If we could absorb and implement Jesus' teaching in this discourse, it would revolutionize our self-concept and our relationships with fellow believers. It would change our churches and advance our testimony to the world (cf. John 13:35).

Jesus' discourse in Matthew 18 flows from his concern for his church. Its members were to be humble as a child. They were to abandon their silly, self-deceptive, grown-up pride. They were to be careful not to corrupt the king's other "little ones." In fact, we may find great security in the knowledge that the Father values his "little ones" so greatly that he protects them with wrathful possessiveness. This protective God is *our* Father. Should we stray into sin, he will pursue us and rejoice at our restoration. The humility of his "little ones" is precious in his sight. Their "littleness" defines greatness in God's kingdom.

Moreover, we "little ones" have a responsibility to the other "little ones" in God's family. We are not only to avoid causing one another to sin, but we are also to steer back to the path in love those who have sinned. God esteems his humble children so highly that he mobilizes the whole family to preserve them.

God calls us to forgive continuously the other "little ones" who offend us, just as we ourselves are continuously forgiven. No offense by any of God's children—against him or against one another—will lower our value in his eyes. Forgiveness is a foundational and pervasive characteristic of all who know God. He expects his church to love and forgive with the same love he has shown (John 13:34–35).

The greatest person in God's eyes is the humblest penitent. God says, "I choose to treat this 'little one' as my most treasured possession. You must treat him accordingly!"

How different the average church would be today if we saw ourselves and one another through the king's eyes. What would become of the infighting, the politics, the sacred cows, the superiority and inferiority complexes? How differently would we appear to the world around us?

On first reading, Matthew 18 may seem like a collection of unrelated teachings and parables. Upon further study, however, we begin to see a single theme: how to relate to one another in love within the church. In fact, the various teaching segments and parables are intended to balance each other, keeping the members of the church from going too far into laxity or severity in dealing with one another.

When we read this chapter carefully, we realize that the "little children" (18:1–6,10), the "lost sheep" (vv. 12–14), the "sinning brother" (vv. 15–20), and the "indebted servant" (vv. 21–35) are different ways of referring to fellow believers in the church. In fact, each of us, at some time in our lives, has probably been aptly described by each of these pictures. Such a person is always a beloved child of God. He is to be treated as such by the other children, until that person proves that he really does not want to live by the family principles (18:17).

Statements from this chapter have been taken out of their context by some people. But they take on new meaning when placed back into the context. For example, verses 18–19 have nothing to do with special prayer power. Rather, they describe the Father's endorsement of church discipline decisions regarding his beloved, rebellious children.

Here is how Jesus' teaching flows in answer to his disciples' question. Each major section of Jesus' discourse in 18:5–35 flows from his initial answer (18:2–4) to the disciples' opening question (18:1):

- The greatest in the kingdom of heaven is a weak, vulnerable child who needs the wrathful, possessive protection of Jesus (18:5–9).
- The greatest in the kingdom of heaven is just the opposite of what you might think. He is a restored rebel, who was brought back to Jesus (18:10–14).
- The greatest in the kingdom of heaven is the person who shares in Jesus' tireless, patient, zealous pursuit after rebellious little children (18:15–20).
- The greatest in the kingdom of heaven is the person who forgives as he himself has been forgiven—endlessly and unconditionally (18:21–35).

Ⓐ The Humble Will Be the Greatest in the Kingdom (18:1–4)

SUPPORTING IDEA: *The Father most highly esteems the most humble of his children.*

For more on the elevation of childlike faith, see Matthew 11:25; 19:13–15. For a similar correction of the disciples' misperception of "status" in the kingdom, see 20:20–28.

Beginning here, the theme of humility runs throughout chapter 20, leading up to Jesus' humble mode of transportation into Jerusalem (riding on a donkey). These chapters fix firmly in the reader's mind the picture of a Messiah who commands and models humility and servanthood. This happens just before Matthew reveals Jesus the righteous judge in the purification of the temple (21:12–13), and the ensuing climactic conflicts in 21:14 through chapter 23. Matthew skillfully fills out the fully balanced character of the Messiah-King (which his followers are to imitate). Jesus shows us how to be "as shrewd as snakes and as innocent as doves" (10:16).

18:1. At that time is an idiomatic expression, and it should not be taken as it would be in twentieth-century English. It means "about that time." If Jesus presented the discourse soon after the events of 17:24–27, perhaps the disciples' opening question sprang out of Jesus' mention of the privileges of kingdom children (17:25–26).

The disciples' question revealed a serious misconception about the kingdom of heaven. They assumed God's kingdom would be like any other kingdom on earth—one in which rank, status, power, and authority were the marks of greatness. Jesus' discourse corrected this error.

18:2–3. Jesus' response to the disciples showed how selfish and foolish their question was. They were thinking childishly, but Jesus showed them that mature faith is the opposite. Mature faith is childlike humility. In fact, elsewhere in the New Testament, Peter seemed to suggest that the more mature a disciple's faith becomes, the more brotherly kindness and love it demonstrates (2 Pet. 1:5–9). The child Jesus called to him served as an object lesson for the disciples. It was a memorable image to help them learn the nature of true maturity. Little children are the most helpless and powerless members of society. But Jesus infused their childlike qualities with value and greatness.

Jesus' **I tell you the truth** might be translated as "Listen up!" In fact, the disciples had not been listening well when he taught the same paradoxical principles in 5:3–12 and 16:24–25.

One way to summarize Jesus' first statement is to say that there is a sign on the gates of God's kingdom reading, "No grown-ups past this point," or "No big-shots allowed!" Jesus was not rejecting the positive aspects of adulthood but the self-sufficiency, pride, sophisticated denial, and self-deception that are learned with years of practice in a sinful world. These negative qualities are not the only reason for God's judgment, but they constitute the "unforgivable sin" of 12:31–32—a stubborn, self-righteous refusal to accept the forgiveness necessary for entry into God's kingdom. At the root of true maturity is simplicity, not sophistication.

18:4. This second statement served as a poetic restatement of the first (18:3), but it also clarified the specific childlike quality believers are to imitate—humility. All the complicated mental gymnastics adults use to avoid facing the truth take us farther from the kingdom. The person who comes to Jesus in simple humility, recognizing Jesus' greatness and his own lowliness, is the greatest in God's kingdom. This person enters the kingdom by grace and serves in such a way as to inherit reward. A person like this warms the heart of the Almighty. He will be used by God to accomplish the greatest good for the kingdom.

The child Jesus called was standing in their midst even as Jesus spoke (**this child**). He was so simple in his trust of Jesus that he came when called, not knowing what Jesus wanted him for. He simply obeyed. He had not yet learned the art of self-assertion, pride, self-deception, and disobedience.

Ⓑ The Father Jealously Protects the Believer's Soul (18:5–9)

SUPPORTING IDEA: *The Father will judge anyone who causes a child of his to sin.*

To make a break here is somewhat artificial. Jesus' flow of thought was continuous through at least 18:14. We recognize the continuity of 18:5–9 with the preceding in the use of **a little child** (18:5) and **these little ones** (18:6). But there is also a shift in emphasis here, from the central character of God's child to the Father's protective warning against any who would corrupt his child. Jesus answered Peter's opening question (18:1) by saying, in essence, "The greatest in the kingdom of heaven is a weak, vulnerable child who needs protection."

18:5–6. Jesus revealed his attitude toward his followers by teaching how we are to treat one another. Specifically, we should treat one another exactly as we would treat Jesus if he were living among us in the flesh. **Welcomes** implies every aspect of caring for other persons—accepting them, loving them, providing for them—as a gracious host "welcomes" a guest (Matt. 10:40–42). **In my name** means "for my sake" or "as though he were me." For a more expanded treatment of the concept that ministry to a believer is ministry to Jesus, see Matthew 25:31–46.

The opposite of welcoming a believer is causing another believer to **sin** (meaning to "plant a snare, cause to stumble, offend"). In this context, when a believer stumbles, he sins. Jesus did not remove responsibility from the believer for his own sin, but he placed even greater responsibility on the person who influences the stumbling believer. Jesus' condemnation of the person causing the sin is weightier than that of the stumbling sinner, for he will pursue the latter, seeking his restoration (18:12–16). But Jesus predicted destruction for the former, who not only committed his own sin, but also endangered the souls of others (18:6–9).

Verse 6 includes one of the clues that clarifies the identity of the **little ones**. They are those **who believe in me**.

Passages such as Romans 14 and 1 Corinthians 8 and 10 explain the specific ways believers can cause other believers to "sin" or violate their own consciences. Certainly no one should influence a follower of Jesus to do something that is wrong, but Paul's teaching warns against using our freedom to cause a brother to do what would be wrong for him, even if it is permissible for us.

It would be better for him is paralleled in 18:8–9, although the wording is different. The comparisons are intended to heighten our respect for the Father's protective wrath concerning the well-being of his **little ones**. What could be worse than drowning in the depths of the sea, cutting off a hand or a foot, or plucking out an eye? The Father's wrath over the corruption of a believer would be worse.

The **millstone** was literally "a millstone of a donkey," or one so large a human could not turn it. The millstone contrasts with the stumbling block placed in the path of the "little one." If any fool puts a small block in a believer's way, causing him to sin, God's wrath would be worse than hanging a huge millstone around the offender's neck and drowning him **in the depths of the sea**. A smaller stone and just a few feet of water would accomplish the same end. But the size of the millstone and the depth of the water serve to amplify the severity of the judgment—a judgment that is **better** than facing God's wrath.

This is a vivid picture of temporal (as opposed to eternal, 1 Cor. 11:29–30) judgment, not unlike God's severity with Ananias and Sapphira (Acts 5:1–11). Later in this discourse, we will learn that we are obligated to protect believers by directing them from the path of sin (18:15–20) and by forgiving their offenses against us (18:21–35).

18:7. Woe means that God's judgment is about to fall. It is as though God had his hand raised, ready to come down in wrath at any moment. Jesus pronounced impending judgment on the world for **things that cause people to sin**. The secular world is filled with temptations for believers. One day this world will be destroyed. The inevitability of temptations in the world does not excuse one's sin. Jesus' second "woe" is a pronouncement of impending judgment focused on the corrupting individuals.

18:8–9. Jesus used similar words over and over with different audiences, or sometimes with the same audience at different times to make the same point. We find statements identical in meaning to these two verses in 5:29–30. The wording differs in several details, but the message is the same.

Because these warnings were addressed to the community of believers, we might conclude that a believer can lose his salvation and be sent to hell. Indeed, the warning is intended to sober believers concerning the seriousness of stumbling. But the eternal punishment would only be carried out on a person who proved, by his sin, that he had never been a child of God.

C The Father Zealously Pursues the Straying Believer (18:10–14)

SUPPORTING IDEA: *Even when we sin, the Father spares no effort to restore us.*

Again, note that the division here is somewhat artificial, since Jesus' flow of thought was continuous. His warning in the first part of 18:10 sprung out of the warnings of 18:6–9. But in the latter half of 18:10, he began to explain the extent to which the Father goes in protecting his "little ones." This is the overriding theme of 18:10–14.

18:10–11. The phrase **See that** is literally "see," meaning "be sure that, give attention to." **Look down on** means "to think little of" or "to despise." We are commanded to treat one another with a sense of value. How might someone be in danger of looking down on one of Jesus' "little ones"? From the context of the discourse, it might be through causing the believer to sin (18:5–9); by failing to confront a brother's sin or by confronting with a vengeful motive (18:15–20); or by failing to forgive a brother (18:21–35). The Father views all of these actions as "child abuse," and he will not tolerate them.

Jesus then gave one reason we are to view fellow believers as valuable. His mention of the believers' **angels** is an indirect warning of judgment against those who would mistreat his children. Matthew's Jewish readers typically understood that every Jewish person had a "guardian angel."

The word **always** means that the believer's angel always has the immediate attention of the Father. And **see the face of my Father** implies being in the Father's presence in personal, close relationship—receiving the Father's constant, full attention. Such is the Father's care for his **little ones**. (Both Luke 1:19 and Rev. 8:2 refer to angels in God's presence, and Acts 12:15 mentions Peter's "angel.")

18:12. Jesus explained the Father's protectiveness and love for his children in another way. **What do you think?** was a common way for a Jewish teacher to start his students' minds working over a mental problem, as he introduced a new concept or teaching (17:25; 21:28; 22:42).

We know from the context (e.g., 18:6,15) that the sheep's straying represented the believer's falling into a pattern of sin, departing from the pattern of righteous living suited to God's children.

The parable of the one lost sheep is somewhat hyperbolic, focusing attention on the lost sheep over the ninety-nine who stayed in place. Jesus' purpose was to correct the misconception that the believer who sinned was less valuable in the Father's eyes than the rest. In reality, the Father values all of his believers equally. Jesus made it a point to emphasize the value of the one straying sheep.

This emphasis also drew attention to the Father's grace. God wanted the universe to know that he is a God who pursues his own and rescues even those who rebel against him.

One way Jesus emphasized the Father's love for a straying believer was by highlighting the trouble to which the Father (the Shepherd) went to restore the sinning believer: (1) he left the ninety-nine behind; (2) he searched through dangerous "mountain" terrain; and (3) he continually searched until the sheep was found.

18:13. The word **if** expresses uncertainty. It renders the outcome of the Father's (the Shepherd's) search far from certain—**If he finds it.** Some straying believers will return to the path of righteousness and the fellowship of the community (18:15–17a), but some will continue their own way, away from the community, away from the Father, into self-destruction (18:17b). We must share responsibility for the loss of brothers because of failure to fulfill our responsibility to them (18:15–20).

The tension of the uncertainty regarding the believer's restoration makes the joy at the restoration of a single person even greater. Jesus drew special attention to the Father's rejoicing with the phrase **I tell you the truth.** He further heightened the Father's joy by comparing it with his joy at the continued faithfulness of those who follow the path of righteousness. His joy with the ninety-nine faithful ones was not meant to be minimized. It was assumed that he was already greatly pleased with them, but he loved to display his saving grace toward those who were most undeserving (cf. with Paul's exaltation of God for saving even "sinners—of whom I am the worst," 1 Tim. 1:15–17).

18:14. Jesus continued his emphasis on the value of the individual believer, especially one who rebels. The Father's "will" is his permissive will, that is, his heart's "desire," which he sometimes allows *not* to be fulfilled (2 Pet. 3:9). This is in contrast with his sovereign will, which is always fulfilled (Eph. 1:11). A straying believer who returns fulfills both God's sovereign will and his permissive will. A believer who does not return fulfills the perfect wisdom of God's sovereign will, but he breaks the Lord's heart by going against the longing of God's permissive will.

Be lost is from a verbal root meaning "destroy utterly." This is clearly applied to a true believer, since the **little ones** are those "who believe in me" (18:6). Some interpret this to mean that a believer can lose his salvation. However, if we accept the irrefutable teaching of the New Testament on the eternal security of the believer (e.g., John 10:28–30; 11:25), we must assume this "destruction" refers to the straying believer's death at the end of his earthly life, after which he will find an eternal welcome in heaven but little or no eternal reward (1 Cor. 3:12–15; 9:24–27; 11:30).

In the next portion of the discourse (18:15–20), Jesus explained how we can participate in his "pursuit" of a straying fellow believer.

DPatiently and Truthfully Pursuing the Straying Brother (18:15–20)

SUPPORTING IDEA: *Believers must take seriously their role as the Father's agents in pursuing his straying children and seeking their restoration.*

Our cooperation in seeking to restore sinning believers is not optional. These are commands. Failure to follow Jesus' instructions regarding church discipline—either by neglect or by confronting with wrong motives or in the wrong manner—is one of the greatest sins of modern Christianity (Matt. 6:14–15).

18:15. "Church discipline" is commonly thought to refer only to those "official" cases in which the sin is extremely serious and the entire church becomes formally involved in the effort to correct the sinning brother or sister. In reality, church discipline is more biblically understood as covering every effort by any individual or group of individuals in the church to turn a straying believer back to righteous living.

For this reason, Jesus addressed first every church member's responsibility to go privately (**between the two of you**) to the sinning brother to **show** him his sin ("bring to light, expose").

This is the gentlest of the four steps of church discipline for several reasons: (1) It is based on the foundation of a relationship between the confronter and the straying brother. This increases the likelihood that the confrontation will be perceived as a loving act. (2) It is done in private to preserve the dignity of the straying brother. The smaller the number of people involved, the more likely the brother's embarrassment will not be a hindrance to his further growth. (3) The confronter's main task is to **show** the straying brother his sin. We must go into every confrontation assuming the best—that what we might perceive is a willful sin is possibly a matter of negligence, or that we have wrongly perceived the person's actions, and that the straying brother or sister will respond correctly. (4) **Go** is in the Greek present tense (imperative mood), implying a gentle, patient series of confrontations.

The motive is love, and the goal is to make it as easy as possible for the straying brother or sister to receive the message and make the change. We are to make every effort to avoid public or private humiliation. This is every church member's responsibility, and we are to remain focused on the central purpose of restoration. Maintaining the focus to correct the straying believer in a spirit of love will guide us in selecting the best words, setting, timing, and manner for the confrontation. To do this properly takes time and prayer.

The relationship between the two brothers also implies that there is a prior history between the two, through which a spirit of trust and acceptance has developed. Therefore, effective church discipline requires an investment before the first step. We must be involved in one another's lives—sharing life experiences, showing trust and transparency, learning one another's nonverbal language, priorities, dreams, and fears. Our successful involvement in the Father's pursuit of the straying brother depends on our prior investment in the relationship.

After explaining the first step for confronting a sinning brother, Jesus acknowledged the better of two possible responses. He might actually **listen**, in which case **you have won your brother over.** We are to read into this statement all the joy of the Father over the rescued sheep in 18:13. And we are to assume that this is a much more likely outcome than many believers think possible. Done correctly in the environment of a trusting relationship, one-on-one confrontation will often result in a positive response. Let us start by believing in the power of God to turn a heart and the longing of every believer for the fulfillment and security of holy living.

18:16. In 18:15b, Jesus acknowledged the second and worse response toward a straying brother—continued resistance. In this case, the next step is to take **one or two others along.** Including the original confronter, this increases the number of confronters to two or three. This is important, as Jesus showed from Deuteronomy 19:15 (also Num. 35:30; Deut. 17:6). These numbers are based on the requirement, under Mosaic Law, that no accusation should be taken seriously unless it was confirmed by the testimony of more than one witness.

The purpose of the additional witnesses is primarily: (1) to bring added loving persuasion to the straying brother so he will realize the seriousness of his sin; (2) to prepare for the possibility of the straying brother's continued resistance (in this event, there would be third-party **testimony** concerning what happened in the confrontation); and (3) to provide one or two "referees" or moderators in the continued confrontation between the original confronter and the straying brother. It is possible the witnesses might conclude that the accuser was wrong.

Again, the hope is that the two or three witnesses will be able to cooperate in the Father's zealous pursuit of the straying brother in order to bring him back from the danger of destruction (18:12–14).

An important question that Jesus did not address is how long the moderators should wait for the brother to respond before progressing to step 2 (and between later steps, as well). This will probably vary from situation to situation, but there must be a balance between gracious patience (allowing the brother sufficient time for a change of heart) and unwavering truthfulness (not waiting so long that the straying brother and other observers conclude that the sin in question is not serious).

18:17. If every effort to turn the straying brother back to righteous ends in futility, the only alternative is to **tell it to the church.** What Jesus had in mind for the gathering of believers who should hear about the brother's sin can be debated. In the first century, where communities were close-knit and the local churches were small house gatherings, everyone would naturally be a party to this problem. Because all might be affected by the brother's sin, all church members should be warned of its danger. This way, all might be instrumental in helping bring the offender back to righteousness.

However, in our society today, many relationships—even within the church—are superficial. Especially in larger churches, there may be situations that would warrant a public announcement only to the segment of the local church that needs to know about the brother's sin and that is in a position to respond to it.

At least the following church members should be included: (1) anyone who is likely to be harmed or misled by not knowing about the sin or by failing to recognize its sinfulness and seriousness; (2) anyone who should be warned by the sinning brother's negative example; and (3) anyone who can be instrumental in bringing the straying brother back to righteousness. The **two or three** starts with as few as possible for adjudication. And the local "church" is the highest ecclesiastical court on earth. In between could be other groups (e.g. a small Bible study group, a large Sunday school class, a group of elders). The primary goal of church discipline is not public embarrassment but the recruitment of the entire church to help in the Father's pursuit of the straying believer.

In the event that the believer continues to resist the appeals of all his brothers and sisters, he is to be removed from the fellowship. He has refused submission to the church (Heb. 13:17). Therefore, he is to be treated as an unbeliever, which is precisely the position he has taken.

Just as the Lord is open to receiving a repentant Pharisee (Matt. 3:7–8; John 3:1–21; 7:50–52; 19:38–42), so also Jesus should be seen here as leaving the door open for even a hardened heart such as this to soften and return.

The Bible insists that every Christian be accountable to the local assembly. The Bible knows nothing of an isolated, individual Christian. The issue is not technology but theology. Christ insists the members of his body *act* like it!

18:18. This and the next two verses are a natural extension of Jesus' teaching on church discipline, although they are often taken out of context by modern believers. To this point, Jesus had been emphasizing the responsibility of the church to confront sin in its midst and to bring the sinning brother back. Matthew 18:18–20 emphasizes the church's authority in taking such action.

I tell you the truth was intended to recapture the disciples' attention afresh on the same topic. Jesus had a new emphasis they needed to grasp to fulfill his instructions.

Jesus' wording was almost identical to that in 16:19. The primary difference is the switch from the singular (addressed to Peter in 16:19) to the plural (addressed to all the disciples here). In 16:19, Jesus' comments about "binding" and "loosing" related to the church's authority to open doors through the wielding of God's revealed Word. The issue here was the fellowship of believers in the local church. Jesus was emphasizing the church's authority to shut the door to the community of faith in the face of the sinning brother who resisted every effort the believers made to restore him to holy character. Just as the church has authority to close that door, it also has authority to open it again, should the believer repent.

The future perfect tense here should be translated, "shall have been bound/loosed in heaven." In other words, the church discipline decisions the church makes—when it follows Jesus' guidelines carefully and maintains a right attitude—are in keeping with what has already been decided by God in heaven. This does not imply that the Lord communicates his decisions to the believers in every situation. As we follow Jesus' guidelines and pursue the brother with the loving heart of the pursuing Father, we can rest assured that our decisions on earth are in keeping with his in heaven. He has given us all the guidance we need, and his Holy Spirit is with us to help us fulfill his instructions.

The Father's endorsement of our decisions on earth is especially critical in Matthew 18. Our disciplinary actions toward the sinning brother are actually our participation in the Father's zealous pursuit of his "little one" (18:12–14). If we fulfill his will and serve as his instruments in loving pursuit of his runaway child, we may rest assured that our actions and decisions are in keeping with his. He has entrusted his dear child to us; we must handle that child with care.

18:19–20. These two verses are among the most misunderstood in the Bible. They are traditionally taken to mean that God pays special attention to the prayers of believers when two or more gather or agree together. But such an interpretation is wrong for two reasons: (1) it takes the statements out of the context of church discipline and the pursuit of the straying brother; and (2) the conclusions that it leads to regarding prayer is contrary to Scripture.

Nowhere in the Bible does God imply that he listens any differently to one person praying than he does to two, ten, or five hundred. If he does hear two or more people better than he hears one, then we must assume that Jesus' prayers lacked effectiveness when he went off alone to pray (14:23; 26:36–44). James made the point that the prayer of a single righteous person is powerful enough to heal a sick person by drawing on the power of the God who listens to each of his children, together or individually (Jas. 5:14–18).

This promise guarantees guidance for the two or three (actually a figure of speech recognizing the part for the whole) who confront a straying believer. This is also a promise to the church to claim wisdom and act with authority in the restoration process toward the sinning person. In other words, when this process is pursued as Christ outlined it, his presence and power are assured.

Agree is from *sumphoneo* (literally, "sound out together"), meaning "harmonize." **Anything you ask for** in this context means an appeal to God for support of the witnesses' actions to restore the sinning brother or to excommunicate him.

By his reference back to a few details from 18:15–17, Jesus was implying a reference to all of the details. So, in this "if" clause, Jesus was saying, "The condition upon which God will base his endorsement of your disciplinary activity is your pursuit of your brother, with the zealous love of the Father in your hearts, and with careful attention to the guidelines I have given." If we follow these guidelines, the fulfillment of God's will concerning the sinning brother **will be done for you by my Father in heaven.**

By his promise to be present **with them,** Jesus claimed a role belonging only to the Almighty (cf. Joel 2:27; Zech. 2:10–11). His promise was another claim to deity.

E Humbly and Mercifully Forgiving the Sinning Brother (18:21–35)

> **SUPPORTING IDEA:** *We are obligated, because of the Father's infinite mercy toward us, to treat with unconditional mercy our fellow believers who sin against us.*

Jesus completed his discourse about the value and treatment of his children with one more caution applied to our relationships with fellow believers who sin against us. As we deal with straying believers (18:15–20), we may be tempted to become merciless toward them, especially when they sin against us. In abandoning mercy, we forget that the Father has shown us great mercy. In this regard, we are no better than our sinning fellow believers. Jesus illustrated through a parable the attitude we are to display toward those who are "indebted" to us in their sins against us. It is an attitude that he displayed lavishly toward us, and we are to imitate this attitude in our relationships with others.

Forgiving our sinning brothers and sisters is a part of our duty toward God's children, just as it is our duty to pursue them for restoration to righteousness. To fail to forgive fellow believers is to abuse God's children, and so incur the Father's wrath. Forgiveness is a foundational characteristic of the family of God.

18:21–22. Peter again spoke for the Twelve. His question could easily have sprung out of Jesus' teaching on church discipline (18:15–20). Peter may have wondered how long he should forgive his sinning brother before casting him out of the church, especially when the sin was against him personally. According to some Jewish tradition, a brother was forgiven three times for the same offense. The fourth offense, however, need not be forgiven, because it would be evidence that the brother had not repented. Peter thought he was being generous in forgiving **up to seven times.**

But the king showed that Peter, even in his "generosity," was thinking human thoughts, not the thoughts of God (16:23). There is some debate over whether Jesus' response should read "seventy times seven" (490) or **seventy-seven,** but the exact number is not important. The numbers involved are presented for emphasis only. "Keep on forgiving endlessly; don't carry a grudge" is what Jesus was saying.

18:23. **Therefore** was Jesus' way of introducing the parable to illustrate the principle he stated in 18:22. He told the disciples first that they were going to learn something about the kingdom of heaven (18:1–4), and he set the scene by introducing the characters (a king and his servants) and explaining the king's desire **to settle accounts with his servants**—to collect from them what they owed him. The king represents God, and the servants represent fellow believers.

18:24–25. It was not uncommon for servants and indebted free men to be sold as slaves to cover debts they could not pay (Lev. 25:39; 2 Kgs. 4:1). In Israel, these slaves were freed every fiftieth year, in the year of Jubilee, in accordance with the Mosaic Law. In some cultures, even their families and possessions were sold if the debtor did not bring enough money to cover the debt. Such was the case with a certain servant of this king. He owed an astronomical amount. No free laborer, let alone a slave, could ever hope to repay this amount in a thousand lifetimes.

18:26. The servant **fell on his knees before him** (8:2; 9:18; 15:25), displaying humility and desperation and casting himself on the mercy of the master. The servant's plea for patience and his promise to **pay back everything** were so unrealistic that they could only be the words of a desperate man. His promise might be compared with a factory worker today pledging to pay off the national debt of the United States by himself. It could not be done.

It is important to keep in mind here that we are not dealing with forensic forgiveness (justification, salvation), but family forgiveness. This deals with sin committed since entering into the family of the king. The issue is brother-to-brother forgiveness.

18:27. The **servant's master** (that is, the king of 18:23) felt his heart going out to the man. He **took pity on him, canceled the debt and let him go.** The servant was undeserving, but the king acted with mercy (withholding punishment that was deserved) and grace (giving a great gift that was not deserved).

So it should be among brothers and sisters in God's family. All of a Christian's sins are forgiven and forgotten forever (see Ps. 103:12; Jer. 31:34). What this parable reinforces, therefore, is the Christian's duty to forgive others (Matt. 6:12,14–15; 2 Cor. 2:10; Eph. 4:32) in the same way he has been forgiven. This entire passage addresses forgiveness within the family of God.

18:28. The word **but** contrasts the first servant and his relationship with a second servant. The two were alike in only one way—the debt each owed gave the creditor power over the debtor's life. But in every other respect, the situations were opposites, highlighting the contrast between the first servant and the king. The servant had not understood family principles. But he was about to learn.

The amount the second servant owed the first was insignificant when compared with the debt the first servant had just been forgiven. One hundred denarii was one hundred days' wages. The first servant had owed more than half a million times as much to the king! Rather than imitating the mercy of the king, the first servant mistreated the second servant (**began to choke him**) and demanded repayment of the debt.

The second servant's debt to the first was not insignificant. It would take some time for any of us to pay more than a quarter of our annual earnings while also paying for daily living expenses. The debt was substantial, and the first servant was certainly entitled to what he was owed.

Similarly, when a brother offends us, it is logical to think that we are entitled to just recompense. There is legitimate restitution. But what we forget, when we fail to release a brother from an offense by forgiving him, is that relationships in the family of God go beyond strict justice. God himself started this pattern by forgiving us a debt we could never hope to repay. This should cause us to forgive others for good reason—we now belong to him. Jesus essentially bought back ("redeemed") our life. So we should live as he says—or, more significantly, as he *lives*.

18:29–30. The actions and words of the second servant were almost identical to those of the first servant in 18:26. This servant also **fell to his knees** in humility, asking for patience and offering to repay the debt. But the first servant refused to give the second servant a chance to repay the debt.

We tend to forget our king's grace, often refusing to forgive even the most trifling of offenses against us. Such behavior among God's family is infantile. It is time for us to grow up! When we refuse to forgive our brothers, we hold punishment over their heads, and they are affected by our decision. But the person who is truly imprisoned is the one who refuses to forgive. Long-term bitterness is a grinding burden.

18:31. The other servants of the household recognized the cruelty of the first servant toward the second. This grieved them deeply. How deeply do we grieve when we see bitterness and grudges between fellow believers? Such discord in the family of God causes great sorrow to the Father. As we share his heart, we will not be able to stand by and watch indifferently. **Told** is a strong verb which means "explained in complete detail." These servants reported the matter to the king.

18:32–33. The angry king held one more audience with the first servant, this time to bring him to account for failing to follow the merciful king's example. God the Father values his children for different reasons. Like this king, the Father does not want any of his children harmed or taken out of his service through mistreatment by others.

We will answer to the Father for our stewardship of the relationships he has entrusted to us—particularly those with other children in his family. Keep in view here the Father's zealous oversight of his "little ones" earlier in Matthew 18. He is protective of all his children—sin and all—and this includes mistreatment from other children in the family.

18:34. The king was so angry at the first servant's mistreatment of the second that he rescinded his previous order to release the first servant and forgive his debt. He imprisoned the servant and **turned him over to the jailers to be tortured.** The parable reveals the anger of the king and his refusal to tolerate an arrogant lack of forgiveness among his family. But notice there is nothing said here about eternal damnation. These are family issues. Family forgiveness restores what was lost (relational intimacy) and is unrelated to what can never be lost (imputed righteousness and therefore eternal salvation).

18:35. Jesus' closing application was sobering. **Each of you** brings the focus to the level of individual responsibility. We can imagine Jesus scanning the faces of the disciples as he closed his discourse. We can also imagine him looking out through the words of Matthew into our hearts with his warning lingering in our conscience. Jesus insisted that his servants be characterized by forgiveness.

In this parable Jesus spoke in hyperbole about his anger toward an arrogant, rebellious child. The language may be exaggerated to cause us to take the teaching on forgiveness seriously. This passage warns about the consequences of failing to forgive others. The point is that every Christian has a duty to be forgiving toward others, just as the Father has been forgiving toward us.

MAIN IDEA REVIEW: *The Father esteems and protects each of his precious children—even when they sin. We must esteem and protect them with the same loving mercy.*

III. CONCLUSION

Every believer has a responsibility to seek the restoration of a sinning brother or sister to righteous living. If the sinning believer will not respond after private confrontation, two or three loving brothers or sisters must go together to try to persuade him. If the sinning brother or sister will not respond to the two or three, the entire church must be employed in the effort to persuade and restore the sinning believer. If the sinning brother or sister will not respond to the church, the church must acknowledge this choice, and remove that person from their fellowship. If we pursue the sinning brother or sister with a heart of mercy and truth and follow the guidelines of Jesus, we can be confident that our decisions and actions are guided by the Father.

PRINCIPLES

- The children of God's kingdom exude a childlike humility.
- Our greatness in God's kingdom will depend largely on how we humble ourselves (James 4:10).
- A hospitable heart toward God's people is hospitality toward Jesus himself.
- Anyone who causes a fellow believer to sin will be subject to God's wrath.
- Temptations in the world are inevitable, but the world will be judged for its temptations.
- There are angels who protect us and help represent us in God's presence.
- The Father will make every effort to restore a believer who strays into sin.
- The Father rejoices over each believer who is brought back from sin.
- The Father's desire is that no believer follow the path of sin to self-destruction.
- We have been entrusted with authority to open and close the door to the community of faith.
- Our debt of sin before God is infinite, and we are powerless to pay it.
- God provided an infinite payment for our sin—his Son—completely at his discretion and initiative, not because of any merit of our own.
- Any sin of others against us is small, in comparison to the debt of sins the Father has forgiven us.
- The Father is angered when we do not forgive one another.

APPLICATIONS

- Accept from God the free gift of salvation.
- Take radical action to prevent sin and avoid God's judgment.
- Do not look down pridefully and disdainfully on any believer.
- Forgive one another, as the Father has forgiven you.
- Show mercy toward fellow believers, not judgment.

IV. LIFE APPLICATION

That God May Be Exalted

In the heart of London is the Metropolitan Tabernacle. Its pulpit was once occupied by the famous preacher, Charles Spurgeon. Along the walls of the pastor's study hang portraits of the pastors who have faithfully served the Metropolitan Tabernacle. Most served long tours of duty.

Spurgeon's time as pastor coincided with some interesting historical events. He opened the Tabernacle the same year the American Civil War began. During Spurgeon's ministry, Karl Marx wrote *The Communist Manifesto* and Charles Darwin his *Origin of Species*. But Spurgeon was a bold preacher and did not retreat when his preaching led to controversy. He was also a colorful character. Once reprimanded by a colleague for his cigar smoking, Spurgeon countered, "If I ever find myself smoking to excess, I promise I shall quit entirely."

"What would you call smoking to excess?" the man asked.

"Why, smoking two cigars at the same time!" was Spurgeon's answer.

Used mightily of God, Charles Spurgeon preached to thousands in London each Sunday and was known for his numerous books of sermons. Yet his ministry had a humble beginning. He started by passing out tracts and teaching a Sunday school class as a teenager. He would also give short addresses to the Sunday school. When he was invited to preach in obscure places in the countryside, he used every opportunity to serve God. He was faithful in the small things, and God trusted him with the greater things.

"I am perfectly sure," he said, "that, if I had not been willing to preach to those small gatherings of people in obscure country places, I should never have had the privilege of preaching to thousands of men and women in large buildings all over the land."

Like Spurgeon, the follower of Christ must learn humility. It was the way of Jesus, and should be evident in his followers. He must always give the glory to God for what he accomplishes in our lives. However small or humble the task or job, we should faithfully perform it. Faithfulness in seemingly small things is only preparation for the larger opportunities God has waiting for us. We would all do well to remember our Lord's rule, "Whoever exalts himself will be humbled, and whoever humbles himself will be exalted" (Matt. 23:12).

V. PRAYER

Merciful and gracious Father, forgive my grudging attitude toward those who have wronged me. As you have forgiven my debt of sin, help me to be merciful and forgiving toward other people. Amen.

VI. DEEPER DISCOVERIES

A. Highlighted Values

Three themes are woven throughout this discourse on the ethics of Christian personal relationships—humility, purity, and mercy. These three values are critical to a healthy church community. Throughout the discourse, Jesus taught principles of healthy relationships within the church. Humility, purity, and mercy support and guide these healthy relationships. Jesus had announced the founding and building of his church (16:18). Now he instructed its members on how to treat one another, especially when a member strays or sins.

Humility is especially evident in 18:1–4,21–35. Just as a child's faith is one of dependency and trust, so we are to imitate this mature attitude toward our Father. And as one debtor to another, we are to recognize our own forgiven status in our dealings with those who offend us.

Purity stands out in 18:5–9,15–20,32–35. This refers not only to individual purity, but to the purification of the body as a whole. This is necessary when Christian brothers or sisters continue to spread corruption. Jesus was concerned for the restoration of the individual, but sometimes this value must be weighed against potential damage to the family by continued rebellion in our midst.

Mercy is highlighted in 18:10–35. Confronting a believer who is on a self-destructive path is a merciful act, if it is done in the right spirit.

These values interrelate with each other beautifully:

- Mercy flows out of humility. Pride causes us to look down on others and to fail to see their need. Pride is centered on a person's own needs and wants. Only a humble person can look beyond self to see the needs of others.
- Mercy is also the balance to purity. Neither negates the other. Both must coexist. Mercy without purity is permissiveness. Purity without mercy is rigid self-righteousness.

B. The Flow of the Discourse

The message of Matthew 18 might be summarized as follows: The greatest in the kingdom is the believer who is as humble as a child (18:1–4). But beware lest you be guilty of causing one of these innocents to sin (18:5–9), because the Father guards each one, even if he or she strays into sin (18:10–14). If one of God's beloved children sins, deal with that person patiently but truthfully, pursuing him in cooperation with the Father's zealous pursuit (18:15–20). But never allow yourself to deal with a sinning child of God without mercy, or you will face the discipline of a merciless judge (18:21–35).

C. The Discourse's Self-Interpretation

A careful student of this discourse will not only seek to understand each segment on its own but also to see how the various segments shed light on one another. For example, the parable of the lost sheep (18:10–14) clarifies the heart motivation with which we should carry out church discipline (18:15–20). A loving confrontation guards us against vengefulness or heartless moralism, allowing us to pursue the straying brother in cooperation with the Father's pursuit of the same straying sheep. On the other hand, the teaching on church discipline (18:15–20) helps us identify the "lost sheep" (18:10–14) as a sinning brother, and helps us understand more fully the nature of the sheep's lostness. These two passages together make a stronger statement about the Father's heart of mercy toward his disobedient children than either passage could make on its own.

D. What Sins Should We Confront?

Here are some principles to follow as we face this question:

Examine your own heart first (Matt. 7:1–5). Check for an impure motive and to ensure that you have the right to speak on the issue you are confronting. With this caution, the confrontation will be more fully justified and you will carry it out with better preparation and purer motives. Be open to the possibility that there may be no sin at all but a difference in personal preferences or convictions. Perhaps there is some kind of pain in your own heart that was triggered by the other person's word or action.

Some believers will see brothers or sisters sin and think, *I am just as sinful. What right do I have to show them their sin?* We must be careful to balance our right to confront with our responsibility to confront. The Father does not expect us to be totally holy before we confront a brother. Instead, he wants us to come to each other in humility, recognizing that we are all debtors showing other debtors where to find forgiveness (18:21–35). After the self-examination and preparation described above, we are commanded to help bring back the straying brother.

Go prepared to listen first (Jas. 1:19–20). Many confrontations should begin with these words, "Here is what I see in your behavior. Is there anything I am not understanding correctly?" What might seem like an obvious sin at first may turn out to be something totally different and innocent. Refrain from jumping to conclusions until the brother or sister has a chance to share his or her story. On the other hand, do not let them make excuses or justify real sin. You will not be doing them a favor if you let them get away with a self-destructive course of action. When in doubt, err on the side of grace, which is the power that fuels true life change (Titus 2:11–12).

Choose only the most critical issue of the moment for confrontation. Any human will respond better to a loving confrontation on one issue than to an overwhelming barrage of accusations on many fronts. If you see several things wrong in a person's life, raise only the one that needs most immediate attention. Be patient and forbearing with other areas that need future growth. If the person is already dealing with one issue, wait until he or she is ready to handle the others before raising them.

In some cases in which trust needs to be developed, the way to a bigger issue may be to raise a lesser issue first. Deal with this issue in a way that demonstrates your loving intention. Give the person a taste of the fruit of holy living. Then move on to the bigger issue.

Anything that hinders a brother's or sister's ability to live in spiritual wholeness might be a topic for confrontation. Our body, mind, and spirit belong to the Lord, and we are accountable to use them for him. But the most critical things to be aware of are the spiritual problems that create distance between the believer and his or her Father. The seriousness of the confrontation should match the seriousness of the problem to be corrected.

E. Summary

This chapter reveals the character of Jesus, particularly his mercy toward his followers and his zealous protection of the purity of the church.

It also prepares Christ's followers for right relationships, attitudes, and procedures concerning sin within the church. This is important at this point in Matthew because Jesus' disciples are still in need of much preparation.

VII. TEACHING OUTLINE

A. INTRODUCTION

1. Lead Story: You Are Asking the Wrong Questions
2. Context: Matthew 18, the fourth of Jesus' five discourses in Matthew, is about life and relational values in the church. The placement of this discourse in Matthew was determined by two factors: (1) the

readiness of the disciples to think toward the church age, as indicated by Jesus' announcement of the church's beginning (16:18); and (2) the nearness of Jesus' death and departure from earth, motivating him to prepare his disciples for the church's proper operation and its members' proper attitudes toward one another.

3. Transition: The disciples asked, "Who is the greatest in the kingdom of heaven?" Jesus spent the rest of the Matthew 18 discourse telling them, "You are asking the wrong question."

The disciples needed to overturn their concept of "greatness," and so do we. If we could practice what Jesus taught in this discourse, it would revolutionize our self-concept and our relationships with fellow believers.

B. COMMENTARY

1. The Humble Will Be the Greatest in the Kingdom (18:1–4)
2. The Father Jealously Protects the Believer's Soul (18:5–9)
3. The Father Zealously Pursues the Straying Believer (18:10–14)
4. Patiently and Truthfully Pursuing the Straying Brother (18:15–20)
5. Humbly and Mercifully Forgiving the Sinning Brother (18:21–35)

C. CONCLUSION

1. Wrap-up: The Father esteems and protects each of his children, even when they sin. We must also esteem and protect them with the same loving mercy.

2. Personal Challenge: How different the average church would be today if we really saw one another through the king's eyes. What would become of the infighting, the politics, the sacred cows, the superiority and inferiority complexes? How differently would we appear to the watching world around us?

VIII. ISSUES FOR DISCUSSION

1. What was the central message of the parable of the lost sheep?
2. What four steps did Jesus say believers should be prepared to take in restoring a straying believer to righteous living and fellowship in the church?
3. Does God listen more intently to hundreds of people praying than he does to the prayer of a single believer?
4. What was the central message of the parable of the unforgiven servant?

Matthew 19–20

The King Approaches the Final Battle

Matthew 19–20

IN A NUTSHELL

The Jewish leaders' opposition to Jesus is moving toward a climax. This chapter returns to the theme of divorce and remarriage introduced in the Sermon on the Mount. To test Jesus, the Pharisees ask him a question about divorce. In his reply, Jesus emphasizes the permanence of marriage as God's original design. God's Old Testament provision for divorce was temporary and based on the rebellion of fallen man. Jesus follows this confrontation with teachings about the demands and rewards of being a disciple of his, of kingdom grace, and coming death and resurrection. God designed marriage to be a lifelong commitment. It is the most permanent relationship in the home, as the two spouses become one flesh. Marriage partners should continually depend on God's strength to maintain this union.

The King Approaches the Final Battle

I. INTRODUCTION

Parking-Lot Humility

*T*he following letter was received by a pastor I know following a busy Easter weekend at a church with multiple worship services. One of the parishioners noticed and honored his servant-leadership as illustrated by his behavior in the church parking lot. The witness wrote these words:

> It happened this way: it was the end of a very busy weekend for the senior pastor of a growing church. He had just completed sharing the gospel message for the seventh time in a span of less than forty-eight hours. It was obvious to me that he had poured himself into the preparation, the presentation, and the proclamation of the Easter story. As much as I was blessed by the music and the message, I witnessed something that spoke to me in a way that words could never communicate. And it was this act that caught my attention.
>
> As I was putting my family into the car to go home, I saw this same man—the leader of the church, the man who stood in front of four thousand people over the weekend, the most visible representative of the church to visitors, the one who had every right to demand special treatment—I saw him walk out by himself to the farthest point of the parking lot to his car! As I looked around I did not see very many who witnessed this act of servanthood, but I was glad that the Lord allowed me to see it. It was a simple thing and yet it was something that spoke volumes to me—perhaps even more than his teaching. If anyone had earned a right to park next door to the church, it was the senior pastor. And yet he humbled himself to the point of giving one more close parking place to somebody else on what would be a very busy Sunday and a very full lot.

When I read that letter, it motivated me to want to be more like that. In a day of reserved parking spaces, corporate parking spaces, executive parking spaces, "employee of the month" parking spaces, and "reserved for pastor" parking spaces, this behavior reflected a different priority. In a day when people clamor for credit, it is important that Christians not forget how to be servants. Jesus loved to highlight the reverse of earthly values in his kingdom.

Earthly "greatness" is turned on its head—"the first shall be last." True kingdom greatness is reflected in the humility of "the least of these."

II. COMMENTARY

The King Approaches the Final Battle

> **MAIN IDEA:** *The humblest servant, most dependent on the grace of God, is the greatest in God's eyes.*

We have seen Jesus' preparation for the cross since 16:21, but now he began his physical journey toward Jerusalem. Humility continues to be the key theme throughout these two chapters—a theme already established in Matthew 18 (esp. v. 4), and culminating in the king's humble means of transportation into Jerusalem (21:5).

The journey to Jerusalem has a somber tone to it. This mood is interrupted and balanced with notes of hope and grace. Jesus took time for the little children (19:13–15). Once again, he promised that all the disciples' sacrifices would be abundantly repaid in eternity (19:28–29). He displayed the grace of God in the parable of the workers (19:30–20:16). He ended his passion prediction with the ultimate triumph of the Resurrection (20:19). And he demonstrated his love and acceptance of the two blind men (20:29–34).

Matthew 19:1 marked the end of Jesus' Galilean ministry. In Matthew, this northern campaign had comprised virtually all of his ministry to this point. In 4:12–17, Matthew emphasized the significance of Jesus' ministry in and around Galilee. In Matthew 19–20, the time is right for Jesus to come out of the back country. He had been avoiding the spotlight, guarding time primarily to develop his disciples. They had passed some tests (16:15–17), but they had failed many (e.g., 8:23–26; 14:28–30; 16:5–11,22–23; 17:14–21). Through every experience, they had come away with new understanding (8:27; 14:33; 16:12; 17:13). The training of the Twelve was progressing.

Geographically, the journey of Matthew 19–20 began with Jesus' departure from Galilee (19:1) and ended with his setting out on the last fifteen-mile leg from Jericho uphill, southwest to Jerusalem (20:29).

A The King Affirms the Marriage Commitment (19:1–12)

> **SUPPORTING IDEA:** *Lifelong marital faithfulness is God's intention, requiring our dependence on his supernatural strength.*

The last major conflict of Jesus with the religious establishment grew out of their second demand for a sign in 16:1–4. And we will not see another such conflict until 21:15–16, after the purging of the temple. It is almost as though Matthew wanted to remind us that Jesus' enemies were still as active and obstinate as ever. They had not gone away. This timing in the narrative is especially appropriate; Jesus had been addressing Christian relationships in Matthew 18 (marriage is the central such relationship), and had now turned toward Jerusalem. This isolated challenge foreshadowed the final week-long battle Jesus would endure in Jerusalem (Matt. 21–27).

This passage returns to the theme of divorce and remarriage, introduced in the Sermon on the Mount (5:31–32). While the message is much the same, the purpose and emphasis is different. In 5:31–32, Jesus used this issue as one example among many to clarify what he meant by "surpassing righteousness" in 5:20. In 19:1–12, he drew attention to the divorce issue itself. The Pharisees began with a tough question on divorce, but Jesus turned the focus to marriage, dealing with divorce and remarriage as side issues. Sin causes us to fall short of the intended permanent marriage bond.

19:1–2. The first part of 19:1 is actually the closing of the Matthew 18 discourse (cf. 7:28; 11:1; 13:53; 26:1). Judea was the province that included Jerusalem. The wording of 19:1b is confusing, but it means that Jesus crossed to the east side of the Jordan River from Galilee, then proceeded south through Perea (east of Judea, across the Jordan), later crossing back to the west side of the Jordan near Jericho (see 20:29). This was the route most Jews followed between Judea and Galilee.

19:3. The Pharisees had been outwitted by the king at every turn, so they came at him again with another **test**. And it was a dangerous one. John the Baptist's dealing with the issue of divorce had cost him his head. The verb **test** is from *peirazo,* meaning "to test, tempt." It is the same verb Matthew used of Satan tempting Jesus in 4:1,3; the Pharisees and Sadducees demanding the second sign in 16:1; the Pharisees, Sadducees, and Herodians together trying to trap Jesus concerning taxation (22:18) and the greatest commandment (22:35). Their "test" was an action of malicious intent.

19:4–6. Jesus avoided the Jewish leaders' controversy and elevated the discussion. Because they had asked Jesus for a legal interpretation, he referred to the law, laying the basic foundation on which all answers to the divorce question must rest. Marriage is an institution created by God. When a man and woman pledge their lives to each other, it is God who makes them one. Therefore, people have no business destroying that union.

Haven't you read implies that the answer should have been obvious. Jesus was unveiling the Pharisees' true motives, which was to trap him. In effect, he was saying, "You know better than to ask this question."

Jesus quoted from Genesis 1:27 and 2:24. His point in the first quote was to emphasize the Creator's involvement in the marriage process. This was *God's* plan, not man's. It had to do with God's image (Gen. 1:26–27), not man's. Christians would do well to understand that their marriage is not so much about them as it is about God. Such revolutionary thinking is not very American, but it is very biblical. Marriage should reflect God's image, not guarantee our personal "happiness." The permanent marriage bond is in keeping with God's original design for men and women.

The second quote from Genesis 2:24 emphasized the one-flesh union of marriage (cf. Eph. 5:22–33), in contrast with the former state of the man and woman, who were members of separate families. The three verbs in this quote are significant. **Leave** (also in 4:13; 16:4; 21:17) is stronger than other synonyms translated "leave." It implies a deliberate abandonment, sometimes permanent (as in this case). When a man or woman leaves behind his or her parents for a spouse, there is no going back. That season of life is over for good.

Because of the cultural expectations, Jesus referred to the man's "leaving" without mentioning the same responsibility for the woman. The woman's leaving was assumed. As in the beginning (Gen. 2:23), she takes her husband's name and draws her identity from him. Clearly, she gives up her previous family and identity. It is important to their relationship that the man do the same.

Next, **be united** means "to cleave, join closely, glue, cling, unite." These words point to the oneness of the married couple. It is not the man and woman who do the uniting, but this is something *done to them*. The clear implication in this context is that God is the one who unites them. Marriage is not their doing; it is his. Jesus was indicating that the marriage relationship is the most permanent relationship in the home, different and deeper than that of parent and child.

Finally, **become** is from the verb "to be." There is no way to express the union of two people more vividly than to say that they **become one flesh.** This is true in a figurative sense, for the two still have individual bodies. But there is also a literal sense here: (1) the sexual union unites the bodies of a man and woman, and any children who result from that union are a "single-flesh" incarnation of the married couple's commitment; (2) the bodies of the husband and wife belong to each other (1 Cor. 7:4); and (3) there is a sharing of spirit and soul in marriage—a union that is mysteriously real.

In our day, Satan makes his most strategic attack on the image and glory of God by his influence in the destruction of the marriage vow. Christians need to raise their eyes from themselves, forget *any* justification for divorce, and learn to live together like God requires. We should sacrifice self-gratification for the will and glory of the Father.

In 19:6, Jesus drew his evidence together into a conclusion. Man must not **separate** the union created by God. Your marriage does not belong to you. It is his. Divorce is always the human destruction of a divine creation.

19:7. This unqualified answer did not satisfy the Pharisees. They did not understand how Jesus' concept of absolute wrongness of divorce could be compatible with their understanding of Moses' instructions regarding divorce. However, the inconsistency lay not in Jesus' answer but in the Pharisees' interpretation of Mosaic Law. Their "quotation" was actually a misquote from Deuteronomy 24:1–4. In the Old Testament context, the statements about a man giving his wife a certificate of divorce and sending her away were conditional statements, not commands as the Pharisees had quoted them. The Pharisees said that Moses "commanded" these things, and Matthew put in their mouths the verbs **give** and **send . . . away**, both carrying the strength of commands.

19:8. Jesus corrected the Pharisees' misinterpretation of Deuteronomy 24:1–4, clarifying that Moses permitted divorce but he did not command it. But he went one step further, turning their own question into an indictment against them. Placing the first-century Pharisees in the same category with rebellious Israel of Moses' day, Jesus said that Moses **permitted** divorce **because your hearts were hard.** Moses knew that hardhearted people would continue to divorce their spouses, so he passed on God's guidelines to protect those who were victims of divorce.

The second half of 19:8 states God's original intention, preparing for 19:9. **But** contrasts God's will concerning divorce (that there be none) with his permission of divorce through Moses. **From the beginning** refers to God's original plan. God's clear intention was that there be no divorce at all. He actually hates the concept (Mal. 2:16).

Jesus' point was that anyone who saw divorce and remarriage in terms of what may or may not be permissible was already out of line. Divorce is not some morally neutral option open to God's people. It is fundamentally sinful, and it grows out of the hardness of the selfish human heart.

19:9. Jesus' wording in this verse was similar to that in 5:32. In fact, phrase for phrase, the meanings of the two statements are equivalent until we get to the outcome of wrongful divorce. Jesus said the man who divorced his wife was the person who committed adultery, whereas, in 5:32, it was the divorced wife and any future man she might marry who committed adultery.

There are several controversial issues related to this verse, all of which have some bearing on its exact interpretation. See the further discussion in "Deeper Discoveries."

19:10. No matter how one interprets Jesus' stance on divorce and remarriage, it was far stricter than the disciples (or anyone else) expected. They had lived all their lives in a society where divorces were granted liberally. The prevalence of arranged marriages and the tendency for women to be viewed as property may have contributed to the number of divorces. To learn that there was no easy way out of an unsatisfactory marriage caused the disciples to rethink the marriage commitment. They considered that it might be better to avoid the risk of getting into a bad marriage by staying single. The disciples' conclusion, given Jesus' high standards, was, **it is better not to marry.** Jesus had made his point.

19:11–12. Jesus affirmed the sobriety with which the disciples had begun to see the permanence of the marriage commitment. He agreed that marriage was not something to be entered into quickly, without forethought, or with the expectation of an "easy out."

He also acknowledged that **not everyone** would accept **this word.** The people who can accept the idea of celibacy over the risk of a marriage ending in divorce are **those to whom it has been given.** This refers to those who are enabled by God to remain single without giving in to sexual temptation. Such a disciplined calling is hard enough today, let alone in that culture in which marriage was considered a person's obligation to family and society.

Jesus then acknowledged the various reasons that a person might be celibate. He said some people were **eunuchs.** A eunuch means literally "an emasculated man." By implication, it also applied to anyone who refrained from marriage and sexual relations. First, such a person might be impotent from birth. Second, a eunuch might be a person who was castrated. This was commonly done to slaves or servants who served in a royal court where the women of the household might be in danger of the servants' sexual interest. Those two categories of celibate men were commonly known to the disciples. But Jesus introduced a third category—those who chose to refrain from marriage to give more attention to advancing **the kingdom of heaven.** Jesus and Paul (1 Cor. 7:32–38), and probably John the Baptizer, are examples of such men. Those Jesus referred to in 19:12c should, of course, be understood to be figurative in the sense that they chose not to engage in sexual activity.

Jesus finished with a challenge to his listeners, some of whom may not have been willing to **accept** his teaching. Such a teaching about the value of celibacy ran contrary to Jewish cultural norms and expectations. It was thought that everyone should marry for the sake of the ongoing community. Jesus' teaching here would have required the rearrangement of a believer's core values.

Jesus was *not* saying that celibacy was holier than matrimony or that it was a requirement for kingdom ministry. He did note it was a limited calling. The apostle Paul affirmed as much (1 Cor. 7:9; 9:5).

B The King Makes Time for Children (19:13–15)

SUPPORTING IDEA: *The kingdom of heaven belongs to those with the humble faith of a child.*

This brief passage advances the theme of humility introduced in Matthew 18. These humble little children stood in contrast to the arrogant Pharisees of the preceding passage (19:1–9), and the prideful rich young man in the following passage (19:16–30) who expected to earn his way into eternal life.

19:13. The laying on of hands and the prayer mentioned here refer to the practice of holy men placing their blessing on individuals. It was natural that parents who were impressed by Jesus would want their children blessed by him. However, the disciples, still not alert to Jesus' values even after the Matthew 18 discourse, acted according to worldly assumptions. It was assumed in that day that children were not as valuable as adults, so they were not important enough to take up Jesus' time. The disciples **rebuked those who brought them.**

19:14–15. But Jesus contrasted the disciples' worldly values with his own. To Jesus, each individual was of great value regardless of age (e.g., 9:18–26; 15:21–28; 17:14–18), gender (e.g., 9:18–26; 15:21–28), social status (e.g., 8:1–4; 9:27–34; 20:29–34), or nationality (e.g., 8:5–13, 28–34; 15:21–28).

In keeping with this conviction, Jesus rebuked the rebukers. His orders were redundant for emphasis: **Let the little children come to me and do not hinder them.** Jesus was equally accessible to everyone.

Then Jesus gave a reason for his desire to welcome the children. **Such as these** means "people of all ages who share the humility of a child" (see 18:2–4). Jesus expressed a special welcome to those who come to him in simplicity, without prideful self-consciousness, whether they were children or adults (cf. 11:25–26). Those who admit their dependence on Christ and his forgiveness will possess the kingdom of heaven (cf. these qualities with those in the Beatitudes, 5:3–12).

The Messiah-King stooped to impart his blessing on the children by laying his hands on them (19:13). Then he moved on, nearer to Jerusalem and the cross. This final comment by Matthew, **he went on from there,** brings into focus the contrast between Jesus, the meek lover of children, and the looming shadow of the cross. How could such a gentle man be found guilty of death? Perhaps Matthew wanted us to see the gentle, sacrificial lamb of Isaiah 53:7–9 (cf. 1 Pet. 2:21–25), being led toward the slaughter.

C The King Clarifies the Demands and Rewards of True Discipleship (19:16–30)

SUPPORTING IDEA: *Eternal life cannot be earned; it must be received as a gift from God.*

The closer Jesus got to the cross, the higher he raised the stakes for those who would follow him. Much as the disciples' question of 18:1 revealed their misunderstanding of "greatness" in the kingdom, so also this man's question

(19:16) revealed his misunderstanding of the "goodness" required for entrance into the kingdom.

19:16. The man respectfully addressed Jesus as **Teacher.** It is apparent from the conversation and his response that the man was sincere in his question about the way to get eternal life, but he was mistaken about how this might come about. He expected to earn eternal life by his own righteous acts **(what good things must I do?)** rather than through God's gracious endowment of righteousness (Rom. 3:9–31).

19:17. Jesus responded by driving the discussion toward the nature of true "goodness." His initial response seemed to bring his own goodness into question. However, by the time he finished the discussion, it was evident that this was one more claim to deity. It was not the goodness of Jesus that was in question here, but the man's assumptions regarding the goodness required for eternal life. Eternal life requires *absolute* goodness, and **there is only One who is good** enough to earn it on his own (see Pss. 106:1; 118:1,29; 1 Chron. 16:34; 2 Chron. 5:13).

Jesus final statement of 19:17 might be parpahrased like this: "If you insist on pursuing this impossible, self-dependent avenue toward eternal life, I will tell you just how good you must be. To begin, perfect righteousness requires absolute obedience to the Old Testament commandments." Of course, that is impossible. That was Jesus' point in the Sermon on the Mount (5:20). Even the best of Pharisees did not come close. Jesus contrasted the reality that only God is absolutely good with the man's foolish expectation that he could be good enough for eternal life.

19:18–19. The man's next question revealed his misunderstanding still further. He did not understand that God required absolute perfection. He seemed to presume that God graded on a curve and that his "goodness" was better than many. Jesus let this man know that anything less than perfection is no "good" at all. A righteous man would have to keep *all* of the commandments perfectly. The man, grasping for possibilities, assumed that there must be some special set of commandments that made a person particularly righteous.

Jesus listed some of the commandments. His listing of the fifth through the ninth of the Ten Commandments, together with **love your neighbor as yourself** from Leviticus 19:18 (cf. Matt. 22:34–40) was intended not as an exhaustive list of all commandments necessary for eternal life but as a representative sample. The man would need to keep *all* of the Old Testament commandments. Even this "short list" would be understood as impossible for anyone.

19:20–21. The young man still did not grasp Jesus' true meaning. He claimed to have kept all the commandments. Yet he knew that such observance was not enough. He asked, **What do I still lack?** No matter how good a person's life may be, if he examines his conscience honestly, he will know that there is still something lacking about his own righteousness (Rom. 2:12–15).

Jesus' answer went straight to this man's self-righteous god—money. He read him perfectly. He knew where his heart and treasure lay (Matt. 6:21). To make such a sacrifice would be to exchange earthly wealth for **treasure in heaven** (cf. 6:19–20). But Jesus also knew that this outward action would require first an inward transformation that was humanly impossible. Jesus attempted to drive the man to the point of seeing his real need.

19:22. But the man did not grasp Jesus' point. He had no sense of sin. And he certainly was not willing to give up his false god. Therefore, because the rich young man was not willing to have his heart transformed, **he went away sad**. He wanted wealth in both worlds, but Jesus' statement demanded that he choose between the two. As much as he wanted the wealth of eternal life, he could not give up his **great wealth** to obtain eternal treasure.

This should not be taken to mean that wealth automatically disqualifies a person from eternal life. Rather, the worship of wealth over God is the problem. There are rare individuals who are able to possess much wealth while keeping God on the throne of their lives, ready at any time to give it all up for him (e.g., Job). Paul made this same distinction in 1 Timothy 6:10, clarifying that it is the "love of money," not money itself, that is "a root of all kinds of evil."

19:23–24. After the young man left, Jesus saw a teachable moment for his disciples. He turned to them and made a statement about the lesson they needed to take from this episode.

I tell you the truth grabbed the disciples' attention and alerted them that Jesus was about to say something of great importance: **It is hard for a rich man to enter the kingdom of heaven**. Note that Jesus did not say such a thing is impossible; merely unlikely, because of the lure of earthly wealth. The rich young ruler had bought into a form of what is today called prosperity theology, which teaches that God blesses those who follow him with material riches.

But Jesus pressed home his argument as his restatement heightened to the point of impossibility. Such a thing is even harder than putting a camel (the largest animal of that region) through the eye of a needle.

19:25–26. The disciples were conditioned by their culture to believe that wealth was a sign of God's blessing on a person's life (Deut. 28:1–14). Therefore, they were **astonished**. Matthew used the specialized, superlative Greek adverb *sphodra,* amplifying the disciples' astonishment to an extreme. If the wealthy—so blessed by God—can never enter the kingdom, **Who then can be saved?**

The phrase **Jesus looked at them** added further emphasis to what he was about to say. The key to the whole dilemma was the One who is the source of righteousness. People in themselves do not have what it takes to enter the kingdom! But **with God all things are possible**. What a person cannot do to save himself, God does by providing a gracious entrance. Salvation is a super-natural gift.

19:27. Then Peter, once again speaking the minds of the Twelve, said, **We have left everything to follow you!** Peter was searching for Jesus' seal of approval for the disciples' sacrifice. He was also looking for some reassurance that the sacrifices of the Twelve would be recompensed. And Jesus gave him that reassurance. Indeed, the Twelve had left everything—family, home, possessions—to follow Jesus. Jesus acknowledged as much in his response (19:28–29).

What then will there be for us? Some might consider Peter's question to be selfish, but it revealed the reality of human nature that we are driven by incentive. And Jesus acknowledged that. Jesus did not rebuke Peter for his question. On the contrary, he offered an encouraging answer. He granted Peter a glimpse of the reward that awaits all who sacrifice for the sake of the king and his kingdom. His answer must have astonished them: **you . . . will also sit on twelve thrones, judging the twelve tribes.** Christ's rewards for his faithful followers are incredible, multiplying many times any sacrifices they make. This was a magnificent statement of magnificent reward.

Believers should not feel guilty about anticipating eternal reward. If it were a shameful thing, God would not have promised it so prominently throughout Scripture. The truth is that we need motivation, something to press on toward (Phil. 3:12–14). The eternal perspective, seeking God's prize, is the only mature perspective (Phil. 3:14).

19:28–29. Jesus underscored the faithfulness of the promise he was about to make with his words, **I tell you the truth.** His additional words, **you who have followed me,** included all the diligent hardship and sacrifice Jesus had predicted would be the lot of his true followers. We hear in Jesus' words warmth and affirmation for his followers. And that includes **everyone who** sacrifices for **my sake.** There is not only eternal life, but enormous rewards (**a hundred times as much**).

The word **renewal** is from *palingenesia* (also Titus 3:5), meaning "rebirth" (*palin*, "again," plus *genao*, "to give birth"). Jesus was referring to the future day when he would, after eliminating Satan and his influence, take over this earth and restore it to its original purpose (cf. Dan. 7:13–14; Rev. 3:21; 20:1–6).

Using his title **Son of Man** in all its messianic fullness, Jesus gave his disciples a glimpse of his future glory as the king **on his glorious throne.** Aside from his transfiguration before Peter, James, and John, this was the fullest revelation of his future glory that Jesus had given his disciples.

Jesus promised that the Twelve would share with him in ruling (this is the present meaning of **judging**) the twelve tribes of Israel. (This is the clearest statement in Matthew of at least one of Jesus' reasons for choosing twelve disciples.) Part of the faithful disciple's reward is authority in his kingdom (cf. believers' future authority in Luke 22:30; 1 Cor. 6:2).

Jesus had already assured his followers that discipleship implies sacrifice. Now he promised that any sacrifice made **for my sake** would be more than repaid. In between **houses** and **fields** Jesus listed even greater sacrifices— members of one's family, even **children** (cf. 10:21–22,34–37).

But the reward for such sacrifice will be the repayment of **a hundred times as much** in some form or another. In the church, the Lord gives us a foretaste of this payment. If a person is rejected by his family for being a Christian, he finds many more "fathers and mothers, brothers and sisters" in the family of God.

The true follower (in contrast to the rich young ruler) will **inherit eternal life**. The use of the term *inherit* here provides the sense of the new family (after one has been rejected by his old family). An heir is a son of the family from whom he inherits.

19:30. Jesus began to caution the disciples not to use a human yardstick when measuring eternal rewards. God's estimation of worthiness is quite different from ours.

The chapter break here is unfortunate, for the flow of thought is continuous. Many people who seem to be deserving of reward will receive less than is expected (though no less than they deserve). And many whom we might judge as undeserving will prove, in God's economy, to be **first**, receiving great reward.

D The King Explains Kingdom Grace (20:1–16)

SUPPORTING IDEA: *Human measures of worthiness are far from God's gracious attitude toward people.*

While Jesus shifted to a different point in this parable, it was related to his point in his conversation with the rich young ruler and the disciples. Our entrance into heaven depends on God's grace, not on our righteous works. In the same way, our reward in heaven will be based on God's reckoning, not our human calculations. Rewards are indeed meritorious, but they are calculated from God's perspective.

Jesus' statements of who would be first and who would be last open and close this parable (19:30; 20:16). It has already been illustrated in Jesus' acceptance of the children (19:13–15) and in his rejection of the wealthy young man (19:16–26). It will again be illustrated immediately following the parable (20:17–19) as Jesus predicted the "lastness" of his imminent suffering and death. Then he also predicted the reversal from the "lastness" of his apparent defeat in death back to the "firstness" of his triumphant resurrection. The theme will find further illustration in the request of the mother of

James and John, and in Jesus' acceptance of the two blind beggars in 20:29–34.

20:1. The word **for** tells us that this parable is an illustration and explanation of the key statement in 19:30. As in most of his parables, Jesus was teaching something about the kingdom of heaven—the way things work under the rule of the Messiah-King. Here he introduced the main characters: the landowner (representing God) and the hired laborers (representing believers). The landowner needed men to plant, tend, and harvest his crops.

Early in the morning is important, because time is an important feature of this parable. A typical workday for field workers in the ancient Near East began at approximately 6 A.M. (sunrise) and ended at around 6 P.M. (sunset). The average workday was likely ten-plus hours. So the landowner of the parable was scouting for workers before 6 A.M.

20:2–5. The men whom he hired to begin twelve hours of work at 6 A.M. formed the first and most prominent of five groups he would hire throughout the day. They agreed to work for the customary rate of one denarius for a full day's work, and then they started work in the vineyard.

We should be careful in our attempts to discern who these full-day workers (or any of the other four groups) represent. We may be tempted to think this first group represents those who have been Christians for most of their lives, whereas the later groups are those who come to Christ later in life. Or we might think the full-day workers are those who are especially faithful in their lifetime as a Christian, while the later groups are not so faithful. Such interpretations distract us from Jesus' main point—that God's way of compensating for righteous working may differ from what we expect. God's sense of "fairness" is not the typical self-serving human perspective. He does not compare us to one another but to our fulfillment of our own stewardship (see 1 Cor. 3:3–5).

The landowner needed still more workers, so three hours later (**the third hour** was 9 A.M.) he went again to **the marketplace** (where most commercial transactions took place, and where men hoping for work would gather) and found more laborers available. He hired them, promising, **I will pay you whatever is right**. Because these men would be working only nine hours (three-fourths of a workday), they would have expected three-fourths of a denarius as their wages at the end of the workday.

He did the same thing at noon (**the sixth hour**) and 3 P.M. (**the ninth hour**). These groups of workers would be working six hours (a half-day) and three hours (a quarter-day), respectively, and so would have naturally expected proportionately less pay than those who started at 6 A.M.

20:6–7. At 5 P.M. (**the eleventh hour**), with only one hour of the workday remaining, the landowner hired yet a fifth group of workers—the second most prominent group in Jesus' parable, because they stood in the greatest contrast with those hired at 6 A.M. These laborers he also sent into the field to work. The point is clear. These "last" workers, for whatever reason, were "last" by normal human performance standards. Jesus was about to challenge normal human reasoning and standards when it comes to kingdom rewards.

20:8–10. The word **evening** means sunset at 6 P.M., when the workers could no longer see to work. **The owner of the vineyard** is the landowner of 20:1. The **foreman** is mentioned only to give a sense of reality to the story, since the landowner himself would not have gone out into the field to call in the workers at the end of the day.

The landowner specifically instructed the foreman to pay the workers in reverse order (**beginning with the last ones hired and going on to the first**). It is assumed that the pay the foreman gave out was also according to the landowner's instructions.

The last group hired—those who worked only one hour—were paid first, before the eyes of all the workers hired earlier in the day. To everyone's astonishment, these one-hour workers were paid a full denarius—twelve times what they would have considered justly earned! The three-hour, six-hour, and nine-hour workers are not mentioned here, but we are to assume that they also received a denarius. Jesus jumped immediately from the one-hour workers to the twelve-hour workers to make obvious the contrast between the two.

The twelve-hour workers were encouraged by what they had observed, assuming the landowner had decided to be disproportionately generous to all the workers. They certainly expected more than one denarius, which, to their disappointment, was exactly what they were paid.

20:11–12. We can identify with their disappointment. They fell victim to the problem of expectations that were higher than reality. They, like so many of us today, had developed a sense of comparison and entitlement. So they grumbled to the landowner: **You have made them equal to us who have borne the burden of the work and the heat of the day**. The full-day workers perhaps looked down on the one-hour workers because they had been passed over as unworthy in the early hiring (20:7).

Jesus revealed here the way we as humans think about what is fair and just. When we see rewards handed out in heaven, we are sure to be in for some surprises. Some of the people and ministries that we have deemed insignificant will be celebrated, while many of the more prominent people and their ministries will receive little recognition. It is not Jesus' purpose here to explain the criteria he uses for such decisions, but only to warn us against false assumptions and expectations.

Jesus made the point that heaven's rewards are based upon: God's standards and our faithfulness to our calling in both attitude and action (1Cor. 4:5). There will be no negotiating or technicalities to consider.

Christians must avoid using other people as a yardstick for comparison. Only Christ himself is an accurate yardstick, and we all fall short of his "stature." This underscores our need for God's grace toward all. We must hold our human thinking in check.

20:13–15. The landowner focused on one of the twelve-hour workers, emphasizing the responsibility of each individual believer to keep his thinking in check. **Friend,** he addressed the worker, setting a calm, reasonable tone. The landowner then explained that he had been fair to the twelve-hour worker, paying exactly what was right and what they had agreed upon at the beginning of the day.

If not for the people who had worked fewer hours, the twelve-hour workers would have gone home satisfied with exactly the same amount. The landowner urged them to focus on their original agreement, not on the other workers. One denarius was their **pay**—exactly what they were entitled to—no more, no less.

Jesus drew a contrast between the landowner's fairness with the twelve-hour workers and his desire for generosity to the one-hour workers. This contrast was drawn not to indicate the landowner was being inconsistent but to emphasize that differing responses were the prerogatives of the landowner. If the landowner had underpaid any of his workers, they would have had reason to accuse him of injustice. But there was no law against overpaying workers. The employer was free to do with his money as he wished. This points out that the Lord is both sovereign and gracious.

Finally, the landowner addressed the root of the problem—their eye was **envious** (cf. Deut. 15:9; 1 Sam. 18:9; Matt. 6:22–23) because the landowner was **generous.** Their perspective was wrong.

This parable highlights both the justice and the grace of God. Neither is to be taken for granted. When God chooses to reward or punish according to what is justly due a person, no one has a right to complain. On the one hand, his rewards are "recompense" or "pay back" (Matt. 16:27; 2 Cor. 5:10; Col. 3:24–25). On the other hand, the God of Scripture is a God who delights to lavish blessing on his children (e.g., Eph. 1:3–14). But we must be careful not to presume upon his generosity. His gifts are not something we deserve; they are given freely at his discretion. If anyone receives the "raw end of the deal" (by our reasoning), it would be God, who gives much more than he "owes."

20:16. Jesus wrapped up the parable with the principle with which he started (19:30). So implies that this principle is the point of the parable. If we do not fully understand the justice behind the "last being first" and the "first being last," we must reserve judgment and thank God for being consistently just and abundantly gracious. We must never consider God unjust.

Applying this to the issues raised in Matthew 19, Jesus was saying that we can be assured that the sacrifices of his followers will always be recompensed fairly and abundantly. Final determination is up to the Father (cf. 20:23).

E The King Again Foretells His Death and Resurrection (20:17–19)

SUPPORTING IDEA: *The king is the best example of humble servanthood.*

20:17–19. It is no accident that Jesus' third formal prediction of his suffering, death, and resurrection followed immediately after the extended explanation of the principle that "the last will be first, and the first will be last" (see 19:30–20:16; cf. 16:21; 17:22–23). He told of the humiliation of his betrayal, the mockings and beatings he would endure, and his death. He who was supremely first over all creation would submit to being treated as the lowest of criminals. (This is the first specific mention of crucifixion, which was a punishment of ultimate humiliation, reserved only for the most despised criminals.) But out of the "lastness" of apparent defeat, the king would rise triumphant over death. Philippians 2:5–11 describes this dual paradox in greater detail: The One obedient to "death on a cross" would be the One who has a "name that is above every name."

At this point in the journey, Jesus and his companions were about to go **up to Jerusalem.** The tension between Jesus and the religious establishment, headquartered at Jerusalem, had been building throughout Matthew's Gospel. Before long the conflict would come to its tragic but triumphant end.

The word *up* alludes to the fact that Jerusalem was situated on a ridge at 2,550 feet above sea level. From any direction, Jerusalem was "up." But especially from the crossing of the Jordan River, near its entrance into the Dead Sea, at about 1,200 feet *below* sea level, the climb was substantial. This would have made for at least a 3,700-foot elevation gain. Perhaps Jesus and his disciples had just crossed the Jordan, or perhaps they were at Jericho, on the way to Jerusalem (see 20:29).

Jesus was preparing his disciples for what would happen during the next week in Jerusalem. As was his custom when discussing such frank matters, Jesus spoke privately with the Twelve. As in 16:21, Jesus connected his suffering with Jerusalem, but this time their arrival in that city was imminent. As in 17:22, Jesus used his title **the Son of Man,** again associating the Messiah with suffering.

In 16:21, Jesus listed "the elders, chief priests and teachers of the law," but here he mentioned only **the chief priests and the teachers of the law,** still representing the Sanhedrin. Whereas in 16:21, he said that he "must be killed," and in 17:23, that "they will kill him," Jesus expanded on his death in this passage. First, **they** [the Sanhedrin] **will condemn** [give judgment against] **him to death**. This was Jesus' first mention of his trial, although his mention of the Sanhedrin in 16:21 might have led the disciples to assume a trial. Second, Jesus mentioned for the first time that the Jewish leaders would **turn him over** to the Gentiles. Because the Jews, under Roman law, had no right to carry out a death sentence (26:66), they would have to rely on the Romans to perform their dirty work.

For the first time, Jesus gave the details of his passion. Jesus' remarks were painful for the disciples, but they pointed out Jesus' sovereignty in all these things. He was going into a difficult time, but he went as a king and never as a victim. He would be **mocked** and **flogged** (using a whip of leather thongs, with jagged bits of metal or bone that would rip the flesh of the victim's back) and **crucified**. The disciples would have cringed at all three of these words, but especially at *crucifixion*. This was a slow, torturous death which usually lasted for days—the most humiliating punishment used by the Roman Empire. It was reserved only for the lowest criminals. And crucifixion was also a sign of God's curse (Deut. 21:23; Gal. 3:13). Jesus finished his comments with the triumph of the Resurrection—a note of hope during their sobering climb toward Jerusalem.

The sovereign king was carrying out his mission to perfect fulfillment. The reality of Jesus' suffering and the disciples' share in his suffering would play a prominent part in the next segment of Matthew's Gospel (20:22–23,28). The disciples' words and attitudes revealed that they had failed to comprehend the gravity of Jesus' prediction.

F The King Corrects Lingering Misconceptions about Kingdom Greatness (20:20–28)

SUPPORTING IDEA: *Our human efforts at earthly greatness display our ignorance and misunderstanding of kingdom greatness.*

Matthew's inclusion of this event serves at least two purposes. First, it makes a connection between Jesus' suffering (20:17–19) and that of his followers (20:22–23). Second, it shows that the disciples still had not learned Jesus' lessons regarding greatness and humility in the kingdom. The event provided more opportunity for Jesus to expound on the need for humility and sacrificial servanthood in the kingdom (20:25–28). Jesus would then proceed to demonstrate the same kind of humble servanthood in the healing of the two blind men (20:29–34).

20:20–21. James and John were the sons of Zebedee (4:21). Their mother was not likely to be acting on her own here; there may have been some complicity with her sons. Perhaps James and John were guilty of maneuvering for status and rank within the kingdom of heaven. The mother respectfully bowed down to Jesus, preparing to make a formal request. When he invited her to make the request, she asked, **Grant that one of these two sons of mine may sit at your right and the other at your left in your kingdom.** Her reference to Jesus' kingdom was to its ultimate, triumphant fulfillment. This was a different picture than Jesus had in mind. The person on a king's right hand was his second in command, and the one to his left was third.

It is possible that James and John had told their mother about Jesus' promise that the Twelve would rule Israel on twelve thrones (19:28). Only two thrones could sit beside the king's. The woman and the two disciples were assuming that greatness in God's kingdom was based on status, rank, power, and authority. They also made the mistake Jesus warned against in 19:30–20:16: they were seeking to influence God's bestowal of reward.

20:22. Jesus confronted their misunderstanding by alluding to the fact that the path to such authority lay through the same kind of suffering he would undergo. By asking for the positions of greatest authority, they were asking for the most bitter cup of suffering. Of this implication they were ignorant: **You don't know what you are asking.**

Jesus alerted them to the connection between great authority and great suffering by asking, **Can you drink the cup I am going to drink?** The two answered, **We can.** These two disciples were prepared to follow Jesus. But it is unlikely that they understood Jesus was speaking of his death on the cross (20:19). A cup was often associated with judgment (Ps 75:8; Isa. 51:17–18).

20:23. Jesus acknowledged their earnest intention, noting that they would indeed suffer: **You will indeed drink from my cup.** James was eventually martyred (Acts 12:2), and John was exiled (Rev. 1:9). But Jesus corrected yet another misunderstanding. Not only was the bestowal of reward not in the hands of the believers; the distribution of those two thrones was at the discretion of the Father. Jesus implied his own obedient submission to the will of the Father (cf. 26:39,42).

Jesus apparently did not choose this private conversation as the opportunity to correct the Zebedee family about eternal rewards and greatness. Rather, he informed them of the implications of their request and that such decisions belonged to the Father.

20:24. Somehow the other ten disciples heard of the Zebedees' request. They **were indignant.** There was more than pure anger here; there was wounded pride. If the disciples had learned Jesus' lessons on humility, there would have been no pride to wound. The ten were apparently sorry only that they had not requested the same privilege first. Jesus chose this opportunity to teach further on the true values of the kingdom of heaven, especially since all twelve disciples had exposed their prideful hearts.

20:25. Jesus called his students for another session in his classroom. He first showed them that their attitudes were like the Gentiles. **You know** drew on their own experience or common knowledge. In the unbelieving world, it is assumed that power and authority define greatness. The **rulers** and **high officials** were examples of worldly greatness. The way they demonstrated their "greatness" was to **lord it over** others and to **exercise authority.** Jesus was not criticizing authoritative or hierarchical structure but the "strutting."

Such behavior is born out of insecurity and pride. The person who "bosses" others around is trying to prove to himself that he is as great as he hopes. It is only an illusion, for such a person is actually fearful and weak.

20:26–28. Jesus transitioned into the contrasting truth of kingdom greatness with his words, **Not so with you,** implying, "You are sons of the Almighty. What are you doing dabbling in these puny efforts at worldly 'greatness' when you could be experiencing true greatness."

In 20:26–27, Jesus phrased his words in a parallel structure, a kind of poetry. The pronoun **whoever** leaves the door to true greatness open to anyone willing to follow the path Jesus prescribes. **Among you** brings to mind the family of God. Just as in Matthew 18, Jesus was speaking of relationships within the believing community.

The **great** and the **first** bring to mind Jesus' previous teachings in 18:2–4; 19:30–20:16. Jesus had compared the humility of a true follower to that of a child; here he compared such humility to that of a **servant** (*diakonos*) or a **slave** (*doulos*). The possessive pronoun **your** in both cases is plural, implying that the great believer is servant or slave of all fellow believers. This is equivalent to saying, "The first will be last" (19:30; 20:16), but Jesus' words here were more graphic. The person who is truly great, by heaven's definition, is the one who chooses an attitude of submission to others in the family of believers.

Not everything another believer might ask of us is for the good of all. We are to serve the genuine good of other believers, not simply do what they want us to do. This means that the truly **great** believer will sometimes encounter misunderstandings from others and disappoint and even anger others by right choices. Some believers might even begin to take pride in their "humility." Our hearts are so self-deceptive that we must always remain open to examination by the loving scrutiny of the Lord. We are accountable to brothers and sisters whose discernment we trust.

All of Jesus' teaching assumes that true humility is based on a healthy self-image. Only the person who is at peace with his true worth in God's eyes is able to act toward others without trying to prove his or her worth. Convinced of one's self-worth, the believer is able to move on in an attempt to demonstrate the worth of others (cf. John 13:1–17).

Jesus could provide no better model than himself. Here he used the title **the Son of Man** to avoid the use of the pronoun "I," which might have been construed by the disciples as boastful. Although the Messiah-King came with every right to be served, his purpose was to serve them. He gave up his rights and took on a responsibility he was not obligated to take. This responsibility would extend ultimately to our eternal souls, purchased by the sacrifice of his life as **a ransom** [a substitute] **for many** (see "many" in Isa. 52:13–53:12).

G The King Stoops to Serve Two Blind Beggars (20:29–34)

SUPPORTING IDEA: *The greatest in the kingdom will stoop to serve the least.*

20:29–31. How long Jesus and his disciples had been in Jericho, on the way from the Jordan crossing to Jerusalem, is unknown. They may have passed through quickly, or they may have stayed there for some days.

Jesus once again gathered a large crowd. His reputation was greater and more widespread than ever. The crowd was convinced that the king would give them liberty from Rome, possibly during this visit to Jerusalem. Among the crowd were pilgrims traveling to Jerusalem for the approaching Passover celebration.

Beggars were considered outcasts in Jewish society. Matthew, writing to Jews who desired two witnesses, mentioned both men. Mark and Luke referred only to one beggar, probably the speaker of the two. He was identified in Mark 10:46 with the nickname "Bartimaeus," or "Son of Excrement." Even though Old Testament law provided for the needy in Israel, few holy men would have anything to do with beggars. They feared they might be made unclean if they associated with beggars. Jesus had already performed one healing similar to this in 9:27–31. But this episode was unique in its purpose for Matthew's story. These two "low-lives" were among those whom the Son of Man had come to serve (20:28).

The blind men called out, **Lord, Son of David, have mercy on us!** The messianic title anticipated its use by the crowds in 21:9,15 as well as Jesus' teaching about it in 22:42–45.

The crowd **rebuked** the men, telling them to be quiet, lest they disturb the important holy man. But these were desperate men. No social taboos would rob them of this opportunity for healing.

20:32–33. Jesus stopped and called the beggars. The crowd looked on in astonishment. His question, **What do you want me to do for you?** was not because Jesus was unaware of the obvious. He wanted the men to verbalize their faith in him. They stated their deepest desire: **we want our sight.**

20:34. The phrase **had compassion** is from *splanchnizomai*, also found in 9:36 (see comment there); 14:14; 15:32; 18:27. The king's heart compelled him to action on behalf of others. Jesus ministered through touch, demonstrating his lack of fear of the uncleanness or lowly status of these men.

Immediately the two men regained their sight and joined his followers, undoubtedly praising God all the way to Jerusalem. This healing and the enthusiasm it must have caused in the crowd provided the momentum for Jesus' triumphant entry into Jerusalem.

The Messiah-King was on the verge of entering "the city of the Great King" (Matt. 5:35; Ps. 48:2). He was about to ascend to the sanctuary of Yahweh, which only the blameless may do (Ps. 15). He was about to purify his own house, the temple (21:13), and was preparing to perform the central messianic act of salvation (Isa. 53). The crowd and the disciples were to know beyond any doubt who was entering Jerusalem and the source and extent of his authority.

> **MAIN IDEA REVIEW:** *The humblest servant, most dependent on the grace of God, is the greatest in God's eyes.*

III. CONCLUSION

God views all people—regardless of age, gender, social status, or nationality—as of equal value. The greatest person in God's kingdom is the humblest servant toward fellow believers. We must follow Jesus' example by stooping to serve those considered least worthy by worldly standards.

PRINCIPLES

- God's intention for marriage is lifelong faithfulness.
- There is a mysterious but authentic spiritual oneness in marriage.
- Because of the reality of man's sin, God has provided guidelines to limit the breaking of the marriage covenant.
- Unrepentant, gross sexual immorality may be reason to allow divorce; but even then, divorce is not a mandate. Reconciliation is God's intention.
- Some people have been gifted by God to remain single for greater investment in the kingdom.
- Kingdom citizens are characterized by the humble faith of a child.
- Eternal life cannot be earned. It can only be received as a gift.
- True kingdom disciples exhibit devotion to the king.
- The devotion of a true kingdom disciple is made possible by the supernatural enabling of God.
- Any false god hinders people from entering God's kingdom.
- Any sacrifices we make for the king and his kingdom will be abundantly repaid.

- God's evaluation of a believer's works will determine a person's reward.
- God will never reward believers unjustly; everything we receive is far more than we deserve.

APPLICATIONS

- Resolve to remain faithful to your spouse.
- Avoid immorality.
- Follow our Lord's example of humility in your service to him.
- Remain faithful in your devotion to God.
- Don't evaluate yourself in terms of others.
- Prepare to suffer as a follower of Christ

IV. LIFE APPLICATION

A Humble Servant

D. L. Moody founded several schools for the training of underprivileged children at Northfield, Massachusetts. Often, when students arrived at the train station, Moody would take his horse and buggy and meet them. One rainy day a man and two women arrived at the station and looked around for someone to take them to the hotel. Seeing a man in a buggy, the man insisted that the driver take him and his party to the hotel. Moody explained that he was waiting to take a party of girls to the seminary.

The visitor was offended and insisted that "these girls are not the only people to be served! Now, you just take us right up to the hotel!"

Meekly the driver obeyed, left them at the hotel, and drove off before he could be paid.

"Who was that driver?" the visitor asked the bellboy.

"Mr. D. L. Moody," the boy replied.

The visitor was shocked because he had come to Northfield to ask Moody to take his daughter into the school. The next day the man apologized, and Moody had a great deal of fun over it.

Dwight L. Moody understood the servanthood attitude Jesus wants us to show toward others. True greatness comes from serving others in God's kingdom, not from advancing our own agendas or interests.

The greatest example of humble servanthood is the Lord Jesus Christ. His sacrifice on the cross to pay for our salvation was the greatest single act of servanthood in history. Let us follow the example of his humble service in our lives, helping others. Any and all sacrifices of servanthood we make in the kingdom will be rewarded by the king.

V. PRAYER

Gracious Father, teach me the meaning of true greatness and make me a servant of others (especially my spouse) in your kingdom. Amen.

VI. DEEPER DISCOVERIES

A. Divorce and Remarriage in Israel (v. 3)

In first-century Israel, divorce and remarriage was as controversial as it is today. The Rabbi Hillel school of thought held liberal views on the topic, allowing divorce for any reason. Hillel allowed divorce for a poorly cooked meal, or even if the husband saw a woman whom he considered more attractive. But the Rabbi Shammai school of thought was much stricter, allowing divorce only for serious reasons, particularly adultery.

Even in Israel, where Mosaic Law gave women more dignity and protection than the surrounding cultures, it was the man who took the action of divorce. Today, however, when cultural expectations of men and women are different, this question applies to women as much as men.

B. Sexual Immoriality (v. 9)

There is debate over the meaning of the Greek word *porneia* ("sexual immorality"), here and in 5:32. Many recent commentators believe the word to refer to the cluster of incestuous or illicit sexual relationships listed in the Mosaic Law (see Lev. 18:6–18). If this interpretation is accurate, there is no allowance for divorce in any legitimate marriage (heterosexual, nonincestuous). The fact that neither Mark nor Luke include any such "exception" clause in their Gospels is a telling argument. Matthew's writing to a Jewish audience is sufficient explanation for its presence here.

However one may interpret *porneia*, a careful student of Scripture should not see a single act of marital infidelity as sufficient to justify divorce. Most biblically sound church leaders, who must apply these passages to specific instances of sexual immorality and divorce, will not jump to the assumption that a one-time indiscretion of one spouse against another qualifies as Jesus' *porneia*. To the contrary, it is clear that God, while he does not condone sexual immorality in any form, also hates divorce (Mal. 2:16). And he encourages forgiveness, redemption, and restoration. That is precisely what Matthew 18 is about. A thoughtful reading of Scripture will bring the reader to the conclusion that God is always in favor of reconciliation.

A wise church leader will define *porneia*, in practical terms, as an ongoing unrepentant practice of sexual immorality. This is evidence that the offending spouse has willfully and repeatedly abandoned the marriage vow of exclusive devotion to his or her spouse. In this case, the offended spouse may be justified in divorcing the other. In the Old Testament, such sin would have terminated the marriage through the stoning of the adulterer.

Jesus made it clear in this passage that the allowance for divorce, even if justified, is only an allowance, never a mandate.

A related issue was whether remarriage to a different spouse was permissible after divorce. It is clear from both Matthew 5:32 and 19:9 that no person who had wrongly divorced his or her spouse had the biblical right to marry another. Some argue that this was because, in God's eyes, the original marriage bond was still intact since wrongful remarriage was defined as **adultery**. As long as one's ex-husband or ex-wife was alive (Rom. 7:2–3) and had not married another person (Deut. 24:1–4), the only remarriage choice for such a divorced person was to reconcile with his or her previous spouse (although 1 Cor. 7:10–17 may also allow abandonment as an exception). It was assumed in the first century that a divorced person would remarry. Therefore, the only way to avoid the adulterous sin of a wrongful remarriage was not to go through a wrongful divorce.

However, in the case of a biblically justified divorce, we are to assume that the offending spouse is not justified in remarriage, but that the offended spouse *is* allowed to remarry.

Some who have wrongfully remarried may wonder if they are continually living in an adulterous relationship. This dilemma is contrary to 1 Corinthians 10:13, which says that God will never put a believer in a situation where he or she has to sin. He will always make a "way out" from sin. So the sin of adultery in a wrongful remarriage is a one-time sin, at the beginning of the new marriage. From that point on, the new husband and wife are committed before God to preserve their relationship for life. Neither spouse in the new marriage has the option of going back to a previous spouse. Such would be "detestable" (Deut. 24:1–4). This understanding supports Moses' original reason for including the Deuteronomy 24 principle. People must understand the divine nature of marriage as an institution and never treat it lightly.

C. Summary

In this chapter, Jesus expanded on his theme of humility in the kingdom, introduced in 18:3–4, by means of further teaching and live illustration. Contrary to the expectations of the disciples and the crowds, the reader is being prepared for the king's greatest act of humble servanthood—his sacrificial death "as a ransom for many" (20:28). The theme of humility also brings balance to the king's role as judge, which he will display in the purging of the temple (21:12–13) and in his condemnation of the hypocritical leaders (esp. Matt. 23).

The geographical movement of Matthew 19–20 from Galilee to Judea was also symbolic of Jesus' movement toward the cross. The time of preparation was over, and it was time to do battle in earnest. The disciples, while far from perfect, were ready. The final countdown to the victorious tragedy had begun.

VII. TEACHING OUTLINE

A. INTRODUCTION

1. Lead Story: Parking-Lot Humility
2. Context: Jesus has been mentally preparing himself and his disciples for the cross since 16:21, but now he begins his journey toward Jerusalem, where he will arrive in triumph in Matthew 21. He knows that the real triumph will come after crossing the valley of death. This is what he has already told his disciples twice (16:21; 17:22–23) and alluded to other times (e.g., 17:9,12), and he will again announce this clearly in 20:17–19.
3. Transition: The events of Matthew 19–20 take place during Jesus' journey toward the cross at Jerusalem. Humility continues to be a key theme throughout these two chapters—a theme already established in Matthew 18, and culminating in the king's humble means of transportation into Jerusalem (21:5). We see humility and servanthood taught openly in 19:13–15 (the little children) and 20:20–28 (the request of the mother of James and John and Jesus' ensuing teaching). We see humility implied in 19:16–29 (Jesus' challenge to the prideful expectation of the rich young man, who wanted to earn salvation) and 19:30–20:16 (the parable of the workers). And we see humility and servanthood modeled by Jesus in 20:17–19 (passion prediction) and 20:29–34 (healing the two blind men).

   Jesus' twice-repeated "first will be last" and "last will be first" statements (19:30; 20:16; similarly in 20:26–28) serve as the central message of Matthew 19–20. The student of these chapters will see Matthew's intent and the impact of Jesus' life and teaching by searching for examples of "lastness" and "firstness."

B. COMMENTARY

1. The King Affirms the Marriage Commitment (19:1–12)
2. The King Makes Time for Children (19:13–15)
3. The King Clarifies the Demands and Rewards of True Discipleship (19:16–30)
4. The King Explains Kingdom Grace (20:1–16)
5. The King Again Foretells His Death and Resurrection (20:17–19)

6. The King Corrects Lingering Misconceptions about Kingdom Greatness (20:20–28)
7. The King Stoops to Serve Two Blind Beggars (20:29–34)

C. CONCLUSION

1. Wrap-up: The humblest servant, most dependent on the grace of God, is the greatest in God's eyes.
2. Personal Challenge: The greatest in the kingdom is the humblest servant toward fellow believers. We must follow Jesus' example by stooping to serve those considered least worthy by worldly standards, especially those within "the household of faith," the church.

VIII. ISSUES FOR DISCUSSION

1. What lesson did Jesus teach his disciples through the example of a child?
2. Why did the rich young ruler refuse to follow Jesus?
3. In Jesus' parable of the vineyard workers, how many different groups of workers did the landowner hire to work in his vineyard? What lesson did Jesus teach through this parable?
4. What did the mother of James and John have in mind when she asked Jesus to "grant that one of these two sons of mine may sit at your right and the other at your left in your kingdom"?

Matthew 21–22

The King Puts the Hypocrites in Their Place

"*It is only when men begin to worship that they begin to grow.*"

C a l v i n   C o o l i d g e

Matthew 21–22

I N   A   N U T S H E L L

In these chapters the conflict escalates as Jesus takes the offensive and enters Jerusalem. Upon his arrival, he receives a king's welcome. He then challenges the corruption he sees in the temple, reclaiming his place of worship. Threatened by his authority, the Jewish leaders soon devise a scheme to trap Jesus. However, in spite of their efforts to subvert him, Jesus proves his absolute authority and establishes himself as the Messiah.

The King Puts the
Hypocrites in Their Place

I. INTRODUCTION

Crunch Time

*E*arly in the Vietnam war, a section of jungle called War Zone D was one tough stretch of enemy-infested ground. It was a "secret" zone about which allied intelligence knew almost nothing—except to stay away. Conventional allied infantry units never went near it. Finally, allied intelligence decided to invade the enemy's sanctuary.

But no ordinary unit would do. This operation required another level of intensity and experience. This was a mission which would demand the best. Chosen were thirteen handpicked American Green Berets and a company-sized element of their highly trained and trusted Cambodian guerillas.

Through several weeks and dozens of firefights without artillery support or any chance of reinforcements, these noble warriors fought fifty-one combat engagements, directed tactical air strikes on twenty-seven critical targets, and raided numerous base camps of much larger enemy units. They focused on their mission and stayed at it until it was accomplished.

Life is like that. When it is crunch time, it is time to step up the intensity. The mission requires it. Whether it is a seasoned championship team in the finals, a gifted musician on a farewell tour, or the Army Rangers at Point du Hoc on June 6, 1944. When the mission faces its most critical moments, the seasoned veterans know what to do. Jesus and his disciples had come to crunch time.

In these final chapters of Matthew, Jesus was on a mission. He was set. The opposition had set up roadblock after roadblock, and Jesus simply drove through them. He refused to be a victim. He insisted on being what he was— the king himself, directing the entire operation up to and including his own sacrifice. It was time to march on Jerusalem. In Matthew 21–22 Jesus stepped into "War Zone D" in the capital city.

II. COMMENTARY

The King Puts the Hypocrites in Their Place

MAIN IDEA: *Jesus is indeed the Messiah-King, having absolute authority and deserving worship and submission from all his subjects.*

Conflict predominates in Matthew 21–23. To this point, Jesus had tried to avoid outright conflict, while, at the same time, warning people openly about the poison of the Jewish leaders. When conflict had come, it did so at the initiative of the hypocrites, and Jesus responded to their attacks.

However, at this point Jesus launched a serious offensive. He took the initiative, entering Jerusalem as king and purging the temple (21:12–13). From that point on, the initiative went back and forth. The Jewish leaders took the offensive, challenging Jesus' authority (21:23–27); then Jesus pressed his advantage mercilessly with a volley of three parables aimed at the hypocrites (21:28–22:14). Next, Jesus' opponents banded together in their best coordinated effort, attempting to trap him with three challenging questions (22:15–40). Jesus deftly parried each of their blows, then retook the offensive, striking with the claim of his own identity (22:41–46). He then silenced his enemies with the scathing indictment of the "seven woes" in chapter 23.

The spiritual battle with Satan, introduced in 4:1–11, is rejoined with vigor in these chapters. The threefold attack of the Jewish leaders in 22:15–40 may be intended to remind us of Satan's threefold attack against Jesus in the desert. We will understand these later battles in a new light if we see Satan as the mastermind behind them, using the evil, self-absorbed leaders as his pawns.

Just as Satan attacked Jesus three times, so did the religious leaders (22:15–40). Jesus also responded to the chief priests' and elders' challenge to his authority (21:23–27) with a series of three parables which focused on the religious leaders' failure.

One notable feature of Matthew 21–22 is the frequent use of Old Testament Scripture:

- In 21:5, Jesus fulfilled another messianic prophecy.
- In 21:9, the crowd quoted the Old Testament in praise of the king.
- In 21:13, 42, Jesus used the Old Testament to warn of God's judgment on the evil Jewish leaders.
- In 21:33, Jesus used Old Testament imagery to set up a parable about Israel and its leaders.

- In 22:24, the Sadducees used Scripture in the second of three testing questions (much as Satan used Scripture in his second temptation; 4:5–7).

- In 21:16; 22:32,37,39, Jesus used Scripture to answer challenges from his opponents (much as he used Scripture to answer Satan's temptations; 4:4,7,10).

- And in 22:44, Jesus used Scripture to lay claim to his rightful identity as the Christ.

At the peak of the spiritual battle, the sword of God's Word becomes prominent (Eph. 6:17). Matthew 21 is a picture of Jesus fulfilling the messianic Psalm 118. At every turn, whether on the offensive or the defensive, the Messiah-King demonstrated his authority with personal confidence and decisive victory.

Anyone observing this battle with an open mind would have come away with the conclusion that Jesus was indeed who he said he was—the Christ, the Messiah, the king. But the hypocrites' minds were far from open, so they walked away after Matthew 23 with their egos badly wounded from their resounding defeat. But their wills became more firmly fixed than ever on destroying this Jesus. If they could not defeat him in a battle of words (spiritual truth and principle), then physical force would have to be used.

Ⓐ The King Enters His City with Triumph and Meekness (21:1–11)

SUPPORTING IDEA: *Jesus is indeed king; he has a fierce commitment to the truth; but he is a king who brings peace with a gentle spirit.*

Jesus' triumphal entry into Jerusalem had been foreshadowed with growing anticipation ever since 16:21, where we find Jesus' first passion prediction. There he mentioned Jerusalem as his goal. Jesus mentioned Jerusalem again in his third passion prediction (20:18). James, John, and their mother may have been anticipating the triumphant king setting up his kingdom upon his arrival in Jerusalem (20:21). The cries of the two blind men, using the messianic title "Son of David," pointed to the entry (20:30–31). And the clearly messianic healing of the blind men built momentum toward the triumphal entry (20:34; cf. Isa. 35:5–6).

From a human standpoint, this marked the high point of Jesus' earthly life, prior to his death and resurrection. The crowds, swollen by pilgrims coming for the Passover feast just a few days away, were swept up in anticipation of a decisive battle to oust the Roman oppressors, which they thought would be led by the promised Messiah. Five days later a crowd comprised of many of these same people would be shouting for the king's execution (27:17–25).

What the people failed to understand was that the king had come to defeat a much greater enemy than Rome—an enemy that knew no national boundaries or respected no political or sectarian differences. It was an enemy whose defeat would have repercussions far beyond the end of this life. Jesus had come to defeat Satan, our own sin, and the claim of death.

21:1–3. The name **Bethphage** means "House of Unripe Figs." This was a village on the southeast slope of the Mount of Olives, east of Jerusalem. The mountain was several hundred feet higher than Jerusalem, providing a spectacular view of the city.

Jesus now drew upon his divine omniscience to prepare for his proper entrance into the city. He sent two disciples into the village, foretelling their discovery of a donkey and her colt. He instructed them to untie them and bring them to him and to be prepared for any objections from observers. The Lord had already prepared the hearts of the animals' owner, so that, at the mention of **the Lord needs them**, the owner would send the disciples promptly on their way with his animals.

21:4–5. Here Matthew added a parenthetical comment to show Jesus' fulfillment of another messianic prophecy—this one from Zechariah 9:9 (about 500 B.C.).

21:6–8. Matthew stated that the two disciples obeyed Jesus, and the two animals were brought to Jesus. The disciples laid their coats (their cloaks or outer garments) on the donkey and the colt, providing a crude saddle. Jesus sat on the colt, riding a humble animal as a king did in times of peace. Most of the people in the crowd took their cue from the disciples' example. They laid their coats across Jesus' path in the road, as though to give him the "red carpet treatment." Others cut branches from nearby trees to extend the "carpet" into the city. John 12:13 tells us the branches were "palm branches," thus our celebration of "Palm Sunday" five days before Good Friday and seven days before Resurrection Sunday, or "Easter."

21:9. The crowd milled around the king, some preceding him as heralds, some following as adoring loyalists. The picture is of a royal procession.

As the crowd moved along, they shouted words of praise, celebrating the arrival of Israel's Savior, the Messiah-King. **Hosanna** is literally a plea to "save," but by this time it had become an expression of praise for God's salvation. As had been acknowledged twice by blind men (Matt. 9:27; 20:30–31), and speculated upon by the people who witnessed an exorcism (12:23), now the identity of Jesus as the promised royal **Son of David** was proclaimed with praise.

For a short time, the people would acknowledge Jesus' true identity as the sovereign Son of David, but they would fail to identify him also as the sacrificial Son of Abraham. They knew he had come to restore his kingdom, but they missed the fact that he was also here to redeem his people. They anticipated the sovereignty but overlooked the sacrifice. Jesus would not exercise the rule without the redemption.

The phrase **Blessed is he who comes in the name of the Lord** was taken from Psalm 118:26. Psalm 118 is a "psalm of ascent," sung as the people ascended toward the temple in Jerusalem for worship, inviting others "with boughs in hand" to "join in the festal procession" (Ps. 118:27). Jesus was about to ascend to the temple on the highest point of the city. This psalm is also that from which Jesus would take his quote concerning "the stone the builders rejected" (Ps. 118:22–23; Matt. 22:42–44), predicting judgment on the "builders" or leaders of Israel.

This second expression of praise worshiped Jesus as the one who **comes in the name of the Lord**—the one who comes representing Yahweh, in this case Yahweh himself. Jesus would put this same quotation to different use in 23:39.

This portion of the psalms of ascent (Pss. 113–118) was referred to as the Great Hallel, and it was sung by the people during the Passover season. A third shout from the crowd, **Hosanna in the highest!** implied praise to Yahweh, who is the highest and who dwells in highest heaven.

21:10–11. As the royal procession passed through the city gate, **the whole city was stirred.** Jesus had not frequented Jerusalem recently (none of his previous Jerusalem experiences are recorded in Matthew). While his fame must have been heard here, he was not as readily recognized as he would have been in the north. But his identity was made known wherever the procession traveled in the city. When city dwellers and merchants inquired about his identity, his enthusiastic followers made him known as **Jesus, the prophet from Nazareth in Galilee.** Jesus had spent most of his ministry in the northern province of Galilee. His hometown was Nazareth in that same province (2:22–23). Thus, he was known by his town of origin. At the mention of his name and origin, most people in Jerusalem probably perked up with recognition. Many more must have joined the procession on the way to the temple.

B The King Reclaims His Place of Worship (21:12–17)

SUPPORTING IDEA: *The king is also the judge, guarding his honor.*

The triumphal entry established Jesus as the Messiah-King, the Son of David, who was entering his city and ascending to his temple. It was the king who entered the temple and challenged the corruption he found.

21:12. The practice of selling sacrificial animals in Jerusalem originated as a good and helpful idea. Jews coming to worship from all over Israel and other parts of the known world needed animals to sacrifice (birds for the poor people, larger animals for those who could afford more). Most of them traveled days—some even weeks—and it was easier to carry money to buy a sacrifice at their destination than to herd an animal along and carry supplies for its upkeep on the journey.

But there was no reason to carry on any of this business inside the temple itself. We can also assume that the priesthood gained a healthy profit from sales in the temple and that Jesus' disruption was an attack on one of their sources of wealth. It is likely that financial corruption was the order of the day; animals were sold and the money exchanged at exorbitant prices. The Jewish leaders were misusing the **house of prayer** for worldly profit.

Jesus' actions did not put an end to this practice. Most of these merchants were probably back in place the next day, especially with the Passover approaching and the business it would bring. Jesus' confrontation had prophetic significance, warning of coming judgment.

21:13. The Messiah-King spoke to his subjects, who were misusing this place of worship. Not only was it **written**, but he himself had written, "My house will be called a house of prayer" (Isa. 56:7). The broader context of Isaiah 56:3–8 was especially significant in view of the temple cleansing. The Lord was reassuring both eunuchs (who were, by Mosaic Law, not permitted into the temple, Lev. 21:20) and Gentiles that, when all was set right, they would be gathered into the community of worship together with the faithful of Israel. In fact, the full quotation from Isaiah 56:7 is: "My house will be called a house of prayer *for all nations*" (emphasis mine). This emphasized the inclusion of Gentiles. Matthew shortened the quotation to draw attention to the contrast between the purpose of the temple for prayer and its use as a market.

In contrast, **you** (not only the merchants, but also the priests who endorsed their presence) had made the temple **a den of robbers**. We can assume the meaning of *robber* was drawn from the misuse of the temple for personal and commercial gain. Certainly, greed and profiteering had come to mark the temple area.

21:14. It was nothing new in Matthew to see Jesus performing healing miracles. But it was all the more fitting that the Messiah should fulfill the prophecy of Isaiah 35:5–6 by healing the blind and the lame in his place of worship. This brief summary statement was another part of Matthew's presentation of the Messiah-King's advent in Jerusalem.

21:15–16. The Jewish leaders did not miss the implications of what was happening. They saw the triumphal entry, the messianic praise of the crowd, Jesus' authoritative cleansing of the temple, his pronouncement of judgment, and his healing miracles. Even the children Jesus had esteemed were proclaiming praise to the Messiah, **the Son of David**. It was too much for the hypocrites. They became **indignant** (also in 20:24; 26:8).

Their assumptions concerning Jesus' identity led the chief priests and scribes to believe that pointing out the children's "error" would cause Jesus to be horrified at their actions. Surely he would command the children to stop. Any Jewish teacher would have been horrified to be proclaimed "Son of David." For anyone other than the Messiah to accept such acclaim was equivalent to blasphemy.

But the Son of David saw no problems with the children's praise. When his attention was drawn to it, he affirmed its appropriateness, supporting it with a quote from Psalm 8:2. His **have you never read** revealed his enemies' lack of understanding of the Old Testament Scriptures, on which they were supposed to be experts (cf. 12:3; 19:4; 21:42; 22:31). Jesus used the children's praise to show how obvious it should have been that he was the Son of David.

21:17. Having accomplished his grand entrance, the king **left** the priests and scribes. Matthew used the Greek verb *kataleipo,* meaning "to leave behind." It is a stronger verb than *leipo,* implying a purposeful departure, possibly in disgust or righteous anger, after the confrontation. The same verb *kataleipo* was used in Matthew 16:4 when Jesus left his challengers to cross the Sea of Galilee, and in 19:5 of a man leaving his parents. There was calculated determination in Jesus' action. In the flow of Matthew's argument, this is most significant. Jesus (in light of the leaders' rejection and opposition) had now deliberately abandoned the chief priests, the scribes, the temple, Jerusalem, and everything else related to official Israel and its false religion.

Accommodations in Jerusalem were limited because of the influx of Passover pilgrims. Jesus had friends in Bethany (Mark 14:3; John 11:1) two miles east of Jerusalem (John 11:18), and he stayed with them that night.

C The King Acts Out the Drama of the Fruitless Fig Tree (21:18–22)

SUPPORTING IDEA: *Jesus will judge those who put on a show of worship and obedience while revealing their true character through a lack of spiritual fruit.*

According to Mark's chronology, Jesus cursed the fig tree on Monday morning while on his way to cleanse the temple. Then the disciples noticed the withered tree on Tuesday morning as they returned for the day of confrontation (21:23–23:39). Matthew arranged events in a different order than Mark to place the temple cleansing after the triumphal entry and to keep the story of the fig tree together. This practice was fully accepted in that culture, and it served Matthew's thematic development well.

21:18–19. Jesus returned to Jerusalem. Along the way he became hungry. As was the right of any Jew or sojourning alien under Mosaic Law, Jesus decided to eat figs for breakfast when he saw a fig tree growing by the road. Jesus assumed the tree had fruit when he saw its leaves. But the leaves had sent a false message. There was no fruit. The tree's promise was empty.

In anger, Jesus cursed the tree, proclaiming that it would never bear fruit again. The tree obeyed the word of its Creator, and it withered **immediately.** We might wonder if the pressure was beginning to get to Jesus. He cursed an inanimate object (this is the only destructive miracle attributed to Jesus, unless we count the drowning of the pigs in 8:32). But that was not the case. The scene makes perfect sense and takes on great significance when we put it into its context.

In the preceding passage, the king had pronounced judgment on Israel and its leaders for their idolatrous behavior (21:12–13). With the fig tree, Jesus acted out a parable or "mini-drama" to illustrate the reality of Israel's fruitlessness and its doom. Just as the leaves of the fig tree advertised fruit, so the Jewish leaders claimed to be fulfilling God's purpose. However, the advertising was a lie. Under the "leaves" of their showy religion (6:1–18; 15:8–9) their hearts were barren and unbelieving. They had missed their opportunity to repent and to bear true fruit, and so the king pronounced their judgment. There would be no more opportunities for these hypocrites—they would never bear fruit but would die through the judgment of God.

21:20–21. The disciples were **amazed** at seeing the fig tree wither before their eyes. Even at this stage of their training, they still were puzzled by Jesus' power. They asked how the fig tree could have withered so quickly.

This was a teachable moment, very similar to that in 17:19–20 (the exorcism the disciples could not perform). In fact, Jesus used some of the same imagery to teach the same lesson—that any believer with true faith can do great things by drawing on the power of God. Faith is the basis for answered prayer (21:22).

Jesus grabbed the disciples' attention, alerting them to the importance of what he was about to say: **I tell you the truth.** The necessary ingredient was faith (taking God at his word), which the disciples lacked. Jesus clarified his meaning by mentioning the opposite of faith—**doubt.**

With that kind of faith, the disciples would be able to wither fig trees and more. Jesus and his disciples were probably crossing the Mount of Olives as they approached Jerusalem. Jesus probably pointed to the mount when he said **this mountain,** giving the disciples a visual image that illustrated the power of God available to the person with true faith (cf. "this mountain" in 17:20). The disciples could envision the Mount of Olives being lifted and cast **into the sea** at the word of a faith-filled believer.

Jesus meant us to assume that mountain-moving faith should not be exercised in such frivolous ways as rearranging the earth. In fact, faith cannot be exercised in any way except according to God's will. It is not the faith which moves mountains, but the power of God in response to the expression of faith. True faith is always in keeping with God's will and is based on intimacy with God and an understanding of his heart and will.

21:22. Jesus' closing comment reinforced the power of God in response to faith. Prayer is an expression of our powerlessness and dependence on God. The weaker we realize we are, the greater the working of God's power through us (2 Cor. 12:7–10). The mature believer has strength that comes from God. The believer in humble dependence becomes a vessel for God's power. A person who asks in accordance with God's desire will have his requests granted.

The faith Jesus implied here is an attitude of submission to his will, confidence in his wisdom, and assurance of his love. This is faith that the Father can take our requests and sort them out according to our best interest and his glory. With such an attitude, we will gradually grow to share the mind of Christ, to desire his desires and to ask for his requests.

D The King's Authority Is Questioned (21:23–27)

SUPPORTING IDEA: *The king's authority will threaten those who desire to usurp his authority for themselves.*

With Jesus' return to Jerusalem and the temple (21:23), Matthew launched into the final verbal battle between Jesus and the Jewish religious leaders. This battle extended through Matthew 23. This first challenge to Jesus' authority would be met with a threefold answer and rebuttal in Jesus' three parables (21:28–22:14), turning the tables on the hypocrites.

Again, according to Mark's more detailed chronology, all of the conflict from this point through Matthew 23 seems to have occurred on Tuesday, after Palm Sunday and before the Passover and Christ's crucifixion. Matthew included several grammatical connecting devices to indicate the unity of this series of conflicts.

21:23. Jesus returned to the temple since this was the place in Jerusalem where people came to hear the Scriptures taught. And teach he did. But Jesus also returned to do battle, knowing that his opponents were waiting for him.

The chief priests and the elders of the people interrupted his teaching to challenge his authority. Both groups belonged to the Sanhedrin, the executive, legislative, and judicial branches of the Jewish government. **These things** that Jesus was doing included his purging of the temple on the previous day, but they may also have included other events (the triumphal entry, his acceptance of praise as the "Son of David," his teaching in the temple, and his miraculous healings). They asked him to state the authority by which he did these things and the source of his authority (**who gave you this authority?**).

21:24–26. Their request was similar to that of the two groups who had demanded an attesting sign from Jesus (12:38–45; 16:1–4). In all three instances, the minds of the challengers were closed to the truth. Jesus' response was the same in all three cases: he would not comply with their request. Even though they were asking for a verbal response, not a miraculous demonstration, Jesus knew they would not accept his answer. He would not give them fuel for the fire they were trying to build.

Instead, Jesus asked them a question, promising an answer for an answer. Suddenly the attackers were on the defensive. Jesus asked them, in front of the audience he had been teaching, to declare their opinion about the source of John the Baptizer's baptism (that is, his entire ministry)—**Was it from heaven, or from men?**

The religious leaders were smart enough not to answer immediately. They were skilled in the art of debate, and they knew the kinds of traps that could be set. So they went into deliberation privately. To acknowledge that the Messiah's forerunner had been sent by God (that his authority came **from heaven**) would be to admit that he had been right and that Jesus, whom John preceded, was indeed the Messiah. If they gave this answer, they would give Jesus an open door to ask them why they had not believed John as a prophet from God. To reject God's prophet was to reject God himself.

The answer they wanted to give was that John's authority was of human origin (**from men**). If the debate had not been in front of a crowd, they might have given this answer. But they were afraid of the crowd: **for they all hold that John was a prophet.** The people were smarter than their leaders; they saw the truth. The leaders had blinded themselves to John's authority and the identity and authority of the Messiah-King. If the leaders publicly rejected God's prophet, the people would recognize them as phonies and they would lose their influence.

21:27. So the chief priests and elders answered, **We don't know,** leaving Jesus with no compulsion to answer their question. Keep in mind that the events described in this passage took place after the turning point of 13:10–17. Jesus began at that point to create hurdles over which people had to jump to understand his teachings. Those who had ears to hear would make the leap and embrace his truth. Those whose hearts were hardened would remain ignorant.

This was the reason Jesus did not give the Jewish leaders a straight answer in 21:23–27. If they really wanted a truthful answer, they would have admitted to the authority of God behind Jesus' teachings and miracles. Jesus knew they were not open to the truth, so he placed a hurdle between them and the answer to their question. They had to acknowledge that John's authority came from heaven. Their refusal to answer was acknowledgment of their resistance to the truth—that Jesus' authority came from God.

E The King Desires Obedient Deeds More Than Words (21:28–32)

SUPPORTING IDEA: *Jesus will accept those who obey him and reject those who only claim to obey him.*

Jesus then turned the tables and went on the offensive, indicting the Jewish leaders on three counts with three parables.

First, while they claimed to be doing God's will and discharging their responsibilities, they were actually in blatant disobedience (21:28–32). A person's actions speak more convincingly than his or her words.

Second, the Jewish leaders had gone beyond neglect of their spiritual responsibility to the point of abuse and persecution of those sent by God, including God's own Son (21:33–46).

Third, in refusing their God-given responsibility, the Jewish leaders were also refusing to accept God's gracious blessing—the privilege and honor of serving as his instruments and the eternal reward to follow. This was the final insult to God. They were throwing his gift back into his face (22:1–14).

Each of the three parables also served to answer the question of Jesus' authority (21:23). Those with ears to hear could have heard Jesus' answer in the parables. In the first parable (21:28–32), Jesus was the unmentioned (third) Son who promised to obey and then followed through faithfully. In the second parable (21:33–46), Jesus was the Son sent by the landowner and killed by the stewards (21:37–39), as well as the capstone of God's people and his plan of redemption (21:42–44). In the third parable (22:1–14), Jesus was the Bridegroom, in whose honor the entire celebration was being held (22:2; cf. 9:15).

Jesus can be seen as a Son in all three parables: a Son who is obedient, a Son who is rejected, and a Son who is honored (cf. Phil. 2:5–11).

21:28–30. Jesus' main point was to show that those in the current Jewish leadership had disqualified themselves from being Israel's leaders. **What do you think?** was a common introduction by a teacher when he wanted the students to engage their minds in solving a problem.

Jesus would provide the interpretation of this parable in 21:31–32. Note that the father (representing God) gave both sons the same instructions. There was no prejudice or favoritism on the part of the father. Both sons started on a "level playing field," having the same opportunity to obey or disobey. The two sons both ended up doing the opposite of what they said they would do. The emphasis is not on the initial statement of intention, but on the actual actions.

21:31-32. Jesus' question emphasized that God's bottom-line concern was not a person's verbal claims but what he actually did: **Which of the two did what his father wanted?**

Actions are more significant than words. This was so obvious that even Jesus' opponents answered correctly. It was the first son—the one who initially said no but who ultimately obeyed—who did the will of the father.

Jesus introduced the interpretation and application of his parable with **I tell you the truth.** Tax collectors were considered traitors by the Jews because they sold out to the Roman oppressors, collecting taxes from their fellow countrymen and usually demanding extra money to line their own pockets. This often left families destitute. Prostitutes were similarly despised. For Jesus to say that **the tax collectors and the prostitutes** would have greater claim on the kingdom of God than the religious elite must have been a shock. Sinners were being welcomed into the kingdom, while the hypocrites only pretended to know God.

As in his previous discussion (21:25), Jesus referred again to the ministry of John the Baptizer. In a sense, John served as the barometer by which Jesus judged the spiritual climate. Jesus used people's responses to John as a test of their spiritual receptiveness. These references by Jesus gave great significance to John's ministry.

In 21:32, Jesus made three statements. The first statement indicted the religious believers for their disbelief in God's prophet John. The second statement, by contrast, vindicated the tax collectors and prostitutes by their belief. The third statement returned to the religious leaders, indicting them again for not taking the second chance God had given them. The leaders should have been humbled by the example of faith in the tax collectors and prostitutes. They should have been shamed by the faithful response of the tax collectors and prostitutes. They should have repented or changed their minds regarding John (and Jesus). But pride won out over humility.

Jesus' wording made it clear that the religious leaders were left with no excuses. God had made the opportunity for faith available to them. John came **to you;** that is, God took the initiative in sending his prophet. And John came in **the way of righteousness;** he lived and taught righteousness. There were no grounds for rejecting him. He should have received a hearing from all who claimed Yahweh as their God. His message was the way to righteousness before a righteous God.

Jesus had struck the first of three blows against the credibility of the leaders of Israel—against their qualification to serve as the shepherds of God's people. In spite of the religious show they put on and their claims to be obedient to God, they had rejected the mission God had given them (see Ezek. 34). They were guilty of neglect and abuse of God's flock.

▣ The Rejected Son Is Actually the Exalted King (21:33–46)

SUPPORTING IDEA: *Jesus, though rejected by the disobedient, will become the most valuable part of God's plan and will judge those who rejected him.*

Jesus continued with his second blow against the credibility of Israel's leaders. Although they fancied themselves to be big-time leaders and rulers of Israel, he charged, they were actually only custodians of God's vineyard.

21:33. Listen to another parable was Jesus' way of tying this second parable into the series of three. As in earlier parables, he used the image of a **landowner,** a man responsible for his land, its crops, and the workers who worked it. The language of this verse makes a direct connection with the "Song of the Vineyard" in Isaiah 5:1–7 (see also Ps. 80:6–16). The details of the construction of the vineyard (the wall, the winepress, and the watchtower) are drawn from this Old Testament passage. Any Jewish listener would clearly see the connection.

In the Isaiah passage, Yahweh is "my loved one," and the vineyard is Israel. Although Yahweh had provided everything necessary for Israel to obey him and produce good spiritual fruit, Israel had produced only bad fruit, going its own way time after time. The song served as the Lord's case against Israel, bringing the evidence before the world and inviting us to conclude for ourselves who was right and who deserved punishment. He would announce that punishment at the end of Matthew 23.

Jesus' parable provided the sequel to Isaiah's Song of the Vineyard. This was the same vineyard and the same landowner. But the new focus was on those to whom the vineyard had been **rented,** the custodians. In Jesus' parable, the vineyard was assumed to produce well, but the stewards of the vineyard were the problem.

The **farmers** (or **tenants**) represented Israel's first-century leaders, who had been entrusted by God with the task of shepherding his people. Ezekiel 34 provided a job description for a shepherd as well as God's indictment of that generation's leaders for neglecting their responsibilities and abusing the sheep. The landowner's journey represented the time until Christ's return at the end times. This was a period of stewardship, and a reckoning would come.

21:34–36. At **harvest time** (literally, "the fruit season"), the tenants were expected to send a portion of the harvest to the landowner as rent payment. This part of the parable represented the accountability of Israel's leaders before God, not only at the end of time but throughout their period of responsibility.

The landowner sent his **servants** (apparently three of them) as representatives to collect his portion of the harvest. The land and all it produced were his, and he had every right to collect. God also has the right to call his stewards to account at any time—to determine whether they have fulfilled their covenant commitment.

But the tenants failed to fulfill their agreement and refused to pay the rent. They mistreated the master's representatives; this was the same as mistreating the master himself. The servants represented God's prophets sent to Israel, whose job was to call Israel (especially its leaders) to account for their disobedience. The beating, killing, and stoning of the three messengers represented Israel's rejection of God's messengers (and God himself) over the centuries. One of the most recent examples of this rejection was their treatment of John the Baptizer (17:12–13).

The landowner persisted, sending an even larger group of servants, but with the same results. The tenants persisted in their rebellion, in spite of the landowner's repeated opportunities for them to respond as they should. God had provided multiple opportunities through many representatives to Israel, but Israel's leaders continued in rebellion.

21:37–39. Then the landowner sent his closest and best representative—**his son.** The mistreatment of his servants had been a slap in the face, which deserved punishment. But this final gesture by the landowner was a measure of the landowner's patience and grace toward the tenants. The thought that they might mistreat his own son was inconceivable.

But the tenants were so conceited that they fooled themselves into believing they could obtain the son's inheritance by killing him. Their mistreatment of the son was emphasized by the detail with which it is described **(took him and threw him out of the vineyard and killed him).**

The gravity of mistreating God's Son—his ultimate messenger (John 1:1,14,18)—heightened the foolishness and evil of the Jewish leaders. Jesus was deserving of highest respect, but the Jewish leaders took the art of self-deception to new heights. They thought they could get away with killing the Messiah to maintain their power and influence.

Implied here was another prediction of Jesus' sacrificial death. For months Jesus had been telling his disciples about his coming suffering at the hands of Israel's leaders. This was much closer than they realized, and Jesus was on a course with his mission.

21:40–41. Finally, the landowner himself decided he would go to his tenants. At this point, Jesus invited his critics to finish the story, asking what a landowner under these circumstances would **do to those tenants.** In their answer, the critics pronounced their own sentence—execution and replacement. Jesus' opponents were guilty of the worst kind of sin—leading God's flock astray and abusing them for personal gain and then killing God's messengers, his prophets, including his Son.

In their place, God would raise up stewards of his kingdom who would reap fruit and bring it to him; namely, his church (see comment on 21:43). In their greed, the hypocrites had thrown away the riches belonging to a faithful steward. They tried to play God and lost.

The leaders' response included a play on words by the use of **wretches** and **wretched.** A literal translation of the passage would be, "The bad ones, he will destroy them badly." *Destroy* here is an amplified verb meaning "to destroy utterly." The Jewish leaders were passing judgment on the tenants in the parable, stating that their evil character deserved severe punishment.

21:42. Jesus pointed out to the Jewish leaders that they had just pronounced judgment on themselves. **Have you never read in the Scriptures** was Jesus' way of telling the teachers of Israel that they should have known better. Jesus quoted Psalm 118:22–23. Although he changed metaphors, he continued to speak to the same topic—rejection of the Messiah by Israel's leaders.

Psalm 118:22 makes a surprising statement. The stone that the experts considered unusable ended up as the most important stone in the whole building plan: **the Lord has done this, and it is marvelous in our eyes.** The phrase "the Lord had done this" emphasized the foolishness of the Jewish leaders. They had changed the blueprint that had been drawn up by the perfect, almighty architect. The way that God would carry out his plan would be awesome and surprising. God would allow observers to believe, for a time, that Jesus was successfully rejected by the Jewish leaders. But then the greatest of all reversals—the Resurrection and the founding of the church, the body of Christ—would provide the grounds for even greater amazement.

21:43. Jesus then confirmed the hypocrites' own unwitting self-condemnation (21:41). The kingdom would be taken from them and given to faithful stewards. In this statement, with the mention of **fruit,** Jesus returned briefly to the agricultural word picture, before turning again to the picture of a stone in 21:44.

These leaders would forfeit the kingdom, and the stewardship would be handed over to **a people** (literally, "a nation") **who will produce its fruit.** The Jewish leaders were attempting to keep what was not theirs (power and control of the people, self-elevation, ill-gained wealth) instead of leading Israel according to the will of its master. Therefore, the kingdom would be taken away from them. Soon the church would take over operations (as announced in 16:18–19; 18:18–20), giving glory and service to God and producing spiritual fruit for him. Two thousand years of church history have proven that even the church does not do this perfectly. But the new covenant, sealed by Jesus' blood, allows God to work through the imperfect church to accomplish his perfect plan. His Spirit now lives in believers, planting his law directly in their hearts and unifying them in a way that was impossible before.

The stewardship would reside in the hands of the church. But God was not finished with Israel. He grafted the church into Israel's roots, but he will see to it that his covenant with Israel and his calling of the nation will be fully realized upon a day yet future (following Daniel's seventieth week and its tribulation). This is the Holy Spirit's argument in Romans 9–11 (esp. ch. 11).

21:44. Jesus then returned to the "stone" imagery of 21:42, using language from Isaiah 8:14–15. He had described himself as a potential "stumbling block" for those who did not believe in him (11:6). Such a skeptic **who falls on this stone will be broken to pieces.** And if the skeptic's resistance is so deeply entrenched that God takes the initiative in bringing judgment and the stone falls on him (cf. Dan. 2:34–35,44–45), the judgment will be horrendous.

21:45–46. The chief priests and Pharisees were the same as "the chief priests and the elders of the people" who had challenged Jesus' authority in 21:23. Jesus had completed his second of three blows against their credibility and authority. Not only had the leaders neglected their mission, but they had also rejected God, killing his prophets and even God's own Son.

The hypocrites could take a hint. They knew Jesus was accusing them of mismanaging God's kingdom and that he was pronouncing judgment on them. They should have repented in the face of the truth, but instead they decided to remove the truth and continue in their denial. They were still thinking that if they could kill Jesus, they would win. They were tragically mistaken. How blind is the insanity of unbelief, especially when marked by hatred and bitterness.

They wanted to **arrest** Jesus, but the local farm hands were smarter than the "enlightened" Jewish leaders. The crowds recognized Jesus as the prophet whom he was. Jesus' popularity prevented the leaders from arresting him at that time because **they were afraid of the crowd.** Even though the Jewish leaders feared the crowds and decided to wait until after Passover to deal with Jesus (26:5), Jesus was still the king. He was the one who insisted that the leaders' evil work be done during Passover. In this way, the king himself guaranteed the actual fulfillment of the Passover. His death took place on the Passover since he was the true Passover Lamb of God (cf. Exod. 12; 1 Cor. 5:7).

G The King Will Receive Honor from the Most Unlikely Subjects (22:1–14)

SUPPORTING IDEA: *Jesus will reject those who refuse his invitation into honor and privilege, replacing them with true worshipers—those restored from sin by his grace.*

The hypocrites got the message, but Jesus was not finished. There was one more aspect of their disobedience that needed to be confronted. This is a poor place for a chapter division, as it falls in the midst of Jesus' threefold indictment of the religious leaders. Matthew 22:1–14 is the third of Jesus' trilogy of parables.

There are many parallels between this parable and the preceding parable of the tenants and the rejected son (21:33–46). However, the key difference is that the preceding parable dealt with the kingdom steward's rejection of his *responsibility*, while this parable dealt with the rejection of the *privilege and honor* of participation in the kingdom by those who had been called into it.

The latter may be considered an even worse offense against God than the former. The hypocritical Jewish leaders had not only rejected their responsibilities; they were turning their back on the privileges of their inheritance. This parable dealt with their deliberate choice to be disinherited.

22:1–2. Jesus proceeded to reveal one more truth about the **kingdom of heaven** and those who had mishandled it. The main character of this parable is **a king**, representing God the Father. **His son** represented Jesus the Messiah. Although not an active character in the parable itself, he is central to its meaning, serving as the reason for the **wedding banquet.** The feast represented the future (eschatological) union of the bridegroom (Jesus) with his bride (God's redeemed people).

For a person to participate in this celebration presupposed that he had placed his faith in the Messiah and become a part of his people, the Messiah's bride. The invitation to the feast was an invitation to discipleship and salvation. It was also an invitation to enjoy the king's blessing—the "food" of the feast as well as the honor of being invited.

22:3–4. As in 21:34–36, the king sent two groups of servants as messengers. The first group went out **to those who had been invited to the banquet to tell them to come.** These people, representing Israel, God's chosen people (its leaders in particular), knew they were supposed to attend the celebration—they had already been invited. The messengers (representing God's prophets) informed them that it was time to attend. But the invitees refused to accept the invitation.

In this case, the invitation also carried the force of a command. To disregard this invitation or call was not an option; rejection of the call went beyond discourtesy to the point of rebellious disobedience. Israel had not been invited but *commanded* to pay the price and reap the blessing of kingdom citizenship.

The king was patient enough, even in the face of such discourtesy, to send a second group of messengers to the people. This group represented the Lord's patient pleading with his rebellious people over the centuries through prophet after prophet (see 21:34–37). The message they carried to the people was, "I have gone to a lot of trouble and great expense to prepare this banquet. Dinner is on the table. Come celebrate with us!" Participation in the feast, in honor of the king's son, was both a responsibility and a privilege. The king was appealing, "Come honor my son and enjoy the honor of my blessing."

22:5–6. The second group of messengers received two responses—apathy and aggression. Some people invited to the wedding feast thought they had more important things to do. They chose to ignore the messengers and tend to their fields and businesses—the everyday pursuits that had taken possession of their hearts (6:19–24). God was just as displeased with those who ignored him as he was with those who opposed him.

The other wedding guests responded like the tenants in the previous parable, mistreating and killing the messengers. The one significant difference between the action of the wedding guests and that of the tenants in 21:36 was that the wedding guests had no motive for mistreating and killing the king's servants. The murder of the messengers and the message of rejection to the king and his son were irrational, since the king intended only good by his invitation.

God's offer of a covenant relationship with Israel carried a price for those who accepted it, but the blessing and honor that the kingdom citizen received would far outweigh the cost of discipleship. God offered redemption, forgiveness, salvation, and reward. Those who rejected God's grace were displaying blindness to the point of insanity. They returned a curse for God's blessing.

22:7. Because of their perverted attitude, the king sent a third messenger. In the previous parable, the third messenger was the landowner's son. In this story, the third messenger was the king's army. They would serve as messengers of judgment on the irrational rebellion of the original wedding guests. The armies destroyed the murderers and burned their cities. This signified God's judgment of those who reject his covenant relationship.

22:8–10. Meanwhile, the celebration was waiting; the son was yet to be honored. So the king sent out his messengers again—but to a different set of invitees this time. The original invitees **did not deserve to come**. Their self-absorption and irrationality had displaced their loyalty to the king and his son. The new guests were those who would be honored with such an invitation. These were the riffraff, the outcasts of society, that the messengers would find along the byways (the Gr. phrase is variously interpreted as **street corners**, "main highways," or "forks in the road," all of which would be places to find many people). **Anyone you find** was carefully worded with indefinite force to include every possible prostitute and tax collector (cf. 9:9–13; 21:31–32).

The messengers went out **into the streets** and invited **all the people they could find, both good and bad.** Whereas those who should have been "good" (Israel, God's chosen people) had shown themselves to be evil, the king treated all who were evil as though they were good. The impartiality of the king represented the impartial grace of God, inviting all people of all nations into the kingdom during the church age. By extension, we can identify the king's servants or messengers now as the believers in the New Testament church (esp. the apostles).

It was as shocking then as it is now that God accepts the worst of sinners unconditionally. As long as a sinner shows a willingness to accept God's grace by faith, God will transform him or her into a kingdom citizen. With such a group of people the king filled his **wedding hall**. It was a blend of good and evil, Jew and Gentile, slave and free, wealthy and poor. Truly, the Lord will fill his kingdom with "all nations" or all peoples.

22:11–12. Jesus had already made an important point, but he was about to clarify exactly who could take part in his celebration of faith. After the guests had gathered in the wedding hall, the king inspected them and discovered a man not dressed properly. The **wedding clothes** (sometimes supplied by the host) were not a particular style of garment. But they were the cleanest and best clothes each person had to wear (cf. Rev. 19:6–8).

This man was displaying disrespect by wearing less than the best available to him. The king addressed the man as **Friend**, implying that he was open to an explanation. But when questioned, the man had no answer. He was guilty of failure to honor the king's son in a proper manner. The garment probably referred to the righteousness of Christ provided through his death. To refuse it would be to refuse Christ's sacrifice. To refuse Christ is to refuse life.

22:13. This disrespectful man was recognized as ill-prepared as every imposter will be. At the king's command, he was bound (a vivid picture of the man's inability to participate) and thrown into **the darkness**. This represented exclusion from this celebration in the kingdom of light and truth. The **weeping and gnashing of teeth** indicated extreme pain and sorrow.

22:14. Jesus' closing statement had a proverbial tone. Note that he did not say that *all* men and women are called. But **many are invited**. God had issued to a wide audience his invitation (command) to join with him in covenant relationship. **But few are chosen.** Not everyone who is invited will be among the chosen. The adjective *chosen* suggests that the faith decision is not totally in our hands, but it is a response to God's sovereign election. In particular, the unbelieving religious leaders were among those called but not chosen.

The doctrine of election, taught throughout Scripture (e.g. Rom. 9), has already been mentioned briefly in Matthew (11:27). The word **chosen** (or "elect") is a word Jesus would soon use to refer to his followers (24:22,24,31).

The parable's basic lessons are clear. The king issued a gracious invitation to people he wished to view as friends. They rejected the invitation. Their rejection sparked a severe judgment from the king. Their rejection caused the king to extend the invitation even further to anyone who would come. Participation was carefully screened. Israel was invited, but the nation refused the invitation. Its refusal served to open the gates wide. But though the gates were thrown wide open, those actually chosen were limited by specific criteria—the righteousness of Christ.

With this, Jesus rounded out his trilogy of parables which condemned the Jewish leaders for their rebellious disbelief. They had: (1) neglected their God-given trust (21:28–32); (2) tried to commandeer the kingdom for their own ends, persecuting and killing God's messengers the prophets, and even his Son (21:33–46); and (3) thrown away the honor and privilege of a covenant relationship with God, thereby dishonoring the Almighty and the Son.

Round 1: The King Validates Civil and Spiritual Government (22:15–22)

SUPPORTING IDEA: *Jesus proves his authority in the arena of political debate.*

The diverse groups from among Jesus' opponents (i.e., Pharisees, Sadducees, and Herodians)—normally hostile toward each other—joined forces to plot against Jesus. They attempted one final series of verbal attacks, expecting to embarrass Jesus in public. This would show him to be a fraud. It was illegal for the Jews to perform an execution; they would have to appeal to Roman authorities on the grounds of an imperial offense in order to have Jesus executed.

We will see first a joint attack by the Pharisees (a religious sect that opposed Roman rule in Israel) and the Herodians (a political party that supported Roman rule through the Herods) in 22:15–22. Next, the Sadducees would join the effort, bringing their trickiest question to bear (22:23–33). Finally, the Pharisees would return with a final attempt (22:34–40). All of those tricks Jesus would turn back before taking the final offensive (22:41–23:39).

22:15–17. The Pharisees plotted to put together a verbal trap for Jesus (the verb "to ensnare, entrap," is used only here in the New Testament). The Herodians and probably the Sadducees were involved in the plotting, for their threefold attack in 22:15–40 was carefully coordinated. The Pharisees and Herodians approached Jesus first, beginning with hypocritical flattery. They addressed him as **Teacher,** partly to gain favor with the crowd, and partly to catch Jesus off guard. They claimed to know that Jesus was **a man of integrity** and that he taught **the way of God,** when in reality they believed him to be a heretic.

They also pointed out Jesus' commitment to truth without consideration for the rank or social status of those who might agree or disagree with him. Jesus was known for being impartial toward all people and forthright in his teaching. They were hoping to coax Jesus into saying something politically incorrect.

Their statements about Jesus' impartiality were intended to force him to take one side or another, thereby showing partiality. The question was whether it was **right** under Old Testament Law to pay the poll tax (we presume) to Caesar, the Roman emperor. The two groups that asked the question were on opposite sides of the issue. If Jesus answered, "Yes, it is right," then he would show partiality toward the Herodians, who supported Roman rule. Then the Pharisees would accuse Jesus of sympathizing with the Romans. This was not a crime, but it was not a popular position among the Jews.

If Jesus answered, "No, it is not right," then he would show partiality toward the Pharisees, who opposed Roman rule and saw Roman taxation as robbing from God. Then the Herodians could arrest him and bring him before Herod Antipas on charges of treason against the Roman Empire.

In either case, they thought, Jesus would show himself to be partial. He would also alienate part of his following, and he might incriminate himself under Roman law.

22:18. Jesus revealed that they were not really interested in his answer—only in trapping him in public. Jesus was a student of people—particularly his enemies—and their motives were obvious, no matter how much flattery they lavished on him. They were **hypocrites** because they pretended to be sincere inquirers after truth, when they were actually trying to trap him. His question **why?** revealed their true motives to the crowd. It also showed that such testing was unnecessary and inappropriate. Jesus had displayed more than enough evidence about his identity.

22:19–21. Jesus asked for the coin used to pay the poll tax, a denarius. Then he answered their question with a question, **Whose portrait is this?** (Portrait is the Greek word *eikon,* from which we derive the English *icon.*) **And whose inscription?** The critics gave the obvious answer that the image and inscription were Caesar's.

Jesus answered by saying there was nothing wrong with giving to each authority what was rightfully his. That is, it was right to give to the Roman Empire what was rightfully theirs, as indicated by Caesar's image and inscription on the coin. Such payment of tax was not robbery from God.

On the other hand, we also have an obligation to give to God what he demands. The two claims by the two authorities were not in conflict with each other. Obedience to both was not contradictory. Both God and civil government were valid authorities (cf. Rom. 13:1–7; 1 Pet. 2:13–17).

Jesus had remained impartial as well as committed to truth. He had sided with neither party in the debate over taxation, showing validity behind both sides.

22:22. Jesus' challengers were **amazed** at his answer, **so they left him and went away.**

▌Round 2: The King Validates the Resurrection (22:23–33)

SUPPORTING IDEA: *The king proves his authority in theological debate.*

22:23–28. The phrase **that same day** showed the chronological flow and coordination of the first and second verbal attacks. This time the Sadducees, the majority sect in the Sanhedrin, came to Jesus with their own question. The fact that they **say there is no resurrection** was important in this context. It showed how far removed they were from their allies the Pharisees—normally their opponents—who questioned Jesus before and after this particular incident. More importantly, it explained the theological assumption behind their question.

The Sadducees began by addressing Jesus with a title of respect, **Teacher,** just as the Pharisees and Herodians had done earlier (22:16). The quote of the Sadducees in 22:24 was an accurate paraphrase of the Mosaic Law in Deuteronomy 25:5–10. They applied this law to a hypothetical situation, taken to an extreme. Suppose seven brothers, each in turn, married the same woman and all died childless. Finally the woman also died. Whose wife would she be **at the resurrection?** They assumed there was no answer to this question, and that the resurrection was a myth.

22:29–30. Jesus answered their question by attacking their false assumptions about marriage and the resurrection. Then he pressed the attack by going deeper, revealing that their disbelief in the resurrection was faulty (22:31–32). Jesus pointed out that the Sadducees were **in error.** They did not understand the Scriptures. Their assumption that a resurrection would imply a continuation of marriages from this life was unsupported in Scripture. Jesus' clarification that **at the resurrection** men and women were no longer bound by marriage is found nowhere else in Scripture. But if Jesus' opponents had had "ears to hear," then they would have recognized Jesus as the author of all, including marriage, the resurrection, and all truth. He had every right to proclaim the truth on any topic, whether it was supported by the Old Testament. Since there was no marriage in heaven, the Sadducees' question was invalid. The answer was that no one would be the woman's husband at the resurrection.

This, together with Ephesians 5:22–33, can lead us to the conclusion that God's primary purpose for marriage is to paint a picture on earth of the heavenly marriage between the Messiah and his bride. When the actual marriage of Christ and the church takes place in heaven, there will be no more need for human marriage. It will be displaced by the greater reality toward which it pointed while we were on earth.

Men and women in heaven will be **like the angels,** who do not marry or produce offspring. From evidence through the Bible, we may assume that angels are without gender. However, when they took physical form, they seemed always to appear in a male form.

The Sadducees were also in error because they did not understand **the power of God.** This related primarily to God's power to raise people from the dead. The Sadducees' denial of the resurrection was not merely a theological position. It was outright disbelief that God can do what he claims. What a rebuke Jesus delivered to these so-called religious leaders: **You do not know the Scriptures or the power of God.**

22:31–32. Jesus then got down to the real issue—the reality of the resurrection of the dead. **Have you not read?** pointed out that the religious leaders—the shepherds and teachers of Israel—should have known better. The truth had been made plain in God's Word (cf. 21:42). In fact, Jesus heightened his challengers' accountability by saying that God spoke the truth **to you,** implying the corporate solidarity of all generations. The truths that God spoke centuries ago still speak to us today.

Jesus used a quotation from the Pentateuch to answer the Sadducees, knowing their high regard for the Pentateuch. His quote from Exodus 3:6 was taken from the words of God, speaking to Moses through the burning bush. This was centuries after the life and death of Abraham, Isaac, and Jacob. Yet, for God to be the God of these three men centuries after they had died implied that they were alive at the time God spoke to Moses. That is, they had been resurrected to new life: **He is not the God of the dead but of the living.**

22:33. As with the crowd at the end of the Sermon on the Mount (7:28–29), this crowd was also **astonished** at the authority with which Jesus dealt with his opponents. Not only did Jesus wield Old Testament Scripture accurately; he revealed new truth that the Old Testament had not revealed (22:30). Jesus had turned his challengers' trap into an embarrassment and an accusation against themselves.

Round 3: The King Elevates Love for God and People (22:34–40)

SUPPORTING IDEA: *Jesus proves his authority in the debate over practical spirituality.*

Now we come to the third and final verbal challenge from Jesus' opponents. After this, the Jewish leaders would fall back on their last resort—physical violence or conspiracy to have Jesus arrested and executed.

22:34–36. The Pharisees had regrouped after Jesus turned their first trap against them in 22:15–22. Seeing the same thing happen to the Sadducees, the Pharisees **got together**, seeking power and courage in numbers. The one **expert in the law** whom they chose to ask the testing question must have approached Jesus with some trepidation. For the third time in three challenges, the questioner addressed Jesus as **Teacher.**

This time the question was simple but profound: **Which is the greatest commandment in the Law?** Matthew used the simple adjective "great" (*megas*), but it carried superlative force ("greatest") in this context. The question demonstrated the way the religious leaders looked at the law. In their tradition, they had reduced the law to 365 negative and 248 positive commandments. They spent much time trying to prioritize these innumerable technicalities. They thought they could trap the Lord of the law.

22:37–38. Jesus drew his answer from the most memorized and recited passage in all the Jewish Scriptures: Hear, O Israel! The LORD our God, the LORD is one. Love the LORD your God with all your heart and with all your soul and with all your strength" (Deut. 6:4–5).

Jesus quoted the Septuagint almost verbatim, but he substituted **mind** (*dianoia*) for the similar sounding "might" (*dunameos*). We are to take this list as an emphatic way of saying, "Love God with everything you are in every way possible." But it was not without significance that our Lord deliberately substituted "mind" here rather than some other term. Christians need to take a lesson from this. We should learn to *think* critically and biblically.

Jesus emphasized his answer by identifying this commandment as **the first and greatest commandment.** This commandment was greatest because of the statement in Deuteronomy 6:4 which preceded it: "Yahweh is your God, Yahweh alone" (paraphrased). To honor Yahweh as the one true God is to love him exclusively, from among all others who claim to be gods.

22:39. But Jesus went beyond the critic's question and added a second command, which is **like** (*homoios*, "resembling") the first, this time drawing from Leviticus 29:18 (cf. Matt. 19:19): **love your neighbor as yourself.** This commandment and the first complement each other, so Jesus mentioned them together. They are not to be separated. It is impossible to love God without loving people, for his law and heart's desire is to love others. The measure by which we know if we are truly loving people is if we love them as much as we love ourselves (cf. Eph. 5:28–31).

22:40. Finally, Jesus defended his choice of these two commandments by observing that **all the Law and the Prophets hang on these two commandments** (or "depends" on them). Every Old Testament commandment and teaching fulfilled the commands to love God and to love people.

Ⓚ The Knockout: The King Defends His Own Identity (22:41–46)

SUPPORTING IDEA: *Jesus establishes himself as the Messiah—the Son of David and Son of God.*

Jesus was not satisfied with having fended off his critics' three verbal attacks. It was time for him to take the offensive again, this time with decisive finality. In 22:41–46, Jesus put forth a defense of his own identity as Messiah, silencing his opponents (22:46). He then pressed forward into a final, climactic indictment of the hypocritical Jewish leaders in Matthew 23. Jesus' aim was not only to vindicate himself, but also to reveal the hypocrites for what they were.

Jesus was through dealing with silly questions. He went to the heart of the matter and the root of every question—the person of Christ—the Messiah. If people were wrong about Christ, they were wrong about everything.

22:41–42. The Pharisees were still together (22:34) after their final attempt to trap him. Before they could escape, Jesus asked them a question to reveal the depth of their denial and hypocrisy: **What do you think about the Christ? Whose son is he?** The Greek word *Christ* and the Hebrew word *Messiah* are synonyms, both meaning "anointed one" and referring to the promised prophet, priest, and king. The Pharisees answered, **The son of David.** It was common knowledge that the Messiah would be a descendant of David, so the Pharisees answered accordingly. (Old Testament passages identifying the Messiah as a descendant of David are Isa. 9:7; 11:1,10; Pss. 2;89;132; Jer. 23:5.)

22:43–45. Jesus then asked a follow-up question. He asked them to interpret Psalm 110:1 in light of the identity of the Christ as David's son. This verse describes Christ's posture in heaven until he comes to reign on the earth (Heb. 10:12–13). In the psalm, David says, "Yahweh said to my Lord" (literal translation of the Hebrew text). In the English translations of this verse, the first usage of the word "Lord" is usually printed in capital letters, to show that it translates the Hebrew name of God, Yahweh. The second usage has only the first letter capitalized, showing that it translates the Hebrew title *Adonai*, meaning "Master, Lord."

Jesus was careful to point out that David's psalm was written under the inspiration of God's Spirit, so there was no mistake in what he had written. Jesus was drawing attention to the fact that by the phrase **my Lord**, David was referring to someone other than himself. He was referring to the Christ or Messiah, whom the Pharisees had just said was a son of David. Jesus' final question for the Pharisees was, "How can the Messiah be both David's Lord and David's son?"

Jesus' implication was clear: The Messiah, the Son of David, was more than a special person. He was also Yahweh the Almighty himself. It followed that Jesus himself was this Messiah. If the Pharisees answered his question, they would have to acknowledge his true identity. Once again, Jesus claimed deity for himself.

Jesus could have been content with quoting only the first line of Psalm 110:1, which shows David calling the Christ **my Lord**. But he had a purpose in going on to quote the next two lines of the psalm. In the New Testament, Psalm 110 is the most frequently quoted Old Testament chapter. The entire psalm is a declaration of the supreme authority of the Messiah. Quoting this first verse of Psalm 110, Jesus highlighted both the Messiah's position of authority at Yahweh's **right hand** and his defeat of his enemies (**until I put your enemies under your feet**). The Pharisees had made themselves Jesus' enemies. To acknowledge him as Messiah by answering his question meant they would have to acknowledge his supreme authority and their own defeat "under his feet."

22:46. Therefore, the Pharisees remained silent **from that day on**. Jesus had brought all verbal arguments to a close. He passed all their tests; they flunked his. But he was not yet finished. For the Pharisees, the worst was yet to come.

MAIN IDEA REVIEW: *Jesus is indeed the Messiah-King, having absolute authority and deserving worship and submission from all his subjects.*

III. CONCLUSION

Every instruction of the Bible—every expectation of the king regarding his subjects' conduct—is a way of expressing love toward God and other people. Loving God and loving people is the believer's central purpose in life.

PRINCIPLES

- Our king is meek in spirit, possessing tremendous power, but wielding it gently, for purposes of peace.
- Our king is a prophet, speaking the truth of God without error.
- Our king zealously guards his worship.
- Our king's identity is so obvious that even children proclaim it.
- Our king will judge the fruitless life, particularly when it advertises fruit but is found barren.
- Even weak faith, when exercised according to God's will, can accomplish the seemingly impossible.
- Our king's authority threatens those who claim authority falsely.
- Our king values obedient deeds over claims to obedience.
- Our king will reward worthy stewards who obediently manage his kingdom.

- Those who expect to be in the kingdom will be rejected if they reject a right relationship with the king.
- Our king validates both civil government and spiritual government.
- Human marriage is for this life, not the next.
- The resurrection is a reality.

APPLICATIONS

- Do not replace your worship of God with mundane, earthly pursuits.
- Pay what is rightfully due civil government.
- Pay what is rightfully due to God.
- Be bold in your righteous requests of God.
- Obey more than talking about obeying.

IV. LIFE APPLICATION

His Rightful Place

The word worship is a contraction of an old expression in the English language, "woerth-scipe," denoting the ascription of reverence to an object of superlative worth. In short, worship is reverence, honor, praise, and service to God.

A more expanded theological definition of worship is given as follows: "An act by a redeemed man, the creature, toward God, his Creator, whereby his will, intellect and emotions gratefully respond to the revelation of God's person expressed in the redemptive work of Jesus Christ, as the Holy Spirit illuminates the written Word to his heart."

The hymn, "O Worship the King," written and published in 1833 in a hymnal entitled *Christian Psalmody,* is one of the finest from the early nineteenth century Romantic Era. Some have referred to it as a model hymn for worship. It has few equals in expressive lyrics in the exaltation of the Almighty. Each of the epithets expressed in the hymn refer to God—King, Shield, Defender, Ancient of Days, Maker, Redeemer, and Friend.

When Jesus cleared the temple of the moneychangers, he was demonstrating his authority to do so. It was his place of worship, and the worship of God was being desecrated, taking a backseat to the greed and unethical dealings of men. Jesus made his own kind of change. He drove the moneychangers out of the temple.

To worship God is to recognize God's authority and obey him. The Jewish leaders had refused to acknowledge Jesus' authority as God's Son. They were more concerned in being obedient to their legal system than worshiping

God. The heart of Christian worship is the power of Christ's presence. But here the leaders were allowing this corruption to take place in God's place of worship.

Napoleon Bonaparte is credited with saying, "If Socrates would enter the room we should rise and do him honor. But if Jesus Christ came into the room we should fall down on our knees and worship him."

In the life of faith, the believer must submit to the authority of Jesus and worship him. Does Jesus have a rightful place of worship in your heart?

V. PRAYER

Lord God, I desire to be a true worshiper of the king. Purge my life of all pride and hypocrisy as I bow before him in love and adoration. Amen.

VI. DEEPER DISCOVERIES

A. Zechariah's Prophecy (vv. 4–5)

Zechariah 9 begins an oracle predicting the destruction of all Israel's enemies and the ensuing peace in Jerusalem. All of Israel's chariots, war horses, and battle instruments would be taken away (Zech. 9:10), and Jerusalem's king would enter peacefully, "righteous and having salvation" (Zech. 9:9). The king would be gentle, since there was no longer any need for war, and he would arrive by the humble means of a donkey and her foal (Zech. 9:9).

It was common practice for a king to ride a donkey rather than a war horse in times of peace (e.g., 1 Kgs. 1:33). In that same context, Yahweh told of "the blood of my covenant with you" providing the means for the freeing of Israel's prisoners and their restoration to hope and prosperity (Zech. 9:11–12).

This Jesus was the deliverer of God's people in a threefold way. He would ultimately rescue them from their national enemies. But in the meantime, he would rescue them from their sin and from the abuse of their evil shepherds (the religious leaders).

Jesus' humility has been taught and displayed throughout Matthew 18–20, and now Matthew said that his humility showed him to be the king. This first coming as the sacrificial Son of Abraham (the Lamb of God) was on the back of a humble donkey. At his second coming, as the sovereign Son of David (Lion of Judah) he would ride a war horse (cf. Rev. 19:11).

B. Den of Robbers (v. 13)

Den of robbers is a quote from Jeremiah 7:11. Jeremiah 7–9 was a judgment oracle against Judah, after the fall of the Northern Kingdom (Israel) to Assyria. The focus of the warning was on Judah's idolatry and misuse of the temple (among other sins, such as injustice and oppression of aliens and the needy). Judah had been committing idolatry, then coming hypocritically to the temple, assuming its presence to be some kind of validation of their actions. They found false security and safety in the temple, even as they went through the motions of worship to Yahweh.

But Yahweh warned, as he had often done before (Jer. 7:21–26), that judgment was on its way. He foretold the ruin of Jerusalem and the surrounding region and the scattering of the Jews into other nations. Both of those events would happen to first-century Israel in A.D. 70—a judgment to which Jesus alluded in Matthew 11:12; 24:2. This reference to the temple as "a den of robbers," along with Jesus' disruption of the merchants' tables and chairs, was an ominous warning of coming judgment.

C. Sadducees and Pharisees on the Resurrection

The Sadducees held that only the Pentateuch was inspired Scripture. Therefore, since the resurrection was not explicitly taught in those five books, resurrection was not possible. They felt that the Old Testament teaching regarding Levirate marriage (all within the Pentateuch) made the idea of a resurrection ridiculous. The Pharisees (and Jesus) based their belief in the resurrection on Isaiah 26:19, Daniel 12:2, and other passages outside the Pentateuch (cf. Job 19:25–27).

For the argument of the Sadducees to make sense, we must understand the practice of Levirate marriage. In Israel, it was important that every man's name be carried on through male offspring. This was tied to the importance of the Promised Land. Only male heirs could inherit a portion of the land. Daughters assumed a new identity through marriage, and they shared in the inheritance of their husbands. In families where there were only female offspring, the father's name could be carried on through the daughter's families. If there were no children, the inheritance went to the nearest male relative (Num. 27:1–11; Josh. 17:3–5).

According to Deuteronomy 25:5–10 (see also Gen. 38:8), if a man with a brother died without a son, the brother was obligated to marry his widowed sister-in-law to give her and her deceased husband a son. This son would carry on the deceased husband's name and receive his inheritance. Any brother who neglected this duty was despised throughout Israel.

D. Summary

The months and years of preparatory ministry were completed. There was no longer any reason for Jesus to keep his identity and his authority out of the spotlight. In fact, he boldly stepped into the spotlight, stating through his actions and his words that he was indeed the Messiah-King.

This claim could not go unchallenged by the religious establishment. Their authority was threatened by the advent of the Messiah. Jesus welcomed every attack from the religious leaders, publicly revealing their foolishness, malice, and disqualification. This set the stage for their final desperate action—to find any reason, whether true or false, to arrest and execute Jesus.

VII. TEACHING OUTLINE

A. INTRODUCTION

1. Lead Story: Crunch Time
2. Context: Conflict predominates in Matthew 21–23 as we see spiritual warfare between Jesus and his opponents. Satan was behind it all. To this point, Jesus had tried to avoid outright conflict while warning people about the poison of the Jewish leaders. Previous conflict had been at the initiative of the hypocrites, and Jesus had responded to their attacks.
3. Transition: Jesus took the initiative, entering Jerusalem as king, and purging the temple (21:12–13). From that point on, the initiative went back and forth between Jesus and his enemies (21:23–27; 21:28–22:14,15–40,41–46). Jesus finished his enemies off with the scathing indictment of the "seven woes" in chapter 23.

   The spiritual battle with Satan, introduced in 4:1–11, was rejoined with full vigor in these chapters. Matthew may have intended the threefold attack of the Jewish leaders in 22:15–40 to remind us of Satan's threefold attack at the beginning of Jesus' ministry. We will understand these later battles in a new light if we see Satan as the mastermind behind them.

B. COMMENTARY

1. The King Enters His City with Triumph and Meekness (21:1–11)
2. The King Reclaims His Place of Worship (21:12–17)
3. The King Acts Out the Drama of the Fruitless Fig Tree (21:18–22)
4. The King's Authority Is Questioned (21:23–27)
5. The King Desires Obedient Deeds More Than Words (21:28–32)
6. The Rejected Son Is Actually the Exalted King (21:33–46)
7. The King Will Receive Honor from the Most Unlikely Subjects (22:1–14)
8. Round 1: The King Validates Civil and Spiritual Government (22:15–22)
9. Round 2: The King Validates the Resurrection (22:23–33)
10. Round 3: The King Elevates Love for God and People (22:34–40)
11. The Knockout: The King Defends His Own Identity (22:41–46)

C. CONCLUSION

1. Wrap-up: Jesus was indeed the Messiah-King, having absolute authority and deserving worship and submission from his subjects.
2. Personal Challenge: We need to respond to the King of kings, not look for ways to get around what we know is right. This involves the awareness that he calls everyone to himself. Are you busy preparing your garments for the Marriage Supper of the Lamb?

VIII. ISSUES FOR DISCUSSION

1. What prophecy did Jesus fulfill when he rode into Jerusalem on a donkey with her foal?
2. Why did Jesus find it necessary to cleanse the temple when he came into Jerusalem?
3. What message did Jesus deliver when he cursed the fruitless fig tree?
4. What three parables did Jesus direct against the Jewish religious leaders in this chapter of Matthew?
5. What was the central message of Jesus' teaching about the rejected building stone?

Matthew 23

The King Pronounces Judgment on the Hypocrites

Quote

"*It is impossible to calculate the moral mischief, if I may so express it, that mental lying has produced in society. When a man has so far corrupted and prostituted the chastity of his mind as to subscribe his professional belief to things he does not believe, he has prepared himself for the commission of every other crime.*"

Thomas Paine

Matthew 23

 IN A NUTSHELL

Having silenced his critics, Jesus warns the hypocritical leaders by pronouncing the most severe judgment in the Scriptures. The seven "woes" (or accusations) are a collection of criticisms of the hypocrisy of Israel's Jewish leaders. These woes reach a climax as Jesus shows a solidarity between the current Jewish leaders and their predecessors who murdered the prophets of God.

The King Pronounces Judgment on the Hypocrites

I. INTRODUCTION

Hypocrisy Confronted

It happened during my high school days at a state leadership camp. It was unforgettable. For the first time in my memory, I had stood up—in public—to confront hypocrisy.

Several hundred high school student-body officers were being trained for their senior tenure. About a dozen of us were housed in one cabin just about right for a couple of guys to doze off, a couple to read, and the rest of us to engage in developing a healthy "group dynamic." In other words, we told stories and hooted at their craziness into the wee hours.

One stretch involved an hour or more of "can-you-top-this" jokes and stories. I found myself unable to participate so I lay quiet in the darkness, hoping the others would think I had fallen asleep. One voice in particular, from the top bunk on the west wall, seemed to dominate the off-color conversation.

When the conversation shifted to things that mattered, the guys began to discuss "religion," real spiritual issues, and eventually their own hearts. It was amazing. Christ and the Christian faith became the center of discussion.

But the majesty of that healthy dialogue was broken when the same voice from the top bunk on the west wall chimed in. Unable to remain silent and wanting to be included with the "in" crowd, he declared: "Oh, yeah, I am a Christian too!"

His loud "about face" disturbed me. To go from off-color jokes to spiritual bliss in one easy breath was more than I could handle. Suddenly I heard my own voice breaking the silence: "Well, if I claimed to be a Christian and had just finished spouting off a bunch of off-color stories, I sure would not be advertising my faith."

My heart was pounding! I had done it! What was going to happen now? As it turned out, not much. The cabin went dead silent. I was sure the other guys could hear my heart pounding. But I do not recall anyone saying another word that night. Nor the next day. My impetuous, angry comment had just ended it all. Camp broke up. We returned to our homes. And that was the end of that; or so I thought. Years went by—through college, then the military and Vietnam, followed by seminary. I never thought another thing about the incident.

Fifteen years later I was walking on the sidewalk of a seminary campus when a voice from across the lawn called a loud hello. The guy asked if I had been at a particular high school leadership camp and involved in a certain conversation. I realized that was the person from that top bunk on the west wall. He proceeded to rehearse the exchange that night and described the discomfort of the silence that followed. "Yes, that was me," I admitted.

Then, in a wonderful moment of confession and a genuine statement of gratitude, he thanked me for my comments in that cabin on that night long ago. He told me that the shock of having his hypocrisy pointed out had begun his turnaround. Those uncomfortable moments in that cabin fifteen years ago had played a significant role in his commitment to Christ. He was now on a seminary campus, studying for vocational Christian ministry. It was a wonderful conclusion to a long-forgotten story.

There comes a time when we need to confront hypocrisy. In the flow of Matthew's Gospel, that time had arrived. Jesus was going to confront the hypocrisy of Israel's religious leaders. In a loud voice, blunt and truthful, the Lord of heaven confronted the hypocritical religious leaders.

Confronting hypocrisy may turn the hypocrite around. But even when it does not, it serves to protect others who might become victims of the hypocrisy.

II. COMMENTARY

The King Pronounces Judgment on the Hypocrites

MAIN IDEA: *Beware of hypocrisy. It will receive God's severe judgment.*

Jesus had arrived on the stage of history (Matt. 1–4); demonstrated his authority as Messiah-King (Matt. 5–10); met with rejection (Matt. 11–12); continued to walk the difficult path of truth in the face of opposition while preparing the disciples to carry on after him (Matt. 13–20); and moved into the spotlight with royal dignity, proving victorious in verbal and spiritual combat with his opponents (Matt. 21–22). Having silenced his critics (22:46), Jesus warned the crowd and his disciples of the poison of their hypocritical leaders, bringing the battle of words to its conclusion. This is the most biting, pointed, and severe pronouncement of judgment in the Bible. It came directly from the Savior's lips and was directed at self-centered spiritual hypocrisy.

After the introductory warning to the listening audience (23:1–12), Jesus pronounced the "seven woes" that form the heart of this chapter. The first six fall into natural pairs. The seventh woe brings a dramatic conclusion to the list, foreshadowing Jesus' own death sentence at the hands of the leaders he was warning others about.

Throughout this angry castigation, Jesus repeatedly addressed his opponents as "teachers of the law and Pharisees, you hypocrites" (23:13,15,23,25,27,29; see also 23:2). Most of the scribes, or teachers of the law (experts in the Old Testament law), belonged to the sect of the Pharisees, probably because of their pharisaical obsession with minute details of the law. But Jesus used these comments against hypocrisy to represent *any* corrupt members of the Jewish leadership, regardless of their theology or position.

Up through 23:31, almost every verb describing the Jewish leaders' hypocritical actions is in the Greek present tense or is part of a construction carrying a present, continuous force. The behavior Jesus described was habitual, repetitive, and continually characteristic of these Jewish leaders.

Underlying all of Jesus' accusations was the question of what a person does with the Messiah. Jesus could easily have given positive examples with each of the woes, contrasting his positive model with the negative model of the hypocrites. Each departure from true righteousness was a way of rejecting the Christ, God's promised king. This rejection was the hypocrites' greatest sin. They would prove this soon in their persecution of Jesus, in a fashion similar to that described in the seventh woe.

It is important to keep this scathing chapter in its context. Matthew 23 is more than a climax of arguments with religious hypocrites. It follows on the heels of the major moment of truth of 22:41–46. Jesus' identity was not a matter for endless dialogue. It was the center of everything that mattered. To be wrong about Jesus is to be wrong about everything. So Jesus took apart these religious leaders who tried to deny or confuse his identity. The tone of Matthew 23 is judicial. These false religious leaders and those who followed them, corporate Israel, would be condemned and destroyed.

Ⓐ The King Warns Israel of the Self-Absorption of Its Leaders (23:1–12)

SUPPORTING IDEA: *Hypocrisy is primarily interested in elevating self.*

This introductory section to the "seven woes" was Jesus' warning to the crowd and to his disciples not to follow the hypocrites' example. He urged the common people to follow God's instruction as it was written and accurately taught, not as it was warped by the Jewish leaders. Jesus was challenging the people to pursue a righteousness greater than that of their leaders (cf. 5:20; 6:1–18).

23:1–3. The religious leaders from 21:23–22:46 were still part of Jesus' audience, but he turned to address his disciples and the sizable crowd. The temple courts, where he was speaking, were a popular place during Passover week. He had spent most of the day in debate with the leaders, publicly demonstrating their lack of qualification for their role and responsibilities. He then turned to the onlookers to help them understand how to live under such poor leadership.

Moses' seat referred to Moses' role as teacher and leader-judge of Israel (e.g., Exod. 18:13). The current leaders were the successors to Moses, as Israel's leaders. God's people needed leaders to teach God's Word, to help the people interpret it accurately, and to challenge them to apply it in their daily living. There is a place for bowing to authoritative teaching. Certainly much of what the first-century leaders taught was accurate and helpful. Jesus commanded the people to **do everything they tell you.** The **teachers of the law and the Pharisees** in particular were generally more conservative in their respect for the Word of God, taking it at face value. But people often learn from example more than by word. This aspect of the hypocrites' leadership was abysmal.

23:4. Through the man-made laws of the Pharisees (Matt. 15:1–9), they introduced burdens of obedience that were impossible for people to carry. Yet, they mercilessly held the people to these burdens.

The **shoulders** were the place for carrying weighty burdens, putting the entire strength of the body under the burden. In contrast, the **finger** represented the weakest part of the body. The hypocrites put forth no effort to aid their followers in pleasing God, which was the fundamental purpose of God's Word. This was no mere mistake or oversight on their part; they were **not willing** to move the burdens. Theirs was a prideful, status-seeking ministry. Jesus' attitude was just the opposite.

23:5–7. Not only were the hypocrites unsympathetic, but they were also insecure. They constantly advertised their "spirituality" and status in an effort to feed their weak egos through the attention of others. Their insecurity masqueraded as arrogance. They did everything in their power to cause others to think they were superior to the average Jewish citizen. They did their "good" deeds purely for applause. They even fooled themselves into believing they were righteous.

Phylacteries were small boxes attached to the left arm or the forehead and worn during prayer. They contained small portions of Scripture that the Pharisees wore, in a legalistic interpretation of the Shema, particularly Deuteronomy 6:8: "Tie them [these commandments] as symbols on your hands and bind them on your foreheads" (see also Exod. 13:9; Deut. 11:18). They literally wore phylacteries on their heads and wrists. God, through Moses' use of a figure of speech, was instructing the people to become servants of the Word of God. But these status seekers made a physical uniform out of it. The hypocrites would broaden their phylacteries, because the more noticeable the box, the more spiritual they seemed to be.

The **tassels** were blue-and-white cords that Jewish men wore on their outer garments (Num. 15:38–41; Deut. 22:12), and later on the prayer shawl. God had commanded the wearing of the tassels so the Jews would be reminded that God had redeemed them and thus remember to obey his commandments. The hypocrites would lengthen their tassels, because the more noticeable the tassels, the more spiritual they seemed to be.

Banquets and **synagogues** were only two examples from daily life where many people gathered. These places were prime opportunities for advertising false spirituality. Virtually any event was an opportunity for public honor and recognition. The **place of honor** and **important seats** were reserved for the most spiritual—those with highest authority and greatest wisdom. These people loved to be seen and to parade their spiritual accomplishments in public ways.

Jesus said that the hypocrites **love** (*phileo*) these attention-gathering methods. They would do anything to get attention. Recognition was their god, replacing the God they should have been loving with all their heart, soul, and mind (Matt 22:37–38).

23:8–10. These three verses about the use of respectful titles sprung out of the preceding comment about the hypocrites' love of respectful greetings, particularly the title **Rabbi.** Jesus' teaching was not a prohibition of the use of titles but an exhortation to humility. Titles have a necessary place, when used appropriately. But the wise and righteous person should be so humble as to feel embarrassed when addressed with a title of honor, knowing that his wisdom and righteousness are gracious gifts from God. **You** is emphatic, drawing a contrast between the behavior of the righteous and the hypocrite.

As the opposite of the hypocrites' love for the title **Rabbi,** Jesus exhorted the person of integrity not to seek such a title, repeating "Rabbi" again as a specific example. Only One has the right to be called our teacher—the Messiah himself. All the rest of us—leaders and followers alike—are the Messiah's students, and therefore **brothers,** learners among learners. When compared with Jesus, the rest of us find ourselves on a level playing field. Realizing this will keep us humble.

Teachers were often referred to as **father,** out of affection and respect. Jesus restated the same message as in the previous verse, using a parallel title. This time the reason to avoid such a title was that ultimately only One has the right to be called our Father—God in heaven. Anyone who claims the title "father" out of pride and for self-elevation finds himself in competition with the Almighty.

In 23:10, Jesus used a third Greek synonym, **teacher**, to repeat the same warning, this time stating clearly there was only one such **Teacher, the Christ** (Messiah). Was this prideful for Jesus to claim such an exclusive status for himself? Of course not. It would be prideful only for someone who was not the Christ, but for Jesus it was his perfect right, even his responsibility.

23:11–12. Compare the text of Matthew 23:11 with the almost identical wording in 20:26–28. The greatest was the person who stooped to serve others. This humble servant was the one with true self-respect, having nothing to prove. But the hypocrites displayed their lack of self-respect by demanding respect from others, seeking to be served and noticed. Compare this passage with James 4:6,10—where the humble are promised they will be lifted up, and Proverbs 25:6–7—which teaches about choosing seating at a banquet (also Prov. 15:33; 22:4; 1 Pet. 5:5–6). All leadership, even at the highest levels, is to be servant-hearted.

The person who exalts himself will be humbled in judgment when his true low status in the kingdom is revealed. By contrast, the person who voluntarily humbles himself, through service and avoidance of undue notice, will be exalted (cf. 18:3–4; 19:14).

Notice that everyone will either experience voluntary humility now or involuntary humiliation in eternity. There is no third alternative. Jesus was instructing the laypeople and his disciples in positive righteousness. But he was also condemning the hypocritical leaders.

B First and Second Woes: Leading People Astray (23:13–15)

> **SUPPORTING IDEA:** Hypocrisy affects us as well as the well-being of others.

The "seven woes" (23:13–36) form the heart of this chapter, illustrating the Jewish leaders' hypocrisy by means of detailed examples, which Jesus raised to public awareness in 23:1–12.

The first two woes are sobering because of the leaders' God-given stewardship of the people's spiritual well-being. Rather than handling their trust with integrity, they had neglected and abused God's people, as had hypocritical leaders of the past (Ezek. 34). The leaders had been given a weighty responsibility. Their violation of this trust incurred a weighty judgment.

23:13. *The first woe.* The word **woe** (*ouai*) is used in Scripture as either an expression of grief or judgment. Here "woe" is an expression of righteous anger and a pronunciation of impending judgment. Jesus himself is the judge who will judge every person. We see here a dose of his indignation at sins that are among the worst possible—willful rebellion and dragging others down as well. (See Jesus' other uses of "woe" in 11:21; 18:7; 24:19; 26:24. Isaiah 5:8–22 and Hab. 2:6–20 also presented a series of "woes," as Jesus did here.)

A paraphrase of Jesus' accusation might be, "Because of your hypocrisy (and therefore failure to experience the truth), you are slamming the door of the kingdom in the faces of seeking people."

The verb form here is in the present tense, implying that the Jewish leaders used every opportunity to keep people out of the kingdom and to keep the door permanently closed. They used their position as teachers to lock the door. In particular, they were closing it to **those who are trying** to enter. People who sought to please God and to enter his kingdom were being misguided.

The primary tool by which the hypocrites kept people out of the kingdom was their own example: **You yourselves do not enter.** They led evil lives, and the people followed them. Here we see again the zealous protectiveness of the Good Shepherd for his sheep (18:10–14).

23:14–15. *The second woe.* This pronouncement of judgment highlighted the zealous evangelistic activity of the hypocrites. They would travel the world (**over land and sea**) for only one **convert**. A convert was a Gentile who was won to faith in Yahweh, the God of Israel.

But the new convert would have been better off if he had not been found by the Jewish evangelist. By following the evangelist's hypocritical example, the convert surpassed his teacher in hypocrisy and evil. As a result, he incurred an even harsher judgment. The new convert may have even convinced himself that he was following God, but he was actually following Satan. God intended Israel to be his ambassadors to the world to bring people to him, but these representatives of Israel were leading people into rebellion.

Ⓒ Third and Fourth Woes: Perverting God's Law (23:16–24)

SUPPORTING IDEA: *Hypocrisy is self-deceptive, leading to rationalization of sin.*

Jesus had already confronted Israel's leaders with their avoidance of God's law by adherence to their counterfeit replacements—laws made by men (15:1–9). These evil men were the authority to whom the laypeople looked for spiritual guidance. The people trusted their leaders to speak for God.

Outwardly, the leaders put on a great show of strong commitment, making their vows and paying their tithes. And they taught these things fervently to the people. But as quietly as possible, they slipped through their own hypocritical loopholes. In the guise of obedience, they were actually committed to the quest to disobey.

23:16–19. *The third woe.* This is the only one of the seven woes that does not begin with the formula address, "teachers of the law and Pharisees, you hypocrites." Instead, Jesus addressed them as **blind guides.** This accusation emerged from their ability to mislead the people. But it was also related to their perversion of the law because they taught this man-made perversion to the people, who believed it to be from God. The leaders had blinded themselves by their hardened hearts, and they were guiding others into the same danger.

Jesus provided two prime examples of ways the hypocrites used oaths to get away with lying. (For the significance of oaths and swearing, see comment on 5:33–37.) Swearing **by the temple** called upon the God who dwelt there to curse the promise maker if he should fail to keep the promise. But when the time came to fulfill the promise, the hypocrite would claim that the oath was not binding, since it did not specify the *gold* in the temple treasury. For these hypocrites, it was the "wealth" of the temple that gave the temple its significance. Their original oath misled the other party into believing they were sincere, when they never intended to keep the promise. God was especially indignant about such misuse of oaths, because his name was brought in as a "seal of approval" on the hypocrite's lie. This was an example of using God's name in vain (the third commandment, Exod. 20:7).

Jesus interrupted his own flow of thought to proclaim such hypocrites as **blind fools.** This designation was justified because they had missed the purpose of the temple. It was not the gold that gave the temple its significance. Rather, God's presence gave the gold its special significance, setting it apart from all other gold in the world.

This was a clear example of the result of legalism. When we are reduced to legalistically "parsing" our verbs in order to twist their intention and protect ourselves, we are lost. The legal/justice system of the United States has become so pharisaical in methodolgy that the real victim is justice itself. We have forced ourselves to define truth in levels. Somehow truth "under oath" is more truthful than truth that is not sworn. We have truth, semi-truth, and true truth. We have become "legally accurate" but morally bankrupt. We have come a long way from letting our "yes" be yes and our "no" be no. And our culture is dying because of it. It is the inevitable end of pharisaism. We have made a mockery of truth and character.

As another example, Jesus accused the hypocrites of claiming an oath **by the altar** to be invalid (at the time the promise was supposed to be kept) because their oath did not specify **the gift** on the altar (23:18).

The altar was a structure in the temple that contained a fire on which the animal sacrifices were burned as acts of worship by God's people. The hypocrites in their arrogance believed their gifts could give significance to God's altar.

For the third time in this "woe," Jesus called the hypocrites **blind** (23:19). They failed to realize that no offering from a sinful person could give significance to God's altar. Rather, the sacred altar in God's temple made the offering **sacred** and therefore acceptable to God. The acceptability of our gifts and our worship is made possible by a gracious concession from God. We are guilty of great arrogance if we think that we, on our own, are the source of anything acceptable to God. Anything we give him is only giving back what he has already provided (1 Chron. 29:14).

23:20–22. Jesus corrected the mistaken thinking behind wrongful oaths by providing three examples of the right understanding. First, an oath **by the altar** need not be any more elaborate than that, for it calls upon the holiness of God's altar and the sanctified sacrifice upon it. This is a different way of saying, "Let your 'yes' be 'yes' and your 'no' 'no'" (cf. 5:36). Jesus was not telling us to stop making oaths but to keep our word by saying what we mean and meaning what we say.

Some people would swear falsely **by heaven,** but fail to keep their vow as they would with the vows by the altar and the temple. Jesus clarified that swearing by heaven calls upon the holiness and authority of God's throne and God himself **who sits on it.** In fact, as we have seen often in Matthew, "heaven" is often a euphemism referring to God himself. Many people who swore **by heaven** were swearing by God, calling on him to be a party to their oaths.

Not only were the Jewish leaders guilty of lying and breaking promises, but they also perverted God's law according to their desires. They passed off their man-made version as though it were God's Word to cover up their own dishonesty and greed. In so doing, they committed a third sin—leading the people to believe their falsehood instead of God's truth. The responsibility of leadership carried with it a greater judgment.

23:23–24. *The fourth woe.* The same could be said about Jesus' fourth accusation, which, like the third, showed how the Jewish leaders had perverted God's law to allow them to disobey its true intent.

The hypocrites tithed (gave ten percent) of everything, right down to the herbs in their pantry—**mint, dill and cummin** (see Old Testament laws on tithing in Lev. 27:30; Deut. 14:22–29). As with their vows and zealous evangelism (23:15), this looked quite righteous to the undiscerning observer, so the leaders received much respect.

But their tithing served only as a smoke screen, distracting people from noticing that they had neglected **the more important matters of the law— justice, mercy and faithfulness** (cf. Deut. 10:12–13; Mic. 6:8). They made it appear that they were paying "full rent," when in reality they were only keeping up the "newspaper subscription." The implication is that they were guilty of committing injustice and acting unmercifully at the expense of others and for their own profit.

Jesus did not say the hypocrites were wrong in their tithing. Rather, he said they should have given greater attention to these **more important** matters of the law while also giving attention to their tithing and other requirements. Compare this with "I desire mercy, not sacrifice" (Hos. 6:6, quoted by Jesus in Matt. 9:13; 12:7).

As in the third woe, Jesus again called the Jewish leaders **blind guides**. Their self-deception about the various Old Testament laws also deceived the people who followed them, so no one knew how to go about pleasing God.

Jesus' hyperbole in verse 24 was humorous. His hearers would have chuckled at the picture of the Pharisees straining out a small insect (**gnat**) while swallowing a huge **camel**.

In their self-serving greed, the leaders of Israel had perverted the law into a man-made version that allowed them to get away with a show of obedience while avoiding true obedience. And they led others into similar disobedience.

Ⓓ Fifth and Sixth Woes: Hiding Evil with Hypocrisy (23:25–28)

SUPPORTING IDEA: *Hypocrisy emphasizes the external show but minimizes the internal corruption.*

The fifth and sixth woes revisited the debate of 15:1–20 over cleanness and uncleanness. In fact, the picture of a cup or dish (fifth woe) was the same as that used in the earlier passage. The sixth woe took the same principle to a more graphic extreme, using the image of dead bodies in a tomb.

The leaders looked holy on the outside, luring people into their confidence. But they were actually a deadly trap, because their true status ("inside") was that of unrighteousness and uncleanness. And anyone who followed them would be defiled by the association, just as a person is made unclean by a cup with a filthy interior or by contact with a dead body (Num. 19:11).

23:25–26. *The fifth woe.* As in 15:1–20, Jesus argued that it was the **inside** of the cup or dish that should be clean. This is the part that comes into contact with the drink or food that goes into a person's mouth. The **outside** should also be clean, but its condition is not so critical. So also a person who looks righteous to an observer but who is truly unrighteous inwardly is thoroughly unclean and a danger to those around him. These sins in particular drew attention to the self-centered attitude of the leaders and their pattern of preying on their followers for their own advancement. The inside of the cup was intended to represent the individual's character.

Jesus' challenge (23:26) to the hypocritical leaders was to begin housecleaning on the inside, confronting the sinful attitudes of their hearts. If the inner person is righteous, righteousness will flow out, resulting in outward righteousness as well.

23:27–28. *The sixth woe.* According to Old Testament law (Num. 19:11), anyone who came in contact with a dead body was ritually unclean for a week. That person had to perform the appropriate sacrifices to complete restoration. Contact with a dead body was among the most abhorrent of experiences to the religious Jew. Jesus expressed this by adding that the tombs were full of dead men's bones as well as **everything unclean**.

Just as a beautifully decorated tomb housed an unclean dead body, the outwardly righteous hypocrite housed a filthy, sinful soul, capable of defiling others around him by his example and his teaching. Jesus selected **hypocrisy** and **wickedness** as terms to describe all the sin inside the Jewish leaders. These were broad terms, covering virtually all sins these people might commit. Any sin would be covered up by false righteousness ("hypocrisy"), and all sin was violation of the law ("wickedness").

Ｅ Seventh Woe: Murdering God's Prophets (23:29–36)

SUPPORTING IDEA: *Hypocrisy lashes out defensively at the truth and any messenger who bears the truth.*

Jesus' seventh woe stood by itself, whereas the first six were paired. It is climactic, presenting the worst of the hypocrites' sins—the persecution and murder of God's prophets (cf. 21:34–39; 22:6). It is also the most lengthy of the seven. The theme of persecution of the prophets is in the emphatic final position and therefore receives much attention.

The present tense predominated in the first six woes. But the seventh woe spoke not only of the Jewish leaders' present disobedience (23:31), but also looked back to their past and ahead to their future. Jesus linked the current leaders with those in the past who also persecuted and murdered God's prophets (23:29–32,35; cf. 2 Chron. 36:15–16; Jer. 26:20–23). He also predicted their continued persecution of God's spokesmen (23:32,34), further justifying their future judgment (23:33–36).

23:29–33. *The seventh woe.* As with most of the first six woes, Jesus began by describing the external behavior of the hypocrites, which appeared to others to be righteous. The **prophets** and **righteous** (cf. Matt. 10:41; 13:17) referred to God's martyrs of the past, murdered by the **forefathers** of Israel, during the days when Israel was in rebellion against God. It was no problem for the first-century leaders to **build tombs** and **decorate the graves** of dead prophets. Those prophets could no longer prophesy about the sin of the first-century leaders.

In direct contrast with the reality of their inner resistance to God's truth, they put on a show of denying such resistance, claiming they would never have participated in the persecution of the prophets of the past (**the days of our forefathers**). But Jesus said: **you testify against yourselves that you are the descendants of those who murdered the prophets** (23:31). Jesus was purposefully ambiguous on the meaning of the term *descendant*. He used it in the sense that the current leaders were literal descendants. But he also used it in the sense that a descendant was a follower or disciple of the **forefather**, implying a consistency of heart belief and outward behavior—"like father, like son."

In 23:32, Jesus shifted the view toward the future, challenging the leaders to go all the way and prove their identity with their **forefathers** by their behavior. **Fill up . . . the measure** means "to keep on sinning, and so prove yourselves to be just as evil as they are." This was not only a prophecy, but a pronouncement of judgment. Sometimes the way God judged the evil was by allowing them to continue on deeper into their sin, thus condemning themselves (cf. Rom. 1:18–32; also Isa. 6:9; Jer. 44:25; Amos 4:4–5). **Then** shows that this pronouncement of condemnation was a result of the guilt they already had, by their own admission (23:29–31).

John the Baptizer had called the Pharisees and Sadducees a "brood [offspring] of vipers" in 3:7. Jesus reinforced the charge, calling them **snakes**. They were sly and clever, fooling the crowds as the serpent fooled Adam and Eve (Gen. 3:1–6). And they were deadly. Because of their deceptive and malicious corruption of God's people, they were subject to harsh judgment. Jesus' question, **How will you escape being condemned to hell?** is rhetorical. The understood answer is, "There is no escape for you."

23:34–36. The word **therefore** carries the meaning, "Since you are already guilty of following in your forefathers' bloody footsteps." Jesus warned that they would be provided with further opportunities to kill God's messengers, that there would be no doubt about their guilt.

Jesus claimed that he was the One who was sending the messengers. Implied here was Jesus' claim to deity. The prophets were from God, so Jesus was claiming to do what only God does. And he was already beginning to do it. The Twelve and their spiritual offspring would be the first fulfillment of Jesus' promise (5:10–12; 9:37–38; 28:18–20).

Jesus had already predicted his own death by crucifixion (20:19). Some of the messengers to come would suffer as he was about to suffer. Others would be killed by other means. Jesus predicted flogging and persecution from city to city (10:17,23) in his warning to his disciples. The Twelve were certainly among those whom Jesus predicted he would send.

These messengers would be sent, and they would be persecuted. Their persecutors would be counted among the murderers of all history, the segment of humanity who is guilty of **all the righteous blood that has been shed on earth.** Expanding on this last phrase, Jesus provided the names of the first righteous martyr and one of the latest in Jewish history. Abel was the first recorded murder (possibly the first human death), and his death at his brother Cain's hand was because of Abel's righteousness (Heb. 11:4; 1 John 3:12), which sparked Cain's jealousy (Gen. 4:1–15).

Jesus finished the seventh and most sobering woe with his pronouncement of judgment. **I tell you the truth** assured the listeners of the validity of his prediction. **All this** included the persecutions and the judgment for them. **This generation** (cf. Matt. 11:16; 13:39,45; 16:4) should be taken quite literally in this case, since judgment on Israel did come in the form of the A.D. 70 devastation. Israel had broken covenant with Yahweh as completely in the first century as in any previous century, by murdering the greatest prophet, the Messiah, God's Son. As in centuries before, punishment would certainly come. This generation of false religionists living in the time of Christ would inherit all the guilt of their forefathers (cf. Jer. 16:10–13).

Jesus had just pronounced a finality to his dealing with Israel. He had determined that judgment for all the unfaithfulness of the nation through the centuries (Abel to Zechariah) would fall upon "this generation." He was about to announce that **your house is left to you desolate**—a statement that shocked the disciples. Jesus would deal with their questions and this impending future judgment in Matthew 24–25.

F The King Laments Israel's Desolation (23:37–39)

SUPPORTING IDEA: *Hypocrisy leads to emptiness and destruction.*

In these final words, Jesus still addressed Israel, the murderers of the prophets. But now the tone of wrathful condemnation gave way to grief and even some degree of compassion. These words are both a lament and an appeal for repentance.

23:37. We might imagine **Jerusalem, Jerusalem** coming from Jesus' lips accompanied by a strong display of emotion. The prophets and other messengers had been sent out of love for the good of Israel. But the recipients of God's grace had despised his love, killing and stoning those sent to win the prodigal people back (see Stephen, Acts 7:59).

Jerusalem was portrayed here as the "mother" of the people of Israel, **your children.** Jesus, God incarnate who had supervised all of history, including the many preceding centuries of Israel's rebellion, expressed his persistent compassion for his people. **How often** implied Yahweh's repeated attempts to reason with his people and rescue them from their own self-destructive rebellion.

Even in the first century, the image of the mother **hen** protecting her chicks carried the same connotation as it does today. This was the kind of affection Jesus has always had for his wayward people, always wishing to **gather** them together in unified obedience, in covenant relationship with him, and in forgiving grace. No matter how deeply his people had sinned, the Lord wanted them back.

But they were **not willing**. Even Jesus does not force compliance. What grief this must have caused him. What a demonstration of love, that he would subject his emotions to our wills, allowing himself to experience pain and suffering at our rebellious whim. That is authentic love.

23:38–39. The word **Look** means "watch, see for yourselves." And he continued into another prophecy of judgment that was not entirely distant future. Even now, the **house** (possibly the temple itself, but also implying the "family") of Jerusalem (the capital representing all Israel) **is left to you desolate.** Israel was on the verge of losing something important to its survival. Within a few years (A.D. 70) Jerusalem would be in ruins.

Jesus explained the nature of this desolation in 23:39 ("for" leads us to expect an explanation). **For I tell you** arrested the audience's attention one more time for a final critical announcement: **you will not see me again.** That was to say, "Your chances to accept me, the Messiah, while I am physically present, have ended." But the Messiah's absence was not permanent. They would again see him, when they (Israel) would say, **Blessed is he who comes in the name of the Lord** (quoted from Ps. 118:26, also quoted by the welcoming crowd in 21:9).

Some commentators make reference here to Zechariah 12:10–13:1, where it was foretold that Israel would mourn for the one they pierced, and that "on that day a fountain will be opened to the house of David and the inhabitants of Jerusalem, to cleanse them from sin and impurity" (Zech. 13:1). This is a reference to Israel's future role near the close of history.

Jesus turned and walked away from the temple, but his shocking words rang in the ears of the disciples. They were moved to ask, "When will this happen, and what will be the sign of your coming?" (24:3). Jesus answered their questions in the fifth and final discourse (Matt. 24–25), the Olivet Discourse, from the Mount of Olives just outside Jerusalem. This great discourse prophesied the coming kingdom and the time of reward for Christ's followers.

MAIN IDEA REVIEW: *Beware of hypocrisy. It will receive God's severe judgment.*

III. CONCLUSION

We must respect and obey the accurate teaching of God's Word, even when we cannot fully respect the teacher. We must also distinguish between a teacher's words and his example. We must see that our own words and actions convey the same message of truth.

PRINCIPLES

- Seeking the attention and approval of others to promote oneself is prideful and wrong.
- In God's kingdom, the person who serves is the most highly esteemed.
- The proud will be humiliated in the future while the humble will be exalted.
- We set ourselves up for judgment when we lead people astray.
- Righteousness must begin with the inner person, not with external obedience alone.
- God is persistent in his attempts to reclaim rebellious people.
- God will judge persistent rebellion.

APPLICATIONS

- Do not seek the approval of men. Strive to please God.
- Carefully listen to God's Word and obey it.
- Never pervert God's Word for personal convenience or gain.
- Never shy away from the central requirements of God for his people.
- Beware of those who seem righteous on the outside but are unrighteous in their hearts.
- Listen to God's messengers of truth. Be careful not to reject them because you do not like the content of their message.

IV. LIFE APPLICATION

Hypocrisy—a Multifaceted Evil

Salt Lake Olympic Committee officials were forced to acknowledge that they had funneled almost $400,000 in tuition assistance, books, and living expenses to thirteen unnamed individuals, six of whom were relatives of members of the International Olympic Committee, which chose the site to host the 2002 Games.

As the story began to unfold, the officials characterized the payments as humanitarian aid to deserving residents of impoverished third world nations, and said they represented only an insignificant portion of the almost $15 million in private money the committee spent on Salt Lake City's Olympic bid.

But that fiction was blown apart by a longtime IOC member who described a systematic pattern of vote-buying in the Olympic site-selection process in which agents deliver blocks of votes and charge winning cities $3 million to $5 million. A special committee has been appointed by the IOC to study the Salt Lake City payments. The suggestion of bribery, said a former Salt Lake City Mayor "strikes at the credibility of the whole operation. . . . It just besmirches the whole process."

What had appeared to have been a fair vote for Salt Lake City was now tainted with the prospects of illegalities.

British novelist W. Somerset Maughham once wrote, "Hypocrisy is the most difficult and nerve-racking vice that any man can pursue; it needs an unceasing vigilance and a rare detachment of spirit. It cannot, like adultery or gluttony, be practiced at spare moments; it is a whole-time job."

That describes the Jewish leaders who were opposing Jesus. By Matthew 23, the opposition to Jesus was in full swing. His enemies were out in the open and actively confronting him. They would not quit.

The severity of Jesus' judgment upon the Jewish hypocrites underscores the severity of their sin. The seven woes illustrate the details of their hypocritical ways. Their sin was a choice, and it was multifaceted and extensive.

As citizens of the kingdom of God, we must not only beware of the hypocrites in our midst, we must also guard against hypocrisy in our own lives. Righteousness begins in the inner person. Feed your mind, heart, and will with the truth of God's Word. It is the best deterrent to the sin of hypocrisy.

V. PRAYER

Sovereign Lord, make me aware of my hypocrisy and pride, convict me of these sins, and lead me to repentance and authentic faith and discipleship. Amen.

VI. DEEPER DISCOVERIES

A. The Last Old Testament Martyr

The books of the Hebrew Old Testament are arranged in a different order than our English Bibles. Thus, Zechariah is the last martyr listed there (2 Chron. 24:20–22). Though the Zechariah murdered in the temple (Jehoiada's son) was a different Zechariah than the son of Berekiah (see Zech. 1:1), Matthew used a common Jewish method of combining multiple references with certain similarities as descriptive of the entire matter. Another possible explanation of the apparent confusion is to assume that Berekiah was the grandfather of Zechariah son of Jehoiada, and that Jesus referred to the grandson as the **son**, using the word "son" to mean "descendant," as was commonly done in that day.

B. Summary

This chapter was the climax and culmination of the series of confrontations that appeared throughout Matthew and began in earnest in 21:23. Jesus' audience and Matthew's readers needed to understand the seriousness of the Jewish leaders' sin. Matthew was accounting for Israel's rejection of the Messiah, his judgment of the nation, and the disappearance of Israel from the prophetic map in the age to come.

Jesus indicated that Israel was to be judged to the point of desolation. The king was finished with the nation until they acknowledged him who "comes in the name of the Lord." Israel would no longer carry the torch of his eternal truth to this world. That privilege was being passed to the church.

The final theme of judgment on Israel set the stage for the Olivet Discourse (Matt. 24–25).

VII. TEACHING OUTLINE

A. INTRODUCTION

1. Lead Story: Hypocrisy Confronted
2. Context: Jesus had arrived on the stage of history (Matt. 1–4); demonstrated his authority as Messiah-King (Matt. 5–10); met with rejection (Matt. 11–12); continued to walk the difficult path of truth in the face of opposition while preparing the disciples to carry on after him (Matt. 13–20); and moved into the spotlight with royal dignity as he was victorious in verbal and spiritual combat with his opponents (Matt. 21–22). Having silenced his critics (22:46), Jesus warned the crowd and his disciples of the poison of their hypocritical leaders. He concluded by announcing the coming judgment on the nation.
3. Transition: After the introductory warning to the listening audience (23:1–12), Jesus pronounced the "seven woes" that formed the heart of this chapter. The first six fell into natural pairs, with the seventh bringing a dramatic conclusion to the list and foreshadowing Jesus' own death at the hands of the Jewish religious leaders.

B. COMMENTARY

1. The King Warns Israel of the Self-Absorption of Its Leaders (23:1–12)
2. First and Second Woes: Leading People Astray (23:13–15)
3. Third and Fourth Woes: Perverting God's Law (23:16–24)
4. Fifth and Sixth Woes: Hiding Evil with Hypocrisy (23:25–28)

5. Seventh Woe: Murdering God's Prophets (23:29–36)
6. The King Laments Israel's Desolation (23:37–39)

C. CONCLUSION

1. Wrap-up: Beware of hypocrisy; it will receive God's severe judgment.
2. Personal Challenge: We need to ask ourselves whether we are going through the motions of religion or whether we are following Jesus Christ. We need to realize how seriously he takes hypocrisy and how subtly it can creep into our lives.

VIII. ISSUES FOR DISCUSSION

1. What were the "seven woes" that Jesus pronounced against the hypocrites in this chapter of Matthew?
2. How were the Pharisees using phylacteries?
3. How were the Jewish religious leaders leading people astray?
4. According to Jesus, what punishment would fall upon the Jewish religious leaders because of their persecution of God's prophets?

Matthew 24

The King Foretells the Future

I. INTRODUCTION
Be Prepared

II. COMMENTARY
A verse-by-verse explanation of the chapter.

III. CONCLUSION
An overview of the principles and applications from the chapter.

IV. LIFE APPLICATION
Are You Ready?

Melding the chapter to life.

V. PRAYER
Tying the chapter to life with God.

VI. DEEPER DISCOVERIES
Historical, geographical, and grammatical enrichment of the commentary.

VII. TEACHING OUTLINE
Suggested step-by-step group study of the chapter.

VIII. ISSUES FOR DISCUSSION
Zeroing the chapter in on daily life.

"*In* preparing for battle I have always found that plans are useless, but planning is indispensable."

D w i g h t   D .   E i s e n h o w e r

Matthew 24

IN A NUTSHELL

This chapter is part of the final of Jesus' five discourses in Matthew, and is referred to as the Olivet Discourse (Matt. 24–25). It focuses on the details of the coming judgment on the Messiah's opponents and Christ's return. Here Jesus gives his disciples a glimpse of the end of the age. Jesus commands his followers to be ever ready for his return— a strong motivation to remain faithful and obedient to his Word.

The King Foretells
the Future

I. INTRODUCTION

Be Prepared

"*Be* Prepared." That slogan is as old as the Boy Scouts but as fresh as the morning. And it is always good advice. We humans have a way of charging off into life hoping everything will work itself out as we go along. But wisdom thinks ahead, anticipates contingencies, and makes specific plans for potential developments. The more critical the mission, the more careful the planning. As any good Boy Scout knows, asking "What could happen?" keeps him more alert to things going on around him.

I will never forget one patrol in the U.S. Army Ranger school. We were in the pipeline to Vietnam and we knew it. All of us were anxious to gain maximum profit from this finest training in the Army. We took our lessons seriously, except for one soldier on one patrol. It was a difficult nighttime operation, with waterborne rubber rafts down the Yellow River in Florida's panhandle. Night was bad enough, but water complicated matters, especially when the rafts were "powered" only with hand-held paddles, and the river's current was swollen with winter run-off.

In the spirit of "be prepared," the Ranger cadre had trained us for waterborne operations. For one thing, we were to remove the normal slings from our weapons and replace them with a nylon cord tied with a special quick-release knot. In case the boat overturned, we would not be hindered by the rifle extended awkwardly over our head and shoulders. One quick pull on the quick release and we were free, with weapon in hand, to maneuver to the bank. We took our knot-tying seriously. This was true except for one trooper, who thought the chances of an emergency were slim.

Later that night, moving swiftly with the current, our raft was swept under some overhanging brush near the bank. And, as it turned out, the only soldier to get into trouble was the one who failed to tie his knot properly. As the rubber raft passed swiftly under the brush, a large branch inserted itself between this guy's rifle and his shoulder. The stout branch lifted him out of the boat and bounced him like a fish bobber in the swift current. He was "hung up," and there was nothing he could do about it except take the full force of the current square in the face. He was immobile, helpless, and actually in danger.

The rest of us managed to get the raft stopped. Using the bank's overhanging brush as tow ropes, we pulled ourselves back upstream to the hapless fellow. We cut him loose, dragged him into the raft, and gave him a glaring look or two before moving out. When he recovered sufficiently from the trauma, he sheepishly apologized for his lack of preparation.

Be prepared. The purpose of all Bible prophecy, such as that in Matthew 24, is to motivate us to live well today. *It is not to satisfy our curiosity about the future. It is to intensify our purity in the present* (see 1 John 3:3). Jesus was determined to prepare his disciples for their critical mission. And his word motivated them to live faithfully to gain future reward in the coming kingdom. In Matthew 24 he gave his followers a glimpse of the future. But he did not do it so they could get excited about future events. He did it so they would become thoroughly motivated to follow his commission in the present.

In the midst of an ongoing debate about the best interpretation of 24:4–41, we must be careful not to lose sight of Jesus' central purpose. Certainly we must strive for the most accurate interpretation of Jesus' prophecies. But regardless of the position we take on such issues, there is no mistaking Jesus' main challenge to all believers: "Be ready at all times. Do not let down your guard. Keep doing the work of the kingdom, preaching the gospel throughout the world. Do not become obsessed with the future, but invest yourself in the present in order to be prepared when the future arrives and you stand before the king."

In answering the disciples' questions (24:3), Jesus downplayed the future in favor of a focus on the present (although he certainly acknowledged that an accurate view of the future is important). But many students of this discourse take exactly the opposite course—following their fascination with the future while ignoring their present conduct.

II. COMMENTARY

The King Foretells the Future

> **MAIN IDEA:** *In light of the future reality of hardship and ultimate salvation, we must stay ready for Christ's return (and his rewards) at all times by living in loving obedience.*

The place of the Olivet Discourse in Matthew. Matthew's placement of the five discourses has been carefully planned throughout his Gospel.

The Sermon on the Mount (Matt. 5–7) was linked with Jesus' launching of his public ministry (4:12–25). It laid the foundation of God's kingdom people and provided a verbal display of Jesus' authority (the theme of Matt. 5–10; see esp. 7:28–29).

Matt. 1–4	Matthew 5–25 Jesus' Discourses (Sermon Teaching)					Matt. 26–28
Opening Narrative *or*	5–7 Sermon on the Mount *or*	10 Commission of the Twelve *or*	13 Kingdom Parables *or*	18 Teaching on the Church *or*	24–25 Olivet Discourse *or*	Closing Narrative *or*
The Introduction	The Kingdom Constitution	The Kingdom's Foundational Leaders	The Pursuit of the Kingdom (in the King's Absence)	The Relational Principles in the Kingdom	The Kingdom's Future	The Climax

The Matthew 10 discourse followed the theme of authority from the preceding chapters. The king delegated that same authority to his disciples and sent them to the lost sheep of the house of Israel.

The parable discourse (Matt. 13) was Jesus' response to the rejection he received in Matthew 11–12. The parables of the discourse were enigmatic only to those who continued to reject him. For those who had "ears to hear," the parables built their understanding of the kingdom, preparing them for the church age.

The Matthew 18 discourse followed on the heels of Jesus' pivotal announcement that he would build his church (16:18), providing principles on how to build his church. Jesus would soon leave his ministry in the hands of the Twelve; this discourse prepared them with specifics on how to proceed with his church.

Jesus' final discourse, the Olivet Discourse (Matt. 24–25; named after its setting on the Mount of Olives) followed immediately after the conflicts between Jesus and the leaders of Israel (Matt. 21–23). The discourse clarified God's judgment on the Messiah's opponents and prepared the Messiah's faithful followers for the end.

Structure of the discourse. Matthew 24–25 is a single unit, but it falls into two distinct portions—prophecy and preparation. In 24:1–41, Jesus foretold details of the coming judgment and his return. In fact, in all of Matthew, this was Jesus' strongest and most detailed emphasis on future events. Then there was a turning point at 24:42 ("therefore"), after which Jesus prepared his people to be ready when the judgment came. The first portion of the discourse consists mainly of factual details about the future, while the second portion consists of commands, illustrated by five parables, showing believers how to live to be prepared for the future judgment.

Chronological and thematic setting. The series of confrontations in 21:23–23:39 probably occurred on Tuesday. If we take the implied time reference in 24:1 at face value and if we assume the Olivet Discourse was presented on a single occasion, then the time setting for the discourse may be Tuesday evening. However, this does not seem to fit as well with another clue in 26:1–2 (which follows the pattern of the closing transitions of the other four Matthew discourses), where Jesus had just finished the discourse and then said that the Passover (beginning Friday evening) was "two days away." This places the discourse more likely on Wednesday, or possibly Thursday.

In any case, the important point is to understand that Matthew linked the Olivet Discourse thematically with the preceding series of conflicts (21:23–23:39), especially with the climactic conclusion concerning Israel's persecution of God's prophets and his consequent judgment (23:29–39). In 23:38, Jesus prophesied the desolation of the temple, the city of Jerusalem, and all of Israel. Then Jesus foretold the details of the destruction of the temple and Jerusalem as well as other future events. This connection was so intentional in Matthew that he omitted the intervening story of the poor widow's offering that Mark (12:41–44) and Luke (21:1–4) included.

Fulfillment of Jesus' prophecy. There is much debate over the exact events Jesus was foretelling. There are portions that seem to point directly to the siege and destruction of Jerusalem and the temple by the Romans in A.D. 70 (esp. 24:2,15–20). But there are other portions that are most naturally interpreted as referring to the end times (e.g., 24:14,21-22,30-31) still to come. Some commentators believe the entire discourse relates to the A.D. 70 destruction, interpreting Christ's "coming" as a figurative reference to his coming in judgment at that time.

At the other extreme are those who interpret the entire discourse as foretelling the end times, with no reference at all to the A.D. 70 destruction. Then there are an almost endless number of variations in the middle, attempting to show which portions of the discourse apply to the A.D. 70 destruction, which apply to the end times, which apply to other historical fulfillments between the two, and which have multiple fulfillments at different points in history.

The best solution should probably begin with the assumption that Jesus was looking ahead toward several acts of judgment, spread throughout history, and foretelling them as a conflated, composite unit. Some details of Jesus' prophecy have been and will be fulfilled at more than one point in history. This is not without precedent in biblical prophecy. For example, Daniel's prophecy of the "abomination of desolation" was fulfilled at more than one point in past and future history (see comment on 24:15).

This composite interpretation of the discourse makes more sense if we see historical events the way the Bible sees them. With our linear Western logic, we are sometimes limited in how we see history. We want to know exactly when an event begins and when it ends as well as the order in which everything happens. Such details were not as important to the Eastern-thinking biblical authors. We want crisp, clean lines, while the Bible, in keeping with its Eastern setting, sometimes speaks in terms of gradual transitions and blended distinctions.

Now, in light of this understanding, we can see that God's acts of judgment in fulfillment of Jesus' Olivet Discourse prophecy are a single judgment event in his thinking. But this judgment, in its prophetic entirety, would take centuries to complete, while the task of world evangelization is also being completed (24:14; also "they will gather his elect from the four winds," 24:31). The destruction of Jerusalem and the temple in A.D. 70 were fulfillment of his prophecy. This is true of other historical occasions that bring Jesus' words into historical reality.

The disciples' question (24:3), to which the discourse is Jesus' answer, was in three parts, although the disciples may not have intended the three parts to be as distinct as they appear to be. They asked: (1) about the timing of the temple's destruction; (2) how to recognize the second coming of the Christ; and (3) how to recognize the end of the age. In their minds, those three would come as aspects of one event, since they could only conceive of the temple's destruction as a sign of God's final judgment.

This pattern is a key to understanding prophetic or eschatological truth. Just as Jesus' first advent was a complex of events (birth, life, death, burial, resurrection, ascension), so with the second advent (rapture, return to earth, reign). Even certain eschatological events themselves may be viewed as a complex of parts. For example, there is a resurrection, but it has several stages. There is a judgment, but it is in several stages. There is an "already" aspect to some things, to be followed later by the "not yet" aspect. Jesus is the "firstfruits" of our resurrection (cf. 1 Cor. 15:22–23). And the judgment of A.D. 70 is the precursor to the Tribulation to come.

Indeed, Jesus may also have seen these as components of a centuries-long judgment event, and he answered the disciples' three questions accordingly. From our historical perspective, after the fall of Jerusalem in A.D. 70, we have more knowledge to help sort out the components that refer to the fulfillment of Jesus' prophecy at different points in past and future history.

One cannot read this passage (24:15–21) without being overwhelmed by its scale. There is something ominous here. This is not history as usual. It is a unique period in all of history (Matt. 24:21; Dan. 12:1). Both the comprehensive thrust and the specific details of these verses cry out for much more than the destruction of one city (Jerusalem) at one time (A.D. 70).

Likewise, there is more here than a general description of history unfolding over the centuries. What makes the Great Tribulation unique is that it represents the wrath of man, the wrath of Satan, and the wrath of God all impacting this planet at the same time. There is much more here than generalities.

Many of the difficulties in this passage are solved by taking the prophecies of 24:4–28 as applying first to the A.D. 70 destruction of Jerusalem. Jesus could say that all of these things would take place before "this generation" would pass away. But the fulfillment of these prophecies—especially the appearance of false Christs and prophets, and the various manifestations of the Tribulation—continues for centuries, as precursors eventually of Christ's return (24:29–41). Some of these elements are specifically treated in other key prophetic passages throughout Scripture. They allow us to assemble a scenario that makes sense of the enormous scale of Jesus' comments here. But first a look at the whole.

Jesus' central purpose in the discourse. The disciples wanted to go straight into the privileged life in the eschatological kingdom, skipping the intervening hardship. But this was not to be—and the challenge remains for us also. We are to steward our time wisely and our opportunities for kingdom advancement wisely, investing ourselves in "risky" (faith-filled) obedience, as did the first two servants in 25:19–23. The opposite of this is to bide our time, playing it safe, maintaining a comfortable life until the joys of heaven become ours.

This passive disobedience is disgusting to the Lord. It incurs his harsh anger, as reflected in his response to the third servant in 25:24–30. We must invest our lives in the kingdom's interests, not simply spend them on our own.

The purpose of every prophetic statement in Scripture is to stimulate holiness. The purpose of prophecy is never to satisfy our innate curiosity about the future. Rather, it is our present obedience that must be the emphasis of our study of prophecy. We are told about the future so that we may change our behavior in the present, in preparation for the future and its rewards. Any time we read prophecy, we must ask ourselves, "What difference should this make in my life now, that I may be more ready for the future?"

ⓐ The King Foretells the Fall of Jerusalem and the End of the Age (24:1–22)

SUPPORTING IDEA: *God's plans for his followers will go forward, in spite of the hardship and opposition in the world.*

This portion of the discourse included Jesus' most direct answer to the disciples' question about the timing and the sign of the temple's destruction and the end of the age (24:3). He listed several signs of the end. Some of these signs would happen well before the end and some of them would be indicators that the end was near.

Some commentators see 24:4–28 as a single unit, beginning and ending with warnings about false Christs and false prophets. Because of this, Jesus' central concern throughout this portion seems to be the ability of his followers to discern and avoid the traps of these counterfeits.

24:1. Matthew's mention of Jesus coming out of the temple was intended to connect the following with the preceding. He foretold judgment that would fall because of Israel's rejection of God and his prophets (23:29–39).

As Jesus and his disciples walked away from the temple, the disciples pointed out to him its impressive beauty. We know from writers of the day that the temple was a beautiful creation. When Herod the Great was named king over Israel, ruling on behalf of Rome, he sought the favor and acceptance of the Jewish people. His crowning achievement was the lavish reconstruction of the Jerusalem temple, which was finally completed just six years before it was destroyed by the Romans in A.D. 70.

24:2. In spite of the temple's outward beauty, Jesus was more concerned with the inward condition of God's people. Israel had broken its covenant with Yahweh, this time by rejecting the Messiah. Of little consequence was the time interval before his judgment broke through the dam of his forbearance. Judgment was certain to come. So Jesus did not see the beauty that should have been reflective of a submissive people and an accepting God. Rather, he saw horrible destruction wrought by the rebellious hearts he had been debating that week in the temple courts. In fact, the purpose of the Great Tribulation to come would be the purging of God's covenant people Israel in preparation for the Messiah-King's return to the throne of David.

Just as the disciples had drawn Jesus' attention to the temple buildings, so Jesus drew their attention to them: **Do you see all these things?** It was as though he was saying, "Take one last good look, because you will not have much longer to see it." As he had so many times before, Jesus alerted the disciples to what he was about to say (**I tell you the truth**). Jesus' wording emphasized the destruction of the temple. This emphasis is very obvious in the Greek text, which uses the strong negative *ou me,* and the strengthened verb *kataluo,* "to destroy." That destruction by the Romans (A.D. 70) was so thorough that the precise location of the sanctuary is still unknown today in spite of exhaustive archaeological attempts to locate it.

24:3. Jesus went to the Mount of Olives, across the Kidron Valley from the temple hill of Jerusalem. The Mount of Olives was several hundred feet higher than the temple mount. It provided a spectacular view of the entire city of Jerusalem. This location was especially appropriate for a discussion of the future because it was the site to which the Messiah would return in the end (Zech. 14:4).

Jesus sat down on the Mount of Olives, probably to initiate a teaching session because a teachable moment was about to come at the disciples' initiative. The disciples were still reeling from Jesus' shocking revelation about the temple's destruction. In their minds, such a tragedy could only be linked to the **end of the age** and Christ's return in final judgment. They probably found themselves speculating about whether they were to experience such evil times.

The central purpose of Jesus' discourse was to challenge the disciples' improper motives behind their question. They wanted to participate in the final kingdom reality while avoiding the intervening hardship. Their single question was a compound question. They asked when the temple's destruction would happen and how they would recognize its coming (**the sign of your coming and of the end of the age**).

Basically, the disciples wanted to be ready in case they were about to find themselves in the maelstrom of history. Jesus had announced his return on at least two occasions (16:27–28; 23:39), and this may have been a recurring theme in Jesus' private teaching with them during the latter part of his ministry.

The rest of Matthew 24–25 is Jesus' answer to this question. It is his presentation of the events that lead up to the climax of his second coming to set up his kingdom on the earth for a one-thousand-year reign (cf. Rev. 20:1–4).

24:4–8. Jesus first warned, in general terms (24:4–14), of several characteristics of the period of time before he would return. There would be counterfeit messiahs, wars and rumors of wars, famines, pestilence, earthquakes, martyrs, false prophets, increasing evil, and the preaching of the gospel worldwide.

Watch out that no one deceives you conveys the meaning of "watch out, be sure." "Deceive" is from the Greek word *planao,* meaning "cause to stray." Jesus wanted the disciples to understand that the destruction of Jerusalem did not necessarily mean the end of the age had arrived. Without his careful explanation, this would have been confusing to these first-century disciples.

One way the disciples could have been misled was by the claims of the **many** whom Jesus promised would come **in my name**; that is, claiming to be the Messiah. They would take the title *Christ* (Gr. equivalent to the Heb. *Messiah,* both meaning "anointed one"; see comment on 1:1–17). And they would be convincing; they would **deceive many.** Because these counterfeits would be so difficult to detect, the disciples would need to be especially alert.

Another way the disciples might be misled would be to take news of wars as a sign of the end of the age (possibly as "fulfillment" of the "prophecies" of the false Messiahs). In fact, **hear** (the present infinitive of *akouo*) is combined with "be about to" (the Gr. future tense of *mello*), implying that the news and rumors of war would keep on coming, no matter the season of earth's history. Jesus was painting the picture of a person persistently paranoid that the end is coming at the slightest possible indication (not unlike some current television preachers).

But Jesus again used the present tense with the imperative statement: **but see to it that you are not alarmed**. This comfort was to be applied repetitively, every time a troubling rumor of war came along. Jesus' message was, "Keep on seeing that you are not troubled, every time a rumor of war comes your way, as they often will in this troubled world." While war is a continual reality on earth, war alone is not sufficient evidence of the Lord's return and the end of the age.

Verse 7 is a further explanation of Jesus' comment on war (24:6). Nations and kingdoms will find themselves in continual conflict with one another. Moreover, there will also be famines and earthquakes. Famine was foretold in the Pentateuch as a sign of God's judgment for covenant disobedience (Lev. 26:18–20,26–35; Deut. 28:23–24,38–42,47–48,53–57). **Such things** implies these and many other possible signs of tragedy and destruction. War, famine, and earthquakes fall into a category of events that, while not necessarily unrelated to the end, are only tiny ripples in the pool of history. They are far removed from the central event of God's final judgment. Jesus described them as **the beginning of birth pangs** (cf. Isa. 13:8; 26:17; Jer. 4:31; 6:24; Mic. 4:9–10). This phrase has three implications.

First, "beginning" implies that patterns of war, famine, and earthquakes do have some connection with the end. But they do not necessarily indicate that the end is near. Adding to this concept is the idea of "birth pains," which begin some time before an actual birth.

Second, birth is one of the most painful experiences in a woman's life. Jesus' choice of word picture indicates that, when the end does come, it will be very painful for all of humanity. These sorrows are continually experienced in history. But as is true with the birth process, the pains will increase in frequency and intensity until Jesus returns in his power and glory.

Third, birth is one of the most joyously fulfilling experiences of a woman's life, bringing about the emergence of something precious, beautiful, and highly valued. Jesus' word picture looked beyond the tribulation of God's judgment to the emergence of the fully realized kingdom with Christ in his glory.

24:9–12. The preceding list of "signs" (24:4–8) was frequently interrupted with Jesus' cautions against taking them too seriously. However, as Jesus continued to list more details of the future, he omitted the words of caution, leading us to believe that the signs he listed here would indicate the approach of the end. **Then** may have been a shift in intensity. Still, the signs seemed to be general in tone. They would mark a gradual progression toward the end of the age.

Jesus' description of the persecution of believers (24:9) is a graphic picture of our present age, which can be described generally as one of opposition and persecution. **Handed over** implies capture and deliverance to those who inflict suffering (*thlipsis,* "tribulation"; elsewhere in Matt. 13:21;

24:9,21,29) and death. Just as Jesus' followers would begin to come from all nations, so also would his enemies. These would also be the enemies of his followers. Because Jesus' disciples would confront the world's values and sin, all nations would hate them, remaining complacent in their pride and self-direction. All of this persecution and hatred would be **because of me**.

Suffering, death, and ostracism were part of following Christ. It was natural that **many** would **turn away** from him, seeking to avoid the suffering of discipleship (24:10; cf. 5:10–12; 10:17–18,24–25; 16:24–25). Not only would they fall away from Jesus, but these same apostates would **betray** and **hate** believers. Jesus clearly stated that the apostate followers of Jesus would become party to the persecution of believers, along with the rest of the unbelieving world. These things are happening to Christians today in many parts of the world.

Verse 11 sounds similar to verse 5 above, describing **false prophets** instead of false Christs. A prophet was a spokesman for God; therefore, a false prophet was one who falsely claimed to be God's spokesman. This was a more subtle form of deception, since there was only one Christ. However, there can be many prophets from God, and it was easier to pass oneself off as a prophet. Jesus said there would be **many** such deceivers and that they would **deceive many people**. The person who attempts to remain faithful to Christ may find great difficulty in discerning between so many claimants to God's true revelation. The false prophets would be clever in their deception, winning great followings. The true disciple of Christ must always remain alert.

A literal translation of verse 12 is, "And because of the increase of lawlessness, the love of the many will be made cold or will be extinguished." The verb **cold** means "to cool something hot or to extinguish a flame." It is used only here in the New Testament. There had been many seasons in history during which lawlessness increased greatly, and there would be many to come (Gen. 6:1–7; Book of Judges; Book of 2 Kings; and in the future, 2 Thess. 2; 2 Tim. 3). The United States seems to be on a fast track into just such an era of anarchy. One of the consequences of the abandonment of God's principles is the hardening and deadening of people's love for one another and especially for God.

The deadening of people's love for other people manifests itself in the devaluing of life, a greater focus on one's own pleasure and protection, and a decrease in sensitivity to the needs of others. People's hearts for others grow numb when they are battered with injustice and unrighteousness. A person's capacity to love others is damaged by misuse and abuse.

The deadening of people's love for God is demonstrated through a loss of conscience. Right becomes wrong, and wrong becomes right (Isa. 5:20), and people lose the capacity to recognize this perversion. Society sees an increase in "senseless" crimes (such as shootings in schools) and wonders how anyone could become so hardened and unfeeling as to lash out in these ways. The cause is society's abandonment of God's values.

All four of the signs Jesus had given in 24:9–12 were symptoms of a society heading toward self-destruction: (1) universal persecution of the righteous; (2) joined by those who once numbered themselves among the righteous; (3) widespread following of false teachers claiming to be God's spokesmen; and (4) the numbing of hearts and consciences due to the abandonment of God's righteous values. As with the signs of 24:4–8, these were not absolute guarantees that the end was imminent. History had taken every great society ultimately to this stage on the way to its own destruction. But judging from Jesus' words and the warnings of other New Testament writers (e.g., 2 Tim. 3:1–9), these symptoms would be predominant throughout the world when the end actually did approach.

24:13–14. Jesus cautioned against signs that did not indicate the imminent end (including the destruction of the temple) and then described signs that would become predominant closer to the end. He then came to the partial answer to the disciples' question (24:3). His answer was twofold; it concerned the end result for the righteous individual and for the world.

First (24:13), salvation through the societal troubles described in 24:9–12 would be determined on an individual basis. Those who fell away from following the Messiah would find themselves among the Judas-like betrayers described in 24:10. But each one who **stands firm to the end** in spite of persecution, false teaching, and the hardening of society's conscience would enter into the eternal kingdom of heaven with the Messiah. In the shorter term, as this prophecy related to the destruction of Jerusalem, those who persevered would live on to spread the gospel (24:14). We find similar exhortations in Daniel 11:32,34–35; Matthew 10:22; 12:32; 13:21, 41; 2 Timothy 2:3,10–13; 3:11; Hebrews 10:32; 11:27; 12:2–3; James 1:12; 5:11.

Second (24:14), the final general sign Jesus gave concerning the end of the age was that **this gospel of the kingdom will be preached in the whole world** (cf. Luke 24:47).

Jesus' next phrase, **as a testimony to all nations,** answered two questions. First, it clarified what Jesus meant by **the whole world,** namely, **all nations.** He used the word meaning "race, nation." This term was often used to mean "the Gentiles." The term refers more commonly to cultural and ethnic boundaries rather than political boundaries.

The second question Jesus answered has to do with the purpose of preaching this gospel of the kingdom throughout the world. A **testimony** (*marturion*) was a legal term, referring to the sharing of information on a particular topic. In this case, it had to do with Jesus and his kingdom. The testimony served two purposes simultaneously: (1) it could win the listener over, and (2) it could condemn the guilty. Implied here is Jesus' distinction between those who listened and those who did not (11:15; 13:9,43). **End** here means the end of the age.

24:15–20. The general descriptions were over. At this point Jesus got noticeably deliberate. These next ten verses make specific references to key prophetic Scriptures. The **abomination that causes desolation, spoken of through the prophet Daniel** and **great distress, unequaled from the beginning of the world until now** are two such unmistakable clues.

One specific sign of the end would be the "abomination (*bdelugma*, meaning "detestable thing") that causes desolation" (*eremosis*, meaning "devastation, destruction, depopulation," related to *eremos*, "desert"). Jesus took this phrase from Daniel 8:13; 9:27; 11:31; 12:11, where it was used to mark a particular turning point in the events of the end times. Specifically, this "abomination" was some kind of defiling, destructive incident in the temple, which would end the practice of daily sacrifices. Jesus specified that the abomination would be **standing in the holy place**; that is, the second most sacred room in the temple.

The "holy of holies," the innermost and most sacred room, contained the ark of the covenant in Solomon's day. However, it was empty in Jesus' day because the ark had been lost centuries before. The holy place, just outside the holy of holies, held the altar of incense, the table of showbread and ten lampstands in Solomon's temple (only one lampstand in Jesus' day). Most commentators take "the holy place" to represent the entire temple complex.

A third and far greater desecration was yet to come. Both of those earlier desecrations were preludes to the ultimate desecration at the hands of "the man of sin" who was yet to come. The apostle Paul wrote of this Antichrist who will set himself up as a god at the end time (2 Thess. 2:3; Rev. 13:14–15).

Although the A.D. 70 "abomination" was almost certainly in Jesus' mind (cf. 24:2,16–20), both he and Daniel looked ahead to another such abomination in the temple, which is yet future to us. This implied, of course, that the temple will again be rebuilt on the temple mount in Jerusalem, where the Muslim Dome of the Rock has stood for the last thirteen centuries.

The warnings of 24:16–20, which related to Jewish geography and Jewish culture, prophesied most directly of the A.D. 70 destruction of Jerusalem, along with the persecution of the Jews by Rome. Jesus warned that when the "abomination" occurs (or when it seems imminent), the inhabitants of Judea (the province of Jerusalem) should **flee to the mountains**, where they could hide from persecutors (24:16).

The destruction would come so quickly that those on their flat housetops (often used for prayer) would need to descend immediately down the external stairway and escape without retrieving any supplies or valuables. Those working out in the fields would need to flee to a hiding place (24:17–18).

Those who delayed would be caught in the destruction. We do know that in A.D. 70 many Christians did flee all the way to the "hiding place" at Petra.

The ultimate fulfillment of these prophetic elements, still future, will take place when the Antichrist occupies the most holy place. Daniel 9:27 describes these events. This evil prince will "confirm a covenant with many [Israel] for one 'seven'" (or one period of seven years). In the "middle of the 'seven' he will . . . set up an abomination that causes desolation." Second Thessalonians 2:4, referring to this same event, describes this ruler setting himself up as a god in the temple.

Of course, the fact that Israel has reestablished itself as a national political entity and occupied the holy temple site again has many scholars anticipating the end times very soon. No other nation has experienced two thousand years of cultural dispersion and retained their national integrity. God is not yet finished with the Jewish people. And the Great Tribulation to come in the seventieth and final of the "seventy weeks" (periods of seven years) predicted for Israel by the prophet Daniel (Dan. 9:24–27) will see the nation purged and prepared for the return of its Messiah-King.

This period of "tribulation" is a specific period of time beginning with the abomination and ending with the second coming of Christ (Rev. 11:2; 13:5). It is during this time that the terrible judgments of Revelation 6–19 with its seals and trumpets will destroy great portions of the earth. This time of trouble will be without precedent in world history.

24:21–22. So the disciples might not underestimate the horror of this Great Tribulation, Jesus explained that it would be the worst suffering in all of history—**unequaled from the beginning of the world until now** (24:21). He added further emphasis, saying that this Tribulation would have the potential of destroying all life, leading some modern students to think of nuclear war. But whatever the means necessary to bring about such unparalleled destruction, it is evident that such a Great Tribulation is still future to us. So there is much more in mind here than the destruction of Jerusalem in A.D. 70. As bad as it was, that destruction has been multiplied in intensity on a number of occasions in the twentieth century alone.

The world has yet to see the **great distress** which will never be observed again (24:21). Jesus said as much when he indicated that those days would necessarily be **cut short**, implying divine intervention (24:22). Christ will intervene to prevent complete genocide and the wholesale destruction of the human race.

But even in judgment, the Lord will display mercy, particularly **for the sake of the elect** (plural of *eklektos,* "select, chosen ones"). These are those who have placed faith in him and followed him as his disciples. The use of the term *elect* also highlights the Lord's sovereign choice as to who these people will be. It is he who draws the faithful to himself; none of us come of our own will. This Tribulation will not reach its full destructive potential because of the Lord's intervention. By his hand, **those days will be shortened.** Because Jesus shifted into his segment answering the question regarding the timing and signs of his coming, we may infer that the Tribulation will be interrupted by Jesus' return. He will end the destruction on earth.

B The King Foretells His Second Coming (24:23–31)

SUPPORTING IDEA: *The certainty of the Messiah's return is our motivation to continue in faithful obedience in the present.*

People will be desperate for a Savior while in the midst of the greatest tribulation earth will ever know. Jesus now gave his disciples some guidelines for discerning when he was likely to return. Just as Jesus' disciples must have trembled at the fearful images of the Great Tribulation, so their hearts thrilled as he described the glory of his coming.

24:23–26. So that God's chosen followers ("the elect," 24:24) might not be fooled by false Christs and false prophets, Jesus forewarned us about them. **False Christs** would be those claiming to be the Messiah himself, while **false prophets** would be those claiming to have truth revealed by God—possibly in a hoax supporting one of the false Christs.

At the time of the Great Tribulation, there would be reports that the Christ (the Messiah) had come. And indeed there would be imposters (the **false Christs and false prophets**) who would provide **great signs and miracles** that people will take as validation of their authenticity as God's Christ or prophet (cf. the Jewish leaders' demand of a sign from Jesus in 12:38; 16:1; see also Jesus' description of miracle-working imposters in 7:21–23). These imposters would be so convincing that they would **deceive even the elect.** It is important to remember that miracles themselves do not guarantee that something is of God. Jesus had already made that point clear to the disciples (Matt. 7:21–23).

The followers of the **false Christs** would invite people to come see the imposters **in the desert,** or **in the inner rooms.** But Jesus commanded his followers not to follow such guidance and not to believe those who invited them. Jesus the Messiah came in this manner the first time, as one group of people could find in the desert or in a house. But his second advent would be quite different.

24:27–28. The word **For** tells us why we should not believe the Messiah will be seen in a single location on earth. When he comes, the whole world will know! Unlike his first advent—through natural birth into a human body and thirty-four years of life as a man—the **coming of the Son of Man** (here Jesus used the title with its full messianic impact) will be like **lightning,** which **comes from the east** and **is visible even in the west.**

The picture is that of a bolt of lightning, flashing all the way across the sky, from horizon to horizon, in an instant. Jesus was about to tell us more about his coming (24:29–31), but this alone distinguished him from all the imposters at the end of the age. They would be mere men, lingering about in one place or another, while he would come suddenly and visibly, and he would not be limited to a single location.

Coming (*parousia*) is a word that appears here for the first time. It becomes an important word for the apostle Paul, who used it to describe the second coming (e.g., 1 Cor. 15:23, 1 Thess. 2:19; 3:13). Other New Testament writers used it as well (e.g., Jas. 5:7–8; 2 Pet. 3:4; 1 John 2:28).

24:29. This verse jumped to the very end of the Tribulation and pointed out that it would be marked by signals of cosmic proportion. **Immediately after the distress of those days**, which will be interrupted by the Messiah's coming, still more signs will make Christ's coming unmistakable. **The sun will be darkened, and the moon will not give its light.** This sign had been prophesied often in the Old Testament in connection with God's final judgment (Isa. 13:10; 24:23; Ezek. 32:7–8; Joel 2:10,31; 3:14–16; Amos 5:20; 8:9; Zech. 14:6; Zeph. 1:15; see also Acts 2:20; Rev. 6:12–17; 8:12). **The stars will fall from the sky** (literally, "from heaven"; see Isa. 34:4; Rev. 6:13). **And the heavenly bodies will be shaken** is not a direct Old Testament quote. Jesus used it to summarize the preceding celestial phenomena.

The Messiah's coming will be accompanied by supernatural manipulations of celestial bodies—or at least manipulations of their appearance, or their ability to give light. These signs in the sky will be such that all people of earth can see them and realize that the Messiah is coming. If only one of these signs were given, it might be explained away as an eclipse or a meteor shower. But all of them together can be caused only by the hand of God.

The second coming of Christ to establish his kingdom on earth will be a majestic event that will extend over many hours. The earth and its occupants will be forced to watch, amazed, as the armies of the hosts of heaven descend to the earth in the vicinity of the Mount of Olives (Zech. 14:4).

24:30. Whether **the sign of the Son of Man** that **will appear in the sky** is an additional sign or a repeated mention of the phenomena of 24:29, the point is that his coming will be unmistakable. This probably refers to Christ himself appearing in the heavens. Perhaps this should be read, "the sign that is the Son of Man," implying that he himself will be the final sign as he descends visibly to earth. This interpretation is supported by the remainder of this verse. He will come in such an obvious way that **all the nations of the earth** will see him.

Using a direct quote from Daniel 7:13, Jesus described **the Son of Man coming on the clouds of the sky.** These may be literal clouds or the cloud of God's glory, as often seen in the Old Testament. Only the divine Messiah could come in such a fashion. Thus, it is natural that he would be coming **with power and great glory.** His arrival will be terrifying to all the people on earth, particularly those who oppose him. They will **mourn** because his coming implies their judgment.

24:31. The only people not mourning at the Messiah's return will be **his elect** (24:22,24). The **loud trumpet call** brings to mind the royal herald, who announced the coming of a king with fanfare with his trumpet. As he comes, the Messiah will send out his angels to gather his faithful disciples **from the four winds** (i.e., the four points of the compass), **from one end of the heavens to the other.** These phrases imply "from every part of the earth" since the gospel will have gone out to all nations (24:14). Jesus' use of the angels as "harvesters" of the faithful echoes his teaching in 13:39–43,49–50.

The trumpet is an Old Testament image. It was used sometimes in connection with the Lord "gathering together" his faithful, as in Yahweh's fearful appearance on Mount Sinai while Israel cowered at the foot of the mountain (Exod. 19:16); the gathering of worshipers to the holy mountain in Jerusalem (Isa. 27:13); and the march of Yahweh's army (Zech. 9:14; see also Deut. 30:4; 1 Cor. 15:52; 1 Thess. 4:16; Heb. 12:19; Rev. 8:2; 11:15).

This section (Matt. 24:15–31) was intended to answer the disciples' question about the sign of the end of the age and Jesus' second coming.

C The King's Certain Return at an Uncertain Time (24:32–41)

SUPPORTING IDEA: *The Messiah is certain to come, but we cannot know when he will come.*

Having described questions about the turbulent end of the age and his own glorious return, the king continued to answer, in more detail, the disciples' question (24:3) regarding the "sign" of his coming. When it comes to knowing the time of Jesus' return, the answer is twofold. First, the signs he had already provided gave some idea of the general "season" in history in which he will return (24:32–35). They also underscored the certainty of his return. Second, we must understand that no one but the Father knows the exact "day or hour" of Christ's coming (24:36–41). This uncertainty led naturally into Jesus' teaching on how to be prepared at all times for his return (24:42–25:46).

24:32–33. The second half of the Olivet Discourse (24:42–25:46) is characterized by application and heavy use of parables. Jesus' brief use of the **lesson from the fig tree** foreshadowed the latter portion of the discourse, beginning to edge the listener toward application of the teaching Jesus had provided.

An observer could watch a fig tree begin to produce leaves (and green fruit) in late spring as a sign that **summer is near.** In the same way, an observer of history who knows the preceding teachings of Jesus was now equipped to **know** when the Messiah's coming is **near, right at the door.** This implies immediacy, but still not a specific time.

24:34–35. Jesus alerted his disciples to the importance of his next statement with **I tell you the truth.** He promised that **this generation will certainly not pass away until all these things have happened.**

Jesus underscored the faithfulness and reliability of his teaching (24:35). His words will stand even after **heaven and earth . . . pass away.** Jesus' words are firmer than earth's bedrock, more sound than the foundations of heaven (cf. Ps. 119:89–90; Isa. 40:6–8). Christ's words are more certain than even the existence of the universe.

The disciples would put their lives repeatedly on the line. Jesus knew they needed strong assurance that his review of future history was accurate and that their hardship for his sake would be worth the cost.

24:36. The disciples were equipped to know, by the signs, the general season of the Messiah's return. Those signs were as reliable as the word of the One who gave them the signs. But they were not to go so far as to think they could know the exact **day or hour** of the Christ's coming. **But** draws the contrast between what they were able to know and what they were not.

Not only were the disciples to remain ignorant of the exact timing of the Christ's coming, but **not even the angels in heaven, nor the Son** knew the time. This particular detail belonged to **the Father.** The contrast between **Son** and **Father** draws attention to the Son's submission to the Father's will. The Son trusted and obeyed the Father even though there were critical details which God did not reveal to him.

That the time of the Christ's second coming is unknown motivates most of Jesus' applicational teaching in the remainder of the discourse (24:42–25:46). He used the uncertain timing to challenge his followers to be ready at all times, in case he should return.

This teaching is also a warning to those who claim to know the time of Christ's return. Such claims have been made for centuries, and, as each one passes, the Messiah has still not come. One would think that people would learn from experience, if not from Jesus' own teaching. These speculations are foolish and disobedient. They ignore Jesus' teaching to believers to be obedient and ready at all times.

24:37–39. As an illustration further clarifying the inability of anyone to know the time of **the coming of the Son of Man,** Jesus drew upon history—the time of Noah. The sinful people of that day were unprepared for God's judgment. They were **eating and drinking, marrying and giving in marriage.**

Their worldly lifestyle was an ongoing pattern. It would have gone on without interruption if God had not brought the Flood.

The people continued in their self-indulgence **up to the day Noah entered the ark.** They had an entire century to observe Noah and his sons building the ark and to hear Noah's testimony concerning God's anger at their sin and the coming judgment. But they did not recognize the warning until it was too late. The judgment of the Flood **took them all away,** because they remained stubborn and ignorant of their coming doom.

Echoing the opening phrase of 24:37, Jesus closed with, **That is how it will be at the coming of the Son of Man.** Those who heeded Jesus' warnings and watched for the signs would be saved. Those who ignored them would find sudden judgment coming upon them before they could realize what was happening or why. Notice that this verse has nothing to do with the rapture of the church. The ones taken are not the believers but the unbelievers, as was true in Noah's day.

24:40–41. By way of specific illustration and application, Jesus gave two examples from the contemporary lifestyle of his day. The two men working in the field and the two women grinding grain at the mill represented the average citizen. The message of this was, "Everyone needs to heed these warnings." One of each pair was prepared because he or she knew Jesus' teachings, had watched for the signs, and had remained obedient.

The other in each pair was unprepared, because he or she had either been ignorant of Jesus' teaching or else simply ignored them and not lived according to the righteous standards of the king and his kingdom. Such people were **taken** from the scene when the king returned to rule. Jesus' point was: *be prepared.* His arrival will be sudden and unpredictable.

The use of the present tense of "to take" (*paralambano*), "and "to leave" (*aphiemi*), was purposeful in order to convey the suddenness and unpredictability of the action, even though the context makes it clear the actions will happen in the future.

With this statement, Jesus completed the prophetic portion of the Olivet Discourse. He then moved into the preparation part of his teaching to help people get ready for these future events by living correctly in the present.

Always Be Ready for the Return of the King (24:42–51)

> **SUPPORTING IDEA:** *The uncertain timing of the Messiah's return should motivate us to remain faithful so we are ready whenever he comes.*

Here we come to another unfortunate decision on the part of the scholars who chose the chapter and verse divisions in our Bibles. It would have been better to start Matthew 25 here. This is where Jesus transitioned from prophecy to practical preparation in our daily living. Matthew 24:42–51 includes a practical command and the first two of a series of five illustrative parables that teach us how to live today in light of the future. Watchfulness, coupled with faithful service, is the key principle.

24:42. Therefore means, "because the time of my return will be sudden and unpredictable." This is the central turning point in the discourse. As Noah spent time and energy preparing for the Flood, so people living prior to Christ's return must spend themselves in being alert and ready for his coming.

The command is, **Keep watch** (cf. 1 Cor. 16:13; 1 Thess. 5:6; 1 Pet. 5:8; Rev. 3:2–3; 16:15). The reason for this exhortation to continual diligence was in the preceding teaching (24:36–41), which Jesus summarized in the next clause, **because you do not know on what day your Lord will come.** "Your Lord" is significant, drawing attention to the fact that we do not belong to ourselves. Rather, it is our master and creator who will return. He will call us to account.

24:43–44. Verse 43 is a brief parable illustrating the importance of readiness at all times. Jesus emphasized its importance with the introductory **But understand this.** Each of us is like an **owner of the house** who is about to be robbed. Not only is he unaware of the time of the robber's coming, but he does not even know he is a target. If the ignorance persists, it represents the ignorance of a person who fails to heed Jesus' warning about the future.

Now the head of the house, if he is informed, will be aware of the likelihood of being robbed, just as we know that Jesus is returning and that judgment will accompany his coming. But he does not know the time a robber might come, just as we do not know the time of Christ's return. **So you also must be ready** (24:44). Not only is the Son of Man coming at an unknown hour, but even at a time that would seem least likely to us (**when you do not expect him**). If we are taken by surprise, it is not because God is out to trick us but because of our own apathetic self-deception or negligence.

24:45–47. Jesus then began a second parable (24:45–51), illustrating in greater detail the principle that we should be ready at all times for his return. This parable adds more understanding to the nature of our task on earth, specifically in our relationships with other people. Jesus used the imagery of a servant relating to other servants.

The challenge is to be like a **faithful and wise servant** of God, being a steward for him in whatever he entrusts to us. The master's **household,** including his possessions and other slaves, was very close to his heart. A wise servant will find obedience in his own best interest. It is only **wise** to do what is right with what God has given us.

It is a precious thing God entrusts to us—the stewardship of other lives as well as wealth. He wants us to live by loving others as ourselves (22:39). Anything else is neglect of responsibility and abuse of others.

The master is certain to return. Blessed is the servant who is faithful at all times and who is found obedient whenever the master returns. In fact, the master will entrust this faithful servant with **all his possessions** because the servant was faithful with some of his possessions.

24:48–51. If, on the other hand, the servant is evil, he will take his chances on whether the master will come soon or not. Assuming the master **is staying away a long time**, he will act selfishly and abusively toward the other servants and keep bad company.

The **servant** of God who tries to live licentiously for a time, planning to clean up his life before the Lord returns, will find himself in a trap. Not only is it obedient to stay the course of faithfulness, but it is a lot less work than trying to reform a corrupt life.

Because the evil servant is lulled into a sense of false security, the master will be certain to come **on a day when he does not expect him and at an hour he is not aware of.** The evil servant deceived himself and had no excuse when the Lord returned with judgment. To **cut him to pieces** means "to cut a person in two. This was a form of judgment used in ancient times. The picture is one of severe judgment. The **weeping and gnashing of teeth** indicates deep remorse by those who will suffer such great loss.

MAIN IDEA REVIEW: *In light of the future reality of hardship and ultimate salvation, we must stay ready for Christ's return (and his rewards) at all times by living in loving obedience.*

III. CONCLUSION

The coming of the Messiah will be unmistakable, accompanied by miraculous signs in the sky and his visible return. Do not be fooled by anything less. Watch for the signs, that you may become aware of the "season" of history in which the Messiah might return. But we should not expect to know exactly when the Messiah will return. Our task is to be continually obedient and faithful, always ready for the Messiah's return.

PRINCIPLES

- History is filled with many horrible things—wars, famines, earthquakes—but we must be careful not to assume that these things mean the end is near.
- We as believers will encounter persecution, including persecution by those who formerly claimed to be believers, as well as hatred from nations and a growing abandonment of God's righteous values.
- No man knows when the Son of Man will return.

APPLICATIONS

- Be careful about placing confidence in past successes or religious monuments rather than in continued faithfulness to the Lord.
- Be discerning of false teachers; they can be convincing, thus deceiving negligent believers.
- In spite of all the hardships, we must endure faithfully to the end.
- Serve as God's instruments to take the gospel to all peoples of the earth.
- Find hope in the promise of the final gathering of the faithful out of the world.
- Be always alert and ready for the return of Christ.

IV. LIFE APPLICATION

Are You Ready?

Many years ago, while traveling out-of-town, a businessman attended a Sunday morning worship service at a large church in Texas. As is customary during most church services, a portion of the time was devoted to important announcements, which the pastor stood up to deliver. One of the announcements was with regard to the sermon topic of that evening's worship service. The sermon title was "Jesus Is Coming!" Its focus would be on Jesus' return and the need for Christians to be ready for this event.

As the pastor wound up his invitation to attend the evening service, he quickly concluded by adding, "Remember, 'Jesus Is Coming!' at seven o'clock this evening." Immediately chuckles could be heard across the large sanctuary. The pastor, after realizing how his statement must have sounded to some of his listeners, simply smiled and moved on.

Although humorous, his statement was somewhat of a stopper for the businessman, he found himself visualizing the possibility of seeing Jesus that evening. The pastor's unintended remark made solid contact with the vistor. It's a question we all do well to ask: Am I ready?

Matthew 24 teaches that we are to watch for the signs of his coming. Our task is to be continually obedient and faithful, always ready for his return. Are you ready?

V. PRAYER

Lord, it is enough for me to know that you will return some day. I trust the details of your coming to the Father and to his timing. In the meantime, make me an obedient and watchful servant of yours in your kingdom. Amen.

VI. DEEPER DISCOVERIES

A. The Temple

The temple was more to Israel than a beautiful building of worship. It was the sign of God's presence and blessing on the nation. When the temple was defiled or destroyed, it was a sign that God's back had been turned against Israel for its covenant disobedience. The worst thing that could happen to Yahweh's covenant people was to lose Yahweh himself (see the false confidence in the temple by covenant breakers in Jer. 7:4–15, the context of Jesus' "den of robbers" quote in 21:13). Jesus' statement would have shocked the disciples and any other Jews who might have been listening.

B. The Abomination of Desolation

The "abomination" was one of the signals with multiple fulfillments. It clearly referred to the defilement of the temple (Dan. 11:31) under Antiochus Ephiphanes (168 B.C.), the Syrian ruler who sacrificed a pig to Zeus on the temple altar in Jerusalem. Then it was desecrated again in A.D. 70 with the destruction of Jerusalem and the temple by Rome. The Roman legions raised Rome's standards on the temple site, elevating the supposedly divine emperor Caesar in the place of Yahweh.

C. "This Generation" and "All These Things"

Some take the Greek word *genea* to mean "race," referring to the human race. Thus, his promise would be the same as that in 24:22—that he would preserve at least a remnant of the human race to the end of history when **all these things** will be fulfilled. While this is a possible interpretation, it does not add anything to our understanding of the passage.

But we can keep the above interpretation of "all these things" (to include the end times) *and* accept the meaning of *genea* as a literal "generation" by interpreting "this generation" as the generation alive in the end times. This again implies a promise not to destroy all human life existing at the time (cf. 24:22). It may mean that these events will occur in such rapid succession that they will take place within one single generation. Probably all of these interpretive elements are accurate as "all these things" include a wide assortment of prophetic aspects—the Antichrist, the tribulation period, and the second coming of Christ in great glory.

It is possible that "generation" means "race," referring to the Jewish people or Israel as a nation. Perhaps it means that they will not cease to exist, that God will fulfill his covenant program with them. This would explain the phenomenon of Israel's maintaining an identity in spite of nearly two thousand years of national obliteration.

VII. TEACHING OUTLINE

A. INTRODUCTION

1. Lead Story: Be Prepared

2. Context: Matthew's placement of the five discourses has been carefully planned throughout his Gospel.

   The Sermon on the Mount (Matt. 5–7) was linked with Jesus' launching of his public ministry (4:12–25) since it laid the foundation of God's kingdom people and provided a verbal display of Jesus' authority. The Matthew 10 discourse followed the theme of authority from the preceding chapters as the king delegated that same authority to his disciples.

   The parable discourse (Matt. 13) was Jesus' response to the rejection he received in Matthew 11–12. The parables of the discourse were enigmatic only to those who continued to reject him. For those who listened "spiritually," the parables built their understanding of the kingdom, preparing them for the church age. The Matthew 18 discourse followed on the heels of Jesus' pivotal announcement that he would build his church (16:18), providing principles on how to build his church. Jesus would soon leave his ministry in the hands of the Twelve; this discourse prepared them with specifics on how to proceed with his church.

   The Olivet Discourse (Matt. 24–25; named after its setting on the Mount of Olives) followed immediately after the conflicts between Jesus and the religious leaders (Matt. 21–23). The discourse clarified God's judgment on the Messiah's opponents and prepared the Messiah's faithful followers for the end.

3. Transition: Matthew 24–25 is a single unit, but it falls into two distinct portions—prophecy and preparation. In 24:1–41, Jesus foretold details of the coming judgment and his return. In all of Matthew, this was Jesus' strongest and most detailed emphasis on future events. Then there was a turning point at 24:42 ("therefore"). In 24:42–25:46, Jesus prepared his people to be ready when the judgment came. The first portion of the discourse consisted of factual details about the future, while the second portion consisted of commands. These commands were illustrated by five parables that showed believers how to live today in order to be prepared for the future judgment.

B. COMMENTARY

1. The King Foretells the Fall of Jerusalem and the End of the Age (24:1–22)
2. The King Foretells His Second Coming (24:23–31)
3. The King's Certain Return at an Uncertain Time (24:32–41)
4. Always Be Ready for the Return of the King (24:42–51)

C. CONCLUSION

1. Wrap-up: In light of the future reality of hardship and ultimate salvation, we must stay ready for Christ's return at all times by living in loving obedience. When he returns, we must give account for our lives and service.
2. Personal Challenge: Are you living your life in light of the reality that Jesus could come back at any moment? What specific differences does that belief make in your life?

VIII. ISSUES FOR DISCUSSION

1. What is the purpose of all Bible prophecy?
1. According to Jesus, what would happen to the beautiful temple in Jerusalem?
2. What did Jesus have to say about false prophets and false Christs in this chapter of Matthew?
3. What did Jesus mean by his statement, "This generation will certainly not pass away until all these things have happened"?

Matthew 25

The King Challenges His People

The main thing is that the main thing always remain the main thing.

German Proverb

Matthew 25

IN A NUTSHELL

Chapter 25 is the second part of the Olivet Discourse. It presents three parables Jesus delivered to teach his followers how to live in the present in light of future certainties. Jesus challenges his followers to remain faithfully obedient until his return and to use their gifts to minister to the needs of fellow believers.

The King Challenges His People

I. INTRODUCTION

Be Goal-Oriented

*T*hey were crosstown high school rivals, looking back on generations of dog-eat-dog competition. It was the biggest game of the season. And both teams were shot through with adrenaline. A basketball legend would be built this night.

The first half of play ended with only a single point separating the teams. Rules at the time still required a center jump at the start of the second half. Our guys controlled the tip and ran their fast break to absolute perfection—a textbook break all the way. The center tipped it to the head of the jump circle. The big forward handled it and passed it over his head like a bullet to the guard breaking down the side. The guard rifled it to the other guard breaking down the opposite side. He dribbled the ball once, and laid it up perfectly into the little white square on the backboard just above the hoop. The ball kissed the glass and dropped for two points. The crowd went nuts.

Then stunned silence. Everyone noticed it at the same time—fans, players, coaches, and referees. Wrong basket! Incredible! Our guys had done everything right, except for one thing. They forgot which goal was theirs. And they lost the game that night by one point. As it turned out, they had put the winning difference in the goal of the other team.

We can understand the game perfectly. We can execute the plays masterfully. But if we forget the main thing—the goal—we can lose. The main thing is that the main thing always remain the main thing.

And it is that way with prophecy. We can study the details from now until Jesus comes back, but prophecy is not about studying future details. Its main purpose is to challenge us to live well in the present. The Bible gives us a glimpse of the future to motivate us in the present. Jesus was teaching us that there is a vast difference between *investing* and *spending* your life. Most Christians just spend theirs. Jesus is disgusted with such passive disobedience. He wants us to invest our lives in the kingdom of the future. The apostle John said just that: "Everyone who has this hope in him purifies himself, just as he is pure" (1 John 3:3). The primary purpose of biblical prophecy is to motivate us to holy living here and now.

The central point of Matthew 25 is essentially the same as Matthew 24, since both are part of the same unified discourse. The parables of Matthew 25 are intended to teach us how to live today in light of tomorrow's certainties. The second parable (25:14–30) brings out the variety of giftings and abilities in different people, enabling them to manage different responsibilities within the kingdom. It also makes the point that each person is responsible to be 100 percent faithful with everything he or she is given by God. And the amount of fruit we bear, compared with someone else, is not necessarily reflective of our degree of faithfulness.

The closing judgment account (25:31–46) focuses on the fact that caring for Jesus' followers is the same as caring for him. It also brings out, more clearly than anywhere else in the book, our future accounting for the way we have used our opportunities for kingdom ministry in this life. So, in light of our prophetic future, let us strive to live well now.

II. COMMENTARY

The King Challenges His People

MAIN IDEA: *In light of the future reality of hardship and ultimate salvation, we must stay ready for Christ's return at all times by living in loving obedience, and he will reward us for it.*

Matthew 25 should have started with 24:42. That is the turning point in Jesus' Olivet Discourse. In Matthew 24:4–41, Jesus provided doctrinal exposition on future events, in answer to the disciples' question about the timing and signs of the destruction of the temple, and about Jesus' coming and the end of the age (24:3). But from 24:42 through chapter 25, Jesus builds on the preceding doctrinal foundation with a series of five parables exhorting his disciples to be alert and busy about the work of the kingdom. Because he might return at any time, we will want to be found ready to face him.

So, as we begin Matthew 25, we find ourselves already into the application portion of the discourse. The first two parables have already been presented in 24:42–51: the parable of the thief (24:43), emphasizing the suddenness of Christ's return and our need to be on the alert; and the parable of the servant (24:45–51), emphasizing the importance of caring lovingly for others, that Christ might find us obedient whenever he returns.

The last three parables make up Matthew 25. They continue to exhort Jesus' disciples toward watchfulness (an enduring theme based on the uncertain timing of his return, 24:36–41). But each story makes its unique contribution to the theme. The first (ten virgins, 25:1–13) presents the theme of wisdom in being prepared for Christ's return, and especially emphasizes the long delay before his return as well as the unexpectedness when he does return.

The second parable (ten talents, 25:14–30) illustrates a theme introduced by Jesus in 13:12. It focuses on the variety of responsibilities entrusted by Christ to his disciples before his return as well as the variety of abilities to handle his trust and the variety of rewards for our faithful stewardship.

The third story (sheep and goats, 25:31–46) is not technically a parable. It gives us an actual glimpse of a scene in true future history, before the judgment seat of God. But this passage serves much the same purpose as the four parables of 24:42–25:30, and it belongs in series with them. It emphasizes the importance of caring for Jesus' followers, which is the same as caring for him.

Jesus' disciples revealed by the nature of their question (24:3) that they were hopeful of getting past all the hardship and into the eternal kingdom. But Jesus used this discourse to answer their question and to correct their perspective. They were focused on the end result. In maintaining this focus, they lost sight of the task to be completed before the Messiah's return. Jesus used the parable to bring their focus back to the present. He taught them about the future to motivate them toward present obedience.

▲ The King Says, "Do Not Delay or Put Off Faithfulness —I Am Coming" (25:1–13)

SUPPORTING IDEA: *Be prepared for a long obedience.*

25:1. This parable, like most of Jesus' other parables, taught another aspect of reality in the kingdom of heaven. The **virgins** were the bridesmaids invited to be a part of the wedding ceremony. This was a great honor. They represent all who have been invited to be citizens of God's kingdom—some of whom, as we shall see, will indeed enter the kingdom and some of whom will not. The bridegroom is the Messiah, and the wedding celebration pictures the eschatological wedding feast of Christ.

All ten bridesmaids **went out to meet the bridegroom**, and the foolish ones were disappointed at the end of the story. This seems to indicate that they represent people who want to be a part of the kingdom. Even the unbelieving want to be in heaven for eternity, but they are not wise enough to choose the correct path. It was an evening wedding, meaning that the bridesmaids had to carry lights during the processional to the groom's house.

25:2–4. The ten bridesmaids separated themselves into two groups by their own wisdom or foolishness. This represents the self-sorting of the faithful and the unfaithful in real life.

The five **foolish** (the Gr. word *moros* from which we derive our word "moron" for dull, inattentive, unthinking) bridesmaids were introduced first. They took insufficient oil with them to keep their lamps burning for the wedding procession. Although they wanted to participate in the celebration, they displayed a lack of respect for the bride and bridegroom through their neglect of their responsibility to come prepared. They demonstrated their unworthiness of the honor of participating in the celebration. The faithless will not enter heaven. By their lack of preparation in this life, they reveal a lack of respect for the Messiah. How a person sees Jesus is the key to his or her eternal destiny.

The five **wise** bridesmaids demonstrated their respect and love for the bride and bridegroom by coming well prepared with oil to keep their torches burning throughout the procession. Similarly, the faithful will enter heaven. By their preparation in this life, they reveal a love and respect for the Messiah.

The lamps and the oil in the parable have no direct parallel in reality. They serve only as elements necessary to the wedding theme of the parable. The key point of comparison between the parable and real life is the need for preparation and readiness and the respect for the "bridegroom" that readiness implies.

25:5–9. The bridegroom's delay represents the stretch of history between the Messiah's first coming and his return. Jesus acknowledged that the length of time before his return would be difficult to endure. All ten of the bridesmaids—both the wise and the foolish—fell asleep while waiting for the bridegroom. This is understandable for anyone under those circumstances. The sleep did not imply spiritual negligence; the wise bridesmaids were so well prepared that they could afford to sleep. But the foolish bridesmaids should have used the time to get the oil they needed.

At midnight, which implied a long wait, the bridegroom's arrival was finally announced. The bridesmaids were called out to meet him, with their lamps burning. All ten bridesmaids prepared their lamps for the procession, but the five foolish bridesmaids realized they did not prepare adequately.

The exact details of the wedding procession are not important to the parable. The bridesmaids' readiness or lack of readiness, in light of the bridegroom's delay, is at the center of the story.

The foolish bridesmaids begged the wise bridesmaids to share their oil. But the wise ones told the foolish ones that they had to obtain their own oil. It was too late to prepare. The unfaithful will discover too late that they have spent their lives foolishly, failing to trust and respect the Messiah-King. An additional important insight is taught here: Preparedness cannot be transferred or shared.

25:10–12. The foolish bridesmaids attempted to make up for their lack of preparation at the last minute. But they were too late; the bridegroom had arrived. He found only the five wise bridesmaids ready for him. They went on without the foolish ones. The door was closed, not to be opened for anyone else, primarily because of the insult the foolish bridesmaids had paid to the bride and bridegroom. The closed door speaks of being shut out of the kingdom.

When the five foolish bridesmaids finally arrived at the **wedding banquet,** they begged to be allowed in. But the bridegroom, offended at their lack of respect, denied them entrance. His **I tell you the truth** implied that there was no negotiating; he would not change his mind. The time had passed. And his words, **I don't know you,** disowned any past or future relationship with the five. His response cut them off from him and his bride for life.

For those who have failed to acknowledge the Messiah-King throughout their lives and realize only at the last minute the consequences of such foolishness, all their last-minute attempts to make things right will be too little, too late. They have already demonstrated the overriding quality of their character—unbelieving rebellion.

25:13. Jesus' closing exhortation is the central application point of the parable, using almost exactly the same wording as when Jesus first introduced the command in 24:42. As in 24:42, we find again the present tense with the imperative mood of the verb *gregoreo,* which means, "be staying continually awake, constantly keeping watch." And the same reason is given—we **do not know the day or the hour** of Christ's return. Our preparedness for Christ's coming demonstrates our personal trust and respect for him.

B The King Says, "Invest Your Life for Me" (25:14–30)

> **SUPPORTING IDEA:** *Believers must live continually on the edge of faith-filled obedience, investing everything they have and are for the kingdom.*

The preceding parable emphasized that we must always be ready, but it did not reveal anything about the specific ways to live. In this parable, and in the final account of the judgment (25:31–46), Jesus gave his disciples some practical direction about how to live in readiness for his return.

This parable demonstrates how saving faith in the Messiah will manifest itself in practical terms. This parable seems to go beyond the first three in that it takes the watchfulness to new levels of practical obedience and, therefore, to reward. The true disciples' readiness will involve careful stewardship of assets during the king's absence in anticipation of reward.

25:14–15. This parable begins immediately with the word **again** (*hosper,* meaning "just as, even as," an abbreviated version of the introductory formula in 25:1). This is another parable teaching something about the kingdom of heaven. A man (representing Jesus) was about to set out on a journey (representing the time before Jesus' return; cf. 21:33). While he was gone, he needed to be sure that **his property** was well cared for, so he called **his servants** and entrusted (*paradidomi,* "hand over") his possessions to them before leaving.

Every Christian is entrusted with some responsibility for the kingdom. Some will take this seriously and invest their lives wisely, and others will squander this responsibility. The part of the kingdom entrusted to each of us is precious to the Lord. He is hurt by the mishandling of a lifetime of opportunity; but he rejoices over a lifetime well spent. He has placed in our hands what is his own. This is a sobering thought—to be stewards of kingdom resources.

One unique element in this parable is the different property entrusted to each servant—five talents to one, two talents to the second, and one talent to the third, **each according to his ability**. The Lord knows us, and he knows the full potential of each person for serving the kingdom. He designed that potential into each of us when he created us. No one is entrusted with more than he can handle, but neither is he entrusted with less than he can handle.

The person entrusted with little will be required to do all he can with the little he has been given. All of us are to live up to our full potential, by God's strength, with his wisdom, for his kingdom. This stewardship is comprehensive. It includes time, talents, spiritual gifts, energies, personality, experiences, attitudes, and material resources.

25:16–18. The phrase **At once** implied prompt obedience on the part of the first servant (as well as the second; note **so also** in 25:17). These two servants did not miss a single opportunity to bring their master a return on his investment. They **put his money to work**, meaning they invested for a profit. Each doubled the amount entrusted to him during his master's absence. There was no doubt that the first two servants worked hard for the master.

Investing resources (e.g., money, energy, abilities) has always been a risky business. Even the wisest investor risks losing increases if something happens at the wrong time (e.g., a famine, a war). Implied in the two faithful servants' actions here was a certain amount of risk. But it was obedient risk. They were expected to do what was prudent—what would normally turn a profit, based on their wisdom drawn from life experience.

Believers also are required to obey Jesus in all things, even when risk is involved, even when we do not see the end results. This is not the same as foolish extravagance or taking risks to test the Lord, without the likelihood of a return on the investment. It does not mean taking chances without thinking ahead. But it implies a life lived on the edge of faith. Such a consistently obedient, faith-filled life pleases the Lord and accomplishes his kingdom purposes.

In contrast, the third servant—who had received one talent—played it safe by burying his talent and waiting for his master's return. His life failed to realize any impact or gain for his master. He demonstrated an appalling lack of understanding of his master. He clearly did not know him very well. Too many so-called "believers" fail to believe the Lord enough to obey him, revealing a lack of faith through passive spirituality and failure to step out in "risky" obedience.

25:19–23. The phrase **after a long time** was Jesus' acknowledgment that there would be quite a time gap before his final coming. It also implied significant opportunity for kingdom gain by those he has entrusted with kingdom resources. Now it was time to settle their accounts, and the servants brought the master's property to him.

Jesus used the threefold pattern of story telling, which was so common in that age. The first two repetitions established a pattern, and the third became a contrasting departure from this pattern. The first two servants brought the original quantity he had given them, plus a 100 percent profit. Between the two of them, they had turned seven talents into fourteen. The master gave the identical response to each of the first two servants. Even though the second servant had earned only two talents, in contrast to the five of the first, each had lived up to 100 percent of his potential.

The master's **well done** was the greatest reward a loyal servant could have hoped for. He called each of them a **good and faithful servant.** The two adjectives together describe a person who is reliable because of his loyalty and good character, as evidenced by the investment of his ability. In addition to verbal praise, the master rewarded each of the first two servants with even greater responsibility (cf. 24:47). They had been **faithful with a few things,** so he would entrust them with even more (**many things**). And finally, he invited them both to **share your master's happiness.**

The point is clear. When the king returns, he will require an accounting from all of us. Those who have consistently invested their lives obediently and wisely, according to heaven's priorities will have a return to offer the king. This return may include personal growth and maturity, souls brought into the kingdom, spiritual infants who have been raised to maturity, needs compassionately ministered to, wounds healed, conflicts reconciled, truth lovingly told. The investment we will have made for this return will be all we have been entrusted with in this life: our time, wealth, opportunities, relationships, natural talents and spiritual gifts, a mind and a conscience, as well as God's Word, God's Spirit, and God's church.

The **well done** awaiting such a servant is the music of eternity—full reward for the person who has been truly loyal to the master. But much more awaits the good and faithful servant of the Messiah. The faithful servant will have even more privilege and responsibility as well as a share in the master's happiness. By living their lives fully vested in kingdom interests and growth, they had gained an entrance into the kingdom (cf. 2 Pet. 1:5–11).

25:24–25. Finally, the third servant came to answer to the master for the opportunity he had received. Presenting the master's one talent to him—no more, no less—the servant explained that he kept the talent safe out of fear—

fear of the master's hardness, expecting return where he had made no invest-ment (**harvesting where you have not sown and gathering where you have not scattered seed**). The servant feared the master's wrath if he should lose the master's talent, so he buried it safely to return what was his. He toiled to "keep his nose clean," so to speak. This servant did not know the heart of his king. He did not contribute to the kingdom's advancement.

The first two servants acted out of loving loyalty, but the third acted out of selfish fear. The first two were motivated by the hope of pleasing the mas-ter; the third by fear of displeasing him. The two motives sound the same, but the end result is quite different. A certain "fear of the Lord" is critical to holy, faithful living (Prov. 1:7; 1 Pet. 1:17). But this is not paralyzing fear. Healthy fear is accompanied by a knowledge of the love of God, while paralyzing fear knows nothing of God's love. This man wasted his investment and failed to advance the kingdom.

25:26–28. The master's response to the third servant revealed that the servant's motive was actually evil, disloyal, and unloving. **You wicked, lazy servant** stands in dramatic contrast to "good and faithful servant" (25:21,23), implying that the servant's laziness was not because of a lack of ability or opportunity. The servant's "safe" behavior and apparent desire not to dis-please the master were smokescreens for his self-serving and disobedient heart. In reality, he refused to take any risks or do any work. He did not spend himself in the kingdom's interest. He was selfish, lazy, and arrogant.

The master used this servant's own words against him. He explained that his demanding character should have challenged the servant all the more to invest the talent. This was obviously the master's will—to gain some return. Even a small return from interest would show some degree of loyal obedience.

The master commanded that the third servant's small amount of respon-sibility be taken from him and given to the first servant, who had shown great responsibility. Our God is a God of high standards, demanding much from his servants. But he never demands more than we can produce because we are empowered by his love, wisdom, and power.

This servant's limited knowledge of his master—he knew only the man's stern side but not his love—was his excuse to handle his master's wealth irre-sponsibly. Many believers today know only a God of rules and wrath, so they float passively and attempt to excuse their sins of omission. God has given them ample opportunity to learn of his love (11:29), but their own undisci-plined hearts make them blindly foolish, and they squander their lifetimes. They call themselves Christians, but they are biding their time, trying to "stay out of trouble," awaiting glory in heaven. Perhaps Jesus sensed this behind the disciples' question (24:3).

In our lifestyle of comfort in Western culture, we are too easily lulled to sleep. We fail to live the life of obedient, faith-filled "risk," and so we fail to bear kingdom fruit, displeasing our Master. Such action will come back to haunt us at the judgment seat of Christ.

25:29–30. Before proclaiming the evil servant's recompense, Jesus put into the master's mouth the central point of the parable. **Everyone who has** implies faithfulness with what has been entrusted to them. This will be rewarded with even greater trust—privileged responsibility and reward—from God. Such faithful servants will **have an abundance.** Every need and desire will be met, and more.

But **whoever does not have** implies self-centered unfaithfulness with what was entrusted. This will be recompensed with the removal of all that has been entrusted to him, since he had proven untrustworthy. It is clear that this servant will not share in the rewards of the king (8:12; 22:13). He had squandered his lifetime of opportunity.

Ⓒ The King Says, "Receive My Followers as You Would Receive Me" (25:31–46)

> **SUPPORTING IDEA:** Minister to the needs of others—especially fellow believers—as though they were the Messiah himself.

This final section of Jesus' discourse involves evaluation or judgment. Jesus spoke in the previous two parables about judgment coming on the unprepared. In this last parable he focused on all the nations. **When the Son of Man comes in his glory** reminds us of Daniel 7:13–14 and of the future reign of Christ (Rev. 5:9; 20:4–6).

While this passage has parabolic elements (the shepherd, the sheep, the goats, and the process of sorting), it is not a parable but an apocalyptic glimpse into the day of judgment—a real event in future history. The simile of 25:32–33 serves to help us understand how the judgment will be carried out.

This passage is intended to be part of the series that began in 24:42. It serves the same purpose as the preceding four parables—to motivate us toward obedience, in preparation for the future.

More specifically, this passage provides a clearer explanation of how we are to be ready and on the alert, awaiting the Messiah's return. We are to fill our lives with care for the needs of others, especially the needs of fellow believers, realizing that every unbeliever is a potential "brother" of the Messiah. This is truly the work of the kingdom.

This passage builds on the principle in 25:26 that failure to utilize our gifts for the Master (sins of omission) as well as overt acts of evil (sins of commission) will be judged. Sins of omission are as serious to God as sins of commission.

While this passage may seem to advocate salvation by works, note that faith in the Messiah is the basis for these acts of mercy. These works are the evidence of saving faith, not the means to salvation. They are done "because of" one's salvation, not "in order to" gain it.

It is fitting that the Olivet Discourse should end with a judgment scene. This is also the final story in Jesus' formal teaching ministry, as recorded by Matthew. Jesus will soon leave behind all the potential "sheep and goats" of earth. It will be up to them to respond to him one way or the other—in acceptance or rejection—before his next coming.

25:31–33. In clear view here is **when the Son of Man comes**, introduced already in 24:3,27,29–31,37,39,42,44. Jesus was referring one final time to the disciples' question concerning the time of his coming (24:3). The Messiah's coming will be accompanied by **all the angels**, implying power and glory (cf. 16:21) as well as alluding to the gathering of the faithful (24:31). Further adding to the majesty of this picture is the fact that **he will sit on this throne in heavenly glory.** The Messiah will be seen in full display of his absolute authority in view of **all the nations** (cf. 24:14; also see Isa. 2:4; Mic. 4:3 for judgment of the nations).

In 25:32–33, we come to the **sheep** and **goats**, a simile that helps us envision the literal judgment scene. We are to envision people being separated from one another, but it will happen in the same manner as **the shepherd separates the sheep from the goats.** Sheep and goats were sometimes herded together down a chute that was wide enough for only one animal at a time. A shepherd would sit atop the fence, swinging a gate back and forth to guide each animal through the appropriate opening to join its own kind.

The right side was considered the side of honor and authority, as when a person was seated at the right hand of a king (Matt. 20:21,23; 22:44; 26:64). This was the side of the sheep, who, because of the greater value of the sheep and their placement on the Messiah's right, were already identified as Jesus' faithful disciples of all ages. On the left, the position of lesser honor, were the goats. These are clearly identified as the faithless.

From this point on to the end of the passage, there is no more mention of sheep or goats. From now on, the two categories of people are **those on his right,** or "the righteous," and **those on his left.**

25:34–36. The remainder of the parable, except the concluding statement (25:46) is divided into two symmetrical halves. First, the king addresses those on his right, **the righteous,** according to 25:37. He addressed them as **you who are blessed by my Father.**

When God does the blessing, because of the power of his word, what he speaks is equivalent to what he does. So God's blessing on a person is essentially a bestowal of some kind of benefit. Jesus was addressing these people as "you whom my Father, by the authority of his word, has already given spiritual and material blessing and favor; blessing and favor which will continue to be yours." This stands in contrast to the ones who are **cursed** in 25:41.

The king's invitation was **Come,** the same word used to command the first disciples to follow him (4:19), to invite the weary to find rest in him (11:28), and to call the guests to the wedding feast (22:4). It also brings to our minds the invitation of Revelation 22:17. This invitation is to inherit **the kingdom prepared for you since the creation of the world** (Matt. 25:34). Finally, the children of the kingdom, who have already proven themselves to be kingdom citizens, will come into their full inheritance (cf. Matt. 19:29; Rom. 8:17; 1 Cor. 6:9–10; 15:50; Gal. 5:21; 1 Pet. 1:3–5; Rev. 21:7)—the complete realization of the Messiah-King's rule.

The mention of the kingdom's preparation **since the creation of the world** (cf. John 17:24; Eph. 1:4; 1 Pet. 1:20) emphasizes the election of the faithful. Since the beginning of time, indeed, from eternity past, God has chosen these people and planned a place for each of them in the kingdom.

In 25:35–36, the king described the behavior of these kingdom citizens. When he was in need, they were the ones who acted in compassion to meet his need. His listing of six needy conditions—hunger, thirst, alienation, nakedness, sickness, and imprisonment—is not exhaustive but representative of all needs that a person might have. Each of these needs is central to survival and quality of life.

Food, drink, clothing, and health are related to the needs of a person's body. Being a **stranger** (Gr. *xenos,* "foreigner, alien") is also related to physical well-being. Because an alien usually had no job or other means of support, there was a strong tendency to view him with prejudice, and even to abuse him. Because of their needy state, foreigners were protected, along with widows and orphans, by Old Testament law (e.g., Lev. 19:10,33–34; Deut. 27:17–19). Someone who was **in prison** was, likewise, unable to earn a living for himself or his family. In fact, such a person was dependent on others to bring him food, because the law enforcement system usually did not provide it for him.

25:37–40. Note that **The righteous** answered in surprise; they did not remember when they had met all these needs of the Messiah. The king began his answer with **I tell you the truth,** indicating the absolute truthfulness of his next statement.

Not all of the righteous served the king to the same degree, but all served with a right heart. The answer continues, **whatever you did for one of the least of these brothers of mine, you did for me.** By **brothers** (a generic Gr. term that could also include "sisters"), Jesus meant his followers (his disciples of all ages; see Jesus' new definition of his family in 12:50; cf. 28:10), since we share with him the same Father.

Anyone who met the need of even the most insignificant of Jesus' followers was ministering to him. Jesus identified this closely with his family on earth (Acts 9:4–5). On **the least** among the believers, see Matthew 11:11; 18:4; 20:26–28; 23:11. On Jesus' identification with believers conducting their evangelistic mission, see Matthew 10:11–14,40–42. On equating love for people with love for God, see Matthew 22:37–40.

Jesus defined more clearly one important component of remaining on the alert and being ready (24:42,44; 25:13) for the Messiah's return. We will be faithfully doing the kingdom work if we care for the needs of those around us.

25:41–43. For the second half of the conversation, the king turned to those on his left. He addressed them as **cursed** (in contrast to the "blessed" of 25:34). Even before announcing his charge against them, he pronounced their sentence. First, **Depart from me** (in contrast with "Come" in 25:34) . . . **into the eternal fire prepared for the devil and his angels.** The opposite of heaven is separation from God. Just as the eternal kingdom has been prepared for the righteous (25:34), so also the eternal fire of hell (cf. 3:12; Rev. 14:10; 19:20; 20:10,14–15; 21:8) has been prepared. The king said that hell was originally meant for the devil and his angels (i.e., demons), and it appears that, by following Satan, the unrighteous will share in an eternal punishment that was at first meant for them. The old Adversary is finished! The battle of the ages is over!

The king listed the same six physical needs as in 25:35–36, but this time he explained that the unrighteous neglected to meet those needs of his.

25:44–45. The unrighteous were just as surprised as the righteous were (25:37–39). They did not remember seeing the king in need. But using almost exactly the same solemn language as in 25:40, the king declared that their neglect of his needy brothers (his followers/disciples), even the least, was the same as neglecting him (cf. Jesus' confrontation of Saul in Acts 9:5, "I am Jesus, whom you are persecuting").

These faithless ones are, according to the terminology of 24:42,44; 25:13, those who have fallen asleep and have dropped their guard, and who are unprepared for the Messiah's return.

25:46. Jesus completed the judgment scene and the discourse by summarizing the eternal destinies of the two categories of people. The unrighteous would **go away** (a permanent departure) into **eternal punishment**, but the righteous would enter **eternal life.** The use of "eternal" to modify both "punishment" and "life" contrasts the two destinies and emphasizes their permanence. By the time each person stands before the king, his or her eternity is established and cannot be changed.

MAIN IDEA REVIEW: *In light of the future reality of hardship and ultimate salvation, we must stay ready for Christ's return at all times by living in loving obedience, and he will reward us for it.*

III. CONCLUSION

All of us will stand before the judgment seat of the king to answer for our treatment of others, especially fellow believers. Minister to the needs of others as though you were ministering to Jesus the king. To ignore a need you can meet is equivalent to ignoring Jesus the king.

PRINCIPLES

- No person can share his heart preparedness with anyone else.
- Faithful investment of your life will earn both your Master's blessing and an eternal share in his joyous heaven.
- The Lord has high standards for obedience and faithful stewardship, but he enables us to achieve these things by providing his wisdom, love, and power.
- You will be rewarded for your faithful work by receiving even greater responsibility and privilege.
- The punishment for negligence of kingdom investment is harsh.

APPLICATIONS

- Be obedient for the long term. Life, while awaiting the king, is a marathon, not a sprint.
- Decide today to prepare for a life of obedient readiness.
- Apply yourself to the kingdom's work with 100 percent faithfulness.
- Obey promptly.
- Do for the kingdom what God has uniquely prepared you to do.

IV. LIFE APPLICATION

Watching and Waiting

The surprise was complete. The attacking planes came in two waves; the first hit its target at 7:53 A.M., the second at 8:55. By 9:55 it was all over. By 1:00 P.M. the carriers that launched the planes from 274 miles off the coast of Oahu were heading back to Japan.

Behind them they left chaos, 2,403 dead, 188 destroyed planes, and a crippled Pacific Fleet that included eight damaged or destroyed battleships.

At 6 A.M.(Hawaiian time) on December 7,1941, the first Japanese attack fleet of 183 planes took off from aircraft carriers 230 miles north of Oahu. Ironically, at 7:02 A.M., two Army operators at a radar station on Oahu's north shore picked up approaching Japanese fighters on radar. They contacted a junior officer who disregarded their sighting, thinking that it was B-

17 bombers from the United States west coast. The first Japanese bomb was dropped at 7:55 a.m. on Wheeler Field, eight miles from Pearl Harbor. No one was prepared for what was occurring. The rest is history.

At Pearl Harbor, the consequences for not being ready for an enemy attack were devastating. There were signs that went unheeded. Had the U.S. military been ready to spring into action, the losses at Pearl Harbor might have been greatly reduced.

The element of watchful waiting applies to the return of Christ. For the believer, being ready for Christ's return involves more than not being caught by surprise. It also involves living a life in faithful obedience to God, investing our resources in the kingdom of God. Jesus will someday return. Those who are found faithful and living in obedience to God will be will be rewarded. Are you among the ready?

V. PRAYER

Lord, while I await your coming, keep me busy at worthwhile tasks, serving the needs of others in your kingdom. Amen.

VI. DEEPER DISCOVERIES

A. Talent

Some interpreters estimate that a talent was worth about fifteen years' wages for a common laborer. The value varied from period to period and place to place. In any case, these three servants were being entrusted with a big responsibility. The master was putting an important part of his valuables in the hands of these three men.

B. Separation of Sheep and Goats

How does this judgment of "the sheep and goats" fit into the larger eschatological picture? Jesus did not mention any resurrection from the dead of the people of all ages. This would be necessary for the great white throne to take place (Rev. 20:11–15) and for what comes after the millennial reign. So, it seems that this is not to be the "final" general judgment of all who have lived. It appears, therefore, to be the king's "sorting" (prior to setting up his millennial kingdom on the throne of David) of all people who are alive on the earth at his second coming. It does fit naturally into the prophetic understanding of a premillennial scenario.

C. Summary

These three stories bring the Olivet Discourse to its practical conclusion, giving Jesus' disciples some important specifics on how to live in continual readiness while awaiting his return. Without these stories, we would be left wondering exactly how to obey the command of 24:42: "keep watch."

The theme of final judgment and Jesus' references to himself as the coming king prepare the reader of Matthew for the climactic narrative of Matthew 26–28. Although Jesus will suffer humiliation and death, the truths of his teaching reveal the victory and the accounting that will come after his suffering, death, and resurrection.

VII. TEACHING OUTLINE

A. INTRODUCTION

1. Lead Story: Be Goal-Oriented
2. Context: Matthew 25 should have started with 24:42. That is the turning point in Jesus' Olivet Discourse. In Matthew 24:4–41, Jesus provided doctrinal exposition on future events, in answer to the disciples' question about the timing and signs of the destruction of the temple and about Jesus' coming and the end of the age (24:3). From 24:42 through chapter 25, Jesus built on the preceding doctrinal foundation with a series of five parables, exhorting his disciples to be continually alert and busy about the work of the kingdom. Since he might return at any time, they would want to be found ready for his coming.

   The Olivet Discourse is divided between exposition and exhortation, doctrine and application, or, in this case, prophecy and practical preparation of the believer for future events.

3. Transition: As we began Matthew 25, we found ourselves into the application portion of the discourse. The first two parables have already been presented in 24:42–51: (1) the parable of the thief (24:43), emphasizing the suddenness of Christ's return and our need to be continually on the alert; and (2) the parable of the master (24:45–51), emphasizing the importance of caring for others, that Christ might find us obedient whenever he returns.

   The last three parables, which make up Matthew 25, continued to exhort Jesus' disciples toward watchfulness (a theme based on the uncertain timing of his return, 24:36–41). But each story had its own unique contribution to the theme. The first (25:1–13) presented the theme of wisdom in being prepared for Christ's return, especially emphasizing the long delay before his return as well as the unexpectedness when he does return. The second parable (25:14–30) illustrated a theme introduced by Jesus in 13:12. It focused on the variety of responsibilities entrusted by Christ to his disciples before his return. It focused as well on the variety of abilities we are given to handle his trust and the variety of rewards for our faithful stewardship.

The third story (25:31–46) was not technically a parable, for it gave us a glimpse of a scene in true future history, before the judgment of God. But this passage served the same purpose as the four parables of 24:42–25:30, and belonged in series with them. It emphasized the importance of caring for Jesus' followers, which is the same as caring for him.

B. COMMENTARY

1. The King Says, "Do Not Delay or Put Off Faithfulness—I Am Coming" (25:1–13)
2. The King Says, "Invest Your Life for Me" (25:14–30)
3. The King Says, "Receive My Followers as You Would Receive Me" (25:31–46)

C. CONCLUSION

1. Wrap-up: In light of the future reality of hardship and ultimate salvation, we must stay ready for Christ's return at all times by living in loving obedience.
2. Personal Challenge: Are you investing your life for the Lord and Master, Jesus Christ? Or are you just passing the time without serious thought or action regarding the kingdom? Do you look forward to Christ's return?

VIII. ISSUES FOR DISCUSSION

1. What is the central message of the parable of the wise and foolish bridesmaids?
2. In the parable of the talents, what mistake did the third servant (the one who was given one talent) make?
3. What is the central message of the parable of the talents?
4. What is the central message of the parable of the sheep and goats?

Matthew 26

❧❧

The King Marches Downward to Death and Upward to Victory

Matthew 26

I N   A   N U T S H E L L

In his final block of narrative (chaps. 26–27), Matthew presents the Passion. For the fourth time, Jesus predicts his death; but this time he adds that it will be by crucifixion and take place during the Passover celebration. Key themes in chapter 26 are Jesus' final evening with his disciples and the Last Supper, his arrest in the garden of Gethsemane, and his trials before the Sanhedrin and Pilate. Many of Matthew's underlying themes converge in this chapter. What is clear is that God is in control of all these events, however tragic they may appear to be.

The King Marches Downward to Death and Upward to Victory

I. INTRODUCTION

Roses out of Ashes

*T*his is a story about standing strong in spite of betrayal.

More than fifty years ago my mother-in-law stood before the altar and recited her wedding vows. On that beautiful day, she could never have guessed what would ensue. The man she married was not all he made himself out to be.

It was not long before the problems began to surface—loud shouting, hurtful names, physical abuse. Over time, and with four years between, they had two daughters, the first of whom would become my wife. Unfortunately, the two little girls would often have to cower in their bedroom while the ugly shouts of anger and the bumps and thumps of physical abuse filled their home. The walls of the home—with a dent here and a hole there—bore the physical evidence of his violence.

Eventually, the abuse spread to the children. My wife remembers him spinning the cylinder on his gun. His threats to kill them and "spread your blood over the county" sent shudders through their little hearts. They could not fall asleep at night without the fear that he would enter the room.

Ultimately, he moved out, abandoning his family without so much as a dollar of support.

With no man, no marriage, and no childhood for her young daughters, "Mom" could have felt very much the victim. But she refused to look at herself that way. In spite of her being completely betrayed and abused, Mom never lost sight of her commitment to her Lord. Single and pregnant with a third child, Mom carried on. If the kids were going to eat, she would have to work, full-time now. And there was not much available in the little valley where they lived. No matter. It was the right and loyal and godly thing to do.

Yes, Mom was special. And God blessed her faithfulness. All three of her children are effective, responsible adults. Her son is a pastor. Her two daughters married pastors. And her grandchildren are walking with the Lord today. Out of disaster God has built a heritage.

And that is precisely what God is doing in the next two chapters of Matthew. Out of the trauma of betrayal, the humiliation of trial, the pain of beatings, and the terror of crucifixion, Jesus marched with determination toward his Father's intentions. What looked like a terrible trip to death was actually a magnificent climb to the peak of God's intentions. In perfect faithfulness and obedience, Jesus walked down the lonely road toward death, only to emerge on the other side victoriously. He was always a king and never a victim.

II. COMMENTARY

The King Marches Downward to Death and Upward to Victory

MAIN IDEA: *The Messiah, our Sovereign Savior, remains loyal to the end, while others fall away.*

The first four chapters of Matthew serve as a narrative introduction to the flow of Matthew's Gospel. Chapters 5–25 trace Jesus' ministry, using the five discourses as organizational structure. Chapters 26–28 serve as a narrative conclusion and as a magnificent climax to the ministry of Messiah. Here Jesus filled out, to the fullest, the role of the sacrificial Son of Abraham.

The King Predicts His Enemies' Plot (26:1–5)

SUPPORTING IDEA: *Jesus continued in the face of death, letting nothing hinder his obedience to the Father.*

Having securely sealed his case for Jesus' identity as the Messiah, Matthew embarked on the final progression of events leading up to the Messiah's victorious death and resurrection. Jesus' prediction (26:1–2) and the Jewish leaders' plotting (26:3–5) are the beginning of the end of his first advent.

26:1–2. The first part of 26:1 (**When Jesus had finished saying all these things**) is the formula that ends all five of Jesus' discourses in Matthew (cf. 7:28; 11:1; 13:53; 19:1; 23:39), so it serves as the transitional phrase ending the Olivet Discourse (Matt. 24–25).

As you know draws on the disciples' awareness that the Passover was just two days away. Jesus used this event as a reference point for his betrayal and crucifixion. The Passover began at sunset Thursday. Jesus' final triumphant work of his earthly ministry, death for redemption, was only days away.

Jesus' mention of the Passover in connection with his death also served as a statement concerning the significance of his death. As was made clear later (the Lord's Supper, Matt. 26:26–29; cf. 1 Cor. 5:7; Heb. 7–10), Jesus the Messiah is the ultimate Passover sacrifice for the forgiveness of his people's sins (Matt. 1:21; 20:28).

In this prediction, Jesus again used his messianic title **the Son of Man**. The phrase **Will be handed over** is in the present tense, possibly indicating that the beginnings of his betrayal were already set in motion. And he stated the exact method of his death—crucifixion. Even though he had told the disciples previously that he would be crucified (20:19), they must have been shocked at the thought of the Christ dying a disgraceful death. Crucifixion was a form of execution reserved only for the worst criminals.

Notice the lack of any mention of his resurrection. This placed the emphasis even more on Jesus' death as the Passover lamb.

26:3–5. The chief priests and the elders of the people were members of the Sanhedrin, and they represented the key leaders of Israel. This was Matthew's first mention of **Caiaphas**, the high priest, the person with highest human authority in all Israel. His only other appearance in Matthew was when he presided over Jesus' mock trial before the Sanhedrin (26:57–66). This private gathering to plot a **sly way** to arrest and kill a man who had not yet stood trial was cruel and underhanded.

But as much as they wanted Jesus out of the way, they cautioned one another not to arrest him **during the Feast** (Passover), lest Jesus' popularity lead to a riot when the people saw their Messiah taken away. During the Passover season, Jerusalem probably swelled to five times its normal population with thousands of pilgrims attending from all over the Mediterranean basin. Any political or religious spark in that crowd could set off a riot.

Jesus—always a king and never a victim—intended to orchestrate the events so he would die at Passover. Jesus' statement in 26:2, followed by the contradictory plotting of 26:3–5, provided a distinct sense of divine sovereignty over the whole affair.

This Jewish plotting provided fertile ground for Judas' approach to the Jewish leaders in 26:14–16.

B The King Is Lovingly Prepared for Burial (26:6–13)

> **SUPPORTING IDEA:** Loyalty to the Messiah requires extravagant worship, as we give unreservedly of ourselves.

Jesus' anointing by the unnamed woman is enclosed by two brief paragraphs related to the plotting against him (26:3–5,14–16). There are obvious clues within the "anointing" passage which pointed to Jesus' imminent death, but Matthew's placement of the story makes the connection even stronger.

26:6–7. During this week, Jesus was apparently spending the nights with friends in Bethany (21:17). This town was two miles east of Jerusalem, on the ridge of the Mount of Olives. On one of these days, he was at the home of **Simon the Leper.** Simon must have been one of the hundreds of people whom Jesus had healed during his ministry. **Reclining**, or sitting on cushions on the floor, was the posture people used for dining. As Jesus rested in this home, an unnamed woman came to him with a valuable gift of perfume. In an act of extravagant worship, she poured it on his head. This "anointing" was an appropriate way to honor the Messiah. It was often done for special guests or rabbinical figures. The anointing oil used on Jesus was very valuable, worth perhaps a year's wages.

26:8–9. Jesus had taught about caring for the poor (25:34–45). Thus, the disciples' **indignant** reaction to this woman's **waste** of resources that could have benefited the poor was understandable. But their error lay in their lack of appreciation for who was in their midst. Jesus was the Messiah-King, who alone deserved such extravagant worship.

26:10–13. The disciples apparently scolded the woman and Jesus told them to leave her alone: **Why are you bothering this woman? She has done a beautiful thing to me.** Such an act of worship would have been inappropriate with others. But not in the case of Jesus, God's Son.

Jesus referred to the short time of his stay on earth. The Messiah should have been the guest of honor, welcomed and respected not only by Israel but by the entire world. He had been on earth a few short years, and he would die in a matter of days. There would always be opportunity to minister to the poor, but the opportunities to minister to the Messiah in the flesh were limited. Timing is always an issue in the spending of kingdom resources.

When a body was prepared for burial, it was wrapped in layers of cloth, with spices and perfumes sprinkled between the layers. Jesus claimed that this woman's anointing was to **prepare me for burial**, figuratively speaking. Jesus used every opportunity to teach his people.

Solemnly affirming his words with **I tell you the truth**, Jesus promised that this humble woman's loving gift would become world-renowned. The story of her act of worship would be taught along with the gospel **throughout the world . . . in memory of her.**

Imagine a story from your life being translated into every language and then taught as part of Scripture throughout the centuries! This woman had honored Jesus, and he returned honor to her. Such is the blessing of the Messiah upon those who worship him from a true heart.

What honor and blessing awaits you as you begin to give extravagantly of yourself to the king? Compare this gain with what you lose by withholding yourself. We serve a generous king, and he seeks generous worshipers (John 4:24).

𝖢 The King's Betrayer Is Paid (26:14–16)

SUPPORTING IDEA: *Disloyalty comes cheaply.*

26:14–16. Judas Iscariot had already been introduced in the original listing of the disciples (Matt. 10:4), together with the one notorious act that would forever be associated with his name—his betrayal of Jesus. Matthew's mention of Judas as **one of the Twelve** was intended to draw a gasp of disbelief from the reader.

Judas knew who to approach, **the chief priests**, and he knew they wanted Jesus. Judas had watched these leaders suffer humiliation before the people many times, as Jesus defeated them with truth and his authority. Judas asked their price for his help to betray Jesus to them.

Ⓓ The King Communes with Friend and Enemy (26:17–29)

SUPPORTING IDEA: *Jesus wants us to remember continually his loyal and sacrificial love.*

This portion of the narrative includes three brief paragraphs revolving around the Passover meal: Jesus' careful preparation for the meal (26:17–19), his revelation that a betrayer was in their midst (26:20–25), and the institution of the Lord's Supper (26:26–29). This emphasis on the Passover strengthened the symbolism of Jesus as the Passover lamb (cf. 26:2).

26:17–19. The phrase **the first day of the Feast of Unleavened Bread** (27:17) was another way of referring to the day of the Passover. The feast derived its name from the fact that no yeast was used in the cooking for these meals. This commemorated Israel's hurried departure from Egypt (Exod. 12). They had to leave on such short notice that they did not have time to leaven their bread, so they ate the first Passover meal with unleavened bread. This was some time before sunset on Thursday. Thus, the Passover meal would be eaten at or after sunset that evening, just as Friday began.

At the disciples' inquiry, Jesus directed them to a particular man's home in **the city**, referring to Jerusalem. The man apparently knew who **the Teacher** was, and would gladly welcome the Messiah into his home. Jesus' words, **My appointed time is near**, indicated his awareness of the triumphant completion of his work of suffering, which would begin that night.

The reason Matthew included these details was to show Jesus' careful preparation for this meal. The king himself was making these arrangements.

The lamb was selected, the leaven was burned, and then the lamb was sacrificed and roasted. The whole process was an elaborate ceremony that lasted several days. The order of the meal was a carefully prescribed tradition that had begun nearly fifteen hundred years before. A prayer of thanksgiving was offered over the first of four cups of wine. A preliminary course of bitter herbs was eaten. A ceremonial question was asked and answered about the meaning of the meal. Throughout the meal, at prescribed times, certain parts of the great Jewish Hallel (Pss. 113–118) were sung.

26:20–24. The words **evening came** refer to the setting of the sun and the beginning of the Passover celebration.

In the middle of the meal, Jesus made a statement that shocked the disciples. Jesus' announcement of a betrayer in their midst met with denial, tinged with self-doubt. They all knew they were weak, but it was hard for them to conceive that they could betray their Lord. Their denials took the form of a question that expected a negative answer: **Surely not I, Lord?** Matthew noted that they were **very sad**, a word that amplified their grief to the extreme. The disciples were beside themselves with sorrow. Jesus' response to their denials was an allusion to Psalm 41:9. This psalm of David praised Yahweh for protecting him from the most treacherous of his enemies.

Matthew recorded Jesus' words in 26:23 in such a way that Jesus is seen as emphasizing the travesty of a person who shared his meal serving as his betrayer. Matthew's point was the unimaginable depth of the betrayal, not the identity of the person who betrayed.

In 26:24, Jesus made it clear that, on the one hand, **the Son of Man will go just as it is written about him.** But, on the other hand, **woe to that man who betrays the Son of Man!** The Messiah-King's death as the sacrificial Son of Abraham must take place. But this did not relieve the betrayer of his guilt. God's sovereignty does not remove human responsibility. Even though the outcome would be the salvation of all who would believe, it would be better for the betrayer **if he had not been born**—so severe would be his judgment.

26:25. Judas joined the chorus of denials, hoping that Jesus' answer to his **Surely not I, Rabbi?** would be "No, of course not." This would indicate that Jesus did not know of Judas's plans. But Jesus' response took Judas's question and turned it into a confession: **Yes, it is you.**

Judas's use of the respectful **Rabbi** was a smokescreen that hid his disrespect for Jesus. Judas was just like the hypocrites who built Jesus up with false compliments even as they were trying to take him down.

26:26. John was the only gospel writer who recorded Judas's departure from the meal (John 13:30). Apparently Judas's presence at the Lord's Supper was not an important detail to Matthew. He wanted to focus our attention on the Supper.

Jesus' comment, **Take and eat; this is my body,** must have caused a stir among the disciples. Matthew did not record Jesus' further elaboration on the significance of the bread, but the symbolism of sacrificial provision was unmistakable. This new rite had direct links with all of redemption history. Just as Israel's deliverance from bondage in Egypt was remembered in the Passover, so all of Messiah's people were to remember his death in this communion ordinance.

26:27–29. At one point in the meal, Jesus took the cup of wine, again gave thanks, and gave it to his disciples, commanding them, **Drink from it, all of**

you. On this occasion, Jesus shocked the disciples by breaking the order of the centuries-long liturgy and offering the cup of his own blood. Thus, Jesus rendered the earlier Passover ceremonial meals obsolete and introduced a brand-new ceremony, the communion. But his further explanation must have surprised them: **This is my blood of the covenant, which is poured out for many for the forgiveness of sins** (27:28). The disciples had witnessed the pouring of an animal's blood on the temple altar as the required Mosaic sacrifice for the sins of Israel (e.g., Lev. 4:7,18,25,30,34). But Jesus introduced something new to their understanding. It would no longer be an animal's blood that would cover sins, but his blood—the blood of the Messiah-King. The blood of animals sealed the old covenant between Yahweh and his people (Exod. 24:8; Zech. 9:11). The blood of the Messiah would seal the new covenant (Matt. 1:1–17,21; Jer. 31:31–34; Ezek. 36:25–27; Heb. 7–10).

Jesus concluded the institution of the ordinance with a solemn affirmation (**I tell you**), vowing not to celebrate this symbolic meal until the eschatological feast **with you in my Father's kingdom** (26:29). This verse anticipates Christ's future reign on the throne of David. We are commanded to celebrate this meal regularly on earth to remember what Jesus has done for us. But he will take part in it again when he can celebrate the final reunion with all his people. This reality emphasizes the symbolism of unity when we celebrate communion together as members of his body.

We feel this same sense of anticipation as we wait for our adult children to arrive "home for the holidays." We can imagine the heart of the king waiting for the ingathering of his entire family before participating again in the meal himself. It has been anticipated nearly two thousand years now by our reckoning. Imagine how long it has been in the reckoning of the Father's heart! What a grand family meal it will be!

E The King Predicts Abandonment by His Best Friends (26:30–35)

> **SUPPORTING IDEA:** *We must not underestimate our own ability to betray Jesus.*

Judas's treachery had already been revealed. But Jesus then told the remaining eleven disciples that they would also become disloyal, though not to the point of betraying him to his enemies. Jesus' careful delineation of these events was one more indication that he was not a blind victim. His was a sovereign and voluntary sacrifice.

26:30–32. Jesus and his disciples sang the last of the Hallel (probably Pss. 115–118). When Jesus and the eleven were finished with the meal, they went out of Jerusalem to the Mount of Olives. This path was familiar, as they seemed to have spent the nights of this week with friends in Bethany, on the other side of the Mount. But this time Jesus stopped on the Mount, not continuing to climb on toward Bethany.

Despite all Jesus' warnings and predictions, the disciples still did not understand what the next twenty-four hours held for them or their master. Jesus told the eleven that all of them would **fall away**. The reason would be **on account of me**—because of their association with him and the danger that would befall them. **This very night** is emphatic. There was no doubt, and their failure would come sooner than they realized.

Jesus explained that their abandonment would be a fulfillment of Zechariah 13:7. Jesus was foretelling the suffering he was about to undergo. While he remained faithful and endured, his disciples, like shepherdless sheep, would be **scattered** in fear.

The word **But** introduces the contrasting note of hope (26:32). Jesus once again foretold his resurrection, adding for the first time a glimpse into the days after he would be raised. **I will go ahead of you into Galilee** suggested that they were to meet him there after his resurrection. Of course, the disciples did not know enough at the time of Jesus' death to go on to Galilee. In fact, the Lord did not want them to go before they had proof of his resurrection—the empty tomb. At that time he would remind them of his instructions (28:7,10).

After spending most of three years in the Galilean ministry, there was a warm ring of familiarity to the name Galilee, almost as though they would be going home for a final meeting before his ascension. The Messiah spent most of his ministry out of the spotlight in the geographical backwater, emerging into the spotlight only when the time was right and only when he would accomplish his greatest work. His short postresurrection period on earth would also be spent out of the spotlight. His last appearances would be reserved primarily for those who were already his followers.

26:33–35. Each of the eleven disciples felt as strongly as Peter, and they told Jesus so (26:35). But it was Peter, their spokesman, whose verbal contradiction of Jesus' prediction was recorded by Matthew. Peter took his promise of loyalty to great heights; he would stand by Jesus even if he had to do it alone (**even if all fall away . . . I never will**).

We can read sorrow, and possibly affection, into Jesus' words, as he solemnly affirmed to Peter: **I tell you the truth, this very night, before the rooster crows, you will disown me three times.**

Peter was within a few hours of this denial. Not only would Peter *not* stand by Jesus, but he would go so far as to disown him three times before morning. The disciples expected to get at least a little sleep before morning (Passover was customarily a late night observance for most people). This cut down even further the likelihood that Peter would have the opportunity to deny Jesus three times during that time.

All of the eleven affirmed that they would go to their deaths with Jesus before denying him. The disciples recognized that Jesus faced danger, though they still did not understand that it was almost upon them, and they promised to face it with him. The linguistic construction of Peter's protest indicates he could not imagine Jesus was actually going to die.

⚏ The King Finds Comfort with His Father (26:36–46)

SUPPORTING IDEA: *The only way we can remain loyal in spite of our weakness is to stay alert to danger and to depend continually on God through prayer.*

Four truths stand out in the Gethsemane passage. First, the disciples continued to fail to understand the danger that awaited them that night. Second, Jesus was alone in his anxiety and grief, since the disciples kept falling asleep on him. Third, Jesus was fully human, longing for the emotional support from his friends. Fourth, Jesus remained loyal to his Father's will, in spite of his knowledge that he was about to endure the agony of crucifixion. In his death on the cross, he was to endure unthinkable separation from his Father. Jesus' death was like no other death, heroic or otherwise. This was not martyrdom. This was self-sacrifice.

26:36–38. The place called **Gethsemane**, on the west slope of the Mount of Olives, faced Jerusalem. The name means "olive press," so it may have been an olive grove with its own press. Jesus left eight disciples in one place, while he and his inner circle of disciples—Peter, James, and John—went a little further for the purpose of prayer. Knowing the physical, emotional, and spiritual torture he was about to bear, Jesus began to be **sorrowful and troubled.** Matthew used these words to communicate the extreme emotional distress Jesus experienced.

Jesus' own words further explained his emotional state: **My soul is overwhelmed with sorrow to the point of death** (cf. Ps. 42:5–6,11; 43:5). Jesus was on the verge of dying from a broken heart, so extreme was his emotional distress. In deep sorrow, the Messiah-King instructed his three closest friends to stay near and **keep watch** with him, probably to support him through their own prayers. He—fully God—put his own emotional well-being in the hands of his creatures!

26:39. Then, moving just a little further on, the king **fell with his face to the ground**—a posture communicating desperate entreaty—**and prayed** to his Father. He prayed **if it is possible**, knowing that his request could not be granted if he were to remain obedient. But Jesus' model is a comfort to us. We need to pour out our hearts honestly to God (Ps. 62:8), even if we know our deepest "want" is not what he will grant. God desires us to be able to come to him feeling the safety of total honesty. He is competent to handle the cries of our souls.

Jesus' request to be spared suffering and death was the desperate cry of a Son's heart to his Father. And his Father accepted it, as a loving Father—but without granting it. And the Son accepted his Father's love, but without receiving his specific request. A Son's loving request and a Father's loving wisdom; let this be a model for our own prayerful exchanges with the Father.

This cup refers not only to Christ's suffering and death (Isa. 51:22; Jer. 25:15–16; Ezek. 23:31–34) but even more uniquely to the Father's wrath upon sin. It was an anticipation of Matthew 27:46 and the Father's turning his back on him. Jesus' extreme grief was rooted in the fact that he was about to become the object of his Father's wrath—an experience that many people on earth will encounter in eternity, but which no one but the Son of God could possibly anticipate ahead of time.

The Father's holy wrath was about to crush the Son (see Isa. 53:10), when the Son had done nothing to offend him. Here Jesus was facing more than humiliation, torture, and physical death. He was about to enter hell. We can only begin to imagine how fearful this prospect was to him. He and the Father had always been one. No wonder he cried out in desperation!

But we are not to confuse Jesus' honest expression of desire with a willful decision to disobey. In the same breath, Jesus continued, **Yet not as I will, but as you will.** As always, the Son remained thoroughly submissive to his Father. There was no other way to fulfill the eternal plan that the Father, Son, and Spirit had foreordained from eternity. His mission was to defeat the adversary by restoring the kingdom and to redeem a rebellious people.

26:40–41. Returning to the three disciples, Jesus found them sleeping. He rebuked Peter on behalf of the others, using plural verbs throughout verses 40–41. His question did not expect an answer: **Could you men not keep watch with me for one hour?** The disciples' sleeping showed that they were unaware of the spiritual danger and that their guard was down. This time when Jesus commanded them to **watch and pray**, he was referring to more than staying awake physically. They were on the verge of entering into the temptation to deny and abandon him, and they needed God's help to stand fast.

Jesus acknowledged their uninformed willingness to remain loyal when he said, **The spirit is willing.** But they were unaware of how weak their flesh was. Without prayerful dependence on God and continual spiritual watchfulness, the flesh would win at the first moment of weakness.

26:42–44. Then Jesus left them to pray again to his Father. This time the words Matthew recorded demonstrate less distress and even greater resolve to obey. The wording of **may your will be done** is a more complete thought than the fragmented wording of the prayer in 26:39.

After some time, Jesus again returned to the three. But again they were sleeping, **because their eyes were heavy.** Matthew acknowledged their human limitations, even as Jesus seemed to do by his decision not to rebuke them the second time. Still with a heavy heart, the Son sought the companionship of the Father a third time, not having found it in his disciples.

26:45–46. For the third time Jesus returned to his disciples. **The hour is near,** he declared. There was no longer any time for sleeping or prayer. He awoke them with a rebuke that might be taken as a question: **Are you still sleeping and resting?** Jesus was not satisfied with their faithfulness.

Jesus' word **Look** may have drawn the disciples' attention to the sound of the approaching crowd, or perhaps to the light of their torches. The time he had been warning them about—the time for action, the time when **the Son of Man is betrayed into the hands of sinners**—had arrived. **Sinners** refers to those who had rejected his authority as Messiah and who were about to arrest, try, and execute him as a common criminal.

With the moment of crisis at hand, Jesus spurred his disciples to action: **Rise, let us go.** Again he drew their attention to the reality around them—to the approaching crowd, led by Judas Iscariot. Things were now moving too quickly for the disciples. Thanks to his time of watchful prayer, the Messiah-King was ready for what lay ahead. Most people would have taken this opportunity to escape, but his purpose did not lie in escape. Jesus went boldly to meet his enemies.

Ⓖ The King Has Them Right Where They Want Him (26:47–56)

SUPPORTING IDEA: *Loyal obedience sometimes means exercising the strength to do the difficult thing.*

26:47. Jesus' enemies arrived **while he was still speaking.** Matthew again referred to Judas as **one of the Twelve,** to draw attention to the irony that one of Jesus' closest associates would be turning on him. He came leading a **large crowd armed with swords and clubs.** Perhaps they thought they would have to overpower an armed revolutionary. If any of the **chief priests and the elders of the people** were among this crowd, they must have been few in numbers. This was consistent with their desire to exercise caution about incurring popular disapproval (26:5). Instead, these armed guards were sent **from** the Jewish leaders to do their dirty work for them.

This was an unexpected opportunity for the Jewish leaders. Because Jesus was usually surrounded by a crowd, they did not expect to have an opportunity to apprehend him until after the Passover festival (26:5). But Jesus deliberately chose to come out to Gethsemane with his disciples. This created the opportunity for his enemies to arrest him. The king was sovereign even over the timing of his arrest.

26:48–50. Judas had arranged a sign with Jesus' enemies, hoping to identify Jesus in the darkness. The **signal** was to be a **kiss**, a customary greeting between members of the same sex in that culture. Judas **at once** went to Jesus with a greeting and a kiss.

Judas could not have expected Jesus not to know what he was doing. But the eleven were unaware of Judas's treachery, and perhaps he could fool them. Judas, however, was the fool. Before the men **seized** him, Jesus declared, **Friend** (referring sorrowfully to the friendship that had been betrayed), **do what you came for.**

26:51–54. The phrase **with that** was intended to draw surprise from the reader at the next step of narrative action. **One of Jesus' companions** was (according to John 18:10) none other than Peter. But we should not make much of this knowledge of the identity of the sword-wielder, since Matthew (as well as Mark and Luke) chose not to include it.

This rash disciple struck out in an effort to defend his master. He cut off the **ear** of the high priest's servant, although he was probably aiming for the man's neck. Matthew's point was to show that the eleven were apparently ready to fight to the death. But they were not ready to see the king give in meekly to what must have seemed like disappointing defeat to them.

Jesus rebuked the sword-bearing disciple, telling him to put his **sword back in its place, for all who draw the sword will die by the sword** (26:52). Jesus would provide the disciples with more effective weapons, suited to a different type of battle, to win a victory much greater than a military triumph. He wanted them alive to carry on the spiritual battle until the gospel of the kingdom was preached to all peoples of the world (24:14).

Jesus further explained why such retaliation was inappropriate. He had the power to end this fiasco any time he wished (26:53). He did not need others to defend him. He expressed continued submission to **my Father,** through whom he could request an angelic army. But, at the same time, he asserted that if he were to make such a request, the Father would grant it **at once.**

A legion consisted of six thousand soldiers. So the number Jesus used **(twelve legions)** was equivalent to an army of 72,000 angels. Because a single angel was capable of defeating an entire army (e.g., 2 Kgs. 19:35), Jesus had at his disposal an infinitely larger power than was needed to handle the mob. This was not the time for a fight. God's perfect plan would be carried out this night.

Finally (26:54), Jesus reminded the disciples that there was a purpose to all that was happening. He was not struggling to escape, because he was here to fulfill the Father's eternal purpose. This had been revealed centuries before through **the Scriptures. . . that say it must happen in this way.**

26:55–56. Turning from his confused disciples, Jesus addressed his captors, shaming those who had come in treachery and deceit to arrest an innocent man. They had had many opportunities to arrest him in the temple. He had been there teaching regularly. Jesus confronted their true motives by demonstrating that it was these hypocrites who had much to hide, coming out to this lonely place to capture him in the middle of the night, **with swords and clubs.** This was inappropriate and unnecessary. It was by his design that they were here to arrest him, and it was his plan to go with them to trial and to the cross.

Jesus had planned this event from eternity past and had written about it through **the writings of the prophets** (Isa. 53; Zech. 12–13; cf. Matt. 26:54). And now it was being fulfilled exactly as he had planned (26:56).

This was the last response the disciples expected from the king. They had watched him heal the sick, raise the dead, and cast out demons. They had seen him calm the sea and walk on water. Before their eyes he had provided food for thousands. And he had put the hypocritical leaders in their place, embarrassing them time after time. Why now was he so easily "giving in"? What happened to the authority he had displayed?

In their perplexity and confusion, the disciples **deserted him and fled.** In fulfillment of Jesus' prediction (26:31–32), these men lost their nerve. They relied on human courage rather than spiritual preparation. Their downfall was their failure to follow Jesus' advice to keep watch and remain dependent on God in prayer (26:41; cf. 24:42). They had been so distracted by their own preconceived ideas that they did not recognize Jesus' exercise of authentic authority when they saw it. Neither did they recognize that the path to victory was through the valley of sacrifice (16:24–28).

Now the king was alone, and he would face the rest of his passion without a single human companion at his side. Even his communion with the Father would soon be severed. He was beginning the bleakest season of his existence. Yet, the king was still in control, marching victoriously downward to death.

◫ The King Is Found Guilty of Speaking the Truth (26:57–68)

> **SUPPORTING IDEA:** *Sometimes loyal obedience involves silence; sometimes it involves speaking the truth.*

26:57–58. The temple guards took Jesus into Jerusalem to face **Caiaphas, the high priest,** and the rest of the Sanhedrin (**the teachers of the law and the elders**). They had **assembled** in the middle of the night, in the home of the high priest. This was not their normal gathering place. They were meeting illegally, plotting a murder without a trial, and doing it during a special feast—all of which were against pharisaical laws.

While this was happening, Peter was attempting to redeem himself and keep what remained of his promise to stand by Jesus even to death (26:33,35). He followed Jesus at a distance, committed enough to trespass on the high priest's property, but not wanting to be discovered. To Peter's credit, he risked coming into the high priest's **courtyard** (an unroofed, open space surrounded by the buildings) and sat down with the **guards** (those who served the Sanhedrin). He pretended that he belonged there. He wanted **to see the outcome** (what would happen to Jesus). He may have been waiting for Jesus to exert himself in miraculous military power.

26:59–62. The key leaders of Israel under the high priest and the leaders of the Sanhedrin were running the show, with Caiaphas supervising and stepping in at key points. Participating in this kangaroo court was **the whole Sanhedrin.**

Together they **were looking for false evidence against Jesus.** This was a violation of the ninth commandment, "You shall not give false testimony against your neighbor" (Exod. 20:16). Matthew used the imperfect tense of "seek" **(were looking)** along with 26:60. They kept on trying to bring forward **many false witnesses.** But **they did not find** any testimony they could make stick.

Finally implied that they had tried for some time to make a convincing case, but Jesus had broken no laws. They began to achieve some degree of success when they found two witnesses who agreed that Jesus had made a statement that could be misconstrued as blasphemy against the temple.

They quoted him as saying, **I am able to destroy the temple of God and rebuild it in three days.** But Jesus never actually said those words. This accusation would return in mockery on the lips of those who watched Jesus die (27:40). Years later, this same accusation would be used against Stephen (Acts 6:14).

These false witnesses attempted to convict Jesus of a capital crime—one worthy of the death sentence. If justice was done and the false witnesses were shown to be liars, each of them should have received the death penalty under Jewish law (Deut. 19:16–21). However, these false witnesses felt safe. The men with the authority to convict them of false testimony were the ones who wanted them to give false testimony.

26:63–64. But Jesus **remained silent,** in fulfillment of Isaiah 53:7. Just as no sign would change the hardened hearts of the hypocrites in Matthew 12:38–45 and 16:1–4, so no answer would change their opinion of Jesus. In fact, by remaining silent, Jesus allowed them to convict themselves—by their persistent efforts to find some shred of evidence against him.

When Jesus refused to answer and the attempts of the chief priests failed to convict Jesus, Caiaphas took the lead. **I charge you under oath by the liv-**

ing God was the priest's trump card. According to Jewish law, the priest had the authority to force a person to testify. If Jesus remained silent, he would violate the law. His decision to answer showed his respect for civil law and authority. His answer also showed that the time was right, in his sovereign plan, to speak and so move one more step closer to the cross.

The question Jesus was charged to answer was, **Tell us if you are the Christ, the Son of God.** Jesus had already answered that question many times for all who were willing to hear. And he had backed up his claim with authoritative words and miracles. But given the stubborn refusal of the Sanhedrin to accept him as the Messiah, his admission to being the Messiah would be blasphemy.

The time was right. And the question was right. It was the heart of the one asking that was wrong. Jesus spoke. Jesus' answer was **Yes.** But he added wording (as with Judas in 26:25) that made the high priest's own words the answer to his own question: **it is as you say.**

Jesus turned to address the entire Sanhedrin. **In the future** looked ahead to the day when he would be the judge and all of them would stand trial before him. Jesus stated that they would see **the Son of Man sitting at the right hand of the Mighty One.** God's **right hand** is the position of authority and honor.

Then Jesus quoted the key messianic "Son of Man" passage (Dan. 7:13). Jesus affirmed his identity with authority—both in the boldness with which he spoke and with the authority of the Scriptures to back up his claim.

26:65–66. This affirmation was what they had been looking for. The high priest **tore his clothes** as a sign of revulsion and moral indignation at Jesus' **blasphemy.** Jewish law considered blasphemy a terrible sin, worthy of death (Lev. 24:16). But the Messiah had not blasphemed. He had the right to claim to be himself.

There was no more need for witnesses, since the entire Sanhedrin had now witnessed Jesus committing the "crime" of blasphemy. Caiaphas asked for their verdict: **What do you think?** They answered immediately, **He is worthy of death.** With that, as far as Jewish authority was concerned, the Messiah's sentence was pronounced.

26:67–68. The job was not yet finished. Now the Jewish leaders had to convince the Roman authorities that Jesus deserved death under Roman law. Now that Jesus was convicted under Jewish law, the hypocrites allowed themselves to gloat over their victim. Their abuse and mockery further deepened their own guilt. Spitting in a person's face was one of the deepest insults possible. It was also against Jewish law. They **struck him with their fists** and **slapped him.** Only Mark 14:65 and Luke 22:64 recorded that Jesus was blindfolded, but Matthew implied it, for he recorded the leaders' mocking challenge, **Prophesy to us, Christ! Who hit you?**

⫿ The King's Best Friend Denies Him (26:69–75)

SUPPORTING IDEA: *Disloyalty can catch us unaware. Stay alert and pray!*

26:69–70. Meanwhile, Peter sat in the courtyard. Jesus and his disciples had been a public spectacle all week, and it would not have been unusual for someone in the courtyard to recognize Peter from the crowded temple gatherings. A **servant girl** came to Peter and challenged him, **You also were with Jesus of Galilee.** The addition of Jesus' place of origin, Galilee, was probably intended as an insult.

But Peter **denied** his association with Jesus. In fact, he pleaded ignorance about the whole matter: **I don't know what you're talking about.** His denial was directed toward all who might have heard the girl's challenge (**before them all**). This may imply that more than the servant girl were questioning him.

26:71–72. Peter evidently became uncomfortable under the scrutiny of those who had just challenged him, so he moved to a different location: **out to the gateway** of the enclosed courtyard. He still wanted to find out what happened to Jesus, but he hoped not to attract any more attention. Another girl saw him there and recognized him. Rather than addressing Peter directly, she spoke to the other people in Peter's hearing, possibly trying to get someone to investigate and detain Peter.

A second time Peter denied his relationship with Jesus, this time **with an oath.** An oath in Jewish culture made God a party to the assertion, calling down the judgment of God if the words spoken were false. This was an ultimate oath of denial. Peter invited God's curse on himself if he was not telling the truth when he said, **I don't know the man!**

26:73–75. Some of the same people came to Peter again and said to him with greater certainty, **Surely you are one of them**, meaning one of Jesus' disciples. Although Peter had said very little, they picked up on his northern accent: **for your accent gives you away.**

Things were getting tense for Peter. They were on to him now, and any minute they might act on their suspicions and arrest him. In an attempt to convince them once and for all, Peter began to **call down curses on himself.** He **swore to them**, repeating the words of his second denial, this time with even more force: **I don't know the man!**

Immediately a rooster crowed. This reminded Peter of Jesus' prediction that he would deny his master three times before a rooster crowed (26:34). It was his deep sorrow at betraying his master, more than fear, that caused Peter to flee from the courtyard, weeping **bitterly.** All of this probably happened well before dawn.

Peter had been so sure of himself and his loyalty (26:33,35), but he failed to recognize the weakness of the flesh. He did not depend on God for strength and wisdom (26:41). We would do well to heed Peter's example, becoming less confident in ourselves and more dependent on God. It is the most basic and the most difficult lessons to learn in Christian living.

MAIN IDEA REVIEW: *The Messiah, our Sovereign Savior, remains loyal to the end, while others fall away.*

III. CONCLUSION

No matter how strong our intentions, we are susceptible to becoming disloyal to our king. Undivided loyalty requires a recognition of our own weakness, a constant awareness of possible danger, and continual dependence on God through prayer.

PRINCIPLES

- Steadfast, loyal obedience is more important than our lives.
- Loyal worshipers give unreservedly of themselves.
- Loyalty is very expensive and very valuable.
- Even those closest to us are capable of becoming disloyal, and we to them.
- We can anticipate our reunion with the king in his kingdom!
- Jesus longs for our companionship. He is a friend of his humble creatures.
- Even the most tragic of circumstances can be used to accomplish God's sovereign purposes.

APPLICATIONS

- Remember the Lord's sacrifice for us through the regular celebration of the Lord's Supper.
- When the truth must be spoken, speak it in spite of the cost.
- Never forget how much the king endured for you.
- When no words will help, stay silent.
- Trust God and stay the course, even in the midst of difficult trials.

IV. LIFE APPLICATION

Loyalty to the End

When we press the buttons of a remote control unit, whether aimed at a video recorder, CD player, or television, we are never surprised that the commands we give our entertainment centers work every time. Why? We know they are programmed to function certain ways.

The transmitter unit (hand-held remote control unit) and the receiver unit work together as a single unit. The encoder microchip in your hand sends a series of electrical impulses in binary code that the decoder microchip in the VCR or TV receives and translates. They are completely in sync with each other. The result is that we can, with a single finger action, remain in our overstuffed chairs with full confidence that our machines will obey our every command.

When it comes to people being in sync with each other, however, they are nothing like machines. With machines, it's easy—it's a matter of programming them to obey certain guidelines and laws. They do not exercise options. With people, it's difficult—it is a matter of choices and obedience to authority.

As we read Matthew 26, we see the Father and the Son in complete synchronization with each other in terms of mission and will. The Son was in loyal obedience to the Father to the end. While those around him were succumbing to the pressure and abandoning him, Jesus remained comitted to his mission.

There is a lesson here for us. God can use even the most tragic circumstances to accomplish his sovereign purposes. Whatever your burden or circumstances, feed on God's Word. Stay in sync with his revealed will and follow the leading of his Holy Spirit. Resolve to follow our Lord's example and obediently stay the course.

V. PRAYER

Loving Father, I realize I am just as capable as Peter of denying you. Lead me to lean on you and your power—not on my own human strength—as I seek to be a loyal servant in your kingdom. Amen.

VI. DEEPER DISCOVERIES

A. Judas' Betrayal of Jesus

Thirty pieces of silver was an average price paid to compensate for a dead slave (Exod. 21:32). Much of the prophetic imagery of Zechariah 11:12–13 is found here and later in this narrative (Matt. 27:3–10). The sinister agreement was sealed. From that point on, Judas's job was to watch for an opportunity to **hand . . . over** the Messiah to the religious leaders. Like a fool, Judas had betrayed himself. The old English couplet says it well: "Still, as of old, man by himself is priced; for thirty pieces, Judas sold himself, not Christ."

Why did Judas betray Jesus? Money may have been one reason, but this was probably not the main one, considering the small payoff. He may also have feared for his own safety as the Jewish leaders became more threatening toward Jesus. Perhaps he was disillusioned, along with most of the Jewish population, with the way the Messiah was conducting himself. They expected a powerful military leader to oust the oppressive Romans, and Jesus came as a spiritual Messiah.

B. The Blood

The blood was thought to carry the life of the animal, which belonged to God as the redemption price for the life of the human sinner—a life for a life (Lev. 17:10–14). The symbolism of Jesus' exchange of his life blood for our lives, requiring our voluntary acceptance of his sacrifice for us (symbolized by our drinking it), seems obvious to us today. But the idea was shocking to the disciples. They obeyed out of loyalty rather than understanding. Only later would the significance of Jesus' instructions become clear (1 Cor. 11:17–34).

C. "My God, My God"

In his prayer, Jesus displayed the same pattern that his forefather David often used. We see in many of the psalms honest expressions of anger, grief, and feelings of abandonment from David's heart (e.g., Pss. 22; 60). But these outcries were honest expressions of what was happening inside the man. By the end of the psalm, David was confident in the Lord's faithful presence, ready to move on in obedience. The release of prayer is critical for all of us, especially when we are experiencing extreme emotions. Honest prayer gives the Holy Spirit an opportunity to bring us back into touch with reality, equipping us for further obedience.

D. The Structure of Matthew 26–27

This two-chapter narrative drama, known as the passion narrative, is a single unit. It consists of these sections: (1) events leading up to Jesus' arrest, including his final evening with his disciples (26:1–46); (2) Jesus' arrest and trials before the Sanhedrin and Pilate (26:47–27:26); and (3) Jesus' suffering, death, and burial (27:27–66).

Of course, the Messiah's death is of critical significance, but the true climax of Matthew's Gospel comes with his victorious resurrection in Matthew 28. It is the Messiah's final and greatest miracle, closing Matthew's case for Jesus' identity. The drama of Matthew 26–27 builds toward this conclusion.

Keep in mind that the chapter divisions of the Bible were not inspired by God as is the Scripture itself. It would probably have been more reflective of Matthew's narrative development to make three chapters out of Matthew 26–27, according to the outline given above. One unfortunate result of the division as it stands is that the second of the three narrative portions is divided down the middle. The flow of Jesus' trials is broken. Do your best to maintain Matthew's flow of thought from this chapter to the next.

E. The Crisis and the Sovereign King

One key theme in the passion is that even as Jesus goes to the cross as the sacrificial Son of Abraham, he is still the sovereign Son of David, the king. He is betrayed and arrested, tried and convicted, crucified and buried, all because they are according to his agenda. This is demonstrated by the number of fulfillment passages and Old Testament allusions throughout the narrative. It is also shown by his conduct—steady movement toward the cross, even when he could have chosen a different course—and by his words.

F. Summary

The entire book has been building to the narrative of Matthew 26–28. In Matthew 1–25, Matthew established Jesus' identity and authority. He laid the groundwork for the fledgling church. And he shed light on Jesus' purpose in coming to earth.

In Matthew 26, Jesus' identity is the key question. His opponents refuse to accept him as the Messiah, which is the basis for their pressing for his death. It is only by his sovereign authority, as demonstrated in Matthew 26, that he progresses toward the cross at Passover and the completion of God's plan to restore the kingdom and redeem a people. It is through his death that he will make the church possible.

VII. TEACHING OUTLINE

A. INTRODUCTION

1. Lead Story: Roses out of Ashes
2. Context: It is probably in keeping with Matthew's thinking to see Matthew 26–28 as a concluding narrative which balances the first four chapters of the book. At the same time, the final narrative is also the climax of the book. The narrative drama of Matthew 26–27, known as the passion narrative, is a single unit. It consists of three sections: (1) events leading up to Jesus' arrest, including his final evening with his disciples (26:1–46); (2) Jesus' arrest and trials before the Sanhedrin and Pilate (26:47–27:26); and (3) Jesus' suffering, death, and burial (27:27–66).
3. Transition: In Matthew 26, Jesus' identity is the key question. His opponents refuse to accept him as the Messiah, which is the basis for their pressing for his death. It is only by his sovereign authority, as demonstrated in Matthew 26, that he progresses toward the cross and the completion of God's plan to restore the kingdom and redeem a people. It is through his death that he will make the church possible.

B. COMMENTARY

1. The King Predicts His Enemies' Plot (26:1–5)
2. The King Is Lovingly Prepared for Burial (26:6–13)
3. The King's Betrayer Is Paid (26:14–16)
4. The King Communes with Friend and Enemy (26:17–29)
5. The King Predicts Abandonment by His Best Friends (26:30–35)
6. The King Finds Comfort with His Father (26:36–46)
7. The King Has Them Right Where They Want Him (26:47–56)
8. The King Is Found Guilty of Speaking the Truth (26:57–68)
9. The King's Best Friend Denies Him (26:69–75)

C. CONCLUSION

1. Wrap-up: The Messiah, our sovereign Savior, remains loyal to the end, in spite of the failures of others.
2. Personal Challenge: Jesus remained loyal to the end. Judas and Peter failed. Who will you imitate? Are there times and situations in which you have denied Jesus by your actions or words? Have you sought forgiveness and restoration for that?

VIII. ISSUES FOR DISCUSSION

1. Why was it appropriate that Jesus' arrest and crucifixion should happen at the time when the Jewish Passover was being celebrated in Jerusalem?
2. Why do you think Judas betrayed Jesus?
3. Why was Jesus so distressed in his prayer to his Father in the Garden of Gethsemane?
4. Why do you think Peter denied Jesus?

Matthew 27

The King Sacrifices
Everything for His People

"*B*e of good cheer, Ridley. Play the man. We shall this day light such a candle, by God's grace, in England, as I trust shall never be put out."

B i s h o p   H u g h   L a t i m e r ,   a t   h i s   e x e c u t i o n   a s   a   m a r t y r

Matthew 27

 I N   A   N U T S H E L L

*C*hapter 27 is a continuation of the previous chapter. Matthew gives an account of Jesus' sentencing and crucifixion. It is here, because of his love for us, that Jesus sacrifices his life to take the shame and guilt of the sin of all people. It is far more than a historical event; it is an act of eternal significance. An overriding theme in this chapter is Jesus' sovereign control over the circumstances of his trial and his choice of the time of his death. The details surrounding Jesus' burial and the tomb set the stage for his resurrection.

The King Sacrificies
Everything for His People

I. INTRODUCTION

On an October Morning

*S*everal years ago my wife and I visited our son in England, where he was pursuing his graduate studies. Late one afternoon I found myself wandering along the cobblestones of Broad Street in Oxford. Imbedded in countless dark stones forming the road's surface were twenty-four white stones. They formed a simple cross on this thoroughfare of the Western world's most prestigious university city. As the bustling traffic surged by, heedless of crosses and white stones, my mind sought to push back the years to the scene memorialized by the marker.

It was a crisp October day in 1555. Two men, refusing to recant their personal faith in Jesus Christ, would die a terrible death that morning. They would be burned at the stake.

What crossed their minds as they walked through the doors of dreary Bocardo Prison and into the sunlight of their last moments on earth? We cannot know all that was in their thoughts; but we have more than stones in the pavement to mark their passing. We have some of their recorded words. As they approached the stake, Hugh Latimer turned to Nicholas Ridley and said, "Be of good cheer, Ridley. Play the man. We shall this day light such a candle, by God's grace, in England, as I trust shall never be put out."

Two men who determined to focus on sacrifice for something much bigger than themselves. They loved God. In spite of the certainty of excruciating pain and a terrible death, they focused on obeying the living God. They followed the example of their Lord, who, in spite of the horror of abandonment by his Father, determined to obey that others might live forever.

II. COMMENTARY

The King Sacrifices Everything for His People

MAIN IDEA: *Jesus the Messiah gave his life for our sins.*

Matthew 27 is a continuation of the narrative begun in the preceding chapter. See the introduction to Matthew 26 for the purpose, structure, and some of the key elements in this two-chapter narrative.

The theme of Jesus' sovereign control over circumstances continues in his trial before Pilate (27:11–14) and his choice of the time of his death (27:50).

ⒶThe King's Betrayer Gets His Due (27:1–10)

SUPPORTING IDEA: *Recognition of one's disloyalty may result in realization of wrong but not necessarily in saving faith.*

27:1–2. The hasty gathering of the Sanhedrin recorded in 26:57–68 served only to bring the case to a preliminary decision. At this gathering was a fuller representation of the seventy members than they were able to gather on short notice the night before. This gathering broke their own law that required an intervening day before passing sentence.

They hurriedly **bound him, led him away and handed him over to Pilate.** The king experienced another in a series of betrayals—this time by the so-called spiritual leaders of his own people. Matthew made no mention throughout the entire Jewish trial process of the Pharisees or Sadducees. This was clearly a bipartisan effort.

27:3–5. Judas was once again labeled as the one **who had betrayed him.** Judas learned of the verdict (**that Jesus was condemned**) and possibly watched as Jesus was led away to Pilate. This caused him to feel **remorse.** This did not necessarily mean that Judas came to a saving faith in the Messiah, but it certainly indicated that he wished he had not betrayed him. It also implied deep emotional distress. At the very least he realized he had been instrumental in the death of an innocent man. This was too much for Judas to bear. Messiah or not, this man had been his friend and teacher.

Because of his remorse, Judas carried out the two final actions of his life. The Sanhedrin had just sent Jesus off to Pilate, accompanied by a select contingency from their number. Others went to the temple to carry out their duties on this Passover day. There Judas met them and attempted to return the thirty silver coins **to the chief priests and the elders.** He confessed to them, **I have sinned . . . for I have betrayed innocent blood.** Judas's adjective, "innocent," is found elsewhere in the New Testament only in Pilate's claim of innocence in regards to Jesus' blood (27:24).

The chief priests and elders disassociated themselves from Judas by replying, **What is that to us? That's your responsibility.**

Knowing that he would receive no sympathy from his coconspirators, Judas acted on his own. The blood money was now repulsive to him, so he **threw the money into the temple and left. Then he went away and hanged himself** in an act of despair.

27:6–8. The chief priests picked up the silver coins, knowing that it was **against the law** to put **blood money** into the temple treasury. So they decided to use the money to buy **the potter's field** as a cemetery for **foreigners.** They were more concerned about religious technicalities such as blood money than that they had spent the money to murder an innocent man. They passed it off as an act of religious faithfulness. Because Gentiles could not own any of the Promised Land, they had to be buried in publicly-owned cemeteries when they died in the land.

Matthew added an editorial aside, noting that this explained why **to this day**—up to the time of Matthew's writing, decades after Judas's death—that field had been called **the Field of Blood**. It had been purchased with Jesus' blood money.

27:9–10. In purchasing this field, the Jewish leaders fulfilled an Old Testament prophecy concerning the Messiah, further supporting the validity of Jesus' claim to be the Messiah. The "apparent problem" in this passage, is that most of the words of Matthew's quotation come from Zechariah 11:12–13, but Matthew clearly identified its author as **Jeremiah the prophet** (this is strongly supported by manuscript evidence). It is not surprising that the Jewish leaders did not see the similarities between their situation and the prophetic details. The fuller Old Testament picture paralleling Judas's and Jesus' blood money was only seen when Matthew pulled together the themes of Jeremiah 19:1–13 and the wording of Zechariah 11:12–13. In God's providence, their blindness extended to more than the identity of Jesus. These rebels served as tools of the Lord to carry out his will, foreordained centuries before.

B The King Goes Before Pilate (27:11–26)

> **SUPPORTING IDEA:** *Jesus the Messiah submitted to unjust conviction because of his love for us.*

Jesus' conviction by both Jewish and Roman authorities reflected the responsibility of all nationalities for his death, because he took on the sins of people from all nations. But even here, where the decision regarding Jesus' fate rested with Pilate, the Jews were portrayed as the driving force behind Jesus' crucifixion. Some have accused Matthew (a Jew), of anti-Semitism. Not true. Matthew recorded historical events as they happened. Some Jews, including the disciples, and especially Matthew, were faithful to Jesus.

27:11. Jesus stood before the Roman governor Pilate, who had jurisdiction over all Judea. The goal of the Jewish leaders was to convince Pilate that Jesus was guilty of a crime that Pilate would consider worthy of death. They presented their charges. Then Pilate gave the defendant an opportunity to make his case. At the heart of Pilate's questioning was Jesus' claim to be the Messiah. So Pilate asked forthrightly, "Are you the king of the Jews?" We have not seen this messianic title since the Magi used it in 2:2. Now we will see it twice in this same chapter. It was used mockingly by the Roman soldiers (27:29), and once as the "charge" posted on Jesus' cross (27:37). Matthew in both his opening (Matt. 1–4) and closing (Matt. 26–28) narratives emphasized Jesus' role as the true king of Israel.

Jesus' response, **Yes, it is as you say**, was exactly the same as his response to Judas (26:25) and Caiaphas (26:64). Jesus answered *yes* in a way that turned Pilate's question into a confession of truth.

These are the last words of Jesus that Matthew recorded before Jesus' "My God, My God, why have you forsaken me?" (27:46) and his loud cry as he yielded up his spirit (27:50). We know from the other three Gospels that Jesus said more to Pilate and to those who witnessed his suffering. Matthew's purpose was to record the essential facts with little embellishment. Perhaps Matthew was also emphasizing Jesus as the silent Suffering Servant of Isaiah 53:7.

27:12–14. Jesus' silence was important in these three verses. Pilate gave the chief priests and elders an opportunity to make their case. They charged him with many things, possibly including several violations against both Jewish and Roman law. Matthew mentioned Jesus' silence twice to be sure the reader did not miss it. Pilate gave Jesus the opportunity to respond to the Jewish leaders' hostile testimony, but Jesus remained silent.

Matthew brought emphasis to Jesus' silence by his wording, including the use of a double negative: **But Jesus made no reply, not even to a single charge**. Jesus could have made a defense against all the accusations, but he refused to do so. His mission was to proceed. In Pilate's experience, accused people who stood before him did their best to defend themselves. Therefore, Jesus' silence caused **great amazement**.

27:15–18. To this point, there apparently had not been a crowd waiting outside. It was early morning, and the Jewish leaders had hurried Jesus into Pilate's presence for a quick verdict. But in 27:17, Pilate addressed a different audience than he did in 27:11–14—**the crowd . . . gathered** outside Pilate's official residence. At this point Pilate's private court hearing moved outside. Apparently the "judge's seat" from which Pilate conducted public hearings was located somewhere outside his residence.

In keeping with the Roman policy of respecting local religions, and also as part of Pilate's attempt to stay in favor with the people he governed, he had developed the custom of recognizing the Jewish feasts by releasing the people's choice of one prisoner at this time of year. Here it was the Passover, and Jesus had certainly been a popular teacher. Pilate would leave the decision up to the people, who would certainly choose to release Jesus. Barabbas was the people's other choice. He was identified as a **notorious prisoner**. The word used to describe him was used often of insurrectionists. Barabbas was notorious, but he was viewed as a hero rather than a villain.

So Pilate put the choice to the people, **Which one do you want me to release to you: Barabbas, or Jesus who is called Christ?** (27:17). The addition of the title "Christ" may have been intended to sway the crowd toward

Jesus as the obvious choice. In 27:18, Matthew gave us a glimpse into the workings of Pilate's mind. The reason he presented this choice to the people was because he knew the Jewish leaders had handed Jesus over for execution **out of envy**. He knew the Jewish leaders were afraid of losing their influence to this teacher, who claimed to be the Messiah, the king of the Jews. They were envious of his popularity. Pilate had no love for the Jewish leaders. He may have wanted Jesus' innocence established to spite the Jewish leaders. So Pilate bypassed the leaders and went straight to the people.

27:19. Somewhere in the midst of these proceedings, while Pilate was **sitting on the judge's seat**, Pilate's wife sent a message to him, warning him not to **have anything to do with that innocent man**. Her reason for the warning was that **today** (probably meaning the preceding night) she had **suffered a great deal . . . in a dream because of him**.

Did Pilate's wife know of Jesus' righteousness by reputation or observation? Or had the Lord given her a supernatural revelation through a dream? We cannot be sure. Either is plausible. But the reason Matthew included this detail was because of its effect on Pilate.

We are not told that Pilate heeded his wife's warning, but perhaps his handwashing in 27:24 reflected his respect for her words. What he should have done—not just because of her warning, but because of the lack of solid evidence against Jesus—was to release Jesus. But Pilate, like many cowardly politicians, left the decision in the hands of the people, hoping they would make the reasonable choice.

27:20–23. But the chief priests and the elders had been hard at work making their twisted case with the crowd. By the time Pilate asked for a choice from the people, they had been swayed toward the release of Barabbas. They demanded Jesus' execution. Pilate faced a dilemma. Jesus' guilt had not yet been established, but Pilate, in his weakness, turned over to the crowd the right to determine Jesus' sentence: **What shall I do, then, with Jesus, who is called Christ?** (27:22). They demanded, **Crucify him!** (27:22).

Pilate attempted to reason with the crowd. Matthew's choice of the Greek word *phemi* ("declare, say") implied that Pilate's questions were more like assertions, defending Jesus' innocence, than attempts to draw answers from the people: **What crime has he committed?** But Pilate's persistent pleas for reason were drowned out by the crowd's louder and more persistent cries: **Crucify him!** The governor had lost control of the situation. His weakness and the mob tendencies of the crowd were playing into the hands of the Jewish leaders.

27:24-25. Now it was too late for Pilate to do what he should have done in the first place—release Jesus and avoid a riot. If he executed Jesus, he would appease the people. If he did anything else, the frenzied crowd would become more and more unruly until they got what they wanted.

Pilate was accountable to his Roman superiors to keep the peace in Judea. Rome wanted the people to be calm and subdued. A riot would have gotten Pilate into serious trouble. A weak man, bowing at the altar of "political correctness," denied the truth and skewed reality. The result was the advancement of evil. But what people intended for evil, God used for ultimate good.

When Pilate saw that his attempts to reason with the crowd were futile, he **washed his hands in front of the crowd.** As he performed this ritual, he declared, **I am innocent of this man's blood.** This was wishful thinking on Pilate's part. The verdict and sentence against Jesus were his responsibility, but he relinquished both to the discretion of a mob. Despite Pilate's declaration of innocence, he shared the guilt for Jesus' wrongful death.

It is your responsibility! he told the crowd. Both Jewish and Roman authorities had made decisions that sealed Jesus' fate. And all of them tried to avoid responsibility, even as their own consciences screamed, "Guilty!"

The people rose to Pilate's challenge. They were convinced that Jesus was the worst villain ever to walk the earth. They cried out in self-righteous indignation at the thought of such an evil man going free: **Let his blood be on us and on our children!** They were willing to claim full responsibility, implying that God's curse would fall on the generations to follow if they were wrong.

27:26. Pilate released Barabbas to return to his life of crime. **Then** contrasted the freed villain with the innocent man. Jesus was flogged. This was a shredding of the victim's back by repeated blows with a whip, made of leather thongs imbedded with sharp bits of metal or bone. Many prisoners had died from such punishment. It is no wonder that Jesus was unable to bear the crossbar all the way to his cross (27:32). He probably had barely enough strength to stand.

Then Pilate **handed him over** to be crucified. The king had been betrayed again.

The King Is Mocked and Beaten (27:27–32)

SUPPORTING IDEA: *Jesus the Messiah was willing to endure the mockery of others because of his love for us.*

27:27–31. Now the Gentiles joined in on the mockery against Jesus (cf. 26:67–68). It was Pilate's soldiers who inflicted the remainder of Jesus' physical suffering. They first took Jesus into the **Praetorium,** the governor's official residence, where he had held court. A cohort consisted of six hundred soldiers.

There the soldiers joined in the mockery of Jesus. They **stripped him and put a scarlet robe on him.** For their "king" they **twisted together a crown of thorns and set it on his head.** They completed the mockery by placing a **staff** in his hand and kneeling before him in mock worship: **Hail, king of the Jews!** The robe, the crown, the staff, and the feigned worship combined to create what was a comical picture to these men—a half-dead Jew who claimed to be their king, their Savior, their Messiah! But the king stood fast, refusing to exercise his power. He had a mission to accomplish.

Their mockery turned to physical mistreatment as they spat on him and beat him with a **staff** (27:30). Finally, they took off the robe and put on his own bloody garments. Then they started to the crucifixion site (27:31).

27:32. When a person was crucified, the vertical pole was already at the site of the crucifixion. The victim was forced to carry his own horizontal beam, which would be attached to the vertical pole. On the way out of the Praetorium, the soldiers realized that Jesus was too weakened from his beatings to carry the horizontal beam. They found a man named Simon from Cyrene (a Mediterranean port on the coast of modern day Libya, in northern Africa), and they **forced him** to carry Jesus' crossbar to Golgotha. Simon was either a settler in the Jerusalem area, or, more likely, a pilgrim attending the Passover.

D The King Is Crucified (27:33–56)

SUPPORTING IDEA: *Jesus the Messiah took on the shame and guilt of our sin because of his love for us.*

Mark 15:25 informs us that Jesus was placed on the cross at about 9 A.M. All that had been done to him since his conviction by the Sanhedrin had happened during the first three hours of daylight on this Passover day.

Throughout this passage, Matthew used the Greek present and imperfect tenses to indicate that the behaviors described here were samplings of a continuous stream of abuse against Jesus. This emphasized the duration of Jesus' ordeal. Since this was one of the most important events in history, Matthew slowed the narrative, providing several details about Jesus' crucifixion and the events surrounding it.

27:33–34. The soldiers brought Jesus to a hill called **Golgotha**, the rough Greek transliteration of its Aramaic name, which Matthew translated as **The Place of the Skull**. This was beside a well-traveled road where the passersby in and out of Jerusalem could see the execution of criminals.

It was customary to offer a crucifixion victim some wine before nailing him to the cross. This was a gesture of humaneness, to ease the pain. But the soldiers played one more cruel trick on Jesus, mixing **gall** (possibly a bitter herb) into the wine. Jesus tasted it, but was unable to take this contaminated refreshment. He refused to drink any more.

Another interpretation of this event is that the gall was a drug that deadened the pain, and that Jesus refused it. Perhaps he wanted to experience the full torture of crucifixion or he wanted his head to remain clear so he would not fall into temptation through this ordeal.

27:35–37. Matthew mentioned Jesus' actual crucifixion almost as an aside. His readers would have been much more familiar with the process than we are today. Here is what they knew about that heinous form of execution.

While Jesus hung on the cross gasping for breath, the soldiers gambled for his clothes. This was in fulfillment of the prophecy of Psalm 22:18. Then they sat down and **kept watch over him,** in case someone might try to rescue him. The Greek present participle of **sitting** and the Greek imperfect tense of **kept watch** communicated the duration of this ordeal.

As a deterrent to other potential criminals, a sign was always posted at the top of the cross, over the victim's head. This sign informed passersby of the crime for which the victim was being executed. Over Jesus' head was posted the charge of which he had been found guilty: THIS IS JESUS, THE KING OF THE JEWS.

To claim to be the king of the Jews was equivalent to claiming to be the Messiah, which the Sanhedrin had declared to be blasphemy and worthy of death. However, the charge was written by the Romans, and its intended meaning had more to do with the crime of treason or insurrection. To claim to be a king over any of the peoples in the Roman Empire was to challenge the authority of Caesar. Whenever the Romans heard of anyone claiming to be the Messiah in Israel, their greatest concern was that he might try to lead Israel in a revolt against them. Insurrection was a capital crime under Roman law.

Matthew intended us to see the irony that this dying man was not only the king of the Jews but the king of all creation. Never was there a greater contrast than that between the treatment Jesus deserved and the treatment he received. He deserved the worship of all heaven and earth, but he hung naked and beaten, laboring for each breath on an instrument of torture and shame.

27:38–44. Jesus was not alone in his suffering. Two **robbers** were crucified with him, one on each side. In his darkest hour, the Messiah's company consisted of the worst outcasts of society (cf. Isa. 53:12). Many people came out to watch the spectacle, taunting and mocking the king.

The mockers used words from Psalm 22:6–8, the psalm that foretold several details of the Messiah's suffering. The phrase, **those who passed by,** described the continuous stream of people, many of whom did not recognize who this was on the cross until others told them. They **hurled insults** at him. As they verbally abused Jesus, they were continually **shaking their heads** in an expression of shame (27:39).

They hurled such insults as, **You who are going to destroy the temple and build it in three days, save yourself! Come down from the cross, if you are the Son of God** (27:40). They did not understand that the One capable of saving himself by coming down from the cross exercised his power to stay on the cross. Love and supreme control won our salvation.

In the same way, the chief priests, the teachers of the law, and the elders mocked him, saying things like these: **He saved others . . . but he can't save himself. He's the King of Israel! Let him come down now from the cross, and we will believe in him. He trusts in God. Let God rescue him now if he wants him.** They completed this insult with a reference to Jesus' own claims, **For he said, "I am the Son of God."** This taunt was an adapted quotation.

Psalm 22 is messianic. The Christ would cry out the words of the Psalm's first verse in Matthew 27:46. Indeed, this was the Son of God, and the Father delighted in the Son, never more than at this moment (Isa. 53:10). Jesus' deliverance would come later.

The insults came not only from below, but also from the two crosses at Jesus' side. The two robbers also **heaped insults on him.**

In the midst of this physical torture, the king was immersed in the emotional strain of incessant verbal abuse. Only the sovereign king of the universe could have kept himself on the cross. Truly, he was the Almighty.

27:45–46. Jesus endured this suffering and abuse for three hours, from 9 A.M. until noon. Then, at noon an even worse torture fell upon Jesus. The Father turned his back on his own Son. The perfect communion of eternity past (cf. Matt. 11:27) was broken. The Father, in essence, had to say, "I do not know you" to the Son (cf. 7:23; 25:12). The king had been betrayed and denied by Judas and all the rest of his friends, by the shepherds of his people, and by the Roman authorities. Now he was left alone by his own Father. At that point he began to bear the hell (separation from God) of punishment for a world of sins.

This three-hour period was so black that creation itself became dark as well. From noon to 3 P.M., normally the brightest and hottest time of day, darkness covered the land. Creation mourned its Creator's spiritual death (separation from his Father) and turned its back on the One the Father now turned away from because of the sin he became.

God directed Matthew to give the reader the exact words Jesus spoke, in the Aramaic language of his family and his people. Matthew wanted the significance of Jesus' death on the cross to be clear. That significance was revealed in these Aramaic words, **Eloi, Eloi, lama sabachthani?** For the sake of his Greek readers, Matthew provided the Greek translation, which means (in English), **My God, my God, why have you forsaken me?** The Messiah was completely alone, bearing the guilt of all sinners. It was an indescribable abandonment.

At about 3 P.M., near the end of the three hours of darkness, Jesus cried out these words—the desperate cry of an abandoned Son to his Father. Still, he remained the sovereign king, as evidenced by the fact that he remained on the cross. The words of Jesus' cry came from Psalm 22:1, echoing the desperate words of his forefather David. But the note of triumph and vindication at the end of the psalm (Ps. 22:25–31) would not come for Jesus until Sunday morning.

27:47–49. Some of the observers who heard Jesus' cry, **Eloi, my God**, thought it was a shortened form of **Elijah**. They assumed Jesus was calling out for the aid of the miracle-working prophet. At the sound of Jesus' desperate cry, one of the bystanders took pity on him, **immediately** ran to fill a sponge with sour wine, and raised it up for Jesus to drink. **Now** introduced the behavior of the rest of the people who watched. Perhaps it contrasted the mercy of the one who gave Jesus the wine with the apathy of the crowd. The rest of the bystanders wanted to see if Elijah would come and save him: **Let's see if Elijah comes.**

27:50. Matthew recorded the final utterance of Jesus on the cross without giving us the actual words he said: **Jesus . . . cried out again in a loud voice.** As his final act of that Passover Friday, the Messiah **gave up his spirit** (Gr. *aphiemi*, meaning "send away, let go"). The king proved sovereign even over the timing of his own death. This loud cry was a shout of triumphal completion. John seemed to indicate as much in his Gospel (John 19:30).

27:51–53. At the moment of the Messiah's death, God provided three miraculous signs. **At that moment** draws the reader's attention to the signs, testifying to their reality.

In the temple, the Holy of Holies was the innermost sanctuary, the place where the ark of the covenant rested and where the presence of God was said to abide. This place was so sacred that only once a year (on the Day of Atonement) only one man (the high priest) was allowed to enter. He offered the blood of a special sacrifice to atone for the sins of all Israel.

The room outside the Holy of Holies was called the Holy Place. Between the two rooms hung a thick curtain, separating all of humanity from the presence of God—except the high priest, once a year. At the moment of Jesus' death, this curtain was **torn in two from top to bottom**. Matthew recorded the direction in which it was torn to show that it was done at God's initiative. And the tearing opened the way for anyone to enter the presence of God, through the substitutionary sacrifice of the Messiah.

During the centuries of Israel's existence, it was unheard of for common people to consider approaching God. The penalty for such arrogance was death. But now God was inviting anyone to approach him. For the first time, provision had been made for God to accept sinful humans as forgiven, having been made as righteous through the sacrifice of his Son.

The second sign, the earthquake and splitting of rocks, was closely associated with the first sign. Perhaps it reflected the immensity of the "earthshaking" revolution that had just taken place with the splitting of the curtain. Through the death of the Son of God, the way had been cleared for sinful creatures to enter the company of the holy God.

The third sign served as a testimony to many people in Jerusalem concerning what had just happened. Some of the tombs from around Jerusalem were opened, perhaps by the earthquake. **The bodies of many holy people who had died were raised to life.** These were **holy people**, those set apart for a special purpose. The earthquake happened at the time of Jesus' death. But 27:53 uses the time reference, **after Jesus' resurrection.** Did the resurrected saints wait three days until Sunday, and then enter Jerusalem to appear **to many** as confirming witnesses to the reality of Jesus' resurrection?

27:54. The **centurion** (cf. 8:5–13) was the Roman officer in charge of the soldiers guarding Jesus and the two robbers. The spectacular signs of the earthquake **and all that had happened** had their intended effect on the centurion as well as the other soldiers who were **with him.** They became frightened and expressed their recognition that the words of the mockers were true: **Surely he was the Son of God!**

Those pagan soldiers knew little of the Jewish faith. They probably did not realize the scriptural implications of the titles thrown at Jesus when the observers taunted him. But they knew what a god was. And they knew that the Jews believed in a single, all-powerful God. They also knew the implications of a Son of God enough to proclaim the title with awe at the supernatural wonders they saw at the death of Jesus. One of Matthew's themes was Jesus' recognition by Gentiles (cf. 2:1–12; 8:5–13; 15:21–39; 27:17–23). Thus, the men he recorded as proclaiming the true identity of the Messiah at the turning point of all history were pagan Roman soldiers.

27:55–56. To this point, all the observers Matthew had mentioned had been critics and mockers (except possibly the one who gave him the wine, 27:48). Here, immediately after recording the death of the Messiah, Matthew explained clearly for the first time that not all of the witnesses of Jesus' crucifixion were unbelievers and enemies. **Many women** had kept their distance during the event, probably mourning his death. Originally from Jesus' home region of Galilee, they had **followed Jesus from Galilee.** These women were the logistical support for Jesus' troupe, as they had traveled south from Galilee to Jerusalem.

These unsung heroines serve as models of quiet, humble servanthood. We should learn from their examples.

But Matthew's primary reason for mentioning these women becomes more apparent when we compare the listed names of three of them with the later events recorded by Matthew. Among the **many** was, first, **Mary Magdalene** (from the city of Magdala, probably on the west shore of the Sea of Galilee; cf. 15:39). Second, Matthew listed **Mary the mother of James** (possibly one of the disciples, the son of Alphaeus, 10:3) **and Joses** (unknown in Matthew except for his mention here).

The third woman mentioned was **the mother of Zebedee's sons** (James and John; cf. 20:20–21). She was mentioned most likely because of her previous appearance. She may have been the leader of the women. But the two Marys are mentioned here in anticipation of their two additional appearances in connection with Jesus' burial and resurrection. These women were given the honor of being mentioned among those who stood by Jesus through his crucifixion. They were also Matthew's first and primary witnesses of the empty tomb and the resurrected Jesus. They also served as Jesus' messengers to the disciples about his resurrection (28:10).

In a culture where women were largely seen and not heard, Matthew gave unusual honor to women. He mentioned women in Jesus' genealogy (1:1–17, the opening narrative), and now here in the latter part (the closing narrative) of the story.

The disciples were absent probably because of the possibility of their being identified as his associates and therefore presumed revolutionaries.

▣ The King Is Buried (27:57–61)

SUPPORTING IDEA: *Jesus the Messiah died and was buried, proving that he paid for our sin and that his resurrection was the miracle the Bible claims it to be.*

Matthew's description of Jesus' burial is brief and to the point. But it is also critical. The fact that Jesus was dead and buried is the foundation on which the validity of the Resurrection is based.

27:57–58. The mention of **evening** signified the nearing of sunset, the beginning of the Sabbath and the end of the Passover day. **Joseph** of Arimathea (probably a town in northern Judea) is mentioned only here in Matthew (and once in the parallel passages of each Gospel) because of his generosity in giving his tomb for the Messiah's burial. Joseph was one of the few **rich** men (cf. Isa. 53:9–12) who managed to be loyal to the Messiah (cf. Matt. 6:19–24; 19:16–26). With popular opinion against Jesus and the apparent victory of the Jewish leaders, anyone associated with Jesus was in potential danger. But Joseph remained loyal, proving he had **become a disciple of Jesus.**

Matthew omitted the fact that Joseph was a prominent member of the Sanhedrin. This detail, mentioned in Mark 15:43 and Luke 23:50–51, heightened even further the sense of danger to Joseph and the depth of his devotion to Jesus. Joseph had probably remained a secret disciple, at least up to this point.

Joseph had witnessed Jesus' crucifixion and death and **going to Pilate, he asked for Jesus' body.** Pilate granted his request (27:58). Joseph had to be a very prominent man in order to gain an audience with Pilate.

27:59–60. Joseph took possession of Jesus' body and wrapped it in a **clean linen cloth.** The logistics involved suggests Joseph had other people to help him. Joseph had paid for this tomb to be cut into the rocky hillside, expecting to be buried in it himself. It was a **new tomb**; no one else had ever been buried there. He placed Jesus' body in the tomb and had a **big stone** rolled against the door.

27:61. Mary Magdalene and **the other Mary** (the mother of James and Joses, 27:56) witnessed this burial. They sat **opposite the tomb**, grieving the Messiah's death. This detail was important not only to show the women's love for Jesus but also to show that they knew exactly where Jesus had been buried. They knew where to come on Sunday morning (28:1).

⬛ The King's Tomb Is Sealed (27:62–66)

> **SUPPORTING IDEA:** *Despite the enemy's attempts to keep the Messiah down, he will be victorious.*

This brief passage is important because it supports the reality of Jesus' resurrection, showing that the religious leaders tried to keep Jesus' body in the tomb. Despite Pilate's provision of a well-trained Roman guard and the seal of the Roman Empire on Jesus' tomb, the king would prove that he was still in control. Nothing—not even the long arm of Rome's "sovereign" power—would be able to prevent his victorious return to life.

27:62–64. The next day was the Sabbath, which was **the one after Preparation Day**, meaning the day after the Passover Friday. The time of this conversation could have been any time between sunset Friday and sunset Saturday. The Jewish leaders probably approached Pilate at daybreak on Saturday morning, when he gave audience during the early morning hours.

Matthew had referred to "the chief priests and the elders" throughout the passion narrative. But here he said that **the chief priests and the Pharisees** met to confer with Pilate. The Pharisees were part of both groups that had demanded a sign of Jesus (12:38; 16:1). Both times they had received from Jesus the promise of "the sign of Jonah" (12:39–40; 16:4). So it was fitting that they were part of the group that remembered Jesus' prediction of his resurrection after three days. Addressing Pilate respectfully, this group recalled for Pilate one of the claims of what **that deceiver** had said: **After three days I will rise again.**

They asked that Pilate make the grave **secure until the third day.** Then, if Jesus' body were stolen after the third day, no one could say his prophecy had been fulfilled. Jesus himself had set the time frame, and the prophecy would have to be fulfilled in detail if it were to prove valid.

Their fear was that Jesus' disciples might try to steal his body from the tomb so they could claim that he had risen. A risen martyr would hold greater power over the people than the Messiah had while he was alive. Martyrs of the past were respected for their devotion. The miracle of the "resurrection" would validate Jesus' claim to be the Messiah more powerfully than any of his other miracles. Therefore, to the Jewish leaders, **this last deception** (the false claim of a resurrected Messiah) would **be worse than the first.**

27:65–66. Pilate granted their request, giving them a Roman guard. A normal Roman guard was made up of sixteen soldiers. Roman soldiers were well-known for their discipline. The penalty for negligence while on duty (falling asleep or abandoning their post) was execution. These men were not going to let any band of disciples take the body of Jesus.

Pilate ordered the Jewish leaders to post the soldiers at the tomb to make it **as secure as you know how.** This was in both parties' mutual interest. So they took the soldiers to the tomb, placed a seal across the gap between the stone and the outer wall of the tomb, and posted the guard before the tomb. These men would be relieved at regular intervals throughout Saturday and Sunday. Monday would be the fourth day, and then it would be too late for anyone to attempt to fulfill Jesus' prophecy about his resurrection.

MAIN IDEA REVIEW: *Jesus the Messiah gave his life for our sins.*

III. CONCLUSION

Jesus is the true king, no matter how the skeptics might mock him. Because the king does not do something does not mean he is powerless. His purposes go beyond our wisdom. No efforts of the enemy can thwart God's sovereign plans.

PRINCIPLES

- A sin that seems in our best interest at the time is certain to turn sour as we live with its consequences.
- Justice is more important than the "letter of the law."
- All of us are guilty of Jesus' execution. We have his blood on our hands.
- Denying guilt does not remove it.
- The Son of God was forsaken by the Father so that we might be accepted by him.
- We have free access to God through the blood of Jesus.
- Humble service receives highest honor.
- It is possible for a rich person to be a disciple of Jesus; but only some have the ability to handle great wealth while worshiping the true God.

APPLICATIONS

- Resist temptations to sin, claiming God's promise of strength.
- When speaking the truth, we need not speak more than is appropriate to the situation.
- When no words will help the situation, remain silent.
- Beware of the fickleness of your heart. All of us can turn quickly against the Lord, especially under pressure from others.
- Serve God with humility, not for selfish gain.
- Remember daily the price Jesus paid for your salvation.

IV. LIFE APPLICATION

Submission and Sacrifice

Frances Jane Crosby, better known as Fanny Crosby, truly captured the spirit of the American gospel song movement. It is estimated that Fanny Crosby wrote more than 8,000 gospel song texts in her lifetime. Her hymns have been, and still are, being sung more frequently than those of any other gospel hymn writer. Her many favorites have been an important part of evangelical worship for the past century.

It is amazing that anyone, and especially a blind person, could write on this variety of spiritual truths and experiences. For a considerable period during her life, while under contract to a music publisher, she wrote three new hymns each week. She used over two hundred pen names besides her own. Many of her original texts are still being uncovered and no doubt will be published in the near future. Often the themes for her hymns were suggested by visiting ministers wishing to have a new song on a particular subject. At other times musician friends would first compose the music and then ask Fanny Crosby for the words. Well-known hymns to her credit include "Blessed Assurance," "All the Way My Savior Leads Me," and "Rescue the Perishing."

Fannie Crosby died at the age of ninety-five. Engraved on her tombstone at Bridgeport, Connecticut are these words taken from Jesus' remarks to Mary, the sister of Lazarus: "She hath done what she could."

We read in Matthew 27 of the sacrifice of Jesus on the cross, where he gave his all to save mankind from the consequences of sin. In this ultimate of all sacrifices, he completely submitted himself to God's will and mission. Fannie Crosby was a model believer who invested her life completely for the kingdom of God. In spite of her challenge of physical blindness, she had a keen spiritual vision. She gave all she was for the cause of Christ.

Have you submitted your all to God's kingdom? Are you prepared to make the necessary sacrifices to further his kingdom?

V. PRAYER

Loving Father, I bow in amazement at the cross on which your only-begotten Son died. Thank you for his love and sacrifice. Send me forth to tell others about your amazing grace. Amen.

VI. DEEPER DISCOVERIES

A. Captial Punishment

The Jews were dependent on the Roman authorities to carry out an execution, as the Jews were not authorized to do so. They needed to convince Pilate, the Roman governor over Judea, that Jesus was deserving of death under Roman law. Since Pilate probably only took cases early in the morning, the Sanhedrin had to hurry the process along and get Jesus to him as quickly as possible that morning. This Friday morning was the continuation of the Passover. It was permissible, under Jewish law, to execute criminals on such feast days in the most extreme circumstances.

But in no case was it permissible to perform an execution on the Sabbath, which would begin at sunset this Friday evening. Because Jesus had forced their hand, the Jewish leaders apparently felt the pressure of concluding this affair before the Sabbath began. This left them only the daylight hours of one day to have Jesus convicted by Pilate and executed.

B. Crucifixion

The victim's horizontal beam was attached to the vertical pole while they were both lying on the ground. The victim was forced to lie down with his back to the cross. Spikes were driven through his wrists into the horizontal beam. His feet were also nailed with spikes to the vertical pole. Then the entire cross was raised upright, with the victim nailed to it, and dropped into a hole.

The victim's weight rested upon the spikes through his wrists and feet. But as painful as this was, the spikes did not kill the person. When the victim was hanging with his arms above him, breathing was a problem. To breath adequately, he had to raise himself up by his nailed feet and wrists, take a breath, and then let himself relax again as he exhaled. Eventually, the victim weakened so much that he could not take a breath and he suffocated. It generally took two or three days for the victim to die. That is why the soldiers usually broke a person's legs–to hurry up the process.

C. Did Judas Come to Saving Faith (27:3–5)?

There is debate over whether Judas ever came to saving faith in the Messiah. Most likely he did not. His remorse probably had more to do with betraying an innocent friend than with a personal commitment to Jesus as the Messiah. Also, Jesus' comment about his betrayer in 26:24 seem to indicate condemnation. The major point of Judas's story, though, is the danger of greed, jealousy, fear, and a lack of openness to God's plan. He threw away the money he received for his betrayal. He ended through suicide the life he feared losing through association with Jesus. The position of influence he may have desired turned into a reputation of infamy, so that his name is now associated with betrayal. And his rejection of the Messiah led to his own destruction.

D. Summary

This chapter describes the most important event of history. Along with the Resurrection, it is the central event of Matthew's Gospel. Chapter 27 completes the passion narrative begun in Matthew 26. The details about Jesus' burial and the securing of the tomb set the stage for the Resurrection.

VII. TEACHING OUTLINE

A. INTRODUCTION

1. Lead Story: On an October Morning
2. Context: Matthew 27 is a continuation of the narrative begun in the preceding chapter. See the introduction to Matthew 26 for the purpose, structure, and some of the key elements of this two-chapter narrative.
3. Transition: The theme of Jesus' sovereign control over circumstances continues in Jesus' handling of his trial before Pilate (27:11–14) and his choice of the time of his death (27:50). This chapter includes the greatest event in history—the Messiah's death on the cross. Its reality is at the heart of the salvation message. The cross is the centerpiece of Scripture.

B. COMMENTARY

1. The King's Betrayer Gets His Due (27:1–10)
2. The King Goes Before Pilate (27:11–26)
3. The King Is Mocked and Beaten (27:27–32)
4. The King Is Crucified (27:33–56)
5. The King Is Buried (27:57–61)
6. The King's Tomb Is Sealed (27:62–66)

C. CONCLUSION

1. Wrap-up: Jesus the Messiah willingly gave his life for our sins.
2. Personal Challenge: Jesus was not only willing to sacrifice for us, but he was willing to *be* the sacrifice for us. He gave his life for us. Are you willing to give your life to him?

VIII. ISSUES FOR DISCUSSION

1. Why did the Sanhedrin take Jesus to Pilate for a trial after they had already declared him guilty?
2. How would you describe the personality and character of Pilate?
3. Why was Jesus silent before Pilate?
4. Describe Jesus' treatment by the Roman soldiers and the bystanders at the cross. How was this a fulfillment of prophecy?
5. What do you think Jesus was feeling on the cross when he asked, "My God, my God, why have you forsaken me?"

Matthew 28

The King Commissions His People

I. INTRODUCTION
A Sober and Dutiful Commissioning

II. COMMENTARY
A verse-by-verse explanation of the chapter.

III. CONCLUSION
An overview of the principles and applications from the chapter.

IV. LIFE APPLICATION
Power over Death

Melding the chapter to life.

V. PRAYER
Tying the chapter to life with God.

VI. DEEPER DISCOVERIES
Historical, geographical, and grammatical enrichment of the commentary.

VII. TEACHING OUTLINE
Suggested step-by-step group study of the chapter.

VIII. ISSUES FOR DISCUSSION
Zeroing the chapter in on daily life.

"*The general who advances without coveting fame and retreats without fearing disgrace, whose only thought is to protect his country and do good service for his sovereign, is the jewel of the kingdom.*"

Sun Tzu

Matthew 28

IN A NUTSHELL

Jesus conquers death! As he had predicted, Jesus rose from the grave on the third day. The empty tomb is proof that we serve a risen Savior. His resurrection brings to completion his saving work on the cross. Because of his conquest of death, we have hope of eternal life. After postresurrection appearances to many, the risen Christ commissioned his followers to continue his disciple-making ministry until he returns. He promised his presence and authority in carrying out this mission.

The King Commissions His People

I. INTRODUCTION

A Sober and Dutiful Commissioning

*O*n June 5, 1967, I stood with several of my friends in the annex of Edman Chapel at Wheaton College. In moments, we would be graduating from college. But we would now mark another, even more, significant moment—our commissioning as officers in the Regular Army of the United States of America. As part of the commissioning ceremony we raised our hands and took a solemn oath, swearing to defend and protect the Constitution of the United States.

Following the oath, the professor of military science stepped forward to one shoulder and my young wife stepped up to the other. They each pinned on my shoulders a small gold bar, signifying my rank as a second lieutenant. It was a proud and sober occasion. Commissions are to be accepted. Commissions are to be obeyed. Commissions are to be fulfilled! And, to the best of our ability, we young officers were determined to give it our best.

We were in the pipeline to Vietnam. While others chose not to volunteer for military service, while some broke the law to avoid it, and while still others gathered to protest it, we submitted ourselves to a responsibility we felt deeply.

Lives offered. Lives taken. Lives changed. All on the strength of a commission. A commission inspired by a sense of duty. A commission that has impacted every day of our lives from that day forward to this very day. Commissions are like that when they are taken seriously.

Jesus was about to do some serious commissioning. His disciples were about to graduate from a school of their own. And the Lord of the universe pronounced an even more demanding commission upon those who would follow him. It would impact all of life, every day, for the rest of their lives and eternity. This was the *Great Commission*.

II. COMMENTARY

The King Commissions His People

MAIN IDEA: *The risen Messiah has commissioned us to continue his disciple-making ministry in his authority throughout his world.*

Matthew's resurrection narrative is rivaled in brevity only by Mark's. This leads us to believe that, as important as the Resurrection (and the passion) were to Matthew, he saw the most important part of his contribution as the central heart of his book (chs. 5–25), where he built the bulk of his case for Jesus as Messiah.

The final emphasis of Matthew was the Great Commission to kingdom *ministry.* Throughout Matthew, Jesus had demonstrated ministry and trained his disciples for ministry. He watched them succeed at ministry a little (and fail a lot), provided teaching for the foundation of the church ministry, and gave his life and rose from the dead as the heart of the gospel ministry. Now he had handed the baton to the church. We are left with the challenge to imitate his model of character and ministry, continuing to do the work he began.

The theme of authority was also prominent throughout Matthew. In the Great Commission, Jesus pointed to his authority as the means to our fulfillment of the worldwide task. We are to go making disciples in the authority of the One who spoke authoritatively, healed authoritatively, exorcised demons authoritatively, commanded nature authoritatively, confronted evil authoritatively, and conquered death authoritatively. We are to do it as people under authority.

Just as Matthew's Gospel moved geographically from Galilee toward Jerusalem, now the reverse is true. Movement back toward Galilee (away from the heartland of Israel's false religious system) is strongly emphasized in Matthew 28 (cf. 26:32).

A The King's Tomb Is Empty (28:1–7)

SUPPORTING IDEA: *We serve a risen Messiah.*

All of 28:1–10 served as proof to the two women, the disciples, believers of all ages, and the entire world that Jesus was alive. This implies that every person in the world is accountable to a living Lord and will one day answer to him either as Savior or judge.

28:1. It was now dawn on Sunday morning. This resurrection morning is the foundation for the church's selection of Sunday as the new day of worship, although there is no basis for taking it to be "a new Sabbath."

The **Sabbath** ended at sunset the night before. It was now permissible for **Mary Magdalene** and **the other Mary** (the mother of James and Joses, 27:56,61) to care for Jesus' body, although Matthew did not state this as their purpose. He merely wrote that they **went to look at the tomb.**

We know from the mention of the two women in 27:61 that they knew exactly which was Jesus' tomb. Therefore, no one can claim that the Resurrection was a case of mistaken identity and that Jesus is still buried in some other tomb that they overlooked.

28:2–4. These verses provide a flashback to events that had happened before the women arrived. When Matthew resumed the narrative in the "present," as the women arrived at the tomb (28:5), they saw only the aftermath of what had happened in 28:2–4.

First, there had been a **violent earthquake.** This was nature's way of expressing the force of what was happening. **For** seems to indicate that the angel's descent and moving of the stone was the cause of the earthquake. This was an **angel of the Lord,** a common phrase for God's powerful beings. He descended **from heaven,** which was his point of origin. This was also a reference to the Almighty who had sent him.

The **stone** that would have taken several men to move was nothing to this mighty being. After he had rolled away the stone, he **sat on it.** This symbolized God's conquest over all barriers to his will. The angel sat waiting for the women to arrive. He was also on a specific mission.

The stone did not need to be moved for Jesus to emerge. We know from the other Gospels that his resurrection body was capable of traveling through walls and closed doors. Rather, the stone was rolled away so others could look in and witness the empty tomb (**see the place where he lay,** 28:6).

The angel's appearance was described in terms similar to those attributed to the transfigured Jesus (17:2). He shimmered **like lightning,** and **his clothes were white as snow.** The angel demonstrated the glory of heaven and the God of heaven.

The angel's power and brilliant appearance caused the tough, disciplined Roman guards to shake with fear, and they **became like dead men.** They may have fainted from the shock. Or their intense fear may have caused them to fall to the ground paralyzed with terror.

The guards probably got up and fled as soon as they collected their wits. They did not seem to be present when the angel or Jesus spoke to the women (28:5–10), and they "went into the city" of Jerusalem some time that morning (28:11).

28:5–7. When the two women arrived, they were also terrified by the appearance of the brilliant being sitting on the stone. The angel said, **Do not be afraid.** Matthew used a construction that usually implies a command to stop doing something that was already being done. The women were to stop being afraid.

The angel next gave the reason they need not fear: **I know that you are looking for Jesus, who was crucified.** Jesus will forever be known as the crucified one (cf. 1 Cor. 1:23; 2:2; Gal. 3:1). The salvation he wrought through his death, the victory he won, and the obedience he displayed will stand for eternity.

The news the angel brought them was also reason to stop fearing and start rejoicing: **He is not here; he has risen, just as he said.**

As proof of the angel's startling announcement, he invited them to look into the open, empty tomb: **Come and see the place where he lay.** Matthew used the Greek imperfect tense to show that he had been lying there for some time. In Matthew's abbreviated account, he did not record whether the women actually looked into the tomb, but we can be sure they did. This strengthened their faith and prepared them to serve as eyewitnesses to the disciples.

Once they had become convinced by their own observation that Jesus was gone, the angel gave them these instructions: **Go quickly and tell his disciples: He has risen from the dead.** These two women were given the honor of taking the news to the disciples. As it turned out, this was a difficult job. Some of the disciples doubted (28:17).

Jesus had gone elsewhere and would be waiting for them. He had gone ahead **into Galilee. There you will see him.** This was God's gentle reminder of the instructions Jesus had given the disciples less than three days before (26:32). They would not find Jesus lingering around the place of his burial. There was no use looking for him in Judea. The king was in sovereign control as he had always been.

𝔅 The King Appears (28:8–10)

SUPPORTING IDEA: *We serve a Messiah who deals with each of us personally.*

28:8–9. The women didn't need to be told twice to **go quickly** (28:7). They were compelled to leave the tomb, **afraid** of what they had just experienced, and drawn on by great **joy** at the unbelievable news they had heard. They **ran to tell his disciples.**

But along the way they stopped short. **Suddenly** Jesus, the risen king himself, **met them** and said, **Greetings.** The greeting Jesus used was typical, similar to our *hello*.

Imagine the women's awe as they approached him, fell to the ground, **clasped** and held his feet (note he was tangible), and **worshiped** him. The picture is one of speechless wonder, mixed with overwhelming adoration.

28:10. Fear was still mixed in with their other emotions. Jesus repeated verbatim the first words of the angel (28:5), **Do not be afraid.** His tone was authoritative and comforting, conveying the strength of security. Jesus then gave essentially the same instructions that the angel had given: **Go and tell my brothers to go to Galilee.** He also repeated the same promise the angel had given: **There they will see me.**

Now the women went on their way with even more to tell. Not only had a heavenly visitor reported Jesus' resurrection and shown them proof, but the king himself had appeared to them!

C The King's Enemies Lie Once More (28:11–15)

SUPPORTING IDEA: *As we conduct the Messiah's ministry, we will have to deal with the enemy's lies about the Messiah.*

28:11. Matthew reported this episode between the soldiers and the members of the Sanhedrin as taking place while the two women hurried away to report to the disciples.

The phrase **some of the guards** indicated that some of the Roman soldiers hid from the authorities after the fright they had experienced. But some of them knew they would be in big trouble with the governor when he discovered they had abandoned their post. The penalty for sleeping on duty or abandoning one's post was execution. So they came quietly into Jerusalem to **the chief priests,** the head conspirators, to tell them **everything that had happened.** This may also have been an attempt to figure out a way to save their necks.

28:12–14. The chief priests gathered other members of the Sanhedrin (**the elders**) together and conferred on how to handle this new development. Matthew portrayed the entire body as unified in their denial.

Their official solution? **They gave the soldiers a large sum of money.** Then they asked the soldiers to spread a lie. They were to **say** ("keep on saying," Gr. present tense) that Jesus' disciples came during Saturday night and stole his body while the guards were asleep.

The guards were reluctant to agree to this solution. "What if the governor hears our false report? He will have us all killed!" So the Jewish leaders, the masters of deception, assured the guards that if Pilate heard the false rumor and sought to execute the guards, the Jewish leaders would intervene on their behalf: **We will satisfy him and keep you out of trouble.**

It is important to note that the Jewish leaders and the soldiers did not try to *deny* the empty tomb but only to *explain* it. Anyone who assumes that Jesus remained in the grave should consider this historical reality. The concocted story was desperate, raising more questions than it answered.

28:15. The soldiers agreed and kept their end of the bargain. This false and ridiculous story of the disciples' theft and the guards' sleep was **widely circulated,** and it remained in circulation even at the time of Matthew's writing of his Gospel decades later. In fact, this remains a popular explanation of the Resurrection among skeptics even today.

Whether the guards' failure was discovered by Pilate, and whether the Jewish leaders went so far as to intervene for them, we don't know. It was not important to Matthew's purpose.

D The King Sends His People with His Authority (28:16–20)

SUPPORTING IDEA: *The presence and authority of the Messiah will accompany us as we carry out his disciple-making ministry.*

The brevity of Matthew's resurrection account allowed him to get quickly to the final application of his Gospel. This closing passage served as a resurrection appearance, testifying to the truth of Jesus' resurrection. It also provided the central purpose for all believers.

Our lives belong not to us but to the One who died to purchase our freedom from sin and death. Along with our freedom, he purchased our availability and usefulness to him as tools for the conduct of his ministry. We rob him of his right when we fail to fulfill his marching orders.

The entire Gospel of Matthew serves to equip us for the fulfillment of the Great Commission.

- Matthew gives the historical basis for our status as disciples of the Messiah and citizens of the kingdom of heaven. Matthew gives us our true identity.

- Matthew shows us the person with whom we have begun a deeply intimate and loyal relationship.

- Matthew reveals this master's unbending demands and his unending grace, contrasting him with the many other masters who clamor for our loyalty. None of these false gods will reward us for faithfulness as he does. None of them care for our well-being.

- Matthew demonstrates the authority with which we are sent out so we might fulfill our disciple-making ministry with confidence. This confidence is not in ourselves but in the Lord and Savior who promised to be with us.

- Matthew promises us the reward that awaits the good and faithful servant, motivating us to faithfulness in our earthly kingdom task.

- Matthew sets before us a detailed example, in the Messiah himself, showing us exactly how to carry out our commission.

- Matthew provides, through the teachings of the Messiah, the basis for the right character of kingdom citizens as well as guidelines for right relationships within the church family.
- Matthew gives us a message of warning and hope for a world heading for destruction. We must proclaim this message fearlessly and lovingly. Some people will become disciples because of our proclamation of Matthew's message.

Seen from the perspective of the Great Commission, Matthew's Gospel is a training manual for life and ministry. We will become true disciples of the Messiah, effectively reproducing other disciples, if we abide with him and live out what we learn from him.

The Great Commission also ties together Matthew's Gospel by bringing to completion the covenant theme implicit in 1:1–17. The sacrificial Son of Abraham has now completed his work. The sovereign Son of David is now restored to his full majesty. Now the Son of David, the king, sends us with his authority. We as the spiritual offspring of Abraham must join with him in fulfilling God's covenant promise—that through Abraham God would bless all peoples of the earth.

28:16–17. Some time during the forty days of Jesus' post-resurrection stay on earth (probably soon after they heard the news that Sunday), **the eleven disciples** and many more of Jesus' followers proceeded to Galilee, where Jesus had instructed them to go (26:32; 28:7,10). Here Matthew's focus was back on the eleven, the foundation stones of his church.

Jesus had apparently specified a particular mountain as their meeting place. (Note mountains as locations for other important events in Matt. 5:1; 14:23; 15:29; 17:1; 24:3; 26:30.)

At the end of the journey, presumably on the designated mountain, **they saw him.** Imagine their joy! It was only natural that **they worshiped him.**

But some doubted (the word *doubt* means "to duplicate," "to be of two minds," or "to waver, hesitate"). All wanted to believe, but their faith was weak. Some experienced the internal tug-of-war between "two minds"—the one wanting to follow their fledgling faith and the other wanting to follow "reason." Even those presented with clear evidence for the truth can still have doubts.

But the word **some** implied there were others who believed everything they saw. These were the followers of the Messiah-King who would continue on into Acts, willing to take any risk in obedience to their master. This was true faith in action, living on the edge of "risky" obedience.

28:18–20. The Great Commission passage is reminiscent of Acts 1:6–11. In Matthew, Jesus issued a similar commission in different words with a different emphasis. However, the setting in the Acts passage was in Jerusalem. It coincided with Jesus' ascension into heaven at the end of the forty days. Jesus probably met with the disciples in Galilee and then instructed them to return to Jerusalem. All of this was done in preparation for their receiving of the Holy Spirit (Acts 1:4–5) and their continuation of his Spirit-empowered ministry in Acts 2 (in Jerusalem).

Matthew did not record Jesus' ascension into heaven, as it likely would have distracted from his emphasis in 28:18–20. He wanted the Great Commission to linger in people's minds as they finished his Gospel. Jesus had a big job in mind for his followers. **All** is a key word in 28:18–20. It emphasizes Jesus' divine identity: *all* authority, *all* nations, *all* things.

Before issuing his commission, Jesus laid the foundation for the success of their future ministry: **All authority in heaven and on earth has been given to me**. This was critically important. Without the Messiah's authority, the mission of the disciples and our mission today would be doomed to failure. The reader of Matthew's Gospel should know well by now the nature and power of the Messiah's authority.

The heart of the Great Commission is 28:19–20, the last words of Matthew's Gospel. Matthew knew the principle that "last words are lasting words." He chose carefully, under the Spirit's direction, the words he wanted to linger in his readers' minds. **Therefore** identified Jesus' authority (28:18) as the reason the disciples must carry out his orders.

The central command is **make disciples**. At the heart of our mission is the reproduction in others of what Jesus has produced in us: faith, obedience, growth, authority, compassion, love, and a bold, truthful message as his witnesses. They were learners commanded to produce more learners.

Jesus' disciples were to reproduce other disciples **of all the nations** (the word translated **nations** is the plural of *ethnos,* meaning "peoples, ethnic groups," as in 24:14). He was hinting that their fulfillment of their commission would ultimately lead to his second coming. It is significant that Matthew ended his Gospel with one more reference to the Gentile mission, challenging the Jewish Christians to lose their prejudices and unify the church. This also challenges us to break down any artificial boundaries erected by our culture. We must minister impartially. Jesus was an equal-opportunity Savior.

We see three participles here that are subordinate to the central command to make disciples. Each of these clarifies the way in which Jesus' disciples are to make disciples.

First, in the emphatic first position, even before **make disciples**, is the aorist participle **go**. In the context, this Greek participle is best rendered, "when you have gone." "Going" is one of the three means by which to fulfill the central command to make disciples. *Going* means more than traveling across geographical borders, although this is part of Jesus' meaning. The point is that we believers are active; we are not inert. *Going* means crossing boundaries to make disciples—going across the street, going to dinner with an unbelieving friend, going into the inner city, going beyond one's comfort zone to make the gospel accessible to the lost. Living life is "going" with a purpose, every day.

Going also implies our support of people who are literally going to other cultures. We must support global outreach financially and support the people going emotionally and personally as well as through prayer. We are a part of their team. In all these ways we "go," in fulfillment of the Great Commission.

We also "go" when we support efforts to equip indigenous ministers in different cultures. We help equip them to lead people of their own culture and language. This enables them to fulfill the Great Commission at home and in cultures where they will find a better reception than we would.

Second, we come to the participle **baptizing** (present participle of *baptizo,* meaning "continually immersing them"). Because baptism was so closely associated with the decision of faith (cf. Acts 2:38; 8:36–38; 10:47–48), it may be best to see **baptizing** as Jesus' way of summarizing the evangelistic half of the disciples' ministry. The third participle, **teaching** (Matt. 28:20), represents the other half of the disciples' ministry—the edification of those who are already believers. Baptism is an initiating rite that "immerses" the believer into a whole new world.

Baptism is not a step to salvation. Rather, it is an initial step of obedience that results from a person's decision to trust the Messiah. Baptism represents the identification of people with this new way of life and faith. Baptism should be experienced as soon as possible after a person trusts Christ.

Jesus specified that we are to baptize disciples **in the name of the Father and of the Son and of the Holy Spirit.** The use of the singular **name** implies clearly that this listing of three persons should be thought of as one name. Here is a clear affirmation of the doctrine of the Trinity—one God, three distinct persons. The believer who chooses to submit to baptism into this name identifies with God's name as well as the spiritual family of all others who are identified with this same name.

This is a good summary of the evangelistic task of the church. It is bringing those who identify with the world into a new identification. It is seeing themselves anew as citizens of God's kingdom, as children of God, as brothers and sisters of the Messiah, and as brothers and sisters with the rest of the family of believers. Our mission is to bring people to a point where they see themselves differently—because they have become different through the transforming work of God's grace.

Third, the participle **teaching** (present participle of *didasko,* meaning "keep on teaching them") completes the series of three means by which we fulfill the Great Commission. This represents the other half of our mission— the edification or building up of those who are believers.

Jesus instructed us not only to teach content, but to train people into obedient action: **teaching them to keep everything I have commanded you.** The teachings of Jesus recorded in Matthew are the essence of the practical teaching we are to pass on to new disciples. There is much more teaching from Scripture beyond Matthew that the church needs. But his teaching in Matthew serves as a strong foundation.

By fulfilling the teaching portion of the Great Commission, we take believers at every stage of spiritual maturity to the next stage of growth. This can range from the infancy of a brand-new believer to various levels of spiritual adulthood. Every believer should progress toward the perfect character of Christ (Eph. 4:11–16), but none will arrive there short of eternity. So we must see ourselves as learners in a family of teachers, who themselves are also learners. The believer who is most mature will be most ready to listen and learn, even from the newest member of the family (cf. Matt. 18:4).

Matthew's last words are a concluding promise from the Messiah-King. **Surely** adds a note of assurance, similar to Jesus' "I tell you the truth." A paraphrase of the phrase **I am with you always** would read, "I myself am continually with you always until the end of the age." Among other things, Jesus claimed omnipresence, again laying claim to deity (note "Immanuel, God with us" in 1:23). He will be with us every step of the way. **I am with you always** reminds us of the great promises to saints of old like Moses (Exod. 3:12) and Joshua (Josh. 1:5).

This promise complements Jesus' claim to universal authority in Matthew 28:18, and it undergirds the believer's confidence in fulfilling the Great Commission. If we take out the three subordinate participial clauses from 28:18–20, boiling the commission down to its grammatical essence, we end up with this: "All authority has been given to me in heaven and on earth. Therefore, make disciples of all the nations; and surely I am with you always, to the end of the age."

MAIN IDEA REVIEW: *The risen Messiah has commissioned us to continue his disciple-making ministry in his authority throughout his world.*

III. CONCLUSION

As Christians we should have no partiality or prejudice in our view toward others, especially as we seek to lead them to the king. Our task is to win people to Christ, helping them to find a new identity with God and his family. We must also teach one another practically, with the goal of encouraging others to obey all of Jesus' teachings.

PRINCIPLES

- The king is alive.
- We have hope of eternal life because of his conquest of death.
- The risen Jesus deals with us personally.
- Even in the face of undeniable evidence, people may still hesitate to believe.
- All the authority of Jesus goes with us and empowers us, wherever we go, as we fulfill our mandate to make disciples.
- The risen king is always with us.

APPLICATIONS

- Think daily of Jesus' resurrection and what it means to you.
- Learn to communicate the certainty of Jesus' resurrection with others.
- Obey Jesus' command to make disciples of all nations.
- Rely on Jesus' promised presence and power as you make disciples.

IV. LIFE APPLICATION

Power over Death

In 1673, French explorers Louis Joliet and Father Jacques Marquette passed through an area along the bank of the Illinois River known today as Starved Rock. At the time, they found a group of Native Americans known as the Kaskaskias, a sub-tribe of the Illiniwek. Marquette returned there two years later to found the Mission of the Immaculate Conception—Illinois' first Christian mission.

When the French claimed the region (and, indeed, the entire Mississippi Valley), they built Fort St. Louis atop Starved Rock in the winter of 1682–83 because of its commanding strategic position above the last rapids on the Illinois River. Pressured from small war parties of Iroquois in the French and Indian Wars, the French abandoned the fort by the early 1700s and retreated to what is now Peoria, Illinois, where they established another fort. Fort St. Louis became a haven for traders and trappers until it was destroyed by fire around 1720.

In the 1760s, Pontiac, chief of the Ottawa tribe upriver, was slain by an Illiniwek while attending a tribal council in Southern Illinois. According to the legend, during one of the battles that subsequently occurred to avenge his killing, a band of Illiniwek, under attack by a band of Potawatomi (allies of the Ottawa), sought refuge atop a 125-foot sandstone butte. The Ottawa and

Potawatomi surrounded the bluff and held their ground until the hapless Ill-iniwek died of starvation, giving rise to the name *Starved Rock*. Today, it is protected ground as part of the Illinois state park system.

As with so many monuments, Starved Rock is a monument to a group of people who succumbed to death—some of whom may have bravely endured until the end for the sake of others. All such monuments and cemeteries are testimonies to the corruptive effect of sin on the world—death. Sadly, some in our world accept death as life's final, inevitable event.

What a contrast we see in the account of the empty tomb of Jesus. His empty tomb is a celebration of life! The cross involved immense suffering and the ultimate sacrifice of our Savior. Yet, death was not the final chapter in his life. Jesus conquered death! And because of his sacrifice and resurrection, we, too, may be freed from the consequences of sin. We should constantly keep in mind the fact of the resurrection and its meaning for our lives.

V. PRAYER

Lord, all authority in heaven and on earth is yours. And I accept your commission to "go and make disciples of all nations, baptizing them in the name of the Father and of the Son and of the Holy Spirit, and teaching them to obey everything I have commanded you." Amen.

VI. DEEPER DISCOVERIES

A. The Timing of the Resurrection

Some people have difficulty with Jesus' prediction that he would spend "three days and three nights in the heart of the earth" (12:40). But this is eas-ily explained. The phrase "a day and a night" was a Jewish idiom referring to a day. Jewish time reckoning considered any part of a day (even an hour) to represent the whole day. Thus, we can see how the time between Jesus' death and his resurrection could be considered "three days and three nights."

The time between his death at about 3 P.M. Friday and sunset (about 6 P.M.) was the first day (or, according to Jewish idiom, "a day and a night"). From sun-set Friday to sunset Saturday (the Sabbath) was the second day (literally "a day and a night"). Then the time between sunset Saturday and the Resurrection, before dawn Sunday morning, was the third day (or "a day and a night").

B. Summary

The resurrection account presents the crowning miracle in Matthew's long catalogue of authoritative miracles and teachings, sealing his case for Jesus as the Messiah.

The Resurrection also brings to completion the saving work of the Messiah on the cross. The sacrificial Son of Abraham died on Friday, atoning for the sins of all who believe. The sovereign Son of David arose in conquest over death on Sunday, assuring his conquest of death in our lives as well.

The Great Commission is the key application of all of Matthew's Gospel, telling us how to apply all we have learned from his account of Jesus' life.

VII. TEACHING OUTLINE

A. CONCLUSION

1. Lead Story: A Sober and Dutiful Commissioning
2. Context: Matthew's resurrection narrative is brief. This leads us to believe that he saw the most important part of his Gospel as the central heart of his book (chs. 5–25). Here he built his case for Jesus as Messiah. The Resurrection is certainly critical to his case, as it is the crowning miracle in his account, which is full of miracles and other expressions of Jesus' authority. But he saw no need to embellish the historical reality of the Resurrection.
3. Transition: The final emphasis of Matthew is the Great Commission to kingdom ministry. Throughout Matthew, Jesus had demonstrated ministry, trained his disciples for ministry, watched their progress at ministry, and provided teaching for the foundation of the church's ministry. He gave his life and rose from the dead as the heart of the gospel ministry. Now he has handed the baton to the church. We are left with the challenge to imitate his model of character and ministry, continuing to do the work he began.

   The theme of authority is also prominent throughout Matthew. In the Great Commission, Jesus pointed to his authority as the means to our fulfillment of this task. We are to go, making disciples in his authority.

B. COMMENTARY

1. The King's Tomb Is Empty (28:1–7)
2. The King Answers (28:8–10)
3. The King's Enemies Lie Once More (28:11–15)
4. The King Sends His People with His Authority (28:16–20)

C. CONCLUSION

1. Wrap-up: The risen Messiah has commissioned us to continue his disciple-making ministry in his authority throughout his world.

2. Personal Challenge: We have received a commission from the One who has all authority in this world. As believers, we have been commissioned to help others understand who their Lord and Savior is and to give them the opportunity to become his disciples. What are you doing with your commission?

VIII. ISSUES FOR DISCUSSION

1. Why do you think Jesus met with his disciples in Galilee after his resurrection?
2. How does the Great Commission of Jesus tie together the entire Gospel of Matthew?
3. What is different about the Great Commission passage in Matthew and a similar commissioning of his followers by Jesus in Acts 1:6–11?
4. How does Jesus' Great Commission hint at the church's future mission to the Gentiles?

Glossary

advent—Christ's coming through the virgin birth to minister and provide salvation. His advent will also occur in the clouds for final judgment.

angel—A messenger from God, either heavenly or human, who delivers God's message of instruction, warning, or hope.

apostles—Men chosen by Jesus as his official messengers; this term refers generally to his twelve disciples.

baptism—The immersion or dipping of a believer in water symbolizing the complete renewal and change in the believer's life and testifying to the death, burial, and resurrection of Jesus Christ as the way of salvation.

church—The community of those who believe in and follow Jesus Christ; used to designate a congregation, a denomination, or all Christians.

covenant—A contract or agreement expressing God's gracious promises to his people and their consequent relationship to him.

cross—Two wooden beams shaped as a letter *t* or *x* used as an instrument to kill criminals by the Roman government; the wooden beams on which Jesus was killed and thus a symbol of Christian faith and responsibility.

crucifixion—A form of execution by affixing a victim to a cross to die; Jesus' death on the cross for sinners.

eternal life—The quality of life that Jesus gives his disciples and unending life with God given to those who believe in Jesus Christ as Savior and Lord.

evangelism—The central element of the church's mission involving telling others the gospel of salvation with the goal of leading them to repentance and faith in Christ.

fasting—Going without food as a sign of repentance, grief, or devotion to God; often connected with devotion to prayer.

forgiveness—Pardon and release from penalty for wrongdoing; God's delivery from sin's wages for those who repent and express faith in Christ; the Christian act of freeing from guilt and blame those by whom one has suffered wrong.

Gentiles—People who are not part of God's chosen family at birth and thus can be considered "pagans."

Godhead—The unity of the triune God: Father, Son, Holy Spirit.

gospel—The good news of the redeeming work of God through the life, death, and resurrection of Jesus Christ.

Gospels—The four New Testament accounts of the life of Jesus Christ. Matthew, Mark, and Luke are called Synoptic Gospels because they relate many of the same events and teachings of Jesus. John is the Fourth Gospel and tends to be more theological in nature, telling events and teachings not in the Synoptics.

heaven—The eternal dwelling place of God and the redeemed.

hell—The place of everlasting punishment for the lost.

Herodians—An aristocratic Jewish group who favored the policies of Herod Antipas and thus supported the Roman government.

high priest—The chief religious official for Israel and Judaism appointed as the only person allowed to enter the Holy of Holies and offer sacrifice on the Day of Atonement.

holy—God's distinguishing characteristic that separates him from all creation; the moral ideal for Christians as they seek to reflect the character of God as known in Christ Jesus.

Glossary

Holy of Holies—The innermost and most sacred area of the tabernacle and temple, where God was present and where sacrifices were made by the high priest on the Day of Atonement.

Holy Spirit—The third person of the Trinity; the presence of God promised by Christ and sent to his disciples at Pentecost representing God's active presence in the believer, the church, and the world.

incarnation—The act of the divine Son Jesus becoming human and enduring all the experiences which tempt us and cause us to suffer, thus qualifying him to be the agent of God's saving plan for humanity.

Jerusalem—Capital city of Israel in the Old Testament; religious center of Judaism in the New Testament; also name of the heavenly city John describes in Revelation (New Jerusalem).

kingdom of God—God's sovereign rule in the universe and in the hearts of Christians.

law—God's instruction to his people about how to love him and others. When used with the definite article "the," *law* may refer to the Old Testament as a whole but usually to the Pentateuch (Genesis through Deuteronomy).

Messiah—The coming king promised by the prophets; Jesus Christ who fulfilled the prophetic promises; Christ represents the Greek translation of the Hebrew word "messiah."

minister—The loving service of Christians to each other and to those outside the church in the name of Jesus.

miracle—An act of God beyond human understanding that inspires wonder, displays God's greatness, and leads people to recognize God at work in the world.

mission—The God-given responsibility of the church and each believer to bring God's love and the Christian gospel to all people through evangelism, education, and ministry. The word "missions" is used especially to refer to work done by Christians outside their own culture.

parable—A short story taken from everyday life to make a spiritual point; Jesus' favorite form of teaching.

passion—The suffering of Christ during his time of trial and death on the cross.

Passover—The Jewish feast celebrating the Exodus from Egypt (Exod. 12); celebrated by Jesus and his disciples at the Last Supper.

repentance—A change of heart and mind resulting in a turning from sin to God that allows conversion and is expressed through faith.

resurrection—The raising of Jesus from the dead to eternal life; the raising of believers for eternal life with Christ; the raising of unbelievers to eternal punishment.

righteousness—The quality or condition of being in right relationship with God; living out the relationship with God in right relationships with other persons.

Sabbath—The seventh day of the week corresponding to the seventh day of creation when people in the Old Testament were called on to rest from work and reflect on God.

Sadducees—A religious group which formed during the period between the Old Testament and the New Testament when the Maccabees ruled Judah.

scribe—A Jewish teacher of the law who studied and copied Scripture.

second coming—Christ's return in power and glory to consummate his work of redemption.

Son of Man—The title Jesus most frequently used for himself that emphasized both his divinity as the prophesied One in the Old Testament and his identification with people.

sovereignty—God's freedom from outward restraint; his unlimited rule of and control over his creation.

transfiguration—Jesus' appearance in full glory to Peter, James, and John.

tribulation—Severe affliction or oppression experienced by God's people interpreted by some scholars as a period of persecution and suffering immediately before the second coming.

Trinity—God's revelation of himself as Father, Son, and Holy Spirit unified as one in the Godhead and yet distinct in person and function.

unpardonable sin—Persistence in refusing to accept Christ as Lord and Savior which prevents a person from receiving God's forgiveness; blasphemy that reflects such a condition.

virgin birth—The miraculous birth of Christ in which Mary remained a virgin as she conceived and bore Jesus through the intervention of the Holy Spirit.

worship—Reverence, honor, praise, and service shown to God.

Yahweh—The Hebrew personal name of God revealed to Moses; this name came to be thought of as too holy to pronounce by Jews; often translated Lord or Jehovah.

Bibliography

Barclay, William. *The Gospel of Matthew.* Rev. ed. Philadelphia: The Westminster Press, 1975.

Bauer, Walter, F. Wilbur Gingrich, and Frederick W. Danker. *A Greek-English Lexicon of the New Testament and Other Early Christian Literature.* Chicago: University of Chicago Press, 1979.

Blomberg, Craig L. *Matthew.* The New American Commentary. Vol. 22. Nashville, Tenn.: Broadman & Holman, 1992.

Bruce, F. F. *New Testament History.* Garden City, N.Y.: Anchor Books, 1972.

Carson, D. A. "Matthew." *Expositor's Bible Commentary.* Vol. 8. Edited by Frank E. Gaebelein. Grand Rapids, Mich.: Zondervan Publishing House, 1984.

Dillow, Joseph C. *The Reign of the Servant Kings.* Miami Springs, Fla.: Schoettle Publishing Co., 1992.

Douglas, J. D., ed. *New Bible Dictionary.* 2d ed. Wheaton, Ill.: Tyndale House Publishers, 1982.

Ellisen, Stanley A. *Three Worlds in Conflict.* Sisters, Oreg.: Multnomah Publishers, 1998.

France, R. T. *Matthew.* Tyndale New Testament Commentaries. Vol. 22. Grand Rapids, Mich.: Eerdmans Publishing Company, 1985.

Hagner, Donald A. *Matthew.* Word Biblical Commentary. Vol. 33a and 33b. Dallas, Tex.: Word Books, 1993.

Hendrickson, William. *The Gospel of Matthew.* Grand Rapids, Mich.: Baker Book House, 1973.

Hughes, Robert B., and Carl J. Laney. *New Bible Companion.* Wheaton, Ill.: Tyndale House Publishers, 1990.

Keener, Craig S. *IVP Bible Background Commentary: New Testament.* Downer's Grove, Ill.: InterVarsity Press, 1997.

Mounce, Robert H. *Matthew.* New International Biblical Commentary. Vol. 1. Peabody, Mass.: Henrickson Publishers, 1991.

Pentecost, J. Dwight. *Thy Kingdom Come.* Wheaton, Ill.: Scripture Press Publications (Victor Books), 1990.

Richards, Lawrence O. *Expository Dictionary of Bible Words.* Grand Rapids, Mich.: Zondervan Publishing House, 1985.

Tenney, Merrill C., gen. ed. *The Zondervan Pictorial Encyclopedia of the Bible.* 5 vols. Grand Rapids, Mich.: Zondervan Publishing House, 1976.

Walvoord, John F. *Matthew: Thy Kingdom Come.* Chicago, Ill.: Moody Press, 1994.